Governance and Politics of China

● trading of
vouchers

bargaining

COMPARATIVE GOVERNMENT AND POLITICS

Published

Maura Adshead and Jonathan Tonge
Politics in Ireland

Rudy Andeweg and Galen A. Irwin
Governance and Politics of the Netherlands (3rd edition)

Tim Bale
European Politics: A Comparative Introduction (2nd edition)

Nigel Bowles
Government and Politics of the United States (2nd edition)

Paul Brooker
Non-Democratic Regimes (2nd edition)

Robert Elgie
Political Leadership in Liberal Democracies

Rod Hague and Martin Harrop
* Comparative Government and Politics: An Introduction (8th edition)

Paul Heywood
The Government and Politics of Spain

Xiaoming Huang
Politics in Pacific Asia

B. Guy Peters
Comparative Politics: Theories and Methods
[Rights: World excluding North America]

Tony Saich
Governance and Politics of China (3rd edition)

Eric Shiraev
Russian Government and Politics

Anne Stevens
Government and Politics of France (3rd edition)

Ramesh Thakur
The Government and Politics of India

Forthcoming

Tim Haughton
Government and Politics of Central and Eastern Europe

Robert Leonardi
Government and Politics in Italy

* Published in North America as **Political Science: A Comparative Introduction (6th edition)**

Comparative Government and Politics
Series Standing Order
ISBN 0–333–71693–0 hardback
ISBN 0–333–69335–3 paperback
(outside North America only)

You can receive future titles in this series as they are published by placing a standing order. Please contact your bookseller or, in the case of difficulty, write to us at the address below with your name and address, the title of the series and one of the ISBNs quoted above.

Customer Services Department, Macmillan Distribution Ltd
Houndmills, Basingstoke, Hampshire RG21 6XS, England, UK

Governance and Politics of China

Third Edition

Tony Saich

First edition 2001
Second edition 2004
Third edition 2011

Published by
PALGRAVE MACMILLAN

Palgrave Macmillan in the UK is an imprint of Macmillan Publishers Limited, registered in England, company number 785998, of Houndmills, Basingstoke, Hampshire RG21 6XS.

Palgrave Macmillan in the US is a division of St Martin's Press LLC, 175 Fifth Avenue, New York, NY 10010.

Palgrave Macmillan is the global academic imprint of the above companies and has companies and representatives throughout the world.

Palgrave® and Macmillan® are registered trademarks in the United States, the United Kingdom, Europe and other countries.

ISBN 978–0–230–27992–6   hardback
ISBN 978–0–230–27993–3   paperback

This book is printed on paper suitable for recycling and made from fully managed and sustained forest sources. Logging, pulping and manufacturing processes are expected to conform to the environmental regulations of the country of origin.

A catalogue record for this book is available from the British Library.

A catalog record for this book is available from the Library of Congress.

10 9 8 7 6 5 4 3 2 1
20 19 18 17 16 15 14 13 12 11

Printed in China

Contents

List of Maps, Boxes, Figures and Tables

Map

Boxes

Figures

Tables

Preface to the Third Edition

The third edition of this textbook is substantially revised and updated to cover the years of leadership of President Hu Jintao and Premier Wen Jiabao, who have strived to maintain economic growth while trying to redistribute the benefits of that growth more widely and to deal with the environmental consequences of rapid transformation. The textbook has kept the same basic structure as previous editions and certain basic facts and institutional structures need to be described in order to understand the context within which policies are made and carried out. All the chapters have undergone substantial revision not only to bring them up to date but also in some cases to include new topics or perspectives. For example, Chapter 4 now has a full description and analysis of politics under Hu and Wen. Chapter 5 includes a more extended discussion of the important role that the CCP's organization department plays and the party training schools. Chapter 6 contains new material on what Chinese citizens think of their government and its performance. Chapter 7 includes new information on how citizens rate the performance of their local government officials. Chapter 8 has been rewritten to focus more on contemporary participation and protest, how government policy has often sparked protest and how new technologies are playing a major role in bringing such protest to light. In Chapter 9, we have added a section on how China's intellectuals and artists are responding to the rapid changes in their polity and society. Chapters 10, 11 and 12 update the three main policy areas. Chapter 10 is restructured to focus more specifically on urban pension and rural medical reforms to provide more depth in analysis while raising challenges that are relevant to social policy more broadly. Chapter 12 now covers China's increasing engagement in Africa. Chapter 13 includes a new section on the environmental challenges and resource constraints that China faces as well as adding some ideas on future scenarios for development.

I should thank Steven Kennedy, my publisher at Palgrave Macmillan. His persistence and good humour overcame my reservations about writing an introduction to Chinese politics. He was always helpful with creative advice and suggestions. He must have the patience to test a saint. I would also like to thank Keith Povey and his staff for their tremendous editorial assistance.

I would particularly like to thank my academic home, the Ash Center for Democratic Governance and Innovation, Kennedy School of Government, Harvard University, and the students in my courses since 1999 in which I tried out many of the ideas in this book. My understanding of contemporary China has been shaped by a number of teachers and friends, of whom David S. G. Goodman, Stuart R. Schram, and the late Gordon White deserve special mention. I trust that the references in the text do justice to the influence of the work of other colleagues. I would like to thank three anonymous referees for their comments. I did not agree with all they wrote but they saved me from making a number of mistakes and caused me to amend some judgements.

My formative experience of China was spent in Beijing and Nanjing at the end of the Cultural Revolution in 1976–77. This experience opened my eyes to the complexity of Chinese reality and to take nothing at face value. Many of the ideas expressed in the book were shaped by this early experience and by my five years as Representative of the Ford Foundation in China (1994–99). I learned an enormous amount from our Chinese grantees and staff at the Beijing Office. I enjoyed wrestling policy issues with Mary Ann Burris, Phyllis Chang, James Harkness, Joan Kaufman, Stephen McGurk and Nick Menzies. In addition, Pieter Bottelier and Arthur Holcombe were always a source of advice. However, it is to my Chinese colleagues too numerous to mention that I owe my greatest debt. Since moving to the Harvard Kennedy School, I have had the good fortune to interact with many government officials, scholars, and students from China and they have helped shape my views, especially with respect to the discord between official rhetoric and social realities.

Nancy Hearst did a terrific job with the bibliography and picked up a number of errors that saved me from embarrassing myself even further. I would like to thank Nancy for all her help to the family and myself over the last 20 years or so.

Last I would like to thank Alex and Amanda – to whom this book is dedicated.

TONY SAICH

Updated material for this title is available on the publisher's website at http://www.palgrave.com/politics/saich/

Romanization, Chinese Units of Measurement and Statistics

The system of romanization for Chinese characters used in this book is the *Pinyin* system, as used by the PRC and scholars in the West. It may be adopted by Taiwan, which has traditionally used the Wade-Giles system. Students will come across this system not only in publications from Taiwan but also in most of the works written before 1979. Also, there are numerous names with familiar spellings in English that belong to neither of these two systems. Two names have been used in their more familiar spelling – Chiang Kai-shek and Sun Yat-sen.

Chinese measurements

Jin Weight measure equal to 0.5 of a kilogram.
Mu Measure for land equal to one-sixth of an acre. Often spelt *mou*.
Yuan Chinese currency unit. The value varies but in the year 2010 there were 6.8 *yuan* to the US dollar and 10.3 to the pound sterling.

Statistics

The statistics used in the text unless otherwise stated are all taken from Chinese official sources.

The terms 'the survey' or 'our survey' or 'author's survey' refer to a survey taken of approximately 4,000 residents of China drawn from a cross-section of geographies. The survey was conducted in 2003, 2004, 2005, 2007 and 2009. It does not include migrants or ethnic minority regions. It was conducted with the help of the Horizon Market Research Company.

List of Abbreviations

ACFTU	All-China Federation of Trade Unions
ADB	Asian Development Bank
AFP	*Agence France Presse*
AMC	Asset Management Committee
APC	Agricultural Producers' Cooperative
APEC	Asia-Pacific Economic Cooperation Forum
ARF	ASEAN Regional Forum
ASEAN	Association of Southeast Asian Nations
CC	Central Committee
CCP	Chinese Communist Party
CDIC	Central Discipline Inspection Committee
CIC	China Investment Corporation
CMAC	Central Military Affairs Commission
CPPCC	Chinese People's Political Consultative Conference
CPSU	Communist Party of the Soviet Union
DPP	Democratic Progressive Party
DRC	Development Research Centre (of the State Council)
EBF	Extra-budgetary funds
EU	European Union
FBIS-CHI	*Foreign Broadcast Information Service – China*
FDI	Foreign direct investment
FEER	*Far Eastern Economic Review*
GDP	Gross domestic product
GLF	Great Leap Forward
GMD	Guomindang (Kuomintang, Nationalist Party)
GNP	Gross national product
GONGO	Government-organized NGO
ILO	International Labour Organisation
IMF	International Monetary Fund
IPO	Initial public offering
ISP	Internet Service Provider
Jin-Cha-Ji	Shanxi-Chahar-Hebei
Jin-Ji-Yu-Lu	Shanxi-Hebei-Shandong-Henan
LDP	Liberal Democratic Party
MLSS	Minimum Living Standard Scheme
MOCA	Ministry of Civil Affairs
NATO	North Atlantic Treaty Organization
NGO	Non-governmental organization
NPC	National People's Congress

NPL	Non-performing loan
OECD	Organisation for Economic Co-operation and Development
PLA	People's Liberation Army
Politburo	Political Bureau
PPP	Purchasing power parity
PRC	People's Republic of China
ROSCA	Rotating savings and credit associations
SAR	Special Administrative Region
SARS	Severe Acute Respiratory Syndrome
SASAC	State-owned Assets Supervision and Administration Commission
SCMP	*South China Morning Post*
SETC	State Economic and Trade Commission
SEZ	Special Economic Zone
SFDA	State Drug and Food Administration
SFPC	State Family-Planning Commission
Shaan-Gan-Ning	Shaanxi-Gansu-Ningxia
SME	Small- and medium-sized enterprise
SOE	State-owned enterprise
SWB: FE	*Summary of World Broadcasts: The Far East*
TOEFL	Test of English as a Foreign Language
TVE	Township and village enterprises
UN	United Nations
UNDP	United Nations Development Programme
UNESCO	United Nations Education, Scientific and Cultural Organization
UNITA	National Union for the Total Independence of Angola
UPI	*United Press International*
US	United States
VAT	Value-added tax
WHO	World Health Organization
WTO	World Trade Organization
WWF	World Wildlife Fund

The People's Republic of China

Chapter 1

Introduction

The convocation of the 2008 summer Olympics in Beijing provided a perfect point for observation of China's development, revealing both its strengths and its weaknesses. The Chinese leadership heralded the Games as a major success that confirmed the country's emergence on the world stage as a major force. One could argue that seeking acclaim through such a well-trodden path as hosting the Olympics signalled China's acceptance of the current world order and its desire to be seen as a reliable partner. By contrast, those who fear China's economic rise will represent a threat to the established order will have been awed by the choreography of the opening ceremony, the resources mobilized by the Central state to invest in the infrastructure, the ruthless efficiency with which old neighbourhoods were bulldozed away, the people moved, and the patriotic fervour that the Games produced. This awe of China's rising power was confirmed by the splendour and military might on display for the 60th anniversary of the founding of the People's Republic of China (October 2009). For critics, such displays look like classic cases of mobilization of state resources to promote propagandistic aims. Careful observers of the Olympic opening ceremony will have noticed that there was no history between 1949, the founding of the PRC, and when reforms began in the late 1970s. China's leaders still do not know how to confront their own tumultuous past. The clashes in a number of countries as the Olympic Flame passed through revealed different perceptions about China's performance on human rights protection and its policies in Tibet. The large-scale clashes between Han Chinese and Uighurs in the northwestern province of Xinjiang in mid 2009, which left almost 200 dead, cast doubt on the official view that different ethnic groups lived in harmony.

Whatever one's take on these questions, there is no doubting that economic growth over the last 30 years has radically changed every aspect of China's society and that the country is now a major player on the world stage. As the world's manufacturing hub, not only have Asian economies shifted to integrate with the export-driven economy but also China's economy is intertwined with those of the US, the EU and Japan. There are few, if any, global problems that can be resolved without China's active participation. The economic weight and population size will mean that China's legitimate national interests will have to be taken into account in global forums and its decision-makers will have to learn to shoulder a major role in future global politics and agenda setting.

1

Since the Olympics, the global financial crisis has rained on China's parade but the economy was affected far less than those in the US and Europe, helped to no little extent by a massive stimulus package. GDP growth for 2009 came in at 8.7 per cent, having dropped to 6.2 per cent in the first quarter, still the envy of many, but the lowest growth for many years (9 per cent in 2008; 13 per cent in 2007). China's premier predicted growth of 8 per cent for 2010, the minimum acceptable level, Chinese officials warn, if sufficient numbers of jobs are to be created to prevent social instability. This need to re-emphasize economic growth has caused conflict with other concerns of the Hu Jintao–Wen Jiabao leadership that had committed themselves to more sustainable develop- ment and an emphasis on social equity and sharing the fruits of reform more widely than had been the case in the 1990s. The previous develop- ment model concentrated more exclusively on high growth rates, with preferential treatment for the coastal areas and export-processing enter- prises with the belief that there would be a 'trickle-down' effect which would bring poorer areas of the country and communities into the economic mainstream. As elsewhere in the world, 'trickle-down' economics has not proved as effective as hoped for and the rising inequalities have now become a major political concern.

The institutional structures, development strategy and challenges are dealt with in the following chapters. Four concurrent transitions have shaped the tremendous changes that China has undergone. Hussain (2002) describes three concurrent transitions that have shaped the demands for social welfare policy; we have adapted these to four that help explain the complexity of the transition in China post-Mao. The first is a demographic transition with the shift from low to high life expectancy and from high to low fertility resulting in an ageing popula- tion. China's leaders are gambling that economic growth will mitigate the worst consequences of society growing old before it becomes rich. This is unlikely, however, and the ageing burden will weigh heavily on China's economy and society, which will feel the negative effects of higher dependency ratios and greater expenditures on elderly care. The second and third are economic transitions; one might be termed a 'normal' economic transition, with millions shifting from low-produc- tivity agricultural labour and heavy industry to employment in higher- productivity manufacturing and service sectors. This follows the similar development pattern of other successful countries in East Asia. It has also moved hundreds of millions of people to old and newly constructed urban environments. Parallel to this transition and unlike its East Asian neighbours is the shift from a centrally planned economy to one that is more influenced by market forces. This has brought enormous benefits but also has created new problems of unemployment as inefficient state- owned enterprises (SOEs) have closed down or shed workers. To these three transitions we can add a fourth: the transition from a belief in the paramount importance of the collective in delivering individual benefits and the subordination of individual will and desire to a situation where individual choice, wants and needs dominate. Socialism rests on the principle that the individual can derive more from the collective than he or she can by working alone. Markets place individual choices and their regulation at the centre. Reforms have seen a shift from the collective as the organizing focus to one based on individual choice. This creates a problem for the Chinese Communist Party (CCP) as its ideology is based on the former premise and it has been struggling to offer effective guidance in the new society. The resultant conflicted morality with a raw capitalist outlook under the rhetoric of an existing socialist system presents a problem for any future leaders as there is no civil society that might provide a bond in the event of CCP collapse. For the individual it creates confusion as official rhetoric bears little resemblance to reality as lived on the streets. The result can be distrust of government, an attitude of putting oneself first and a moral vacuum. These four transitions have brought enormous benefits to China's people but also they have created new challenges for China's leaders to resolve. Subsequent chapters deal with the impact of these transitions and changing social norms.

The Chinese leadership has continually confounded those critics who have seen its imminent demise and questioned its ability to deal with the consequences of socio-economic progress. If anybody had said to me when I was studying in China during the last throws of the Cultural Revolution (1966–76) that the country would witness such monumental progress, I would have dismissed them as crazy. Yet, the problems facing China during the next phase of its development are daunting. To do justice to this complexity in an introductory text is no easy matter. In the chapters below I have tried to present some of the complexities of governing the most populous country in the world. The danger is that almost anything one writes seems too simple but too many qualifications tend to confuse as much as clarify. It is a difficult line to tread. I hope that the book will be of interest not only to those beginning to thread their way through the maze of Chinese politics, but also to those who already know the basics as well as to students of comparative politics, transitional regimes, communist and post-communist politics and the politics of development.

There are a number of specific problems with writing an introduction to Chinese politics. First, few have knowledge of the country before starting a university or other programme. China barely figures as a subject on the syllabus at secondary school, although its economic growth is slowly forcing it onto course choices and study of the language is expanding. In addition, the general assumption that the institutions, theories and practices developed within Europe and the US are the norm of politics means that the study of countries such as China are often pushed to the periphery of the syllabus.

Second, China is changing so fast that it is difficult to keep abreast of developments. When I began to study China in the early 1970s, with the exception of the fact that one could hardly visit there, it was an easy task. There was so little information available and very few original Chinese sources. One could be an 'expert' on almost any aspect of China with little effort. Then came reform, China opened up, fieldwork in China became possible and publishing exploded. Now it is hard to keep up in one's own field let alone grappling with areas that are relevant but peripheral. The pace of change and abundance of information set a challenge to highlight what is significant and enduring and to ignore what is irrelevant and ephemeral. China is a maze of intricacies, complexities and contradictions. In 2007 and 2008 the Seventeenth Party Congress and the Eleventh National People's Congress (NPC) met, new leaders were appointed and subsequently a number of new policy initiatives have been launched; others will certainly follow.

Third, all political systems experience a disjuncture between political practice and rhetoric and between social reality and the desires of the political centre. This disjuncture is even greater in China. When the UK Prime Minister or the US President makes a speech about their vision for their respective countries, no one believes that this reflects entirely political and social reality. Such pronouncements provide a policy blueprint or political aspiration that is contested within the bureaucracy and by the local political authorities and society. Such visions represent an ideal type of the kind of society that the leaders would like to see. In the past some observers of the Chinese political scene took what leaders said to represent social reality and saw the political system as geared to implementing the pronouncements of the CCP's General Secretary. Perhaps the fact that China's ruling party still calls itself a *communist party* conjures up a vision of a totalitarian political system that really does function with one heart and mind from top to bottom. Reality is quite different. Contrary to much press reporting and general perceptions, the political centre does not control the system throughout and there is significant deviation from central policy across bureaucracies and at the local level. In some senses, real politics in China is local politics. It is at the local level that problems have to be solved concerning economic policy and social equity. Policy implementation can vary enormously even within one province in accordance with the local distribution of power. This pluralism of policy outcome has led to different analyses of the Chinese state as being essentially predatory, corporatist, clientelist, or bureaucratic-authoritarian. Making sense of this seemingly contradictory country is what makes the study of its politics and society so endlessly fascinating.

This complexity is one of the main themes that runs through the book together with the notion that history and institutions matter. Reform did not begin with a blank slate in 1978 and even the best macroeconomists have to deal with the fact that policy implementation is predicated on responses drawn from historical and cultural repertoires and mediated through political institutions that have been inherited from the Maoist years. The focus is on the politics and governance of China during this process of transition. The use of the term 'governance' moves us beyond the functioning of government institutions and administrative departments to the broader issues of how individual citizens, groups and communities relate to the state. It includes processes and institutions, both formal and informal, which guide and restrain the policy challenges. Included are issues of accountability and transparency and the potential role of actors within civil society and the international community.

Three main themes emerge from the chapters below. First, the economic reform programme has been more consistently successful than many outside observers have predicted over the years, but it is now facing significant challenges. The CCP has shown a remarkable capacity to adapt to the rapidly changing environment, and its performance has looked particularly impressive when compared to developments in post-Soviet Russia. However, the question now arises as to whether the limits of the current development strategy have been reached. Many of the problems now confronting China's leaders are those of delayed reform. Much of the initial success and popular support stemmed from the fact that there were relatively few losers and those who did lose out were politically marginalized. It is now apparent that as reform moves to the next stage and China integrates further into the world economy, there will be significant losers, including those workers and institutions that have formed the core of the CCP socialist system. To date, the shake-up of the state-owned sector and the resultant job losses have not led to a major challenge to CCP rule. The easy reforms have been completed and China has benefited enormously from a process of catching up with its East Asian neighbours. The Chinese leadership has now to deal with ensuring that development is sustainable, that environmental damage does not erode the economic gains and that institutional adaptation can keep pace with changes elsewhere in the system.

Muddling through might no longer be sufficient. Most of the problems and challenges stem from inadequacies in the system of governance. Corruption is present at all levels of government, has increased greatly in scale under reforms and is fuelled by the lack of budget transparency and the close relationship between political power and economic actors. Attempts to improve the environment are undermined by the skewed incentives for local government agencies and the weakness of the environmental watchdogs. Governance is also a problem in the commercial sector where corporate governance is poor and one senior reform economist described China's nascent stock markets as 'casinos'. None of these problems is insuperable but does require the CCP to accept greater oversight of its activities by independent organizations and society. To date, it has been reticent to allow this. While state dominance of the economy has declined significantly, the private sector is still treated as second-class, finding it difficult to obtain the necessary financing to expand operations. This is important as the non-state sector has been the major provider of jobs in recent years. The service sector needs to expand but this requires a significant shift in resources to invest in education. Without this, China will suffer from a continual shortage of skilled labour that will leave much of the country on the lower rungs of the production chain and it will not be able to follow the development trajectories of Japan, South Korea and Taiwan. While most analysts focus on the question of state enterprise reform, this is a temporary problem and a political problem for the CCP given its traditional power base and privileging of an urban proletarian elite over other workers and farmers. The real challenge for the CCP remains as always in the countryside. Here it needs to resolve the problem of land management and ownership.

Second, China, like many transitional economies, has not been able to deal well with the social transition, and the development of social policy has lagged badly behind economic development. In major part, this derives from the CCP's bias towards what it sees as productive forces, and the health and education level of its population are not factored in sufficiently. Yet failure to tackle social policy effectively could lead to undermining the progress made with economic reforms. The demographics of China, while currently favourable, will become problematic over the next 10–15 years. Unless China's leaders are able to get to grips with pension and other welfare reforms, the economic advancement for many in this generation could be undone in the next by an unaffordable welfare burden. The outbreak of SARS in 2002–03 and the fear that it might spread to the rural areas highlighted the weakness of the health infrastructure for the countryside.

China's new leaders must also deal with the distribution of the benefits of reform. One distinctive feature of China's development in comparison with other East Asian polities is its toleration and even encouragement of inequality as a driving force for change. The development strategy has favoured the coast over the inland areas, the urban over the rural, and male over female. The inability to develop the hinterland will act as a brake on economic growth as it will limit the size of the domestic market; thus, the campaigns to 'Develop the West' and 'Revive the Northeast'. It will also provide the potential for social conflict as the politics of resentment may arise. The urban bias of current policy needs to be changed and the structural impediments that block rural dwellers from benefiting fully from the reforms need to be removed. While women have enjoyed the general benefits of reform, more freedom of choice and rising prosperity, they have been disfavoured by comparison with men. They have been encouraged to retire early, are the first to be laid off from SOEs, bear the brunt of the family-planning programme, and shoulder a disproportionate amount of the rural labour. It is not surprising that women have no effective representation in the political system.

The third theme is that while there has been substantial adaptation of institutions, there has been insufficient genuine political reform. New institutions have been set up to manage the new economy and a legal system has been revived and extended to preside over it. Social organizations with varying degrees of autonomy have been established to meet people's material and leisure needs and, to a much lesser extent, their spiritual ones. However, with the exception of the village election programme, little has been done to make the system more accountable. The CCP still rules as an autocratic elite often out of touch with the consequences of its own economic policies. As good Marxists these elite should recognize that substantive change in the economic base must impact on the political superstructure. The truth is that Marx is irrelevant to their visions of the political future and those who may read more liberal tracts on the need for checks, balances and accountability keep quiet for fear of being branded a 'bourgeois liberal'. By default, theories of authoritarianism hold sway. At the local level, at its worst this system can lead to rule by corrupt, despotic cabals who see the local population merely as a source of revenue. The 2009 arrest in Chongqing, a major municipality in southwest China, of some 2000 people for gang-related activities raised alarm bells about the penetration of gangs into the local government and power elite. Not only were there three billionaires in the group but also some 50 government officials, six district police chiefs and several who were elected deputies to the local branch of the people's congress. Without further reform, it is hard to see such a system providing the kind of stability that will produce long-term economic growth.

Chapter 2

Diversity within Unity

Some years ago, I was in a jeep driving down a mountain road in rural Sichuan and was held up by a long queue of traffic meandering down the hill to a new bridge that was being dedicated. Getting out of the jeep I wandered down to the bridge to witness an elaborate ceremony complete with the lighting of incense and various actions to ward off the evil spirits. Somewhat facetiously, I began to ask those waiting what the Communist Party must think about this ceremony as it clearly represented an example of 'superstitious practice' so soundly denounced during the Cultural Revolution (1976–77) and still denounced today, albeit with less severity. I was greeted with puzzled faces before one person replied that the man in the exotic robes leading the ceremony *was* the party secretary. As the most important person in the village, he had no choice but to dedicate a new bridge that would link it to the world outside and bring greater wealth.

The event set me thinking about the relationship between the party, the state and society and between China's tradition and modernity. Did the party secretary believe in the ceremony and its power to conjure up good spirits to protect the bridge or was he simply going through the motions to increase credibility among the local population? Was the party secretary importing the power of the party into the village community or bringing heterodox beliefs into the party or both? The traditional nature of the ceremony contrasted with the objective of building the bridge that would integrate the local community with the world outside. The bridge provided the link to the market that is the driving force for development in the post-Mao years. Such small events are daily occurrences throughout rural and urban China and they cause us to question any notion of China as a monolith. China comprises a patchwork of local cultures and histories that the Chinese Communist Party (CCP) and its nationalist and imperial predecessors have tried to weld into a unitary entity. While the CCP may have tried to penetrate society more thoroughly than its predecessors, the last 30 years have revealed the residual power of local cultures.

More recently, I was walking out of the tranquillity of the cradle of the communist revolution in Yan'an, where Mao had moved his red army in the late 1930s, only to be besieged by the trinket sellers who are the products of China's economic reform; from Mao Zedong's China to Deng Xiaoping's in a few paces. The market responds to the desires of consumers rather than to those of communist ideologues, something

8

clearly seen by the books on sale. While those sold inside Yan'an, such as *Mao Zedong Enters Yan'an*, tell the official story of the revolution, the books on sale outside, often under the counter, tell a different tale. They range from Mao Zedong's notorious womanizing, through the inner secrets of who destroyed whom in the party's new headquarters (Zhongnanhai in Beijing), the corruption of a former mayor of Beijing, to unofficial biographies of former general secretaries, Hu Yaobang and Zhao Ziyang. These are the CCP's hidden histories, those the conservative party veterans do not want their people to know about, but they are the ones that the people with interest and money want to buy. Rather than a revolutionary world full of selfless heroes, they tell stories of betrayal, corruption, and greed. Whose history, whose politics? This warns us not to take official pronouncements at face value but to peer behind the public façade to discover the reality of how the Chinese polity really works.

This chapter and subsequent ones seek to introduce the reader to the diversity of China, its land and its peoples, and how CCP policy since 1949 has affected them.

A land of diversity

As the two anecdotes reveal, China is a very complex land where multiple realities are operating beneath a façade of a unitary nation-state. However, this does not mean as some have claimed that China may fall apart into its regional components as a result of the reforms (Segal, 1994) or that a *de facto* federalist structure is emerging (Wang, 1995). Rather we should be careful about any generalization we make and be aware that the same policy will impact on different areas and different groups in China in a variety of ways, sometimes with unexpected results.

China's land, climate and peoples exhibit broad diversity. China's land mass is roughly equal to that of the USA (9.6 million square km) but is home to a population of around 1.32 billion (just over four times that of the USA), meaning that every fifth child is born in China. However, this population is not spread evenly across the land and, while the images of teeming cities full to bursting are correct, there are massive expanses of China where one can roam the hills or desert for days and barely see a soul. While the population density is 622 per sq. km. for the country as a whole, the figure is over 2000 per km^2. for the eastern coastal regions and under 100 per km^2 for the far Western provinces (Donald and Benewick, 2005, p. 24).

This population spread has always been the case with the predominantly peasant population concentrated along the river deltas and basins of the east, providing the bodies for the development of the mega-cities of Shanghai, Tianjin, Beijing, and further west, Chongqing (see map). By contrast the high Tibetan-Qinghai plateau is home to a sparse, scattered population engaged in pastoral activities. The plateau lies some 4000 meters above sea level and occupies a full 20 per cent of China's land mass. Radiating out from the plateau are the major rivers of China, Southeast Asia and the Asian sub-continent. The Yangzi, Yellow, Mekong, Red, Ganges, and the Brahmaputra all find their source here on this desolate plateau. Beyond the plateau there is a series of smaller descending plateaus and basins that eventually give way to the major plains of the east such as the Yangzi Delta, the North China Plain and the Northeast (Manchuria) Plain.

The huge oceans to the east, the plateau to the west and the surrounding mountain ranges have protected China throughout its history. This combined with the continuation of some form of the Chinese state over two millennia contributed to an insular attitude to alternative modes of thought and an ethnocentrism that the dominant Han Chinese felt was justified by the heritage to which they were the unique heirs. This insularity is reflected by the name of China itself, *Zhongguo*, which literally means the middle or 'central' kingdom. Yet even here there have been variations. China has witnessed periods of extensive dealings with foreigners such as in the Han (205 BC–AD 220) and the Tang (AD 618–907) dynasties. These were periods of extensive trading when foreign products were well received in China and when Chinese goods reached far-flung corners of the globe. This trade was even accompanied by the influx of foreign systems of thought. Most noticeable was the increasing influence of Buddhism, which arrived from India from the late Han period onwards. The later Qing period (AD 1644–1911), despite some attempts to keep foreigners out, and the Republican period (1911–49) were both influenced by foreign trade and the influx of new ideas. The Taiping Rebellion (1850–64) with its strange mix of half-baked Christianity, iconoclasm and traditional notions of peasant rebellion mounted a major challenge to Confucian orthodoxy (Spence, 1996). The May Fourth Movement (1915–19), in part a response to the decision to cede the German concession of Shandong to Japan following the First World War, also witnessed a major attack on the Confucian tradition and revealed an intellectual fascination with a whole host of foreign ideas ranging from liberalism to Marxism to anarchism (Chow, 1960). Indeed, during the reform period from the late 1970s, the CCP has tried to make use of the more cosmopolitan trading of China's coastal regions as a key element in its economic programmes. Policy has favoured a development strategy that relies heavily on coastal trade and investment by revitalizing historic links with the overseas Chinese communities in Southeast Asia and beyond.

Given that China has such an expansive and varied land-mass, it will come as no surprise that there is enormous climatic variation, much more so for the winters rather than the summers. While most of the country lies in the temperate zone, there are wide variations of climate. The Northeast freezes, with temperatures dropping as low as minus 25–30 degrees centigrade, and even the capital Beijing can still get the occasional winter day of minus 10–15 degrees, although the average temperature for January hovers just a few degrees below zero. By contrast, Kunming in the Southwest province of Yunnan is known as the city of eternal spring, Guangzhou (Guangdong) enjoys winters with around 15 degrees and the island of Hainan has a balmy tropical climate. This north–south climatic divide led the CCP to decree that south of the Yangzi River public buildings would not be heated in winter. I have never been so cold in my life as in the winter of 1976–77 when studying at Nanjing University just south of the Yangzi River. We used to look forward to occasional trips across the Yangzi by ferry to sit in the local post office north of the river that was allowed heating. Rising affluence has changed this, with those now able to afford heating able to purchase it as they please, as long as supplies are available.

The forces of nature have not been tamed as fully as in more advanced countries, and this has resulted in different problems. Rainfall is variable and each summer one is treated to the news that while certain areas have been subjected to flooding (Jiangxi, Zhejiang, Hunan, Jiangsu) other areas are suffering from severe drought (Hebei, Henan, Shanxi); people refer to 'north – drought, south – floods'. South China depends on the vagaries of the monsoon for its rainfall whereas most of the North and West of China do not receive its effects. The severity and diversity of these problems may be illustrated by the fact that in 1981 millions of people in north-central China faced quite severe food shortages because of extensive drought; in the western province of Sichuan, 1.5 million people lost their homes because of floods. The water shortages of the North have been exaggerated by the industrial development and urbanization of recent years and the water table of the North China Plain has been dropping precipitously. This has led to the ambitious government programme to divert water from the abundant rivers of the South to the North. This will provide some relief but not enough and China needs to adopt policies that will price water more realistically and that will promote water conservation.

These climatic and topographic variations have caused a rather varied environment for agricultural production. It is only in the areas around the Yangzi River and the South that the flooded paddy fields are commonplace. In fact, most of China is dependent on dry-field cropping of wheat and millet. The staple for most in the North is noodles and steamed bread rather than the rice that many associate with being

Chinese. This dependence on staple grains has meant that traditionally the overwhelming majority of China's population has settled along the fertile plains and basins that provide suitable arable land. By contrast the grasslands of Inner Mongolia and Ningxia, the Far Northwest and Tibet are home to livestock with vast stretches of land for grazing. The periphery in the Northeast and Southwest is home to China's main remaining forest cover. This forest cover has been declining rapidly, it now covers only 14 per cent of the land-mass, and perhaps as much as 90 per cent of the remaining coverage is threatened. The current coverage is considered insufficient for economic needs and for everyday use. While the government often blames local practices such as swidden (slash and burn) agriculture in Southwest China for the decline in the remaining forests and the subsequent soil erosion and flooding, it is clear that the major culprit in recent times has been the government itself through its massive forestry industry. Although the authorities have moved aggressively to cut down on illegal logging, the practice continues but on a much smaller scale. One unexpected consequence of the crackdown has been the intensification of logging in neighbouring countries in order to meet Chinese demand. With the decline of forest cover and the expansion of arable land and urbanization, there has been a decline in China's great biodiversity and wildlife. Animals such as elephants, tigers and the golden monkey are to be found only in small parts of remote Yunnan, while the giant panda can be found only in declining numbers in a few Sichuan reserves.

These more remote areas are home to most of China's 55 recognized national minorities (there were 400 to 500 applications to be recognized, Blum, 2000, p. 74). While these minorities comprise less than 10 per cent of China's total population (still around 100 million), the remainder being the Han Chinese, they occupy over 60 per cent of the total land-mass. This includes the very sensitive border areas of China including the Xinjiang, Tibet, Inner Mongolia, and Guangxi Zhuang Autonomous Regions that touch against Russia, Mongolia, Kazakhstan, Kyrgyzstan, Tajikistan, Afghanistan, Pakistan, India, Nepal, Bhutan, Myanmar, and Vietnam. Yunnan, home to 25 minorities, borders on Myanmar, Laos, and Vietnam. China has had difficult relations with virtually all of these countries over time. These peripheral areas have always been important to Chinese security concerns and provide a buffer zone to protect the 'Han-core' from possible invaders. Beijing's concern about these areas is increased by the fact that they possess enormous natural resources and they are the last areas into which China's growing population can expand (Grunfeld, 1985).

This concern with security from external threat explains in part why Beijing is so concerned with consolidating its rule over the border areas and has adopted various policies to encourage more Han to move into them so that they form the majority population group in many such areas. However, regions such as Tibet and Xinjiang have also been the site of considerable domestic opposition to CCP rule and tensions have increased because of the settlement policies. Both have experienced sporadic resistance to Beijing's rule and both are viewed with suspicion by the Centre. In Tibet, many still pledge their allegiance to the exiled Dalai Lama, who fled to India in 1959 after the People's Liberation Army (PLA) crushed the Tibetan revolt. In March 2008, on the forty-ninth anniversary of the failed 1959 uprising against CCP rule, a major riot broke out in Tibet with much of the violence directed against Han people. While the CCP blamed the unrest on the exiled supporters of the Dalai Lama, it seemed to be sparked by the economic inequality that has developed between local Tibetans and Han and other outsiders under reforms. In Xinjiang, Beijing fears that people might forge links with radical Islamic groups that have been more active since the break-up of the Soviet Union. July 2009 witnessed ethnic unrest in the province and again Beijing blamed the situation on groups in exile. Until the CCP develops policies that allow greater religious freedom and permit the spoils of economic growth to be distributed more equitably to the local communities, the threat of unrest will persist. The CCP has adopted a paternalistic, not to say patronizing, attitude to these communities. Before the demonstrations in Tibet, at the annual NPC meeting, the party secretary of Tibet stated that 'The Communist Party is like the parent to the Tibetan people, and it is always considerate about what the children need'. He also noted that the central party committee is the 'real Buddha for Tibetans' (Reuters, 2 March 2007).

However, the Tibetans (5.4 million) and the Uighurs (8.4 million), the main ethnic group in Xinjiang, are not united groups internally. With respect to Tibet, the CCP has had some success in trying to circumvent the authority of the Dalai Lama by developing local Buddhist leaders more sympathetic to Beijing. The Panchen Lama, the second most important religious leader, did not flee to India and was used by Beijing to mediate with Buddhist groups domestically. However, the former Panchen's death in 1989 and the debacle of finding a successor combined with the heavy hand of repression from the late 1980s seem to have undermined Beijing's attempts to build Tibetan loyalty. A further blow to Beijing came in December 1999 when the young religious leader who the CCP was grooming to mediate on its behalf with the Tibetan community fled to join the Dalai Lama in India.

The tension between Han and non-Han peoples is a legitimate topic for discussion in China; indeed it was legitimated by Mao in 1956 when he referred to it as one of the Ten Great Relationships that marked the post-1949 political landscape. However, in some cases it is the tensions between the different minorities that have their own cultural and historical origins which are more important. In the border areas of Yunnan, some villagers will never have come across Han Chinese. In fact, many minorities in Yunnan such as the Bai (1.9 million), Miao (8.9 million), and Hani (1.4 million) are more likely to complain about the way the Yi (7.8 million) dominate the ethnic minorities' administrative networks in the province. This, they feel, enables the Yi to dispense a disproportionate amount of largesse to their own group.

Many of the ethnic groups living in the Yunnan border region are closely related to groups in Myanmar, Laos and Vietnam and indeed the border is quite porous and seems to have become more so since the reforms began. Cross-border trade and work is common. While the main roads have border posts and each village has a border office, there is little attempt to stop this casual movement. In the village of Mengla you can see the hills of Myanmar across the fields and the border is secondary to economic activity for many. The local head of the village had a four-wheel drive Toyota jeep with Thai number-plates, indicating the extent of his business travels. When asked about whether he needed to affix Yunnan plates to the car, he replied that as he had been head of the border patrols and knew the local police he could drive wherever he needed to go in Yunnan with the Thai plates and, besides, much of his work was over the border. His optimism was not entirely justified as at least once he was stopped by the police on his way to the provincial capital of Kunming. Yet, even in such a remote point, decisions made far away in Beijing can exert an enormous impact on the local economy [see Box 2.1].

Box 2.1: Decisions Taken on High Can Reach the Farthest Corners

A walk up the mountains to the remote regions above Yunnan province's Mengla is like travelling back in time. A bumpy dirt road gives way to narrow, slippery paths that wind up the steep inclines. Life in these villages – among the 200,000 across China that still lack roads – has changed little over the past 50 years. These hills are inhabited by the Hani, a minority people bypassed by reforms. Yet, in the mid 1990s, the main village had experienced a mini-economic boom when it became a main transit point for the shipment of bauxite brought over the border from Myanmar for refining on the Chinese side. This had led to a widening of the village square, the setting up of a number of roadside restaurants, a Karaoke bar and a brothel as well as a couple of places to stay. It looked as if this business would finally bring the village out of poverty. However, after a couple of years, Beijing decided that such economic activities entailing cross-border movements might endanger its security concerns. As a result the shipments stopped, the road emptied, the restaurant customers dwindled, and the prostitutes had to limit themselves to serving the needs of the local border patrol.

Many of the minorities, despite their special status, are for all intents and purposes assimilated. This is the case with China's two largest minorities, the Zhuang (16.2 million) and the Manchu (10.7 million) and to a lesser extent with the Muslim Hui (9.8 million). The Zhuang live primarily in the Guangxi Zhuang Autonomous Region that borders on Vietnam. Despite their distinctive Dai language, a language common to a number of other groups in the Southwest, they have effectively adopted a Han lifestyle. It was the Manchus who established the Qing dynasty (AD 1644–1911) and were the last imperial rulers before the Republic was established in 1911. Many have suggested that their survival as imperial rulers derived from the Sinification of their practices. While a Manchu language survives, it is used by very few. The Hui are an interesting group with the largest concentration in the Northwest (the Ningxia-Hui Autonomous Region) but they also live in many cities such as Xi'an (Shaanxi), Kunming (Yunnan) and even in Beijing. They speak the national language (Mandarin or *guoyu*) and are indistinguishable from their Han neighbours except for their cuisine and worship at the mosque.

Last but not least, we should note that the broad classification of Han Chinese conceals great diversity within the group itself. Even the national language is a fairly recent construct and many of the Han Chinese actually speak other languages. These are more commonly referred to as dialects as the written script is the same. In reality they can be as different as English and German. The national language is derived from the language spoken around Beijing. The CCP as a part of its drive to bring unity and to increase literacy both simplified the written characters and promoted the use of the national language in schools and through radio and television. As a result, those who have enjoyed basic schooling can speak some of the national language. Whenever I am in non-Han villages one of the easiest ways for communication is to seek out school-age children and to ask them to act as interpreters for their parents and grandparents, many of whom may speak only a few words of the national language at best. In one village, a couple of hours' bike ride from the tourist destination of Yangshuo, I chatted with one of the village elders through his grandson as interpreter. He was particularly interested in trying foreign cigarettes. My colleague offered him one that he finished in one puff and dismissively discarded; not a patch on his home-grown tobacco, a whiff of which would seriously damage your health. He seemed blasé in the presence of foreigners, unusual at the time. I asked him if many foreigners came to the village. He thought for a second, drew on his cigarette and replied in a matter-of-fact tone, 'Oh yes, one came here about forty years ago.'

The home language even for many Han is quite distinct, with about 30 per cent (some 350 million) speaking something other than the national language at home. In Guangdong the language is Cantonese (*yue*) while *Minnan* is spoken in various dialects throughout Fujian, *Gan* is spoken in Jiangxi and *Wu* in Shanghai. Before communications improved it is said that travelling up the Yangzi Valley one would have to change languages at each county town. This may be apocryphal but it indicates how fragmented local Chinese society was until the twentieth century. An important part of the nation-building process for the CCP has therefore been to build a common language. In this it has been fairly successful with, at least, the written script understood by all those who are literate. The official figures for 2008 (persons over 15 years of age) claim that 92.2 per cent of the population is literate, with Beijing leading the way at 96.9 per cent and Tibet bringing up the rear at 62.2 per cent. Nationally, the illiteracy rate among men is 4.0 per cent and among women 11.5 per cent. For those who cannot read there has been a continual bombardment of officially approved news through radio and television. In the Cultural Revolution, there were even the communal loudspeakers that dictated the pace of one's life from when one woke up until one went to sleep. I remember lying in bed one morning trying to work out what was different and why I felt so relaxed before I realized that someone had cut the wires on the campus speakers. It was bliss to lie in bed and not listen to the blare of early morning wake-up routines and homage to the 'Great Leader', Mao Zedong.

So long as the leadership speaks with one voice this system has been remarkably successful in providing acceptance for the official narrative. In 1991 I was visiting relatives in Shashi, a town of some 3 million inhabitants, a few hours up the Yangzi from Wuhan. They were considered free-thinking liberals in Shashi and thus I was surprised when we talked of the 1989 student-led demonstrations in Beijing and they referred to them as chaos and a counterrevolutionary uprising rather than using the milder phrases of liberals in Beijing. When I asked them how they knew this, they replied that it was true because they had read about it in the *People's Daily*, the CCP's official media organ, and seen it on Central Television. In the same way, the CCP was successful in getting most of its citizens to believe that the NATO bombing of the Chinese Embassy in Yugoslavia in May 1999 had been a deliberate act of provocation by the USA. The use of the media to build up patriotic sentiment at the time of the Olympics in the summer of 2008 was another example of how effective the media can be. However, the rise of new media provides China's citizens with alternative information sources and presents the old propaganda system with a new challenge (see Box 2.2). Blogs and instant messaging have become commonplace and many do not carry approved information or analysis. Nationalists have used new media to push the leadership to undertake sterner policy positions towards Japan and the US than it may have done otherwise. In response the CCP has employed an army of people to monitor the internet and also to write pro-party messages and to attempt to guide discussion. This latter group has been ridiculed as the '50-cent party' for the payment they receive for each pro-government posting.

The aforementioned linguistic affiliations and local ties have, if anything, strengthened with the reforms. Within the locality these ties are reinforced by various local festivities and deities and even, for many, by the local cuisine. There is a clear cultural divide between the North

---

Box 2.2: SARS and the Media

The outbreak of SARS in 2002–03 reveals the problems that the CCP has in controlling the message but also reveals how quickly the propaganda system can adapt to new challenges. While some thought that the experience might lead to a shift in official reporting, as they did when the major Sichuan earthquake struck in 2008, there is little evidence of a systemic shift. In January 2003, initial reporting of a new disease by Guangdong authorities ridiculed the idea that there was a problem and a February press conference took the same view. Earlier, provincial health authorities in Guangzhou had informed doctors of a new disease but requested that the public not be informed. It was instant messaging that forced the provincial leadership to make some kind of public acknowledgement. According to Guangdong Mobile the message 'There is a fatal flu in Guangzhou' was sent over 120 million times in the space of three days. Officials responded that there was a disease but that it was completely under control. It wasn't. This was the regular pattern. Eventually, a retired army doctor, irate at the cover-up tried to notify the Chinese press of the problem and when unsuccessful passed the information to foreign outlets. The international coverage made it impossible for the government to maintain the stance that there was a small problem but basically everything was under control. Belatedly on 20 April a press conference was held that appeared to signal a significant change in government attitude and openness. However, the traditional propaganda system soon moved into gear with a new campaign to mobilize people's support for the struggle against SARS while bringing in restrictions on reporting. This was more familiar ground and the media was filled with patriotic accounts of individuals struggling against heroic odds and making personal sacrifices to defeat SARS, including patriotic ditties such as 'Angels in White Coats'. Traditional CCP language now took over and sure enough, on 1 May, Hu Jintao declared that China was engaged in a 'people's war' against SARS for which the 'masses' should be mobilized. Constraints on the media were soon put back in place and the limited openness around SARS did not spread to other areas. Publications were requested to stop reporting on sensitive issues and media outlets and academics were warned not to analyse how government had dealt with SARS. Some of those who had reported honestly came in for criticism and official rebuke.

Source: Saich, 2006.

of the country and the South. The southern parts of China were effectively integrated into China in only the later part of the Song Dynasty (AD 960–1279, Blum, 2000, p. 82). The North is the political capital and operates under a more bureaucratic culture while the South represents the more open, cosmopolitan trading culture. The rise of a nationalist discourse in the mid 1990s and anti-American tracts such as *The China That Can Say No* (Song et al., 1996) and *Behind the Scene of Demonizing China* (Li et al., 1996) also led to a rise in publications that stressed local identity and cultural essence. Books appeared on what it is to be Shanghainese or Sichuanese and even related local cooking to identity. The spicy food of Sichuan and the chilly taste of Hunan cooking contrast markedly with the fish and steamed food of Guangdong or Shanghai, or the noodle soups of Shaanxi. Hunan even had Mao Zedong patronize the phrase that you could not be a revolutionary if you could not eat peppery food.

It is also in the South that lineage and clan play an important role in rural life, much more important than in the North. In many villages I have visited in the South, large lineage halls have been restored or built anew and clearly form the most important organizing point for political and socio-economic exchange. This re-emergence of more overt traditional power structures has made the implementation of party rule more difficult. In many villages the party group is ineffective and often where effective the party secretary and lineage head are one and the same. A number of officials involved with the programme to introduce direct elections into China's villages complained that the election is decided by the most important lineage and there is little the party or the higher-level administrative authorities can do to alter this.

These local identities are reinforced by religious practice and customs. While China is officially an atheist country, the CCP has had no choice but to tolerate religious practice so long as it is not seen as a challenge to state power. The CCP has adopted a series of secular official celebrations that mark key dates of the revolution or communist tradition (such as 1 October – National Day or 1 May – International Labour Day) but the most important festivals have to do with Chinese tradition (Chinese New Year – a week in January or February or Qing Ming, grave sweeping – early April) and local custom. Local religious worship and traditional practices have blossomed since the reforms began but organized religion that stresses an allegiance beyond the CCP is viewed with suspicion and usually repressed. This is the case not only with Tibetan Buddhism because of the presence of the Tibetan government-in-exile under the leadership of the Dalai Lama but also with Christianity. Not surprisingly it is difficult to get a number of how many people practise these religions. Official statistics estimate around 100 million religious believers but a 2007 survey by Shanghai University of 4500 respondents found 31.4 per cent declared themselves as religious, which would translate into some 300 million people nationwide. Most of these were Buddhists, Taoists or believers in a variety of local deities. In fact, there is a clear tendency among many of the new urban elites to profess Buddhist beliefs and it seems that the numbers of Christians on university campuses is increasing. The survey found 12 per cent declared themselves to be Christian, which would translate into 40 million believers (http://news.bbc.co.uk/2/hi/asia-pacific/ 6337627.stm). Donald and Benewick (2005, p. 84) cite 18 million registered Protestant Christians and 12 million Catholics (including those in the underground churches). They also estimate 100 million Buddhists. The CCP refuses to recognize the authority of the Catholic Church and cracks down hard on those who profess allegiance, often arresting priests who accept the Vatican's authority. Instead, practising Catholics are required to belong to the Chinese Catholic Patriotic Association, an organization that follows the ranks and salary scales of the state administrative system. CCP suspicion of Christianity is compounded by the association of the missionaries with imperialism before 1949. As a result all missionary activity is banned in China but it is not very hard to find active missionaries in both the cities and the countryside. The number may exceed 10,000 and there is a large underground trade in bibles. Some missionaries have been involved in rural development projects and the local authorities have tolerated their work as long as they do not become too public with their beliefs.

Buddhism is widespread, with probably in excess of 100 million practitioners. There are three main variants: Tibetan Buddhism (with four major sects), Theravada Buddhism and a mixture of Chinese folk traditions and Buddhism. However, practitioners may also follow another religion, such as Daoism, thus making it difficult to assess the true numbers (Blum, 2000, p. 88). Figures are similarly inexact concerning followers of Daoism and folk religion but are in the realm of 250 million (Donald and Benewick, 2005, p. 84). The CCP's attitude towards local religion is also ambivalent. It denounces what it sees as 'superstitious' practices and in the Cultural Revolution it destroyed not only places of worship but also sought to stamp out practices such as ancestor worship and fortune telling. However, unless there is a perceived political threat, it now tolerates a wide range of locally based religious worship. In fact, there has been a debate about the value of belief within the CCP and in recent years a more positive view has been apparent.

Some of these local practices can be quite striking. In Yunnan, I have watched a video of the exorcism of spirits that had possessed the body of a young, female researcher from the Yunnan Academy of Social Sciences and have witnessed ceremonies to welcome young men into manhood [see Box 2.3]. The young anthropologist in the video had been carrying out research in a remote mountain area and the village elder took pity on her when she was about to return to the city possessed by a bad spirit. Normally, he did not care about city folk and did not mind them carrying evil spirits away. He felt that she was a good person and as a result was willing personally to oversee the lengthy process to exorcise the evil spirits before allowing her to return.

The local CCP party has to make accommodation for these religious practices. Perhaps this is seen best in those areas where overseas Chinese investment has been vital to local economic health and where these investors have allied with the local population to demand the restoration of local lineage houses or temples. In Wuxi, overseas Chinese have donated money to erect an enormous gold leaf Buddha that looks over the local lake. It is the dominant site of the locality. However, it was not constructed without controversy. The local propaganda bureau set the building of the Buddha as one of the three great tasks for completion in 1997, one of the other tasks being to strive to ensure the successful return of Hong Kong to Chinese sovereignty. This caused uproar when reported to the Propa-

---

Box 2.3: The Party, Religion and Worship

In one mountain village, I witnessed the performance of a traditional ceremony to welcome a young man into adulthood. At the entrance to the village I was met by a middle-aged man who introduced himself as the local party secretary and before exiting he guided me to where the performance would take place. Shortly, the ritual began with an elaborate demonstration in front of the boy who was about to be initiated. The ritual was led by a man draped in a tiger skin and wearing a crucifix and who occasionally slipped into a language that none could understand. The fact that only he could speak this language added to his power among the village community. After a few minutes, I recognized the man as the village party secretary who had greeted me; a clear example of the fusion of religious and political power at the local level. I also slowly recognized that the strange language into which he occasionally lapsed resembled Latin and I was later informed that in the past Jesuits had been active in the village, although they had now gone and not returned. Indeed, while Jesuits have been active in some villages in rural Yunnan, the Protestants seem to have been more successful among non-Han groups in recent years. We then joined a parade to where the young boy would complete his ritual. At one point, all passers were challenged at spear point to make a gift. The final part of the ceremony entailed the boy climbing onto a small tower perhaps some 10 feet high. Once on the tower, he had to clasp his hands together and fall backward off the tower to be caught by his colleagues in a large blanket. When unwrapped, if his hands were still clasped, he had passed into manhood. Fortunately they were. We were told that in the past the fall had been much more arduous, with the young men rolling backwards down a hill that was a couple of hundred feet high. This sanitized version was much safer.

ganda Department in Beijing, which claimed that the erection of a Buddha representing a backward superstition could in no way be equated with the 'glorious task' of regaining sovereignty over Hong Kong. The Wuxi party authorities were forced to withdraw it from the glorious three tasks for 1997, but the Buddha was finished the next year!

Should, however, traditional practices link up across localities and be perceived as a threat, the CCP will move swiftly to crack down. This was the case with a *qigong* (a type of exercise and breathing regime) related sect called the *Falungong* (Skills of the Wheel of Law) that came to prominence after a large gathering of its followers surrounded the party headquarters in Beijing in April 1999 following criticism of its organization. This woke up China's senior leaders to the potential of such faith-based movements to inspire loyalty. This concern and the humiliation that senior leaders felt at being caught by surprise led to a draconian crackdown on the organization and a subsequent campaign to discredit it as a superstitious cult. Thousands of its members have been arrested and it has also led to the investigation of a number of similar organizations.

The impact of CCP policy

The CCP's vision of a modern state and its policies have had a marked impact on the physical structure of towns and countryside as well as on people's lives. The CCP came to power in 1949 with a vision of the future which was inspired by that of the Soviet Union. To be modern was to be urban, industrial and with production socialized. The CCP despised the private sphere, and policy through the early-1950s was to eradicate what remained of private industry in the urban areas. Yet, at the same time, there was a suspicion of the cities as carriers of indolence, corruption, and other traits that ran against the perceived revolutionary heritage.

The effects of post-1949 CCP policy produced a uniform, drab urban environment. With the exception of a few cities, such as Beijing, Xi'an and Pingyao that have an imperial heritage or Shanghai with its conflu-ence of colonial styles, virtually all other cities have adopted the dour, grey architecture of the Soviet era. City walls in many cities, even including much of Beijing, were ripped down to make way for the new, wider roads and work-unit apartment blocks. Those who favoured urban planning that would have afforded greater protection to China's historical heritage were often drowned out by those who favoured the Soviet-style plan. In the anti-rightist campaign of the 1950s and the Cultural Revolution, defenders were denounced for their bourgeois and/or feudal thinking. Much of what remained of the old cities was torn down to accommodate the building boom of the 1990s. Some even calculated that more of old Beijing was lost to the real estate developer in the 1990s than in any other decade that century, which included the Cultural Revolution, Japanese invasion and civil war.

The desire rapidly to build up the industrial base also had a major impact on the urban landscape as the CCP sought to develop the heavy industrial sector. Smokestack factories became a familiar part of many cities, with little notion of zoning and protection of green areas. Scenes of the new urban industrial China were proudly displayed on the propaganda posters of the time. Even depictions of rural China would include a smoking chimneystack. In part the industrialization of the First Five-Year Plan (1953–57) built on the inheritance of the past. The Northeast became the industrial powerhouse with its legacy from Japanese control of Manchuria with chemicals, steel, and coal prominent. This made the urban Northeast one of the privileged areas of the Maoist period, privilege that has steadily eroded since reforms were introduced from 1978.

The second main area for heavy industrial development was Sichuan, especially Chongqing. This had two origins. First, the Guomindang (GMD; the Nationalist Party with which the CCP fought two civil wars to gain power) with its retreat to Chongqing after the Japanese invasion of 1937, moved significant industry to the Southwest. This inheritance was built upon by the CCP with the post-1949 policy to industrialize the hinterland as well as security concerns. Following the Sino-Soviet split (1960), Mao became increasingly concerned about war with the Soviets and even the possibility of nuclear conflict. This led to the policy to develop the industrial 'third front' that was based in Sichuan and the further Southwest and built on earlier investment in the Northwest (Naughton, 1988, pp. 351–86). There was a massive redeployment of investment, almost 50 per cent, from the mid 1960s to the mid 1970s to build an industrial base and nuclear facility that could resist Soviet attack. It provided Sichuan and Chongqing with significant problems of outdated industry in the 1990s.

In the countryside the CCP first abolished the old landlord system and, as a result of peasant expectations and pre-1949 policy, land reform was carried out with land redistributed to the household. However, by the mid 1950s steps were taken towards collectivization in order for the state to extract the funds necessary to feed its industrialization programme. The division of China into 50,000 rural communes brought uniformity to political administration in the countryside that lasted until the early-1980s when they were dismantled and a return of household farming was promoted. The promotion of the communes brought a far greater uniformity to the visual impression of rural life than the varied topography would suggest. It also allowed the CCP to push nationwide policies while ignoring the law of comparative economic advantage. The most damaging of such policies was the promotion of 'taking grain as the key link' to accompany the industrial policy of 'taking steel as the key link'. The former led many communes to turn over ill-suited land to grain production. Slopes were cleared of tree cover and grazing land was ploughed under to meet mandatory grain production targets. Not only did this depress local incomes, it also caused significant environmental damage (Shapiro, 2001).

The other major policy that transformed the physical image of the countryside was the promotion of small-scale industry during the Great Leap Forward (GLF) (1958–60) as a concerted programme for rural industrialization. The most notorious result was the 'backyard steel furnace' that produced a huge volume of steel, much of it useless and consuming scarce resources. Other experiments such as the creation of small electric power generators and chemical fertilizer plants provided the legacy for an equally dramatic transformation of the countryside in the 1980s and 1990s with the massive growth of township and village enterprises (TVE).

The Maoist lack of concern and the privileging of production over all other factors enhanced the degradation of the environment. This perspective was enthusiastically adopted by Mao Zedong, who saw nature as something to be conquered and tamed and did not appreciate that there are natural limits which resource endowment places on growth. Not only did the development strategy favour rapid exploitation of natural resources to build up the heavy industrial base but also the associated policy of below-cost pricing for water, coal and other inputs contributed further. Walking by office buildings with lights burning in the weekends and past bathrooms with constantly running taps that could not be turned off even if one tried showed the irrelevance of water or electricity prices to workplace and domestic budgets.

The rapid economic growth and urbanization of the years after 1975 have come at the cost of enormous environmental damage, and natural resource constraints are a potential brake on China's future development. The political economy of the reforms has in many ways been inimical to the development of an effective policy to control environmental pollution (for a critical analysis see Economy, 2004). According to the World Bank (1997g, p. 2), the damage caused by air and water pollution amounted to $54 billion a year, a staggering 8 per cent of GDP in 1995. Of this amount, $33 billion was calculated to come from urban air pollution and $4 billion from water pollution.

The economic reforms introduced since 1978 have also had a significant impact on the physical look of both urban and rural China while binding the two closer together than in the Mao years. The reforms have released the tight grip of the party and state over local society and have allowed space for the return of local enterprise and even limited private entrepreneurship. Cities in contemporary China are certainly livelier and less homogenous than in Mao's China. The drab Stalinesque town centres have been transformed in many cities with the rise of gleaming, glass-fronted skyscrapers housing luxury offices, shopping malls, and the ubiquitous McDonald's. These are the new symbols of moderniza- tion and much of the old architecture and housing that survived the Maoist blitz has been bulldozed to make way. While it is true that much of the housing was sub-standard, the redevelopment and loss of family homes to move to sterile new apartments far from the city centre have met with resistance and sit-ins.

Historical heritage has often been bulldozed away in the name of a new concept of progress. Kunming was chosen to host the International Flower Exhibition in the late 1990s and this led to a frenzy of develop- ment and demolition. As a result, many of the charming old lanes around the Cuihu lake area were demolished to make way for new buildings. When I asked a local official why they preferred demolition to restora- tion, he replied that the old lanes represented the past and backwardness and the foreigners who would come to the Exhibition would think of China as a poor country if they saw them. As a result, communities were broken up and dispersed in the name of modernity. The new buildings represented the future and the modern. Unfortunately, to Western eyes, the building material of choice in Southwest China is white tile, making most buildings look like inverted public lavatories covered with opaque deep sea-blue glass. In hosting the World Expo in 2010, the Shanghai authorities organized training sessions for neighbourhoods on correct behaviour. They were particularly concerned about laundry, especially underwear, hanging out on the streets to dry and the habit of old men to roll up their undershirts in the hot weather to reveal their torso. These were explained as things that would give a bad impression to foreigners and might be interpreted as 'backward' habits.

The new architecture also reinforces the reified view of state power with many new gleaming, marble-decked buildings constructed to house the local party, government and judicial authorities. In Wuxi, an affluent reform-minded city in Jiangsu a couple of hours from Shanghai, I asked local officials about this phenomenon. I wondered aloud whether they thought that such ostentatious signs of state power and public spending were appropriate in the modern world and whether local citizens felt disturbed to see so much expenditure on civic buildings. The local offi- cials were dumbfounded and amused by my question. It had never occurred to them to think about this and when they did they replied that it was indeed appropriate as it was the party that had provided the correct guidance and policies for China to take off. They may be correct and such graphic demonstrations of state power are a universal phenom- enon. Certainly there seemed to be no popular angst about such public extravagance. Interestingly, sitting on the hills overlooking the famous lake of Wuxi is not only the Gold Buddha, representing the return of belief, but also the enormous villa that belonged to one of China's top capitalists, Rong Yiren, who also served as President of China, representing the return to credibility of private capital in China. So there in one city, the architecture represents three facets of modern China that have to find a new *modus vivendi*, state power, popular religion and private capital.

Even in poorer provinces such ostentatious building for party and state is common. The Guiyang government, capital of the southwestern province of Guizhou, has built a lavish complex of buildings and open plaza to house the party and government complex. The offices for the Guizhou provincial administration remain in the old buildings downtown. A senior official of the provincial government asked me what I thought of the complex and I replied that I was not convinced this was the best way to spend the people's money, commenting that it was very difficult for Western governments to build such altars to their power these days. He agreed and noted that the then Vice-President of China, Zeng Qinghong, had been equally critical of the new construction but they were powerless to stop the municipal government from spending the money as they saw fit.

The new icons of urban modernity tower above a more varied urban environment that is a product of the reforms. I remember in 1976 the delight with which we greeted a street seller in central Beijing who was selling homemade toys for a few cents. Now the streets teem with so many vendors that one is more likely to run away and seek refuge from the hawkers and traders. The gradual release first on rural markets and later for rural produce to be sold in the cities has led to a much more diverse urban street life. The markets, restaurants and discos are signs of the new entrepreneurship or official organizations moonlighting to make a bit of extra money. The restaurants and nightclubs are filled with the beneficiaries of reform: the private entrepreneurs, those involved in the new economy, the managerial elites, and the politically well connected. Periodic curbs on government entertaining are met with horror by the owners of these establishments.

The reforms have also changed what is for sale in the stores. In the Cultural Revolution by and large one bought what one could get if one had the money and the correct ration coupons. Entering the department store was not a particularly energizing experience as choice was limited, quality was poor and service distinctly surly. Two phrases that you quickly became acquainted with were *mei youle* (don't have it) and *mai wanle* (sold out). Now film and rock stars are used to promote new products and open stores. Competition has caused even the state-run stores to become more entrepreneurial and to offer service with a grudging smile rather than a scowl. Most of the luxury goods that were kept back in special stores for senior officials and foreigners are gener-ally available for anyone who has money.

Reform has even changed the content of official bookstores such as the Foreign Languages Bookstore on Beijing's main shopping street. Its transformation has been a bell-wether of reforms. In the 1970s and 1980s its main stock was the collected works in foreign languages of China's leaders, posters of revolutionary icons such as Stalin and Enver Hoxha, and English language textbooks that carried revolutionary parables or stories of friendship between Chinese and foreign citizens. When I have visited in recent years, there was barely a collected work in sight and no revolutionary icon to be found. In their place were Harvard Business School textbooks and manuals on how to make money or manage financial transactions. The posters had been replaced by a wide choice of Western novels, cassettes and CDs introducing the latest sounds and fashions. Learning English by revolutionary parable has been replaced by learning English through business management.

The urban one-child per couple policy has affected shopping. Toy shops and department stores are now the icons of happy family life with parents lavishing relatively large sums to pamper the 'new emperors' of modern China. As one old party wag commented, they were the hope for greater party accountability in the future. In his view they had been so spoilt and so dominated household spending and priorities that there was no way that they would listen passively and unquestioningly to party directives when they grew older! They were more likely to demand results to improve the quality of their life and provide greater accountability.

Not all have money to spend in this new urban China. There have been beneficiaries but there have also been losers – workers in inefficient state-owned enterprises, the aged with no family dependants, some migrants and farmers engaged exclusively in grain production. The increasing pressure of marketization and the need to cut costs and increase profits caused a rapid increase in lay-offs from the old SOEs in the 1990s. While the worst effects for many have been cushioned either through supplemental income from the state or the retention of low-cost housing and medical provision, there is no doubt that it has been a hard transition for some. The favoured Northeast and Sichuan of the Maoist period have become the rust-belts of the early twenty-first century. It is noticeable that provinces such as Liaoning and Jilin that used to be among the wealthiest in the Mao years have become relatively poorer in the reform period. By contrast Guangdong, one of the poorest provinces under Mao, has become the wealthiest under reform.

Many older workers are bewildered by the changes and are unlikely to find work in the new economy where quite different skills are required than those learned by the traditional working class. Official unemployment figures (just over 4 per cent for 2009) significantly underrepresent the true levels and the regional variation. One survey by the Chinese Academy of Social Sciences calculates urban unemployment at around 9.4 per cent for 2008. In northeastern cities such as Mudanjiang, unemployment may even have run as high as 40 per cent to 60 per cent during the worst period. Certainly anecdotal evidence would suggest much higher rates. Peddlers in the streets in such towns and the hostesses and prostitutes working in the hotels and clubs tend to be local rather than outsiders as is the case in larger cities such as Beijing and Shanghai.

The impact has fallen unduly heavily on women. In most SOEs, they are the first to be laid off and would be the last to be taken back. In many state organizations, women are being persuaded to take early retirement - usually around 45 and, on occasion, even earlier. The chance of finding new, legal employment is slim. The elderly and the single have also been vulnerable. With workplaces shedding their social welfare responsibilities and a new system only slowly coming into place, old age or divorce can appear more threatening than in the days of cradle-to-grave socialist care for the elite of the urban industrial working class.

A rise in the divorce rate has been a by-product of reforms and there has been much hand-wringing in the Chinese press. While some see it as a breakdown of social mores, others have heralded it as a positive sign of modernization, pointing to the higher divorce rates in the 'developed West'. The divorce rate had risen from 0.44 in 1985 to a high of 1.71 in 2008 with extra-marital affairs being the main cause of divorce. The northeast provinces have comparatively high divorce numbers and Sichuan the highest, perhaps reflecting the economic distress of those areas. Similarly high are the more affluent provinces of Jiangsu and Shandong. The rates might seem low but for a society coming out of the Mao years of enforced social conformity and repression of sexual desire (unless you happened to be Mao himself) it has been seen as a disturbing increase. The early rise in divorce rates related to people shaking off political marriages that they undertook during the Cultural Revolution. In those years, rather than feelings of love, correct class background and political stance were more important for finding urban marriage partners. It led to many loveless marriages in urban China for the now 50-somethings, leading not only to rising divorce rates but also to increases in extra-marital affairs as well as the enormous popularity of books and films like *The Bridges of Madison County*.

I have sat through many discussions by older urban residents of nostalgia for the old days. Forgetting the famine of the Great Leap Forward and the chaos and violence of the Cultural Revolution, they reminisce of the 'golden days' when life was secure, there was basic healthcare and the streets were safe. For many, reforms have meant bewildering choices, loss of security, rising crime and declining personal safety, and a younger generation who treat their elders with less respect. Many such people have been attracted by the 'leftist' manifestos published by former Maoist party veterans. These criticize the 'capitalism' and 'materialism' and new inequalities of current policy and call for a return to stricter discipline, party control and central state planning. Others have been attracted to a variety of religious and popular movements such as *Falungong*. This is just the tip of an iceberg as many seek to find something that brings meaning to their life in such a turbulent world.

It is the migrants who have received popular and official blame for the increase in crime, dirt, and disease in urban China. While such hyperbole is usually unjustified, migrants are a feature of the post-Mao reforms. There have been previous waves of migration post-1949 but at the end of 2008, the migrant population was estimated at over 225.4 million of whom 140 million had found work outside of their home county (*China Daily*, 26 March 2009). The decline in farming incomes and the pull of better-paid work in the cities have led many young men, and increasingly women, to abandon the harsh conditions of rural labour for higher wages in the cities. The construction boom of the 1990s was a major source of employment as was the expansion of township and village enterprises and the foreign-invested manufacturing enterprises that have mushroomed in the Special Economic Zones (SEZ). One further link between the urban and the rural has been the rapid expansion of rural industry in the form of township and village enterprises. In 1978, TVEs employed 28.1 million people and this has risen steadily to a high of 154 million in 2008. In Jiangsu and Shandong, TVEs employed 41 and 33 per cent of the workforce respectively.

However, life in the cities while perhaps not as harsh as in the countryside has not been easy either. Migrants tend to live in sub-standard or shanty-housing or in dormitories provided by their employers. In the former, they often group together in native-place villages. A major problem for the migrants is that their place of registration is still considered to be in the countryside and thus they have been frustrated with respect to medical and education access despite policy reforms (Ming, 2009).

As noted, the migrants have been important to the growth of not only the non-state sector but also the development of the new growth areas of China along the coast. The CCP has promoted this strategy of coastal growth while allowing a progressive running down of the old industrial areas. This began with the promotion of trade as a key component of the new policy and the licensing of the four SEZs in 1979 that provided a series of incentives for foreign enterprises and joint ventures. They were set up primarily to absorb overseas Chinese investment, thus turning Hong Kong millionaires into billionaires. The programme expanded from the four zones (Shenzhen, Zhuhai, Shantou, and Xiamen) under Zhao Ziyang by the late 1980s to a coastal zone development strategy. Shenzhen, the first major zone over the border from Hong Kong, was just a small, sleepy village when I first passed through in 1976. On the train ride from the border with Hong Kong to Guangzhou one passed endless rice paddies, small clustered village hamlets and the occasional water buffalo pulling a plough or swishing its tail while bathing lazily in the river. A decade later, Shenzhen was Asia's newest metropolis with an urban centre full of towering skyscrapers rising from the former paddies. It is now the most crowded city in China with around 14 million residents in 2008 (of whom only 30 per cent have permanent resident status). It is also said to be home to 20 per cent of China's PhDs (*Shenzhen Daily*, 13 June 2007).

Very few rural areas have undergone such a dramatic transformation but official figures state that the incidence of poverty has dropped from 250 million at the start of the reforms to only 23.6 million in 2005. It should be noted that there is the emergence of an urban poor, with 23.34 million in 2008 receiving the minimum living support. As these figures suggest, the reforms have been equally dramatic in their effect on rural China. The communes have been abandoned and farming returned to a household basis. As a result, the wide fields and expanses of land have been divided up into small parcels that are often guarded as crops ripen. The breakdown of communal farming has led to an increase in theft of crops in the countryside.

Migration has also affected the demographics of many rural villages and many who have remained behind have pulled out of farming where there is a viable alternative. While still some 54 per cent of China's population is registered as living in the countryside, farming families are increasingly reliant on non-farm sources of income. This may come from remittances from migrants or wage labour in TVEs or household business. Even for those who remain in agricultural production there has been a shift away from the Maoist obsession with grain production to other products that fetch a higher price in the urban markets. Generally, with the low returns for grain production, most only keep fields to fulfil their quotas. For a country that has such a heavy pressure on the available land, it is disconcerting to see so much good agricultural land being abandoned either because families do not want to farm it or cannot because of migration or redeployment to more profitable non-agricultural work.

The composition of those farming has also changed. In many villages, males have moved in search of off-farm employment as have many women of pre-marriage age. This has left farming in many areas to the elderly and married women. Because of the low status and income from these activities, there has been discussion as to whether we are witnessing the 'feminization' of not just agriculture but also poverty. Many villages seem to comprise only the elderly, children, the sick, and married women dealing with all the household and production affairs. A 2008 study by the Chinese Academy of Social Sciences stated that in 90 per cent of China's villages there was no young and healthy labour remaining and that it was doubtful whether the young people would return from the cities.

Migration and other social changes have also led to the increase of sexually transmitted diseases and HIV/AIDS. For example, the incidence of syphilis has increased from 0.17 per 100 000 in 1989 to 13.3 in 2006 (an annual increase of 30.7 per cent, State Council AIDS Working Committee Office, 2007, p. 8). The figures for HIV/AIDS are not especially high with a prevalence of only 0.05 per cent but the disease has spread from original at-risk populations (intravenous drug users and commercial sex workers) to the population at large. Migrant male workers who have contracted sexually transmitted diseases have brought them back to the village where there may be no adequate healthcare. The spread of HIV/AIDS has also been linked to poverty. Ethnic minorities represent 9 per cent of the population but 40 per cent of the absolute poor and 36 per cent of reported HIV/AIDS cases (information from Joan Kaufman). While HIV/AIDS is now spreading among the heterosexual community and from sexual activity with prostitutes, much of the spread has come from needle sharing by drug addicts and the sale of blood to 'blood snakes' by the poor. China's coercive and social systems are ill-equipped to deal with this situation and an epidemic of major proportions is looming.

Yunnan is typical. In small rural towns in the province, HIV/AIDS first began to spread among intravenous drug users and subsequently to sex workers. In border towns such as Ruili the explosive mix of drugs and prostitution has caused a major epidemic to develop. I have visited villages in the surrounding area that have been devastated by the death of many of the males through contraction. One major problem with tracking the spread of a new disease such as this is that local health workers often fail to recognize it. In addition, there are bureaucratic and systemic imperatives that can lead to the spread of the disease being hushed up. Local authorities are worried that any adverse publicity would not only bring opprobrium from higher authorities but also would discourage foreign investment. The same fears have prevented local authorities from investigating and exposing the extent of the spread of HIV/AIDS through the sale of contaminated blood.

With reforms rural China has become more varied than in the past, with greater freedom for households to decide on what to produce, where to sell it and how to deploy their labour force. However, reforms have not favoured all in the rural areas and the extension of household-based farming and markets to areas where they are inappropriate has had adverse effects. For the absolute poor, many of whom live in remote mountainous areas, liberalization and the increased use of market forces have been of little benefit as they have little if anything to sell. In fact, with increased prices for agricultural inputs and the collapse of medical access, their living standards have almost certainly declined. In addition, with financial pressures increasing on local authorities many have resorted to raising illegal fees and levies that fall on the poor disproportionately.

The CCP's vision of modernity has also intruded into rural life. Clearly, the CCP still sees the future as urban and industrial. Policy has always privileged these areas but other policies have also impacted on rural life. In particular, the CCP sees nomadic or other traditional farming practices as 'backward'. As a result CCP policy has tried to organize nomadic and shifting cultivators into more permanent habitats. More permanent settlements, of course, make it easier to control activities and to pursue unpopular policies such as family planning.

The CCP has to rule over this increasingly diverse society while trying to guide China into further integration with the world economy. This is a daunting challenge. The CCP has also to provide an explanation to its people of where the country is heading and offer some kind of a moral compass. This is hard to do not only because of the diversity but also because ideological orthodoxy appears to run counter to the direction in which the economy and society are heading. It is hard for General Secretary Hu Jintao, or any other senior leader, to provide a genuine vision of China's future as at best it would suggest a radically transformed role for the CCP and at worst perhaps no role at all. If the future is an economy increasingly dominated by market forces and integrated with the world economy, is a CCP that still professes commitment to socialism and the state-owned sector while harbouring suspicion of foreign motives, the most effective organization to manage this? However much practice may move away from Marxism, the ideology remains a crucial component of the CCP's self-legitimation (Kelly, 1991, p. 23). To abandon adherence would be impossible.

The gap between official rhetoric and social practice has widened significantly under the reforms and is perhaps even greater than in the Soviet Union and Eastern Europe in the late 1980s. While China's leaders claim 'only socialism can save China' the students laugh that 'only China can save socialism'. The leadership has adopted a number of linguistic phrases that seek to explain current reality while retaining allegiance to socialism. The latest is that China is a 'socialist market economy' while the phrase of 'Chinese-style socialism' has been used to cover a multitude of policies that are difficult to describe as being conventionally socialist.

While Chinese society has become less ideological and even more pluralistic, CCP ideology sets limits to how far reform can go. Party leadership has retained its commitment throughout to socialism however much the definition of its content may have changed. The reforms have not been intended to introduce either democracy or a capitalist economic system but rather to find a way for socialism to survive (on this point see Huang, 2008). This explains the residual commitment to the SOE sector, the slow, grudging approval given to the private sector and the attempts to make foreign investment support the CCP's socialist objectives. Whether such an approach to development is still tenable is one of the major challenges the CCP faces in the twenty-first century. With the commitment to the World Trade Organization (WTO), there must be serious concern as to whether the socialist core can be retained and even whether certain senior leaders wish to retain it. In a prescient observation, Kelly has remarked that one outcome of transition may be the 'installation of a New Authoritarian regime that dispenses with Marxist state ownership and its attendant social welfare functions but retains the self-legitimating apparatus of Marxist ideology' (Kelly, 1991, p. 34).

Certainly, within society and even among party members there is little faith that socialism can provide a guiding light for China. Socialism is very rarely raised these days in discussions with foreigners and when mentioned is usually met with an embarrassed giggle by those sitting around the table. When bored listening to the development plans of local officials, I often ask them about the relevance of socialism to their plans. They usually pull up short and mutter something about social stability, party guidance and that the kind of socialism being pursued was one with Chinese characteristics. The appeal to the primacy of social stability and the appellation of Chinese characteristics seemed to justify most things one wanted to do.

Whether such linguistic conundrums can suffice in the future is hard to say. It is clear that many party members and citizens have a highly instrumental view of the party. As long as it has sufficient patronage to deploy and continues to deliver the economic goods there is little incentive to seek alternatives or to rock the boat. This makes legitimacy highly conditional and the party has struggled to provide deeper reasons for attachment, best seen in its promotion of nationalism. One significant legacy of Deng's reforms is that the overwhelming majority of people do not have to worry about the CCP anymore and it does not interfere directly in their lives. This is an important advance from the Mao years and even those of the 1980s when political campaigns in which all were supposed to participate were commonplace. Withdrawal could be interpreted as lack of support and punishment could be harsh. Now campaigns generally only affect the 76 million or so party members and even then many do not have to take them seriously.

Some citizens have not been willing to withdraw into a private realm of activity but have joined a variety of religious and spiritual organizations. A very small number have even joined underground political and labour organizations. Such individuals have clearly transgressed the limits of the permissible and such organizations are broken up and key individuals arrested when discovered. Many more inhabit a grey zone of local religious organizations, clans, lineages, gangs or social organizations that operate at the margins of the politically acceptable.

Providing governance over this diverse people and territory is an increasingly complex challenge. The chapters that follow provide an introduction to the way the CCP has governed to date and the challenges it faces in the immediate future. It looks at the organization of the party and the state at the central and local levels, the shifting nature of participation and protest and how the relationship between state and society has changed over time. The final chapters review the key areas of economic, social, and foreign policy before looking at important future challenges.

Chapter 3

China's Changing Road to Development: Political History, 1949–78

After 22 years of conflict with its nationalist rivals domestically and Japanese invaders, the Chinese Communist Party (CCP) took control of Beijing in January 1949 and Shanghai in May the same year. By 1950 the Guomindang (Nationalist) forces retained control of only the island of Taiwan. Though CCP leader Mao Zedong told the Chinese people that they had stood up, the country which the CCP now controlled in their name was economically backward, predominantly agrarian and contained considerable opposition to communist rule. Victory returned the CCP to the cities they had been forced to abandon following repression by the nationalists. CCP leaders now had to return the revolution to the cities, build an industrial base and a working class whom they were supposed to represent, create new political institutions and train officials to staff them. Pockets of opposition remained from troops loyal to the nationalists with whom the CCP had fought two civil wars (1927–37 and 1945–49; see Box 3.1) and there was armed fighting with Tibetans who resisted incorporation into the People's Republic of China (PRC). In addition many, especially in the cities and the south, were suspicious of the CCP's motives and intentions. The economy had suffered badly from the dislocation and destruction not only of the civil wars but also the Japanese invasion (1937–45), and the country was suffering from rampant inflation.

Given this inheritance, the achievements by the mid 1950s were impressive. The country, with the exception of Taiwan, was unified, the rural revolution completed, inflation tamed, and solid economic growth achieved. For many older CCP members the early 1950s era is remembered as the 'golden age' of steady progress and social stability. One might have thought that China's search for a suitable form of state to help the nation modernize and take its rightful place in the world would have ended and institutionalization would have been completed. Yet, only a few years later the CCP led its people through a series of disastrous movements that ripped apart the ruling elite, caused social dislocation and famine on a massive scale, and culminated in the Cultural Revolution (see Box 3.2). In fact, even in the early 1950s tensions lay just below the surface that were derived from the pre-1949 CCP legacy

34

and the application of the Soviet economic model. This chapter first reviews the framework of the debates and tensions within the revolutionary inheritance, and then how Mao and the CCP moved from triumph to disaster, from state-building to state destruction.

Box 3.1: Key Dates of the Communist Revolution 1911–49

1911 Uprisings bring down the Qing dynasty and Sun Yat-sen is proclaimed President of the Republic of China

1912 14 February, Sun steps down and Yuan Shikai, a former Qing official, takes over

1919 4 May, students protest against their government and the Japanese in response to provisions of the Versailles Treaty at the end of the First World War

1921 23 July, the CCP opens its founding Congress

1923 June, Third CCP Congress agrees to collaboration with the Guomindang (GMD)

1926 July, Chiang Kai-shek with CCP and Soviet support launches the Northern Expedition to unify China

1927 12 April, Chiang Kai-shek's soldiers massacre communists in Shanghai and a purge of communists begins in many eastern and southern cities

1928 April, Mao and Zhu De unite to form the Jinggangshan base

1933 January, Party Centre flees to the Jiangxi Soviet

1935 15–18 January, enlarged Politburo meeting at Zunyi criticizes past military policy and elects Mao to the Standing Committee of the Politburo

1936 December, kidnap of Chiang Kai-shek by his own troops facilitates formation of second united front

1937 January, CCP moves its headquarters to Yan'an
7 July, clash between Japanese and Chinese troops at Marco Polo bridge near Beijing provides pretext for full-scale Japanese invasion of China

1941 September, the Rectification Campaign is launched

1945 April–June, CCP Seventh Congress convenes marking culmination of Mao's rise to power
14 August, Japan surrenders unconditionally

1946 10 October, with the fall of Kalgan to GMD troops the CCP announces that civil war is inevitable

1949 January, Beijing falls to CCP troops and Shanghai falls in May
1 October, Mao Zedong announces the establishment of the People's Republic of China (PRC)

Box 3.2: Key Political Dates, 1949–65

1950 February, China signs the Treaty of Friendship, Alliance and Mutual Assistance with the Soviet Union
May, Marriage Law promulgated
June, Land Law is promulgated
October, China joins the Korean War

1951 February to 1953, 'Campaign to Suppress Counterrevolutionaries'
August to June 1952, 'Three-Anti Campaign' against official corruption

1952 January to June, 'Five-Anti Campaign' to curb the violation of official regulations by private businesses

1953 October, First Five-Year Plan launched, although formally ratified only in 1955

1954 February, Gao Gang charged with trying to seize state power
September, First National People's Congress meets, replacing the Chinese People's Consultative Conference as the highest organ of state power

1955 July, Mao rejects that collectivization could be subordinated to mechanization

1956 February, Krushchev's secret speech denounces Stalin
April, Mao's talk 'On the Ten Great Relationships'
May, 'Hundred Flowers' Campaign' launched
September, Eighth Party Congress acknowledges success of First Five-Year Plan and approves the second to start in 1958

1957 February, Mao widens 'Hundred Flowers' Campaign'
8 June, *People's Daily* article signals start of 'Anti-Rightist Campaign'
September–October, Third Plenum of Eighth Central Committee (CC) adopts radical measures that pave the way for the Great Leap Forward (GLF)

1958 May, Second Session of Eighth Party Congress ratifies plans for GLF

1959 10 March onward, Crushing of the revolt in Tibet
July–August, Lushan Plenum, Peng Dehuai criticizes the GLF

1960 July, Soviet Union withdraws all its technical personnel from China

1961 January, Ninth Plenum of Eighth CC adopts economic adjustment policies worked out the previous summer

1962 September, Tenth Plenum of the Eighth CC, Mao stresses the continued existence of class struggle
October, Border war with India breaks out

1963 May, Socialist Education Movement intensifies with publication of the 'Early Ten Points'

1965 November, article by Yao Wenyuan criticizes a play written by Beijing deputy mayor Wu Han claiming it a defence of Peng Dehuai

Parameters of policy debate

Two sets of issues framed the policy debates through the 1950s into the 1990s. The first is a set of debates that have been common to all socialist systems operating under a one-party political structure managing a centrally planned economy. The second is a number of tensions that derived from the Chinese revolutionary experience.

The nature of the socialist system (see Kornai, 1992) means that the possibilities for change are limited and the areas of policy debate tend to oscillate along a continuum of a key set of policy alternatives. The main determining features are a centrally planned economy with predominant, if not total, social ownership of the means of production overseen by a hierarchical highly centralized political power structure concentrated within a one-party state and with an atomized society within which the agents of civil society are weak or ineffective. It was only when reformers in the Soviet Union and China began to undermine these pillars that fundamental change became feasible.

This structure results in recurrent debates on a number of specific questions. In the economic sphere, there is the question of the relationship between the government and the state-owned sector of the economy and the extent of the supplemental role to be played by the collective and private sectors. What is the relationship between consumption and accumulation? How extensive a role should foreign trade play in the development of the national economy? Debates in this field focus particularly on the level of trade with 'advanced capitalist countries'. In addition, there have been sharp debates over how best to motivate managers and labourers to work effectively. Should material incentives in the form of bonuses or piece-rates be expanded or should moral exhortation and social recognition be used as a primary form of stimulus?

The cyclical debates have also included the management and administration of the economy. First, in terms of broad economic management there has been oscillation between the role of directive planning and the use of economic incentives to direct the behaviour of economic actors. This is related to specific questions of how much autonomy should be granted to the production enterprises and in which functional areas. A further area of debate is between the division of economic decision-making powers between the central administration and its various local agencies.

In the political sphere, there have been oscillations between the level of authority to be enjoyed by party officials *vis-à-vis* other state administrative cadres and enterprise managers. Just how much specific decision-making power should reside with party secretaries? What is the role of the intelligentsia and technicians in the process of policy formulation and how much academic freedom should they be accorded and in which areas? Last but not least, there are debates about the extent to which any institution or organization outside of the party-state should be permitted to exist.

In addition to these generic debates, the specifics of the CCP's rise to power contributed legacies that framed the post-1949 debates. The Chinese revolution had been fought in the countryside and this raised a fundamental question about whose interests the new regime would serve: those of the social force that brought it to power (primarily the peasantry), or in whose name it was brought to power (the proletariat); or, as some have suggested, its own bureaucratic structures and personnel.

The preference for the proletariat, if not urban China, was clearly understandable from CCP ideology. Even though the CCP had had no effective contact with the proletariat during the years before seizure of power, its leaders never dropped their commitment to an ideology based on its supremacy and leadership over the peasantry, as represented in the Soviet-inspired vision of the future. As soon as conditions permitted, the party reasserted the primacy of urban work over that in the countryside. However, the socialization drive of the new party-state ran against the material interests of both the farmers and the proletariat. This disregard for the interests of the two primary classes the CCP was supposed to represent derives from the party's 'privileged' position in relation to them before 1949. In the absence of an actual proletariat in the revolutionary base areas, proletarian rule in practice meant rule by its vanguard, the CCP. The party adopted the habit of speaking in the name of the proletariat without the nuisance of having to listen to an actual, existing class. This affected CCP rule after 1949 and its autonomy to act. The party often spoke on behalf of all social forces, cognizant that it knew best what was in the real class interest. As a result, after the CCP came to power it enjoyed significant autonomy from the specific interests of all social forces.

This autonomy of the CCP was heightened externally by its relationship to the Soviet Union, the head of the communist movement worldwide. The Chinese revolution was distinct from the 'baggage train' governments that followed the extension of Soviet power into Eastern Europe following the Second World War. The revolution was indigenous and Mao made it quite clear that the CCP was not fighting a war to become the 'slaves of Moscow'. Obviously the influence of Marxism-Leninism as an ideology and the practical help of Soviet Russia cannot be denied, but the end product of Mao Zedong Thought was a distinctive approach geared to and influenced by Chinese realities. The CCP was willing to ignore Soviet advice when it ran counter to national interests and to abandon the Soviet approach to development once its internal inadequacies and its inapplicability to the Chinese situation became apparent. This desire for strong independence was enhanced by China's humiliation at the hands of foreigners in the century before the CCP took power.

Last but not least, there was a legacy of institutional overlap and tensions between individual and institution. In the revolutionary war, institutions were very fluid and often the military was a more visible expression of communist power than the CCP itself. Individuals held positions in multiple institutions without any apparent contradiction. It was impossible to identify a senior CCP official, for example, as having a military background or representing a military interest as all senior CCP leaders had been military leaders before 1949. This bred a some-what cavalier attitude to institutions and their use to achieve other policy objectives.

However, in the CCP revolutionary base area of the Shaan-Gan-Ning in the 1940s more attention was paid to organizational development and the drafting of codes and procedures. CCP stress on organizational stability and ideological orthodoxy went, somewhat paradoxically, hand-in-hand with the accretion of power in Mao's hands. Indeed, it went even further than this, as loyalty to the organization was reinforced through a campaign to promote the individual of Mao Zedong as the font of supreme wisdom in China's revolution, a campaign that built up momentum from July 1943 onwards. At the time, it does not seem to have occurred to other senior leaders that the build-up of a Mao cult negated the stress on collective leadership and loyalty to the CCP as an organization. While his pre-eminence did not necessarily have to lead to the abolition of inner-party democracy and serious policy discussion, it was the major factor preventing the institutionalization of more enduring political structures after 1949.

Economic recovery and the adoption of the Soviet model, 1949–55

The CCP's main aims in 1949 were to revive the war-ravaged economy and to eliminate the remaining domestic opposition. If differences remained within the leadership they were hidden beneath a façade of unity. Before 1949 the CCP held a number of base areas in addition to Shaan-Gan-Ning, and their precarious nature and vulnerability to Japa-nese or GMD attack meant that the party had to rely continually on the support of the poor peasantry and the local elites (see Box 3.3). This made policy more conciliatory even in Shaan-Gan-Ning than it might otherwise have been, with economic moderation and political attempts to placate a wide range of social forces. Post-1949 initial policy followed this approach, with populist measures to remove the most obvious ineq-uities of the old system, a moderate economic policy and harsh treat-ment of those considered enemies of the state. Over time, policy radicalized and increasing sections of the population, including intellectuals, became the focus of CCP criticism. Gradually, the authoritarian strands of the pre-1949 legacy came to dominate over any proto-democratic proclivities. In addition, personal dominance by Mao Zedong over decision-making frustrated the developmental need to build sustainable institutions. As these tensions mounted and the CCP confronted economic failure on a vast scale during the Great Leap Forward, the façade of unity began to crack.

The principles of 'New Democracy', developed by Mao (February 1940) in Shaan-Gan-Ning, with their emphasis on reconciliation and class collaboration, were to guide the new state. Naming the new state the People's Republic rather than a people's democratic dictatorship symbol-

---

Box 3.3: Revolutionary Base Areas

Before 1949, CCP forces were organized in a number of base areas that provided sanctuary, allowed policy experimentation and officials to develop administrative experience. The main base where Mao and the party headquarters were situated was Shaan-Gan-Ning with its capital in Yan'an. The experiences here provided a blueprint for post-1949 society. Policy combined a moderate economic policy and external relations with tough internal party discipline and the 'mass-line' campaigning style of politics. Apart from Shaan-Gan-Ning, there were major base areas in Jin-Ji-Yu-Lu (Shanxi-Hebei-Shandong-Henan) and Jin-Cha-Ji (Shanxi-Chahar-Hebei) regions. The CCP was successful at putting down local roots only where it showed flexibility in adapting policy to local circumstances, where initially it was good at micro-politics. By contrast, attempts to transform local environments to conform to predetermined ideology were unsuccessful. These different base area experiences were often ignored after 1949 and especially during the years of the Cultural Revolution (1966–76) when the focus was exclusively on a CCP history based around the persona of Mao Zedong. When the reforms began in the late 1970s, these varied experiences became important points for alternative policy experimentation. For example, the programme of village elections launched in the late 1980s under the patronage of then National People's Congress leader, Peng Zhen, owed much to his own experiences in Jin-Cha-Ji. Peng hoped that 'controlled democracy' would keep local elites on board and give them a stake in the new politics to prevent them from going over to the enemy. The experiences of Jin-Ji-Lu-Yu are important because key leaders of the reform period such as Deng Xiaoping, Bo Yibo, Wan Li and Zhao Ziyang spent time there. The precarious and fragmented nature of this particular base area meant that policy had to be even more conciliatory than that in Shaan-Gan-Ning. This paramount emphasis on survival meant that a very flexible economic structure was maintained that built on the pre-existing banking expertise of the area and an agricultural policy that very closely resembled that of the 'responsibility system' introduced in China during the 1980s (see Goodman, 1994; Saich, 1994a, 1996).

ized this. Important practical considerations favoured the adoption of a relatively 'moderate' policy. On assuming power the communists suffered from a shortage of properly trained administrative, managerial and technical personnel, and they lacked experience in managing a modern, urban, industrial sector. With priority given to economic recovery it was necessary to ensure that all available scarce resources were not wasted. This foreclosed the immediate introduction of a full-scale socialist transition strategy. The 'moderate' mood was summed up in the slogan: 'three years of recovery and ten years of development'. Policy was to benefit not only the workers and peasants, but also the petty bourgeoisie and those capitalists who had supported the CCP. By contrast, landlords, unsympathetic industrialists, those with foreign interests and those connected with the GMD were to be dealt with harshly.

Policy towards capitalists deemed sympathetic to the revolution provides a good example of the gradualism through which the CCP bound key groups into new forms of state patronage before eliminating them. They were allowed to develop their industries as a prime requisite for the development of a modern economic structure that would then be ripe for socialist transformation. Although this meant the initial maintenance of a mixed economy, only the CCP-controlled state apparatus was capable of providing any real coordination. This allowed the CCP to transform the mixed economy to its own advantage without a major disruption in production and distribution. The state took control over both ends of the production process, providing the industrial enterprises with their raw materials through the national ministries and placing orders with the private entrepreneurs for processed and manufactured goods. The state was therefore able to control what went in and what came out. Once privately owned enterprises were tied up in this way, the CCP began to promote the creation of joint state-private enterprises. This made sense for many of the privately owned enterprises that found it difficult to compete with the state enterprises and that lacked the necessary capital to replace outdated machinery. This movement reached a peak in 1954 and was gradually extended into a programme to 'buy out' the private owners, who were paid interest on their shares at a rate determined by the state. This gradualist policy proved to be very successful for the CCP and as early as 1952 industrial production had been restored to its highest pre-1949 levels.

Social and rural policy attacked gross inequalities of the old system and sought to build or consolidate new bases of support. The two most important pieces of legislation were the Marriage Law and the Land Law, both adopted in 1950. The Marriage Law was intended to improve the position of women in Chinese society by according them equality and freedom in their choice of marriage partner. Practices such as infanticide and the sale of children were outlawed.

The countryside was dramatically transformed but radical socialization was postponed. Policy was based on Sun Yat-sen's view that all had equal rights to land and that land should be given to the tillers. This is not to say that the process was peaceful, and up to 800,000 landlords were killed in the land reform campaign (1950–52), while many more were beaten and humiliated by the villagers they had previously ruled over (Teiwes, 1993). Land reform was modelled on policies adopted in the base areas and was seen as crucial for breaking up the traditional social order and power relationships in the countryside. Further, land reform had the advantage of forcing an identity of interest between the peasantry and the CCP by redistributing land to the rural households. This had been a hard bond for the GMD to break before 1949. The fact that most in the party saw land reform as an integral part of the victory strategy before 1949 meant that it was a stage that could not be skipped over on the march towards socialism. The CCP did not wish to follow the Soviet mistake of a premature rush to rural collectivization before peasant support and trust had been gained. Finally, the CCP did not have sufficient trained administrative and technical cadres to preside over a collective farming structure. As a result, policy emphasized caution and persuasion and, as before 1949, excesses tended to come from spontaneous outbursts by villagers rather than directives from above.

The Land Law sought to bring land reform under close party control in an attempt to restrain peasant 'enthusiasm'. A five-fold categorization based on property relations was drawn up to enable cadres to unravel the complexities of rural Chinese life. The law sought to ensure land redistribution to the labourers and the poor peasants while not alienating the middle and rich peasants. This was done to minimize the disruption of production. The category of 'middle peasant' was the vaguest but essentially a middle peasant was one who worked the land without engaging in exploitation. The land worked did not necessarily belong to the peasant. Landlords' land was to be confiscated or requisitioned for redistribution. The blow of being designated a landlord could be softened if the person had supported the revolution. However, the land of the rich and middle peasants, including those designated as prosperous middle peasants, was to be protected. The bulk of land reform was completed in the 18 months after the 1950 autumn harvest. Several hundred million *mu* of land was redistributed among approximately 300 million peasants, giving them between 2 and 3 *mu* each on average. However, there was considerable variation from region to region, and some areas such as Tibet, with which Beijing had signed a short-lived agreement promising 'national regional autonomy', did not undergo land reform at all. With party organizations weak or non-existent, central leaders did not wish to upset the traditional, religious elite.

It was never likely that the CCP would tolerate a household-based farming system for long. As CCP leaders began to think about pushing ahead with socialism, a rural sector based on private farming and markets was anachronistic. CCP leaders also felt that the small units of land would make rational use impossible, the popularization of new farming techniques difficult and large-scale capital construction projects problematic. In addition, the CCP leadership took on the Soviet notion that bigger was better, that fast growth regardless of quality was paramount and that to be modern meant to be urban and industrialized.

These factors meant that gradualism was abandoned, the reorganization of the rural sector into larger collective units began and the role of rural markets was curtailed. The Soviet-style emphasis on heavy industry meant that little capital was available for investment in agriculture, yet more efficient agricultural production was necessary to feed the industrialization programme. The solution was to cooperativize agriculture. This process began slowly at first in 1952 with the formation of mutual-aid teams that shared seasonal work and other chores, but gradually gathered pace until the crash programme of communization was embarked on in the late 1950s.

Mao's view that the 'peasant masses' were raw material for mobilization in time of need meant that post-1949 policy soon treated them as the primary source from which to extract resources to feed urban development and the rapidly expanding party-state structure. While the peasants were the immediate beneficiaries of the revolution through the extension of land reform, the need to build up capital quickly led the CCP to take them through the process of collectivization (see Box 3.4). This was resisted by many and communization at best benefited few.

Friedman et al. (1991, p. 273) show how by 1952, in the North China Plains, extra-village relations once mediated by the market and travel were attenuated by statist restrictions, and how the farmers gradually lost out to a party-state that sought to penetrate society in order to attack tradition and any potential oppositional organizations. Increased party penetration through collectivization into rural social structures brought the activities of clans and lineages under greater scrutiny and control than ever before.

Apart from the landlords, the 'dictatorship of the proletariat' was unleashed on those deemed by the CCP to be 'counterrevolutionaries'. These included GMD supporters, industrialists who were not willing to toe the new party line and who were too critical of CCP practice. The tense post-civil war situation may have caused the campaigns to turn into witch-hunts but many party members seemed to accept harsh measures as justified. One senior party official who was detained briefly in 1943 by the CCP and again in the early 1950s defended party actions. In his view there were indeed many spies, traitors and saboteurs around

Box 3.4: Stages of Collectivization in the Chinese Countryside, 1952–59

1952–54 *Formation of mutual-aid teams.* Five to eight households combining for work in particular seasons with up to twenty households cooperating on a year-round basis. Animals, tools and redistributed land were in private hands but labour was pooled.

1954–55 *Formation of lower-stage agricultural producers' cooperatives* (APCs). Voluntary associations of roughly 30 households pooling not only labour but also property, land, farm implements and draught animals. Farmers received income in relation to the proportion of the size of the shares of property originally invested.

1956–57 *Formation of higher-stage agricultural producers' cooperatives.* Containing between 100 and 300 households, depending on the terrain. Income distribution was now decided on the basis of work-points earned; 750,000 were set up.

1958–59 *Formation of people's communes.* A total of 24,000 communes were set up to carry out not only agricultural work but also such things as industrial work, trade, education, military affairs, health, village administration and social welfare. In 1962 the number of communes was increased to 74,000. Three levels of ownership were introduced: commune, brigade (equivalent to the higher-stage APC) and the production team (equivalent to the lower-stage APC) as the basic accounting unit.

and this justified harsh, extra-legal measures. For him, the system worked as he was released after investigation with his innocence proven. He was less sanguine about his arrest in the Cultural Revolution. However, the system worked less well for the half a million who may have died in these suppression campaigns.

The harshness of CCP action was given further impetus by China's involvement in the Korean War. Before this, the CCP had little to worry about in terms of organized resistance but war increased the communists' fears while, at the same time, enabling them to mobilize the patriotic support that had initially helped them to power. This fear that external threat might lead to internal revolt led to the 'Campaign for the Suppression of Counterrevolutionaries' that was ruthlessly pursued throughout 1951 until the war reached a stalemate. Two other major campaigns were launched during the early 1950s: the Three-Anti Campaign (August 1951–June 1952) that aimed at the abuse of official position to engage in corruption, waste and bureaucratism, and the Five-Anti Campaign (January–June 1952) that sought to curb the violation of official regulations by private businessmen.

Although the emphasis on the need for reconstruction meant that attention was focused on the solution of immediate problems, one decision was taken that had implications for the longer-term development strategy. In June 1949, Mao outlined the policy of 'leaning to one side' that entailed learning from the Soviet Union. This preference was of major significance when, towards the end of 1952, the Chinese economy began to move from rehabilitation to development. This generated the need for greater centralization and the conscious application of Soviet development techniques, certain of which ran counter to the Chinese revolutionary experience. In October 1953, the First Five-Year Plan was effectively launched, although it was not formally ratified until 1955.

With the benefit of hindsight it is easy to criticize adoption of a Soviet-style plan, but at the time the inherent problems in the model and the specific problems of applying it to China were not so apparent. It was the only socialist model for modernizing an economically backward country and, as far as the CCP leaders were concerned, it had already demonstrated its success. Given the challenges China faced and the economic dislocation, central planning appeared to offer a way to distribute scarce resources rationally and effectively. National planning seemed to imply that the diverse war-torn land was indeed one unified nation. Economic centralization matched the political concentration of power that was taking place and would aid the 'consolidation of the dictatorship of the proletariat'. Further, to carry out the industrialization programme, China needed a considerable quantity of financial and technical aid. Given the contemporary climate of world opinion it was obvious that the Soviet Union was the only source of supply.

Initially in China application of the model also appeared successful and an infrastructure for industrial development was rapidly established. The concentration on industrial development meant that 88 per cent of the state's capital investment went to heavy industry: 649 major industrial enterprises were to be built, of which 472 were to be set up in the interior regions – 156 of the total constructed using Soviet advice and equipment. Growth rates were high: industrial production grew at 18 per cent per annum, compared to a target of 14.7 per cent; heavy industry grew at 12.9 per cent. However, agricultural production lagged behind with a growth rate of only 4.5 per cent per annum (Xue, [1980] 1982). Agricultural growth was high by international standards and in relation to population growth (2 per cent), but there were worries about how sustainable this might be and whether agriculture could support the further ambitious industrial expansion and urban growth. Application of the plan also facilitated political objectives with the socialization of the means of production through the nationalization of industry and the collectivization of agriculture.

It was not long before the kinds of problems that have plagued other Soviet systems also began to emerge in China. The concentration on heavy industry soon led to the creation of bottlenecks in the system as well as imbalance in the economy. The obsession with heavy industry and the fixation on growth rates and gross output figures led to neglect of the quality of production and ignored considerations of whether anyone would actually want to buy what was produced. The incentive structures within the system were weak and this meant that worker and management enthusiasm was low. Over time, rates of return on capital declined as did labour productivity. Last but not least, consumption was repressed as funds were accumulated for capital construction.

The Chinese economy was considerably weaker than that of Soviet Russia when each chose to launch its respective First Five-Year Plan: Soviet output per capita in 1927 was about four times that of China in 1952; in agriculture, Chinese output was about one-fifth that of Soviet Russia. Some wondered how long the unbalanced growth and privileging of heavy industry could be continued in the Chinese context. Indeed, by 1956 Chinese repayments of Soviet loans began to exceed the value of new monetary aid, meaning that China would have to find an effective way to generate investment capital (Lieberthal, 1995/2004, p. 99).

The adoption of the Soviet model of development also meant, to a large extent, the adoption of Soviet management techniques and the creation of a Soviet-style society. While the Soviet model may have had some superficial resonance with notions of order in traditional China, it was at variance with other traditions, as well as running counter to the CCP's own experiences in the revolutionary base areas before 1949. Finally, the Soviet approach to development would lead to the formation of two new elites that proved to be anathema to the populist strain in Mao's thinking. First, there was the new technocratic elite of managers and economic professionals, from whom China's current rulers are drawn, who were needed to design and implement Soviet-style plans and, second, a new political elite of party professionals.

The striking growth rates were not sufficient to allay these concerns and increasingly China's leaders felt that new methods were needed if China was to break out from its economic backwardness. In particular, unless agricultural production could be boosted, the accumulation necessary for industrial development could not be met and the rapidly growing population could not be fed. Instead of shifting development priorities to a major programme of agricultural modernization, Mao chose to expand agricultural output by exploiting traditional farming methods at breakneck speed together with a dash for industrial growth. The resultant strategy was the 'Great Leap Forward' (GLF) and its disastrous implementation led not only to massive famine in China but also severe splits about the way forward within the senior ranks of the Chinese leadership.

The origins of a Chinese path to socialism, 1955–62

Although it was not until 1958 that the CCP made a radical break with previous economic practice, there had been earlier signs of disillusionment, and the years 1955–57 were crucial for the rupture. The socialization of industry had moved apace and in 1955 the pace of collectivization of agriculture picked up dramatically. In the economic sphere the main debates concerned the speed of development, the relationship of socialization to technical transformation, and the question of whether the economic process should be decentralized and, if so, how. Mao's view concerning agricultural transformation was signalled in a July 1955 speech in which he rejected the approach that collectivization should be subordinated to mechanization. Mao felt that China's conditions meant that technical transformation would take longer than social transformation and in 1956 he put forward his 12-Year Plan for Agriculture that proposed socialization as the necessary prerequisite for a rapid increase in production. However, Mao's economic thinking did not immediately gain the support of a majority within the leadership. His plan was shelved with the relatively moderate political climate of 1956, only to be revived again in 1957.

The Eighth Party Congress (September 1956) acknowledged the success of the First Five-Year Plan and approved proposals for a second plan to start in 1958. The new plan again accorded agriculture the lowest priority for allocation of funds but more emphasis was placed on light industry to meet consumer demands. Some decentralization was also introduced to curb the powers of the central ministries but the plan still lay within the Soviet orbit and assumed that socialist transformation required a developed industrial base. Mao, as shown in his views on agricultural development, was moving away from this approach, and it is clear that a serious divergence of opinion was emerging. Given the Mao-centric nature of the Chinese political system, it was clear that once Mao decided openly to throw his political weight behind his views, policy would have to shift.

The ground for a major shift in strategy was prepared with decisions taken at the Third Plenum of the Eighth Central Committee (September-October 1957) which adopted the radical measures that paved the way for the GLF. The decision was taken to decentralize power to the regions rather than to enlarge the power of initiative for individual enterprises as proposed by Chen Yun, a revolutionary veteran like Mao and a key economic planner, although limited decentralization of power was allowed to be carried out within individual units. Chen's strategy would have facilitated the use of material incentives to promote production and might have led to a decrease in the influence of the party in the production process. In fact, this approach formed the starting point for reforms introduced in the late 1970s. Mao feared that such a policy approach would encourage an incentive structure that would encourage the growth of 'spontaneous capitalist tendencies'. Decentralization only to the regions would allow greater flexibility while ensuring continued party control and conformity with central planning. It would permit mobilization techniques to promote production enthusiasm rather than the use of material incentives. These decisions paved the way for the adoption of the radical approach to development embodied in the GLF.

Two other factors contributed to the radicalization of policy. The first was that Mao had already begun to push social transformation in the countryside, sweeping aside the objections of those who felt that steady mechanization must come first. In July 1955, Mao called for one-half of all households to be in cooperatives by the end of 1957. In practice, the speed of transition was even quicker, with all households so organized by the end of 1956 and communization completed even more swiftly.

Second, significant criticism of the practice of CCP rule surfaced. The external origins were derived from the death of Stalin and Krushchev's February 1956 'secret speech' denouncing Stalin's crimes and attributing them to the cult of the individual. The internal causes were derived from resistance by workers and peasants to the rapid pace of socialization. Mao was not willing to go as far as Krushchev in his denunciation of Stalin – to do so might have reflected badly on himself – but accepted that he had made mistakes. It did cause him to think about leadership and he outlined his own methods on correct leadership in the Ten Great Relationships (Mao 1956, in Schram, 1974, pp. 61–83). He reaffirmed that a balance must be struck between democracy and centralism and argued that there would be 'long-term coexistence and mutual supervision' between party and non-party people. This theoretical position, together with Mao's reaction to the 1956 uprising in Hungary and his desire to shake up a party apparatus that he felt was becoming increasingly conservative and institutionalized, led to the launching of the 'Hundred Flowers' Campaign. Mao felt secure that the intelligentsia basically supported his revolution and that, while he decried the nature of the criticism unleashed in Hungary, what was needed in China was not repression of complaint but the encouragement of open criticism of the party apparatus.

The Campaign was launched in May 1956 and widened in February 1957 when Mao invited intellectuals to raise criticisms and suggested that the party, some of whose leaders were frustrating his plans for social transformation, was not above criticism from those outside. The depth of criticism was, however, unexpected and ranged widely, even calling into question the legitimacy of the party and the revolution itself. Mao was bitterly disillusioned with the intellectual elites and on 8 June 1957 the Campaign was brought to a swift close when the *People's Daily* published an editorial denouncing the 'rightists' who had abused their freedom to attack the party and socialism. This marked the start of the 'Anti-Rightist Campaign' under which hundreds of thousands of intellectuals were investigated, demoted, fired or imprisoned.

Perhaps more alarmingly, the socialization drive of the new party-state had begun to run against the material interests of both the workers and the peasants. Evidence suggests that peasant withdrawal from the cooperatives in the winter of 1956–57 was extensive and was dubbed a 'small typhoon' (Teiwes, 1987, p. 140). Research by Perry shows how the socialization of industry was not universally approved of by the new working class (Perry, 1997). By early 1957 reforms had led to a decline in real income for workers and loss of input into decision-making, leading to an increase in strike activity in Shanghai and other industrial centres. Those protesting, on the whole, were rejecting the process of socialization. Thus, while the immediate causes were economic, the ultimate consequences could have quickly become political. This must have alarmed Mao and the Party Centre and perhaps provides an additional explanation as to why the leadership not only launched a crackdown on 'rightists' but also rallied behind a policy to press ahead quickly to complete socialist transformation.

Radicalization in the political sphere was soon followed in 1958 by the 'Great Leap Forward' in the economy marking a radical break with the Soviet model of development. The GLF represented a return to the mobilization techniques for development used in the Yan'an period. The GLF was based on the premise that the enthusiasm of the masses could be harnessed and used to promote economic growth and industrialization. Mao wanted to fast-forward the development process and an express aim of the movement was to overtake Britain's output of major industrial products within 15 years. Better agricultural production would increase the amount of capital that could be accumulated for investment. The strategy rejected the notion that high-level development of the productive forces was a necessary prerequisite for socialist transformation; its theoretical foundations lay rather in Mao's notion of 'permanent revolution'. Permanent revolution would prevent the institutionalization and bureaucratization of the revolution, with continuing or new contradictions resolved by a series of qualitative changes as a part of the process of realizing Mao's developmental goals. Mao questioned the value of administrative planning copied from the Soviet Union and came down heavily against a detailed planning of economic activities by the central government. The advantages of local initiative, such as the innovation and improvement of basic agricultural implements, were to be brought into play. Local initiative was not to be stifled and the gains from mass mobilization were not to be underestimated. This would leave ample possibilities for the people to be mobilized for capital works and for engaging in the transformation of the social relations of production.

An integral part of the strategy was the policy known as 'walking on two legs'. This promoted the dual use of modern, large-scale, capital-intensive methods of production and traditional small-scale methods. Mao hoped that this combination would tap the huge reservoir of hitherto unexploited resources in the rural areas so that they would be capable of providing their own industrial goods, manure and agricultural tools. The most notorious result of this approach was the 'backyard steel furnaces' that produced a huge volume of often useless steel. Other more successful small-scale projects were the creation of small electric power generators and chemical fertilizer plants. This use of intermediate technology remains the greatest legacy of the movement and many of the small-scale production plants formed the basis of the rural industrial take-off of the 1980s.

Hand in hand with the GLF strategy went the programme of communization that created much larger collective units. By the end of 1959, the 750,000 cooperatives (higher-stage APCs) had been amalgamated into just 24,000 people's communes. The communes not only carried out agricultural work but were also responsible for such things as industrial work, trade, education, military affairs, health, village administration and social welfare. Communal living was introduced in some areas to release more labour for production.

While the GLF was not quite the wild act of voluntarism that it is often portrayed as in the West (Lippit, 1975), the campaign style with which it was pursued and the dominating radical political atmosphere very quickly pushed it to excesses. Most communes and industrial units falsified production figures to show that they were more 'red' than their neighbours. This contributed to setting even higher targets in subsequent plans. It is clear that although many people doubted the exaggerated figures, they were afraid to speak up for fear of being criticized. Planning was rendered totally ineffective. The imbalance within the structure of the national economy, combined with inevitable bottlenecks, meant that stoppages in production occurred and many enterprises overextended their productive capacity.

The communization programme also encountered major problems and resistance. Many peasants resented communal living and the confiscation of private plots. Other problems arose from the unwieldy size of the communes and the lack of competent personnel to administer them. Two external factors further contributed to the failure of the strategy. First, during the summer of 1960 the Soviets withdrew their aid following the Sino-Soviet split. Second, floods and droughts were extremely severe. This latter factor enabled Mao and his supporters to shift the blame for failure onto natural disasters claiming that they were 70 per cent responsible. Foreign observers have always blamed the strategy itself and the post-Mao leadership has been less charitable about the catastrophe, blaming the strategy for 70 per cent of the damage.

From 1959 production in all sectors began to fall. Between 1958 and 1962, China's gross national product (GNP) fell by about 35 per cent. Paradoxically, national consumption at the aggregate level fell only marginally, as the share of national income devoted to investment dropped off sharply. Nonetheless, in many rural parts of the country acute shortages of food caused famine on a massive scale and at least 30 million people died as a result (from Pieter Bottelier; on the famines see Becker, 1996). It was obvious that a different strategy had to be found to restore production and, in particular, assure food supply for the population. Serious opposition first became apparent at the Lushan plenum (July–August 1959) and the main critic was the Defence Minister, Peng Dehuai. Peng attacked across a wide range of issues and particularly criticized the speed with which the programme had been implemented, the exaggeration of figures that made planning impossible, and condemned the commune programme. In addition, Peng criticized party practice, claiming that democracy in the party and the party's relations with the masses were being severely hampered by the 'petty-bourgeois fanaticism' characteristic of the GLF. While the strategy was abandoned in 1960 and Mao accepted some blame, such a direct challenge to his rule was intolerable. Peng was denounced as the leader of an 'anti-party clique' and replaced as Defence Minister by Lin Biao. The plenum, in accordance with a prior agreement, replaced Mao as President of the Republic with Liu Shaoqi, to whom powers of policy implementation increasingly passed. This situation was uncomfortable for Mao but ultimately deadly for Liu.

Liu had been the most enthusiastic supporter of the Mao cult in the 1940s but had presided over the removal of Mao Zedong Thought from the Party Statutes in 1956. In the 1950s Liu had favoured a policy that promoted agricultural mechanization before the social transformation proposed by Mao. In the early 1960s, together with Deng Xiaoping, he presided over policies of economic liberalization designed to restore economic health after the ravages of the GLF. Economic policy focused on how to provide correctives to and reversals of the disastrous GLF policy. The period also contained some policy experimentation that formed the initial point of departure for the post-Mao reforms. At the time, the policies promoted provided the basis for the conflicts that broke out in the Cultural Revolution.

The most pressing problem was how to revive agricultural production, and a series of adjustment policies were adopted throughout 1961. The order of priority for economic development was changed with agriculture taking priority over light industry and with the formerly favoured sector of heavy industry placed last. This meant that in rejecting the GLF strategy the Chinese did not resurrect the Soviet development strategy, and a lower growth rate for industry was anticipated than was put forward in either the First Five-Year Plan or the GLF. Further, the communes were reformed and more flexibility over production was granted. Private plots abolished under the radical atmosphere were returned to the farmers who were once again allowed to sell their goods in rural markets. The number of small enterprises assuming responsibility for their own profits and losses was also increased. These changes were encapsulated in the slogan of 'three freedoms and one guarantee'. The communes were not abolished but were greatly reduced in size and the socio-economic functions they had acquired during the GLF were reduced. The basic organization was codified in September 1962 in the 'Regulations of the Work in the People's Communes' (the 60 Articles) and it remained essentially unchanged until the reforms of 1978–83. The number of communes was increased from 24,000 to 74,000, making them more manageable units, and the three-tier structure of commune, brigade and team was reaffirmed, with the team functioning as the basic accounting unit. The size of the teams was decreased so that it comprised only 30 or 40 households. The team became the most important unit in the countryside as it could make the final decisions concerning both the production of goods and the distribution of income.

When provided with an alternative, the farmers tended to reject advanced collective structures. Dali Yang (1997) has shown that after the famine when local leaders and farmers sought any strategy for survival, they chose non-sanctioned ones, especially household contracting for agricultural production. This system took the household as the key economic unit, with it undertaking certain production guarantees with local administrative authorities. While Mao was willing to decentralize certain powers to the production team, re-empowering the household was unacceptable. By contrast, many farmers opted for the household when they had the choice. Rejection of the collective continued even after the crackdown on household contracting began in November 1961; the practice was criticized as representing the 'spontaneous capitalist tendencies of the peasantry'. As late as May 1962, 20 per cent of all rural households adopted a household-based system of responsibility; by the summer this figure rose to 30 per cent. Mao and his supporters at the policy-making centre consistently rejected this preference for household farming and associated market factors as a retrograde step that could lead China astray ideologically. To accept this would have marked a major defeat for Mao and his view of the transition to socialism. This battle over households, markets and socialism was rejoined in the reform debates and policies of the 1980s, and has led Selden (1995, p. 250) to conclude provocatively that:

We must now read the entire history of the PRC at one important level as the persistent – ultimately successful – effort from below to restore the role of markets that socialist party leaders had accepted during resistance but sought to suppress once they were in power.

In the industrial sector a policy of financial retrenchment was introduced to help rationalize production. Thousands of construction projects were stopped or scrapped and investment for capital construction was lowered by 80 per cent. Material incentives were revived as the main stimulant for increasing production and managers were given greater freedom to determine policy in their own enterprises. The workforce was greatly reduced as the 20 million or so farmers who had joined it in the industries were returned to the countryside. To prevent future urban drift the residence system was tightened to keep the rural dwellers in the countryside and to make it difficult for workers to change jobs and virtually impossible to change cities. In return, enterprises and work-units would provide cradle-to-grave care for their employees.

The recovery programme was an impressive success with growth, from a low base, averaging 15 per cent per annum from 1962 to 1966 (information from Pieter Bottelier). However, the economic recovery and the manner in which it was achieved led to policy divisions resurfacing. By 1964, Mao and his supporters felt that economic readjustment was complete. While there had been undeniable economic gains, they had been attained by increasing the urban–rural difference and by increasing the differentials between various groups in society. The programme had proved especially advantageous to skilled workers and technocrats and the social and political tensions that resulted led some to question of whether the programme should be continued. The new priority given to agriculture was not disputed but there were differences over the substance of specific policies. The main source for disagreement stemmed from continued debate over the GLF. Nobody proposed a complete return to the strategy and Mao acknowledged that a more cautious approach to planning was necessary. Even so, Mao was not willing to see all the GLF policies abandoned in favour of ones less concerned about the means through which economic development was to be achieved.

The radicalization of politics and the resurrection of class struggle, 1962–78

In the early 1960s, Mao found he was unable to direct the policy-making process and referred to himself as a 'dead ancestor'. His attempts to preserve something of the GLF experiment appeared thwarted, but in January 1962 speech he signalled that he would not remain in the political wilderness. Like his policy nemesis Liu Shaoqi, he stressed the importance of democratic centralism, but unlike Liu he spoke at great length of the importance of democracy and the continued use of the mass line. For Mao, the mass line would prevent bureaucratization of the body politic and was a way to mobilize the people to reach an objective. It went hand-in-hand with a campaign-style of policy implementation. Mao felt that this approach had been abandoned during the years of economic retrenchment. Crucial for later developments, he put forward the idea that class struggle did not gradually die out in socialist society but continued to exist, a point reiterated at the Tenth Plenum of the Eighth Central Committee (September 1962). Using Yugoslavia as an example, Mao claimed that it was possible for a socialist country to change its nature and become revisionist. Mao's insistence on the continuation of class struggle did not predict the massive upheavals of just a few years later and he made it clear that class struggle should not interfere with economic work but proceed simultaneously. Mistakes made by rural cadres were to be treated as 'contradictions among the people'. Out of the plenum grew the Socialist Education Movement (1962–65).

While the leadership supported the new campaign, it is clear that Liu Shaoqi and Deng Xiaoping were more inclined to control the movement, keeping the party in charge and not letting it run out of control and damage the economic revival. Mao and his supporters felt frustrated by what they saw as deliberate attempts to stop mobilization of the masses to weed out corruption and to keep rural cadres on the revolutionary path. By January 1965 Mao had decided that Liu had to be removed (Snow, 1972, p. 17) and the movement radicalized, paving the way for the Cultural Revolution and the death and humiliation of most of Mao's former 'comrades-in-arms'.

In January 1965 a Central Work Conference issued a document that signalled an important shift in the targets of the movement. The document proceeded from the premise that the struggle between socialism and capitalism was present in the party itself. Consequently the principal target became 'people in positions of authority in the party who take the capitalist road'. The document undermined the capacity of the party to control the movement by adjudging that the masses represented the most effective supervision of cadres, and 'peasant associations' were permitted to seize control temporarily if they decided a local administration had been 'usurped' by capitalist elements. As Mao became convinced that the source of the troubles lay at the heart of the party itself, the lines were drawn for the battles of the Cultural Revolution (see Box 3.5).

The Great Proletarian Cultural Revolution is the most complicated and one of the most misinterpreted events in the history of the PRC (for the best account see MacFarquhar and Schoenhals, 2006). Attempts to understand it have not been helped by simplistic explanations that it was a two-line struggle between socialism and revisionism. It is not even clear what Mao really wanted from the movement, and he changed his mind on crucial issues during its course (see Box 3.6). Lieberthal (1995, p. 112) has neatly summarized a number of factors that underlay Mao's thinking. He certainly wanted to get rid of Liu Shaoqi, who died in desperate circumstances in 1969, but seemed to have no other successor in mind. He also seems to have wanted to shake up the bureaucracy,

---

Box 3.5: Key Political Dates, 1966–78

1966 16 May, Circular marks start of Cultural Revolution
August, Eleventh Plenum of the Eighth CC adopts the 'Sixteen Point Decision', further radicalizing the political atmosphere

1967 February, 'Revolutionary rebels' announce the establishment of the Shanghai commune; Mao rejects it

1969 March, Soviet and Chinese forces clash along the Ussuri River
April, Ninth Party Congress marks the return to top-down rebuilding of party and state

1970 August, Second Plenum of the Ninth CC reveals leadership divisions and subsequently Chen Boda is purged as a 'sham Marxist'

1971 September, Lin Biao's plane crashes in Mongolia
October, China is admitted to the UN; Taiwan's status revoked

1972 February, President Nixon arrives in Beijing

1973 August–September, Tenth Party Congress attempts to forge a new leadership

1974 April, Deng Xiaoping reappears to speak at the UN and by January 1975 is effectively in charge of the government

1975 January, Fourth National People's Congress, Zhou Enlai outlines the 'Four Modernizations'

1976 January, Zhou Enlai dies and Hua Guofeng is appointed acting premier
April, Tiananmen demonstrations used to purge Deng Xiaoping
September, Mao dies
October, 'Gang of Four' arrested

1977 July, Third Plenum of the Tenth CC restores Deng to all his posts
August, Eleventh Party Congress calls an end to the Cultural Revolution

1978 February–March, Fourth National People's Congress announces a new ambitious economic policy
December, Third Plenum of the Eleventh CC announces shift to economic modernization as core of party work

Box 3.6: Changing Views of the Cultural Revolution

'All revolutionary intellectuals, now is the time to fight! Let us be united, hold high the great red banner of Mao Zedong thought, rally ourselves around the party CC and Chairman Mao, break the controls of revisionism and all its plots and tricks, so as to wipe out resolutely, lock, stock and barrel, all the monsters and freaks and all the Krushchev-style counterrevolutionary revisionists and to carry out to the end the socialist revolution' (Nie Yuanzi *et al.,* Philosophy Department, Peking University, 25 May 1966).

'I say to you all; youth is the great army of the Great Cultural Revolution! It must be mobilized to the full.

We believe in the masses. To become teachers of the masses we must first be the students of the masses. The present great Cultural Revolution is a heaven-and-earth shaking event' (Mao Zedong, 21 July 1966, in Schram, 1974, p. 254).

'The Great Cultural Revolution wreaked havoc after I approved Nie Yuanzi's big character poster at Peking University, and wrote a letter to Tsinghua University Middle School, as well as writing a big-character poster of my own ... It all happened within a very short period, less than five months ... No wonder the comrades did not understand too much. The time was short and the Peking University poster was broadcast, the whole country would be thrown into turmoil. Since it was I who caused the havoc, it is understandable if you have some bitter words for me' (Mao Zedong, 25 October 1966, in Schram, 1974, p. 271).

'The Great Cultural Revolution is not a mass movement, but one man moving the masses with the barrel of a gun' (Wang Rongfen, student, Beijing Foreign Languages Institute, 24 September 1966, in Schoenhals, 1996, pp. 149–50).

→

which he did by shattering the central party and state administration leaving the army and radical forces to fill the vacuum. He seems to have seen the movement as one last attempt to keep the revolutionary fires burning, giving the younger generation a feeling for the revolutionary enthusiasm that Mao's own generation had enjoyed. On the policy front there was stalemate in all major areas, although with the exception of education, arts and literature, the early years of the Cultural Revolution did not seem to resolve anything.

What the Cultural Revolution did result in was a shattered social fabric with students required to turn on their teachers, children encouraged to denounce their parents and authority in all its forms held up to ridicule. It unleashed many of the social tensions that had built up under CCP rule and revealed the frustrations of many with the bureaucracy. For a brief period of time even the leading role of the party was called into question, as revolutionary committees were formed to fill the political vacuum left by the collapse of the existing administrative struc-

→   'Smashing the "Gang of Four" is yet another signal victory in the Great Proletarian Cultural Revolution ... The victorious conclusion of the first Great Proletarian Cultural Revolution certainly does not mean the end of class struggle or of the continued revolution under the dictatorship of the proletariat ... Political revolutions in the nature of the Cultural Revolution will take place many times in the future. We must follow Chairman Mao's teachings and continue the revolution under the dictatorship of the proletariat to the end' (Hua Guofeng at the Eleventh Party Congress, 1977, pp. 49, 52).

'The "Cultural Revolution", which lasted from May 1966 to October 1976 was responsible for the most severe setback and the heaviest losses suffered by the party, the state, and the people since the founding of the PRC. It was initiated and led by Comrade Mao Zedong.

[Mao's erroneous "left"] theses must be thoroughly distinguished from Mao Zedong Thought. As for Lin Biao, Jiang Qing, and others who were placed in important positions by Comrade Mao Zedong, the matter is of an entirely different nature. They rigged up two counterrevolutionary cliques in an attempt to seize supreme power and, taking advantage of Comrade Mao Zedong's errors, committed many crimes behind his back, bringing disaster to the country and the people.

Irrefutable facts have proved that labelling Comrade Liu Shaoqi a "renegade, hidden traitor, and scab" was nothing but a frame-up by Lin Biao, Jiang Qing, and their followers.

Chief responsibility for the grave "left" error of the "Cultural Revolution", an error comprehensive in magnitude and protracted in duration, does indeed lie with comrade Mao Zedong. But after all it was the error of a great proletarian revolutionary' ('On Questions of Party History', 27 June 1981).

tures. A set of temporary organizations emerged at the centre to keep the country running, such as the Central Cultural Revolution Small Group, led by Jiang Qing, and the Working Group of the Central Military Commission. Citizens were exhorted to adulate Chairman Mao and his disjointed sayings became the justification for all policy initiatives and actions. More radical elements in the Cultural Revolution even seemed to eschew any intermediary organizations and envisioned a system that comprised 'Mao in Holy Communion with the masses'. For many the Cultural Revolution resulted in a loss of respect and legitimacy for the CCP as an institution. Once the PLA put the students back in their place, many became cynical towards the party and authority and alienated from the political process, a legacy that has persisted to this day. Certainly at the lower levels much of the struggle in the 1960s and 1970s comprised personal revenge rather than principled struggle, though on occasion the two could coincide. Chinese politics since 1969 has been dominated by the fallout from this momentous movement and even the reforms under Deng Xiaoping's tutelage would not have taken off so quickly without the excesses that had made most people tired of the politics of mobilization and class struggle.

Feeling frustrated by the party bureaucracy, Mao turned to an explosive cocktail of the mobilization of students as Red Guards, younger more radical party members who gathered around his wife, Jiang Qing and, crucially, PLA officers loyal to Defence Minister Lin Biao. The movement began in the realms of culture with criticism of veiled attacks on Mao by those who were opposed to Peng Dehuai's dismissal and who were critical of the GLF. Very quickly, calls for more proletarian literature led to a major attack on the party establishment.

The '16 May Circular' of 1966 drawn up by Mao and issued in the name of the CC radicalized the movement. The target was identified as 'the representatives of the bourgeoisie who have infiltrated the party, government and the army' and they were described as 'counterrevolutionary revisionists' who wanted to 'overthrow the dictatorship of the proletariat and replace it with that of the bourgeoisie'. While the PLA waited in the wings, Mao unleashed the students who had begun agitation following promulgation of the Circular. In August Mao gave them and their Red Guard groups his blessing.

In August, at a CC plenum from which opponents were excluded, the '16-Point Decision' was adopted and this reflected further radicalization. The aim of the movement was now the 'overthrow of those persons within the party in authority taking the capitalist road'. An important part of this struggle was the elimination of the 'four olds': the old values and customs that the 'capitalist roaders' manipulated to enable them to dominate the masses. Clearly, if the highest levels of the party were affected they could no longer be relied on to supervise the purification of the lower levels. This meant that it was up to the masses to liberate themselves; under no circumstances was action to be taken on their behalf and the party 'work teams', sent by higher levels for investigation, were criticized for trying to control the movement. Those who held 'incorrect' views were to be persuaded of their errors by reason rather than by force, but in the following months the battling Red Guard groups honoured this more in the breach than the observance. Finally, the decision was referred to the electoral system set up by the Paris Commune that appeared to challenge the whole idea of the ruling vanguard party. The new political organizations that evolved in the struggle were to become 'permanent' mass organizations for the exercise of political power.

Following the publication of this decision, debate and fighting between Red Guard groups and their opponents increased and the movement quickly fragmented and became increasingly unruly. Even Mao very quickly became aware of the need to bring the situation under control and to rebuild some kind of party and state structure. Yet, the Red Guards could not be wished away as easily as they had been created. Many opposed the resurrection of a system that they felt was in essence similar to that which they had been trying to destroy. Even among those groups that supported the return of a modified party and state system, there was considerable disagreement about precisely what form it should take.

With the 'masses' divided and the party-state structure in disarray, the process of restoring order fell to the PLA. Mao had already ensured army support through the appointment of his loyal supporter, Lin Biao, as Defence Minister. The result was military Maoism. Mao, with his 'infallible' capability to map out the correct road to socialism, provided the system with its legitimacy, while the PLA provided the institutional continuity and necessary force to deal with 'class enemies'. For a while, it appeared as if Mao wished to extend the PLA's supposed tradition of plain living and unquestioning loyalty to society as a whole.

Not all in the PLA were happy about this new role. Local PLA commanders were often faced with the difficult task of deciding who were the revolutionary forces. Often they chose to side with the old, local bureaucrats whom they had known for years rather than with the more unruly 'revolutionary rebels'. This put local commanders in conflict with their own central military command. Not surprisingly, the students and other groups who had been promised a new system were disillusioned by these events. Mao had destroyed their faith in the party-state system and now his use of the military destroyed their faith in Mao as the invincible leader.

To run the country, Mao soon rejected the radical ideas of the Paris Commune as the new organizational form and instead the revolutionary committee was proposed. Not all authority was to be considered bourgeois and these committees were to comprise a 'three-in-one alliance' of revolutionary mass organizations, leading members of the local PLA units and revolutionary leading party-state cadres. The first such committee had been set up in Heilongjiang province. By September 1968 the last of the provincial revolutionary committees had been set up and in April 1969 the Ninth Party Congress was convened, marking the abandonment of the attempt to rebuild the system from the bottom up. The need to rebuild was also spurred by the March clashes with Soviet troops along the Ussuri River, clashes that we now know were initiated by China (Goldstein, 2001, pp. 985–97). The clashes following the Soviet invasion of Czechoslovakia, justified by the Brezhnev doctrine that asserted the Soviet right to intercede in the affairs of other socialist countries, gave impetus to Mao's recognition that rebuilding was necessary. This must have convinced Mao of the need to restore order. It also prompted him to improve relations with the United States that culminated in President Nixon's February 1972 visit to Beijing.

While proclaimed as a Congress of 'unity and victory', the unity was fragile at best and it was difficult to see what the 'victors' had won. The turmoil had done nothing to solve the policy differences and had actually created new problems. The Ninth Congress set in motion party rebuilding but differences existed within the leadership about the kind of party it should be, where the new cadres would come from and about the correct role for the PLA. The PLA was the one group really to benefit from the Cultural Revolution and it had acquired a new and vital governing role. Active soldiers headed all but four of the revolutionary committees and almost half of the CC members were from the PLA. The pre-eminence of the PLA was reflected by the appointment in the new constitution of Lin Biao as Mao's chosen successor.

However, rebuilding the party apparatus would mean that Lin would have to supervise the removal from power of his own support base. While the PLA had been important during the phase of destruction, Zhou Enlai and the revolutionary veterans were to play a greater role in reconstruction. Before the military could agree to withdraw they required assurances that the 'left' and the mass organizations would not carry out reprisals for the brutal way in which some had been treated. This was achieved with the removal from power of Chen Boda and his 'leftist' supporters in 1970. Chen had represented the most radical voice at the centre but he was unceremoniously dumped and criticized as a 'sham Marxist'.

The leadership group around Mao and Zhou could now turn their attention to reducing the influence of Lin Biao and the military. Between December 1970 and August 1971 the provincial party apparatus was rebuilt but the military actually consolidated its position during this process. In addition to the fear of reprisals, PLA reluctance to return to the barracks stemmed from the new-found power of centrally directed units such as the air force and navy that had not exercised political power previously and seemed unwilling to part with it. The death of Lin Biao while attempting to flee to the Soviet Union after an alleged *coup d'état* and the purge of his military supporters at the centre decreased military influence. Recent research reveals that Lin and his generals never had any intention of challenging Mao and certainly did not plan a *coup*, while Mao decided relatively late that Lin should go. The Lin Biao that emerges from recent accounts is sickly and passive and did not rouse himself even when he knew that Mao would purge him (Teiwes with Sun, 1996; Jin, 1999). A series of campaigns was launched against Lin, calling on the military commanders to accept party leadership, with the party rather than the army being once again portrayed as the symbol of national unity.

The question of what kind of party should rule China was resolved less easily, and indeed today still remains the core political issue. As the influence of the radicals was curbed and military influence decreased, increasing numbers of officials who had been purged during the Cultural Revolution returned to senior positions. The best example was Deng Xiaoping, who had been criticized as the 'number two person in authority taking the capitalist road'. In fact, it appears that Mao had always intended to bring Deng back once he had been taught a lesson.

This process of rehabilitation gained momentum at the Tenth Party Congress (August–September 1973). The Congress reflected an attempt to put together a leadership that could command sufficient support to allow economic development not to be disrupted, but at the same time could maintain some of the revolutionary momentum of the Cultural Revolution. In this context the Congress abandoned the attempt to resolve the question of succession by appointing a specific individual in favour of appointing a collective leadership by electing five vice-chairs. However, it was clear that the system was excessively dominated by a 'supreme leader', the institutions attacked in the Cultural Revolution possessed no legitimate authority in the eyes of many, the people who staffed the institutions were severely divided about the way forward, thus paralysing decision-making, and many urban residents had become cynical about the whole political process.

By 1974 Mao and his supporters felt the pendulum had swung too far and they appeared ready to launch a new campaign to consolidate the gains of the Cultural Revolution. On 2 February 1974 the *People's Daily* called on people to 'dare to go against the tide and to advance into the teeth of storms' and a campaign of mass criticism unfolded. Premier Zhou Enlai, who was critically ill, was one of the main targets, together with those such as Deng Xiaoping who had returned to power under his and even Mao's protection. Initially, the conflict was contained and another attempt at ensuring collective succession was made at the Fourth National People's Congress (January 1975). At the Congress, Zhou Enlai outlined the policy of the four modernizations (agriculture, industry, science and technology, and national defence), a policy that he had first presented in 1964. The policy envisaged a two-stage programme, with the first objective being to build an 'independent and relatively comprehensive industrial and economic system' by 1980, and the second being to bring the national economy to the front rank of the world by the year 2000. The Congress appointed a coalition that seemed to represent the opposing groups within the leadership. However, it was very fragile, and fell apart shortly afterwards.

The new economic policy ran counter to the sketchy ideas that Mao and his more radical supporters had begun to develop during the 1960s and 1970s. It is difficult to say that their ideas amounted to a coherent theory of economic transition but it is possible to piece together a nascent strategy that had a number of specific policy consequences (see

Christensen and Delman, 1981; Van Ness and Raichur, 1983). In the 1950s Mao had already made clear his dislike of Soviet-style administrative planning and preference for decentralization to local-level governments. This he felt would provide greater flexibility but would ensure policy coordination and offer the opportunity for mass mobilization for capital construction works and to transform the social relations of production. Mao also rejected decentralizing economic powers to the production units themselves as well as an incentive strategy based on material incentives.

In his major critique of Soviet economic thinking, Mao proposed a break with the idea that socialism was an independent mode of production (Mao, in Roberts and Levy, 1977). In his view, socialism was a transitional mode between capitalism and communism. As we have seen, Mao did not see socialism as a phase of harmonious and peaceful development, but rather racked by contradictions between the economic base and the superstructure, and that class struggle still persisted. In contrast to his more orthodox Marxist colleagues, Mao felt less constrained by 'objective laws of economic development' and adopted a more voluntaristic approach, as witnessed in the GLF and the Cultural Revolution. Such an approach would permit people to overcome physical and other constraints on development and could also prevent the revolution from stagnating and even a capitalist restoration taking place.

These ideas were developed by the group later denounced as the 'Gang of Four', in particular Yao Wenyuan (1975) and Zhang Chunqiao (1975). They sought to explain how a socialist economy might regress back to a capitalist one. They identified 'bourgeois rights' and the persistence of capitalist factors, such as commodities and differential wages, as providing a material base for the reproduction of capitalism. Such factors also provided the source of power for a new bourgeoisie to emerge and prosper. Further, the division of labour created an 'intellectual aristocracy' who ruled over the production units, denying the workers access to real power. In their view, it was necessary to enforce the 'dictatorship of the proletariat' to prevent capitalism from being restored and a new bourgeoisie from taking power. Their wrath turned on the policy of the 'four modernizations' and in one of their memorable phrases they claimed they would rather have 'a late socialist train' than 'a capitalist one that ran on time'. To prevent capitalist restoration there would have to be many 'cultural revolutions' to eradicate the remaining capitalist factors.

Their solution had direct policy consequences that affected the lives of hundreds of millions. Intellectuals and those engaged in management were viewed with particular suspicion and were required to undertake regular manual labour and even to spend many years in the countryside to 'learn from the peasants'. This policy even extended to the foreign students in China. Each week the institute leaders would devise manual labour tasks for us students to engage in. We pulled down trees and moved rocks from one end of the campus before moving them back again the next week. We also did a stint on a people's commune just outside Yangzhou, where the Grand Canal meets the Yangzi. We were a drag on the production of the commune and the local farmers had to be bribed to take us on with a few little household items. Perhaps the most important impact of this policy, as with the 'revolutionary travels' of the Red Guards, was to expose to the urban elite just how poor and backward China really was. It convinced many of the need for drastic reforms.

To prevent the power of a new management class from developing, workers' control of the enterprise was to be secured through worker participation in management. This did not mean, however, that the workers ran the factories, but it did provide various institutional mechanisms through which their voices could be heard. In particular, the 'Gang of Four' sought to reduce and even eliminate the material privileges that could succour the 'new bourgeoisie'. Grades on salary scales were to be limited to reduce income differentials and piece-rates and bonuses were to be curtailed or even eliminated. In the countryside private plots were criticized as was production outside of the plan as the 'tails of capitalism'. On the communes, while more moderate voices wanted to keep accounting at the team level, the 'Gang of Four' wanted to raise it to the level of the brigade as this would make the countryside appear more socialist. These and other measures would eradicate a material base for the 'new bourgeoisie' from emerging. This policy put the collective above the individual and was accompanied by an egalitarian distribution policy and austerity in consumption. Austerity was promoted by campaigns to be frugal and adopt plain living (something Mao's wife, Jiang Qing, never took to apply to herself) and was reinforced through an intricate system of rationing. Combined with the emphasis on 'self-reliance' in production under which most areas produced for their own needs, it meant that consumption was limited to a small number of basic goods.

Finally, the 'Gang of Four' took a negative view of the role of international trade in development. The principles of 'self-reliance' extended to foreign trade, with it playing at best a residual role, and all efforts were made to restrict the import of bourgeois ideas. In particular, they attacked Deng Xiaoping's plans to import technology on a large scale and to pay for it through the export of China's minerals. They accused Deng of being a traitor and of turning China into an 'appendage of imperialism'.

Given such divergent views it is not surprising that the political coalition soon fell apart. Two main factors accelerated the collapse of this attempt at conciliation. First, the ill-health of the older generation of China's leaders brought the question of succession to the forefront. Secondly, concrete economic plans had to be drawn up for the new Five-

Year Plan to be implemented beginning in 1976. This brought the differing approaches to development strategy into sharp focus. While Zhou, Deng and their supporters started convening meetings and conferences to draw up programmes for their growth-oriented policies, their opponents launched a series of theoretical campaigns directed against those whom they saw as 'whittling away' the gains of the Cultural Revolution. The latter group enjoyed little influence in the crucial apparatus such as the military and the economic planning system, but instead dominated the education and propaganda systems. Policy practice and party rhetoric began to diverge dramatically. While Zhou and Deng sought to rally production and begin the importing of new technologies, their opponents began campaigns using historical allegory to attack what they saw as 'class capitulation at home and national capitulation in foreign affairs'.

Not for the first time in a communist system, it was the death of the 'supreme leader' (Mao in September 1976) that offered a window of opportunity for a radical break with the past. Developments unfolded swiftly and on 6 October 1976 the PLA elite guard, under instructions from the veteran military leader Ye Jianying, arrested the 'Gang of Four' (Jiang Qing and her closest supporters). The organizational forms experimented with by the 'Gang of Four' failed to gain legitimacy. This fact, combined with the 'Gang of Four's' suspicion of the party and lack of support within its top leadership, meant that they fell back all too readily on the invocation of Mao's name as a source of legitimacy. While they were able to manipulate Mao's vague directives and pro-Zhou and Deng demonstrations in April 1976 to cause Deng's second purge, their grip on power was tenuous. In January 1976, after Zhou had died, it was neither Deng nor one of the 'Gang of Four' who was named acting premier but the little known Hua Guofeng. This indicated that, while Mao may have had reservations about Deng, he was not willing to give free rein to his wife and her supporters.

With the arrest of the 'Gang of Four', the challenge of coming to terms with this economic and political legacy first fell to Hua Guofeng, who pursued a policy of 'Maoism without Mao'. For the economy, Hua favoured the 'quick-fix' approach, setting ambitious planning targets and using the selective import of high-level technology to transform the ailing situation. The basis for this transformation was to be the 1976–85 Ten-Year Plan presented to the Fifth NPC (February–March 1978), a plan that owed much to Deng's alternative policy prognosis from 1975 to 1976. The plan set forward a number of optimistic targets and bore resemblance to Mao's 12-year plan of the mid 1950s that had preceded the GLF. However, Hua reversed the previous sectoral priority, placing the emphasis on heavy industrial development rather than agriculture. Some 120 large-scale projects were to be completed by 1985 and an almost 150 per cent increase in steel production was called for. The Maoist obsession with grain production was retained with the call for an increase in production of over 40 per cent.

This initial post-Mao strategy served only to compound the problems. The importing of modern technology, the 'Great Leap Westward', far outstripped both China's export capacity and its ability to absorb the imports. The trade deficit with 'capitalist' countries grew from US$1.2 billion in 1977 to $4.5 billion in 1979. There was the notorious case of the modern Wuhan steel plant that would have required more electricity to run it than could be generated to supply the needs of the entire city. Many of the large-scale projects could not be completed because of planning errors and a shortage of the necessary skilled personnel

In the political realm, Hua also failed to address the problems of the Maoist legacy. Little attention was paid to political-administrative reform. For the most part, such problems as were recognized were put down to the excesses of the 'Gang of Four', the 'bad workstyle' to which officials had grown accustomed as a result of the Cultural Revolution, and the remaining influences of a 'feudal' way of thinking. No moves had been made to redefine party–society relations or to reduce the excessively leader-dominated system.

Hua and his supporters retained certain ideas from the Cultural Revolution period along with the ambiguities. Further, their attitude towards the party's role in society was designed to complement their optimistic proposals for economic development. Essentially, Hua and his supporters proposed the continuance of the party as a vehicle of mobilization to conduct mass campaigns, both economic and political, to achieve the ambitious economic targets. They persisted with the Maoist ambiguity that while the party was to be in command, the masses were to monitor abuses by its officials. This view caused suspicion of the party to remain while failing to create organizations with legitimacy. It was too dependent on the more 'radical' aspects of Mao's legacy and the creation of a new personality cult around Hua to resist policy shifts to the new economic programme.

Hua Guofeng was never able to come to terms with the problem of leadership. He continued the Mao cult and set about creating one of his own. Politically, it would have been extremely difficult for Hua to have dismantled the excessively Mao-centred system as his own right to rule was based on the claim that he was Mao's hand-picked successor. The increasing emphasis from December 1978 onwards on the need to regularize procedures and the mounting criticism of the 'feudal workstyle' did not augur well for Hua's continued occupation of top party and state posts. The restoration of Deng Xiaoping to his posts at the Tenth Plenum of the Tenth CC (July 1977) had not helped Hua. It was clear to all that Deng enjoyed higher military status and prestige than Hua. No matter how much they may have sought to cooperate, there was no room in the Chinese political system for two dominant leaders. Indeed, Hua gave up the premiership in September 1980 and his position as party chair in June 1981. The quaint poster that was widely distributed of the aged Mao handing the youthful Hua a piece of paper with Mao's inscription 'With you in charge, I am at ease' smacked far too much of the Emperor passing on the Mandate of Heaven to his chosen successor.

By the late 1970s, it was becoming clear to the group of veteran leaders around Deng Xiaoping that solution of the economic, political and social problems required a major overhaul of the system. While the aggregate figures for the economy do not justify the official CCP verdict that the Cultural Revolution represented 'ten lost years', they mask increasing problems and imbalances in the Chinese economy. After a mild economic recovery in the early 1970s, the growth rate declined, and by 1976 the decline began to assume crisis proportions. In 1976, the average growth rate of the national income dropped 2.3 per cent and the growth of total production was, at 1.7 per cent, below the rate of population growth. In part, the serious Tangshan earthquake of 1976 can explain these poor results. However, it is more plausible to explain the seriousness of the results in terms of the paralysis that gripped China's economic decision-making in the years prior to 1976. This economic downturn was combined with a longer-term dissatisfaction about stagnating living standards on the part of much of the population. The government's consistent overconcentration on accumulation at the expense of consumption meant that rationing, queuing and hours spent on laborious household chores were the daily fare for most urban residents. In the countryside, the attacks on private plots of land and free markets as 'capitalist tails' had caused farmer resentment by undermining alternative sources of income. Although the collective functioned effectively in some regions, many farmers saw it as an alien entity that made unfair demands on their time without supplying just returns. It seems no exaggeration to conclude that China's population had probably had enough of tightening their belts in return for the promise of a bright future.

Behind all this was a ticking population time bomb. Mao's 1950s view that a larger population would increase China's strength had meant that the population had boomed from 540 to 930 million by the time of his death. Unemployment and underemployment were serious problems, and it was clear that a major overhaul was required to resolve the problems; the Third Plenum of the Eleventh CC (December 1978) began to articulate a new policy course.

Chapter 4

China under Reform, 1978–2010

The reform era now lasts longer than the period from 1949 until its commencement. It runs from the initial dismantling of the communes in the countryside, to the faltering attempts to reform the urban industrial structure, to the systemic crisis that resulted in the demonstrations of 1989, to the no-holds-barred rush for economic growth of the 1990s, to the adjustment policies of the twenty-first century that have sought to ensure that growth will be sustainable while dealing with the problem of rising socio-economic inequality. Institutional adaptation and policy innovation have been impressive but one thing has remained constant: the paramount position of the CCP. The combination of a more marketized economy combined with an authoritarian political structure has seen the rise of descriptions such as 'populist authoritarianism', 'adaptive authoritarianism', and 'market Leninism' to describe this hybrid system. The current leadership are grappling with the legacies of this reform trajectory as well as dealing with more recent events such as the fallout from the 2008–09 financial crisis.

The reform programme launched under Deng Xiaoping's tutelage in 1978 affected every aspect of life in China and left no institution untouched. The reforms led to a significant liberalization of previous regime practice in terms of party control over the economy and society. However, it was not the intention that this liberalization would lead to democracy and Deng and his followers preferred to combine the introduction of market forces in the economy with tight political control. While the reforms left the pillar of one-party rule untouched, they undermined the other main pillar of a centrally planned economy with predominant social ownership of the means of production. Certainly by the early twenty-first century, this strategy appeared to be a success in economic terms, with the economy averaging 10 per cent per annum output growth, leading to significant rises in incomes. However, the reforms have been deeply contested by those opposed on ideological grounds, or groups that felt disadvantaged by the reforms, or by those who felt that the reforms had not progressed swiftly enough. This chapter reviews the progress of the reforms and the opposition they have generated.

no intention of democracy

The Third Plenum and the Initial Reform Agenda, 1978–84

The criticism of Mao Zedong and the attempts by Deng and his supporters to dismantle the personality cult meant that Mao's name could no longer be invoked effectively to underpin legitimacy. As a result, they chose to promise a bright economic future for all within a relatively short space of time, meaning that CCP legitimacy would be linked closely to the ability to deliver the economic goods. The political breakthrough for Deng came at the Third Plenum of the Eleventh CC held in December 1978 (see Box 4.1). Deng had formed an alliance with pragmatic planners, in particular Chen Yun, accepting their views of an alternative approach to economic development. In this sense, the initial victory at the plenum was Chen's rather than Deng's. Later developments and the official history that ascribes the new line and its development almost exclusively to Deng have tended to obscure this fact. Deng's usurpation of full credit for the original reform programme and its subsequent radicalization angered Chen, and he became Deng's strongest opponent on the question of pace and extent of economic reform. On a number of occasions, Chen upbraided Deng for ignoring the opinions of others, thus defying the principles of collective leadership that Chen claims had been restored at the plenum. The differences between the two never reached a crisis point, unlike Deng's relations with his first two chosen successors, Hu Yaobang and Zhao Ziyang.

The plenum implemented three decisions that had a lasting impact. First, economic modernization was made central to all party work. Ideology and class struggle were downplayed and policy-making became more pragmatic, summed up in the slogan 'practice is the sole criterion for testing truth' (the slogan was launched in May 1978) and the corresponding policy line of 'correcting mistakes wherever they are discovered'. Second, despite the plenum's decision to forget about the past and concentrate on the future, the new 'practice' slogan was used both at the plenum and subsequently to reverse a whole series of previous political judgements. These were used both to undermine the legitimacy of Hua Guofeng, the party chairman, and his supporters, and to establish the credibility of Deng's and Chen's policy positions. Essentially, Mao's increasing radicalism in his later years was denounced while previous attempts to moderate 'economic excesses' through a policy of economic liberalization were praised. To award themselves the mantle of popular legitimacy the demonstrations of April 1976 were reassessed and proclaimed a revolutionary movement that had demonstrated support both for Zhou Enlai and Deng Xiaoping. Third, the plenum formed the source for a new policy direction that gradually increased the influence of market forces in the Chinese economy. This was felt first in the rural sector. The plenum ducked

Box 4.1: Key Political Dates, 1978–96

1978 November, Posters start to go up at Democracy Wall
December, Third Plenum of the Eleventh CC shifts policy to economic reform

1979 March, Deng puts forward the 'Four Basic Principles'
October, Democracy Wall writer Wei Jingsheng sentenced to 15 years in prison

1980 February, Fifth Plenum of the Eleventh CC rehabilitates Liu Shaoqi
May, China joins the World Bank and International Monetary Fund (IMF)
September, Zhao Ziyang replaces Hua Guofeng as Premier

1981 January, Trial of 'Gang of Four' completed
June, Resolution on party history criticizes both the Cultural Revolution and Mao
June, Hu Yaobang replaces Hua Guofeng as party head

1982 September, Twelfth Party Congress adopts new statutes

1984 October, CC document proposes major urban industrial reform

1986 April, Zhao Ziyang presents the Seventh Five-Year Plan that is cautious in tone
September, Sixth Plenum of the Twelfth Party Congress calls for improvement in ideological and cultural
December, student demonstrations lead to the purge of Hu Yaobang (January), and Zhao Ziyang becomes acting General Secretary

1987 October, the Thirteenth Party Congress favours continued economic and political reform

1988 Summer, Beidaihe meeting removes Zhao's right to speak on economic affairs

1989 15 April, Hu Yaobang dies, sparking student demonstrations
3–4 June, PLA troops brutally clear students from Tiananmen Square
June, Fourth Plenum of the Thirteenth CC formally removes Zhao Ziyang and Jiang Zemin becomes General Secretary
November, Deng Xiaoping steps down as head of Military Affairs Commission

1992 January–February, Deng tours South China to kick-start economic reform
September, Fourteenth Party Congress approves renewed economic reform

1993 November, Third Plenum of the Fourteenth Party Congress adopts the document 'Establishment of a Socialist Market Economic System'

1996 March, Taiwan Straits crisis escalates as Li Teng-hui is elected president of Taiwan

two pressing political issues: no assessment was made of the Cultural Revolution nor of the role of Mao. Given that Hua Guofeng and others had risen to power because of these two factors, this was not surprising.

After the plenum, Deng and the more pragmatic economic planners such as Chen Yun and Bo Yibo began to criticize the ambitious economic plans identified with Hua Guofeng and warned of 'economic rashness'. They repeatedly stressed the need to comply with 'objective economic laws', thus rejecting the voluntarism that had plagued policy since the late 1950s. These warnings were reflected in the new economic policies presented to the Second Session of the Fifth NPC (June–July 1979) and at the Third Session (1980) a three-year period of 're-adjusting, restructuring, consolidation and improvement of the national economy' was introduced. Economic priorities were reordered, with heavy industry relegated to last place behind agriculture and light industry. The primary focus was to fix targets for the agricultural sector. Rather than leading the economy, heavy industry would receive only such funds as were necessary for its adaptation to meet the needs of the other sectors (Pairault, 1982, pp. 119–48).

Economic policy revolved around the promotion of market mechanisms to deal with the inefficiencies of allocation and distribution that occurred with the central planning system. Awareness of the 'new technological revolution' increased the Chinese leaders' desire to make their system more flexible and thus more amenable to change. To take advantage of the market opportunities, more power of decision-making was to be given to the localities and in particular to the units of production themselves. Production units were given greater autonomy to decide what and how much to produce, and where to sell. At the core of this system was the ubiquitous contract that was expected to govern economic activity. Correspondingly, material incentives were seen as the major mechanism for causing people to work harder, and the socialist principle of 'to each according to their work' was to be firmly applied. Egalitarianism was attacked as a dangerous notion that retarded economic growth. These reforms of the domestic economy were accompanied by an unprecedented opening to the outside world in the search for export markets and the necessary foreign investments, technology and higher-quality consumer goods.

Change was rapid and dramatic in the rural sector and moderate in the urban sector, while political reform was ineffective and ultimately divisive. The Third Plenum ratified a policy intended to encourage growth in agricultural production by substantial increases in procurement prices and by modernizing agriculture through investments by the brigades and teams (Watson, 1984, pp. 83–108). At the same time, policy was relaxed to let different regions make use of the 'law of comparative advantage'. Reversing the policy of the Cultural Revolution, farmers were given the green light to work private plots and engage in sideline production. To allow the farmers to sell their products, for example their above-quota grain, private markets were again tolerated. Rural towns began to emerge as bustling centres of exchange. The drab, sparsely stocked state-run store was soon supplemented with a street market selling a range of foodstuffs that was far more varied and of better quality. The policy was firmly based on the collective and represented nothing radically new, and was modelled on the policies for economic revival that followed the Great Leap Forward (GLF). The net effect of this policy was, however, to increase dramatically state expenditure on agriculture, with well over 1 billion *yuan* of state subsidies provided for grain supplies to the urban areas. This kind of massive state investment was not feasible over the long term and neither was rapid technological transformation and mechanization. China's leaders were confronted by the same dilemma as in the mid 1950s of how to boost productivity without increasing state spending. This time, the answer was radically different and led to abandonment of the collective through a major restructuring of farmer incentives, away from the use of production quotas and to a focus on the household as the basis of production. This process was encapsulated in the term 'production responsibility system'.

In 1979, farmers in poor areas were beginning to abandon the collective structures and grassroots experimentation took place in contracting output to the household. Gradually this practice spread throughout other areas of rural China. Their abandonment of the collective, while opposed by many local cadres, received tacit support from pro-reform cadres (Zhou, 1996; Zweig, 1997, pp. 12–15 and chapter 2). It is worth noting that as late as 1981 Deng remained agnostic as to whether this was a good or a bad thing (personal communication from Fred Teiwes). As practice at the grassroots radicalized, the centre could do nothing but stand by and make policy pronouncements to try to catch up with reality. In this initial stage of reform it is clear that the central authorities were being led by developments at the grassroots level. However, it is important to point out that not all areas opted for decollectivization when given the choice. For example, while poor areas were going back to the household, one commune in Heilongjiang announced a shift to a wage labour system.

For a while, it looked as if the centre might abandon or be forced to abandon its monolithic approach to policy and allow different organizational models to flourish in different parts of China. By 1982–83, however, decisions were taken to standardize the new system and decollectivization was enforced throughout the country with a speed reminiscent of the collectivization of the 1950s. The new State Constitution (1982) returned the political and administrative powers of the commune to the resurrected townships, leaving the communes as an economic shell. The scale of administration was reduced, with 96,000 township governments replacing 55,000 people's communes. In 1983 the 'responsibility system for agriculture' was officially endorsed with the household as the basis for contracting. This was reconfirmed in 1984 when cropping contracts were extended to 15 years and measures were introduced to concentrate land in the hands of the most productive households. Abandonment of the collective as the key economic unit in the countryside was complete. In 1985, it was made clear that the market was to dominate with the announcement that the state procurement system was to be abolished. Instead of the state assigning fixed quotas of farm products to be purchased from farmers, a system of contract purchasing was introduced with all other products being sold on the market. The aim was to improve the distribution of commodities and reward further efficient producers with the expectation that wealthier farmers would reinvest capital and labour in the land. As discussed below, this did not prove to be the case.

Change in industry and the urban areas was much less dramatic. The embedded institutional interests in the industrial sector made a radical overhaul more difficult to achieve than in the rural sector and, as a result, policy was a stop-go affair with radical proposals bogging down once the effects began to bite. The October 1984 'Decision on Reform of the Economic Structure' promoted policy to bring the kinds of incentives and use of market forces that had proved successful in the rural areas to bear in the industrial sphere. It outlined the need for reform and pulled together the piecemeal experiments into a more thoroughgoing reform blueprint. The key was seen as making enterprises more economically responsible and profit retention was introduced and the system of tax-for-profit, introduced in 1983, was confirmed; losses, in theory, would no longer be covered by the state. To enable enterprises to take advantage of the limited market opportunities, managers were to be given greater power of decision-making with respect to production plans and marketing, sources of supply, distribution of profits within the enterprise and the hiring and firing of workers. It was clear, however, that enterprise reform was to form part of a comprehensive reform strategy. Not surprisingly, these reforms created differences of opinion and the acuteness of the debate about the way forward was sharpened by the overheating of the economy in late 1984 and early 1985.

It is not true to say that the period witnessed no political reform, but it was limited in scope to administrative reform while more radical proposals for change were criticized. The period 1978–80 was a high tide for suggestions for political reform, with not just the Democracy Wall Movement activists but also highly placed party members floating ideas on far-reaching change. Deng Xiaoping indicated his approval for political reform in August 1980 when he called for people's democracy to be developed to the fullest extent possible. According to Deng, it was necessary to ensure that the people as a whole really enjoyed the power of supervision over the state in a variety of effective ways. In particular, they were to 'supervise political power at the basic level, as well as in all enterprises and undertakings' (in Deng, 1984, p. 282). Although Deng's speech was not published officially until 1983, it did set the tone for subsequent discussions about reform, some of which recommended quite far-reaching structural change. This early promise of extensive reform was not followed by sufficient substantive change, thus causing many intellectuals and students to become frustrated. Substantive change was ruled out by the refusal of senior party leaders to accept the kind of structural reform that would lead to a redistribution of power to other groups and organizations in society. Orthodox party members were offended by the attacks on the party-state system that were aired during the Democracy Wall Movement of 1978–79, attacks that were sometimes repeated in the official media (see Wei, 1997). The rise of Solidarity in Poland in 1980 convinced them that too great a relaxation of party power would lead to loss of control. While some were presenting blueprints for a new political structure, party leaders, including Deng Xiaoping, were setting stringent limits to the extent of possible reform. The essential question was how far control could be relaxed to ensure that ideas useful for economic modernization would surface without party dominance being weakened. The experiences of the 'Hundred Flowers', the GLF and the Cultural Revolution caused leaders such as Deng Xiaoping to be suspicious of participation that took place outside direct party control. They thus tried to restore the effective leadership of the party while, at the same time, not negating the contributions that 'articulate social audiences' could make to the modernization process.

In effect, this meant that change was to be brought about by a 'revolution from above'. The party was to define the limits of what was acceptable and it was anticipated that continued party control over the process would ensure stability and stop the possibility of degeneration into chaos. This was best seen in the promotion of the slogan of adherence to the 'Four Basic Principles' that Deng put forward in March 1979. These principles enshrined the leadership of the party and adherence to socialism. Many critical intellectuals and students saw the promotion of the principles as an excuse to hold back on genuine political reform. Indeed the principles were used by ideological conservatives to launch campaigns against heterodox ideas in 1980–81 and 1983–84.

Until 1986, Deng was fairly successful in stopping these divisions from becoming destabilizing and the limited political reforms taken had been to his advantage or had supported his attempts to get the Chinese system moving again. The outstanding political issues from the Cultural Revolution were resolved in 1980–81. In February 1980, at the Fifth Plenum of the Eleventh CC, Hua Guofeng's closest supporters were removed from office and the former president, Liu Shaoqi, was posthumously rehabilitated. Hua relinquished the premiership to Zhao Ziyang in September 1980 and resigned as chair of the party in June 1981, turning affairs over to Deng's protégé Hu Yaobang. In 1981, the year of verdicts, the 'Gang of Four' together with 'supporters' of Lin Biao were sentenced and an official resolution on party history was adopted that was critical of both Mao and the Cultural Revolution.

Further, according to Deng, in 1982 China was in the midst of an 'administrative revolution' and measures were introduced to reduce the size of the bureaucracy, eliminate functional overlap, prevent the over-concentration of power in too few hands and recruit new, better technically trained members into the party. In 1982, the Twelfth Party Congress (September) and the Fifth Session of the Fifth NPC (December) codified the new policy directions and organizational changes by adopting new Party Statutes and State Constitution. Deng called the party congress the most important since that held in 1945 that had paved the way for CCP victory after the war.

Economic troubles and political instability, 1985–91

By 1985, there were problems in both the economy and the political realm, with opposition to the reforms becoming more apparent and bursting out for all to see in 1986 and 1989. By the end of 1984, the rapid pace of rural growth had slowed down and, ironically, the next phase of reform adversely hit the farmers' pockets. In 1985 when the state abolished its mandatory grain purchase, prices on the market dropped significantly. This led to several years of cat-and-mouse games between farmers and state agencies, with farmers cutting back on production or buying on the market when prices were low and selling to the state when it was obliged to pay the higher price. In addition, declining returns were setting in as the one-time boost farmers received from the organizational changes and other incentives worked their way through. With the decline in grain yield and the spiralling state food subsidies paid out to keep the costs down for urban workers, Chen Yun proposed stopping the second phase of reforms. Many farmers were forced back into grain production, which they had abandoned because of its lack of profitability. Not surprisingly, farmers resented the curtailment of their new-won freedoms. Stringent production quotas for grain were reimposed and the attempts to dismantle the state monopoly over distribution were effectively abandoned. Farmers were forced to sell to the state at below-market prices. Further, many farmers left the land either to work in more lucrative jobs in the rural industrial sector, which was by 1984 producing nearly 25 per cent of industrial output, or to migrate to find work in the cities.

In the industrial sector, problems had emerged with the transition to a market-influenced economy. The lifting of price controls and the new incentive system in enterprises led to a major overheating of the economy by late 1984 and early 1985, with a surge in inflation in 1985. As a result, the Seventh Five-Year Plan presented by Premier Zhao Ziyang (April 1986) struck a note of caution, with balanced growth as its theme. According to Naughton (1995, pp. 175–6), it rates as 'one of the most realistic and sound plans ever promulgated in China'. Growth, while lower, was still projected at a healthy 7.5 per cent per annum, with moderate improvements in social welfare and living standards to keep pace with economic growth. According to Zhao, the slowdown in growth rates would 'avert strain on the economy and ensure the smooth implementation of the reforms'. His worries centred on the twin problems of the tardiness with which industrial reforms had been implemented and the fall in grain output that occurred in 1985. In fact, Zhao came under pressure from deputies from leading grain-producing provinces to increase government investment in agriculture and to pay more attention to grain production. In a significant break with the past, the plan suggested guidance for production figures rather than setting mandatory targets. Zhao saw the plan as providing a solid basis for further advance of reforms. He confirmed that enterprise reform should continue, with enterprises being genuinely responsible for profits and losses. Under the phrase of a 'socialist commodity market' he proposed further extension to the market and also that a new form of macro-management be established with the state gradually moving from mainly direct to indirect control of enterprise management.

Nonetheless, opposition was coalescing and the issue of political reform and the student demonstrations of 1986 enabled opponents to manoeuvre to remove reformist party secretary Hu Yaobang. By summer 1986, it was clear that political reform had become a severely divisive issue within the political leadership. During the spring and early summer, critical intellectuals began to raise ideas for radicalizing the reforms, yet by the end of the year their views had been rejected and Hu Yaobang, who was thought to be sympathetic, had been dismissed from his post as general secretary. Disagreements led to the postponement of an expected decision on political reform until the Thirteenth Party Congress (October 1987). In fact, the Sixth Plenum of the Twelfth Party Congress (September 1986) instead of discussing political reform passed a resolution on the need to improve work in the ideological and cultural spheres. These are issues more closely identified with those seeking to limit the extent of political reform. The opponents of more radical reform continued to link wide-ranging changes with bourgeois contamination. The student demonstrations in late 1986 provided these opponents with their chance to launch a counterattack and remove Hu Yaobang.

The student demonstrations began in the city of Hefei, Anhui province, in December 1986 because of official interference to prevent students from standing in local elections. The demonstrations spread rapidly and combined a mix of student grievance over living and study conditions and concerns over lack of progress on political reform. On the whole, the students threw their support behind Deng and Hu and very few voices raised criticisms of one-party rule. Unlike in 1989, the demonstrations found little support within the broader society, partly because students were regarded as being relatively well off and in part because their demands found little rapport with the public at large. This was different from 1989 when the criticism of corruption found a sympathetic response. The turning point of official toleration was when students in Beijing defied a government ban and held a 1987 New Year's Day demonstration in Tiananmen Square (see Munro, 1988).

At the political centre, opposition came from three major groups that were able to ally on occasion to frustrate far-reaching reforms. However, while these groups could frustrate the progress of reforms, they could not roll them back for a consistent period of time. First, there were those who attacked the reforms on primarily economic grounds and who represented the traditional central-planning and economic apparatus. They were concerned about the destabilizing effect of pushing the marketization of the economy too far, too fast. They criticized the overreliance on the market and worried about the 'overheating' of the economy caused in part by the rapid growth of the collective sector, particularly the rural industries. Further, this group feared that policy trends would deepen regional inequalities between China's poor hinterland and its more advanced coastal regions. Finally, they were concerned about the mushrooming of corruption that sprang up as a result of the more liberalized policies and increased contacts with the West. Both issues are of major policy concern to current General Secretary Hu Jintao.

The concern about corruption was echoed by a second group who were worried about the consequences of liberalization for the social fabric of China. These orthodox party leaders consistently insisted that the party must reaffirm its leading role also in the realm of ideology (see Zhao, 2009). They argued that socialism had moral and spiritual goals as well as a material goal, and that only the party could define them. These leaders felt that it was the party's role to dictate the nation's ethical and moral values. In this respect, the party had taken over the traditional role of the state in China. At the Twelfth Party Congress (1982), Hu Yaobang, then general secretary, announced a reversal in the listing of the party's tasks, placing the building of spiritual civilization before democratization, thus making it a prerequisite for democratization. This paved the way for subsequent campaigns for 'spiritual civilization' and against 'bourgeois liberalization' in 1983, 1987 and 1989–90. Further, they saw the 'open-door policy' as a source of problems within the party; a point they were able to get officially accepted in October 1983. An official decision on party consolidation, while stating that the 'open-door policy' had been entirely correct, noted that there had been an increase in the 'corrosive influence of decadent bourgeois ideology and remnant feudal ideas'. It is important to note that one year earlier when Hu Yaobang announced formally that a programme for the rectification of party style and 'consolidation' of party organizations would be launched, he did not cite this as a reason for problems in the party.

Third, there were some senior military leaders who had been closely associated with Mao during the war years and who subsequently provided a rallying point for those disaffected with the reform programme. Such military figures retained a 'leftist' ideology and were concerned by the erosion of Mao's legacy and the tarnishing of his image. Some were disgruntled about the low priority that the military had been accorded within the modernization programme, while others opposed the shift to a less political and more professionalized army. Discontent surfaced among the rank-and-file rural recruits when they saw the new possibilities for making money opening up in the rural areas that they had left behind. The impact of the responsibility system, in the form of providing outlets for making a decent living, caused China to introduce a conscription law in 1984.

Faced with this opposition, Deng Xiaoping was remarkably successful until the end of 1986 in limiting its impact. In 1982, the Central Advisory Commission to the CC was set up. The intention was that the Committee would function as a 'retirement home' for elderly officials, opening up positions in the formal political system for a younger generation more in tune with the demands of the modern world. However, many of those moved to the Commission were not willing to accept a decorative position and 'retire'. Although billed as 'transitional' (it was in fact scrapped in 1992), throughout the 1980s it provided more traditional party leaders with an institutional base from which to launch attacks on the reform programme. The role of the Commission as a focal point for the expression of conservative, orthodox views became more pronounced in late 1987 when Chen Yun became its head following his 'retirement' from the Standing Committee of the Politburo. This undermined somewhat the 1984–85 shake-up of the party and military leadership that had resulted in a major weakening of these groups' influence in formal leadership bodies.

The military's direct political influence was reduced and many elderly officers were replaced by a younger generation more committed to the idea of a less political, more professional military. In December 1984, 40 senior officers of the PLA general staff retired, the largest retirement ever; in January 1985 budget cutbacks were announced; and in April,

Hu Yaobang announced that troop levels would be cut back by 25 per cent, some 1 million personnel. To weaken the PLA's political influence, two other important measures were taken. First, in June 1985, a meeting of the Central Military Affairs Commission (CMAC), chaired by Deng Xiaoping, announced a restructuring of the military regional command structure. Apart from reasons of efficiency, this had the effect of breaking up potential powerful regional ties of key military leaders.

The second important step was the shake-up of the party leadership at the CCP national conference held in September 1985. This saw a sharp reduction in military representation on the Politburo. Of the ten resignations, six were military figures and no military appointees were among the six full new members of the Politburo. The military establishment resisted, however, one important change to personnel. Deng Xiaoping had tried to pass on his post as chair of the Military Affairs Commission to General Secretary Hu Yaobang. While senior military officers were willing to concede ultimately to Deng's authority, they were not prepared to accept his then protégé. This clearly reduced Hu's prestige and prevented him from forging an alliance with reformers in the military. It presaged later events when Deng was similarly unable to install his second chosen successor, Zhao Ziyang, as head of the Commission. Given the fact that control of the military was a key lever to power in China this was a serious blow to the pragmatic reformers and was a worrying sign which later developments confirmed.

The campaign against 'bourgeois liberalization' launched after Hu's dismissal was short-lived and his replacement by Zhao Ziyang seemed to indicate that the attack by the orthodox party members had caused little more than a hiccup in the reform process. This was borne out at the Thirteenth Party Congress held in October 1987 at which Zhao delivered a speech that on balance favoured commitment to continued reform. Despite containing some elements of compromise, on crucial issues Zhao came down on the side of the reformers. Thus he reiterated the necessity to 'uphold the four basic principles' while pursuing reform but the first five items of his work report dwelt on reform and the conservatives' demand for 'the building of a spiritual civilization' came last on the list. Most importantly, Zhao confirmed that China was in the 'initial stage of socialism', a phase that would last for around 100 years. Similar phrasing had been used as early as 1981 (Zhao, 2009, p. 205). The major task of this period was to improve material standards and not to wage class struggle. Such a definition was intended to remove the use of ideology to oppose reform. As far as possible, ideology was to be taken out of decision-making. As China was entering uncharted waters, theory was to be defined as policy developed, thus freeing China's decision-makers from the restraints of Maoist dogma.

In the economic sphere Zhao attacked the two traditional shibboleths of state socialism: central planning and state ownership. A dramatic reduction in the role of the plan in controlling the economy was proposed, giving the green light to the non-public sectors. He also advocated not only the use of commodity markets for consumer goods and means of production but also 'markets for ... funds, labour services, technology, information and real estate'. Moreover, Zhao broke with the principle that the only source of income was 'distribution according to work'. In the future

> buyers of bonds will earn interest, [and] shareholders dividends, enterprise managers will receive additional income to compensate for bearing risks, and owners of private enterprises who employ workers will receive some income that does not come from their own labour.

Zhao brushed aside possible accusations that this was making use of capitalist economic mechanisms, with the simple statement that these 'are not peculiar to capitalism' (Zhao, 1987).

However, Zhao's report showed elements of compromise on crucial economic questions. First, the Maoist obsession with grain production was not totally eradicated; Zhao committed China to major increases in grain production in the coming decade. More importantly, Zhao was cautious on the crucial topic of price reform. It had become increasingly obvious that the industrial reform programme would not succeed without a thorough reform of the pricing and subsidy system. Yet each time the reformers put this on the agenda they retreated rapidly in the face of the inflation unleashed. This would become a major issue after the Congress.

Zhao was also clear that political reform should continue, the issue that had led to Hu's dismissal. He reaffirmed that it was indispensable if economic reform was to continue but he was vague on what should be done. He did, however, call for a redistribution of power both horizontally to state organs at the same level and vertically to party and state organs lower down the administrative ladder. The most important measure proposed was the abolition of leading party member groups in units of state administration and work was begun to eliminate them as well as to eradicate those groups that had functional overlap. He also acknowledged that there was now a limited political pluralism under the leadership of the CCP.

Zhao also indicated that policy would push ahead with trying to reduce party influence in the day-to-day management of enterprises. The Party Statutes were amended to reflect this reduced role and in April

1989 at the Seventh NPC a new Enterprise Law was adopted that tried to limit as far as was politically feasible the scope of party work in the enterprise. Indeed, with respect to the role of the party in enterprise management no clear indication was given to resolve confusion over the division of responsibilities between party secretaries and managers.

However, after the Congress the economy faltered and inflation took off as China experimented with price reform. Initially, it looked as if with Deng's support China might stay the course but by the summer of 1988 Deng started to back away and shifted the blame for the attempts to make a radical breakthrough on to Zhao. The economic situation increased general disgruntlement among the populace while many critical intellectuals were frustrated at what they saw as the lack of political reform. The leadership might have navigated the troubled period without crisis if it had remained united, but the façade of leadership unity began to crack under the strains of management and was blown apart by the massive student-led demonstrations that erupted throughout urban China in the spring of 1989. Zhao tried to use his position as general secretary to limit the ability of the more conservative premier, Li Peng, to divert more radical economic reforms. Having previously been critical of Hu Yaobang's attempts when General Secretary to interfere with Zhao's work as Premier, Zhao found himself doing precisely the same thing (Zhao, 2009). From the summer retreat at Beidaihe in 1988 came rumours that Zhao was to be prevented from speaking out on economic issues. Zhao himself acknowledges these rumours and that opponents stated that as General Secretary he should not 'interfere' in the affairs of the State Council. However, he claims that at Deng Xiaoping's instigation he should continue to run the Central Economic and Financial Leading Group as Li Peng was less familiar with the pressing economic issues (Zhao, 2009, p. 233). Clearly the stage was being set for a showdown.

The catalyst for widespread disruption was the worst inflation in PRC history in 1988 that began to discredit calls for more radical reform and led by 1989 to a programme of economic retrenchment. Key groups were severely disaffected by spring 1989. Farmers were feeling insecure with the fluctuating grain prices and policies, workers were undergoing lay-offs, all urban dwellers were hit by inflation and critical intellectuals felt betrayed by the dismissal of Hu Yaobang and insufficient political reform. The refusal to engage in serious political reform was compounded by the failure of the urban economic reforms and the declining position of the working-class and state employees. Essentially, urban workers were offered a deal that involved giving up their secure, subsidy-supported low-wage lifestyle for a risky contract-based system that might result in higher wages at the possible price of rising costs and unemployment. Many urban workers decided to reserve their judgement. Their reservation was exacerbated by the leadership's indecisiveness about urban reform, which resulted in a stop-go cycle throughout the 1980s. The insecurity mounted when after 1986 the reforms resulted in spiralling inflation without consequent improvements in material standards. Not surprisingly, talk of price reform and reduction of subsidies created a sense of panic. Zhao's attempts to produce rapid economic results created the inflation of 1988 and 1989, which threatened those on fixed incomes. The resultant decline in living standards added many to the urban reservoir of discontent.

Urban anger was increased by the higher visibility of official corruption. Abuse of public position and private accumulation from public function by the late 1980s was the worst since 1949. By 1989, for many urban dwellers the party's incompetence and moral laxity had eroded any vestigial notions that the party was a moral force in Chinese society. Once the students breached the dams, a flood of supporters was waiting to defend the students and attack the authorities. Student agitation had festered on the campuses since 1986 and critical intellectuals had given regular lectures there. The specific cause of the demonstrations was the unexpected death of Hu Yaobang (15 April) during a Politburo meeting at which it was rumoured he had wanted to discuss education and was engaged in a major argument with party conservative Bo Yibo.

The student demonstrations quickly found resonance with large numbers of the urban citizenry. The initial government response was slow and incoherent in part because of the size of the demonstrations and the pending visit of Soviet President Gorbachev, but also because of severe leadership division about how to handle the demonstrations and future policy direction. Repression was unacceptable until all possible avenues had been tried. This was not just because the party was deeply split but also because it was difficult to take violent action against a group that was demonstrating peacefully, singing the 'Internationale' and calling for support of the CCP, further reforms and opening up. Yet entering into dialogue would mean recognition of autonomous organization in society, something that was anathema to orthodox party members. The potential for a tough regime response had been signalled in a *People's Daily* editorial of 26 April issued when Zhao Ziyang was out of the country (see Box 4.3). The editorial condemned the movement as a 'planned conspiracy' directed against the party and constituted a 'political conspiracy' aimed at negating 'the leadership of the CCP and the socialist system'. Despite the early decision to take a hard line, it took another six weeks before the protests could be crushed. Apart from the problem of using force against unarmed students, Zhao Ziyang came to oppose a tough response, favouring instead a limited dialogue.

Box 4.2: Perspectives on Tiananmen, 1989

'The situation for the people throughout the country has now become intolerable. After a long period of bureaucratic dictatorial government, inflation is out of control, and the people's living standards have slipped. To cover up their extravagance, the small group of ruling officials have issued a large number of various types of government and treasury bonds. They are thereby squeezing every penny out of the people. We appeal to people from all walks of life to come together to fight for truth and the future of China.

Police brothers, soldier brothers: Please come and stand on the people's side. Come and stand for the truth. Do not serve as tools of the people's enemies' (Beijing Workers' Autonomous Union, 20 April 1989, in Ogden et al., 1992, pp. 86–7).

'Facts prove that what this extremely small number of people did was not to join in the activities to mourn Comrade Hu Yaobang or to advance the cause of socialist democracy in China. Neither were they out to give vent to their grievances. Flaunting the banner of democracy, they undermined democracy and the legal system. Their purpose was to sow dissension among the people, plunge the whole country into chaos and sabotage the political situation of stability and unity. This is a planned conspiracy and a disturbance. Its essence is to, once and for all, negate the leadership of the CCP and the socialist system. This is a serious political struggle confronting the whole party and the people of all nationalities throughout the country' (*People's Daily*, 26 April 1989).

'Don't believe us. We tell lies' (Banner of protesting journalists, 4 May 1989).

Q 'What did you expect to get when you first joined the movement?'

A 'I expected improvement in the following two aspects. First, as far as democratic consciousness was concerned, I hoped we could get the same effects of enlightenment as those of the May Fourth Movement. Actually, although the Chinese people strongly desire democracy, they lack consciousness of democracy, and do not understand democracy. I hope that through the student movement, we will make progress in our work toward enlightening the people. Second, I hoped that we could set a good example with regard to the skills for promoting democracy. At the beginning, I hoped that our Students' Self-Government Federation's legal status would be recognized, and could play its role in government administration as an opposition group' (Wu-er Kaixi, one of the key student leaders, 3 June 1989, in Oksenberg, Sullivan and Lambert, 1990, pp. 354–5).

'This storm was bound to come sooner or later. This is determined by the major international climate and China's own minor climate. It was bound to happen and is independent of man's will. It was just a matter of time and scale. It is more to our advantage that this happened today. What is most advantageous to us is that we have a large group of veteran comrades who are still alive. They have experienced many storms and they know what is at stake. They support the use of resolute action to counter the rebellion. Although some comrades may not understand this for a while, they will eventually understand this and support the CC's decision' (Deng Xiaoping to Martial Law Troops, 9 June 1989, in Deng, 1994).

With the start of the hunger strike (13 May) and the involvement of organizations that had close ties to Zhao and the reformers, the demands of the movement began to change. From mid May onwards they became more directly political and sharply focused. The secret dismissal of Zhao was followed by the implementation of martial law (20 May) and one last attempt at dialogue was made. With Zhao removed and the motions gone through, the way was open for a tough response. Importantly, the demonstration had spread to include huge numbers of the urban population and now not only the students were forming autonomous organizations but also the workers and critical intellectuals. The orthodox leaders were able to use these developments to push for a brutal resolve. During the night of 3–4 June, troops from the PLA were sent in to clear out all protesters from the Tiananmen Square focal point.

Subsequent events showed both the capacity for the orthodox party faction to frustrate those reforms it opposed, and its lack of strength to roll back the momentum of economic reform for long. The scale of the demonstrations also meant that the leadership had to appear to respond to the criticisms. The veteran orthodox party members such as Chen Yun, Bo Yibo and Yang Shangkun together with Deng had effectively taken over decision-making in late April. Their programme had two main elements. First, the policy of economic austerity was strengthened with the intention of restoring the centrally planned economy to pride of place. Second, tight political supervision over society combined with a major political campaign was introduced to eradicate the influences of 'bourgeois liberalization'. While Deng Xiaoping supported the second, the programme of economic austerity entailed attacks on his own reform programme. Deng always maintained a traditional view of political activity that occurred outside of party control and resisted Mao's attempts to open up the party to criticism from outside forces. In August 1989, the *People's Daily* carried a 32-year-old speech by Deng in which he argued that too much democracy was undesirable for China and made clear that the party would remain paramount. The reforms to reduce the role of the party throughout state institutions were swiftly abandoned.

In late June 1989, the Fourth Plenum of the Thirteenth CC announced the removal of Zhao Ziyang and supporter Hu Qili from the Politburo Standing Committee, with Zhao criticized for 'grave errors and mistakes', including 'splitting the party'. He was not allowed to defend himself at the plenum. Shanghai Party Secretary, Jiang Zemin, was appointed to replace Zhao as general secretary primarily on the basis of the effective way he had dealt with the demonstrations in Shanghai. In terms of institutionalization of politics, the manner of Zhao's removal and Jiang's appointment show how little progress had been made. The crucial decisions were made, contrary to the Party Statutes, by a cabal of veteran revolutionaries at Deng's residence and then sent to party functionaries for official transmittal. Veterans Chen Yun and Li Xiannian had first raised the possibility of Jiang's appointment at a meeting on 21 May and the decision was made on 27 May, after Deng personally moved a motion on the composition of the Standing Committee of the Politburo. They also decided not to announce the decision immediately but to wait for the Fourth Plenum (Nathan and Link, 2001, pp. 260–1, 308–14).

The dismissal of Zhao also opened the way to a critique of the economic reforms, but already by May 1990 there were clear signs that the orthodox attack was being blunted. Critics pointed to their success in bringing down inflation and calming excessive growth as grounds for trusting their economic competence. GNP growth in 1989 was only 4 per cent, the lowest since the death of Mao Zedong, while inflation for the year was calculated at 17.8 per cent but by the end of the year had dropped to around 3 per cent to 4 per cent. Even the collective and private sectors of the economy and the coastal policy for export-led growth came in for criticism. However, the programme of economic austerity imposed in late 1988 and tightened after 4 June 1989 very quickly revealed its limits (Naughton, 1992, pp. 77–95). The austerity programme did not deal with the fundamental structural problems of the economy and, in fact, exacerbated many of them by denying their existence. The economic squeeze dampened demand but did not improve productivity nor remodel the irrational structure as had been promised. Already by early 1990, there were clear signs that the austerity measures were pushing the economy towards a major recession. In October 1989, for the first time in a decade, industrial output fell on a month-to-month basis by 2.1 per cent. In the period January–March 1990, industrial output recorded no growth while that of light industry fell to 0.2 per cent. The previously thriving collective sector was hit hard and by September 1989 the growth in monthly industrial output had dropped from 16.6 per cent to 0.6 per cent. A number of large factories sat idle because of the slowdown in output. In the first two months of 1990 alone, this resulted in 1.5 million urban residents losing their jobs.

Shaken by the economic downturn, and fearing social dislocation, measures were quietly introduced to ease the austerity programme despite resistance by fiscal conservatives at the centre. Many initiatives associated with the disgraced General Secretary, Zhao Ziyang, again became key elements of policy. The role played by the collective and private sectors was recognized and articles began to appear praising their contributions to economic growth. The strategy of coastal development that was closely associated with Zhao was reaffirmed and the reputation of the SEZs was rehabilitated. Government policy also began to deal with the problem of pricing and subsidies. In April 1991, the sharpest price increases for some 25 years were introduced for staple foods, with high-quality rice rising by 75 per cent and wheat prices by

55 per cent. In April 1992, the price of rice was increased again by 40 per cent. These were necessary measures but still not sufficient to allow market forces to work properly in the Chinese economy.

In addition to continuing the programme of economic austerity, the leadership responded, or tried to give the impression of responding, to the movement's political demands. On 28 June 1989, the Politburo adopted a seven-point programme to deal with corruption and a widely publicized campaign followed. This addressed issues such as closing down firms that had engaged in potentially corrupt activities, preventing the children of senior officials from engaging in commercial activities, limiting perks derived from official position such as entertaining, travel abroad, special supply of scarce goods and driving around in imported cars. Further, one of the students' main demands was met when, on 9 November 1989, Deng Xiaoping stepped down from his last official position as chair of the party's Military Affairs Commission. However, it was clear that such a process of internal regeneration alone could not be successful over the long term.

Return to economic reform, boom and moderation, 1992–97

By stealth, the programme of economic retrenchment was gradually being rolled back but Deng Xiaoping obviously felt that policy-making by increment or by default was insufficient and that a clear statement of intent was necessary. When the CCP celebrated its 70th anniversary on 1 July 1991, the chances for a dramatic change of course looked slim. The party remained defensive in the aftermath of Tiananmen and felt threatened by enemies from both within and without. Yet, the party prided itself on the fact that it had ridden out the storm of protest in 1989 and had been spared the consequences of the dramatic collapse of the communist regimes in Eastern Europe and the profound changes then taking place in Gorbachev's Soviet Union. Open dissent had been quashed and inner-party battles kept within acceptable limits. General Secretary Jiang Zemin, in his speech commemorating the party's founding, reaffirmed the hard line by claiming that 'class struggle' would continue for a considerable period of time within 'certain parts' of China. This contrasted markedly with the party line that had dominated since the late 1970s when Deng Xiaoping and his supporters had claimed that class struggle was dying down and that the main focus of work would be placed on economic development. Social harmony was to replace class warfare. In response to the situation in Eastern Europe, Jiang claimed that 'We Chinese communists are convinced the tempo-rary difficulties and setbacks recently experienced by socialism in its march forward cannot and will not ever prevent us from continuing to develop.' As far as the West was concerned, CCP policy was still to focus on resisting the capitalists' presumed attempts to transform China through 'peaceful evolution' (Jiang, 1991, pp. 1–14).

In addition to the need to deal with the structural problems in the economy, two other factors combined to convince Deng Xiaoping and his allies that it was necessary to reassess the hard-line policy and to push China once more along the road to reform. The first was the fallout from the failed *coup* in the Soviet Union (August 1991), and the second was the need to lay down a clear agenda for the Fourteenth Party Congress that would define his legacy. While Deng was bitterly critical of Gorbachev for undermining socialism, he realized that unless the CCP could satisfy the material aspirations of the population, it might be destined for the same fate. Debates about the future direction were brought into sharper focus by the fact that the Fourteenth Party Congress was scheduled to be convened before the end of 1992. Party congresses and the fixing of Five-Year Plans are always times of tense debate in China. Policy differences that could be previously contained often spill over into factional fighting and resultant purges. Once a document that will dictate policy for the coming five years has to be written down, it becomes more difficult to paper over the cracks in the leadership. Political differences become increasingly public as the various policy tendencies strive to set the agenda through newspaper articles and controlled leaks.

The year 1992 proved to be a watershed and led to the dramatic economic boom and building craze that characterized much of the 1990s. However, it also led to another round of overheating, forcing the new leadership under Jiang Zemin to articulate a more coherent plan for economic development than had hitherto been the case. Rather than 'bourgeois liberalism', the main theme of criticism in 1992 was 'leftism', namely those opposed to Deng's reforms.

The most dramatic breakthrough came with Deng Xiaoping's inspection tour to South China in January–February 1992. Deng concluded that continued economic reform was vital for the party's legitimacy. He claimed that if China's economic reforms were reversed, the party would lose the people's support and 'could be overthrown at any time' and he ventured the view that it would certainly not have survived the trauma of Tiananmen. Interestingly, Deng absolved both Hu Yaobang and Zhao Ziyang, his first two choices as general secretary, of faults in the economic arena by stating that they had been removed from power because of not opposing 'bourgeois liberalization' properly. Deng went beyond stating the general need for economic reform by implicitly criticizing those who sought to slow down the pace of change. He claimed that economic reform should not 'proceed slowly like a woman with bound feet' but should 'blaze new trails boldly'. Most importantly,

Deng announced a major change in the CCP's political line. Ever since the events of 1989, the Chinese public had been told that the greatest threat to socialism in China came from 'bourgeois liberals', termed 'rightists'. As far as the party veterans were concerned, these people were responsible for the unrest that had broken out in 1989. This unrest legitimized the attacks on Zhao Ziyang and his supporters as well as on outspoken pro-reform intellectuals throughout the system. Now Deng told his party members that it was the 'leftists', who opposed further reform, who presented the greatest problem for China at the present time, something already signalled by Yang Shangkun in a major speech of October 1991. Deng turned his fire on those who argued that economic reform must inevitably lead to capitalism. According to Deng, a market economy did not necessarily imply capitalism any more than a planned economy implied socialism. He refused to accept their arguments that the danger of 'peaceful evolution' mainly originated in the economic sphere. Deng warned against sinking into another ideological impasse. For Deng, the basic line of rapid reform was clear and it was to be upheld for 100 years.

This relaunch of reform caused Jiang Zemin to submit a self-criticism (March 1992) and paved the way for drafting the party congress documents. The Fourteenth Party Congress adopted Deng's calls for a more rapid economic reform but mediated a figure of 8–9 per cent for the growth rate, reflecting an emerging consensus that too rapid growth would see the return of the old problems of bottlenecks and inflation. The three key aspects of the Congress reflected a victory for Deng, as did key institutional and personnel changes. First, the Congress praised Deng as 'the chief architect of our socialist reform, of the open-door policy and of the modernization programme' and credited him with developing the 'theory of building socialism with Chinese characteristics'. It thus provided a way out of the sterile ideological battles that were waged over what constitutes socialist mechanisms of development.

Second, the document sanctioned sweeping economic reforms under the formulation of a 'socialist market economy'. This gave a greater role to market forces than that offered by any other ruling communist party to date. While the state was to retain the capacity to make 'macro-level adjustments and control', market forces were to be unleashed to eradicate poverty, while the laws of supply and demand were to ensure the rational allocation of commodities throughout the economy. Indeed, Jiang Zemin even proposed that price levers and competition be used to improve efficiency and 'realize the survival of the fittest'. However, the report steered away from precise objectives, leaving the door ajar for debilitating arguments over the specific implementation of the guidelines. The 'open-door' policy also received a clean bill of health and Jiang proposed that foreign capital could be used not only for enterprise technological transformation but also in areas of finance, commerce, tourism and real estate.

Third, the liberal view of economic affairs was paralleled by a strong commitment to political control. The reforms that Zhao Ziyang had suggested at the Thirteenth Party Congress are not mentioned. The only proposals were to trim the size of the bureaucracy and clear up party and government overlap. Whereas the previous congress had proposed eliminating 'party cells' in government organizations, the proposal now was to strengthen them at all levels. The newly elected leadership produced a clear majority in favour of Deng's economic reform programme and only six of the old Politburo were re-elected to the new 20-person body. Importantly, the Congress confirmed the abolition of the Central Advisory Commission, which had become an institutional base of support for Chen Yun's sniping at Deng over economic policy.

After the Congress, the economy continued to boom on a diet of foreign investment and real estate speculation and it seemed as if most of urban China had turned into a massive building site. As the saying went, the national bird of China had become the crane. At the same time, inflation also shot up to around 30 per cent by the end of 1994. Through 1993 and 1994, attempts were undertaken to rein in growth and prevent economic distress from turning into social instability. This time, economic retrenchment did not work; GDP grew at 13.4 per cent as opposed to the projected 9 per cent and accelerated further in 1994. Yet another vicious stop-go cycle was in the making and forced a group of reformers gathered around vice-premier and new Politburo Standing Committee member Zhu Rongji to articulate the most far-reaching plan for economic transformation to date. Almost for the first time the leadership seemed to be setting out a programme that would place it at the forefront of the reform process rather than appearing to react to short-term contingencies. Not surprisingly given the ramifications of the plan, it has been deeply contested and most subsequent political debate has revolved around its implementation. Vested interests have deflected policy in a number of key areas and fears of social unrest have been used to slow down the pace of structural transformation.

In November 1993, the Third Plenum of the Fourteenth CC adopted a key economic reform document that argued a renewed role for the centre in managing key macroeconomic levers (for details see Chapter 10), especially in reversing *de facto* economic decentralization. It proposed an extensive role for the market, modernization of the enterprise system and importantly, for the first time, highlighted the need for restructuring the financial system. To back up the reforms, substantial policy innovation would be necessary to deal with the provision of social welfare, especially in the urban areas.

The policies of retrenchment continued, with the regions resisting and often registering growth exceeding the official projections. However, Vice-Premier Zhu Rongji was slowly able to manipulate the remaining macroeconomic levers to calm growth to 8.8 per cent in 1997 and bring inflation to 0.8 per cent by the end of 1997. While Zhu may not have achieved a soft landing for the economy, he had bought time that, if used wisely, could bring about the kind of transition that would put an end to the stop-go cycles.

From October 1995 onwards there were attempts not only to rein-in a wayward economy but also a society that seemed to be evading political control by the party. The economic spurt unleashed by Deng from 1992 was accompanied by an attitude in society that anything went. Public security organs, PLA units and party members began to neglect other duties in order to join the rush to make money. In October 1995, Jiang Zemin delivered a speech 'More Talk About Politics' that supported attempts to exert more control over society. The speech was followed by the registering of religious organizations and the crackdown on underground churches; the reregistering of publications and more concerted attempts to ban unwanted publications and control content; a new law that set tougher limits on the activities of social organizations and tightened controls over their operations (Saich, 2000a); and new restrictions on research collaboration with foreigners in the social sciences. The attempt to revitalize the party and exert greater control over society became a hallmark of Jiang's rule that became even clearer after the Fifteenth Congress, a trait continued by his successor, Hu Jintao. However, many of the controls have proved impossible to implement for any length of time, testifying to the decline in state capacity and threatening to result in continuing friction between the state and elements of society.

Managing reform without Deng, 1997–2002

It was in this context that the Fifteenth Party Congress and Ninth National People's Congress (September 1997 and March 1998, respectively) were held (see Box 4.3). One additional factor influenced the Party Congress; it was the first time that Jiang Zemin did not have Deng Xiaoping, who had died in February, behind him. In fact, in the couple of years before the Congress, Jiang had been moving cautiously to establish a more independent position while wrapping himself in the mantle of Deng's legacy. Given what happened to all of Mao's chosen successors and the first two of Deng's, a cautious strategy was a wise one.

Box 4.3: Key Political Dates, 1997–2010

1997 February, Deng Xiaoping dies
July, Hong Kong reverts to Chinese rule
September, Fifteenth Party Congress proposes significant advances for economic reform

1998 March, Ninth NPC new Premier Zhu Rongji unveils a dramatic package of reforms

1999 April, supporters of *Falungong* protest criticism by surrounding party headquarters in Beijing, a major crackdown follows
May, NATO bombing of Chinese Embassy in Belgrade
September, Fourth Plenum of Fifteenth CC announces a cautious approach to reform
November, China agrees to terms of WTO entry with the United States
December, Macao returns to Chinese sovereignty

2000 September, US Congress passes Permanent Normal Trading Rights for China
October, Fifth Plenum of the Fifteenth CC agrees to the new five-year economic and social plan that calls for 'relatively rapid economic development' while improving 'qualitative' aspects of growth

2001 March, Fourth session of the Tenth NPC ratifies the Tenth Five-Year Plan
April, EP-3 US plane makes emergency landing in Hainan setting off a crisis in US–China relations
July, Jiang Zemin and Putin sign a new 'Treaty of Friendship and Cooperation' – forever friends, never foes
September, Sixth Plenum of the Fifteenth CC adopts a decision to improve party work-style
December, China enters WTO

2002 November, Sixteenth Party Congress installs Hu Jintao as general secretary

→

While the announcements at the two congresses were dramatic, subsequent events blunted some of the more radical thrusts. Jiang's strategy, ably supported by Premier Zhu, had five main strands. First, there was continued commitment to high economic growth that was seen as essential to maintaining social stability. This meant that more attention would be paid to the worries of sparking inflation and getting to grips with the deep-seated financial sector problems. Second, the leadership made the clearest commitment to date of a mixed economy with theoretical continued dominance of the state sector (Jiang, 1997, pp. 10–37). Third, while the party would continue to refrain from an

→

2003 March, Tenth NPC appoints new government with Wen Jiabao as Premier
April 20, press conference acknowledges the severity of SARS
May–June Hu Jintao visits Russia on way to parallel meeting of the G-8 in France

2004 September, Fourth plenum of 16th CC, Jiang Zemin retires from the Central Military Commission to be replaced by Hu Jintao

2005 Fifth plenum of the 16th CC stresses sustainability and social equity rather than GDP growth

2006 September, Shanghai Party Secretary, Chen Liangyu, removed from his post on charges of corruption
October, Sixth plenum of the 16th CC discusses building a 'harmonious society' by 2020

2007 October, Seventeenth Party Congress convenes and adopts Hu's idea of the 'scientific outlook on development'. Together with the First plenum, a new leadership is elected

2008 Jan–Feb, snow storms devastate 21 provinces causing some $21 billion in economic losses
March, Eleventh NPC confirms new state leadership and discusses administrative reforms
Angry riots break out in Tibet
May, Massive earthquake hits Sichuan
August, Summer Olympics held in Beijing
October, Third plenum of 16th CC focuses on rural development
November, China announces a massive stimulus package for the economy
December, Charter 08 critical of one-party rule signed by 303 activists

2009 September, Fourth plenum of the 17th CC discusses enhancing inner-party democracy
October, Celebration of the 60th anniversary of founding of the PRC
November, US President Obama visits China

2010 March, Premier Wen highlights the need to boost spending and redistribute wealth

overbearing role in the economy and society, the CCP would be strengthened and its guidance enhanced. Jiang and his supporters clearly saw the party as the key institutional actor at all levels and in all crucial areas. At the same time, the appeal of the party was to be broadened beyond its traditional constituency, as was seen later with the acceptance of private entrepreneurs and Jiang's promotion of the 'Three Represents'. Fourth, the pace of integration with the world economy was to be quickened, best exemplified by WTO entry. Fifth, Jiang carried on Deng's preference for a good relationship with the United States wherever possible.

Contrary to the perceptions of many before the Congress, there were no new ideas for political reform. During 1997, political reform seemed to come back on the policy agenda with a number of suggestions for significant change. For a while, it appeared that Jiang was sanctioning these discussions. While he may have been testing the waters, the main intent was to divert the opponents' attention away from enterprise reform, clearly the most important issue for Jiang. The political proposals put forward amounted to little more than improving the functioning of the Congress system, closer involvement of mass organizations and affirming the value of village elections. In addition, Jiang's main contender as a champion of political reform Qiao Shi, head of the NPC, 'retired' from the leadership. Qiao's removal enabled Li Peng to take over at the NPC.

With the onset of the Asian financial crisis and the realization that China's banking system was as perilously placed as many of those that collapsed in the surrounding countries, reformers were able to push ahead with a comprehensive package of new policies that culminated in Zhu Rongji's presentation at the NPC in March 1998. The first measure to be unveiled was an overhaul of the banking system, the centrepiece of which was the reorganization of the local branches of the People's Bank along regional lines to reduce political interference by powerful provincial party chiefs in lending decisions.

At the 1998 NPC meeting, Zhu Rongji announced an integrated set of five major reform measures. First, approving plans proposed a decade before, Zhu announced that China would set up a nationwide grain market to ease the country's reserves. Most importantly, China would reduce the massive amount of government subsidies pumped into the system because of the remaining influences of the Maoist obsession with self-sufficiency in grain. Second, the investment and financing system was to be overhauled to prevent wasteful duplication of capital investment, with the Central Bank stepping up its regulatory functions and commercial banks being allowed to operate independently. Third, housing was to be marketized and 'welfare housing' abolished. For those who did not purchase housing, rents were projected to rise to around 15 per cent of the family income. Fourth, Zhu revealed that a new nationwide medical care reform programme would be introduced in the second half of 1998. Finally, the tax collection system was to be rationalized to prevent the levying of excessive fees and levies by local authorities who had been the source of much resentment and social unrest. In addition, Zhu announced a massive restructuring of the government bureaucracy, with half the officials to be laid off and reassigned to new jobs. In the ensuing five years progress was made in all the areas targeted for reform but the more radical intentions were blunted by interest groups at the centre and the localities. The difficulty of moving ahead on any significant reform shows that the central state is now far from autonomous. Senior leaders lobby on behalf of their ministries to avoid the worst administrative cutbacks, line agencies interpret policy to the benefit of their own sectoral interests and localities seek to pursue their own economic agendas.

Given the enormity of these reforms and the structural and social challenges that they would cause, it is surprising how little overt protest occurred. The fear of unrest did lead to reinstatement of subsidies and 'policy loans' to moderate possible state sector job losses. The leadership also became worried about political activism in China. Apparently after a debate about whether open political activism could be allowed, the leadership decided to move quickly to crush any potential opposition. First, in a direct challenge to its rule, activists across China formed the China Democracy Party that after a delay in 1998 was harshly crushed. By the end of the year (November 1998) its key members had been arrested, others were periodically picked up and harassed. Second, in April 1999, members of a *qigong* sect, the *Falungong*, encircled the party headquarters in Beijing in a quiet show of strength to protest against criticism. After a few months of hesitation, in the build-up to the fiftieth anniversary of the PRC, leaders of the group were arrested, thousands of followers picked up and all publications concerning the movement banned.

External factors also played a role in moderating the speed of restructuring. Not only did the Asian financial crisis that began in 1997 limit China's growth alternatives and help it focus on developing the domestic market but also Jiang and others seem to have been unnerved by the sudden fall of the Suharto regime in Indonesia and the rapid systemic collapse. Here was a man who had presided over a long period of economic growth and who seemed securely in power supported by the military and an authoritarian political system and yet was swiftly swept away by street demonstrations. The potential parallels must have seemed alarming.

Further, the relationship with the United States that had looked so promising in 1998 following the Clinton–Jiang reciprocal visits began to sour in 1999 with revival of frictions over Taiwan, human rights and WTO entry as well as unexpected events. Bad relations with the United States always hamper domestic reform attempts. The accidental NATO bombing of the Chinese Embassy in Belgrade in May 1999 caused large anti-US demonstrations in Beijing and a few other cities. The inauguration of President George W. Bush in January 2001 with an administration determined to take a tougher stance on China did not help and the 'relationship' almost fell apart when a US EP-3 reconnaissance plane collided with a Chinese jet fighter over international waters in the South China Sea (April 2001). This caused a tense stand-off before the US crew were returned and the plane was sent back in packing cases. This marked a turning point for the new Bush administration, which realized that some kind of constructive engagement with China was necessary. Exchanges of visits were set in motion, culminating in President Jiang's visit to Bush's Texas ranch in October 2002. In the intervening period, the 11 September 2001 attacks on the World Trade Center had dramatically changed US foreign policy, with the result that the notion of a 'China Threat' became less important and China was viewed as an ally in the US 'War on Terrorism'.

Such domestic and international uncertainties combined to cause Jiang to ignore calls for more rapid economic transition and even political reform. He preferred to adopt a cautious approach, with tight political control legitimated by a strident nationalism. It was rumoured that Jiang, under pressure from Li Peng and others, announced that political reform should not be discussed for two to three years. When celebrating 20 years of reform in December 1998, Jiang made it clear that radical or 'Western'-inspired models of economic and political reform were not for China. He chose instead to stress the need to maintain stability and crack down on any potential unrest immediately and re-emphasized Deng's use of the 'Four Basic Principles'. In this context, he suggested that the bold reforms of earlier in the year would be moderated for people to adjust to their consequences.

However, Jiang did launch one major initiative with far-reaching consequences. In a speech in February 2000 that was intended both to portray Jiang as a great theoretician and to indicate that the CCP was still relevant to China's future, he raised the idea of the 'Three Represents' (the CCP will represent the advanced social productive forces, the most advanced culture and the fundamental interests of all the people). This became a major campaign and the idea was adopted in the Party Statutes in 2002.

The campaign sought to portray the CCP as leading not only the new and dynamic areas of the economy but also the newly emerged technical and economic elites. It furthered the process of distancing the CCP from sole reliance on the proletariat the party created 50 years before. The proletariat was consigned to the past as the CCP claimed a broader constituency of representation. The campaign suggested that the CCP wanted not only to welcome new constituencies but also to exert leadership over the new burgeoning sectors of the economy. This was accompanied by Jiang's declaration on 1 July 2001 (the CCP's anniversary) that under certain circumstances, private entrepreneurs could become party members, a shift that generated howls of disapproval from the 'old' and some of the 'new left'.

The various party plenums and NPC meetings from 1999 to 2001 confirmed the more cautious approach. Jiang tried to walk a middle line by recognizing the need for a radical shake-up of the state sector without accepting that privatization was necessary. The Fifth Plenum (October 2000) also concentrated on the economy adopting the blueprint for the new Five-Year Economic Plan (2001–05), which was formally approved at the March 2001 NPC meeting. The plan called for achieving average growth of about 7 per cent per annum with the goal of doubling the size of the economy by 2010. Growth under the previous Five-Year Plan had averaged 8.3 per cent. Most importantly, the plan acknowledged the need to improve competitiveness because of pending WTO entry. The new plan also stressed that economic gains would lead to improvements in welfare and would mean that most Chinese would be able to enjoy a comfortable (*xiaokang*) standard of living, a theme that would mark the Sixteenth Party Congress and the policies of the new leadership.

Political reform had disappeared from the agenda but the need to fight corruption was prominent although no structural reform was suggested. This concern with corruption must have been the driving factor behind discussions at the Sixth Plenum of the Fifteenth CC that examined a decision to improve and strengthen party work-style. The decision mentioned the problems of 'material temptations' while the communiqué claimed that winning the struggle against corruption within the party was an essential condition for maintaining its power and authority. However, beyond exhortation to work better and honestly nothing was recommended that would get to grips with the deep-seated structural causes.

Attempting to balance growth with social equity, 2002–10

These discussions provided the backdrop to the leadership succession that took place at a delayed party congress (November) and the Tenth NPC in March 2003. Not surprisingly little was said in terms of new policy other than to reaffirm that greater attention was to be paid to the non-economic aspects of reform and getting to grips with the problems of inequality. Jiang Zemin outlined the important objective of keeping up with the times and building a comfortable society (*xiaokang shehui*) that included quadrupling the 2000 GDP (around $900 per capita) by the year 2020 (Jiang, 2002).

However, the big issue at the Sixteenth Party Congress was election of the new leadership and what continued role Jiang would seek to play. While pre-Congress some talked of the institutionalization of elite politics with Jiang retiring from all posts, while a remarkable step forward in comparison with previous practice, things were not entirely clear-cut. First, Hu Jintao was Deng Xiaoping's chosen candidate identified some ten years previously. Second, Jiang himself muddied the waters by retaining his post as Chair of the CMAC. This was portrayed as contributing to stability and ensuring continuity in foreign policy, especially in terms of dealing with the important but often difficult relationship with the United States. Third, it appears that at the first Politburo meeting after the Party Congress, new General Secretary, Hu Jintao, proposed that important party issues be referred to Jiang and that he would be the only departing leader to continue to receive minutes of the Politburo Standing Committee meetings. This was to continue even after he relinquished the post of President to Hu (March 2003). However, it was clear from the outset that Jiang would not enjoy the kind of long-term influence that Deng had enjoyed behind the scenes. The title of General Secretary does bestow institutional power on its holder and this meant that time was on Hu's side. It should be remembered that when Jiang become General Secretary, he did not have a natural power base but his shrewd politics and use of the prestige that came with the title enabled him to consolidate power. Jiang does not have the personal prestige of Mao or Deng and without a formal position such as the head of the CMAC, he found it difficult to rule from behind the scenes.

Jiang was honoured by amending the Party Statutes to include his 'Three Represents' and also to make it easier for private entrepreneurs to become party members. However, the Congress offered virtually no indication about the new directions in political reform and rehashed dominant themes of the Jiang years: administrative fine-tuning, improvement in the quality of public officialdom, mention of the rule of law, firm party control over the reform programme and a tightening of the party's grip over the state sector. Despite this lack of encouragement, as in previous post-Congress periods there was a flurry of articles and suggestions about reform (see Chapter 13) and the old mantra that 'economic reform needs political reform' from the Zhao Ziyang years was revived.

In March 2003, the leadership transition was completed when Hu Jintao was appointed as President and Wen Jiabao as Premier with a new, essentially technocratic cabinet. It also confirmed the course of economic policy and undertook a further but much milder round of government restructuring. With so much on its plate, the NPC delayed amending the Constitution until its 2004 meeting. Most important in the government restructuring was the establishment of two new commissions to oversee the banking sector and asset administration, and a new food and drug administration that seemed to indicate the new leadership was serious about moving more towards a regulatory model for the state. Of equal significance was the change in name of the State Development Planning Commission to the State Development and Reform Commission that would guide the overall reform efforts.

The new leadership under Hu and Wen has been at pains to portray themselves as more open, efficient and concerned about the plight of the poor. In the eyes of many, Jiang represents the interests of China's new economic and coastal elites, yet even in the latter years of Jiang's rule there was increasing concern about inequality and the potential threat this might pose to stability. The new leadership cannot consider itself lucky and its attempts to concentrate on sustainable development and spreading the benefits of the reforms to those who had not profited so well have been struck by a number of unforeseen disasters. It probably never occurred to Hu and Wen as they surveyed the policy minefields ahead of them that the first test would come from the health sector with an outbreak of Severe Acute Respiratory Syndrome (SARS) that would have a global impact. In November 2002, this new disease broke out in Guangdong province but was initially covered up and eventually infected people not only elsewhere in China, primarily in Beijing, but also in a number of other countries throughout the world. However, once they decided to act in April 2003, Hu and Wen presented themselves as modern managers with a problem-solving orientation who were concerned for the welfare of the people. By contrast, Jiang Zemin and his supporters looked irrelevant and initially were invisible, although they tried to regain some ground by bringing in the 'Three Represents' and stressing that economic development must not be ignored in the attempt to eradicate SARS. The run-up to the 2008 Olympics was disrupted by a number of natural disasters and the post-Olympic lift was soon undercut by the global financial crisis. These unexpected events delayed the ability of the leadership to push ahead as significantly as they might have wished with their policy priorities.

The policy approach may be termed 'populist authoritarianism' and marks one of three distinct discontinuities with the years under Jiang. In the run-up to the conference, a number of Chinese reports played up the fact that both Hu Jintao and Wen Jiabao had spent significant phases of their career in poorer Western provinces. This is in marked contrast to Jiang, Zhu Rongji and Li Peng who worked in the developed metropolis of Shanghai or in the central ministries and bureaucracy in Beijing. The implicit message that the new leadership would show greater concern for those who have not benefited as well from the reform programme was deliberate. It was of symbolic importance that the first two public visits by Hu Jintao as General Secretary were not to the glitzy cities of Shanghai or Shenzhen but rather to Xibaipo, a town southwest of Beijing where Mao Zedong plotted his final push on the capital in 1949, and Inner Mongolia. Hu's numerous references to 'plain living and hard struggle' in the speech he delivered at Xibaipo were clearly intended not only to draw a line of legitimacy from Mao but also to indicate that the agenda for building a comfortable society would include a broader constituency.

Thus, the first discontinuity is that policy rhetoric and even policy practice has become more people-centred with populist gestures combined with attempts to tighten control over state and society in the name of preserving social stability as the key foundation for continued economic growth. At a speech to the Central Party School (February 2003), Hu proposed a new 'Three People's Principles' – that power be used by the people, concern be shown for the people, and that benefits be enjoyed by the people. While the phrase never really took off, it highlighted Hu and Wen's approach of 'putting people first' and a people-centred policy. The policies were pulled together at the Sixth plenum of the 16th Party Congress (October 2006) that was remarkable for its focus on social development and put forward the slogan of 'building a harmonious society', while somewhat awkwardly still acknowledging that economic work was at the core. Hu had first put the slogan forward in 2004 but now it was given more content. Hu kept Jiang and his supporters on board by not rejecting entirely their growth-oriented policies but rather suggesting that they be moderated. Among the policy measures to be pursued were reducing income inequality, improving access to healthcare and education for those in the rural areas and migrants, improving and extending the social security system, moderating environmental impact of economic development, and providing greater feedback opportunities from disgruntled citizens.

The plenum also recognized the need to combat the moral vacuum that many see in China. The Chinese leaders called for a 'socialist core value system' that would lay down 'moral and ideological foundations' underpinning the policies to build the 'harmonious society'. In addition to stressing Marxism, this was to comprise the 'socialist sense of honour and disgrace'. Clearly, the new leadership was not willing to cede moral regeneration to neo-Confucianism alone.

Before the plenum, Hu had launched a major campaign to force allegiance to the new regime. In January 2005, the party launched an 18-month major 'Campaign to Maintain the Advanced Nature of the Party' to outline the norms to which individual party members were expected to conform. The campaign was intended to strengthen socialist ideology and the party's leading role. After the study period, party members were to be judged on their performance to decide whether they could continue their work. However, beyond letting people know the new rules of the game, it is debatable how much impact such a campaign could have in the modern day and age. Most party members that foreigners came into contact with privately expressed a high degree of cynicism about the campaign: jokes so abounded that an official directive was sent out requesting that party members use only the campaign's full name and not shortened forms that could be turned into puns. At worst, some party members were upset that the effort diverted time and attention from pressing issues that needed serious policy attention. At least one enterprising group set up a website, where the appropriate self-criticisms for different-level officials could be downloaded for a fee. All busy officials had to do was put in their names and change some of the details to personalize the report! Perhaps responding to the view that the campaign had little to do with real problems, then Vice President Zeng Qinghong linked the campaign to raising the quality of party organizations so they could serve the people better (*Xinhua News Agency*, 25 May 2005). The stress on funding for Marxist research was met with glee by many organizations that had been starved of cash under reforms and even by others that were not cash poor but could always turn their research to include something on Marxism. However, Hu remained undeterred and at the Fourth Plenum of the Seventeenth CC he claimed that the party's goal for the new century was to 'Sinicize Marxism' (something supposedly completed by Mao Zedong in the previous century!) and render it 'timely and popular'.

This ideological stress highlights the second area where the Hu leadership has differed from Jiang. Despite the invocation of Chinese traditions, Hu has proved to be more orthodox in the political realm than Jiang. However, in this realm economic development and social diversity is beginning to push the party to experiment with measures that improve feedback but stop short of full transparency and accountability. Hu has reaffirmed his credentials as a strong Leninist leader who has sought to clamp down on dissent and to limit the range of ideas expressed in the public sphere. It should be remembered that Hu came to the attention of the central leadership through his imposition of martial law in Tibet in 1989, before the imposition in Beijing. Many Chinese were shocked by the harsh nature of his unpublished speech to the fourth plenum in September 2004 which contained rhetoric and language that had not been prevalent for many years. He attacked the spreading of 'bourgeois liberalization' by foreign and domestic groups and urged a crackdown on political problems. One report of the speech said that he referred to those within the party who advocated political reform as creating turmoil, although the context within which he said this is unclear. He also praised Cuba and North Korea for their control over ideology and the flow of information despite their 'temporary' economic problems, claiming that they had always adhered to a sound political line.

Leadership concern about society slipping out of control has played a role in this tightening and there is nervousness about the levels of inequality and social unrest in China. Last, but not least, the 'coloured' revolutions have disturbed the leadership. This has caused them to worry about the role that an emerging civil society may play as a potential catalyst for change. They have also put foreign foundations under scrutiny, especially as those funded by the US government are seen as being behind the fall of the pro-Beijing authoritarian regime in Kyrgyzstan and the upheavals in Uzbekistan. Such sentiments were increasingly turned into action. Effective from March 2010, the State Administration of Foreign Exchange promulgated a notice that tightened the receipt of foreign funds for domestic independent NGOs (*SCMP*, 12 March 2010). It seems that the purpose was to control incoming funding to prevent any possibility of a foreign-funded social movement from below.

There has been a noticeable tightening over media reporting with more areas put on the taboo list and the party has been struggling to come to terms with new technologies that can deflect the party's message or provide alternatives. This involved significant moves to control the internet, monitor its content and even to post pro-regime messages and try to guide discussions in the chatrooms. In June 2005, all Chinese websites and bloggers were required to register their real names with authorities or risk being closed down by the end of the month. On 25 September, the State Council Information Office and the Ministry of Information Industry issued joint rules on administering news information on the internet. The rules drew together existing regulations but added that the internet could not be used either to incite unlawful assembly or carry out activities on behalf of 'illegal civil organizations'. This was prompted by the capacity of loose organizations of citizens to mobilize through cyberspace.

The problems of controlling an increasingly articulate society and the party's unwillingness to tolerate any signs of organized opposition was reflected in its response to the promulgation of Charter 08 to mark the 10 December 2008 anniversary of the Universal Declaration of Human Rights. This document was initially signed by 303 activists and called for the end of authoritarian one-party rule while laying out a vision of a rights-based society. The document was based on the Czech Charter 77 that called for freedom from the Soviet dominance and rule of the communist party. The spread of the document on the internet and its publicity inside and outside of China soon produced an official response and two of the key drafters were arrested and others either arrested or interrogated. Significant resources were then dedicated to preventing its spread on the internet. In December 2009, Liu Xiaobo, one of the key organizers, was sentenced to 11 years' imprisonment.

In place of any significant reform, Hu Jintao is offering cleaner and more efficient government administration. The party has been stressing that to maintain control it needs to complete its shift from a revolutionary to a governing party and that government capacity needs to be enhanced. Hu has promoted more feedback loops within the party and has carried on supporting the emergence of quasi-elections within the party. At the Fourth Plenum of the Seventeenth CC, inner-party democracy was a theme but the lack of transparency around personnel issues indicated that most party members were still excluded from any meaningful discussions and decisions. One interesting direction is the announcement that direct elections would gradually be expanded for leading positions in 'grass-roots party organizations'. The announcement also suggested that not only party members but also the general public would be able to nominate candidates. Most interestingly it proposed experiments in some counties and urban districts to establish a permanent presence for the party congress rather than just having it come together once every five years.

The third significant difference is that Hu does not share Jiang Zemin's essentially pro-US disposition in foreign affairs. In major part, this derives from China's increasingly global footprint and its need to import the resources necessary to keep its economy moving. Hu seems more suspicious of US intentions and has tried to build alliances with other countries, including those not close to the US. China had made progress in a number of areas and continued to carve out more international space for itself while making clear that it was willing to look beyond the US to build its international relationships. China has latched onto the notion of 'soft power' and has been trying to promote this through the funding of Confucius Institutes overseas to teach Chinese and promote Chinese culture, the expansion of CCTV International, and the increasing amounts of aid that it has dispensed in Africa.

Under the Bush administration American officials initially adopted the habit of saying that the relationship with China was in the best state ever, although later they began to describe the relationship as 'complex'. It is clear that the relationship still has no solid underpinnings; deep divisions remain in the US about whether the 'rise of China' is a threat or an opportunity. The Obama administration seems to see the relationship as an opportunity to solve global problems but events in late 2009 and early 2010 such as the US sale of arms to Taiwan and the meeting between president Obama and the Dalai Lama set back progress. It is clear that not only does the US need to collaborate closely with China to resolve the short-term economic and financial problems but also to resolve longer-term security challenges such as the evolution of the regime in North Korea and global concerns with climate change and global warming. This is recognized by the Obama administration that is trying to find a framework in which it can work collaboratively with China on such issues while not ignoring criticisms of the country's human rights record and policies in Tibet. The difficulty of threading through this policy quagmire was revealed during Secretary of State Hillary Clinton's first visit to China (2009) where she was criticized for downplaying China's human rights abuses in order to get more traction on other issues. President Obama's November visit also focused on a wide array of issues meaning that little concrete was achieved.

The most remarkable development in recent years has been the increase in China's reach as its economic muscles have grown and investments in Latin America and Africa have increased substantially. Much of the investment has been to secure natural resources and minerals to support China's rapid economic growth. This will provide a major challenge to China's foreign policy-makers as it will be hard to maintain its' traditional view of non-interference in the affairs of other countries. Whether China likes it or not the level of investment and engagement in other developing countries will make it a major player in their domestic politics. Policy-decisions taken in Beijing will have significant ramifications for other local economies.

One persistent concern since the reforms began has been the corrosive impact of corruption and Hu's regime has railed against it with similarly little ability to control its spread. In addition, in the same way that Jiang Zemin used a corruption scandal to remove a rival, the Beijing party secretary, Hu did the same to remove Shanghai Party Secretary, Chen Liangyu (in 2006). Chen was known to have clashed with Premier Wen Jiabao over economic policy and was seen as a key member of what is referred to as the 'Shanghai Gang', a group of politicians thought of as close to former leader Jiang Zemin. With ideological battles as justification for purge a thing of the past, corruption has become the latest weapon of choice to remove political rivals. Chen Liangyu was brought down by the Social Security Fund scandal that had been brewing in Shanghai for a couple of years. This was followed by a strong speech by Hu to the Politburo (29 June) in which he attacked corruption as eroding the party's standing and called for deepening democracy, and another Politburo meeting (29 August) at which they dusted off the 1997 regulations that require all officials to provide details of their personal affairs.

The evolving policy platform was pulled together at the Seventeenth Party Congress (November 2007) and the Tenth NPC (March 2008). While Hu was clearly in charge, not everything went his way and his populist policies were tempered by those who favoured a primary focus on economic growth rather than redistribution. In addition, there was one major surprise in the personnel appointments that will affect who will rule China for the next ten years after Hu.

Hu's report (2007) to the Seventeenth Party Congress outlined in broad terms the strategy for the next five years (2007–12) and laid the basis for Wen Jiabao's report to the NPC. One major success for Hu was the incorporation into the party canon of his concept of 'the Scientific Outlook on Development'. It was only at the end of his second term that former General Secretary Jiang Zemin's concept of the 'Three Represents' was included. On this basis, Hu was doing well! The key policy slogans of the new leadership are now incorporated under Hu's policy slogan. The definition of the 'Scientific Outlook on Development' has economic development as its key component and calls on the party to see development as its top priority in governing and rejuvenating the country. The only specific target mentioned by Hu at the Party Congress was a shift of quadrupling GDP by 2020 to quadrupling GDP per capita thus evincing his confidence in the upside growth potential of the Chinese economy. However, Hu follows this imperative with the notion of 'Putting People First', therefore making sure that future development is more balanced and sustainable than in the past. Thus, the concerns with reducing energy consumption and grappling with pollution remain important but local leaders might be able to find their way around tougher voices from the Centre by claiming that continued economic development takes priority.

Hu's concept of 'Building a Harmonious Society' that embodied the ideas of social justice and equity and improving the lot of those who have been marginalized by reforms did not receive significant attention in the report. While most of the elements within this policy initiative are included in the report, the phrase itself received little attention, which is surprising given its prominent use over the couple of years prior to the Congress. This is most probably because use of the phrase has been used by both the 'old left' and the 'new left' to criticize government policy, especially with respect to the rural healthcare system. This has meant that pride of place has been given to Hu's notion of the 'Scientific Outlook on Development'.

Those expecting significant movement on political reform were left disappointed as usual. While much was made of the more open atmosphere at the Congress and that the word 'democracy', although usually prefaced by the word 'socialist', was mentioned around 60 times in the report, there was very little detail about any concrete measures to implement it. It is clear that the leadership want to focus on improving debate and information flow within the party. This will include enhanced feedback loops on the performance of party officials and more canvassing of the public but it will not lead to any fundamental shift in the party's monopoly on power. In fact, most of these measures are designed to ensure that the party does not have to open itself to greater responsiveness to society. One thing that Hu shares with Jiang is his belief in the primacy of the party's role and that they cannot trust government organs and societal institutions to carry out the party's will.

The two Congresses also ratified key leadership changes that give a glimpse to who will be ruling China over the ten years after Hu and Wen step down in 2012 and 2013 respectively. The new leadership elected at the Party Congress gave Hu Jintao a more favourable line-up in the

Standing Committee of the Politburo and in the Politburo itself but there was one major surprise. The elevation of the Shanghai Party Secretary, Xi Jinping, who had replaced the disgraced Chen Liangyu, to the Standing Committee of the Politburo means that he now outranks Li Keqiang, who most had thought would receive the mantle of successor at the Congress. Xi is also the senior member in charge of the Party Secretariat, making him the most likely next Party General Secretary but much can change before the next Congress scheduled for 2012. Xi apparently did extremely well in the informal soundings that were taken of CC members before the Congress and he received a very high approval rate. Xi, a son of one of the earlier leaders of the CCP, and thought to have been close to Jiang is acceptable to most of the factions in the party and is thus a safe choice. Xi's new found popularity is surprising as when elections were held for the Fifteenth Party Congress (1997), he received the lowest vote of the alternate members, in part as a protest against the elevation of 'Princelings', children of senior officials. Xi has worked in Fujian and Zhejiang provinces before moving to Shanghai and is known to be friendly to business and has also promoted the private sector in his previous positions. His work in Fujian has already provided him with much experience of working with Taiwan, something that will be important in the future.

This makes Li Keqiang the more likely successor to Wen Jiabao as State Council Premier in 2013. Generally, it was thought that Li was Hu's favourite to succeed him but Hu himself may have held reservations despite their obviously close relationship. There are two reasons why party members, at this stage, did not endorse Li's succession. The first is precisely because they felt he was too close to Hu (he is seen as a core member of the Chinese Communist Youth League, a power base for Hu), and they might not want to endorse a successor who acts and looks too much like Hu. Second, and more importantly, his achievements to date as a provincial leader have been mixed and he has a reputation of, at best, being an 'unlucky leader' and, at worst, not being able to make hard decisions.

The new generation of leaders, referred to collectively as the Fifth Generation, are better trained to deal with the complexities of the next phase of development. They are less likely to see development in the kind of pseudo-scientific and linear terms that are typical of engineers, who comprise most of the Fourth Generation of leaders. They are more likely to seek solutions from their social science training and feel less need to revert to statements about socialism to buttress their views (although the phrase 'socialism with Chinese characteristics' dominates Hu's report). Compared with the Fourth Generation, on coming to power, the Fifth Generation have had far more international exposure and may have a more sophisticated view of geopolitics. However, they are also products of the reforms and are not likely to take risks that would jeopardize them. Their experiences during the Cultural Revolution will ensure that they stress social stability and their networks and family ties may incline them towards economic nationalism. They are likely to act in what they perceive to be the national interest to maintain growth and preserve access to the necessary energy and raw materials.

The Hu-Wen leadership has strived to moderate the negative effects of economic growth, shift the focus of growth, and channel more resources to the countryside. This policy thrust has been deflected by the global financial crisis that has caused policy to focus once again on accelerating GDP growth to ward off social unrest. The outline of the new five-year programme (no longer termed a plan) presented at the March 2006 NPC confirmed the need to pay more attention to the negative effects of development. This entailed help for those citizens whom the economic reforms have bypassed or have not benefited so well (migrants, the rural poor, and laid-off urban workers), grappling with problems of inequality, trying to improve environmental degradation, and reducing China's energy demand by setting a target of using 20 per cent less energy for each percentage point of output growth. In a symbolic move, from 2004, State Council Document No. 1 was dedicated to rural affairs, a return to the early years of reform. This coincided with comments by Hu and other leading rural policy-makers that it was now time for the cities to support the development of the countryside.

The post-Congress leadership that had expected to concentrate on the Olympics and celebration of 30 years of reform in 2008 and the sixtieth anniversary of the founding of the PRC were knocked off their stride by a series of unexpected disasters domestic and global. Riots in Tibet and Xinjiang used up political capital and put China in the international spotlight, while the snow storms followed by the massive Sichuan earthquake produced international sympathy and allowed the central leadership to mobilize domestic sentiment in advance of the Olympics. However, it was the global financial crisis that threatened to rain on China's big parade and pose long-term challenges.

The shock of the crisis caused China's leaders to refocus their energies on the economy. The leadership had already come to the conclusion that they will have to reform the economic model that has proven successful over the last three decades. There is a limit to the role that two of the main drivers of economic growth to date, state investment and foreign trade, can play in expanding growth further and policies will have to be developed to boost domestic consumer demand as the principal driver of future economic growth. With a slowing of the world economy, the leadership will have to promote policies that can boost domestic consumption as a major engine of growth while ensuring macroeconomic stability. Growth will slow, not necessarily a bad thing, but 80 per cent of China's aggregate demand comes from domestic sources. This has allowed China to weather better than many the expected global downturn. The new development strategy will need to increase reliance on domestic demand and domestic innovation while trying to capture a larger share of the value-added in the global production chains. This should be helped by the process of rapid urbanization and the expansion of the service sector of the economy. Over the short term, in addition to the contraction of the major external economies (EU, Japan and the US), China will have to deal with a liquidity crunch as asset prices decline. Also, rising production costs will push China to rethink its development strategy as a low-cost export-oriented producer.

However, in the short term the leadership resorted to state investment as part of a major stimulus package. In November 2008, China announced a 4 trillion *yuan* ($570 billion) stimulus package and at the March 2009 NPC meeting, Premier Wen pledged to speed up delivery on the plan and also announced that more funding could be made available if necessary. China is in a better position to keep growth going through this large injection than it was during the Asian Financial Crisis in 1997–98. It has a huge reserve of foreign exchange and a healthy current account surplus. The stimulus funds are to be spent over two years in 10 major areas (including rural infrastructure, low-income housing, transportation, water and electricity). The potential amount of investment amounts to about one-third of China's total fixed asset investment in 2007 and is around 15 per cent of GDP. Two major questions are how much of this is new funding and how much will come from the coffers of the Central government. In fact, maybe as much as 90 per cent of the package may have already been earmarked and local governments will have to contribute a significant amount. One concern is that local governments will find ways to evade their contributions or simply shift projects that they were going to fund themselves onto this new budget line. In fact, Premier Wen noted this possibility and on 10 November 2008 actively urged local governments not to hold back. China already has a significant problem with corruption and major infrastructure projects anywhere in the world are magnets for fund diversion.

The adoption of the stimulus package did affect the direction that Hu and Wen had wanted to take reforms. While the massive injection did produce a V-shaped recession for China (economic growth for 2009 was 8.7 per cent), it did reverse the trend to promoting consumption as a more important driver of growth. Concerns about potential inflation and easy credit meant that in January 2010, the leadership began to tighten monetary policy and to try to exert more control over lending. Towards the end of 2009 and in early 2010 it was clear that some had reservations about the long-term impact of this growth stimulus on the economy and it was rumoured that some of the next generation of leaders were worried that they would be left to deal with the consequences after Hu and Wen had retired. Reversing the thrust of the reform period the phrase the 'state advances and the private retreats' (*gongjin mintui*) became commonplace. Subsequent chapters deal with how the leadership is dealing with institutional change, participation and protest and key policy challenges.

Chapter 5

The Chinese Communist Party

While the CCP has resisted all attempts to challenge its political power, the reforms have led intentionally and unintentionally to significant changes in its role in the political system, its relationship to state and society, its capacity to command obedience and its membership. It is clear that the CCP today, while still committed to a Leninist model of political control, is far from the party that set the reforms in motion in the late 1970s. Policy within the party and its relationship with other institutions is more contested than in the past. With 75.9 million members (2008) it is an extremely diverse organization with a wide range of political beliefs represented. This chapter first reviews the party's organizational structure and membership and then looks at the changing role of the party in the political system.

Party organization and membership

Although there are eight other political parties in the PRC that accept the established system, the only one that matters is the CCP. The Party Statutes adopted in September 1982, with minor revisions, outline the current thinking about organizational affairs. They describe a traditional Leninist party structure, more akin to the old Communist Party of the Soviet Union than that outlined in the more 'radical' statutes adopted in 1969, 1973 and 1977. However, reforms have also brought a number of changes to party organization and to membership composition.

The basic organizing principle of the party is democratic centralism that demands that the 'individual is subordinate to the organization, the minority is subordinate to the central committee'. This creates a hierarchical pattern of organization in the shape of a pyramid. At the bottom is the network of some 3.51 million 'primary party organizations' based in work-units, neighbourhoods or in villages and where there are three or more full party members. Above this is a hierarchy of organization running upwards through the county and provincial levels to the central bodies in Beijing (see Figure 5.1). The second important principle is that of collective leadership – this is designed to avoid the tendency towards one-person rule inherent in such a hierarchically organized structure. In fact, the statutes expressly forbid 'all forms of personality cult'. This was a clear response to the earlier dominance of Mao Zedong. Party committees at all levels are called on to 'combine collective leadership with individual responsibility under a division of labour'. The third principle concerns the protection of minority rights in the party and seeks to enable individual members to hold different views from those of the organization and bring them up for discussion at party meetings. If there is serious disagreement, the individuals can present their views up to and including the CC. They must continue to carry out policy while awaiting a decision. However, neither party norms nor internal discipline function according to such rules and regulations and personal networks and factions riddle the party and there is a continual tendency towards personal rule over institutionalized rule.

The most striking feature of leadership in the PRC has been the dominance of the system by a paramount individual. From 1949 until his death in 1976, Mao dominated the party and leadership through a combination of political cunning and ruthlessness when necessary (for an unreliable account by his doctor that gives a sense of Mao's power and personality see Li Zhisui, 1994). After a brief interregnum, Deng Xiaoping dominated the leadership from 1978 until his death in 1997. Neither Mao nor Deng were General Secretary of the party but everyone knew that they dominated the political scene. The First Plenum of the Thirteenth Party Congress (1987) enshrined Deng's paramount position, although this was only made public by Zhao Ziyang in talks with Soviet leader Gorbachev in 1989. From Zhao's accounts of the events of

Figure 5.1 *Organization of the Chinese Communist Party (CCP), 2010*

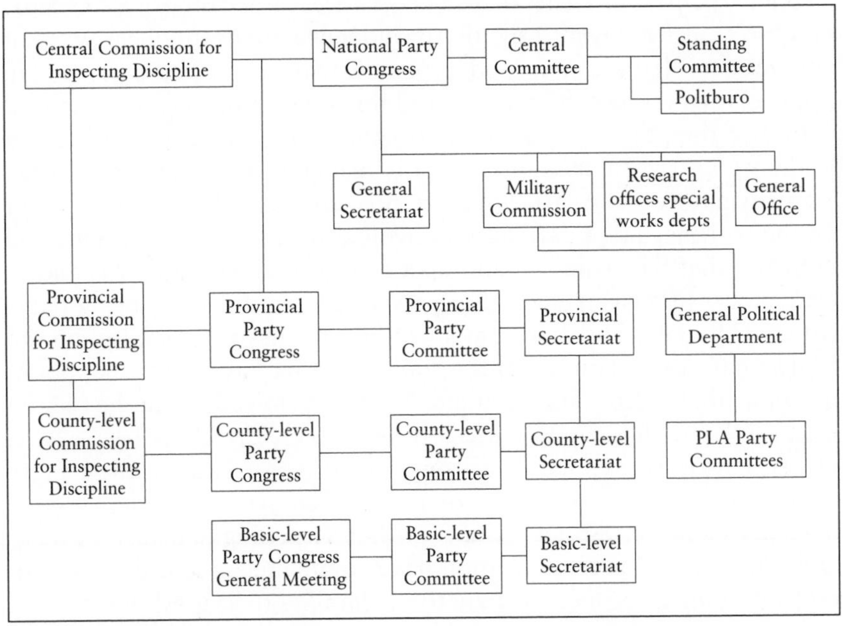

1989, it is clear that real politics was about influencing Deng to bring him onside in much the same way as politics had operated under Mao (Zhao, 2009). Policies in all spheres up until the mid 1990s bore the hallmark of Mao or Deng. Despite the CCP's formal emphasis on the norms of democratic centralism and Deng's stress on the need for institutionalization, it is clear that the party had not devised an enduring mechanism for regulating leadership debate or for dealing with leadership succession.

An important part of leadership legitimacy is the development of a concept or theory that becomes accepted as a part of the party canon. This is reflected by adoption in the Party Statutes. However, it seems the unwritten rule is that the contribution to China's progress and Marxism should not surpass and precede these of the previous 'paramount leader'. Thus, in the preamble to the Party Statutes we have described as the guide to action 'Marxism-Leninism, Mao Zedong Thought, Deng Xiaoping Theory' but Jiang Zemin does not qualify for mention by name though his contribution is referred to as 'the important thought of Three Represents'. Hu's theory of the scientific outlook on development makes it into the version of the Statutes adopted at the Seventeenth Party Congress but only later in the preamble where it states: 'The whole Party must achieve unity in thinking and in action with Deng Xiaoping Theory, the important thought of Three Represents and the Party's basic line, thoroughly apply the Scientific Outlook on Development and persevere in doing so for a long time to come'. Should the CCP be in power for another sixty years, it will be a very long preamble to the Statutes!

While the post of General Secretary carries clear authority, the capability to transfer this into significant influence after retirement was not apparent for Jiang Zemin and probably will not be the case for Hu Jintao. However, despite their more limited charisma and the changed nature of the political system, the organizational structure pushes any leader along the same course. This is heightened by the personalized factional nature of the party structure. So many individuals are dependent on the patronage of a particular individual for their career benefits and influence that they tend to build up a cult around the leader to concentrate power in their hands and to prevent power and spoils being redistributed at a later unspecified moment in time. In particular, certain top leaders have carved out spheres of influence that have affected appointments in that sector. For example, former Premier Li Peng has had a major influence in the power sector where his children have been active. His successor as premier, Zhu Rongji, held major sway in the finance sector and thus it is no surprise that his son enjoyed the leadership role in China's main investment bank. It is not surprising that various blogs and other means of dissemination have complained about the spoils of reforms going disproportionately to the families of senior leaders.

Neither Jiang nor Hu have been able to appoint their successor, again pointing to the reduced influence of the General Secretary (rather than the 'paramount leader'). This is probably a good thing as historically the norm of appointment by paramount leader has not been very successful. It has not proven easy to transfer legitimacy across the political generations. Mao designated two successors (Liu Shaoqi and Lin Biao), both of whom were subsequently jettisoned before in his dotage he picked Hua Guofeng who could never escape the legacy. Similarly, Deng Xiaoping lost two successors (Hu Yaobang and Zhao Ziyang) before acquiescing in Jiang Zemin. Depending on the patronage of one individual is clearly problematic and places constraints on the capacity to develop an independent power base. The 'successor' cannot stray too far away from the policies and networks of the patron for fear of being denounced as a traitor who has betrayed the patron's trust. While Hu Yaobang appealed privately to Deng on a number of occasions to retire, thus opening up the way for Hu to consolidate power, Zhao pursued his claims by taking Deng's retirement for granted. Yet the attempts to develop their own policy positions and networks of support that would survive Deng's death brought them into conflict with their patron.

Jiang Zemin was fortunate that Deng remained alive long enough for him to consolidate his power sufficiently to survive the death of his patron. He also learned from the removal of his two predecessors, Hu Yaobang and Zhao Ziyang, that it was not wise to push one's own policies independent of the paramount leader. Jiang played an extremely shrewd game, revealing that he was an enormously skilful insider politician, in not offending Deng or other factions in the party and appearing to be all things to all people. It was only as Deng's health deteriorated dramatically that he began to stake out his own terrain more specifically.

Yet Jiang was not able to pick his successor and, ironically it seems that Hu Jintao had been singled out by Deng a good decade before he actually took over. This allowed him the time to cultivate the necessary connections to consolidate his position. The need to be cautious for fear of losing the status of 'chosen successor' meant that the outside world knew very little about him before he assumed the position of General Secretary. Jiang's presumed favourite, Zeng Qinghong, suffered by association and was not promoted to full Politburo membership at the Fifth Plenum of the Fifteenth CC (September 2000) as expected and this disqualified him from having a shot at becoming general secretary when Jiang stepped down. The latest heir apparent is Xi Jinping who was surprisingly promoted as Hu's heir apparent at the Seventeenth Party Congress and appointed Vice-President of China at the Eleventh NPC. He was not Hu's choice and now he has to make sure that he makes no obvious mistakes in the years in the run-up to the Eighteenth Party Congress in 2012.

Personal power and relations with powerful individuals are decisive throughout the Chinese political system and society. While this may decline as the reforms become more institutionalized (Guthrie, 1999), most Chinese recognize very early on that the best way to survive and flourish is to develop personal relationships (*guanxi*) with a powerful political patron. Thus, the Chinese political leadership is riddled with networks of personal relationships and is dominated by patron–client ties (see Nathan 1973; Pye, 1981, 1995; Nathan and Tsai, 1995). This system of patron–client ties lends itself easily to the formation of factions within the leadership. The basis of such factions is shared trusts and loyalties dating back decades, rather than policy preferences. This process of faction formation also relates to institutional and regional interests but the nature of the personal ties makes it difficult to identify such interests clearly. The venom with which an individual is denounced is often difficult to understand unless one knows that person's history and relationships. Similarly, on occasion an individual is attacked as a surrogate for a top leader who is the head of one of the patronage systems. This means that we must understand the informal nature of the Chinese body politic to comprehend the nature of policy-making. Dittmer, like a number of other writers, gives primacy to the role of culture in defining the importance of informal relationships in the political process. Informal politics, in his view, prevails at the highest levels (Dittmer, 1995, pp. 1–34; Dittmer, Fukui and Lee, 2000).

The overdependence on personal relationships makes the Chinese political leadership extremely unstable. Despite the impressive appearance of the CCP as an enduring organization, it is in fact vulnerable to very rapid breakdown. When disputes break out among the leaders of the factions and patron–client networks, this has ramifications throughout the system, often leading to large-scale purges of personnel who are deemed to have supported the 'wrong line'. These purges are accompanied by campaigns against particular individuals or groups of individuals who have 'deceived' party members and the masses and led the party away from its correct line. Rather than reasoned debate of policy faults, the most common form of attack is to dole out personal abuse (see Box 5.1). When Hu Yaobang was dismissed as General Secretary in 1987, it looked as if new norms might be emerging as he was allowed to keep his seat on the Politburo and to speak at meetings. However, this did not hold for Zhao Ziyang in 1989.

The response of the leadership to the student demonstrations of mid 1989 showed how this system of individual power relationships built up over decades remained far more important than the rule of law and the formal functions people held. The events also highlighted how in the absence of institutional mechanisms for accommodating serious divisions, the system still desperately needed a Mao-like figure to perform the role of final arbiter in policy disputes. Increasingly, Deng Xiaoping slipped into the same pattern of personalized rule as Mao. This tendency was noticed not only by the Democracy Wall activists of the late 1970s and the student demonstrators of the late 1980s, but also by Deng's opponents at the top of the party. The more orthodox economist, Chen Yun, rebuked Deng for abandoning the notion of collective leadership that had been agreed on in the late 1970s; Chen warned Deng not to set himself up as an Emperor by avoiding listening to the views of others. Such criticism notwithstanding, a secret party decision was taken in 1987 that all important matters had to be referred to Deng for his approval.

With passing of Deng, it is clear that current and future leaders will derive their authority more from the formal position they occupy than from their revolutionary heritage. This means that a slow but sure process of institutionalization is taking place. While Jiang tried to extend his influence after stepping down as General Secretary by retaining his

---

Box 5.1: Criticism CCP-Style: Chen Boda's Denunciation of Wang Shiwei

The denunciation of the critical intellectual, Wang Shiwei, occurred in the Shaan-Gan-Ning base area during a major campaign to enhance party unity. The style of criticism is the prototype for subsequent CCP attacks on critical intellectuals and party members who have run foul of the 'correct party line'. Wang attacked the inequalities that were being perpetuated in the Shaan-Gan-Ning and chided the authorities for saying that life there was better than outside and that the problems were nothing to worry about. The persecution of Wang and his colleagues put an end to a more cosmopolitan strain of thinking in the CCP as Mao drove to exert a new orthodoxy. His accuser, Chen Boda, was a secretary to Mao and was a main source of the Mao cult. He rose to national power in the Cultural Revolution before being purged himself as a 'sham Marxist' in 1971.

Wang Shiwei's thinking contains a strain of Trotskyism that is antimasses, antination, counterrevolutionary, and anti-Marxist, and which serves the ruling class, the Japanese imperialists, and the international fascists ...

In my view, it is too bad that while his [Wang's] clothes are quite clean, his soul is very dirty, base, and ugly. We can find in him various manifestations of all the dirtiest elements that can be found in humanity. His filthy soul rides in tandem with his real life ...

I think that he could be as great as a 'leech'. This kind of leech hides in water; when people walk in water, it crawls on to people's feet or legs, using its suction to get into their skin and suck their blood. It can only be removed when people beat it. We think that Wang's 'greatness' is like [the greatness of] this kind of worm; it is truly 'great' (Chen Boda, 1942, in Saich, 1996, p. 1108).

position as Chair of the Central Military Commission, his real influence waned swiftly. The same is likely to be true for Hu Jintao.

The Party Congress and the Central Committee

In theory, the top of the party pyramid is the National Party Congress, or its CC, which takes over the Congress' functions when it is not in session. In reality, power lies within the Political Bureau (Politburo), its Standing Committee, and to a lesser extent within the secretariat. The Congress should convene once every five years and as a part of the post-Mao institutionalization this has indeed been the case (see Figure 5.2). The number of delegates attending the Seventeenth Party Congress (15–21 October 2007) totalled 2219. Such a large number of delegates meeting over such a short space of time means that it is rarely, if at all, that anything of consequence is seriously debated. However, the symbolic function of the Congress is extremely important in terms of providing a display of power and unity, and more important 'milestones' in the party's history. Importantly, the Congress formally elects, although in reality it approves, candidates to the CC who are proposed by the outgoing Politburo and senior leadership.

When the Party Congress is not in session the CC is, in theory, the leading body of the party. Although it meets more frequently, usually once a year in plenary session, its size (204 full members and 167 alternates at the Seventeenth Congress) again indicates that it cannot be the main focus of decision-making in the party. Debates seem to have become livelier but again plenums are convened primarily to approve a party draft document. These plenary sessions are not necessarily restricted to members and alternates, and may include other important personnel who are involved in the decision to be ratified. The draft decisions were usually worked out by the senior leadership during their summer retreat to the Beidaihe seaside, interestingly abandoned by Hu Jintao in 2003. Plenums normally last a couple of days and decisions taken are usually published in the form of a communiqué.

The fact that it is effectively a rubber stamp to decisions made elsewhere does not mean that the CC is entirely uninteresting for study. First, it is vested with a number of formal powers, such as electing the Politburo and its Standing Committee and the general secretary. When there is division on lists among the senior leaders, CC members can have a marginal impact on the elections. In addition, the CC is important as a transmission belt passing down policy proposals and receiving ideas concerning their feasibility and implementation. Finally, membership on the CC is a good indicator of trends in the political system, and a study of the composition indicates what the leadership considers important at any one time and how this changes over time. In turn, the

Figure 5.2 *Central Organization of the CCP (Simplified), 2010*

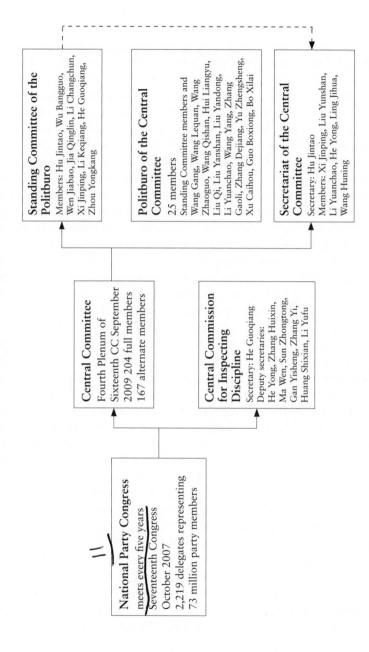

study of any such change over time will reveal the changing requirements of the leadership.

The number of full members oscillates in the range of 170–200, while
that for alternates varies from just over 100 to 150 or more. The position of alternate provides a training opportunity for future promotion to
the full CC. The first on the alternate list will be promoted to the full CC
should a member die or be removed from office. There have been a
number of trends discernible during the reform period concerning the
level of education, regional and gender representation and the level of
military involvement. The education level of delegates has risen and the
average age has dropped since the Eleventh CC was elected in 1977. At
the Twelfth Congress (1982) only 55 per cent had a college education of
any form, the number reached a peak at the Sixteenth Congress (2002–
98.6 per cent) but dropped slightly at the Seventeenth to 92.2 per cent.
By contrast, average age has dropped. By the time of the Eleventh CC in
1977, age had steadily increased, indicating that power had not yet
passed into the hands of a successor generation but merely from one
section of the same generation to another. It stood at 65.9 in 1977
(Goodman, 1979, p. 47). The major turnover during the early 1980s
when Deng forced most of the veterans into retirement meant that the
age at the Thirteenth CC dropped to a low of 55.2 and remained so in
the mid 1950s thereafter. At the Seventeenth Congress, 37 per cent were
under 50 years of age. Also, the CC has become more technocratic over
time, with 56 per cent of the members at the Fifteenth having a professional background in science, engineering, management and finance
compared with 40 per cent in 1992 (Baum, 1998, pp. 153–4).

Regional and functional representation has also changed over time.
At the Ninth CC (1969) the dominance of central officials was radically
reversed, with 59 per cent of members drawn from the provinces as
opposed to only 31 per cent at the time of the Eighth CC in 1956. This
trend reached a high point during the 1970s when the percentage of
those from the provinces in the CC was over 60 per cent. Throughout
the 1980s and 1990s, the situation of the 1950s was restored, with 26
per cent provincial representation in 1992 and 32 per cent in 1997 and
32.8 per cent in 2002 (65 members). Of the CC members and alternates
on the Seventeenth CC, those from the local levels formed the largest
group with 41.5 per cent (Li, 2008); 66.1 per cent of the full members.
With Jiang Zemin's emphasis on fusing party and state power, state
councillors and ministers booked the largest increase in CC seats at the
Fifteenth CC, raising representation from 18 per cent in 1992 to 26 per
cent (Baum, 2000, p. 26); this was maintained at the Sixteenth with 30
per cent (Fewsmith, 2003, p. 7). The military has retained a significant
voice on the CC even though its representation has been weakened at
the highest levels of the party. Not surprisingly, given the destruction of

Comp of
a CC?

the party after the Cultural Revolution was launched, military representatives on the Ninth CC accounted for 50 per cent, a figure that
declined to 31 per cent by 1977 as the civilian apparatus was restored.
This bottomed out at 17 per cent in 1987 but the increased military
influence after 1989 saw representation rise again to almost 25 per cent
but has dropped back again since to around 17 per cent. The one group
consistently underrepresented is women. Under Mao, there had at least
been rhetoric to support the inclusion of women within the leadership
and this was reflected in a 1973 CC that had 10 per cent women. This
declined to 5.3 per cent in 1992 and a low of only 2.5 per cent in 2002!
Representation revived to 6.4 per cent at the Seventeenth Party Congress
(among the delegates women accounted for 20.1 per cent). So much for
holding up half the sky! Ethnic minorities fair somewhat better and with
a 7.8 per cent representation (10.9 per cent of Congress delegates).

The Politburo, Secretariat and General Secretary

The attempts to institutionalize life at the party centre led to changes in
the relationship between the party's leading organs. During the 1980s
and 1990s, institutional power in the party has shifted among the Politburo, its Standing Committee and the Secretariat under the general
secretary, a post restored in 1982 when the position of party chairman
was abolished.

At the Thirteenth Party Congress, Zhao Ziyang announced an important adjustment in the relationship between the Politburo and the Secretariat. The Party Statutes adopted at the Twelfth Party Congress (1982)
legislated that the Politburo, its Standing Committee and the general
secretary and the Secretariat were all to be elected by the CC. This
resulted in the Secretariat and the Politburo acting as competing sources
of power. This is not surprising given that one of the reasons for the
resurrection of the Secretariat was because at the time Deng Xiaoping
and his supporters could not gain a natural majority in the Politburo. In
fact, there was even talk of the Politburo being abolished. In theory, the
Secretariat was to handle the day-to-day work of the party, becoming its
administrative nerve centre. The Politburo and its Standing Committee
would be freed to concentrate on taking important decisions on national
and international issues. In practice, it placed the Secretariat in an
extremely powerful position, as it supervised the regional party organs
and the functional departments of the party that should, in theory, have
been responsible directly to the CC and the Politburo. This access to
information and its control functions meant that it could function as an
alternative power base to the Politburo.

Zhao Ziyang announced a clear change in this relationship, downgrading the Secretariat with respect to the Politburo: The Secretariat

was reduced in size from ten to only four full-members (excluding the general secretary) and one alternate and was made the working office of the Politburo and its Standing Committee. Instead of being directly elected by the CC, its membership is now nominated by the Standing Committee of the Politburo and approved by the CC. A practical indication of the decline of the power of the Secretariat was the announcement that in the future, agendas raised by the State Council for policy-making by the Politburo or its Standing Committee would no longer be 'filtered' by the Central Secretariat. However, in practice, it functioned as Zhao Ziyang's support base in the party centre. Zhao and three of his supporters in the Secretariat were removed at the Fourth Plenum of the Thirteenth CC on 24 June 1989. Similarly, under Jiang Zemin it was useful to use the Secretariat to work around the Politburo and its size started to rise again (seven members at the Fifteenth Party Congress). Under Jiang all members were on the Politburo or its Standing Committee, whereas under Zhao only two members were on the Standing Committee of the Politburo. Under Hu Jintao, it seems to be becoming more functional with two (including Hu) from the Standing Committee, a further two Politburo members and one deputy secretary from the Central Discipline Inspection Committee (CDIC), the Director of the General Office of the Central Committee and the Director of the Policy Research Office of the CC. The Director of the General Office is considered to be a Hu protégé while the Director of the Policy Research Office is thought to be a protégé of Jiang's.

The Politburo and its Standing Committee are the most important organs of the party and lie at the centre of the decision-making process. The Statutes give no idea about the extent of the powers of the Politburo and its Standing Committee, and simply state that they are elected by the CC, that the Politburo convenes the plenary sessions of the CC and that when the CC is not in session the Politburo and its Standing Committee exercise its functions and powers. We know little about the actual workings of the Politburo, except for the fact that its meetings are frequent and that discussion is said to be unrestrained. The increasing size of the Politburo over time (11 members in 1949 and 25 in 2007) meant that in 1956 the Standing Committee was set up as a kind of 'inner cabinet'. This committee has functioned continuously since 1956, and it is the highest collective authority in the party.

Under the reforms there have been attempts to formalize membership of these two bodies on the basis of functional representation, and upper age limits have been introduced. However, membership is subject to fierce lobbying and the stress on institutionalization can give way to more pragmatic concerns. Standing Committee membership should comprise not only the general secretary but also the premier, the heads of the NPC and the Chinese People's Political Consultative Conference (CPPCC) and the CDIC. This used to leave one or two places over which senior leaders would wrangle and try to manoeuvre their protégés into place, although the membership was expanded to nine at the Sixteenth Congress and it has remained so at the Seventeenth. At the Seventeenth Congress, in addition to the functional positions noted above, people have been appointed to oversee the propaganda and public security systems and the likely successors to Hu and Wen (Xi Jinping and Li Keqiang). Interestingly, from the Fifteenth Party Congress onwards no military leader has been appointed to the Standing Committee, a factor that suggests that the civilian leadership wants to assert its control more clearly. This continues a gradual decline in military representation at the highest party levels. When Deng and Mao were alive this was not such a great problem but for Hu and his successors it will be more of a problem given their lack of military experience. At the Fourth Plenum of the Seventeenth CC many had expected heir apparent, Xi Jinping, to be elected the Vice-Chair of the Central Military Affairs Commission but this did not happen. This may have been because of resistance within the military or perhaps because of Hu's reticence to make his succession a *faît accompli*.

The other members of the Politburo are drawn from a combination of functional and factional backgrounds. The Seventeenth Congress saw a significant turnover of personnel, not as dramatic as the Sixteenth when six out of seven old Politburo Standing Committee members retired and fifteen new members were appointed among the additional sixteen Politburo members. At the Seventeenth Congress, ten newcomers were appointed, two of whom were elected directly to the Standing Committee (Xi Jinping and Li Keqiang), and one of whom was promoted from alternate member. The regional party apparatus provides the most substantial block in the Politburo but essentially represents the richer coastal areas of China. It now seems institutionalized that the major municipalities are represented: Beijing, Shanghai and Tianjin. Chongqing was added for the first time thus reflecting its status as a major municipality. In addition, the Party Secretary of Guangdong retains a place. Many of the other members have regional experience having worked in either coastal or central China. The underrepresented area is the West and again Sichuan, the most important province in the West enjoys no representation at the highest levels, despite the campaign to develop the West. It would appear that Chongqing has been identified as the pole to drive growth and investment for the western regions. The reappointment of the Xinjiang secretary has more to do with the centre's intent to maintain its territorial integrity and to resist any moves for autonomy rather than those of poverty and inequality. The Xinjiang secretary is seen as serving a key role as in the fight against 'terrorism'.

This means that to all intents and purposes the new Politburo resembles the old with traditional major municipalities (Beijing, Shanghai and

Tianjin and now Chongqing) and the wealthy coastal province of Guangdong enjoying representation while the inland and poorer areas of China are excluded. Given this, one may presume that the policy will continue to be biased in favour of the 'haves' while rhetoric will continue to be paid to the needs of the 'have nots'. It is clear that regional leadership is now an important stepping-stone to the top. A process seems to be developing of officials who have been successful in the coastal areas then serving a term in the inland provinces before returning to the centre to continue work. Of the 23 civilian members of the Politburo, 19 have served as top provincial leaders, and 8 of the 9 Standing Committee members, the exception being Premier Wen Jiabao.

A few other features are worth noting about the Politburo. The new Politburo maintains the norm of electing members in their early sixties (62 years, compared with 60.2 at the Sixteenth Congress) as opposed to 72 back at the Twelfth Congress in 1982 (Zheng and Lye, 2002, p.2). The trend of a younger leadership is matched by that of a better educated one. While back in 1982 no Politburo member had a degree, 23 of the 25 members of the 2007 Politburo have one. There is also a significant shift under way in the educational background. The Politburo members in the Jiang years and during the first term under Hu reflected the pre-Cultural Revolution emphasis on technical training, imported from the Soviet Union (although none of the current leadership trained there) and this meant that the Standing Committee members were engineers, as were the majority of Politburo members. This helps explain both the increasing policy pragmatism and the general belief that there is a technical solution to society's problems if only the correct formula can be found. In fact, four of the nine 2002 Standing Committee members graduated from Beijing's prestigious Tsinghua University. In the new Politburo (2007), of the 23 who have a degree, only 11 are in engineering, 2 in mathematics or sciences, while the remaining 10 are spread across four in economics, one in political science and three in the humanities (Miller, 2008, p. 5). It may be that this new generation is less likely to see development in the kind of pseudo-scientific and linear terms that are typical of engineers. They are more likely to seek solutions from their social science training and feel less need to revert to statements about socialism to buttress their views. Compared with the Fourth Generation (Hu Jintao, Wen Jiabao, etc.), on coming to power, the Fifth Generation have had far more international exposure and may have a more sophisticated global perspective.

Military representation has been reduced to two full members of the Politburo and in the current Politburo, only one other member can be said to have military experience. That person is, however, Xi Jinping. Last but not least there is only one woman among the Politburo members.

However, institutionalization can be dispensable, as are age requirements if factional politics override. Two examples, one from the Thirteenth Congress and one from the Fifteenth Congress, demonstrate this point. Attempts to institutionalize membership on the basis of functional occupation as stated in the 1982 Party Statutes was abandoned at the Thirteenth Congress. According to the Statutes, the heads of the Military Affairs Commission (Deng Xiaoping), the CDIC (Qiao Shi) and the Central Advisory Commission (Chen Yun) had to be members of the Standing Committee. Deng presumably felt it was better to face ridicule for yet again ripping up the Statutes than to have his strongest opponent, Chen Yun, still in the Standing Committee. As a result, neither Deng nor Chen served. Also, given Deng's and Chen's ages it would have made the policy of introducing 'new blood' look utterly ridiculous. However, rejuvenation can also be broken if other reasons are paramount. This was shown at the Fifteenth Party Congress. While no mandatory age for retirement had been agreed for senior cadres, age limits were used as a mechanism for Jiang to remove his chief rival Qiao Shi by declaring that all over 70 should retire and that he himself was willing to do so. However, party elder Bo Yibo is said to have stressed that the key was unity and rejuvenation and that Jiang as the designated 'core' of the 'third generation' should remain. The others had no choice and reluctantly stepped down (Baum, 1998, p. 151). By contrast, Li Ruihuan, a vocal opponent of Jiang, was manoeuvred out of the Politburo, despite being under 70.

The Organization Department, Discipline Inspection Commissions, and Party Schools

The party has three main mechanisms to enforce loyalty and allegiance throughout the system. The Central Organization Department plays a vital role in selecting senior leaders and overseeing training. While institutionalization is still not enshrined, the need to restore party discipline after the Cultural Revolution has led to the revival of the commissions for inspecting discipline and the party schools. Both systems have been resurrected to overcome the problems of bureaucratism, bad work-style, opposition to agreed party policy and the rampant corruption that pervades the party. This is a nationwide system that covers some 2,500 schools nationwide. The schools such as the Central Party School are expected to educate party members in the way that they should behave and in the running of the party. The Central Party School runs short-term (3-month) and 1-year training programmes for officials, both to create an *esprit de corps*, but also to prepare them for promotion. The party has clearly decided that it, rather than the state, is the most important organization for pursuing reforms and has exerted much effort to train the targeted personnel. Contrary to perception, the atmosphere at the school can be very open and critical. It was, for example, at the

negotiated state

Central Party School that reformer and Politburo member, Tian Jiyun, made his famous speech in April 1992 ridiculing 'leftism' and signalling that China was going to break free from the policies of tight economic control that had followed 1989. After reiterating his support for the thrust of Deng's 1992 southern tour, Tian suggested that perhaps the 'leftists' in the party leadership might want to set up their own SEZ in which salaries and prices of goods would be low, and queuing and rationing would be commonplace. There would be no foreign investment, all foreigners would be kept out, and no one would be able to go abroad. Bootleg tapes of the speech were one of the hottest selling items in China through the spring of 1992. Similarly, but in less eloquent fashion, both Jiang Zemin and Hu Jintao have showcased what would become their reports to subsequent party congresses.

The Central Party School and its affiliates at the lower administrative levels can also play a significant role in generating new policy ideas and its research divisions have acted as a think-tank for the central leadership (Shambaugh, 2008). Parallel to the system of party schools, the government set up an administration school system that concentrates more on the practical aspects of governing. However, it is only at the national level where the National School of Administration (now Chinese Academy of Governance) is separate from the Central Party School. At the local levels the two are merged under what the Chinese refer to as 'one sign, two schools'. This saves money and resources. In 2005, the party set up three new training schools: in Shanghai, Jinggangshan, and Yan'an respectively. The impressive school in Pudong, Shanghai is meant to focus on China's engagement with the global community, the Jinggangshan School is to teach China's revolutionary principles, while the school in Yan'an is to focus on the policies to develop the West. An aspiring leader is now expected to undergo spells of training in all these schools in order to make him or her a well-rounded CCP official. The style of teaching is also changing with the case study method becoming more popular than traditional lecturing. By 2012–15, schools have been instructed that at least 50 per cent of classes should use the case method.

For participants, attending the Party School has a number of advantages. First, it is a mark of honour within the party to be singled out. Second, it gives local officials a privileged inside view of current senior party thinking that will enable them better to second-guess the situation once they return to their locality. Third, it provides an ideal source for networking among up-and-coming leaders. Last, but not least, most participants find it very peaceful, providing them with a few months of tranquillity to read and catch up on the various chores that work had prevented them from completing.

Discipline inspection commissions are important agencies in the attempt to re-establish a system for dealing with discipline and monitoring abuses within the party. This system replaces what the party saw as the arbitrariness and unpredictability of the Cultural Revolution. It was also a clear expression that although the party recognized the breakdown of the Cultural Revolution, it was not willing to entrust monitoring of its membership and its behaviour to non-members and to submit them to any external democratic supervision. In explaining the tragedies and incompetence of the past, the party has always prided itself on the fact that it alone had righted the wrongs. During the reform period the party always resisted any attempts or suggestions to be held accountable to society and the citizenry. This frustrated its attempts to eradicate the corruption that senior leaders, including Jiang Zemin and Hu Jintao, have identified as a threat to continued CCP rule. Indeed it is now common for senior leaders and the head of the CDIC to comment that work-style and relations between the party and the people are issues that have a close bearing on the party's survival. It has also meant that cases of party corruption that are exposed are done so either because the leadership wants to make an example to discourage others, or because of factional in-fighting.

The Commission has concentrated on promoting the restoration of internal 'party life', and has drafted guidelines that would prevent the personalization of politics and restore Leninist norms of collective leadership. In addition, it has tackled such problems as the evaluation of accusations made against Liu Shaoqi in the Cultural Revolution (declaring him to have a clean bill of political health), preparing the materials against the 'Gang of Four', and the investigation of Shanghai Party Secretary, Chen Liangyu, and his associates on charges of corruption. Chen, a political enemy of Hu Jintao, was eventually sentenced to 18 years imprisonment.

The Central Organization Department and its affiliates play a crucial role in maintaining discipline and adherence to the party through their control over members' personal files, their evaluation of performance and recommendation for promotion. Basically, the Department oversees that CCP's *nomenklatura* appointments, these cover all senior ministry appointments, senior judicial appointees, heads of major state-owned enterprises, top university presidents such as Beijing and Tsinghua, the editors of key party publications and other media, provincial leaders and the directors of think-tanks. Not surprisingly it becomes the turf for numerous battles between different factions and groupings in the party. Its influence is pervasive and party members bend over backwards to please and flatter its staff. One senior retired official told me that the CCP really only needs two agencies – the organization department and the propaganda department. He should know as he had headed both of them at different times.

Currently, the Central Organization Department is headed by Politburo member, Li Yuanchao. Even before Li took over, the Department had been trying to devise methods for improving the process of selection and the training programmes that officials are expected to undergo. The Department has a division for leadership and they have been casting the net widely for experiences on methods of leadership assessment. There is a complicated set of performance indicators that are used to assess performance that include factors such as maintaining social stability and managing environmental concerns. However, hard economic criteria such as GDP growth still loom large in any assessment. The Department has also adopted a number of measures such as feedback from colleagues and 360-degree evaluation. Certainly the quality of officials has improved but the attempts at 'scientific assessment' are still trumped on occasion by political interference and the jockeying between different factions. The fact that the buying and selling of official posts is a quite common phenomenon at the local level also suggests that the scientific assessment of one's suitability can be easily undermined by money. I have been in a number of townships where officials seemed to know exact pricing for the various posts in the local administration.

In recent years, the Department has also been promoting internationalization of the training system. It is not unusual for foreigners to be giving lectures at the Central Party School and the Harvard Kennedy School has even organized a week-long training programme for officials at the Shanghai Party School (referred to for the foreigners as the Shanghai Administration Institute). The training has also extended to sending party officials overseas for tailor-made programmes in France, Japan the UK, and the USA.

Central Military Affairs Commission

The Central Military Affairs Commission (CMAC) is the main vehicle through which the party ensures control over the military system. There is also a state commission but its composition is identical and is clearly irrelevant as an independent entity. The state commission was formed in 1982 to give the impression that the military came under control of the state rather than the party. This was done in particular with respect to possible reunification with Taiwan; the military was thus portrayed as one arm of the Chinese state rather than the CCP. The CMAC is clearly more important than the Ministry of National Defence and is the highest policy-making body for military affairs and the highest command organ for military operations. In reality, the Ministry of National Defence is subordinate to the CMAC rather than to the State Council. The Minister of Defence serves as a Vice-Chair of the Commission. The CMAC has existed under one name or another since 1931, when it was established on the instructions of the First All-China Soviet Congress. Personnel appointments to the CMAC give an indication both about the strength of the military in the system and about the paramount leader. Until his death, the CMAC was headed by Mao, then briefly by Hua Guofeng, then by Deng Xiaoping. Now it is a key position for the General Secretary to hold, thus it was occupied by Jiang Zemin who reluctantly relinquished the position to Hu. This multiple office holding reflects a pull-back from the reform attempts of the 1980s when there was a serious attempt to separate the multiple functions.

Membership

While the total party membership is huge (75.9 million in 2008), the CCP has always prided itself on its exclusivity, with membership representing less than 6 per cent of the total population. Its Statutes give no evidence of this exclusivity, and contain detailed rules governing the admission of members and the duties and behaviour required of them. The actual criteria for membership have changed over the years, reflecting shifts in ideology and recruitment policies. In contrast to a number of its forerunners, the 1982 Statutes acknowledge that class background is no longer a significant factor in China and they provide an extremely broad definition of eligibility. This was amended further in 2002 when the category 'any other revolutionary' was amended to 'advanced element of other social strata' to reflect the more inclusive nature of the 'Three Represents'. Thus, membership may be sought by: 'Any Chinese worker, farmer, member of the armed forces, intellectual or advanced element of other social strata who has reached the age of 18 and who accepts the party's programme and statutes and is willing to join and work actively in one of the party's organizations, carry out the party's decisions and pay membership dues regularly.'

To become a probationary member an applicant must be supported by existing members, accepted by a party branch after 'rigorous examination', and approved by the next highest level of party organization. Probation normally lasts for one year during which time the candidate's progress is assessed and education is provided. If all goes well, full membership will then be granted by the general membership meeting of the party branch and approved by the next higher level. Members who violate party discipline are subject to various sanctions, including warnings of varying degrees of severity, removal from party posts, probation and expulsion from the party. The party can also propose to the 'organization concerned' that an offender should be removed from non-party posts. A member subjected to discipline has the right to be heard in his or her own defence and has a right to appeal to higher levels.

Although exclusive, party membership has risen steadily since 1949 when there were only 4.5 million members to reach 73 million at the most recent party congress in 2007 (see Figure 5.3). Despite this steady growth, there has been considerable variation in the nature of recruitment. During the reform period the party has had to undergo a massive process of renewal to bring in the kind of recruits who had the requisite technical skills for development. During the Cultural Revolution, and even before, insufficient attention was paid to the recruitment of the educated and the young. The 'Gang of Four' took the blame for their emphasis on worker, peasant and soldier recruitment that left the party ill-equipped to manage the modernization drive. To build up their own support, they were accused of pursuing a reckless speed of recruitment and promoting new cadres at the 'double quick' ('helicopter cadres'). The new recruits joined at a time when rational rules and regulations were under attack, meaning that these members were unfamiliar with traditional Leninist norms. By the time of the 'Gang of Four's' arrest (1976), 43 per cent of all party members in Shanghai had been admitted during the years 1966–76 and it was claimed that a 'handful of them' did not even know what 'the Communist Party, communism or party spirit' were (*SWB*: FE/6341). The flurry of books published during the 1980s as a part of party education campaigns contained the most basic questions that party members were expected to answer in tests to assess their capability.

Figure 5.3 *Party Membership, 1949–2007*

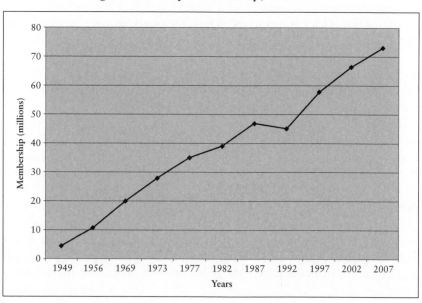

When starting the reforms, poor education levels were a general problem. In 1984 only 4 per cent of members had received a higher education and over 50 per cent were either illiterate or had been only to primary school. Moreover, in 1978 only 27 per cent of members had a senior middle-school education. By the end of 2007, 32.4 per cent of all members had a college education. At senior party levels, the party is now highly educated and technically competent, but at county level and below the problem of elite renewal remains serious. Whereas in 1950 nearly 27 per cent of members were under 25, by 1983 this had fallen to less than 3.3 per cent and had only risen to 4.6 per cent by mid 2002. Recruitment has had an effect and by 1995 those under 35 had risen to 21.1 per cent and to 23.7 per cent by end-2007. Not surprisingly, not only are women underrepresented in the leadership but throughout the party as a whole. In 2007 only 20.4 per cent of members were female but this was up from 11.6 per cent in mid 2002. By contrast, recruitment among the non-Han peoples roughly reflects their percentage of the population as a whole (6.2 per cent in 2002 and 8.01 in 1990).

Although the high standards demanded by the Statutes are not always met in practice, membership can require a high degree of commitment and considerable sacrifice of personal time. On occasion, party members have had the unpleasant task of implementing policies that were widely disliked, for example the enforcement of family-planning policy. Many local party officials have confided to me that their most hated task is overseeing the implementation of this policy (see Box 5.2).

During the Cultural Revolution many members were particularly vulnerable to the violent oscillations of the Maoist political process and were subject to savage criticism. Many members suffered simply by backing the losing side in a particular dispute. Over time such oscilla-

---

Box 5.2: Party Duty and Personal Choice

When I was a student in China at the end of the Cultural Revolution, the Campaign to Criticize Lin Biao and Confucius had just wound down. Politically, the campaign comprised a major attack on Zhou Enlai and his more moderate economic policies; socially it attacked many traditional practices. While chatting, one of the Chinese students told us of her distress at having to go periodically from Nanjing University to the surrounding communes to lecture the farmers on the evils of Lin Biao and Confucius. They were not welcoming, said they had no interest in or idea of what she was talking about, and told her in no uncertain terms to stop wasting their time and get back to the university. She often returned in tears. When we asked her if she could avoid this humiliation, she replied that it was her duty as a party member and while she could claim sickness once or twice, further absence would be noted and a demerit placed in her personal file.

tions have led to dramatically different reasons for joining the party. For many, the attractiveness of party membership diminished as a result of the record of past failures and excesses that tarnished its image. Recent policies for agriculture, the emphasis on encouraging and rewarding the professionally competent and party withdrawal from interference with much of daily life have also made it increasingly possible for some to pursue relatively well-paid and responsible jobs without membership.

However, membership keeps rising, indicating that there must be incentives for joining. Membership still confers great benefits for career advancement and also now the acquisition of economic resources. Politically, the party is still the only game in town and thus remains the locus of political power and few can achieve real political influence without membership and a record of political activism. I have met party members who are Maoists, Stalinists, more Friedmanite than Milton Friedman, Shamans (traditional religious leaders), underground Christians, Anarchists, and Social and Liberal Democrats. With no other political home to go to, virtually all with political ambition will try to enter the CCP to pursue their political agenda.

In the Maoist era, the vast majority of responsible jobs in the state and mass organizations went to party members who often had few other qualifications. Deng Xiaoping's insistence on the need for an elite of competent modernizers in all walks of life has meant that political reliability alone is no longer regarded as a sufficient qualification for a senior appointment. However, party credentials remain necessary for a wide range of sensitive positions and are a major advantage for many other jobs. Moreover, wage scales in China are highly differentiated and those in senior positions enjoy relatively high incomes, commensurate pensions, superior accommodation and access to innumerable perks. There is also a range of 'informal' advantages. Although the precise nature has differed over time, these have always included access to information denied to the general public; an increased ability to obtain 'good' education and to use 'connections' to advance the careers of one's children; opportunities to travel at state expense; the right to use cars in a country where private car ownership was until recently limited; and the opportunity to enjoy a certain amount of wining and dining at public expense. The privileged position of party membership and the access it brings has been a major cause of corruption in China.

The party is now faced with the dual challenge of making membership relevant to today's youth while not attracting only those who see it as a vehicle for personal gain. Jiang and his supporters with the 'Three Represents' campaign tried to make a case for continued relevance, claiming that the party represents the most advanced scientific and productive forces and a broader constituency than the traditional working class. In the rural areas, the party has used the village elections to attract new members who have a degree of popular legitimacy. However, senior CCP members have argued about just how accommodating they should be towards new social forces that are products of reform. In particular, debate centred on the new private entrepreneurs whom orthodox party members saw as having no place in the CCP. As long as the CCP allows no other opposition to exist, it will have to find a way to be more inclusive of such groups or risk their alienation. In July 2001, celebrating the 80th anniversary of the CCP, Jiang broke the deadlock, announcing that under certain circumstances private entrepreneurs would be welcomed to join the party. It is reported that 100,000 private entrepreneurs applied to join the party immediately after Jiang's speech and 10 provinces were set up as experimental sites (Dickson, 2003, p. 104). However, as noted, this was confirming existing practice.

According to Dickson (2008, p. 70) the number of private entrepreneurs who are party members has jumped significantly from 13.1 per cent in 1993 to 19.8 per cent in 2000 and then 32.2 per cent in 2006. However, this jump is attributable in major part to the fact that many SOEs and collective enterprises had been converted to private enterprises and their heads were party members. This has increased the number of what he calls 'red capitalists'. The political consequences are liable to be significant especially at the local level. Certainly party membership has helped many become wealthy. Of China's 100 wealthiest people, 25 per cent are members of the CCP. Even more noteworthy is the statistic that 90 per cent of China's millionaires are the children of high-ranking officials (Dickson, 2008, pp. 22–3, 171).

The role of the CCP in the political system

The most important question for reform of the political system is that of the correct role for the party and its relationship to other organizations. CCP dominance has been felt in all walks of life as the party sought not only to control the legislature and executive but also to dictate the nation's moral and ethical values. Not surprisingly, suggestions for reform have focused on the need to decrease the party's influence over the day-to-day affairs of other organizations. Since fundamental reform in this respect would lead to a decrease in the party's power, it has been strongly resisted. This resistance led to the dismissal of two general secretaries, Hu Yaobang (1987) and Zhao Ziyang (1989). However, by both design and by unintentional effect the reforms have curtailed the party's power in certain respects. In addition, the party has been aware of the changing environment in which it is operating and has sought to adapt its practices. The collapse of the Communist Party of the Soviet Union (CPSU) sent shock waves through the party (see Shambaugh,

2008 for how the CCP responded) and it has had persistent reminders with the fall of authoritarian leaders such as Suharto in Indonesia and the 'coloured revolutions' that have occurred in Central Europe.

The Legacy of the Cultural Revolution

A major challenge in the reform era has been to deal with the legacy left by Mao Zedong from the Cultural Revolution. The Cultural Revolution witnessed an unprecedented attack on a ruling Communist Party. This attack was all the more astonishing since it was initiated and led by the leader of the party – Mao Zedong. At a superficial level, there are obvious parallels with the CPSU under Stalin. Indeed, the conscious attempts to revive party life since Mao's death seem comparable with Khrushchev's attempts following Stalin's death. Certainly, under Stalin the party was emasculated. This is demonstrated by the virtual atrophy of the regular party organs. The Party Congress did not meet between 1939 and 1952 and the CC did not fare much better. The CCP did not hold a congress between 1958 and 1969. In the Soviet Union under Stalin there was a relative eclipse of the party as the supreme institution of power at the centre. As Stalin's personal power moved into the ascendant that of the party declined. Again one can find a parallel with the party under Mao.

However, there are important differences. Despite Stalin's destruction of his opponents in the party (politically and, invariably, physically), the downgrading of the party's importance and the growth of the personality cult, he always claimed to be acting in the name of the party and invoked its name to sanction its actions. Mao in destroying his opponents and, for a while, the party, was willing to invoke his own authority against that of the party. While Stalin turned to the state administration and the public security forces to attain his objectives, Mao appealed to the masses and later the army to break down the old system. While Stalin destroyed the old Bolsheviks and began to replace them with a managerial elite, Mao tried to extinguish the 'new class' and inject revolutionary zeal into the emerging managerial ethos.

Although differences existed between Mao and his supporters on questions of the nature of the ideal form of the party, his thinking on organizational issues influenced the whole programme of party rebuilding until the late 1970s. Mao's attitude to organization of any form was ambivalent. While he saw leadership as necessary to guide the revolution forward, he was suspicious of those who occupied leadership positions. He was constantly aware of the possibility of leaders becoming alienated from the masses and adopting bureaucratic postures. In the 1960s, this trend of thought led Mao to believe that the party itself provided part of the basis for the emergence of a new class dedicated to serving themselves rather than the masses and socialism. If the party as an organization had a tendency towards bureaucratism and if its top leaders could be seduced along the 'capitalist road', purely internal party mechanisms of control could not be relied upon.

Leaders were exhorted to maintain close contacts with the masses, formalized through programmes such as those for cadre participation in manual labour. The masses, for their part, were expected to exercise supervision over the leadership and offer criticism. The internal party control mechanisms that had operated before the Cultural Revolution were abolished. They were replaced by a faith in a leadership committed to revolutionary values and in the power of the masses to point out problems as they arose. The chapter on organizational principles in the party statutes adopted by the Ninth and Tenth Party Congresses (1969 and 1973) referred to the need for 'leading bodies to listen constantly to the opinions of the masses both inside and outside the party and accept their supervision'. The post-Mao stress on the need to re-establish an institutionalized system for maintaining party discipline and the virtual elimination of a role for the masses in determining the party line meant that such references were dropped in the 1982 Statutes. The organizational principles referred only to the need for higher party organizations to pay constant attention to the views of the lower party organizations and rank-and-file members.

Mao's ambivalence meant that he could not provide his supporters with a clear idea of the precise organizational forms that he preferred. Despite the attempts to separate the party as an organization from the individuals in the party who were under attack, the effect was to undermine the party's prestige. This brought to the fore the question of legitimacy. With the discrediting of the party as a source of authority and legitimacy in the Chinese polity, the tendency was to resort to the invocation of Mao's name. The fact that the Cultural Revolution did not, or was not allowed to, develop alternative forms of organization only compounded the problem.

The post-Mao leadership had not only to devise a proper relationship between the party and society but also to deal with the issue of excessive dominance by one person. While Hua Guofeng was unable to come to terms with this, Deng Xiaoping recognized the need to address this legacy and return, as he phrased it, to a 'conventional way of doing things'. By this he meant having the CCP return to a more traditional Leninist role with collective leadership, predictable rules governing the power of the higher over the lower levels and a tight grip on state and society.

The reforms have changed the role of the CCP in significant ways even as it retains its all-powerful role in the system and is willing to crush any potential opposition. This was shown most clearly in the crushing of the student-led demonstrations of 1989, again in December

1998, when leaders of the China Democracy Party were given heavy sentences, and again in late 2008 when it moved against the initiators of Charter 08. The need for change also came from the recognition that a revolutionary mobilizing party would not suit the needs of the new plans for economic modernization and that the CCP was now a ruling party and not a revolutionary party. However, a variety of factors set constraints on the extent of change. For example, the traditional Leninist rejection of organizational pluralism, the fear of internal unrest, the collapse of the CPSU and the fall of Suharto all caused Deng and Jiang Zemin to favour limited change, a development model under which increased market influences in the economy are accompanied by authoritarian political rule. This has led to a fusion of political and economic power, especially at the local levels, and even the incorporation of criminal elements into the party. Minxin Pei (2006) sees this fusion of power at the local level leading to a trapped transition within which local officials have no incentive to push ahead with measures to enhance transparency and accountability let alone more democratic initiatives. Pei sees this form of collusive corruption as spreading and as a direct product of a more gradualist approach to reform.

One hallmark of Jiang's rule, emphasized at the Fifteenth and Sixteenth Party Congresses, was the attempt to reassert party control over state and society. This has continued under Hu even as he has struggled to find ways to make the party more responsive to its changed environment. The strategy has been to try to bind new organizations into traditional forms of party patronage that are inclusive and prevent the development of an autonomous realm outside of party control. This can be seen clearly with respect to the growth of the NGO sector (Saich, 2000a) and the private sector (Dickson, 2003 and 2008). The party built new institutions to tie these to the existing system while at the same time mobilizing existing united front organizations to oversee them.

Talk about political reform was legitimized by Deng Xiaoping in August 1980 when he proposed that a mere tinkering with the system and a removal of what were seen as irregularities in party work caused by the Cultural Revolution were not enough (Deng, 1984, pp. 280–303). This had followed Deng's 1978 observation that party leadership was to be limited to 'political leadership' and was not to substitute for the government and other organizations in the system. He eschewed using the phrase of 'overall leadership' (Deng, 1983, p. 113, from Zhao, 1997, p. 13). The new development strategy adopted at the Third Plenum of the Eleventh CC (December 1978) accentuated the need for change. The policies introduced to stimulate the use of market mechanisms combined with attempts to decentralize economic decision-making were not readily served by a rigid, overcentralized political system dominated by the party and staffed by personnel who felt most at home hiding behind administrative rules and regulations. Leaders such as Deng Xiaoping and his supporters began to realize that the demands of a modern economy required a greater differentiation and clarification of roles for China's institutions.

During the early 1980s, a number of initiatives were undertaken to reform the political system, including the adoption of new Party Statutes and State Constitution, measures to trim the bureaucracy, attempts to improve the quality of the cadre force and steps to promote more effective citizen participation. The party even changed its self-definition. The 1982 Party Statutes refer to the party as the 'vanguard of the Chinese working class' rather than as the 'political party of the proletariat and its vanguard'. The term 'working class' is more neutral than that of 'proletariat', the latter term conjuring up visions of class struggle. This suits the emphasis that was placed on the tasks of economic modernization and the downgrading of the role of class struggle. Also, importantly, the CCP now defines intellectuals as an integral part of the working class. This attempt to reach out to broader groups in society is shown by the fact that the 1982 Statutes claim that the party is the 'faithful representative of the interests of all the Chinese people'. This claim did not appear in any of the previous Party Statutes, not even in those of 1956, Statutes that were also adopted at a time when the main emphasis was placed upon economic development.

However, a major overhaul of the party's role has been resisted and cadres baulked at the idea of curtailment of their power. Even the most reform-minded members of the establishment realized that there would be limits to the permissible. As in other periods of liberalization in the PRC, as indeed in all state-socialist societies, there were differences of opinion about just how much the grip of the party could or should be relaxed. Recognition that the party cannot control everything and trying to define what its leading role means in practice leaves plenty of room for disagreement.

The notion of continued party leadership is enshrined in promotion of the slogan of adherence to the 'Four Basic Principles'. These principles were first put forward by Deng Xiaoping in March 1979 at a Central Theoretical Work Conference, in response to the Democracy Wall Movement of the late 1970s and the heterodox views put forward at the Conference by the party's own senior intellectuals. After initially using the movement in his political struggle against his opponents in the party leadership, Deng had no further use for the movement and wished to set limits to non-party-sanctioned activity. Adherence to the 'Four Basic Principles' indicates that there are limits to the reforms and suggests a range of obligations for those engaged in discussions about political reform.

A further limit to wide-ranging reform was the general consensus shared by senior party leaders that political reform should be dictated by the needs of economic reform. Only such reforms would be initiated as were necessary to keep the motor of economic reform running smoothly. Jiang Zemin and his supporters were swayed by those using arguments about economic development rather than Marxism to justify authoritarian rule, drawing the conclusion from the swiftly developing economies of East and Southeast Asia that the modernization process required a strong centralized political structure, especially in the early phases, to prevent social divisions from undermining it. They hoped that this would help them push through unpopular measures without mass protest. Quite simply, they equated democratization with chaos, and chaos with underdevelopment (Saich, 1992, p. 1159).

Differing Views of the Party's Role

Within the top leadership, opinions on the role of the party in the political system have moved between two main polar points: the pragmatic reforming and the traditional orthodox. These two viewpoints served as points on a continuum around which different opinions clustered at crucial moments. Certainly they were not the only views expressed and Deng Xiaoping, Jiang Zemin, and Hu Jintao have shifted between the two viewpoints as circumstances dictated. For example, in the spring and summer of 1997, Jiang Zemin appeared to be giving licence to wide-ranging discussion of political reform only to endorse a fairly orthodox statement of the party's role at the Fifteenth Party Congress held later that year. Again at the Sixteenth Party Congress in November 2002, he confirmed that China would never copy Western political models, a statement that came after the sentencing of the leaders of the China Democracy Party.

At the Seventeenth Party Congress, while Hu mentioned the word 'democracy' around 60 times, it was usually prefaced by the word 'socialist', and there was very little detail about any concrete measures to implement it. Hu follows Jiang in wanting to improve debate and information flow within the party. This includes the feedback loops on the performance of party officials mentioned above and is encompassed in references to improve inner-party democracy. The current attitude seems to be that if the party can get it right, provide better feedback, clamp down on corruption and promote better-qualified leaders then there will be no need to open up the party to greater responsiveness from society. The following quote from Hu's speech (2007) to the Seventeenth Party Congress shows the conundrum of claiming that while power should lie with the people it should be led by the party in everything:

We must uphold the Party's role as the core of leadership in directing the overall situation and coordinating the efforts of all quarters, and

improve its capacity for scientific, democratic and law-based governance to ensure that the Party leads the people in effectively governing
the country. We must ensure that all power of the state belongs to the
people, expand the citizens' orderly participation in political affairs at
each level and in every field, and mobilize and organize the people as
extensively as possible to manage state and social affairs as well as
economic and cultural programs in accordance with the law.

Hu has closely identified himself with this need to improve inner-party
democracy and the fourth plenum of the Seventeenth CC (September
2009) adopted a decision to promote it more effectively. What it boils
down to in practice is increasing competition for party positions and
creating more feedback loops. The stress on inner-party democracy was
already borne out by the process of election of CC members at the
Seventeenth Party Congress. From mid 2006, the Sixteenth CC sent
about 60 investigation teams to relevant organizations to find out more
about the background of the nominees for the new CC. Over 40,000
candidates had been nominated, a 43.4 per cent increase on five years
before. The Standing Committee of the Politburo convened nine teams
to hear the reports and narrowed down the name list. Finally, 8.3 per
cent more names were presented for the primary election than there
were places to be filled on the CC, 9.6 per cent more for the alternate
members. These were increases over five years before. The turnover for
CC members and alternates was 49.3 per cent. Elections with more
candidates than places (*cha'e xuanju*) have become the norm for CC
membership since the Thirteenth Party Congress (1982).

It was at the Thirteenth Party Congress (1987) that Zhao Ziyang
provided the fullest articulation of the pragmatic view. The term 'pragmatic' is used as the reforms proposed are designed primarily to improve
economic efficiency. Zhao indicated that future reforms would have to
deal with some of the core issues of the party's role and structure as
inherited from the Leninist model, developed during the pre-1949
struggle for power and intensified under the centrally planned economy.
This role and structure did not suit the demands of a more decentralized, market-influenced economy where flexibility, efficiency and the
encouragement of initiative were key values. Zhao made it clear that
political reform was indispensable if economic reform was to continue,
and with an unusual rhetorical flourish stated that the CC had decided
that 'it was high time to put political reform on the agenda for the whole
party' (Zhao, 1987, p. iii).

The proposals called for a redistribution of power, both horizontally to
state organs at the same level, and vertically to party and state organs
lower down the administrative ladder. The party had so dominated, and
continues to dominate, the legislature, the executive and the judiciary as

to make their independence a fiction. The intention was for the party to exercise political leadership but not to become directly involved in the routine work of government. In particular, Zhao proposed that the dual holding of both government and party posts would be stopped, party administrative departments that carried out the same functions as those in the state sector were to be abolished along with the system of party committees ruling over academic and economic organizations. Most importantly, the system of party core groups in government and other non-party organizations was to be abolished. After the Party Congress, these reforms began to be implemented throughout the system, but the harsh atmosphere that followed the crackdown in the summer of 1989 led to a reversal. Both Jiang and Hu have seen it necessary to occupy all three top positions in the party, state and army (general secretary, president and chairman). It seems that Jiang was also concerned that if he was not head of state then it would be more difficult to meet other presidents.

Zhao even acknowledged that there existed a limited political pluralism under the leadership of the CCP. Breaking with the monistic view common to CCP thinking and the idea of uniform policy implementation, Zhao acknowledged both that 'specific views and the interests of the masses may differ from each other' and that '[a]s conditions vary in different localities, we should not require unanimity in everything' (Zhao, 1987, pp. iii–iv). Yet this acknowledgement of a limited pluralism was not intended to lead to the accommodation of factions within the party, something that had been suggested by some reform-minded intellectuals. Such reforms were seen as the only way to maintain party leadership in a time of change.

Similarly, supporters recognized that experts and intellectuals should be given a greater degree of freedom as a prerequisite for their contribution to policy-making. They should be given greater guarantees that they would not be punished tomorrow for what they said today. In turn, market-oriented reforms required that new groups in society be given the chance to participate in the process of both formulating and implementing the reforms. In this changing environment, the pragmatists realized that the party had to find a new role for itself and devise new institutions to mediate between the party and the officially sanctioned sections of society. Pragmatic reformers did not see this as weakening party control, far from it. Such reforms were seen as the way to strengthen party leadership. The clear definition of roles with the removal of the party from administrative work would strengthen its political leadership. This thinking underlay the more pragmatic response to the student-led demonstrations that sought to negotiate rather than to eliminate the voice of the protesters.

While neither Hu Yaobang in late 1986 nor Zhao Ziyang in mid 1989 saw the student protests as a major threat, the traditionalists in the party saw them as a challenge to the very fundamental principles of party rule. Crucially, Deng Xiaoping decided to side with them. Whereas Zhao appeared willing to make concessions to the students' demands, his opponents felt that no retreat was possible as it would lead to a collapse of socialism. Their reaction to the events and their brutal repression of the students served only to highlight their fear of spontaneous political activity that occurred outside their direct control. It is this view of the threat from autonomous organizations that dominates the thinking of the majority of the senior leadership at the present time and that has caused them to move hard against any independent organization, whether it be an openly political organization such as the China Democracy Party or a faith-based movement such as the *Falungong* or the underground religious movements. The rise in social unrest in recent years has contributed to the view that any nascent organization should be nipped in the bud lest it begin to pull together the incoherent and fragmented protests.

Deng always maintained a traditional view of political activity that occurred outside party control and resisted Mao's attempts to open up the party to criticism from outside forces. The general caution derived from his Leninist heritage had been reinforced by experience of the 'Hundred Flowers' Campaign, the Cultural Revolution and the democracy movements of the late 1970s and late 1980s. In all these movements, the party as an institution came under attack and the associated political instability led Deng to conclude that too much democracy was undesirable in China (see Zhao, 2009). To ignore the masses was dangerous as this might lead to greater unrest, a view reinforced by the events of the Cultural Revolution. However, the party itself would decide whether to take any notice of the views expressed, and whether it was qualified to continue in its leadership role was a matter for the party alone. This was an explicit rejection of 'Big Democracy' as proposed by Mao Zedong, under which non-party masses would be allowed to have a say in party affairs. The earlier political campaigns also greatly influenced those such as Jiang Zemin who went through the movements of the 1950s and 1960s as new party recruits trying to work their way up the system. The one notable exception is former Premier Zhu Rongji, who was one of the victims of the anti-rightist campaign. Crucially for Jiang's view is the fact that he owes his position as general secretary to the events of 1989 when he was recruited from Shanghai to run the party. The elders seemed impressed by his firm but non-violent handling of the demonstrations in Shanghai, including shutting down the city's liberal newspaper, and Deng recognized that the Beijing party leadership had been discredited by the crackdown and none could be promoted to general secretary. Similarly, it seems that Hu Jintao came to notice of the senior leaders through his handling of the unrest in Tibet earlier in 1989. His imposition of martial law at an early stage quelled dissent in a manner quite different from the outcome in Beijing. Hu is also old enough to have experienced the turmoil created by the Cultural Revolution. As new generations come to power, such memories may become less of a constraint to reform.

The traditional orthodox view opposes wide-ranging political reform and too much loosening of party control because of the consequences of liberalization for the social fabric of China. Proponents seek to run the party and its relationship to society on orthodox Leninist lines. Efforts to relax the party's grip over state and society are resisted and they seek continually to institutionalize party dominance. In particular, they are concerned about attempts to loosen the control of the party in the workplace. With the decentralization of limited decision-making powers to the work-units, it is felt important that the party retains a strong role in the enterprises to stop the work-units from deviating too much from central party policy. Thus, there is a stress upon the need for party strengthening at the grassroots level and the concern that political and ideological work continues to be taken seriously.

From the 1990s this view dominated, with the result that a number of reforms instigated at the Thirteenth Party Congress were reversed or slowed. Jiang Zemin and his associates made it clear that the party remained central to the reform process and that they trusted the party only to lead reform from within all organizations. This was reflected in a number of measures. First, at the Fifteenth and Sixteenth Party Congresses, Jiang referred to the need for political reform but offered much thinner fare than Zhao had in 1987. Not only did he predictably reject a Western-style political system but also Zhao's earlier stumblings towards acceptance of pluralism. Instead he proposed 'multi-party cooperation and consultation under party leadership' and increased control over the press and media. This formula was adopted in China's first 'White Paper on Political Reform' (State Council Information Office, 2007). Under Hu at the Fourth Plenum of the Sixteenth CC (2004), the Decision adopted displayed a similar hostility to the West stating that 'there has been no change in the strategic conspiracy of hostile force to westernize and cause China to disintegrate'. Such reforms as have been proposed are in terms of strengthening the legal system, consolidating the programme of village elections and continuation of the civil service reforms (a cornerstone of the Fourteenth Party Congress proposals). Both Jiang and Hu have stressed administrative reforms in their speeches, the training of officials and the promotion of mechanisms such as e-governance to improve efficiency.

Generally, from the 1990s onwards party control has been tightened whenever possible. It has become again common practice for senior party figures to take on important state functions and the party core group system in non-party organizations was strengthened and generally the authority of party committees and secretaries was boosted. This was particularly seen in the new law on higher education and with attempts to control the rapidly expanding NGO sector. The draft education law presented in late 1998 surprised reformers by reconfirming the pre-eminence of the party secretary at higher education institutions *vis-à-vis* the president or administrative head. This was seen throughout the university system as a major setback for academic freedom and the vitality of the universities. A number of senior university officials felt that while it might not affect premier universities too badly, as the party secretary would have to be well educated and relatively open-minded to survive, it could be stifling for the less prestigious colleges (interviews, Beijing, September 1999), where party secretaries might be able to pull rank more easily. For the NGO sector not only did the CCP promote new regulations (1998) to try to bind social organizations into a Leninist hierarchy, but it also reactivated the use of party cells within non-party organizations to try to ensure control and monitoring. In early 1998, an internal circular called for the establishment of party cells in all social organizations and the strengthening of party work in those where a cell already existed.

However, it is hard to say whether these measures have significantly restored party prestige and the party-strengthening campaigns have not had an enduring effect. Certainly party membership has continued to rise rapidly and many young, well educated people want to get into the party but often for very instrumental reasons – connections and information that can turned into a successful career or money. The primary reasons for the diminished effect are threefold. First, the increased social space that the party allowed was filled by a range of heterodox ideas and beliefs. The reforms launched from the early 1980s were not only accompanied by sharp debates among the party leadership but also by the public expression of quite unorthodox ideas. The party found it difficult to maintain its system of patronage for certain intellectual groups and social organizations while slowly losing control over the discourse that was filling the public spaces. Increasingly, public discourse was breaking free of the codes and linguistic phrases established by the party. These discourses revealed a weaker party and one whose authority was being slowly undermined. In the villages, for example, party control was challenged by the revival of traditional religious practices, and temples became places for not only worship but also the kind of reciprocity that was previously solely controlled by the party. The party has had to struggle against the revival of local religious leaders, clans, and triads as well as being challenged in some areas by private wealth. For some it has meant taking on multiple roles of being the party secretary and the local religious leader. One thing that is certain is that the party has become more contested and embroiled in daily life.

Second, the party itself lost much legitimacy in the eyes of many because of the extremely high levels of corruption that accompanied the reforms and the close identity of interest between business and official party position. As the historian Meisner (1996) has pointed out, with no commercial middle class when markets were introduced, it was local party officials who acted as the entrepreneurs and who became rich as a result. The pursuit of economic riches without genuine marketization and democratization and where power remains hierarchically structured with information dependent on position resulted in corruption being institutionalized. A system of state, society, party and bureaucratic reciprocities based on networks of favour, kinship, friendship and association has become the operational norm. Public enterprises controlled by the state became in practice fiefdoms plundered by those who ran them, with a market system in which goods and services were less important than power and prestige. The combination of party appointment to controlling positions and a dual economy created a hybrid economic formation that one might refer to as '*nomenklatura capitalism*'. The real good of value in this form of market is information that can be traded for money – or, more often, for further power (Apter and Saich, 1994). Party membership is crucial in this process.

Third, with the emphasis on economic development and the shift in the party's fundamental legitimacy to its capacity to deliver the economic goods, the objectives of party and state were not always synonymous. Neither is the obedience of party members at lower levels guaranteed. The party needed to affect its policy intent through mobilization of both party members and organizations at all levels and the implementation and enforcement by state organs. Local governments in pursuit of local developmental goals may take policy options that at best conflict with party policy and at worst run counter to it. The party cannot count on state organs for automatic policy support. A good example was the privatization of SOEs that was rife at the local level but deeply contested at the centre. This caused a fundamental tension between the party's traditional Leninist vanguard role and its other roles as an integrating mechanism and development agency.

These trends led one analyst to suggest that the party had abandoned its desire for ideological correctness and disciplined grassroots organizations to ensure maximum penetration into society. Instead it became a network of bureaucratic elites whose primary purpose was to retain power to protect their own interests (Zhao, 1997, p. 20). In all probability, the decline in attention to the grassroots comes more from default and lack of capacity than design.

To revitalize the base of the party and to try to find officials who enjoy greater support within the party, grassroots elections have been experimented with that are more open and elections for the CC have more candidates than places. The intent of such experiments is in Hu Jintao's phrase to 'strengthen the governing capacity of the ruling party'. An article by head of the Organization Department, Li Yuanchao revealed the contradiction. The article calls inner-party democracy the party's 'lifeblood' and calls for its expansion (*People's Daily*, 1 November 2007) but the article also stresses that all party members must 'resolutely follow the unified leadership' of the CC. However, in 2004, Li when in charge of the municipality of Nanjing did introduce direct elections for party representatives of local communities. By the end of August 2009, 363 communities had selected secretaries, deputy secretaries and the party committees through a two-step process referred to as 'open recommendation and direct election'. The recommendations were made by party members and party organizations and the two candidates with the most recommendations were chosen to run in the direct election by all party members within the jurisdiction (Rong and Kyriakides, 2009, at www.chinaelections.net). This is seen as one method to replace the traditional mechanism of selection from higher-level party organizations.

The drive to maintain institutionalized party dominance provides stability and assurances as well as status for party cadres. However, at the same time this drive does much to explain the stifling of initiative in the political realm that, in combination with the former dual-pricing system, provided the structural basis for corruption that was heavily criticized not only by student demonstrators but also in the official Chinese press. The concentrated nature of power and the lack of a genuine system of accountability meant that party officials at all levels were in a unique position to turn professional relationships into personal connections for financial gain. Given this structure, the idea that the problem could be resolved by the punishment of a few middle-ranking officials and an ideological campaign to instil correct behaviour in cadres was a non-starter. It is a fundamental problem that affects CCP rule over the long term and will be returned to in Chapter 13.

Chapter 6

The Central Governing Apparatus

Post-Mao policy has led to a revitalization of the state sector, with a renewed stress not only on the state's economic functions but also its legislative and representative functions. Four sets of pressures have pushed this process along. First, there is the performance deficit inherited from the Mao years when government efficiency was low, the state intrusive, law arbitrary if it existed, and citizens' rights subject to the whim of local officials. Second, the emphasis on economic reform required the state to withdraw from its previous overbearing role and reduce administrative interference, and led to a major redistribution of power both horizontally and vertically, with significant *de facto* powers decentralized to lower-level administrative units (see Chapter 7). Third, the information revolution has built on these two factors and has revealed the gap between performance in the public and private sectors. Fourth, there has been pressure to increase levels of accountability, either through village elections that were introduced to fill the institutional vacuum left in China's villages (see Chapter 8) or through the expansion of non-state organizations. This chapter first discusses some of the aspects of governance that do not appear on the organizational charts; second we look at how to evaluate government performance; then we describe the structure of the central state apparatus, the legal and coercive system and the military in the political system.

Institutional integrity and jurisdictional authority have been less important than in many countries. Indeed it is the role of the state, including its judicial organs, to implement party policy. Yet state organs and individuals have a great capacity to distort party policy during the process of implementation. Not just Mao Zedong but also local leaders have intervened in the governing process to amend outcomes to suit their own preferences.

It is no surprise given China's immense size, the large population and attempts to retain a unitary state structure that the organization of government is very complex. While it is an authoritarian system, authority is, as Lieberthal (1992) has suggested, 'fragmented' both horizontally and vertically through the system. As a result, it is also a 'negotiated state' (Saich, 2000a), where local governments and even individual institutions vary in nature depending on the relationship they have negotiated with other parts of the *apparat* (see Chapter 9 for further discussion). The problem is compounded by the fact that formal organization charts often hide as much as they reveal about where real power lies in the system. The question of party dominance was dealt with in Chapter 5 and the relationship between the centre and the localities is covered in Chapter 7. Here a number of other important issues are briefly considered.

First, as noted in Chapter 5, despite the stress in the post-Mao period on the need to move to a rule of law and away from personal dictate, it is still a system where individuals hold immense capacity to circumvent formal regulations. This is true not just at the centre but also at the local levels, and it is difficult to tell the real extent of a person's power from their position on an organizational chart. One example of this is the system of personal secretaries that senior leaders maintain (Li and Pye, 1992). The party elite can choose their own secretaries and thus that person's loyalty will be primarily to the senior leader rather than to any organization as a whole. They often come to form a trusted inner cabinet acting as the 'eyes and the ears' of the senior leaders. Many of them may later go on to develop important political careers of their own.

Second, there are a number of organizations and relationships that do not appear on any chart but that are important for understanding power and control. These are the leadership groups at the centre, the organization of various systems that coordinate work and policy in broad functional fields and the relationship between line command and horizontal command (for a fuller description of these see Lieberthal, 1995/2004, pp. 192–207, 169–70). To coordinate work across a particular field, the central leadership organizes a small group that is usually headed by a member of the Standing Committee of the Politburo. The group may be set up to oversee a particular problem at a particular time or they may be more permanent, such as those that oversee party affairs, agriculture, propaganda, economics, foreign affairs or state security (Hamrin, 1992). These more permanent groups are often referred to in China as being 'gateways' (*kou*) that link the elite to a functional area within the party and state system. In the past, control of crucial 'gateways' was a source of conflict. In the late 1980s when Zhao Ziyang was moved to be CCP general secretary, for example, he fought with Li Peng, the new premier, for control over the economics 'gateway'. Through his control, Li was able to keep him out of the loop on a number of key policy issues (interview with official concerned). By the end of the 1990s, interviews with relevant officials suggested that these 'gateways', with the exception of party affairs and propaganda, had declined in importance. Control over finance and economics had shifted effectively to the groups working under the State Council system, reflecting greater professionalization of the system, and others such as agriculture met only once a year before the main party-work conference.

Below these senior leadership groupings functional bureaucracies are grouped together in what the Chinese call a 'system' (*xitong*), and

Chinese commonly refer to themselves as working in a particular *xitong*. The *xitong* should coordinate policy and attempt to monitor its implementation: no easy task in such a dispersed bureaucratic system. *Xitong* has a narrow and a broader meaning; some use it to refer to all the units within the jurisdiction of a particular ministry or commission, while others might refer to the broader group of functionally related bureaucracies that cross individual ministry or industry lines. While there are many *xitong* in this second sense, Lieberthal (1995) identifies six major ones: party affairs, organization and personnel, propaganda and education, political and legal affairs, finance and economics, and the military. These *xitong* link to the leadership groups at the centre and while they may provide some coordination, they are not entirely effective for either implementation or feedback.

The problems of bureaucratic coordination have resulted in tensions between what Schurmann (1968, pp. 188–94) refers to as a 'vertical' and 'dual' rule that proximates to what the Chinese call *'tiao'* (branches) and *'kuai'* (areas). The dominance of one over the other will affect how central policy is implemented and how authority is exerted. *Tiao* indicates that a ministry at the central level has control over all the units at the lower levels that come under the scope of its jurisdiction. As a result, the flow of information and command runs vertically up and down the system. *Kuai* indicates that the party committee at each level would be the primary point of authority coordinating the activities of the organizations within its geographical jurisdiction. It amounts to a form of dual rule as the unit at the lower level is responsible to the corresponding departments of the line ministry and the higher levels as well as to the party committee at the same level. In the first pattern, it is the line ministry or equivalent that exerts a 'leadership relationship' (*lingdao guanxi*) over those below, whereas in the second it is the party at the same level that enjoys this authority.

Which of these relationships dominates varies over time and one Western author has interpreted post-1949 history as a struggle over the dominance of *tiao* or *kuai* (Unger, 1987). The system of vertical control was adopted under the First Five-Year Plan, but it caused the growth of specialized bureaus at the lower levels that were responsible to the corresponding departments at the higher level but that were resistant to party supervision at the same level. This did not lend itself to the kind of political mobilization preferred by Mao, which was to be led through the party system at the various levels. As a result, in 1956 the Eighth Party Congress adopted the system of branches. In practice this enabled the party to keep control over the state system as the party committee at each level was the only body capable of coordinating the activities of all other units. During the Great Leap Forward, following the 1957 decentralization measures, the party took almost complete control over the state administration at lower levels and ministries of the State Council were effectively cut off from their functional departments at the lower levels. On the whole the dominance of *tiao* leads to the development of large industrial systems, while the dominance of *kuai* supports a policy of local self-sufficiency with the development of autarkic economic systems. The reforms have tried to move China away from this tug of administrative war but the main result has been greater *de facto* independence for the localities to pursue their own development strategies within broadly defined guidelines.

Given this background, one might wonder whether it is worth spending much time on the formal organization structure at the centre. However, as Blecher (1997, p. 117) has pointed out, at the very least the formal institutions shape the overall nature of the state and politics and it is thus important to understand them, how they function and how they interrelate. Second, slowly but surely China has been moving towards a greater institutionalization of the policy process and the central institutions have became a focal point for lobbying by diverse groups and interests as they formulate rules and regulations. Third, the central state has presided over a massive body of legislation to support the economic and social reforms since the 1980s. If China is to complete its transition to a market economy, it will require a competent national government to adjudicate disputes, to interpret the rules, to give concrete form to the emerging norms and to devise new institutional forms.

Evaluation and perception of government performance

Most of the problems that China confronts are related to questions of governance, whether it is the poor implementation at the local level of good national regulations, illegal transfers of land by local administrations, or lack of transparency in the government or corporate sector. However, in comparative terms, China's government does not perform too badly for its economic level and most citizens are relatively satisfied with the performance of the national government, if not their local government.

According to the World Bank's Governance Indicators, China's governing performance has not varied significantly since 1996 when the project began. Four of the six indicators rank in the 50th to 75th percentile. The exceptions are government effectiveness, which is almost at the 65th percentile, and voice and accountability, which rates extremely low (5.8). Control of corruption has declined since 1996 from 54.4 per cent to 41.1 per cent in 2008 (Figure 6.1).

When compared with other large developing countries and those with similar incomes, China's evaluation is favourable. Not surprisingly, China's ranks extremely low on voice and accountability, even lower

Figure 6.1 *Governance Indicators for China 1996–2008*

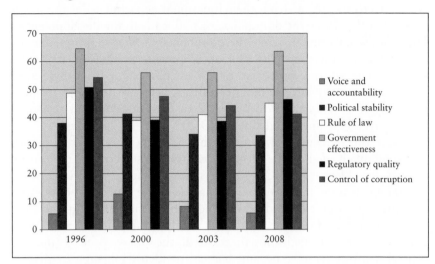

Source: Data from D. Kaufmann, A. Kraay, and M. Mastruzzi, 2009: Governance Matters VIII: Governance Indicators for 1996–2008 available at http://info.worldbank.org/governance/wgi/sc_chart.asp.

than Vietnam, but its government effectiveness ranks higher than the other two large populations in the region, India and Indonesia. Its performance is lower than India on rule of law and control of corruption but is seen as more politically stable. However, comparison with the 'tiger economies' of East Asia shows that China still has a long way to go in terms of government effectiveness. For example, it lags far behind South Korea on all indicators (Figure 6.2).

From 2003, the author conducted a survey of some 4000 respondents on their attitude towards government in China. With respect to citizen satisfaction with government, two trends are noticeable. The first is that respondents 'disaggregate' the state and, while they express high levels of satisfaction with the Central government, satisfaction declines with each lower level of government. Thus, while 95.9 per cent in 2009 were either relatively or extremely satisfied with the Central government, this dropped to 61.5 per cent at the local level (Figure 6.3). In China, local governments provide almost all public services and the fact that satisfaction levels decline as one gets closer to the people is a worrying sign. While the central government proclaims many policies to improve public service provision and rattles the nationalist sabre against Japan and Taiwan, it is the county and the township that has to fund and provide the services.

The second major finding is that satisfaction has risen steadily since Hu and Wen took over leadership. While that for the Central govern-

Figure 6.2 *Governance Indicators for Selected Countries in Asia*

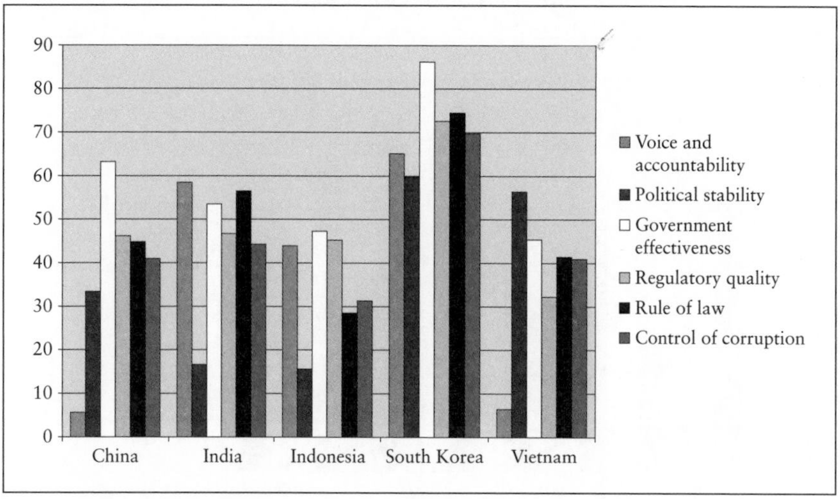

Voice and accountability

Political stability

Government effectiveness

Regulatory quality

Rule of law

Control of corruption

China　India　Indonesia　South Korea　Vietnam

Source: Data from D. Kaufmann, A. Kraay, and M. Mastruzzi, 2009: Governance Matters VIII: Governance Indicators for 1996-2008 available at http://info.worldbank.org/governance/wgi/sc_chart.asp.

ment has not changed significantly, satisfaction with the lowest levels of government has risen from 43.6 per cent in 2003 to 61.5 per cent in 2009. The highest and the lowest income earners are the groups that are most satisfied. This would suggest that those with the highest income feel that they have done well under the current system and thus are relatively satisfied with the way government functions. That there is higher satisfaction levels with the central government by the lowest income earners suggests that they clearly see the policy intent of the Centre as being supportive of their interests, as seen, for example, in the attempts to stamp out illegal fees and levies, to cut agricultural taxes, to regulate better land seizures and to provide better access to health and education. These are, of course, benefits that should apply to all rural dwellers accounting perhaps for the high satisfaction rates generally. This notwithstanding, the trend is distinct from many developed economies, where satisfaction levels tend to rise as government gets closer to the people, indicating that people feel that they have greater control over the decisions of local government and may be able to influence local policy and resource allocation.

While the consequences of these findings may raise concerns about the quality of local governance, they are not necessarily bad news for the Central government. The low levels of satisfaction might be a potential indicator of social instability but the survey suggests that for our sample at least, citizens do not see the problems as lying with the Central

Figure 6.3 *Percentage of Citizens Relatively Satisfied or Extremely Satisfied with Government*

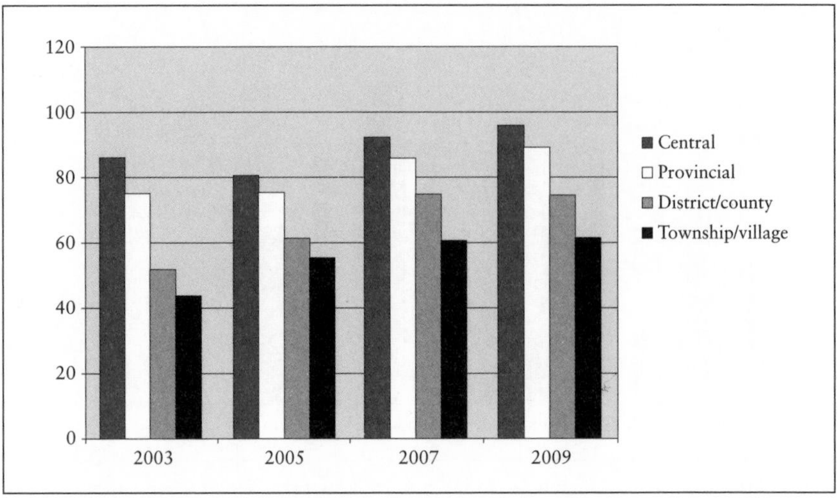

Source: Author's own surveys 2003–09.

government. This accords with the findings of others that while demonstrations, strikes and unrest may be daily occurrences in rural and urban China, the Central government retains a strong source of legitimacy. Many would appear to see the problem with local policy implementation rather than with lack of the Centre's will or systemic bias. In fact, the incentives for local governments to follow central directives in areas such as environmental and social policy are weak, while there is intense pressure on them to generate revenue often through non-sanctioned fees and levies. However, this set of perceptions holds out the possibility that residents will continue to remonstrate against local officials seeing their actions as justified by central policy intent.

Central government

The Constitution

The question of whether it is worth studying the formal aspects of China's political system is even more apparent when one talks about the relevance of the Constitution to actual political practice. While much of the important politics in China is informal and thus parts of the Constitution cannot be taken at face value – for example, rights extended in one part may be contradicted in another – as a whole it does provide a useful guide to the leadership's thinking about the present situation and gives an indication of the way in which they would like to see it evolve. In this sense, like the three previous State Constitutions, the 1982 version and its amendments provide the reader with a good barometer for China's political, economic and social climate (Saich, 1983, p. 113). This is clearly demonstrated with the leadership's evolving acceptance of the non-state sector of the economy. At the NPC meeting in March 1999, the role of the non-state sector was elevated from being 'a complement to the socialist public economy' to 'an important component of the socialist market economy'. Similarly, the change of the phrase 'counter-revolutionary activities' to 'crimes jeopardizing state security' reflected China's attempts to move towards international norms on legal issues. The March 2004 session made two important amendments to guarantee citizens' 'legally obtained' private property and inserted the statement that the 'State respects and protects human rights'.

The PRC has been governed by four Constitutions. The years immediately following the establishment of the regime were a time of radical political, social and economic restructuring and it was not until September 1954 that the first Constitution was adopted detailing the new state structure. Inevitably, it owed much to the Soviet system of government and paralleled that of the party with three levels of government below the centre – the province, the county or municipality and the town or commune. With minor changes, this structure has remained the same since. The first Constitution effectively ceased to operate in 1966–67, when the Cultural Revolution (1966–76) resulted in the disruption of established institutional arrangements and produced new structures and processes that had little, if any, constitutional validity. The second Constitution was adopted in January 1975 and reflected the more radical atmosphere of the Cultural Revolution. This was replaced by the third constitution, adopted in March 1978, which marked the initial attempts to restore the pre-Cultural Revolution system. The current Constitution was adopted in December 1982.

In general the 1982 Constitution reflects the leadership's concern to create a more predictable system based on a clearer separation of roles and functions and a system of clearly defined rules and regulations applicable to everyone. The Constitution defines the nature of the state as 'a socialist state under the people's democratic dictatorship', a concept similar to the 1954 definition of China as a 'people's democratic state'. These two Constitutions were adopted during periods when the emphasis in policy-making was on economic development. Clearly, the intention was to use a definition that incorporated as many people as possible, thus limiting the number of people to be considered as enemies of the state. This accords with the utilization of united front tactics by the pro-reform leadership in the 1980s. Vital to this approach was the downgrading of the importance of class struggle in Chinese society – a decision announced at the Third Plenum of the Eleventh CC (December 1978). Thus, the fiercer definition used in the 1975 and 1978 Constitutions of China as 'a socialist state of the dictatorship of the proletariat' was no longer deemed applicable.

All communist regimes suffer from the problem of party penetration into state affairs. In China this problem has been particularly acute, and during the Cultural Revolution any pretence at distinction between the two was effectively abolished. Thus, at the start of the Cultural Revolution, the organs of party and state at the non-central levels were identical. The revolutionary committee, which replaced the pre-1966 party and state organs, initially combined the functions of both in one committee. Even after 1969, when the party structure was gradually rebuilt, confusion persisted concerning the correct division of responsibilities between the party and the revolutionary committee. To resolve this problem the post-Mao leadership abolished the revolutionary committee and restored the pre-Cultural Revolution system of local government.

The 1982 State Constitution reflected the attempt to free the state sector from the grip of the party. Unlike the more 'radical' constitutions of 1975 and 1978, the power of the party was played down in the Constitution. Reference to the party as the 'core of leadership' was dropped, as was the claim that it was the citizens' duty to support the party. Mention of party control now appears only in the preamble, where its leading role is acknowledged in the 'Four Basic Principles'. Yet, in practice, it is clear that the state's freedom for political manoeuvre remains circumscribed and limited.

The National People's Congress and the Chinese People's Political Consultative Conference

Since its creation in 1954, the NPC has been the highest organ of state power, but prior to this, during the period of the Common Programme (1949–54), the highest body was the Chinese People's Political Consultative Conference (CPPCC). In September 1949 the CPPCC met in Beijing to proclaim the establishment of the People's Republic of China (PRC). The CPPCC was a manifestation of the united front policy, which meant that many of its members were non-communists, but its ultimate purpose was to bring about its own replacement as the most important administrative body. The meeting elected the Central People's Government Council and the Government Administration Council, the forerunner of the State Council, and approved the Common Programme and the Organic Law that provided the principles of organization for the new state structure.

The CPPCC still functions, headed by a member of the Standing Committee of the Politburo – currently Jia Qingling, and has become a lively forum for discussion and policy suggestions on prominent social, economic and foreign policy affairs. It now meets annually, around the same time as the NPC. With the stress on harmony rather than class conflict it provides liaison with other political parties and promotes united front work, providing a discussion forum for some non-party intellectuals and figures prominent in other walks of life who have no party affiliation. The CPPCC provides the party and the NPC with expertise that is helpful for policy-making. Of the 2195 delegates to the Eleventh CPPCC (March 2008), 60 per cent were non-CCP members (and only 4.38 per cent had their functional identity as the CCP) and female representation was 17.7 per cent. The highest percentage was those identified as being related to arts and entertainment (6.57 per cent). This is also a forum that encourages the participation of Hong Kong residents who have significant ties to the Mainland's development; 5.63 per cent of the deputies come from Hong Kong. It is not unusual for them to pay a 'fee' to enjoy membership. The Tenth CPPCC had raised 21,842 proposals, of which 99 per cent were said to have received a response from the relevant authorities or had been dealt with.

For CPPCC delegates, membership provides a voice to influence policy-making over a range of economic and social questions. Evidence suggests that proposals from the CPPCC do have some impact, although it should be pointed out that they do not deal with fundamental questions of policy but rather with technical matters, environmental questions, or social issues. At the Eleventh CPPCC, some delegates raised critical voices about the government's property law and the 2007 decision to raise the stamp duty in the stock market. A topic that is often discussed critically is the family planning policy. While citizen input is virtually non-existent, one woman who raised the idea, at the 2010 CPPCC session, of banning private internet cafes and replacing them with state-run facilities was roundly condemned online. This show of strength of the cyber community even ran to hacking her business website (*SCMP*, 4 March 2010).

In discussions with CPPCC members over the years, they have identified two other values of membership. First, members are allowed to see an array of internal party and state documents that the general public is not allowed to see. Second, membership allows them to pick up subtle and not so subtle changes in the political winds before they are more generally apparent. This can afford them the time to adjust their public views and practices accordingly to head off any potential criticism.

At all levels, state power is vested in people's congresses. The highest organ of state is the NPC, which is composed of deputies elected by the provinces, autonomous regions and municipalities directly under the central government, and by the armed forces. The NPC is elected for a term of five years and holds one session in each year. To date, there have been eleven national congresses held.

The Constitution vests in the NPC a wide range of powers and functions. It has the power to amend the Constitution, to make laws and to supervise the enforcement of constitutional and legal enactments. Formally it has a significant role in appointment of senior state officials. It elects the president and vice-president and shall 'decide on the choice of the Premier of the State Council upon the nomination of the President'. The 1978 Constitution stated that this be done 'upon the recommendation of the CC'. Similarly the NPC shall 'decide on the choice of vice-premiers, state councillors and ministers upon nomination by the Premier'. Some offices, however, are at the NPC's disposal without such constraints. Thus, it is empowered 'to elect' the chair of the Central Military Commission, the president of the Supreme People's Court and the Procurator General (see Figure 6.4). It also has the power to remove from office all those listed above, from the president downwards. The NPC is also entitled to examine and approve the national economic plan, the state budget and report on its implementation, to 'decide on questions of war and peace', and 'to exercise such other functions and powers as the highest organ of state power should exercise'. To give fiction to the importance of the NPC, its head officially ranks as the number two person in the CCP hierarchy, currently Wu Bangguo.

At first glance these powers seem extensive, as indeed they are, but in practice it is not the NPC that controls them. Major decisions and appointments are made by the party, usually ratified by the CC before the NPC and passed on to the NPC for its 'consideration'. Within the party, normally the legal and political group of the CC or a special drafting committee will assess the proposed legislation and present its views to the CC. As O'Brien has noted, from its inception the NPC has lacked the organizational muscle to tell the State Council, ministries or courts what to do (O'Brien, 1990, p. 79). Further, the NPC has too many delegates (2987 at the 2008 Eleventh Congress) and meets too infrequently to really exercise its powers. Thus, the NPC elects a Standing Committee to act on its behalf when not in session. Because of its smaller size (approximately 150 members), it can hold regular meetings with comparative ease. Since 1987, the Standing Committee has met every two months. This body conducts the election of deputies to the NPC and convenes it. The 1982 Constitution adopted important increases in the powers of the Standing Committee; it has been given legislative power and the power to supervise the enforcement of the Constitution. When the NPC is not in session, the Standing Committee can examine and approve partial adjustments to the state plan and budget, and it is hoped that this will provide the state with flexibility and speed when reacting to problems in the economy. The Standing Committee's power of supervision over state organs has also been increased.

That said, it is clear that the NPC has strengthened as an organization; it has institutionalized and strengthened its input into decision-making in ways that are not an overall threat to party dominance, and its outcomes have become less easy to predict, as seen in its higher number of dissenting votes on legislation and personnel appointments. As with other parts of the political system, the party cannot guarantee

Figure 6.4 *Central Organization of the Chinese Government, March 2010*

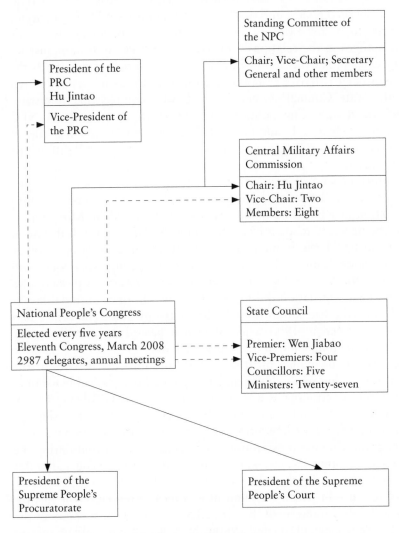

Note: ⟶ = elects - - - ⟶ = decides on recommendation.

absolute support and has accepted a looser form of control than in the Maoist days when the NPC was simply stocked with model workers and peasants, pliant intellectuals and senior party leaders. However, around 70 per cent of delegates are CCP members, 71.3 per cent at the Ninth NPC and 70.3 per cent at the Eleventh.

It seems that this form of looser control was accepted by Jiang Zemin after a brief attempt to exert party control after 1989 (for details see Tanner, 1999, p. 111; 1994, pp. 397–402). In February 1991, a CC document outlined that party leadership was, henceforth, to be limited to establishing overall policy direction, with the Politburo reviewing and confirming draft laws before they were sent to the NPC for final discussion and approval. It was also acknowledged that most articles would not need detailed review and that certain 'less important' laws might not even need to be reviewed by the Politburo. The document also made subtle changes in the relationship between the NPC and the ministries and agencies under the State Council. Through much of the 1980s the NPC had been reactive, responding to legislation as it was submitted from the State Council system. Now it was required that ministries should report significant political laws they were drafting to the NPC leadership in advance. In addition, NPC leaders were placed in charge of working out any problems with such legislation with the Politburo or the Secretariat.

In a further sign of regularization, the March 2000 session of the NPC passed the 'Legislation Law' that sought to bring some clarity to the question of who could make laws on what and when. Most importantly, the new law made it clear that only the NPC could draft law in areas regarding basic human rights, litigation and taxation. In other areas the State Council, local governments and congresses could still legislate. Second, it endorsed the rights of local legislatures to pass laws when national legislation did not exist. However, once national law is passed, then the legislation must be brought into line. The centre had been embarrassed in 1993 when Shenzhen passed its own Company Law after launching China's first stock exchange.

The reforms have also breathed a little life into the debates at the NPC meetings, but while challenging its image of being a 'rubber stamp' it is far from functioning as a Western legislature. As O'Brien (1990, p. 178) has concluded, reform of the NPC system has led to limited inclusion as a substitute for liberalization, not a sign of it. There have been reports in the Chinese press about policy debates conducted during the sessions and voting has become far from unanimous. The particular individual who chairs the NPC still makes a difference but there is an increasing sense in which the chair also comes to represent the institutional and policy interests of the NPC. Thus under the leadership of the orthodox Peng Zhen in the mid 1980s, the NPC acted to hold up reform legislation on the question of bankruptcy and a new enterprise law that was designed to increase the power of managers at the expense of party committees. It was only when Peng was replaced by the reformer Wan Li that the delaying tactics ceased. By contrast, given his previous experiences in the pre-1949 base area of Jin-Cha-Ji, Peng pushed and promoted experimentation with village elections and presided over a draft law regularizing them nationwide.

It is interesting to note that when Li Peng became chair in 1998, while not known for his democratic credentials, he became a champion of both the programme of village elections and the role of the congress system. In this, Li followed in the footsteps of his three predecessors as chair, Peng Zhen (1979–88), Wan Li (1988–93) and Qiao Shi (1993–98). All three made speeches about the need for the NPC to shed its passive role and to provide serious monitoring and evaluation of party policy. Current head, Wu Bangguo, has followed this trend. Peng had been secretary general of the NPC in the 1950s and he voiced support for the assertiveness of the NPC and an increased institutionalized role in policy-making. Following the events of 1989, Wan held the view that 'further policy mistakes and catastrophes could be avoided if the party used the NPC as an institutionalized device for listening to the complaints of the people' (Tanner, 1999, p. 107). The NPC system became a strong platform for Qiao Shi's promotion of the rule of law and the right to engage in elite party politics, significantly a battle in which he ultimately lost to the party general secretary, Jiang Zemin. Jiang himself inevitably stressed the need for NPC delegates to hold to the party line. Under the leadership of Li Peng this received more attention and at the NPC session held in March 2000, he called for deputies to 'support the party's leadership over the work of the people's congress' (*SCMP*, 10 March 2000, internet edition). This 'party-first' concept seemed to roll back some of the increased powers that Li's predecessor Qiao Shi had carved out for the NPC. While Qiao strove to increase NPC capacity to supervise the party as well as the government, Li seemed more content to boost its powers over government and judicial units. In line with Jiang's and Li's wishes, the power of the party cell over CCP NPC legislators was strengthened. This tightening of control was even more apparent at the non-central levels where 23 party secretaries from the 31 provinces or equivalents also headed the legislature, something that Zhao Ziyang's reforms had tried to stop.

The clash of views between the orthodox leaders who still see the NPC as having only a 'rubber stamp' function and those who favour genuine debate was highlighted at a number of NPC sessions. At the March–April 1989 session the orthodox premier, Li Peng, clearly saw the session as simply necessary to provide the seal of approval for his proposals for economic retrenchment. To ensure his objectives were met, he tried to muzzle both China's domestic press and the delegates to the congress. Indeed, China's most strongly pro-reform newspaper was barred from sending reporters to cover the proceedings. The rest of the Chinese press corps was told not to cover the delegates' complaints, only their positive remarks. Delegates were asked not to raise troublesome issues but to confine themselves to patriotic displays of support for central policy. Such attempts to ensure that only the bright things of socialist life were covered is more reminiscent of the Cultural Revolution years than the 'open-door policy' pursued under Deng Xiaoping.

However, these strictures could not prevent some of the discontent coming to public view and the NPC Rules of Procedure passed by the meeting contained a clause that delegates should enjoy immunity during debates. Questions raised at the meeting by delegates reflected a more independent spirit and showed how increasingly difficult it had become to stage-manage such events. The biggest success of the dissenting voices was the temporary halting of the project to build a huge dam across the Yangzi River that would have major social, economic and environmental consequences. Some 270 delegates criticized this project during the meeting and consideration of construction was to be delayed until 1995 at the earliest. Given that this was a pet project of Premier Li Peng, perhaps many felt that this was also a way of making a personal snub. However, shortly after the events of 1989, Li Peng brought the issue back to the NPC, muzzled all criticism and bulldozed the measure through at the March 1992 NPC session. Resentment was even displayed at the special treatment that the coastal areas received. In his work report, Li Peng supported the policy of rapidly developing the coastal regions and a special motion was passed that gave Shenzhen, the city and SEZ over the border from Hong Kong, special privileges in terms of drafting its own legislation. Opposition was shown by the fact that 274 delegates voted against the motion while a further 805 abstained – a record at that time in NPC voting.

While this may have been an initial high tide of NPC assertiveness, events a couple of months later showed that on any vital issue the NPC was a mere sideshow to the decisions made by the senior party leadership. In May 1989, after the State Council had promulgated the imposition of martial law, around one-third of the NPC's senior leaders signed a petition calling for its standing committee to be convened to consider this step (Hu, 1993, pp. 3–34). There was also the hope among many demonstrators that then NPC Chair Wan Li might return from his overseas trip, call the NPC to order and provide a constitutional resolution to the friction that was dividing the party, state and society. On both counts people were disappointed and the NPC was shut out of any meaningful role.

In the 1990s, the NPC picked up its role of occasional assertiveness and was especially robust in monitoring the annual work report of then

Premier Li Peng, demanding numerous revisions. In general, the NPC tried to exert greater scrutiny over the different *apparats* within its jurisdiction. For example, the NPC Finance and Economic Subcommittee heard reports from relevant ministers on economic development. With such senior economists as Li Yining and Dong Furen among its ranks, it is not surprising that ministers and their teams were challenged and heavily criticized.

Negative votes have become more commonplace and the NPC has also been willing to express its disapproval of candidates for vice-premier positions whom it feels lack competence and are clearly being appointed for factional reasons. Even Jiang Zemin's election as president in March 1998 was not unanimous, with 2,882 votes in favour, 36 against and 29 abstentions: not a large number but interesting all the same given the enormous build-up of Jiang's pre-eminent status that had followed the Party Congress (1997). In fact, as most positions only have one candidate, negative votes can tell much about a candidate's popularity. Thus, while Li Peng received 2290 (85 per cent) of the votes at the Ninth NPC, Zhu Rongji received 2890, with only 60 abstaining or voting against (Cabestan, 2000, p. 10). Wen Jiabao in 2003 had only 19 abstentions or votes against. Interestingly, at the Tenth NPC Congress (2003) all those associated with Jiang, including Jiang himself, received lower votes than those associated with Hu Jintao. Thus, in the vote for Chair of the Central Military Commission, Jiang received a 92.5 per cent approval vote while Hu received 99.7 per cent. For President, Hu received a 99.8 per cent approval rate while Zeng Qinghong in the vote for Vice-President received a lower 87.5 per cent. At the eleventh NPC (2008), two people seen as close to Jiang received the highest rate of no votes and abstentions (Li, 2008, p. 10).

The debate on the Property Law in 2006 was the most recent case of proposed legislation not making it through the NPC as initially expected (the Highway Law in 1999 is another example). The passage or rejection of such laws can become part of the broader political struggles. The postponement of discussion of a new law on property rights that was expected to be passed by the NPC raised concerns that reforms to solidify the market economy further were losing momentum. Leftist groups criticized the law claiming that the legitimation of private property would provide protection to officials who had been engaged in the theft of state-owned assets. The political mainstream was blindsided when an attack on the draft was launched by a Peking University professor who suggested that the legislature was behaving like 'slaves' in copying a capitalist law that did not guarantee the inalienable nature of socialist property. In retrospect, the real reason for postponement may have been simple vested interests combined with the fact that it is very difficult to define what could be called property. In part, this relates to a major concern of the leadership over the illegal transfer of land. In the countryside, land is owned collectively, which in practice means that the local political authorities can decide on its use and distribution, a fact that lies behind much corruption and unrest in the countryside. How property rights should be defined in the countryside is a major headache as giving rights to the farmers would not only rob corrupt officials of their spoils but would also undermine the rationale that socialism still operates in rural China as land is collectively, not privately, owned. The draft law had been in the works for 13 years and in 2007, the political leadership prepared itself better and it was passed into law by the NPC.

In addition, the NPC has found a popular cause with respect to law, order and corruption. It has been highly critical of various reports of the heads of the judiciary and the procuracy, reflecting popular disenchantment with the legal system. At the Ninth NPC, the candidate for chief prosecutor received only 65 per cent of the votes. Many voted against him both because of his age (66) and because they felt that a career as minister of railways was perhaps not the best legal training. In addition, nearly half of the delegates voted against the annual work report of the procurator-general, the largest negative vote in NPC history. This resulted in greater consideration being given to the report and delegates' views the following year. Support has improved but is still not unanimous. At the Eleventh NPC, 83 per cent approved the court report and that of the procurator.

How the NPC will develop in the future is, like all things, difficult to predict, but it is the hope of many reformers in China. They feel that the institutional strengthening that has taken place and the professionalization of NPC staff will lead to an even more assertive role on policy-making and implementation, and that it will even begin to hold the party to greater accountability. Periodically since the early 1990s suggestions from party reformers have been submitted, suggesting that direct elections be introduced for provincial level congresses, leading eventually to national elections.

Certainly a rolling back of the NPC's role is unlikely in the immediate future. It has carved out an institutional space for itself that is supported by significant individuals and interests within the system. In addition, as legislation becomes more complex and specialized, more power will move to those with the necessary skills to research and draft more elaborate regulations. The NPC is well placed in this process, with a number of specialized committees including legal affairs, finance and economics, education, foreign affairs, environment and agriculture. Its staff expanded significantly during the 1980s and many of those newly recruited were well qualified and committed to building the rule of law and helping the NPC assert its role more strongly in the political system.

The State Council

The highest organ of state administration remains the State Council, which is the executive organ of the NPC. In theory, it is responsible and accountable to the NPC and its Standing Committee and is, in effect, the government of China. It is able to submit proposals on laws to the NPC or its Standing Committee as well as to formulate administrative measures in accordance with the laws; to exert leadership over the non-central levels of administration as well as the ministries and commissions; to draw up and put into effect the national economic plan and state budget; and to oversee public order and safeguard the rights of citizens. The work of the State Council is presided over by an executive board composed of the premier, vice-premiers, state councillors and the secretary general.

Under the State Council are the various ministries, commissions, committees, bureaus and ad hoc organizations, the total number of which has varied over time. There has been a general tendency for the number of such organizations to expand followed by attempts at retrenchment. As the reforms began the numbers began to increase to accommodate the new economic agencies and those that covered the re-emerging legal system. In part, the ebb and flow of personnel numbers associated with the agencies derived from the lack of an effective retirement system in the 1970s and 1980s. The rise in the number of cadres and of the administrative organs under the State Council became too expensive for the state to cover. From 1982, there have been six major attempts to reduce the size of the bureaucracy resulting in just 27 ministries in 2008. In 1982, the State Council cut 39 ministries as well as importantly ending lifetime tenure of government posts. This was followed by a further reduction of ministries and commissions from 45 to 41 in 1988 (Bo and Chen, 2008). The need to streamline was intensified by the state's deteriorating budgetary situation. In 1991, 36 per cent of total financial expenditure went to administrative and operating expenses. This led Jiang Zemin and Zhu Rongji to continue the attempts to reduce both the size of the bureaucracy and to change its functions from direct governance to more indirect regulation. In 1993, the number of ministries and commissions under the State Council was reduced to 44, with a 20 per cent cut in personnel, and in 1998 the number was reduced further to 29.

The reforms of the Ninth NPC (March 1998) were announced as an institutional 'revolution' to produce a more efficient, well-integrated and standardized administrative system that would meet China's needs. The criticism was that the state was managing too many areas that could be handled better by commercial enterprises or new social intermediary organizations. This overload not only led to a massive wage and administrative bill but also detracted from the government's capacity to carry out its work effectively. The fact that the administrative system had evolved to oversee the planned economy was identified as a primary cause with the result that government had set up a large number of special economic management departments. The overall objective was to strengthen macroeconomic regulation and control departments while reducing the specialized economic departments, social services departments were to be reduced with individuals and social organizations taking on greater responsibility, and legal and supervisory departments were also to be strengthened.

In practice, this meant cutting the existing 44 departments under the State Council to 29 ministries, commissions, administrations and banks, with a further reduction to 28 at the Tenth NPC (March 2003). Twelve actual ministries were dissolved together with three commissions, and four new major ministries were created to absorb some of the defunct departments. In addition, the old State Planning Commission was renamed the State Development Planning Commission and then the State Development and Reform Commission that was put in charge of guiding the overall reform programme. In the domestic trade area, changes were dramatic. First, the State Economic and Trade Commission (SETC) that was set up in 1993 absorbed the ministries of coal, the metallurgical industry, machine-building industry and internal trade, which were all turned into bureaus under its jurisdiction. Having completed this task, in 2003 the Commission itself was abolished with its duties farmed out to various other ministries. In 2003 the formerly powerful Ministry of Foreign Trade and Economic Cooperation was dissolved into a new Ministry of Commerce to oversee both international and domestic trade.

Control over SOEs that had been with the SETC was placed under a new State Asset Management Commission that functioned as a holding company for government stakes in the SOEs. Gradually the Commission has reduced the number of SOEs under its purview (see Chapter 10). The creation of this Commission marked part of an attempt to move to a regulatory state and was accompanied by the creation of a China Banking Regulatory Commission and a State Food and Drug Administration. The former took over certain powers from the central bank to oversee the restructuring of the banking sector and reducing the non-performing loans. The latter is modelled on the US administration that oversees the food and pharmaceutical industries.

At the Seventeenth Party Congress (2007), Hu Jintao put forward the notion of creating a number of 'super ministries' to improve bureaucratic coordination. Despite resistance by some of the agencies concerned, this was acted on by the Eleventh NPC and five 'super ministries' were established. These were the Ministry of Industry and Information, Environmental Protection, Transport, Human Resources and Social Security, and Housing and Urban–Rural Construction. It was clear that this was a beginning and those agencies that had managed to resist this first round might well be affected at a later date. The creation of the Environmental Protection Ministry is recognition that its former status as an 'Administration' did not give it the necessary profile or political voice to deal with the enormous challenges that China faces as a result of its development trajectory. However, it is not yet clear whether the new agency will be able to wrestle pollution control away from other ministries such as water resources and agriculture. The power of vested interests is shown by the fact that the Ministry of Railways has kept its independent position and is not part of the new Ministry of Transport. In addition, much discussion took place about the creation of the National Energy Commission but the powerful Ministry of Energy has kept its independence. More reforms are promised to integrate the finance and agricultural sector more effectively.

It remains to be seen whether this latest round of bureaucratic retrenchment will be more successful than other attempts. Previously, after an impressive start, the numbers have quickly climbed again. However, there are grounds for optimism that while the numbers may creep up again, they will not rise to the levels of the 1980s. The reform attempts of the 1980s were hampered by a number of factors in addition to the lack of an effective retirement system. Most important was that attempts to streamline the bureaucracy were launched at the same time that other demands such as revamping the legal system, regularizing economic activities and dealing with international trade were causing a bureaucratic expansion. In the 1980s a government job was still thought of as the best and there was very little in the way of a private sector to absorb those laid off. Now the situation is quite different. Government is not the only job, although still an extremely popular one, that people aspire to and there are many good alternative opportunities for those sufficiently qualified who want to leave government. Second, a functioning retirement system has been put in place that reduced the incentive for many to stay on the active payroll. Third, after 25 years of reform the role of government in the economy and society has changed and many are cognizant of this fact and feel that a less extensive government apparatus is needed. Last but not least, China can no longer afford to pay for such a large government infrastructure either at the central levels or in the localities. It should be remembered that all these entities at the centre have their agencies at each level of government.

The legal system, coercive control and rights

When the reforms began in the late 1970s, the legal system was effectively at ground zero. What had not been undermined by the campaigns of the late 1950s was destroyed in the Cultural Revolution. The first task in rebuilding the legal system was to devise a system of rules and known procedures for governing people's daily lives to provide reassurance and comfort after what was described as the anarchy and lawlessness of the previous decade. In major part this entailed a resurrection of the Soviet-inspired system that was set up after 1949. However, as economic reform took off, this was equalled in importance and even surpassed by the need to legislate for the new economy. As China opened up more to the outside world there was the pressing need to introduce legislation that would reassure foreign investors and slowly move this area of law towards international practices. This has taken on greater importance after China entered the WTO. As then Premier Zhu announced (Zhu, 2003) in March 2003, the State Council reviewed 2300 foreign-related regulations and policies, abolished 830 of them and revised a further 325.

This combination of factors means that the Chinese legal system operates under a complex set of influences which often contradict one another. The more recent influences come from European law, especially with regard to the state, from US law, mainly felt through international investment and trading practices, and sit aside the longer-term inheritance from Soviet practice and Marxist theory that subjugates the law to the needs of the state. All these influences overlie Chinese traditional practice that has not emphasized a regular legal process in a Western sense, and that has not been overconcerned about formal institutions. Not surprisingly, the end result is that 'China does have a set of institutions for the preservation of social order and governmental authority, but these institutions operate on very different principles from institutions usually called "legal"' (Clarke, 1995, p. 92).

The legal system is simply one specific cog in a bureaucratic machine that is built to achieve state objectives. It enjoys parity with other bureaucratic entities and thus there is no immediate notion that the decision of a court is binding on another administrative agency or across different geographical locations. This means that, once a court decision is made, the judiciary may have to negotiate with other agencies to realize the desired outcome or the court decision may simply be ignored or be unenforceable (see Box 6.1). This kind of system means that enforcement is variable, depending on the power of the administrative agencies concerned. Thus, while enforcement of environmental regulation has remained weak, public security agencies have a greater capacity.

In addition to the bureaucratic fragmentation that often prevents the enforcement of a court decision, there is the fact that all law is seen to be in the service of 'socialism', meaning that the party can override any legal decision and intervene where it thinks appropriate. The binary nature of politics and law, like propaganda and education, in the CCP's view is shown by the coupling of the two characters *zheng* and *fa* in Chinese. Thus, the relevant party committees are political-legal affairs committees and the major specialized legal training university in Beijing is called the University of Political Science and Law.

From 1954 to 1966 a legal system of sorts developed and over 1,100 statutes and decrees were promulgated to add to the handful of very wide-ranging, vague and highly politicized directives of the early years. Attempts to enjoy 'socialist legality' were overridden by party interference in the form of political campaigns, and the legal system as such was dominated by the public security organs. The police agencies were responsible for the maintenance of public order; the investigation, arrest and detention of suspects; and the administration of the prisons and 'Reform Through Labour' camps. Although prosecution was supposedly the function of separate prosecutorial organs, these tended to be subordinate to the police. They also enjoyed legal powers in some instances to imprison offenders without the formality of a trial.

It may not have been law in the Western sense but there were some understood norms that people could grasp. For example, those with a 'bad' class background (landlords) would receive harsher punishment for the same transgression than would a worker or peasant. Similarly, a party cadre could get off punishment more lightly if they confessed their guilt, turned in others and displayed repentance for their 'crime'. There is evidence that many police took their job seriously, went to consider-

Box 6.1: The Problem of Implementing Court Decisions

The Centre for Women's Law Studies and Legal Services of Peking University takes on the litigation of selected cases that the centre's staff believes to be of significant importance for women or that are in some ways representative. One woman came to them who had been abused by her husband and wished to file for divorce. This sounds simple; the Centre took on the case and won the case for the woman. The settlement included the decision that she and the child should have the housing, with the husband moving out. However, the housing was allocated through the husband's place of work and, despite the court order, the workplace did not act. Their reason was that housing was tight, they could not move the husband, and the woman did not have an entitlement in her own right to housing at the work-unit. The woman therefore had to remain living with her abusive husband. The court had no mechanism to enforce its ruling. The Centre did not leave things there. During President Clinton's visit (1998), Hillary Rodham Clinton and Secretary of State Madeleine Albright visited the Centre to highlight China's progress in establishing the rule of law. The case was presented by Centre staff members at the meeting and the problem was very quickly solved in the woman's favour after it was widely reported by the foreign correspondents accompanying the presidential visit.

able pains to collect and sift evidence, and usually arrested someone only after they had built up a solid case. The exception was in political campaigns that soon undermined any attempt to establish norms.

The Cultural Revolution finally destroyed even these small semblances of predictability. The legal organs themselves were early points of attack and were labelled as 'bourgeois' by those who sought to abolish them. One of the important bodies abolished was the People's Procuratorate that had operated between the public security forces and the people's courts, rather like the District Attorney's office in the United States. Its powers were given to the police at the various levels, meaning that to a large extent the arbitrary power of the police became enshrined in the Constitution. However, especially in the first years of the Cultural Revolution, the police themselves also came under attack. In one province alone it was claimed that 281 police stations were ransacked, over 100,000 dossiers were stolen, and large quantities of guns and ammunition seized. For many, police power was replaced by the summary justice of the Red Guards who set up their own 'people's courts' and prisons.

Given this inheritance, it is impressive the extent to which the legal system has been rebuilt and the feeling of security guaranteed for most citizens. However, problems remain, especially with respect to the dominance of the police in the legal system and the interference of the party at all levels of the political system. Not surprisingly, the new leadership exhibited a massive display of revulsion against the anarchism and brutality of the Cultural Revolution period. The first step was to try to heal the political wounds. From 1977 the leadership began a lengthy process of investigation that resulted in the reversal of verdicts on hundreds of thousands of people who had suffered unjust punishments ranging from demotion to death. However, the leadership was careful not to allow criticism of the system as a whole and blame was placed squarely on the shoulders of the 'Gang of Four' for leading many astray. In addition, the leadership was very cautious about allowing investigation of the pre-Cultural Revolution system as a source of troubles. This is the theme of an interesting film, *Legend of Tianyun Mountain* (1980). The film argues that the difficulties that plagued China as it entered the 1980s stemmed not just from the Cultural Revolution, as the 1981 official resolution on party history decrees, but resulted from the 1950s and especially the anti-rightist campaign in which Deng Xiaoping played a prominent role (Pickowicz, 1989, p. 46). What emerges from the film is not identification with the 'good' cadres who had been harshly treated during the Cultural Revolution, but their exposure and replacement as heroes by those persecuted a generation before.

The process of regularization is covered by the phrase 'socialist legality' and the stress on the need to build a 'rule of law'. Thus a system of rules and regulations was to be created to replace the more arbitrary and uncertain situation of the Cultural Revolution. The fact that it was *socialist* legality set certain constraints and retained for the party the major role in deciding what was and what was not a crime. Further, it is clear that when Jiang, Hu, and their advisers use the phrase 'rule of law' they do not mean a system that gives primacy to law above political considerations and party policy. Instead it is a way to manage power, regulate the economy and discipline society in light of the rapidly changing circumstances. In this sense, while it might provide greater predictability it is just another weapon in the arsenal of party control.

The process comprises two main elements. The first has been to resurrect the legal system, enact significant numbers of regulations and slowly to allow professionalization and differentiation of function within the legal system (for an excellent account of this rebuilding see Lubman, 1999). The second has been to protect citizens' rights and use law to show that it is indeed of significance. This second aspect has witnessed slower progress.

In terms of legal rebuilding, the State Constitution adopted by the Fifth NPC (1978) resurrected the procuratorate system and after the NPC session there were concrete manifestations of the drive to restore law and order. This included the establishment of a Commission for Legal Affairs, the resurrection of the Ministry of Justice, the regularization of the people's courts system, the introduction of a series of laws and the re-establishment of law programmes at various key universities. Drafts of seven laws were presented to the Second Session of the Fifth NPC (June 1979), including the organic laws for the people's courts and people's procuratorate and, most importantly, the first criminal code and law of criminal procedure. These laws came into effect on 1 January 1980 to serve as the basis for the new socialist legality. A revised Criminal Procedure Law was passed in March 1996 to take effect on 1 January 1997 and an amended Criminal Law was adopted in March 1997 and went into effect on 1 October 1997. These provide a good window on how far the legal system has changed, and how far there is still to go in building a more impartial legal system.

The code of criminal law and the criminal procedure law were designed to promote the idea of equality of all before the law. The criminal law brought together in one relatively short document the major categories of criminal offence and the range of penalties they were likely to attract but, as Lubman has noted, the law, 'remained faithful to a politicized view of the criminal law' (Lubman, 1999, p. 160). This is reflected in the great attention paid to 'counterrevolutionary' crimes; 24 articles dealt with this problem – included were not only predictable activities such as plotting to overthrow the government or leading armed rebellions, but also using 'counterrevolutionary slogans ... to spread propaganda inciting the overthrow of the political power of the dictatorship of the proletariat and the socialist system'. These were the first official definitions of 'coun-terrevolutionary' behaviour, thus making it formally a crime to work against communism. In the revised law, the need to move towards inter-nationally accepted norms has meant that the crime of counterrevolution has been scrapped and replaced by the phrase 'crimes of endangering national security'. This definition can, in practice, still subsume all that was previously determined to be counterrevolutionary.

The Law on Criminal Procedure made meticulous arrangements for the handling of criminal cases, and carefully defined the rights and responsibilities of the legal organs and those accused. The role of the procuratorate is to exercise authority to ensure the observance of the Constitution and the laws of the state and to protect the rights of citi-zens. It decides whether to approve a request for arrest by a public security department, and also whether the person, if arrested, should be held criminally responsible. This was a marked change from Cultural Revolution practice. The public security organs are responsible for investigation of crimes, detention and arrest of suspects; the courts are to convene the public trials. In the 1980s, a number of amendments expanded police powers of detention and this, combined with the annual 'strike hard' campaigns launched in 1983, sanctioned a much more quota-driven, politicized form of policing once again. The continued role of the party is shown by the fact that all key appointments in both the procuratorate and court system fall under the *nomenklatura* system.

The Law also outlined an array of punishments, ranging from surveil-lance to the death penalty, including the particular Chinese decision of a two-year suspension of death sentence during which time the accused has the opportunity to show if she or he had 'reformed'. It also empha-sized such basic procedures as that where the accused was entitled to a defence and the court could appoint someone to defend the accused if they did not do so themselves, that the accused or the advocate could see the material pertaining to the case and that no one could be convicted on the basis of a statement unsupported by other evidence. In theory, police were, with certain exceptions, expected to arrest people only upon the production of a warrant from the procuratorate. After arrest, a detainee's family was normally to be informed within 24 hours and the procuratorate was to examine and approve the arrest within three days. Trials were to be public unless state secrets were involved and there were to be proper appeals procedures.

The revisions to the law were long in gestation and much fought over, with the public security organs unwilling to give up their powers to greater scrutiny and control by the procuracy and the courts (for a fascinating account of the amendments and the political background see Lawyers' Committee, 1996). The principal revisions were with respect to arrest and detention, defence counsel, initiation of prosecution and trial proceedings, while the regulation of investigation, evidence, appeal and review of death sentences were largely left alone (Lawyers' Committee, 1996, p. 19). The revisions eliminated a major method of police detention, called 'shelter and investigation', which allowed them to hold people indefinitely (initially accounting for 80–90 per cent of arrests). However, the concerns of the police were addressed by relaxing the standards for arrest and increasing the scope and length of pre-arrest detention.

Importantly, the revised law suggests movement towards the norm that there is a presumption of innocence. The amendment was made to state: 'In the absence of a lawful verdict of the people's court, no person should be determined guilty.' This would suggest that, unlike previously, the procuratorate cannot make a decision on guilt. However, the Lawyers' Committee report (1996, p. 63) concludes that the revisions result in 'little movement toward genuine acceptance of the presumption of innocence'. As the report states, many other aspects of the legislation that would facilitate this are severely restricted or simply absent. For example, suspected criminals may still be subject to lengthy pre-trial detention, there is no recognition of the right to remain silent, no exclusion of illegally gathered evidence and no right not to testify against oneself. The right to remain silent has been a major point of contention between the public security forces and reformers, who see its absence as a practice open to abuse and forced confessions.

However, the revised law remains subject to periodic debate and reformers still seek to push China's practices into conformity with international ones. At the 2004 NPC meeting, it was accepted that investigation into further revisions should begin in the next couple of years. This was prompted by China signing in 1997 and 1998 two UN covenants, on economic, social and cultural rights, and on civil and political rights. The former was adopted in 2001 after China joined the WTO but the latter has never been adopted because certain articles in the Chinese law on the notion of a fair trial and review of death sentences are not in line with those contained in the covenant. Especially the excessive use of the death penalty in China has become a focus of reformers and rights' activists in China.

As the above suggests, there has been progress towards greater regularization in law and the protection of individual rights, and it is true to say that most Chinese enjoy more individual freedom of choice than at any time since 1949. The party has taken itself out of much of daily life, and as long as one is law-abiding things are more predictable than they used to be. Party influence in the legal system remains considerable and is not restricted only to political offences. With the setting of quotas in the annual 'strike hard' anti-crime campaigns, there is strong pressure on the police and perhaps even encouragement to flout regulations on due process in order to meet targets. However, as student demonstrators in 1989, members of the China Democracy Party and Charter 08, and of the spiritual movement *Falungong* have seen, once targeted as a political enemy the full force of the coercive state apparatus comes into play. In fact, although 'shelter and investigation' was removed from the revised Criminal Procedure Law, other forms of administrative detention remain available to the police to pick up political suspects and to keep them under lock and key for significant periods of time. The most used is 're-education through labour' that allows detention from one to four years, and while used for misdemeanours it is also used to hold political dissidents. Recently, coming under increasing international scrutiny, China has begun to charge political dissidents under its criminal law, accusing them of tax evasion or consorting with prostitutes. Prior to the Olympics in 2008 or major events such as the Sixtieth Anniversary of the Founding of the PRC it is usual for critics of the system to be persuaded to leave town or to be put under effective house arrest. The most notorious example was that of former General Secretary, Zhao Ziyang, who after 1989 was kept under virtual house arrest despite no official legal charges until his death in 2005.

The rise in political activity outside the party's direct control has eroded somewhat the initial post-Mao concern with individual rights that had been so mercilessly flaunted in the Cultural Revolution. Like other communist states and a number of authoritarian Asian leaders, China has conceived human rights in collective rather than individual terms. In so far as the four state constitutions promulgated since 1949 have enshrined the rights enjoyed in 'bourgeois' democracies, these have regularly been negated by other constitutional provisions, by actual practice or, in some instances, by subsequent constitutional amendments. The PRC has, in fact, gone to great lengths to restrict personal choice and it was only after Mao's death that attempts were made to bring about liberalization and to establish a predictable system.

The post-Mao leadership stress on the equality of all before the law was reflected in the 1982 Constitution with the restoration of the 1954 stipulation to this effect. Indeed the renewed emphasis on citizens' rights (and duties) and on the need to treat people in accordance with known rules and regulations is reinforced by the fact that the chapter on Fundamental Rights and Duties of Citizens is now placed second in the Constitution whereas in all previous Constitutions it stood third after the chapter on the State Structure (Saich, 1983, p. 119). Interestingly, the 1982 Constitution did drop two citizens' rights from the 1978 Constitution. These are the freedom to strike and the freedom of the 'Four Bigs' – the right to speak out freely, air views fully, hold great debates and write big-character posters. The latter freedoms were considered too closely associated with the style of expression associated with the radicalism of the Cultural Revolution. The deletion of the right to strike was clearly influenced by events in Poland and the rise of Solidarity.

The question of rights has become a key point of contention not only domestically but also internationally, all the more so since the events of 1989. China has clearly resented external pressure on its rights record but has still felt compelled to defend it and to imply that it does indeed conform to internationally accepted norms. However, China has a poor understanding of these norms, as witnessed by its decision to sign the two UN covenants on rights (October 1997 and October 1998). China does not seem to have appreciated that by signing the covenants it is accepting that there are international norms concerning the freedom of organization, right to work, procession and formation of political groups that transcend national boundaries. China's leaders appear to have thought that they could sign on and then hold off implementation by retreating behind sovereign borders and talking about different histories and national conditions. The international human rights regime has been one forum in which China has been active in trying to shape guidelines. It has fought to resist scrutiny of domestic abuses while trying to focus attention on the actions of 'hegemonists and imperialists'. China has been a strong advocate of the right to development and has stressed that providing food and livelihood for its people takes precedence over rights of political expression and demonstration; hence, the above-noted adoption of the UN Covenant on Economic, Social and Cultural Rights but still discussion on accommodating the demands of the Covenant on Civil and Political Rights.

China has been particularly adamant in preventing monitoring of human rights by international agencies from leading to criticism of its domestic practices. It was particularly stung by the critical resolution in August 1989 adopted by the UN Subcommission on the Prevention of Discrimination and Protection of Minorities, the first time that a permanent member of the Security Council had been censured on human rights grounds in a UN forum. Subsequently, it fought a hard battle to escape criticism in the annual Geneva meetings of the UN Commission on Human Rights over the objections of the United States and the European Union. To escape this possible avenue of censure, China has moved to situate discussion of its human rights record in less intimidating bilateral forums. China declared its willingness to conduct discussions with countries on a one-to-one basis so long as pressure at Geneva was dropped. This was an effective strategy to marginalize concerted international censure of China's human rights abuses. In an interesting move in 2003, the United States decided not to propose a motion to criticize China at the annual Geneva meeting. After years of getting nowhere, the Bush administration decided a new approach, taking the Chinese leadership at its word that without Geneva there could be fruitful bilateral discussions and progress on specific issues concerning religious tolerance, political detainees and the excessive use of the death penalty. Secretary of State Clinton in her first visit to China under the Obama administration (2009) was careful to point out that human rights was just one issue within a very complex set of bilateral relationships and should not be allowed to dominate the dialogue

However, like the former Soviet Union, China has tried to manipulate the 'international human rights game' and gain international concessions by timing the release of a few political prisoners (see Nathan, 1994, pp. 622–43; 1999, pp. 136–60). As the Soviet Union found, this is a difficult game to play. China's leaders have now acknowledged to the international community and their own people that they accept that certain UN-defined rights are universal, and that like it or not these can be held up to international scrutiny. Not only does this open up China to evaluation in terms of international norms, something it finds difficult to accept, but it also legitimizes debates on human rights domestically, something it finds problematic. Indeed, legal reformers in China have seized on the signing of the two covenants to provide an impetus for reform of some of the most problematic areas of domestic law, including eliminating the excessive use of the death penalty and avoiding the courts by sentencing people to re-education through labour, and amending the criminal law to include things such as the right to remain silent. In fact, as one prominent legal specialist stated while China joined the economic mainstream 20 years ago, it now needed to join the human rights mainstream (interview, September 1999).

The military and the political system

The PLA has formed an important element of state power in China, has stepped in to save the CCP at crucial moments and its support is vital for any aspiring leader. That the role of the PLA has changed under the reforms is clear, but how it will continue to evolve and what the consequences are for the political system are less clear (for an excellent overview see Shambaugh, 2002). The tendency has been towards a more professionalized standing army that still undertakes domestic chores such as disaster relief when the ice storms struck in early 2008 or the massive Sichuan earthquake in May 2008. In many ways it is the PLA that has the national organizational capacity to mobilize in times of natural disaster (see also its response to the terrible flooding in 2005). Representation seems to have been institutionalized with the PLA holding two positions in the Politburo but with no representation on its Standing Committee. While the maxim is that the 'Party controls the gun', commander-in-chief is a crucial position for any civilian leader who wants to become the dominant political leader to hold. This was easy for Mao and Deng because of their prior military experience and connections but has been more difficult for Jiang and Hu. It now seems axiomatic that whoever becomes general secretary should also assume the Chair of the Military Affairs Commission within a couple of years. Of the post-Hu Jintao generation, only Vice-President Xi Jinping has military experience but as of the Fourth Plenum of the Seventeenth CC he had not been appointed as Vice-Chair of the Military Affairs Commission. The military retains a strong policy voice on strategic issues such as US–China relations and those with Taiwan.

Despite this interlocking party–military relationship communication has not always been effective. The outbreak of SARS in 2002–03 provided a good example of poor coordination, with the military hospitals and system clearly not feeling the compulsion to report the number of infections to the civilian authorities. This led to the wider spread of the disease than was necessary. The lack of an effective emergency response system led to an unpardonably long delay in reacting to the downing of the EP-3 US reconnaissance plane in Southern China (April 2001). Even in 2009, Admiral Keating, the top military commander for the Pacific, was complaining that he did not have direct phone contacts for his counterparts in the PLA, increasing the potential for misunderstanding and even conflict. He noted that he tended only to speak with them about disaster relief and humanitarian assistance (*Financial Times*, 1 October 2009). He should not be surprised that he cannot get their phone numbers; most senior Chinese officials' offices are not allowed to have direct access to overseas numbers!

At the same time, the domination of the military by civilian figures has also dragged the PLA into domestic politics against its own interests and perhaps better judgement. This included Mao ordering the PLA to enter the fray of the Cultural Revolution and Deng ordering the military to clear Tiananmen Square of student demonstrators on the night of 3–4 June 1989. Both actions tarnished the reputation of the PLA in different ways. It is improbable that Hu Jintao or his successor could enjoy such automatic support from the PLA, and will have to lobby its leaders, listen to its concerns and find ways to address them, while trying to promote a corps of officers that could be considered loyal. Continued support will depend on results not just in terms of providing the PLA with sufficient hardware and policy input in those areas that it considers vital to its interests, but also more broadly by guaranteeing economic growth and social stability. It will be interesting to see whether Hu will keep hold of the position of Chair of the Military Affairs Commission for a couple of years after he steps down as general secretary, as did Jiang. Jiang's retention of this post did cause some unease within the PLA as, in theory, the military had to answer to someone who was not even a member of the CC. It seems that the PLA was uncomfortable with the dysfunctional nature of being the servant of two masters. This was all the more so as Jiang was seen to keep the post for personal ambition, unlike Deng who had kept the post to push ahead with reforms. The tendency is towards greater institutionalization.

Traditionally the PLA, unlike armies in the West, has been more than a professional standing army and has enjoyed a much wider field of operation than that of a bureaucratic pressure group competing for scarce resources. The role of the PLA – which includes the navy, the airforce and those divisions concerned with nuclear weaponry – in the Chinese political system owes its origins to the pre-liberation struggle. No consideration of the post-1949 communist regime can afford to ignore the importance of the military. Shambaugh (1997, p. 127) has even described the nature of the regime at its outset as one of military conquest. As he writes: 'it is essential to view the CCP's victory as an armed seizure of power following protracted military campaigns'. Not only did many of China's citizens first witness the military conquest of the PLA before they met their new CCP leaders, but it was also the PLA that seized control of many of the factories, enforced land reform and played a leading role in reconstituting regional and local governments.

Certainly, the influence of the military was important before and after 1949, but this should not be taken to mean that the CCP was or is a military regime. However, the militaristic heritage has influenced CCP politics in significant ways, and it has also deeply affected the CCP's language. While Marxism, especially in its Leninist form, is punctuated by the language of struggle, particularly that of class, the terminology of the CCP is one of war: war on class enemies or the struggle to achieve production targets or the battle to overcome nature or disease. This language combined with the mobilization campaigns that accompanied policy initiatives or denunciations of enemies explains, in part, the severe nature of post-1949 Chinese politics.

The positive view of the military in the PRC has been widely held. Individual soldiers or units have frequently been promoted as models for emulation because of their embodiment of the communist spirit. The best-known example of this is Lei Feng, the soldier who was put forward in the early 1960s during the PLA campaigns to study the thought of Mao, again after the fall of the 'Gang of Four' in 1976–77 and finally for young people to learn from after the party had called in the PLA to crush the student-led demonstrations in 1989. Essentially, the messages to be drawn from the study of Lei Feng are to be loyal, obedient, serve the party faithfully and unquestioningly and know and accept your place in the hierarchy.

Before 1949, party and military leaders were often interchangeable and since 1949 many leaders have held concurrent party and military positions. Apart from causing institutional overlap, the liberation struggle has affected the functions of the military since 1949. The conditions during the Long March and in Yan'an and the need to rely on the population to wage guerrilla warfare meant that the PLA became a multifunctional body carrying out education and production tasks. The legacy of the past and the military success led Mao Zedong not only to have a highly favourable view of the military *per se*, but also as a participant in the political system. When Mao sought to purify the ranks of the party and state during the Cultural Revolution he turned to the army for help because he felt that under Lin Biao's leadership it embodied the 'true spirit' of the revolution. The military was seen to embody the plain-living, selfless values that Mao felt the party elite had abandoned.

Since 1949 there have been various attempts by some leaders to downgrade this 'traditional' role of the PLA and to 'professionalize' it by concentrating on its purely military functions. The most concerted and successful of these attempts has been since 1978. The fundamental question remains whether the military in politics acts as a homogeneous group pursuing military interests against those of other *apparats*, or whether the most important leadership differences cut across the different *apparats*. Related to this question are the often-quoted dichotomies of 'red' versus 'expert', and of 'politicization' and 'professionalization'. In fact, the military, especially at the non-central level, has always been involved in politics – but it is important to understand the nature of that involvement and how it has varied over time. Also the use of the singular term 'military' can be misleading because different factions have existed within the military itself.

When Mao became disillusioned with the party and state apparatus, he turned to the PLA under the leadership of Lin Biao to promote the values he wished the whole of society to adhere to. Groups in society were asked to compare themselves to those in the military, the training of militias was increased and a large number of military personnel were transferred to civilian units. Under Lin's leadership the main strategy for the PLA was enshrined in the notion of the 'People's War'. The revolutionary credentials of the PLA were boosted further in 1965 when it abolished ranks and insignia and introduced the 'Down to the Ranks Movement' for officers. Mao was using the PLA to bypass an administration that was reluctant to implement the radical policies of the Socialist Education Movement, and it was not surprising that he turned to them to impose his will in the Cultural Revolution. The collapse of the civilian administration meant that the military was thrust into the prominent leadership role, something that some military leaders clearly felt uncomfortable with. Lin Biao was even designated Mao's successor and leaders from centrally directed units enjoyed power that they had not experienced before, while 20 of the provincial revolutionary committees were chaired by people with a military affiliation.

It was clear that after 1969, the rebuilding of the party and state apparatus would have to entail a diminished role for the military. Lin Biao's fall provided the starting point for a long process of modernization in the military and a change in its political role, first back to resembling that of the pre-Cultural Revolution years but subsequently to one of substantive change. While withdrawal from direct involvement in politics and modernization and professionalization were to become key themes under Deng, it is important to remember that the new era was launched by what in effect was an illegal *coup* in which the PLA played the key role. On 6 October 1976 Politburo member, Wang Dongxing, with the support of Ye Jianying and other veteran revolutionaries, led the elite 8341 Unit of the PLA to arrest the 'Gang of Four'.

Deng shared Mao's favourable views of the PLA but also recognized the need for its modernization, without adding extra financial resources, and for the PLA's withdrawal from the broader political arena to be confirmed. However, Deng also made it clear that military modernization would figure last in the 'Four Modernizations' and that it would have to happen without an increased allocation of financial resources. In 1985, Deng outlined that PLA units would have to diversify their revenue sources as a result of the declining budgets (Shambaugh, 1996, pp. 276–7). This coincided with the moves to reduce the PLA by around 1 million troops, other organizational reforms and a significant change in military strategy. The notion of 'People's War' was dumped and in 1985 Deng put forward the view that China no longer faced imminent attack from the Soviet Union and that there was a need to focus on peacetime production and economic construction.

Initially, PLA economic diversification started with a CMAC directive to engage in self-reliant agriculture and sideline production to try to cover some of the decline in the central government's food subsidy (Yeung, 1995, pp. 159–60). However, it soon led to massive involvement by the PLA in production for civilian consumption, import and export (legal and illegal), the construction of hotels and entertainment centres and even retailing. This involvement expanded yet further after Deng Xiaoping's 1992 trip to the south. PLA enterprises were able to take advantage of military benefits, including a tax rate of only 9.9 per cent compared to 33 per cent for other firms. This engagement in business led to serious problems of corruption and decline in morale that Jiang Zemin had to deal with. By the early 1990s, this entrepreneurial engagement had become extremely significant. The PLA admitted to having 10,000 enterprises, with much higher independent estimates, and commercial earnings in the range of $5 billion by 1992 (Shambaugh, 1996, p. 277). These included 9 major conglomerates and as many as 70 automobile plants, 400 pharmaceutical factories and 1500 hotels (*SCMP*, 31 January 2001, internet edition). In the Shenzhen SEZ in 1992 there were 500 PLA-run enterprises that accounted for 10 per cent of the total industrial output value of the zone (Yeung, 1995, p. 164).

The policy to modernize and professionalize the PLA has been successful. The new strategy for the PLA is to be prepared to fight a 'limited war under high technology conditions'. In addition, as Mulvenon (1997) has noted, the education level of PLA officials has increased, combined with an increasing functional specialization. In his view, the PLA has undergone the shift from the revolutionary generation to a new post-1949 cohort that is more experienced in modern warfare and consequently more inclined to modernization and doctrinal evolution.

This does not mean that the PLA has had no political role under Deng, Jiang or Hu. The nature of this role has changed, however. It is still the case that it would be impossible to become the paramount leader in China without PLA backing. Deng's first two choices as successor, Hu Yaobang and Zhao Ziyang, were not accepted by the military leadership and were never able to consolidate their position on the CMAC. Conservative members of the military played an important role in bringing about their downfall. In addition, it was the PLA that came to the aid of the CCP on the night of 3–4 June 1989 when troops cleared Tiananmen Square of the remaining student and other protesters. While there were rumours of divisions within the military over how to handle the situation, once there was a clear line of command and it was clear that Deng was using his prestige to call them in, discipline held up well.

The events of 1989 caused a temporary reverse in attempts to keep the PLA further away from politics, but there is no evidence that as an institution the PLA had a desire to become embroiled again in elite politics. The king-making capacity of the PLA is something that both Jiang and Hu have appreciated and they have made great efforts to court the military while promoting a new generation of military leaders that will be loyal to them. However, neither could count on the PLA for automatic support in the way that either Mao or Deng could, and continued PLA support will be much more performance-based. This underlies the campaigns for loyalty that have been launched by Hu from 2005 on and that have intensified in 2009.

Jiang Zemin inherited a situation where most of the military leadership was loyal to Deng and where it was engaged in massive commercial transactions that had been legitimized by the economic policies of the 1990s. Jiang's first objective was to promote into key PLA positions people who would owe their position to his patronage. Second, he moved to strengthen party and political mechanisms within the PLA, while publicly lavishing praise on the PLA as an institution and increasing its budget every year. By the Fifteenth Party Congress (1997) for the first time Jiang had a senior CMAC leadership that he had appointed. As noted above, however, at least some elements in the PLA were uncomfortable with Jiang remaining in charge of the CMAC when no longer general secretary. While he was in charge the PLA became a major promoter of Jiang's notion of the 'Three Represents' and its media has glorified the theory and lionized Jiang as its leader and inspiration. How deep such support went is debatable and it is interesting to note that in the election for alternate members of the Seventeenth CC, Jiang's former secretary for military affairs got the lowest vote. We shall see whether Hu's image will diminish as quickly.

While Jiang did manage to gain public loyalty from the PLA, this did not mean that he would not go against their interests when these were considered detrimental to the nation as a whole. One development that caused concern over conflict of interest was the PLA's enormous business empire, the seeds of which were sown in the 1980s but the fruits of which ripened in the 1990s. Many of those who profited were the children of senior cadres and they have been involved in a number of scandals. Not only the civilian leadership has been worried about this and the associated corruption, but senior military figures have also expressed concern about the corrosive effect on military discipline, preparedness and morale. Jiang was apparently also disturbed about the corruption that was involved in some of the PLA 'business' ventures. As a result, Jiang, with the support of key figures such as then Defence Minister, Chi Haotian, decided to remove the PLA from business or at least to reduce its role significantly. In November 1994, a CMAC directive banned units beneath the group army level from conducting business activities, and in July 1998 Jiang made the bold announcement that the PLA would withdraw from its business activities within the year.

The programme of divestiture has been more successful than one might have imagined given the immense financial empire, and showed clearly how senior leaders saw the PLA's dealings as counterproductive. The disengagement was one of the most contentious decisions made by Jiang, and his fortitude surprised many. The revelation of questionable activities of PLA-run enterprises that came to light in the process (smuggling, gun-running, prostitution) has sullied the PLA's reputation. A dramatic fall in smuggling has resulted from this policy and it is no surprise that the customs department announced a 41 per cent increase in revenue in the year 2000 ($27 billion in total). The divested companies were placed under a newly created office, the National Transfer Office, under the SETC. Over the first two years, 6000 companies with assets of around $24.1 billion were transferred but only 900 remain, the others having been closed or merged. Included were nine major conglomerates that accounted for around 75 per cent of the PLA's business empire (*SCMP*, 31 January 2001, internet edition).

To sweeten the pill of this programme, Jiang had to promise an increased budgetary allocation to offset the decline in external revenues and it is clear that different branches of the PLA used this as a means to extract inflated budgets from the state in compensation for supposed business losses. One problem in trying to assess the value of PLA enterprises stems from the fact that the PLA has tried to conceal the true extent of its business operations. In addition, progress was hampered not just by difficulties in deciding what exactly was a PLA business but also by problems of finding jobs for laid-off workers, clearing up the bad debts left behind and accurately assessing the financial liabilities. It seems that some units had tried to palm off loss-making enterprises while finding creative registrations to keep those that were profitable.

The corruption that plagued the PLA engagement in business has persisted but, as Mulvenon (2006) has pointed out, corruption has transitioned from a 'major, debilitating problem in the go-go days of PLA, Inc. in the 1980s and 1990s to a more manageable issue of military discipline in the new century'. This was achieved through the policies of Jiang and the emphasis on military modernization and the strengthening of the commissar system, party cells and the discipline inspection system within the military (Shambaugh, 1991, 1996). Yet, on 7 August 2006, the *Liberation Army Daily* noted that combating corruption within the PLA was on a par with winning wars! The most recent major case to embarrass the military high command was that of Admiral Wang Shouye, the deputy commander of the Chinese Navy. This colourful and enterprising individual is credited with having numerous mistresses and obtaining bribes in the region of between $15 and 20 million. Action was only taken against him when one of his mistresses went public after he failed to acknowledge fatherhood of her child and pay her off. He was removed from his post in January 2006 but the announcement was not made public until June. That the PLA leadership were not aware of his indiscretion earlier seems implausible and one wonders what action would have been taken if the affair had not been made public.

This event has played into Hu Jintao's broader concern about corruption in official bodies and his attempts to foster better morality among Chinese officials. These campaigns have now been extended into the PLA and are clearly to mark Hu's contribution to military development along with the programme of military modernization. As with the CCP, each 'paramount' leader has to have his contribution to the military adopted. Currently military work is described as 'holding high the great banner of Deng Xiaoping Theory and the important thinking of the "three represents", implementing in depth Jiang Zemin's thoughts on national defence and army building, and conscientiously carrying out a series of instructions from Chairman Hu'. One presumes that in the future Hu will graduate from a series of instructions to something more substantial.

Although Hu had spoken of values in the PLA before, in December 2008 he proposed his 'core values of military personnel' extending his concept of a 'socialist core values system' to the PLA (for details see Mulvenon, 2009). Thus, while modernization was to continue, campaigning is not dead and this heralded a major campaign within the PLA for 2009. The objective of the campaign was to extend the values being promulgated in the party to the PLA to ensure obedience. Such a campaign was also deemed necessary because of the increased influence of foreign contacts and ideas that were impacting on the PLA. Such a campaign would also complement Hu's stress on 'building a harmonious society' and help build loyalty to himself as the commander-in-chief. This will have been reinforced by his solo review of the troops at the National Day Parade in October 2009, reminiscent of Deng's earlier review. The Wang Shouye affair has also allowed Hu to extend his move against corruption into the PLA. Starting in 2006, a major anti-corruption drive was launched with a leading group set up to audit the leading military officers. In August 2006, the PLA started to tackle 'commercial bribery' that was said to have stemmed from the marketization of equipment procurement and the outsourcing of logistics support.

In recent years, the PLA has played a more assertive role in policy areas that it considers important and has been one of the main proponents of nationalism and promotion of the national interest. With the collapse of the Soviet Union and the change in the geopolitical situation, it became clear that China would be freer to assert its own national interest without regard to ideology or existing power blocks. Combined with the decline of Marxism-Leninism as providing policy guidance, a more assertive expression of national interest emerged and this was particularly strong in the military. With economic performance now providing the main source of legitimacy, Hu has used nationalism as a way to build up a broader base of support. However, he has had to be careful that this does not turn into a more dangerous xenophobia as it threatened to do under Jiang. Senior military figures have taken a hard line on issues such as the reunification with Taiwan and the relationship with the United States. In 1995–96, after the United States had given a visa to then President Lee Teng-hui of Taiwan, the PLA was the most powerful voice pushing for a more aggressive response. Again during the 2000 presidential elections on Taiwan, the PLA was the harshest group advocating pressure on the United States and Taiwan to make sure that independence would not be considered. Similarly, the PLA as an institution remains the most suspicious of the United States and since the accidental NATO bombing of the Chinese Embassy in May 1999 and the EP-3 incident (April 2001) has been the most difficult organization to persuade of the need to resume normal relations.

Chapter 7

Governance Beyond the Centre

The relationship between the centre and the localities has undergone significant changes with the reforms. This chapter outlines the organization of government away from the centre and then examines the role of the province in the political system. The reforms have also led to significant regional inequality that is providing a major challenge to governance. Finally, the chapter reviews the changing centre–locality relationship especially as it has been affected by fiscal reforms. While the centre tries to exert political control over the localities through the system of party-sanctioned appointments of leading personnel – the *nomenklatura* system – its fiscal capacity and its moral authority have declined. State revenues amounted to only 20.4 per cent of GDP in 2008, down from 36 per cent in 1978, and most localities increasingly have had to deal themselves with the serious problems that confront them. The revenues had dropped as low as 11 per cent. The decline in state revenues created pressures at all levels and in all Chinese government agencies to meet recurrent costs from locally generated sources. Increasingly, political outcomes are determined by local power structures and resource allocation. Within the same province and even in adjacent counties one can see radically different socio-political outcomes deriving from the reforms. What are the consequences of this for the nature of the local state and what are the consequences for governance and policy?

The organization of local government

Since the abolition of the six administrative regions in the mid 1950s, the most important administrative level has been the province and the municipalities. Unlike the former Soviet Union, the PRC has always been a unitary multinational state. Constitutionally, all nationalities are equal and are theoretically free to use their own languages and there are constitutional arrangements for regional autonomy in areas inhabited by non-Han minorities. But there is no right to secede: 'All the national autonomous areas are inalienable parts of the PRC.' The real level of autonomy is, in any case, extremely limited and since the late 1980s, Beijing's fears of resistance to its rule in Tibet and Xinjiang have meant that the limited autonomy that was enjoyed in the early years of reform is now highly constricted. The unrest in Tibet in 2008 and in Xinjiang in 2009 reveals the resentment with these policies. It also reflects the fact that the economic growth has gone disproportionately to the Han Chinese in these two provinces.

The non-central government is administered through 22 provinces (although official PRC sources count Taiwan to total 23), 5 autonomous regions, 4 municipalities directly under the central government, and 2 Special Administrative Regions (SARs). The notion of a SAR was included in the 1982 Constitution with an eye to the return of Taiwan and also Hong Kong and Macao to Beijing's sovereignty. In July 1997, Hong Kong was handed over by the departing British colonial administration and in December 1999 Macao was handed back by Portugal. Administration of these two SARs is covered by Beijing's concept of 'one country, two systems' which guarantees that for a period of 50 years they will be able to keep their previous economic and political systems. Thus, Hong Kong will be able to retain its capitalist economic system under a chief representative (effectively nominated by Beijing) and a partially elected legislature.

Under the provinces and equivalents, there is a three-level administrative network of prefectures, counties and cities, and townships and districts (see Figure 7.1). The prefecture does not constitute a level of political power, and therefore does not set up people's congresses and people's governments but instead has administrative agencies set up by the province. The leading members of these agencies (administrative commissioners and their deputies) are not elected but are appointed by the higher levels. The role of the prefecture remains one of the least researched topics and its functions and influence seem to vary widely. The three levels of government below the centre – province, county and township – are organized in basically the same way as the centre, with government and party organizations paralleling one another. The people's congresses are the local organs of state power and are able to elect and recall members of the people's governments. In June 1979, the people's governments replaced the revolutionary committees that had been set up during the Cultural Revolution. The people's governments at the provincial level are elected for five-year periods while those at the county level and township level are elected for three years. The people's government is the administrative (executive) organ of the People's Congress and is responsible to both the People's Congress and its Standing Committee at the same level, and to the organs of state administration at the next higher level, and is ultimately subordinate to the State Council.

The powers of the local people's congresses have been increased to allow them to adopt local regulations, and at and above the county level standing committees were created to carry out the work of the congresses on a more permanent basis. Shenzhen, for example, became the first SEZ to be granted legislative power by the NPC, quickly followed by

Xiamen. In 1996, this power was also granted to Zhuhai and Shantou. Guangdong seems to be taking the lead and appeared to grant to its three SEZs (Shenzhen, Zhuhai and Shantou) powers to make local laws that would be adopted after a four-month period of review by the legislature. This built on the NPC legislation and the powers were also extended to the provincial capital, Guangzhou (*SCMP*, 19 September 2000, internet edition).

Before 1978 the legislative and administrative organs (standing committees of people's congresses and people's governments) were not separated. Previously, when the people's congress was not in session these powers were exercised by one body, the revolutionary committee. Furthermore, neighbourhood and villagers' committees were written into the 1982 State Constitution as 'the mass organizations of self-management at the basic level'. The election of the committees is covered in Chapter 8.

Figure 7.1 *Levels of Government under the State Council, 2010*

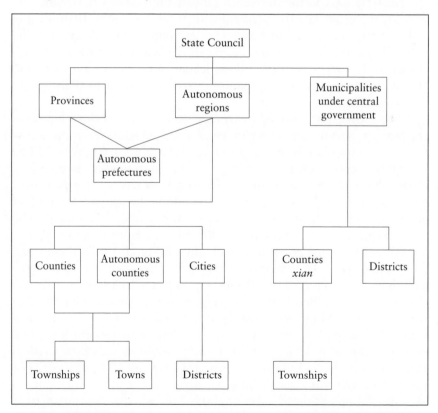

Note: In addition there are the two Special Administrative Regions (SARs) of Hong Kong and Macao that will retain their existing political and economic systems for up to 50 years.

The most important change in local government under the reforms is that the people's communes, set up during the Great Leap Forward (1958–60), no longer function as a unit of either economic or government administration. Now the township operates as a level of government and with the decollectivization of economic life throughout the countryside the commune has disappeared altogether as an organ of substance. The changes were designed not only to strengthen the state at the lowest level, but also to improve economic performance. Under the old system it was claimed that the party committees interfered too heavily in the economic life of the countryside.

The province as a unit of analysis

The provinces and four major municipalities form the most important level of sub-national administration in the Chinese system. This has been the situation since the establishment of provinces (*sheng*) during the Yuan Dynasty in the thirteenth century. In today's China, administratively the province carries the equivalent rank to a ministry in Beijing and its party secretaries and governors are important politicians in the political system, brokering the desires of the centre with the needs and wishes of the localities. It gives these leaders great power and potential but also offers great risks and requires careful management skills to play this role well.

While formally all provinces carry the same rank, it is clear that some are more important and carry more political weight. Variation across the provinces and even within provinces is enormous. Many would be substantial countries in their own right in terms of population, geographic size and endowment of natural resources. Five provinces have populations in the range of 70 million to around 90 million people – Henan, Shandong, Sichuan, Jiangsu and Guangdong. The population of Sichuan was over 100 million before Chongqing was established as an independent municipality in March 1997. By contrast, the population of Tibet numbers only 2.5 million but it is geographically big – 1.2 million km^2. While not as big as the largest province (Xinjiang – 1.6 million km^2), it dwarfs a province such as Ningxia that is a mere 66,000 km^2, let alone the municipality of Shanghai that is a mere 6431 km^2. Yet, Shanghai has economic muscle with an urban GDP per capita in 2007 of 23,623 *yuan* (10,144 rural) compared to Tibet's 11,131 *yuan* (2788 rural) or poor Guizhou's 10,678 *yuan* (2374 rural). The GDP of China's largest provincial economy, Guangdong, was over 90 times that of Tibet in 2007.

The economic might of Shanghai and Guangdong makes them important to the centre. Shanghai has traditionally been a major cash-cow, while Beijing has spent much of the reform period trying to figure out how to get hold of more of Guangdong's recent wealth. They clearly pull more weight in discussions in Beijing than does a poor northwestern province such as Ningxia or Gansu. However, poor Tibet and other sparsely populated border provinces are important to the centre for strategic reasons. They cover 60 per cent of the land mass, house only 6 per cent of the population and are home to many of China's national minorities. Beijing has had cause to wonder about their loyalty in the past and garrisons them heavily for fear of external threat, and in the cases of Tibet and Xinjiang for internal opposition.

Given the sheer size of China and this diversity, despite the formal administrative conformity, it is difficult to make too many coherent generalizations about policy implementation across provinces. Virtually all writers on the subject agree that not only has the relationship between centre and province become more complex since the reforms began but also that with increased control of financial resources there is more capacity for creative local leadership than in the past. The increasing provincial control over vast resources, the decline in the moral authority of the centre, and China's previous history of fragmentation and warlordism have led some writers to surmise about a possible break-up of China (see Jenner, 1992; Segal, 1994). Despite the economic growth of provinces such as Guangdong and the reorientation of a province such as Yunnan towards Thailand and Southeast Asia for foreign direct investment (FDI) and trade, this has been no more than wishful thinking (see Huang, 1995a, pp. 54–68). This concern that was prevalent in the mid 1990s has declined with the fiscal reforms and other measures described below. To date, when the centre has really wanted to impose its will on a significant issue it can, and the provinces have been willing to go along with this.

The only provinces where a breakaway might be a reality are Tibet and Xinjiang. Here, the relationship with the centre is qualitatively different and it has had to resort to violence on a number of occasions to exert control. Despite the process of moving in Han Chinese to dominate the political and economic apparatus of these two provinces, considerable opposition to Beijing's dominance has remained. In both cases this is aided by a history, language and culture that provide an alternative point of reference to Beijing's official story of unity. It is also helped by Tibetan loyalty to the exiled Dalai Lama and in Xinjiang by the various Muslim groups in the newly formed independent states that emerged from the break-up of the former Soviet Union.

The relationship between the centre and the localities is not necessarily one of a zero-sum game, and most may feel that they have more to gain by remaining within a collaborative framework with Beijing than suffering the cost of trying to wriggle free, something that would be impossible in any case unless CCP rule were to collapse. Further, as Goodman (1997, p. 2) has pointed out, it was Beijing's intent that each province should develop its comparative advantage as a fundamental component of the economic reform programme. Indeed, as new research is now indicating, the natural endowments and political skills of provincial leaderships have become key determinants of the development of particular provinces (see especially Goodman, 1997; Cheung, Chung and Lin, 1998 and Hendrischke and Feng, 1999).

With the provinces playing such a critical role in the political system and with their leaders forming an important group, it is not surprising that there should be attempts to integrate those with possible conflicting ideas into the national decision-making framework. This has taken a number of forms. The NPC's annual meetings have become a major venue for meshing central priorities with the needs of individual provinces. Until the new revenue-sharing system was passed in 1994, NPC sessions had become focal points for sharp arguments between provincial delegations and central financial leaders over the division of revenues. Representation at the NPC is organized along the lines of provincial jurisdiction and all sub-provincial delegates operate as a part of a provincial delegation, especially during small group discussions (Cheung, Chung and Lin, 1998, p. 10). At the Eleventh NPC, in terms of delegates per million of population, the best represented was Tibet (7.6) followed by Tianjin (4.4) with the lowest being Henan, Guizhou and Sichuan (1.7) (Bo and Chen, 2008). Even many senior central leaders are appended to provincial delegations, preferably where they may have worked or been born, or sometimes even where they have no connection and may not even have been.

It is clear that experience in provincial leadership is now a key stepping stone to a national position. As noted in Chapter 5, with the exception of Premier Wen Jiabao all members of the Standing Committee of the Politburo have significant provincial-level work experience. At the level of the CC, provincial representation has always been strong but placement in the Politburo only revived from 1987 onwards. When reforms began in 1978, provincial representation on the CC was a little over 40 per cent but it has dropped since to range between 25 per cent and 35 per cent. However provincial leaders remain the most influential group and provincial experience is now necessary for further promotion. This should not be taken to mean, however, that they dominate elite politics and the different provinces encompass a multitude of interests that would preclude them acting as a single interest group. Representation on the Seventeenth CC is 31.8 per cent, if one includes alternate members the percentage rises to 41.5 per cent, the largest group. By contrast 22.6 per cent are drawn from the central ministries, 17. 5 per cent from the military, and only 5.9 per cent from the central party organizations (Li, 2008). Provincial representation has also become institutionalized. With the exception of Tibet and Xinjiang, each province normally enjoys two positions on the CC (party secretary and governor).

In the Politburo, while a quarter of the members are serving in the provinces, 76 per cent of the members have significant provincial management experience. At the start of the reforms, provincial representation was around 20 per cent but it dropped to zero in 1981 (Sheng, 2009, p. 349). It is also clear that there has been a strong bias in promotion for those who have worked in the coastal areas of China rather than those who have been stationed in the poorer inland provinces. Of the Politburo members who have had provincial experience, 69 per cent have worked in the coastal areas while of those with current or immediate experience, 65 per cent are working in the coastal provinces. In part, this is because three of the major municipalities that enjoy Politburo representation are in the coastal area (the exception being Chongqing) and because economic powerhouse, Guangdong, also enjoys representation. Certainly under Jiang Zemin, Shanghai provided a reservoir of talent for the centre but with Jiang's retirement and the disgrace of former Shanghai secretary, Chen Liangyu, this might be changing. Also, General Secretary Hu's provincial experiences have been in the poor west of the country and this combined with his stress on paying more attention to inland development may signal a shift. Li (2008) notes trends within the Seventeenth CC that suggest that more representatives from inland regions might advance at the Eighteenth Party Congress. He also notes that Shanghai has been disfavoured in only having one alternate on the Seventeenth CC, who received the fourth lowest vote. This may show the decline in influence of the Shanghai group and wariness of anyone who may have been associated with disgraced former party boss, Chen Liangyu.

Despite the policy to rotate officials to prevent local cliques building up, it is interesting to note that the number of 'natives' serving in the provincial administration has risen under the reforms. Throughout China in 1965, this group comprised only 35 per cent of provincial leadership but this rose to 41 per cent for provincial party secretaries in 1985 and 44 per cent for governors and vice-governors in 1988 (Chung, 1998, p. 435). Goodman suggests that this trend increased in the 1990s and notes that most of those who have become party and government leaders at the provincial level have significant work experience in the province, heralding a break with past practice (Goodman, 1997, pp. 8–9). This has moderated somewhat but remains a significant trend. At the time of the Seventeenth Party Congress, 24 per cent of provincial heads and 44 per cent of deputy provincial leaders were 'natives'. Of those provincial leaders on the CC, 51.6 per cent were 'natives' of the province they represented (Li, 2008). This tendency may be heightened by the increased use of local feedback for the evaluation of official performance. It stands to reason that a local candidate would have the chance to do better than an outsider. Of course, they are also prey to more negative scrutiny as well.

Ultimately, Beijing has the power of control over appointments and this makes it difficult for any provincial leader to defy the Centre for too long. In fact, Yasheng Huang (1996a, pp. 655–72) has argued that economic decentralization has been accompanied by a strengthening of China's unitary political system. In particular, he highlights the continued role of the Organization Department in the appointment, management and promotion of officials. Thus, the party retains a very powerful institutional mechanism for rewarding and punishing non-central officials. The system is now one of 'one-level downward' management that replaced the two-level downward system in 1983. This means that the Centre directly appoints and removes only 7000 cadres, a reduction of some 6000 from previously. Certainly this is a good mechanism for controlling provincial level officials given that many see their career prospects in terms of transfer to a national ministry or equivalent. One only needs to see the fawning over any visit by the general secretary's local trips or latest pronouncements by provincial party secretaries and even governors to see how powerful this can be in keeping local officials in line publicly.

In the 1990s, Jiang Zemin made it a top priority to reorganize the Beijing municipal leadership and the Guangdong provincial leadership, both of which were seen as too independent. Hu Jintao acted similarly in his first term to break up the influence of Shanghai. In the Beijing and Shanghai cases, the instrument of choice was charges of corruption to remove the incumbent party secretary. In 2006, Shanghai Party Secretary, Chen Liangyu, was arrested on charges of corruption. Jiang eventually was able to install one of his entrusted followers in Guangdong to try to break up the local politics. Especially with Guangdong it is difficult for 'outsiders' to dominate for long over the 'native sons'. In Guangdong the presence of the CCP is historically weak and was first felt as an invading force from the north after 1949. As Goodman has noted, the party apparatus in the province is seen as being less important than the government administration (Goodman, 1997, p. 6). In fact, some of the senior officials sent down from Beijing to bring Guangdong back under central control claimed they felt uncomfortable working there, were shut out from the informal politics and longed to return to Beijing. One complained to me that in many meetings they resorted to discussing in Cantonese, thus shutting him out from what was going on (interview with officials concerned, 1999, 2005, and 2008).

The centre has also set up more indirect means to control the provinces, including developing rules and regulations for local administrations and improving administrative monitoring through better auditing, collection of information and disciplinary inspection (Huang, 1995b, pp. 828–43). These new mechanisms complement traditional control mechanisms such as ideological campaigns or party-school system training programmes. In 1987 to try to control corrupt and other unwarranted behaviour, the Ministry of Supervision (abolished in 1959) was revived and the General Audit Administration was set up to monitor the fiscal affairs of both firms and government agencies (Huang, 1996, p. 662). The Administration has become famous in China for its exposure of misuse of funds, even including in its own agency. Huang also notes that central administrative control over the provinces has increased through the regularity of personnel changes and is demonstrated by the administrative uniformity across provinces and the tenure characteristics. In a prescient study of inflation and investment controls Huang shows how political and bureaucratic centralization shapes the incentive structure of local officials and affects their economic behaviour. When the centre really wishes to implement a policy and moves coherently, local officials will comply even at significant cost to their own economic interests (Huang, 1996). This does not prevent policy resistance and non-compliance, however. Despite continual requests from the centre, environmental regulations are often not complied with nor are those for mine safety. One retired Minister was moved to comment, 'policies made by Zhongnanhai (the political centre) sometimes cannot reach outside of Zhongnanhai' (*Zhongguo qingnianbao*, 15 November 2005). In contrast, the centre also worries that the provinces pass on the blame when unable to resolve problems themselves. In February 2006, Hu Jintao on a local visit asked the localities to resolve the problems themselves and not just to turn them over to the central authorities (*Apple Daily*, 4 February 2006).

That said, the situation has changed significantly from the Mao years. In Chung's view (1998, p. 430) the pre-reform role of the provinces was relatively simple, 'disseminating Beijing's policy directives and monitoring subprovincial compliance with state plans'. They were left largely to rely on their own efforts under the policy of 'self-reliance' that produced a cellular structure. The power of the centre led most to see provincial leadership more as a vital cog in the transmission of the centre's ideas to the provinces – ensuring that political power rested exclusively with the centre (Falkenheim, 1972, pp. 75–83). In an early comprehensive study of the first provincial party secretary, Goodman (1980, p. 72) concluded that 'there is little to suggest that the first secretary has been a local leader rather than an agent of central control'. While there may still be an element of truth in this for the first party secretary, the picture is more nuanced for the provincial leadership as a whole. Some have seen them as policy entrepreneurs or as agents with multiple principals in the capital and in the province (Cheung, 1998, pp. 14-15). Lieberthal and Oksenberg (1988, p. 344) have defined the provincial level as 'a gatekeeper guarding and providing access to the local levels'. It is these latter roles and how the leadership mediates between the Centre and its local constituencies that have received most attention in recent literature.

The provinces have been important to the centre and also to particular leaders in terms of providing incubators for reforms. In fact, Susan Shirk (1990, pp. 227–58) shows that Deng Xiaoping's reform strategy as a whole was dependent on the support of provincial governments that were willing to push ahead with reform in the face of recalcitrance from more cautious bureaucrats in Beijing. A remarkable example was in January–February 1992 when Deng went to south China to kick-start economic reform once again after the pace of reform had been slowed in response to the demonstrations of 1989 and the ousting of Zhao Ziyang.

Consistently, reforms at the local level have provided the basis for national implementation. Thus, Goodman (1986, p. 181) has observed that 'national decision-making was frequently an incremental process involving provincial experimentation before a final decision was reached'. It is well known that what became the household responsibility system was first experimented with by Wan Li, when he was in charge of agricultural policy in Anhui and by Zhao Ziyang in Sichuan. Zhao was so successful in turning around grain production that the Sichuanese thought up the little ditty '*yao chifan, zhao ziyang*' (if you want to eat food, then look for Ziyang – the sound *Zhao* meaning both 'to look for' and being his family name). Both were promoted to the central levels because of their success.

The attitude of the local leadership can influence how swiftly a new policy or reform measure is taken up. Shortly after the attempts to introduce the household responsibility system nationwide, collectives in Heilongjiang announced a switch to a rural wage system, the complete antithesis of the new policy. In fact, a wage system was probably in the interests of the farmers in the northeast who worked on highly mechanized communes; the return to small family farming did not appear to be in their immediate economic interests. Similarly, leaders in Shaanxi opposed the policy until 1982, a couple of years later than other provinces, and also rejected the idea of promoting rural collective enterprises as a major growth engine. Lane (1998, pp. 212–50) puts this reluctance to be inventive in reform down to the legacy of the revolutionary struggle in the province, the lack of central incentive and a general conservatism that meant that local leaders were more attached to the centrally planned economy than their southern counterparts.

The experiment with SEZs provides another good example of both the desire of reformers at the centre to have a local base for experimentation and the importance of local leadership to pursue an opportunity. The zones were set up in the 1980s to receive foreign technology and to be reform laboratories. While Guangdong grasped the opportunity once offered and became a pioneer of reform, recording consistently high growth rates, Fujian's leaders were more cautious though offered the same package. Similarly, they were slow off the mark with Deng's 1992 speech that launched another massive expansion of provincial-led growth (Lin, 1998, p. 420). Apparently, officials in Hunan were kicking themselves for missing the implications of Deng's 1992 speech. He had first made the comments while on an inspection tour there and they were too slow to pick up on the policy shift and to promote it. This lost them favour with Deng, and made them slow off the mark subsequently (interview with officials concerned, May 2000).

The provinces also provide the centre with a reliable organization to fine-tune policy and allow more flexibility with implementation than would otherwise be the case. The provincial people's congresses can promulgate local legislation so long as no national legislation exists or as long as it does not conflict with the objectives of national legislation. The centre also provides the power of discretion to the province to flesh out the details of national legislation and to arrange the schedule for its implementation (Cheung, 1998, p. 10). Thus, for example, while Beijing has decided that there should be a minimum wage, the provinces decide the appropriate level within their jurisdiction, not Beijing. In April 2006 the Governor of Anhui and the Mayor of Hefei called for greater flexibility in policy implementation. The Mayor commented: 'The state has its national development direction, but the key is to combine this with the various local situations so that we can manage development' (*SCMP*, 24 April 2006).

With more at stake, rivalry between provinces has also intensified and it is still the case that many provinces trade more internationally than they do with other provinces in the country. However, there is now a huge difference between the levels at which different provinces engage in the global marketplace. Provinces have often acted to prevent movement of raw materials to other provinces while erecting high tariffs to prevent goods from other provinces entering that might undermine local industry. A classic case was when Guangdong sent trucks to Sichuan to buy silkworm cocoons directly from the producers, while the Sichuan authorities responded by setting up armed blockades to prevent them from leaving the province (Breslin, 1995, p. 68). Similar 'wars' occurred over wool and other vital raw products (see Watson, Findlay and Du, 1989, pp. 213–41; Zheng, 1994, pp. 313–14).

The main tug-of-war between the centre and the provinces has been over the division of finances. This is discussed below in more detail. The Hu Jintao administration has made a number of moves to improve the fiscal autonomy of the provinces and has been discussing whether to allow the provincial governments to issue government bonds. There is strong resistance to local governments issuing bonds as the fear is that it will be difficult to maintain oversight and the possibility for misuse of funds is large. In September 2006, the Central government issued some new rules governing land supply and revenue from mining. The State Council no longer required each project to be sent for approval that intended to use farmland for construction purposes but instead they could be approved by the provincial government and reported on an annual basis. Importantly, the provincial government was allowed to keep money from the sales but they had to be included in the local budget and not kept as 'off-budget' revenues. The rental of land from farmers for construction purposes was explicitly banned. This method was often used to evade taxes and remove the need to seek government approval. All underground sources are deemed as belonging to the state, with Beijing taking 40 per cent of the revenue from coal mining. This was dropped to 20 per cent in the new regulations.

Regional inequality

One major problem for the centre to deal with in this new relationship has been the rapid increase in regional inequalities. The provinces do not have an incentive to redistribute wealth and the centre's disposable funds for redistribution have declined. The new economic development strategy has led to geographic losers and winners. While coastal areas have been able to develop their economies very rapidly, the western inland provinces have not fared so well by comparison. The reforms have reversed the fortunes of a number of provinces that enjoyed relative wealth under the centrally planned economy. Guangdong was one of the poorest provinces in the Mao years but has benefited enormously from the policies of international trade and economic liberalization. Similarly, formerly disfavoured Zhejiang has benefited from the greater freedom given to the private sector. By contrast, the most prosperous provinces of the Mao years that benefited from the emphasis on heavy industry (Liaoning, Jilin, Heilongjiang) have suffered significant relative decline under the reforms. Such provinces have struggled with very high levels of unemployment, ageing industry and infrastructure and social welfare bills that are increasingly difficult to meet.

The inland provinces have lobbied the NPC to increase their resources and to accord them the same kind of privileges that have been given to the coastal areas. This, the centre consistently refused to allow until the mid 1990s when the leadership became more worried about regional inequality as a source of instability. Even with the 1994 reforms that were designed to guarantee Beijing's revenues, it is clearly the case that richer provinces turn over far less of their surplus to the centre than previously.

The concentration of foreign trade and FDI has exacerbated the regional inequalities, contributing further to the greater wealth concentration in the coastal areas. Guangdong alone receives around 25 per cent of FDI (in 2006 the FDI/GDP share was 5.4 per cent), whereas the nine provinces and one municipality in the northwest and southwest of China receive less than 5 per cent of all FDI. Guangdong is home to 23 per cent of the foreign funded enterprises in China, the three eastern municipalities (Beijing, Shanghai and Tianjin) a further 21 per cent, with the northwest and southwest only home to just 12 per cent. Given this background it is not surprising that living standards and consumption vary greatly. The average per capita annual total income for urban households in 2008 was 29,759 *yuan* for Shanghai while for Guizhou it was 12,186 *yuan*. For rural per capita annual net income Shanghai tops at 11,440 *yuan* with Guizhou and Gansu the lowest (2797 and 2724 respectively). If we look at consumption across the region, one interesting feature emerges: the northeast and the central provinces of China are almost as disadvantaged as the west (see Table 7.1). In fact Wen Jiabao shortly after becoming Premier launched a programme to rejuvenate the northeast but it never gained the traction of the 'Develop the West' programme. Further, poor provinces in central China, such as Jiangxi, have pushed for special consideration as they miss out on the funds available to either the west or the northeast. We can see that in urban China, levels of possession of basic goods such as a washing machine have almost levelled out but there remain major disparities for more luxury items such as computers and phones. In rural China, the differences are more noticeable.

These trends have contributed to the major migration flows, leading to the huge surge of job seekers to urban China. Significant numbers have been attracted to the employment opportunities offered in the SEZs, along the coast and in major municipalities in the manufacturing sectors that have developed with foreign investment. This has led to a breakdown of the old residence control system that kept the farmers out of the cities and protected an intricate system of benefits and allowances that favoured the urban over the rural. Currently, the government is starting with experiments to offer some social services for these migrants but they are not effectively integrated into local government service provision. The massive plans for urbanization will require a major rethinking of traditional government service provision that can no longer be based on place of birth. It is interesting to note that Guangdong, where migrants make up some 25 per cent of the population, took the lead in reform in this area. It began to allow farmers who had stable jobs and accommodation to obtain residence permits in small town-

Table 7.1 *Regional Disparities in China (2008)*

	Eastern	Central	Western	Northeastern
Per capita annual income (Rmb) –2007	18,544	12,392	12,130	12,306
Ownership per 100 urban households				
Automobiles	14.35	4.08	6.06	3.76
Computers	74.86	48.24	48.31	45.70
Mobile phones	187.43	153.84	168.57	159.98
Washing machines	95.73	94.94	94.10	91.12
Ownership per 100 rural households				
Motorcycles	68.88	49.16	43.81	53.11
Computers	12.15	2.65	1.45	3.77
Mobile phones	129.87	102.78	91.29	109.11
Washing machines	68.09	46.88	43.92	73.61

Sources: *China Statistical Yearbook*, 2009 (Beijing: China Statistics Press) and http://www.stats.gov.cn/tjs/ndsj/2008/indexeh.htm.

ships, allowing them access to the same social welfare benefits that are enjoyed by other urban dwellers (*SCMP*, 2 June 2000, internet edition). These measures have become national policy (see Chapter 11).

While the central government has continually stressed that more attention has to be paid to the poorer interior, this has not translated into a coherent policy approach, and the powers that the coastal provinces have won will not be given up easily. China is pursuing an extremely inegalitarian development strategy, especially in comparison with its East Asian neighbours that it seeks to emulate. China's central leaders have been concerned by the growing disparities and have launched classic central-planning policies to try to stimulate growth in the western parts of the country. For example, from 1980 more developed provinces or municipalities were 'teamed' with poorer provinces; the objective was to get the richer provinces to invest in the poorer ones or to undertake major infrastructure projects. Provincial leaders have had little choice to go along with this, but it is clearly not a main priority for them and many of the investments are of dubious value. For example, in Xishuangbanna in Yunnan province, Shanghai municipality built a hotel for tourists, many of whom come to see transsexual shows. Most of the profits are repatriated to Shanghai (discussions in Xishuangbanna, November 1998). There are also formal 'twinning' arrangements between coastal provinces and the interior. Thus, for example, Shanghai is teamed with Yunnan, Beijing with Inner Mongolia, Shandong with Xinjiang and Guangdong with Guangxi. Interestingly, the poor province of Guizhou is teamed with the four cities of Dalian, Qingdao, Shenzhen and Ningbo.

The main response to deal with regional inequality has been the 'Develop the West' policy that was launched in late 1999 and confirmed at the Tenth NPC (March 2003) and the 'Revive the Northeast' programme launched in 2004. It comprises 12 provinces but excludes very poor provinces such as Jiangxi. The policy was to rely on state-led funding for infrastructure combined with political persuasion and arm-twisting of the more developed provinces to shift investment to the interior provinces. A Leading Group on Developing the West was set up, headed by the Premier and with an office under the State Council. Initially $6 billion was set aside for use in 2000. The importance was again stressed in the Eleventh Five-Year Plan (2006–10). The intention was to boost infrastructure to attract external investment and to reduce the income gap. In fact, despite the fanfare state commitment has been quite limited. Most of the projects announced were already scheduled and many provinces sought to shift the costs of current projects to the central exchequer. Increased funding is to be provided through state bank loans and those from international financial organizations and preferential loans. If the funding is not diverted from more productive investment it should help. Many analysts feel that the initiative to 'Develop the West' serves rather more political purposes than genuine development needs and there is resentment from those provinces excluded.

Hu and Wen have supplemented this programme with one of their own to 'Revive the Northeast' (see Chung et al., 2009). This programme was launched in 2004 to deal with what had become a problem area under the reforms, especially with the decline in the capacity of the many SOEs in the region. The two programmes reflect the leadership's desire to stimulate development in areas other than the coastal provinces that benefited most during the late 1980s and 1990s. As Chung and his colleagues have noted, there are four major differences between the two programmes. First, while the 'Develop the West' programme is seen as a 50-year project, 'Revive the Northeast' has a shorter duration of some 15 to 20 years. Second, the focus is different with the former to address the problems of poverty through significant investment in infrastructure, while the focus in the Northeast is on reorganizing the industrial structure to put it on a more sustainable growth path. This means that state investment is most significant for the West whereas the Northeast hopes to attract FDI. Last, the Central government has taken the lead on the

'Develop the West' programme while both the Central and local governments are partners in the programme to 'Revive the Northeast'.

It is still too early to assess the success of these programmes. However, an OECD report states that better integration of China's regions is important not only for equity reasons but also as it is becoming an impediment to meeting other development goals. It points out that key features of the initiative such as using 'growth poles' and launching major infrastructure projects without taking into account regional demand and supporting declining sectors of the local economy have not worked elsewhere, and there is no reason to suspect that they will work in China (OECD, 2002, p. 41).

Many of the current problems in the western region stem from previous bad central policy, in major part from Mao's policy of the 1960s to build a 'Third Front' to help China survive a potential Soviet invasion. About 20 million people and many factories were moved from the coast to the hinterland and a large number of industrial and military projects were carried out. They nearly bankrupted the economy in the 1960s and now they sit as millstones round the necks of local leaders who have to deal with falling revenues and large numbers of laid-off state workers. The problems in the northeast stem from the industrial restructuring that has intensified with the reforms and much of the outdated industry has found it difficult to compete.

Not surprisingly, given the economic structure many local leaders have remained more wedded to the old central-planning techniques than their colleagues in the coastal areas. For example, in Yunnan and Sichuan the state-owned sector of the economy remains dominant. It is interesting to note that the country's first national agricultural census published in 1998 reported that there were five times as many farmers engaged in private ventures in the east than in the west, and four times as many individual household enterprises; 33 per cent were engaged in non-agricultural production in coastal areas, compared with 15 per cent in the east (*SCMP*, 9 March 2000, internet edition). This suggests that a radical overhaul of economic structure might be more beneficial, together with major investments in education, rather than pumping money into state-run infrastructure projects. Given the poor construction of many of the major state investment projects to date, and the corruption that has siphoned off money earmarked for development or poverty relief in the past, there is little cause for optimism that this policy will be successful in helping to bridge the gap. In fact, it was reported that Beijing was awash with requests from the interior provinces for large infrastructure development projects that specialists saw as lacking credibility (Interview with officials concerned, May 2000). This problem has also haunted the 2008 stimulus package that China announced to counteract the global downturn. A far more judicious use of investment would be in basic education and healthcare facilities, something to which the Hu-Wen leadership had turned its attention before the financial crisis struck (see Chapters 10 and 11).

Relations between the centre and the localities: the fiscal picture

While the central state apparatus has the capacity to react to problems when acute or perceived to be regime-threatening, its relationship with its local branches has changed significantly and it does not command automatic allegiance. Just how much it has changed has been the topic of considerable debate; however, the topic is not as new as some of the recent literature suggests and ever since 1949 the CCP has fretted over the appropriate relationship between the centre and the localities. Debates have focused not only on how much power could be ceded downwards, but also to which administrative level it should be devolved. In the debates of the mid 1950s, once it was decided that the overcentralized Soviet model was not suitable for China's needs, Mao and Chen Yun differed over whether decentralization should be to geographic regions that would keep the party in control and allow for mobilizational politics or whether more authority should be devolved to production enterprises allowing a more incentive-based economic strategy.

The most important element in the reform period has been the decentralization of powers away from central government agencies to those at lower levels, especially the effective decentralization of the fiscal system. This more than any other factor accounts for local variation. Getting the financial picture right is vital to any discussion of the relationship between the centre and the localities. Before the most recent fiscal reforms, only about one-quarter of all state expenditures occurred at the central level and the major responsibility for financing infrastructure and providing social welfare occurred at the local level. However, government revenue as a percentage of GDP declined to only around 11 per cent in 1995 before beginning a slow revival to 24.9 per cent in 2008.

Changes in the fiscal picture are important as most public goods and services are provided by sub-national levels of government and consequently the expenditure responsibilities are quite out of line with international practice (World Bank, 2002, p. ii). The Maoist notion of 'self-reliance' reinforced the idea that each locality should minimize 'dependence' on support from higher levels and this has influenced significantly the impact of reforms. Sub-national expenditures as a share of public spending are very high, at around 70 per cent and actually hit 78.7 per cent in 2008. This is higher than that of other countries within the region; for example, in Vietnam it is 48 per cent, Indonesia 32 per cent, and Thailand 10 per cent (Mountfield and Wong, 2005, p. 86).

In the first phase of the reforms from 1980 to 1993, the Chinese government operated a fiscal contracting financial system. This was institutionalized in 1988. Under the system, local governments made a lump-sum remittance to the centre and the provinces were responsible for meeting expenditure requirements from the revenues that they retained. The objective was to empower local governments to finance their own priorities, subject to certain budget constraints. This system gave local governments a powerful incentive to encourage economic expansion but limited the centre's capacity to benefit sufficiently from this expansion (Yang, 1994, p. 74). Before the major overhaul of 1993–94 (see below), the reforms had transformed a province-collecting, centre-spending fiscal regime to an essentially self-financing regime for both the centre and the provinces (Zhang, 1999, p. 121). Provinces collected and spent up to 70 per cent of budgetary revenues and while the provincial role for collection had declined in comparison with the Mao years, it had increased for expenditures. Revenue-sharing was de-linked from revenue needs, thus placing local governments on a self-financing basis for the first time, something that was subsequently codified in the 1994 Budget Law (Wong and Bird, 2008, p. 432). The drop in central government revenue restricted its redistributive capacity.

The resultant system was highly inequitable as provinces retained increasing amounts of funds, enabling the wealthier provinces to fund more programmes. By 1993, the sub-national share of total fiscal revenue reached 78.9 per cent of the total (Su and Zhao, 2006, p. 13). By contrast, expenditures by the central government had dropped from 47.4 per cent to 28.3 per cent in 1993. Thus, rather than a decline in state capacity under reforms as some have suggested, there was a realignment between the centre and the localities, with the localities controlling far greater amounts of revenue than they had previously (Yang, 1994).

Government revenue as presented in Chinese statistics comprises two major components: the unitary budget and the extra-budgetary funds (EBF) for both the central and the local governments. The unitary budget comprises the taxes, fees and revenues collected by state financial offices and is subject to formal budgeting by the centre. The Ministry of Finance provides the central supervisory role together with the local authorities (Wedeman, 2000, p. 498). The EBF cover officially sanctioned charges such as surcharges from taxes and public utilities, road maintenance fees and incomes from enterprises run by various administrative agencies. Originally, the largest part of these funds came from the retained profits, depreciation and major repair funds from the SOEs. The EBF became increasingly important during the reforms; in 1992, they amounted to 110 per cent of the budgetary revenue. However, in 1993, the definition of this fund was changed to exclude the portion from SOEs that had comprised 79.9 per cent of the 1990 total (Zhang, 1999, p. 123). The EBF, while reported to higher administrative levels are, to all intents and purposes, subject to control and oversight only by the local authorities (county or township). The local financial bureau manages to fund the plans of the local administration accordingly. Not surprisingly, it is difficult to calculate the real value of the EBF. Official statistics show that the centre controls only 7.3 per cent of the revenues and 6.4 per cent of the expenditures. One can see the impact of the fiscal reforms of 1993–94 when the central government share of EBF revenue dropped from 43.6 per cent and expenditures to 17.2 per cent. These officially sanctioned EBF do not include the various revenues collected locally without central authorization. If one adds these extra-establishment funds that by their very nature do not turn up in the statistics, the total sum of revenues available was the same in the early 1990s as at the start of the reforms; 39.5 per cent as compared with 40 per cent (Zhang, 1999, p. 123). Those observers who have suggested a major decline in the state's extractive capacity have relied on the official budgetary revenue and this has indeed declined by almost 60 per cent. The alarmism that some have sounded about the decline of state capacity is in this sense unwarranted. What is important is the changing nature of the centre–local fiscal relationship and the changing role and importance of the different funds as controlled by the centre and the localities.

In 1994, a major reform of the financial system was implemented to stabilize the fiscal relationship between the centre and the localities. The old system that had operated, with minor modifications, from 1979 had the following features (based on Wong, 2000, p. 54). First, all revenues accrued to the central government with expenditure budgeted by the centre. This meant that the EBF were crucial to local authorities. Second, the revenue system was industry-centred with agriculture irrelevant for the generation of budgetary revenues. Third, the tax system was simple, with few types of taxes. Fourth, not surprisingly, tax administration was straightforward. This system was very redistributive, Shanghai gave up 80–90 per cent of collected revenues while Guizhou financed fully two-thirds of its expenditures from central subsidies.

The 1993–94 reforms were intended to provide the centre with greater fiscal capacity by raising the budget to GDP ratio and the ratio of centrally collected revenues to total budget revenue. For the centre the intention was to raise the ratio of its budget to GDP and the ratio of centrally collected revenue to total budget revenue (Zhang, 1999, p. 131). In addition, the intention was to eliminate distorting elements of the tax structure and to increase transparency (Wong, 2000, p. 55). The objective was to raise the centre's share of state revenue to at least 60 per cent, with 40 per cent as central expenditure and 20 per cent as transfer grants to local governments. The reforms introduced the tax-sharing system, and formalized it in the Budget Law that came into effect on 1 January 1995. This had been on the policy agenda since 1985 but experimentation in nine provinces began only in 1992 (the following account draws from Zhang, 1999, pp. 131–8, and interviews with officials concerned). The intention was to delineate clearly the division of responsibilities between the centre and the localities with respect to spending responsibilities, while allowing the centre a significant role in the redistribution of revenues. This required clarifying the division of spending responsibility, how taxes would be divided between the centre and the localities and how to divide the administration for the collection of central and local taxes.

There are now three sets of taxes. Central taxes include items such as customs duties, income (personal and institutional) and consumption taxes, and profit remittances from central enterprises. Second are the central–local shared taxes, the most important revenue stream including VAT (75 per cent for the centre and 25 per cent for the localities), resource tax (100 per cent of offshore oil to the centre, other resource taxes to the localities) and securities' trading stamp tax (evenly divided for those provinces participating). Third are the local taxes which include business taxes and income taxes from local enterprises that do not fall into the first category, individual income tax, urban land-use tax, property and vehicle tax, stamp duty, and agriculture and husbandry taxes. The centre hoped that this would regularize a system to replace the unseemly squabbling that took place with the localities and usually reached a peak of threats and counter-threats just before the annual NPC session. To achieve its objective the centre had to concede that the provinces would be guaranteed revenues in line with a base year of 1993 with a special transfer payment mechanism for the provinces. Not surprisingly, provincial leaders boosted revenues to gain maximum benefit. The provinces were compensated for any shortfall against the 1993 baseline as well as receiving a payment of 30 per cent of any increases in the central government's revenue from value-added tax (VAT) and consumption tax in that province over the previous year.

This new system has raised central revenues as a percentage of the total but also has had adverse effects on local governments that are dealt with below. The ratio of the budget to GDP has been raised as well as the ratio of centrally collected revenue to total budget revenue. Centrally collected revenue now exceeds that of locally collected revenue – 53.3 per cent as opposed to 46.7 per cent (in 2008) – thus overcoming the initial tendency of the localities to collect only for themselves. Although the centre's take still falls short of the 60 per cent, the improved ratio, together with the general rise in revenues, has provided the centre with an enhanced capacity to support those policies it deems important. Thus

Premier Wen Jiabao has been able to announce more support for free elementary schooling in the countryside, collective healthcare schemes in the countryside, and greater rural infrastructure investment. However, it is important to note that although the balance of revenues has shifted in favour of the centre, the expenditures by local governments have hardly changed since the 1993–94 fiscal reforms. In 1978, 47.4 per cent of government expenditure was by the central government and 52.6 per cent at the sub-national level but by 1993 this had shifted to 28.3 per cent and 71.7 per cent respectively. Subsequently, local government expenditures continued to account for over 70 per cent of total spending (78.7 per cent in 2008). The consequences of this are dealt with in the following section.

The consequences for local governance

There are a number of consequences for local governance. First, some have raised the spectre of unruly provinces and the possibility of disintegration. While unlikely, as noted above, trends do suggest a more nuanced relationship and more local variation in development in accord with revenue generation. Combined with the decline in the party's moral authority and legitimacy, some argued that by the mid 1990s there had been a potentially unhealthy rise in the power of the regions (see, for example, Wang, 1995, pp. 87–113; Yang, 1996, p. 364). There is some truth in this, and Wang's work together with Hu Angang (1999) raises legitimate concerns about the consequences of the significant regional inequality that has been an integral part of the reform strategy.

Montinola, Qian and Weingast (1995, pp. 50–81) have interpreted the trend in a positive light, arguing that what is developing is 'federalism, Chinese Style'. Local governments have primary control over behaviour, policy and economic outcomes with each autonomous in its own sphere of authority. They credit this with placing limits on central control and providing richer localities with substantial independent sources of revenue, authority and political support. At the same time it induces competition among local governments, serving not only to constrain their behaviour but also to provide them with a range of positive incentives to foster local economic prosperity. However, the problems or advantages do not arise from the decline in the fiscal capacity of the state as a whole, but rather from how revenues are collected and controlled. Given the mess that the centre has often made in directing the national economy, perhaps it is just as well that its capacity is curtailed. However, as discussed above, it is not so clear that the centre has lost its capacity to control the provinces and there is considerable evidence that the localities can also devise irrational development plans.

The fiscal inequalities have also led to enormous variation in the provision of public goods and services. The main systemic incentive is for local governments to stress revenue mobilization at the expense of other distributional and growth objectives (Park et al., 1996, p. 752). At the same time, popular expectation of the kinds of services that local authorities should provide has not declined. This has meant that local governments are more reliant on central government transfers and raising their own revenues to meet their obligations. In 2008, subnational levels of government provided 94.5 per cent of spending on education, 98.3 per cent of spending on health, and 94.9 per cent of spending on the social safety net and employment relief and 95.4 per cent on environmental protection. Local government finance has become even more difficult since the government converted all fees into the single agricultural tax in 2002 (and subsequently abolished it), followed by the special products tax and slaughter tax.

The financial pressure has meant that one emerging general imperative shared by economically developed and more resource-constrained localities is the increasingly acute need to derive one's own sources of revenue to cover centrally mandated obligations. The resultant fiscal inequalities that arise from this system are a major cause of the significant variation in the provision of public goods and services. Financial pressures lead to preference for a development plan that maximizes short-term revenue extraction over longer-term needs and is disinclined to distributional and welfare priorities. The main concern of government at all levels is to increase revenues rather than thinking about the correct role of government. The concern over revenue generation is exacerbated by the fact that despite fiscal decentralization, the central government has retained control over the policy agenda. The centre sets many tasks that must be implemented by local governments, and most of these are unfunded mandates.

Cities at the prefecture and county levels should cover all expenditures for unemployment insurance, social security, and welfare, whereas in most other countries the central government will cover social security and welfare, with education and health shared between the localities and the centre (the following discussion is based on Saich, 2008a). The county in China is being developed into the fiscal centre in the rural areas and it is beginning to eclipse the township. This expansion of responsibility has been conducted under the slogan of 'taking the county as the lead' (*yixian weizhu*); spending at the county-level now accounts for about one-quarter of all public expenditures. Most important was the decision in 2001 to shift the fiscal responsibility for teachers' salaries to the county from the township (*People's Daily*, 14 June 2001).

The expenditure responsibilities for the townships are similar to those of the counties, although they often have a weaker financial base and they carry the heaviest load for social spending. The county and the township together account for 70 per cent of budgetary expenditures for education and 55–60 per cent for health (World Bank, 2002, pp. 34, 94 and 111). In Xiangyang county, Hubei, budgetary contributions in 2002 to finance education amounted to 40.6 per cent of total expenditures. Of the government contribution, the township provided 84.6 per cent and the county provided 15.2 per cent, the remainder coming from the province (0.2 per cent) (Han, 2003, p. 12). Prior to the 2001 reform, education had been the largest expenditure for townships: approximately two-thirds of township expenditures nationwide. A study in 2002, just as the new reform was to be implemented, discovered that 78 per cent of compulsory education costs were covered by the town/township and village, with a further 9 per cent covered by the county, and 11 per cent and 2 per cent by the provincial and central governments respectively (Kennedy, 2007, p. 49). Despite the lightening of the burden, the township remains responsible for subsidies for teachers and also for the maintenance and up-keep of the school premises.

Villages, which are not a formal level of government, have significant expenditure responsibilities even though they have no independent fiscal powers. They have inherited many of the obligations of the old collective economy, such as salaries, care of the elderly, and even support for health and education (Wong, 1997, p. 174). These responsibilities drive the village and township leaderships to seek various off-budget revenues from user fees and other unsanctioned levies to support their activities. For example, in three counties surveyed by the Development Research Center (DRC) of the State Council (Han, 2003), expenditures exceeded revenue, thus increasing the need to raise larger off-budget revenue. Nationwide, extra-budgetary funds may total 20 per cent of GDP, whereas in the three counties surveyed by the DRC they ranged from 30 per cent of total income (in Xianyang, Hebei province) to 69 per cent (in Taihe, Jiangxi province). The use of these extra-budgetary funds and self-raised funds (*zichou zijin*) clearly increased as a result of the 1994 tax reforms. For example, the value-added tax is split 75–25 between the centre and the localities. Prior to the reform, Guizhou province had derived fully 45 per cent of its revenue from alcohol and tobacco. The centre now takes much of this revenue.

Despite the rapidly rising social welfare demands, the two major causes of growth in government expenditures are capital spending and administrative outlays. The OECD has calculated that in the 1998–2003 period, capital expenditures contributed 31 per cent of the total growth in expenditure and administrative outlays 21.1 per cent (OECD, 2006, p. 23). The latter burden falls most heavily on local governments that provide 82.1 per cent of administrative spending; they provide only 55.6 per cent of capital investment (OECD, 2006, p. 47).

Many local administrations have great difficulty in meeting their salary bills. The budgets of local governments are often referred to as 'eating budgets' (*chifan caizhang*) as they only cover basic essentials and salaries for bloated staff numbers (Shih et al., n.d.). Even in major cities local governments have difficulties in meeting their administrative expenses. Again we see enormous variation across China. Large municipalities such as Beijing and Shanghai are almost self-sufficient in terms of their capacity to fund their activities: Beijing covers 88.6 per cent of its needs and Shanghai 89 per cent. By contrast, poorer provinces such as Qinghai and Guizhou can cover only half or less of their obligations, at 39.3 per cent and 53.7 per cent respectively, and Tibet only covers 12.9 per cent (Su and Zhao, 2006, p. 15). In Guizhou many counties were unable to meet payroll obligations (Wong and Bird, 2008, p. 455).

The tax reforms of 1993–94 allowed the richer provinces to retain more revenue, thus exacerbating the inequalities. Wong and Bird (2008, p. 437) have calculated that from 1992 to 1998 the ratio of provincial per capita fiscal expenditures in Shanghai grew from 2.5 to 3.9 times the national average, in Beijing it grew from 2.2 to 2.7, and in Guangdong from 1.1 to 1.4. By contrast, in Henan it dropped from 0.44 to 0.42, in Gansu from 0.8 to 0.6, and in Hunan from 0.53 to 0.49. Not surprisingly then, per capita fiscal capacity shows great variation. In 2008, Shanghai's revenue per capita was 12,493 *yuan*, over 13 times that of Guizhou at 917 *yuan*. Shanghai's per capita expenditure was 13,739 *yuan*, as against 2778 *yuan* in Guizhou, a 4.9 differential. These figures reveal Guizhou's reliance on transfers. By contrast, in the United States the poorest state has about 65 per cent of the revenue per capita of the average state, and in Brazil the richest state has 2.3 times the revenue per capita of the poorest state.

The problems are exacerbated at the sub-provincial level by provincial retention of a high level of the revenues generated within the province. For example, the per capita fiscal revenue of the Yunnan provincial government is 14 times that of the county-level governments, and in Guangdong it is seven times. Dollar (2007, p. 14) estimates that the richest county's per capita spending is 48 times that of the poorest. Together, the provinces and municipalities account for 70 per cent of all sub-national-level fiscal revenue, whereas the counties and townships, where the need is great, account for only 30 per cent (Su and Zhao, 2006, p. 22). This means that the fiscal system is highly regressive and local governments in poorer areas often have no alternative other than to eliminate services or to extract high fees from the residents. But even high taxes may not enable local governments to meet their obligations, a situation that has been described as 'predatory fiscal federalism' (Shih et al., n.d.).

This situation has led to a search by local governments for stable revenue sources. In the 1980s and 1990s, the financial pressures and the removal of agriculture as a viable financing source for local government contributed to the expansion of locally owned enterprises, especially township and village enterprises (TVEs), as these were seen as the most stable source for local income. This was the case irrespective of whether the locality concerned was relatively wealthy or poor. The need for funding led most local governments to collect a wide range of sanctioned and unsanctioned fees and levies. They are often referred to as the three arbitraries (*sanluan*): arbitrary taxation (*luan shoufei*), arbitrary fines (*luan fakuan*) and arbitrary expropriation (*luan tanpai*) (Wedeman, 2000, p. 490).

The various demands of the different line agencies come together at the individual household level. Villagers in a poor rural village in Pingchang County, Sichuan, told of how the household had to weigh up the competing demands to plant enough trees to satisfy the forestry bureau, enough grain for the grain bureau, to raise enough pigs to sell to the local state, while being mindful of staying within the family-planning quota and having to provide a certain number of days of *corvée* (forced) labour to the local government. It is clear that for most villagers, especially those in poor areas, despite the development of market exchanges the role of the local state is still the defining factor in their lives.

Dealing with exorbitant fees also leads to invention on the part of farmers. Chatting with a farmer in one poor county in Sichuan we totted up 120 such illegal levies that were levied on his household (interview, November 1995). As a result, farmers adopt a number of strategies for evasion or feign compliance. For example, in this county the farmer had to deliver eight pigs to the local authorities at a fixed price. Obviously he had to deliver some, but could pay a fine for those not delivered. He calculated that he could deliver four and pay a fine for the others, which he sold for a higher price on the free market. This price exceeded the price of the fine and so he figured that both he and the local government were happy.

The advantage of these off-budget revenues is that they do not fall under the 1993–94 tax-sharing agreement with higher levels of government. By their very nature, these funds are hard to calculate, but Bird and Wong (2008, p. 447) calculate that the EBF and extra-budgetary activities of government amounted to between 19 per cent and 29 per cent of total public sector spending. This confirms the view that public sector spending has not actually declined under the reforms. Rather, what has declined is the amount controlled by the Ministry of Finance.

Beginning in the late 1990s, the central government tried to rein in these fees and levies, some of which were illegal and many of which caused farmer discontent. The first step was to convert the various fees and levies into taxes and to reduce the level to a maximum of 5 per cent of farmers' income. Thus, in Beijing municipality, the percentage of 'other revenue' in the budget declined from 42.4 per cent in 1998 to 32.3 per cent in 2000, whereas 'on-budget revenue' rose from 39.4 per cent to 47.4 per cent. The formal 'off-budget' revenues remained relatively constant at 18.2 per cent and 20.3 per cent respectively (Su and Zhao, 2006, p. 25). Once the practice of illegal fees and levies came under increased scrutiny, local governments had to use the land under their jurisdiction to raise more revenue, often converting agricultural land to higher-priced commercial or residential land use.

However, it is possible that the reduction and then the abolition of the consolidated agricultural tax may have had a negative impact on the provision of welfare services. Local governments increasingly relied on such revenues to provide services. In poor and remote communities where marketization has barely begun and where the scope of economic activity will always remain limited, local treasuries have little recourse other than the elimination of services. In many poorer parts of China, rural medical health schemes were abolished and access to schooling drastically reduced. Whereas villagers' committees in poorer areas might be more concerned with how to raise revenues to cover basic welfare requirements, richer villages preside over an extensive income from local enterprises and make decisions regarding village investment in road building, hospital development, etc.

Preliminary evidence suggests that the abolition of the agricultural tax, unless compensated for by adequate transfers, may indeed have a negative impact on service provision if there are not major cost savings. Research by Kennedy (2007) in Shaanxi reveals that there was a sharp decline in the provision of educational and medical services, with poorer townships heavily dependent on the county government for revenue and able to act as no more than an 'administrative shell' and unable to offer basic services. He shows that counties and townships have only suffered a small drop in the number of hospitals and medical personnel, whereas villages have suffered a precipitous decline. Between 2001 and 2003 doctors in Shaanxi villages declined by 23 per cent and healthcare workers declined by 82 per cent. The number of village clinics dropped by 25 per cent.

Christine Wong has also pointed out that the abolition of the miscellaneous education fees and their replacement by transfers to cover elementary education costs may actually end up causing a shortfall in income for local governments. The subsidy from the central government covers only a portion of the revenue that local governments used to derive from various education-related fees and levies. The subsidy is 140 *yuan* for elementary school students and 180 *yuan* for junior middle-school students. However, before the new programme began, the costs were much higher; in one school visited, the cost was 1000 *yuan* per student (Wong, 2007, pp. 14 and 17).

The other major impact of fiscal reform is the continued decline of the township. Although some reformers have called for the abolition of the township as a formal level of government, the preferred policy seems to be to promote a withering away of the township through mergers and conversion into towns (*zhen*). In 2008, the number of township jurisdictions was 40,828, down from 72,153 in 1985 and 47,136 in 1995. Of the jurisdictions in 2008, almost half were towns (19,234). In Guangdong, towns already form the majority, at 1139 out of 1584 township-level jurisdictions. In poorer provinces such as Guizhou and Xinjiang, townships still predominate (691 towns out of 1553 and 229 out of 1002 respectively). The merger of townships has led to the elimination of accessible services for many since the schools and clinics are closed in those townships that lose their appellation. In areas where distances are large, such as Tibet, this means that the former township community may entirely lose its previous access to education and healthcare (discussion with Arthur Holcombe, President Tibet Poverty Alleviation Fund, April 2007).

As we have seen, at the centre, the number of government agencies has been reduced. At the municipal level, the number of different committees and departments is to be reduced from 61 to around 45, from 53 to around 40 at the provincial levels, while in poorer or less populated provinces the cut is to be deeper, to around 30. Those who favour the more radical cut of abolishing the township as a formal level of government propose that there could be just county administrative offices at the township level and thus many departments could be abolished or merged and the whole paraphernalia of the people's congress and people's political consultative conference done away with (interviews, Beijing, May 2002). The county would be a sufficiently large entity that if all fiscal matters were located there it could deal with redistribution issues. However, local government is such an important employer in the countryside, especially in poor areas, that many see township abolition as destabilizing. The intention is that any savings made from downsizing government will go to increase the salaries for those who remain. Given the parlous financial situation, there might not be much extra cash to distribute. Some have complained that if the staff cuts are not sufficiently deep, the levies on farmers at the local level will increase yet further to cover salary hikes.

At the same time as struggling to raise funds, local governments are still under pressure from higher-level agencies to fulfil certain tasks of economic production and social development without receiving funding. Researchers in the Translation Bureau of the Central Committee (Rong *et al.*, 1998) have named the current structure of local government a 'pressurized system' that needs to be reformed to accommodate a more open democratic system of cooperation. In their view, the *de facto* decentralization has meant that higher-level agencies put administrative pressure on lower levels of government, as manifested in the political contract system. This system divides up and sets tasks for organizations and individuals at the lower levels and they are expected to fulfil them within a prescribed period of time. This political contracting and the responsibility system for fulfilling the tasks by local leaders provide an important incentive framework guiding their behaviour. While certain objectives can be missed, some performance targets must be met or promotion will be denied. For example, all local officials are charged with meeting family-planning targets and maintaining social stability while many counties require townships to meet fixed revenue-generation requirements (interviews with local officials).

With most problems having to be resolved *in situ*, local resources and their distribution concern the majority of people's lives. Many local officials may well be party members but they are also members of the local community, and where there is a moderate increase in local accountability through village elections and transparency regulations they have to take this seriously (see Chapter 8). While most observers agree that the economic powers of local governments have been enhanced through control over local industry and EBF, there has been considerable disagreement about the emerging nature of the relationship between the local state and society. This chapter raises some comments on the effect on local officialdom, while the broader question of changing state–society relations is reviewed in Chapter 9. The tendency in the literature has been to dwell on the fusion of political and economic power at local government levels and to suggest that the state is either predatory or displays some variant of local state corporatism or clientelist structure (Oi, 1992, pp. 99–126; 1999). What this has meant to local cadres has also been open to different interpretations. Not surprisingly, those who see local corporatism or clientelism as the dominant paradigm feel that the power of local officials has been enhanced by increased control over resources for distribution to those within their jurisdiction. Chinese researchers under Xu Yong have argued that, despite the village elections, the head of the villagers' committee acts as much as an agent of the state as a representative of the villagers (Xu, 1997). Victor Nee (1989, pp. 663–81) proposed that, on the contrary, the new opportunities in the local economy provided individuals with control over financial and other resources independent of local cadre power. However, the increasingly widespread practice of buying and selling official posts suggests that much can be earned from them. Sayings such as the following have become commonplace in the countryside:

If you bribe your superior 10,000–20,000 *yuan,* you have just checked in. If you offer him 30,000–40,000 *yuan,* you have registered for promotion. If you give him 80,000–100,000, you will get promoted.

The reforms have clearly led to an extremely varied pattern of local development, with local officials enjoying greater financial freedom from higher levels and being less dependent on higher-level approval for career advancement and economic reward. However, as Nevitt (1996, pp. 39–40) notes, the vertical chain of career advancement is more a concern for those at the municipal and provincial leadership level than for those at lower levels of township and village.

What these developments mean is that it is at the local level that one should look for substantive change and that questions of rights, account-ability and transparency mean something for the vast majority of people. It is also at this level that the general impression of a system in stasis is challenged by the vibrancy and inventiveness of solutions to problems. Society has become very dynamic, and not only institutional needs but also the institutional fabric of state–society interactions have become more complex. Much experimentation is taking place with basic level organizations and institutions, which all makes for a very messy kind of China and one that defies simple categorization. The one thing that is certain is that the rapidity of change has been staggering and there is every reason to expect that it will continue.

Perceptions of Local Government Performance

We saw in Chapter 6 how satisfaction with government fell as it got closer to the people and above we have explained just how much of citizens' needs are meant to be met by local governments that are often struggling to raise the necessary funds. From the surveys the author conducted between 2003 and 2009, two sets of findings are interesting. The first concerns citizens' attitudes towards local officials and who they think they represent and second, which kinds of services they would like the government to concentrate on in their work.

The survey asked about residents' attitudes to the ability and style of government in implementing policy and essentially in whose interest they thought local government acted. Thus, in 2003 while 50.8 per cent of respondents deemed local government ability very competent (21.5 per cent deemed it incompetent), again we see satisfaction dropping the closer government gets to the people. The view that government is very competent in executing policy dropped from 64 per cent for those living in major cities to 43.9 per cent in townships, while rising slightly to 47.3 per cent for village officials. These figures improve for 2009 with overall 74.8 per cent of respondents stating that government is competent and with only 9.2 per cent saying that it was incompetent. By 2009, 70.7 per cent found village officials competent. As for government attitude when implementing policies, we see a significant improvement from 2003 to 2009, with 60.1 per cent (39.1 percent in 2003) feeling that local officials were friendly, while 28.7 per cent (38.9 percent in 2003) found them cool and indifferent (see Table 7.2).

The new policies of the government and attempts to encourage local governments to be more responsive and take care of those in need may be having an effect. Although dissatisfaction is still relatively high and satisfaction relatively low, all the indicators have improved from 2003 to 2009. Respondents' attitudes about the way policy is implemented by local governments should raise cause for concern. Irrespective of place of residence, large percentages feel that the behaviour of local officials is bureaucratic rather than being helpful to the concerns of ordinary people (see Table 7.3). By 2009, the only category where a majority for bureaucratic behaviour prevailed was for officials trying to get closer to their superiors. One clear message is that the quality of governance is perceived to be better in major cities than in the smaller towns or villages.

Citizen satisfaction with the provision of specific public services reveals some interesting insights that are helpful for thinking about the changing role of government and what local government should concentrate on to improve satisfaction levels. Across the three years of the survey there was not much variation about the five aspects of local government work that received the highest ratings. Thus, in 2007 these were water and electricity supply, family planning, road and bridge construction, management of primary and middle schools, and traffic management. By contrast, the five areas of government work that caused the greatest dissatisfaction were: combating corruption, unemployment insurance, employment creation, help for families experiencing hardship, and land management. The services that respondents identified where government work is poor and that urgently need improvement

Table 7.2 *Citizens' Impression of the Attitude of Local Government in Executing Policy 2003 and 2007*

	City		Town		Village	
	2003	2009	2003	2009	2003	2009
Cool and indifferent	33.1	21.0	39.5	33.5	40.9	31.6
Warm and friendly	50.0	72.2	35.0	59.8	35.8	54.1
Competent	64.0	82.3	43.9	75.4	23.7	70.7
Incompetent	14.9	11.2	22.3	9.7	47.3	8.3

Table 7.3 *Comparison of Citizen Attitude towards Government Behaviour*

	Bureaucratic behaviour				Concern for ordinary people		
	2003	2005	2009		2003	2007	2009
Stand high above the people	48.2	42.6	39.4	Method of helping ordinary people	30.9	38.7	46.8
Close to those with money	50.1	42.9	43.9	Care about ordinary people with hardships	28.1	37.0	44.2
Move close to superior leaders	54.0	43.5	49.4	Have the idea of taking care of ordinary people	24.5	34.3	39.4
Act in line with slogans	51.2	42.6	37.4	Resolve real problems	26.3	37.2	45.6
Primarily take care of own interests	49.8	41.7	40.3	Bring benefits to ordinary people	23.7	34.2	45.6

were: job creation, unemployment insurance, hardship family relief, medical insurance and environmental health. We also find that family-planning policy, which enjoys the highest level of satisfaction, has the lowest level of importance attached to it.

This would suggest that the areas of work citizens really wish government to concentrate on are job creation and providing basic guarantees to protect against the shocks of the transition to a market economy. Labour and medical insurance are high priorities for all residents. Given that it is unlikely that governments will be able to raise significantly more revenue to finance the provision of public services, it is necessary to meet objectives by reducing costs and focusing more clearly on the kinds of services local government can and should provide.

Chapter 8

Political Participation and Protest

Until the reforms began in the late 1970s, China was distinctive for political participation mobilized by the party leadership to show public support for their policies. This chapter looks at the existing mechanisms for citizen participation, such as sanctioned mass organizations, electoral participation and membership in non-governmental organizations (NGOs), and the evolving role of the internet. The chapter concludes with an analysis of dissent and protest both within the party and outside.

In a formal sense, there has been a very high level of participation in China, especially in the Mao years. Indeed, ever since the founding of the PRC, mass participation has been a distinctive feature of the Chinese political scene. As Oksenberg (1968, p. 63) suggested, it has been a matter of not 'whether' one participated but 'to what extent'. The key question, of course, is how meaningful such participation is. Does such participation impact on the political agenda or is it limited to public expression of support for centrally agreed policy preferences? Here, opinions in the literature differ widely. While the CCP sees maintaining high economic growth rates as its major challenge, an equally decisive issue is how to accommodate the expanding citizen demands and participation. While greater and more meaningful participation is recognized as necessary for economic development, severe differences of opinion have arisen concerning how autonomous that participation should be and what the correct role of the party is in guiding such participation.

The need for participation received strong emphasis in the thought of Mao Zedong. For Mao, it was not sufficient to accept a policy passively – one must be seen to support it actively. In theory, this participation was not to be restricted solely to expression of policy support but was also intended to apply to the process of policy formulation. This notion was embodied in the principle of the 'mass line'. Through the mass line it was hoped to combine the benefits derived from consultation with those at the lower levels and those of a tight centralized control over policy formulation. However, this does not mean that Mao was willing to accept the existence of different, competing groups in Chinese society. Despite this, throughout the 1950s and 1960s Mao appeared ready to open up the system to more meaningful participation, albeit unstructured, than his colleagues in the top party leadership.

Modernization and participation since Mao

The renewed stress on the primacy of economic modernization since December 1978 has produced parallels with other periods when the demands of economic development have required the party to relax its grip over society and to devise mechanisms to incorporate the views of various groups. However, in many respects, and various setbacks notwithstanding, the party has gone further than at any time since 1949 in its attempts to take account of the increasing heterogeneity that its modernization programme has produced. The experience of the excesses of the Cultural Revolution showed China's leaders the kind of problems that could arise if the flow of ideas and information from society was cut off or unduly distorted. Thus, the post-Mao leadership realized that a higher degree of participation by sanctioned groups was both desirable to promote modernization and was inevitable given the proposed rapid changes that they hoped to bring about. However, the experience of the 'Hundred Flowers', the Cultural Revolution, the Democracy Wall Movement and the student movements of the 1980s caused the leadership to be suspicious of participation that took place outside its own direct control. Thus, party leaders have launched a number of movements to restore the effective leadership of the party and to control social space while not negating the contributions that 'articulate social audiences' could make to the economic programmes. This is now challenged by the fruits of the reforms themselves. The reforms have produced a differentiated population that have a wider range of information at their disposal and many of whom are less likely to take 'party truths' at face value. The party has had to develop new skills to compete with the spread of new technologies and to form or revive old institutions to integrate new segments of the population.

There is no intention to make the party or the state apparatus genuinely accountable to the citizens of China. It is a tricky policy to follow and it has been impossible for party members to remain immune from the influence of different social groups and for the party organs to channel fully the activities of the new organizations that have sprung up in recent years. The tacit recognition by the party of the existence of other groups in society should not be interpreted as the emergence of a 'pluralist' political system. It is an attempt to finesse self-regulated and autonomously defined political organizations by incorporating those groups the party leadership sees as important into the existing modified power structures and spaces. The party moves to accommodate the increasingly wide range of articulate audiences to thwart or limit the possibility of alternate political-ideological definitions. This is best seen with the 2001 decision to allow private entrepreneurs to join the party.

There are clear limits to the permissible: the party had to remain in control and activities had to take place within a framework laid down in the relevant state decrees. This was first signified by the promotion of adherence to the 'Four Basic Principles' that were put forward by Deng Xiaoping. Further, democracy in so far as it is promoted is prefaced by 'socialist' and is not interpreted as an end itself but as a means of achieving the party's central task of economic modernization, a position that has not changed substantially. As the party recovered from the trauma of the Cultural Revolution and began to book some economic success, its confidence rose and it began to reassert its role as the guardian of ideology once again.

As noted, both Jiang Zemin and Hu Jintao share this basic approach and from the mid 1990s there have been attempts to channel participation along more structured lines through those institutions that are officially sanctioned. From October 1995, following Jiang's speech 'More Talk About Politics', the leadership has tried to reassert party and state control over business, society and the localities. These attempts intensified after the 1996 Sixth Plenum of the Fourteenth CC adopted the resolution on the need to build a 'socialist spiritual civilization'. The challenge raised by the formation of the China Democracy Party, the existence of *Falungong,* the signing of Charter 08 and the strikes and protests over the lay-offs caused the party to try to reassert its relevance. The China Democracy Party questioned the CCP's right to political monopoly, the support for *Falungong* challenged its right to moral authority, Charter 08 challenged the party to uphold its own statutes and constitutions, and the strikes questioned whether the party could protect the working class it had created during the process of industrialization. To meet this challenge, in 2000 the party launched a major campaign under the name of the 'Three Represents' in a further attempt to display its relevance in a changed world (see Chapter 4). This has been followed by Hu's attempts to return a moral core to the centre of the CCP universe. He has promoted what the leadership refer to as 'putting the people first' and 'building a harmonious society'. Such exhortations need to be accompanied by more institutionalized mechanisms for participation.

Impact on the sanctioned organizational structure of representation

As Chapter 6 has shown, there has been a revitalization of the state sector with the people's congress system and the consultative congresses playing a more lively role than in the Mao years. In addition, official policy has tried to integrate experts into the decision-making process, to influence key groups in society more indirectly by binding them into organizations that are dependent on regime patronage, improve democracy at the grassroots and sanction a limited number of social organizations.

The attention paid to economic growth in place of class struggle has led to a more empirically based approach to the solution of problems in place of an overreliance on ideological criteria. In turn, this has led to greater value being placed on consultation and discussion. It also resulted in the upgrading of the position of intellectuals in ideological and material terms. Gone are the Cultural Revolution references to intellectuals as the 'stinking ninth category', and instead intellectuals are defined as an integral part of the working class. This 'ideological upgrading' has been accompanied by attempts to improve their work, housing and salary conditions, and intellectuals have been given greater freedom within their fields of professional competence. There has been an explosion of professional journals and convening of meetings to facilitate the exchange of views. Professional societies have mushroomed as further forums for the exchange of ideas and as organizations on which the party and state leading bodies can draw for expertise. Many of these organizations have been drawn into inner-party debates through their provision of advice to different policy tendencies within the top leadership. Other organizations have used the newly granted public space to challenge the boundaries of acceptable discourse.

Participation and the Eight 'Patriotic' Political Parties

The revival of the 'united front' approach and the increased reliance on experts has led to a revitalization of the eight other political parties in the PRC. Contrary to the view that these parties would pass away with the generation that spawned them, they have survived and have begun to recruit a growing number of members. However, in 2007 their total number of members was 707,100 compared to the CCP's then 73.3 million. The CCP sees these other parties as providing a useful link to the intellectuals who it cannot draw directly under its own influence and as playing a pivotal role in mediating with influential Chinese abroad. For example, the Jiusan Society is composed mainly of intellectuals from scientific and technical circles and the CCP has sought to take advantage of those connections. These parties provide important legitimacy for the CCP's view that it is not a one-party state but rather one that entertains eight other political parties. This was confirmed in China's white paper on political reform that stated what suited China best was the 'existing system' of 'multiparty cooperation' under which the other eight parties advise and 'supervise' the CCP but do not oppose it (State Council Information Office, 2007).

Certainly members of these other parties have been playing a more active role in government. This process reached its peak with the announcement that two non-CCP party members had been appointed in 2007 as the ministers of science and technology and health. One has no party affiliation at all and the other is the chair of the China Zhi Gong Party. In addition, there were said to be 31,000 non-CCP members in government posts at and above the county level with 177,000 representatives of the people's congress at various levels being non-CCP members (*SCMP*, 16 November 2007).

The Mass Organizations

To head off potential mass opposition, the party seeks to extend its organization, coordination and supervision of as much of the population as possible. Traditionally, the party has relied on what it terms 'mass organizations' such as the trade unions and the Women's Federation, a two-edged sword as it provides a mechanism of participation to officially sanctioned groups but makes the formation of autonomous union organizations or women's organizations impossible. By subjugating sectoral interests to general party policy, the party allows such organizations the autonomy to organize their own activities within a broadly defined framework, and to support the pursuance of legitimate rights of their members in so far as they do not override the common good, as defined by the party. In return, the party expects unconditional support for its broader political, economic and social programmes.

The unions for the most part have been engaged in conflict avoidance, or conflict management, and with mobilizing support for party policy. Many working within the official union movement recognized the problems inherent in this construct and that many workers see them as stooges for the party rather than as their representatives. The party moved hard to crush any attempts to provide independent representation for labour; those who were involved in the 1989 attempts to set up an autonomous labour union received much more brutal treatment and punishment than did the students. The establishment of the Capital (or Beijing) Workers' Autonomous Federation, independent of the official workplace-based unions, was a direct affront to the party's claim to be the sole representative of the working class, and it was interpreted by orthodox party members as a 'counterrevolutionary' organization.

Thus, activists within the union are reduced to exploiting whatever space the party cedes or trying to ensure that policy is implemented at the local level. For example, in the early 1990s the All-China Federation of Trade Unions (ACFTU) successfully took up workers' demands for a five-day week to replace the six-day system, and tabled motions to this effect at the annual NPC sessions. They also tried to work on the protection of workers' rights in the Korean, Hong Kong or Taiwan-run sweat-shops but have usually been thwarted by local political leaders who are afraid of scaring off investors. The adoption of the 1992 Union Law represented a high point for the official union when it was able to convince the party leadership that it needed to present a semblance of autonomy to retain credibility among its members. However, such actions have done little to convince the rank and file of its viability. Over 64 per cent of workers in SOEs turn not to the ACFTU but to informal networks for support when their rights are infringed (Lee, 2000, p. 55). The strength of the Union is further eroded by its declining fiscal base, with many enterprises and members unwilling or unable to pay, trends exacerbated by the large number of SOE lay-offs.

Similar tensions are evident with the All-China Women's Federation. Croll (1984, p. 3) has noted that the common trend is for the Women's Federation to be marginalized politically and for it to be placed on the defensive in representing women's demands, especially where these demands are seen to be conflicting with the overall priorities of political and economic development. These tensions were particularly evident during the preparation for and convocation of the UN World Conference on Women and the NGO Forum held in Beijing in 1995 (see also Zheng, 2010, pp. 103–6). The Women's Federation had to tread a careful line between opening up more political space to improve the situation of women in China and gain credibility with the international women's movement while not alienating the CCP. The CCP was more interested in the prestige of holding a major UN Conference and reversing the international criticism that had followed the crushing of the 1989 demonstrations than highlighting the plight of women *per se*. The tension led to deep divisions within the Women's Federation between those who wished to forge better links with the international movement and its agenda and those who wanted to toe the party line. This came to a head when the party leadership decided to move the NGO forum to Huairou, a small town some 15 km outside Beijing. The CCP forced the Women's Federation leadership to defend the decision, a decision much derided by the international women's movement and many national governments. However, the mere fact of preparing for the Conference integrated the official Chinese Women's Federation and the hastily created NGOs into an international network and focused on key issues that have had an impact in China far beyond the Conference itself. Many of the groups set up for or tolerated by the NGO Forum are still in existence, providing invaluable support for women. But official ambivalence remains. In the 'Beijing plus five' follow-up meeting held in New York in early 2000, the Women's Federation invited a number of NGO representatives to join the official delegation but informed them that they should not speak up at the meetings (interview with members of the delegation).

However, under the reforms the Federation has undertaken a more strident role in defence of women's interests at the national level while at the local level its branches have sometimes been at the forefront of key policy experimentations. Activists have set up NGOs to work under the umbrella of the Women's Federation. For example, the group of women activists gathered around the magazine *Rural Women Knowing All* has undertaken work ranging from sexual health of rural women, to hotlines for migrant women, to raising concerns about the high levels of suicide among young rural women. The effectiveness of this group comes not only from the social commitment of its members, but also because a number of the key figures are senior members of the All-China Women's Federation. The key figure in the group was one of the chief editors of the *China Women's Daily*, the official organ of the Federation. This has meant that the group can use the infrastructure and staff of the Federation to publish their own journal specifically targeted at rural women and to ensure that important policy issues are taken up in the official newspaper. As a result, such issues are immediately in the domain of key policy-makers with respect to issues concerning women. A number of the local federation branches have been inventive in policy implementation; for example, some have set up rural micro-credit schemes targeted at poor women and legal counselling centres.

New Social Organizations

Not only has there been a revival of activity in these more traditional organizations, but new social organizations have also developed. These range from clubs such as philately associations, to the China Family-Planning Association set up by the government Family-Planning Commission to receive foreign donor funding, to groups such as Friends of Nature, which operates as freely as one can in the field of environmental education. Naturally the further the group is along the spectrum of party-state sponsorship towards autonomy, the more vulnerable it is in terms of administrative interference (Saich, 2000a, pp. 125–41). By the end of 2008, there were 229,681 registered social organizations, defined as community entities composed of a social group with common intention, desires, and interests. The majority were registered at the county level.

Not surprisingly, economically developed provinces such as Jiangsu, Shandong, and Zhejiang have the most social organizations. Together with Fujian, Guangdong, and the two municipalities of Beijing and Shanghai, they have 33.4 per cent of the locally registered organizations (227,900). By contrast, the eight western provinces, excluding Sichuan and Chongqing municipality, have only 16.1 per cent. NGO activity increased in Sichuan in the wake of the 2008 earthquake and a number of writers saw this as a major opportunity for NGO expansion and a chance to develop further legitimacy. Initially, this did appear to be the case as massive amounts of donation money flooded in and many informal and formal organizations sought to help in the immediate reconstruction. However, as in other instances once the immediate danger passed and the local state was able to reorganize, the space for the NGO sector was curtailed. In addition, groups that sought to place the blame for the high numbers of deaths of schoolchildren on shoddy construction work that may have resulted from embezzlement of school building funds were quickly shut down. Reporting bans were imposed on this topic.

A more expansive definition would include the converted public service units and the growing number of civilian non-commercial enterprises. After the introduction of regulations to govern them in 1998, this latter category increased rapidly, from 6000 in 1998 to 148,000 by 2005. Of these, the majority was in the fields of education and health: 75,812 and 27,179 respectively (MOCA, 2006, p. 94). These two categories also cover organizations set up by the party and state agencies to handle welfare concerns and the various organizations that have been progressively spun off from government; organizations that operate independently but enjoy government support at some level, such as the environmental group Friends of Nature; or organizations that have grown out of party-state organizations, such as Rural Women Knowing All, mentioned above. The vast majority of these organizations are run by urban elites who undertake work on behalf of the groups they claim to represent, for example migrants or poor rural women. Very few have been organized at the grassroots level or work in a community-based or participatory mode. Yet, slowly by default these kinds of organizations have also been expanding. With greater social space created by the reforms and with the state unable or unwilling to carry the same range of services and functions as before, organizations with varying degrees of autonomy from the party and state structures have been set up. They have been allowed or have created an increased organizational sphere and social space in which to operate and to represent social interests, and to convey those interests into the policy-making process.

The party and the state have devised structures and regulations to bind these organizations to state patronage and to try to control their activities. For example, in 1998 regulations were adopted that sought to incorporate them more closely with existing party and state structures. These included the need to register with a sponsoring state agency that would oversee and be responsible for the organization's activities, while banning 'similar organizations' coexisting at the various administrative levels. There cannot be two national trade unions, for example. This helps to control representation to a smaller number of manageable units and has been used to deny registration for some groups. It ensures that the 'mass organizations' continue to enjoy monopoly representation and cannot be challenged by independent groups seeking to represent the interests of women or workers.

The state's intent is clear: it is to mimic the compartmentalization of government departments and limit the horizontal linkage. This favours those groups with close government ties and discourages bottom-up initiatives. It keeps people with different opinions on the same subject from setting up 'opposing' interest groups. However, many organizations have found ways to evade such controls or to turn the relationship of state sponsorship more to their own advantage. Many social organizations have also been effective in negotiating with the state to influence the policy-making process, or at least to bring key issues into the public domain.

The support of foreign funding has caused concern for the leadership and they have taken notice of the role it played in the 'coloured revolutions' and the overthrow of authoritarian regimes by citizen organization. Thus, new regulations came into effect in March 2010 that require domestic NGOs to present to the State Administration of Foreign Exchange a certificate of registration for the overseas donor and a notarised donation agreement. Many NGOS that are unable to register as a social organization, register instead as a for-profit entity, a much easier process. However, this might create problems for foreign donors that could be expected to pay tax on donations. In the US, this might raise concerns about their tax-exempt status. Specifically excluded from these new regulations are the mass organizations (the Women's Federation and ACFTU) and those that enjoy close government connections (such as the Soong Qing Ling Foundation and the China Disabled Persons' Federation).

Broadly speaking, those groups working in the fields of education, environment and health have been permitted or have negotiated a relatively free space (see Box 8.1). The idea of NGOs working in public service delivery is gaining acceptance. This has been noticeable in areas such as HIV/AIDS and in major cities such as Shanghai. However, there remains ambivalence towards them and their acceptance is still vulnerable to the whims of local officials. Activists and organizations that advocate too stridently may easily run afoul of local governments and find their activities curtailed. This has consistently been the case in Henan province where the transmission of the disease via blood-selling was first revealed. In November 2006, a meeting involving hemophiliac activists was banned by local police. Earlier, in April 2006, Shanghai police broke up a news conference of a group of hemophiliacs who claimed that they had contracted HIV/AIDS through contaminated blood transfusions (Reuters, 25 November 2006). By contrast, officials in Sichuan province called for greater involvement of NGOs in work dealing with the spread of HIV/AIDS. The deputy director of the provincial Disease Prevention and Control Bureau acknowledged that because many of those infected were sex workers or in the gay community, 'it would be very difficult to reach' policy objectives by using 'the traditional method – mobilizing government institutes at all levels' as with other public health crises such as SARS. As a result, he called for existing regulations to be revised and greater scope to be given for the development of the NGO sector (*Xinhuanet*, 1 May 2007). These two examples reveal the differing bureaucratic interests in dealing with HIV/AIDS. Whereas health officials have been generally more sympathetic to contacts with groups such as commercial sex workers and intravenous drug users, public security officials have often taken a tougher line, regarding them as engaged in illegal activities (see Saich, 2008a, for more details).

In rural China, community-based organizations are expanding in number and it is clear that alternatives are emerging to take over functions that were previously considered the preserve of government. Many of these organizations are based on traditional associations such as temples or social networks, including clans and lineages. The role of these informal institutions has been explored by Hu (2007) and Tsai (2001, 2002, and 2007) who show how membership of social networks becomes important given the low investment in public goods by village government. Tsai (2007) terms these 'solidary groups' and shows that if officials are 'embedded' in such groups they will feel more obligated to provide public goods as fellow group members can use the norms and the network to punish them.

Hu (2007) shows the importance of 'village trust' in setting up Rotating Savings and Credit Associations (ROSCA) in Xiangdong village, Zhejiang province. Almost all the villagers have participated in a community-based ROSCA that can be used for a number of different functions. For our purposes, one of the most salient functions is to finance family emergencies such as medical expenses and school fees. Those who join this kind of ROSCA tend to be from poorer families and thus the scale is rather small, with fund payments limited to 1000 *yuan* over three months. Such organizations are important given the problems that rural dwellers face in accessing formal financial institutions. Bad debt in the ROSCAs is rare (with a default rate of less than 1 per cent) and the financial risk is very limited.

Research by Tsai reaches similar conclusions that in some areas social capital substitutes for governmental performance and officials allow social institutions to take over the provision of public goods. In her survey of 316 villages in Shanxi, Hebei, Jiangxi, and Fujian, Tsai discov-

Box 8.1: Green Earth Volunteers and Protecting the Nu River

Environmental concern has been one main avenue for activists to become engaged in with relative safety. It is harder for the authorities to clamp down on actions that call for a more environmentally clean China. One example has been with the campaigns to protect the Nu River that runs through Southwest China. The river is some 2800 km in length and is the largest undammed river in Southeast Asia and one of the last two major rivers in China that has not been dammed. Part of the river flows through an area designated by UNESCO as a world heritage site. Not surprisingly, the plans to build 13 dams along the river and to build hydroelectric plants drew domestic criticism as well as international attention because of the potential impact the dams would have on Myanmar and Thailand. Proponents have defended the project saying that it would help the local people out of poverty, although there seems to be little local support. Particularly active in opposition was the group Green Earth Volunteers that had been founded by a Beijing environmental journalist, Wang Yongchen. It had a volunteer membership of some 50,000. As in a number of other cases, the journalistic connections were important in bringing the plans to public attention while also reporting the event internally. Interestingly, even though reporting about the Nu River was banned from news pages, reporting in pages about the environment, geography or travel was not banned and opponents used these pages to promote their views. The opponents were also helped by the passing of the Environmental Impact Assessment Law (effective September 2003). The campaign that was organized brought together NGOs, scientists, government officials (especially those within the environmental protection agency) and the general public to promote economic development that respected the environment and local communities. This phrased the campaign in the language of Hu Jintao and Wen Jiabao's policies for sustainable development. In April 2004, Wen announced a temporary halt on construction based on the limited and questionable quality of environmental impact assessment conducted by the company involved (although the report was not released for public view). Strong disapproval was reiterated by the minister for water resources in October 2006 but he did acknowledge that building no dams at all was not an option. At the NPC meeting in March 2008, the party secretary of Yunnan Province said that the local government was still intending to carry out a plan to build dams and hydroelectric power stations. This was a couple of months after the official announcement that the scenic 'Tiger Leaping Gorge' would not be dammed. The power company has strong political connections in Beijing, including the son of a former premier and this complicates the matter further. Building preparations continue.

Sources: Interviews with Wang Yongchen and officials involved in the case.

ered that lineage or religious organizations in 54 had organized public projects. She makes an interesting distinction between the role of temples and churches in enmeshing local officials in networks that provide moral compulsion to deliver better public goods. Village temples are described as 'encompassing and embedding' (2007, p. 120), whereas the churches are 'encompassing but not embedding', even more so as local CCP officials are in theory banned from joining the church. She describes the village temples as reinforcing state authority and legitimacy, whereas the history of churches in China means that they are viewed suspiciously and as dangerously connected to foreigners. Also the temples only serve the specific community and do not necessarily make a claim of union with some broader or higher entity. These alternatives for mobilizing community and outside resources are especially important as the incentives to encourage village officials, village elections notwithstanding, to provide public goods are weak and there are very few institutionalized channels for gaining support from higher-level governments to provide public goods in the village (Tsai, 2002, p. 25).

Despite the various concerns there is also growing official recognition that NGOs have a role to play in welfare provision, broadly defined. Indeed, with the state downsizing and many local governments strapped for cash, there may be little choice. Premier Wen Jiabao vowed to turn over responsibility for more activities that the government should not be engaged in to enterprises, NGOs, and intermediary organizations (*China Daily*, 13–14 March 2004). Thus, despite the more restrictive environment for civil society development, China has begun to develop the same categories of organizations that one finds elsewhere. Most fall into the category of mediatory organizations that take on roles that the state can no longer fulfil and they often act as a bridge to society or contribute to state objectives by providing services and enhancing capacity.

Participation at the grassroots and the role of elections

Perhaps the most meaningful form of participation for the vast majority of individuals is that which affects their immediate work or living environment. In China the workplace, which for many is also a social unit, has been a focus of political attention for the leadership. The working class, with their allies the farmers, are supposed to be the 'masters of society', but the truth of this assertion is debatable. In the urban sector, indications suggest that more meaningful participation has been taking place at the workplace and experiments have been expanding to create a role for elections within local communities. In the countryside, there has been the extensive programme to introduce direct elections in the villages, the effectiveness of which is contested. There have been sporadic attempts to move direct elections further up the administrative ladder. Last but not least, new information technologies have increased avenues for participation.

Urban China

In the early years of reform most workers were still employed through the state enterprises and were dependent on them for their welfare benefits, housing and many other services. As reforms have progressed, much housing has been privatized, SOEs have shed workers, the private sector and service sector have expanded significantly, and migrants have moved in on a permanent basis. As a result, the urban workplace is no longer as dominant in people's lives and this, in turn, has had consequences for the ways in which citizens participate.

The main forum for workers' participation is the workers' representative congress that operates mainly in SOEs although also present in other urban work units. According to regulations promulgated in July 1981, the congresses were not to be viewed as advisory or supervisory, but as 'organs of power' through which the workers and staff were to 'run the factories and supervise the cadres'. In reality, control is relative, not absolute, and the functions and powers of the congresses are limited to factors such as the objectives of the state's overall plan, the level of direct interference by the party committee, and the accountability of the factory director. With the massive lay-offs, the congresses did become actively involved in negotiations about the level and the compensation package provided. In fact, for most SOEs the lay-offs have to be approved by the workers' congress. To deal with arbitration in 1987, the State Council resurrected the labour dispute arbitration system, which had been abolished in 1955 (Lee, 2000, p. 47). This law was revised and passed in May 2008. Lacking the right to strike, arbitration is one of the few sanctioned channels for workers to address grievances. The issues covered have expanded through the 1990s and now cover wages, fringe benefits, occupational safety and health, contract disputes and termination of contracts of permanent workers in SOEs. The re-establishment of this system reflected leadership awareness that there was a lack of formally sanctioned channels through which workers' grievances could be expressed and that workers were increasingly tending towards unsanctioned actions such as strikes and go-slows. The increase in the numbers of cases led to the revisions in the original law with an attempt to speed up the process of getting a decision. In addition, the revised law made it clear that labour arbitration was a free service. However, the revised law did not deal with one of the main problems. Arbitration is still based on the individual whereas most problems involve group action. In 2008, the number of labour dispute cases accepted was 693,465, of which 21,880 were collective labour disputes. The number of workers involved in the collective labour disputes was just over half a million. Just over 30 per cent of the total cases concerned remuneration. The economic downturn that followed the financial crisis of

2008–09 saw a rise in arbitration cases in China. For example, in Guangzhou in the first nine months of 2009, there were a total of 60,000 cases, equal to the entire number of the previous two years. Of these cases, 60 per cent were reported as relating to back pay and most of the rest related to redundancy issues (*China Daily*, 13 October 2009). The total number of cases in 2007 was 350,182, of which 12,784 were collective disputes.

Lee's research (2000, pp. 47–8) shows that the provinces or municipalities with the highest number of arbitrated disputes are Guangdong, Chongqing, Shanghai, Fujian and Jiangsu, where economic growth has been most rapid. Elsewhere it is reported that Guangdong handles 25 per cent of the cases nationally (*China Daily*, 13 October 2009). Most of the cases are from the SOE sector, with private enterprises making up the smallest percentage. Not surprisingly, most disputes are economic, with wages, welfare and social insurance payments being the most common cause (see Lee, 2007 and 2010). This confirms work done on other periods of time when it has been possible to monitor labour grievances (Saich, 1984, pp. 157–9). The key question is, of course, the degree of success that workers enjoy in these arbitrated disputes. Here, the picture is mixed. Grievance was redressed in 50–80 per cent of cases, depending on the locality. However, as we have seen in Chapter 6, success in court does not mean the decision is acted upon. In one county in Beijing, of the 441 employees involved in disputes in 1993–94, 66 per cent were later dismissed by employers (Lee, 2000, p. 48).

In terms of residence, the urban residents' committees (*jumin weiyuanhui*) have played an important role, although more in terms of monitoring behaviour and ensuring compliance with policies such as family planning than in providing a mechanism for participation. From the mid 1990s this has been supported by a programme that is referred to as 'community construction' (*shequ jianshe*). In the past, the role of these residents' committees was less important than work-based committees in terms of the everyday life and needs of most urban residents. This is changing with the expansion of the non-state sector of the economy, and with the work-unit providing less in terms of housing and social welfare benefits. With individuals taking increasing responsibility for these, urban residents' committees are of greater importance. The number of residents' committees has declined in the 1990s but has risen again to 83,413 at the end of 2008. Each committee has between three and seven members headed by a director. They cover an area encompassing between 100 and 700 households, but some cover 1000 (Read, 2000, pp. 807–8).

The sense that the street committee and residents' committee would not be able to cope with the burdens placed on them by the reforms led to experiments to create a new organization as a part of community construction that the Ministry of Civil Affairs began to promote from the mid

1990s (Bray, 2005 and Derleth and Koldyk, 2004). The community districts are based on the residents' committees but are larger in area and have a wider scope of obligations. They are required explicitly to take over the social welfare tasks that previously had been the domain of the workplace or the residents' committee and the street office. The residents' committees were seen as too small to operate effectively, while the street offices were too large to function as an effective grassroots organization.

As Bray notes (2005, p. 185), the party moved to replace one form of collectivity with another. Rather than allowing people to interact individually with government agencies and the market, these new organizations were to take over collective aspects of work and service provision that had formerly been provided by the workplace. They fall under the authority of the street offices and while they can raise some funds from the services they provide, for most activities they are dependent on budget appropriations from the street offices. However, the spread of these new organizations has not taken off as planned, in part because the agenda is too ambitious for the available staff and they are underfunded. Also, there is a general bureaucratic inertia as China already has a complex set of organizations in the urban administration and it is difficult to restructure them to integrate effectively with these new communities.

Reformers have seen the residents' committees as playing the same kind of role as the villagers' committees. Like their rural counterparts, they do not form part of the formal state structure but are considered as a grassroots, autonomous mass organization. Experiments have been under way in a number of major cities since 2000. In May 2000, Beijing announced that it would sanction 'open and fair' elections for members of the 5000 residents' committees in the city. Members would be elected for a period of 3–4 years. From the beginning of 2000, experimentation had taken place in 200 of the committees in Beijing, while another 20 cities outside of Beijing were also engaged in experimentation (*AFP* and *UPI*, 24 May 2000). Shanghai held a first round of elections in 2003 targeting a turnout of 20 per cent of voters (31.4 per cent actually participated). For the second round in 2006, the city aimed for a 40 per cent turnout (*China Daily*, 3 August 2006). In 2008, 724 of Shenzhen's committees were directly elected (92.4 per cent up from 47 per cent in 2005). In pushing ahead with this programme, Shenzhen clearly wanted to position itself as a pioneer of political reform to add to its reputation as an economic reformer.

That the electoral process in the urban areas lags behind that in rural areas is clearly recognized. The deputy director of the Ministry of Civil Affairs department in charge of the elections noted that in 2008 only 22 per cent of committees were elected but the intention was to raise this to 50 per cent in 2010 (*SCMP*, 5 August 2008). Little study has been made of these elections in comparison with the village elections and one study of the 2003 Shanghai elections is not very encouraging (Gui et al., 2006). They conclude from their observations that party oversight of the process was very tight, the residents were generally apathetic and there was very little public debate or information available.

Village Elections and Villagers' Committees

The use of direct elections conducted in a fair and free manner would represent a major change in the relationship between the state and society by forcing the former to be more responsive and providing a degree of accountability to the latter. To date, despite the initiatives mentioned above, the most noteworthy step in this direction has been the attempt to introduce elections for villagers' committees (*cunmin weiyuanhui*) since 1987. However, the process of the election has been complex and contested and the impulse to set up villagers' committees was guided primarily by the need to restore some kind of governing structure for China's villages. This formed part of a set of measures to restore governance to the countryside and it included the use of Village Representative Assemblies and Financial Transparency Committees and the open publishing of the village accounts. By the end of 2008, there were 604,285 villagers' committees with 2.8 million members of whom about 56 per cent were CCP members and about 21 per cent were female.

With the dismantling of the commune system, an administrative power vacuum was left at the village level. While the township took over the government functions of the commune, a new organization called the villagers' committee was to take over those of the brigade. Following experiments in 1980 in Yishan County, Guangxi, where villagers began to organize committees to oversee village administration, to address the needs of infrastructure and to deal with public services and order, it gained provincial and national approval. Although this new entity was mentioned in the revised State Constitution of 1982 it was fleshed out only by the Draft Organic Law on Village Self-Governance passed by the NPC in 1987, a definitive version of which was promulgated in late 1998.

It was generally recognized that the political vacuum and crisis in the countryside could be solved only by letting the villages govern themselves (Kelliher, 1997). As with arguments for political reform more generally, the reason given for promoting elections for villagers' committees was instrumental: they would provide better leadership and self-governing villages would enforce unpopular state policies more effectively than was the situation currently. These observations, based on a survey of the literature by Kelliher, are borne out by visits to various villages I undertook through the 1990s.

Inspiration for the elections derived from the system that had been implemented in Taiwan in the 1950s but, more importantly, the CCP's own experiences during the 1930s and 1940s with village elections in the Jin-Cha-Ji Revolutionary Base Area (Saich, 1996, pp. 975, 1017–38). Peng Zhen, who had championed this earlier programme, was head of the NPC in the 1980s and was the main driving force behind the Draft Organic Law. Naturally the specific environment of the 1980s is different but the logic is the same for the establishment of villagers' committees, with state power needing to be reconstructed in many villages after the introduction of the household responsibility system. This process was heavily contested and it took almost four years for the Draft Law to be passed and, despite numerous proposals, it was only in 1998 that a final version of the law was ready.

Once this final version was ratified, it has become a necessary part of work to ensure that elections take place. The committees are entrusted to deal with all administrative matters of the village, including tax collection, budgets, public goods and services, public order, social welfare and dispute resolution. The committees are overseen by a village representative assembly that comprises all village residents over 18 years of age (Lawrence, 1994, pp. 61–8). The assemblies were promoted by a 1990 Ministry of Civil Affairs circular and their role and the requirement that all villages set them up was written into the revised 1998 law. To some extent, this move represents a step away from direct accountability in the village. In some villages these assemblies comprise only the heads of households. These assemblies not only monitor the work of the committee but also in some cases oversee the work of the party committee, monitor all accounts and expenditures and can make policy proposals.

State dominance is apparent in the process of the establishment and development of the villagers' committees. The presentation ritual on visiting a village committee is almost always the same and is delivered by the villagers' committee head, if that person is the party secretary or deputy secretary. On occasions where the head is not a party member, the briefing is usually chaired by the village party secretary, before handing over to the village head to fill in the details. This reveals the complex relationship between the villagers' committees and party committees, a point returned to below. After the geographical and statistical details, the briefing turns to the terrible problems that used to exist in the village: corruption, conflict over resource allocation, marital disputes and last but not least the failure to carry out family-planning policy effectively. The establishment of the villagers' committees are then credited with clearing up these problems and with enforcing effectively state policy in the villages. In fact, it has clearly been a tactic of reformers to show that villages with functioning committees actually result in the people doing what the state wants better. Rarely does one hear arguments based on the fact that they enhance the power of the people rather than those of the state (Kelliher, 1997, pp. 70, 75).

Despite statistics that show that not all those elected are party members; far from it, interference by the party and higher administrative levels is commonplace. In 2007, 56 per cent of committee members were party members; earlier research shows that more village heads are party members. Pastor and Tan (2000, pp. 504, 510) suggest that 80 per cent of village heads were party members. In Shanghai, the figure was 92 per cent while in Zhejiang it was only 62 per cent. The distinction of whether one was a party member before the election or only joined afterwards is important. The elections have provided a source of trusted new leadership for the party and a popular, elected member might be asked to take on the job of party secretary. In all villages where there is a functioning party branch or cell it convenes a meeting to consider the implication of the election.

These figures do not imply total party dominance of the process but it should be remembered that while the village committees only fall under the guidance (*zhidao*) of the township level of government, they operate under the leadership (*lingdao*) of the party. Not surprisingly, there are many cases of the party stepping in to affect villagers' committee affairs. For example, four democratically elected village leaders from Yuezhuang, Shandong Province were arrested when they called for a land redistribution that was opposed by party officials. In fact, they had beaten the candidates favoured by the local party officials and had led a demonstration of some 500 villagers over the land redistribution (*AFP*, 13 November 1999).

It is clear that some township cadres have not been satisfied with the expansion of elections as it has undermined their capacity to intervene directly in village affairs to obtain the outcome they desire. This tendency is reflected in attempts to limit the direct, secret ballot as the main electoral form and propose indirect elections or the use of public meetings to approve the elected by acclamation. These latter forms give the party and higher-level administrative agencies a greater capacity to control the electoral outcome. Even among reform-minded leaders, there is a tendency to influence outcome and not trust villagers to make their own choices. The widespread view among local officials is that the 'quality' of the farmers is too low and that they are a breeding ground for feudal and superstitious ideas and backward practices.

Many reformers who support the elections have publicly stressed the 'statist' component of the elections while privately expressing the hope that the process itself will develop accountability and build a more democratic culture that will gradually be transferred upwards in the administrative system. To date pressure to raise the level at which elections take place has been resisted but, with a more sophisticated populace and a more complex society, a variety of experiments have taken place (see below). The rise in corruption has caused the central party leadership concern as they fear that it may undermine their legitimacy to rule. In this context, it is interesting to note that a number of official accounts have stressed an increased interest in the role that competitive and open elections might play in monitoring, restraining and disciplining local officials. This has been countered by those who have argued that the direct elections have led to vote buying and the domination by clans. At least the former practice, which is said to be on the increase (*Xinhua News Agency*, 4 August 2008), would suggest that some at least think that the elections are worth winning and one official engaged in the work commented, 'why buy votes if there was nothing to gain out of being elected?' In some villages, it is reasonable to conclude that greater public control over local decision-making has increased and that the need to place a record of results in front of the electorate has led to greater accountability of the local officials. The expansion of elections in the villages has also led to concern about the role of lineages and clans in village politics. There is little systematic research on this and the level of influence seems to vary according to place. He (2003) suggests that in a one-surname dominant village one tends to vote for a candidate from one's own village but in multi-surname villages, voters tend to concentrate on the qualities of the candidate. Where the economy is poor, most likely villagers will vote for their own lineage to maintain their own domination. One survey of village heads revealed that 42.3 per cent were from a minor lineage and 51.4 per cent from a major one (He, 2003).

In June 1998, the CC and the State Council issued a joint Circular to accompany the revised law and it placed less emphasis on the 'statist' aspects of the elections. It stated that 'open and democratic management of village affairs is conducive to developing grass roots democracy in rural areas, and will guarantee the direct exercise of democratic rights by farmers'. Particular stress was placed on promoting villagers' capacity not only to participate in management, but also to monitor closely the 'performance of the leadership they have elected'. Further, the Circular noted that all major matters must not be decided or resolved secretly but made public to villagers and suggested that each village have a public board to publicize details of all village affairs. On the party, the Circular calls on village branches and committees to hold regular democratic elections and never to try to delay the elections.

One major problem that has arisen is the question of who has the right to vote. Especially in richer villages much of the wealth is built on the migrant labour that has come for work (Saich and Hu, forthcoming). They are not allowed to vote in the elections as their registration lies elsewhere. This has been a common criticism. People wishing to improve the system have suggested that it would be best to allow people to vote where they live rather than where they are registered. Many migrants working in the cities might not return for elections and, as noted above, many migrants working in the villages are disenfranchised.

Reformers have tried to push the idea that the success of village elections should lead to raising direct elections to the level of the township but the idea seems to have been all but abandoned. Most recent experimentation has focused on introducing elections to the residents' committees, grassroots' party officials, or providing more candidates than positions to be filled. In so far as elections at the township have been held, they have been one of a number of mechanisms to assess the popularity of candidates and higher-level authorities have held on to their 'right' to make appointments at the township level. Dealing with township government is thus more complex and deeply contested. Most importantly, the township forms the lowest level of state administration and thus its officials are state cadres. Their appointment, evaluation and approval procedures are decided within the set of relations between the township people's congress and the county congress, the party committee for the township and that at the county level. Township leaders come under the party's *nomenklatura* list, meaning that the party must oversee and sanction even those leaders who are to be elected through one means or another. The township is thus nested within the party and state networks and is the key interface between state and society. These factors have led to calls to raise the level of elections to be continually frustrated (see Saich and Yang, 2003).

Non-sanctioned participation

Despite the development of such formally sanctioned channels of participation, as well as other mechanisms such as petitioning and letter writing, it is clear that the reforms have given rise to unprecedented political activity outside these channels, some of which has been anti-systemic. Such actions have included use of the 'weapons of the weak' (Scott, 1985), cynical jokes and songs, dissent within the party and major demonstrations and riots to signal economic and political plight. As Cai (2008) has noted, the institutionalization of conflict resolution is 'rather limited'.

Especially in urban China, the younger generation is much more committed than their parents to individualism and self-pursuit and pays scant attention, if any, to official party-state definitions of what is correct, socially defined behaviour. The party has begun to lose control over the discourse that is filling public spaces. Increasingly, public discourse is breaking free of the linguistic phrases established by the party. Urban China is awash with the kinds of jokes, mockery and cynicism that continue to erode the legitimacy of the party. When students at Beijing University talk of two factions, the *ma pai* and the *tuo pai*, they are not referring to the Marxist and Trotskyite factions of party hagiography but to those who play mah-jongg and those who want to pass the test of English as a Foreign Language (TOEFL) in order to go abroad. Even the singing of official, patriotic songs is used to mock the authorities. Immediately after the suppression of the demonstrations in 1989, academics at the Chinese Academy of Social Sciences were encouraged to sing patriotic songs. Not only was the choice by a group of elderly women of the children's song 'I love Beijing Tiananmen' a poignant reminder of what had happened in the nation's capital but the sight of grown women marching singing a children's song critiqued the infantalization of the adult population that the party has sought to bring about. The rise of the internet and mobile phones has given rise to a range of unorthodox messages and communications that often poke fun at the official rhetoric or versions of events (see Box 8.2).

While such anecdotes may not be overwhelming as evidence of party weakness, they do point the way to a partially submerged discourse that is clearly at odds with the official one. As in many other authoritarian

---

Box 8.2: Grass-Mud Horses and River Crabs Do Battle

While the Chinese authorities maintain an extensive network to filter internet content, on occasion they can be taken by surprise. Following the launch of Charter 08 in December 2008, censorship of the internet tightened as the authorities feared the spread of the human rights document and the possibility that online petitions might bloom. In January 2009, an alpaca-like creature said to live in the Gobi desert emerged to do battle. The species was named Grass-Mud Horse (*cao ni ma*), a homophone for an obscenity meaning 'fuck your mother'. The creature was variously described as 'lively', 'tenacious', and able to 'overcome a difficult environment'. The difficult environment was that its grassland was being invaded by river crabs (*hexie*), a homophone for Hu Jintao and Wen Jiabao's 'harmonious society'. This was clearly meant to mean that freedom online was being threatened by official censorship. In some depictions the crab wore three watches, which would sound like Jiang Zemin's 'three represents'. The horse became a short-lived sensation. Toys were sold for 40 or 50 *yuan* and a children's song on YouTube drew almost 1.5 million viewers. The fun of poking a proverbial nose at the censors was closed down in March as officials caught up with what was happening and announced that such materials should no longer be 'promoted' as the issue had been 'elevated to a political level'. International media were criticized for exaggerating the incident as a 'confrontation between netizens and the government'. The association of the Grass-Mud Horse with river crabs was deemed to be particularly distasteful.

Sources: Discussions in Beijing, and *New York Times*, 11 and 20 March 2009.

regimes in the throes of transition, it is the writers and other creative intellectuals who have been at the forefront of bringing this discourse into the public eye and have opened up another world for us to see in China. Official histories and accounts of particular events are a key element of CCP rule; they provide the meta-narrative to legitimize the hegemony of the ruling party. Underground literature during the Cultural Revolution, the 'roots literature' of the mid 1980s and the various styles of the 1990s and beyond have all eroded belief in the official narratives. These literatures reveal 'heroes' who are not necessarily party members, colourful local histories and vibrant sexuality that proves to be just as much a driving force as the ideological fervour displayed in official party writings. With faith in the orthodox eroded and alternatives presented, protest becomes more acceptable.

Protest in Society

There is no doubt that open protest has increased since the 1980s and persisted even after the massive student-led protests of 1989. Hardly a day goes by in China without some workers' demonstration over lay-offs or unpaid wages, farmers' unrest over land issues or excessive taxes, or go-slows or stoppages being reported. The vast majority of these protests are not overtly political and derive from economic grievances that are a product of the reforms. Major causes are the industrial restructuring, the pressures on local governments to raise their own revenues that lead to illegal levies, the manifest increase in inequality and the high-handed behaviour of local officials (see Hsing and Lee, 2010). While the causes may be contemporary, the alliances formed in protest and the symbols used may often resemble the traditional. As Perry and Selden (2000, p. 8) have remarked, 'traditional forms of contention are being revitalized in a new sociopolitical context, sometimes creating new public spaces with new economic bases'. They and others have also remarked on how some protesters have invoked the Maoist notions of egalitarianism and fairness, combined with traditional mores, to critique the inegalitarianism currently promoted. One of my favourite instances concerns a rural leader who rose up in the mid 1990s in Hunan to challenge the state and to demand the restoration of a Taiping Heavenly Kingdom system of equal fields. Through a vision, the leader also revealed himself to be the younger brother of the Taiping leader Hong Xiuquan and thus also a younger brother of Jesus Christ. Whether out of fear or respect many farmers from a score of villages were said to have followed him until the army was sent in to break up the movement. In good classical fashion, the leader was said to have melted away into the mountains and was never caught (interview with Hunan official, January 1999).

As noted, most protest has been confined to narrow material interests. In the urban areas, most collective protests have come from the forced acquisition of homes for redevelopment, the failure to meet payments either for salary or pensions, or from lay-offs. A smaller number of actions have come from citizens who have been duped in some kind of investment or pyramid selling scam. Given the social trends and tremendous scale of transition it is not surprising that social unrest is on the rise. In fact, the government's approach encourages people to be unruly as the political system lacks effective channels for citizens to express genuine grievance. Given that the origins of most social unrest lie with the illegal actions of local governments or those with powerful connections, citizens are unlikely to receive redress through official channels that are controlled by the local party bureaucracy. This drives citizens to extra-legal means such as demonstrations and strikes. Not surprisingly, figures for such unrest are hard to come by but anecdotal evidence and the level of reporting in the papers suggests that they have increased.

The levels of unrest have created concern among the leadership but it is apparent that they do not know how to respond effectively. They have become fixated on ensuring that GDP growth does not fall below 8 per cent as they feel that this might be a threshold for unrest to increase. There does not appear to be any objective evidence to support this view. On the whole, they do recognize that the protests are not political and do not deserve a harsh response. For example, the Minister of Public Security in 2005 while calling for vigilance noted that 'extreme measures' should be avoided and that they were 'internal conflicts among the people'. Even more remarkably, in an interview with the *South China Morning Post* (4 July 2005), Chen Xiwen, who oversees agricultural policy, criticized violent protest but saw the rural protests as a sign that farmers were recognizing how to protect their rights and interests. That said there is no doubt that the leadership remains concerned about the possibility of unrest getting out of hand. This was made clear by a 28 July 2005 *People's Daily* commentary which warned that no illegal attempts to disrupt social stability would be tolerated and that the protection of stability comes before all else. Also, the right of citizens to petition the central government directly has been curtailed. Combined with the message that conflicts should be resolved through the existing system, this is discouraging and puts considerable power in the hands of the local authorities who have been responsible for many of the disturbances in the first place.

The concern of the leadership does merit some justification. A number of major riots have been sparked by an accident that has led to citizen frustration boiling over into violent action. The emotions displayed have often represented feelings that people have about the widening gap between the wealthy and ordinary people and the different kind of justice they might receive and the local corruption that not only causes problems but also leads to cover-up attempts once an incident has taken place. The lack of trust in local authorities and their impartiality was shown in a major riot in Weng'an County in poor Guizhou Province (June 2008). A young village girl was found drowned in a river and, while officials claimed suicide, the family claimed that she been raped by the son of a local official and his friend. The investigation caused dissatisfaction and locals felt there had been a cover-up. The incident was blogged widely and reached international attention. The riots involved thousands of local residents and led to over a hundred office buildings being trashed and some 40 cars set on fire. Eventually, the party secretary was removed together with several other local officials and the provincial party secretary blamed the riot on prior abuse by local officials in dealing with problems over mines, demolishing homes for public projects and the relocation of residents (*Xinhua*, 4 July 2008).

In the countryside, the main bones of contention have been the imposition of illegal levies and fees, land disputes and resistance to unpopular policies such as those for family planning. Rural riots such as in Weng'an have been episodic, usually targeted against local officials rather than the system as a whole. Many seem to hold the traditional view that if higher-level officials know of the problems, they will step in to resolve them. Two events in 2005 brought together the social and the political, however. They both occurred in Guangdong Province – one in Taishi on the outskirts of Guangzhou, and the other in Dongzhou near Hong Kong. At the end of July, 400 villagers in Taishi petitioned to remove the village chief whom they felt had embezzled funds from land sales and factory rentals. This was perfectly within their rights and the villagers brought in outside legal experts and spread their message to both domestic and international media. By late September, pressure from the local authorities including the hiring of thugs to intimidate those involved caused the villagers to withdraw their complaint and the committee put in to review the head's work was replaced. This occurred despite the fact that at one point the action of the villagers appeared to gain the Centre's support. The use of hired thugs revives an old tradition and has become increasingly common in resolving disputes in favour of power-holders.

In December 2005, an incident in Dongzhou involved violence by agents of the state itself rather than hired thugs. According to reports, the cause was expropriation of farmers' land by the local authorities, a common occurrence, this time to build a coal-fired plant (*International Herald Tribune*, 9 December 2005). This initial act for which the residents did not feel that they were adequately compensated was compounded by the concern that pollution from the plant would destroy their livelihood that is derived from fishing. Official accounts claim that the residents had attacked the authorities and that the paramilitary group was within its rights to use lethal force. Official counts tried to keep the death count at three while local accounts claimed that 20 or more were killed. In an important and unusual step, an unnamed local commander was detained as a result of the deaths presumably in the hope that this might appease further protests. Unrest surfaced again in June 2006 when locals took a number of officials hostage (*New York Times*, 27 June 2006). What is important about this incident for our purposes is the combination of protest produced by state action with the use of state force for repression. Blame was placed on the local actions and once the demonstrations subsided, the construction moved ahead, no compensation was paid and 19 villagers were prosecuted, with 7 receiving lengthy sentences. No public investigation was carried out into the shootings.

As is usually the case, the authorities chose to blame either the protestors themselves or 'outside agitators' who sought to pursue ulterior motives. Despite the rhetoric of the Central leadership, local ranks closed to protect the image of the leaders. A new target of this repression has been urban lawyers and activists who have tried to defend local protestors in class action suits against the local government. Local governments have been upset by 'outsiders' coming in to defend citizens against alleged government abuses. Those seeking to use the law have come under increased harassment, including physical violence, and have had legal charges brought against them to stop their activities. For example, in 2006, the blind lawyer, Chen Guangcheng, trying to assist citizens of Linyi City, Shandong in a class action lawsuit for forced abortion and sterilization, was sentenced to over four years in prison for disrupting traffic and 'wilful damage to property'!

The political threat of such urban and rural unrest stems from the party's historic claim to represent these two classes. The party has also been subject to complaints from others whom it would normally count on for automatic support – the elderly and veteran party members. A number of elderly who are members of groups such as *Falungong* have been alienated, as have those who have not been receiving their pensions on a regular basis. In addition, there have been a number of cases of sit-ins organized by the elderly when they have been faced with forced eviction as city centres are redeveloped, often without adequate compensation and consultation with lifelong residents.

One major factor fuelling protest and bringing local abuse to light has been the rise of new technologies (see Chapter 13). Violence that was easily covered up is now put online while it is taking place. This has become a major challenge for the leadership when trying to keep control over its population and to promote the official view of events. The party has developed one of the most sophisticated systems for policing the internet but still, as the Grass-Mud Horse saga reveals, citizens are very inventive. China now tops the world in internet users and the authorities have shown that they are adept at denying access to certain websites or even shutting down regional access, such as during the riots in Xinjiang in 2009, but they are less adept at dealing with micro-blogging and instant messaging (see Box 8.3)

Protest Within the Party

Most protest in contemporary China is not regime-threatening as long as the party itself stays united, continues to eliminate any focal points of opposition and retains a monopoly over representation and coercion. The main systemic threats have arisen when the senior party leaders have fallen out among themselves. Most of the time, party discipline and codes of conduct make it very difficult for an individual or group to oppose the general policy line at a particular time. While local leaders can ignore or deflect central directives, strategies for central leaders are more complex. They must work incrementally to change policy, either

---

Box 8.3: The Waitress and the Party Official

Internet activity has been increasing in a number of cases that have become high profile. For example, when a person who stabbed to death six policemen in Shanghai, the internet was abuzz with support and sympathy not for the dead policemen but for the condemned killer. Officials have been hounded for their extravagant behaviour and internet pressure and public pressure led to a waitress who murdered a party official getting a fair trial and not being convicted of murder. The woman, Deng Yujiao, in May 2009 was washing her clothes in the hotel when she was molested and hit by a government official and colleague who offered her money for certain services. Ms Deng pulled out a fruit knife and lashed out killing the official and wounding his colleague. She called the police and was arrested for murder. Normally that would have been the end of the story but it was taken up on the internet where citizens contradicted official reporting to defend Ms Deng, who they claimed was acting in self-defence. In addition, others raised questions about why an official should be in the hotel demanding 'special services' and asking whether they were to be paid for with government money. News spread fast and support came from a variety of groups including the All-China Women's Federation. The publicity clearly affected the outcome of the case. Ms Deng was found guilty of causing injury with intent but was freed without a sentence as a 'mood disorder' had meant that she was not criminally responsible. This verdict enabled the authorities to release her while giving the dead official some 'face'. One prominent lawyer claimed that the verdict was 'a victory for public opinion'.

Sources: *The Times*, 27 May and 17 June 2009.

by building a new coalition and consensus or through licensing experiments together with local leaders to provide proof of the viability of an alternative policy approach. Opposition to the party line as a whole is much harder, as is public opposition. If one is opposed to the party line there is little recourse other than to seize power and denounce the previous power-holders for deviating from the 'true line'. This is what happened when the 'Gang of Four' was arrested in a coup in October 1976 by troops under the command of veteran Marshal Ye Jianying.

To oppose party policy publicly is difficult, but is more likely to be tolerated if the critique comes from the 'left' rather than from the 'right'. Historically, those individual party members and groups that have criticized the party for not being liberal enough or for not pursuing market-oriented reforms more seriously have either received internal party sanctions that have made further promotion difficult or have been expelled from the party. Party culture has always made criticism from the 'left' safer. This tendency was identified as early as 1937 by Liu Shaoqi when he suggested in a letter to the CC that methods in ideological struggle had always been excessive and had created a situation that blocked 'calm discussion' of problems within the party. Further, he noted that the hallmark of the party was 'leftism', which in turn had exacerbated the factionalism within the party (see Saich, 1996, p. lix). In the 1990s, a senior ideologue, Deng Liqun, sponsored a series of criticisms of the reforms that highlighted the abandonment of socialist principles in favour of free-market economics and greater bourgeois influences. These circulated widely within and outside of the party but Deng received no known sanction. One suspects that if the intensity and severity of the attacks had been from a party member espousing a 'rightist' point of view, that person would have been expelled from the party.

On a number of occasions the CCP has been rocked by dissent where inner-party strife or disagreement has allowed China's broader population to become involved. The first occasion was in the 'Hundred Flowers' (1956–57), launched by Mao as a response to de-Stalinization in the Soviet Union and the Hungarian uprising of 1956. Mao suggested that what was needed was not the repression of complaints but the encouragement of open criticism of the party apparatus. The campaign was opposed by those in the leadership who favoured a more guided and limited form of criticism. Given what they thought was a green light by Mao, citizens unleashed a torrent of criticism about the bureaucratic nature of the system and demanded greater freedoms such as competitive elections, a free press, effective trade unions, academic freedom and an independent judiciary. Mao was not amused and shut the movement down with the 'Anti-rightist campaign'. As we have seen, the outpouring of dissent and political activity in the Cultural Revolution was also at the instigation of Mao in order to unseat his opponents in senior party positions. This time, public criticism came from both the left and the right but both were ultimately suppressed.

Divisions in the Party and Dissent in Society .

In the post-Mao period, there have been two significant bouts of dissent, the first with the Democracy Wall Movement of 1978–80 and the second with the student-led demonstrations of the late 1980s culminating in the events of 1989. Unlike in the Mao years, neither was prompted by a senior leader and both began spontaneously. However, they came at times when the leadership was divided about the way forward and then split about how to deal with the protests. In November 1978, many of the ideas expressed during the 'Hundred Flowers' campaign received a second airing and initially it was tactically useful to Deng Xiaoping in his inner-party struggles. The movement took its name from the 'Democracy Wall' in western Beijing where people congregated to put up wallposters and to express their grievances. The main stimulus to action was the redesignation of the 5 April 1976 Tiananmen Incident as a positive act that represented the people's attempt to remove the 'Gang of Four'. The demonstrations had been used as an excuse to remove Deng Xiaoping from all his posts for instigating a 'counterrevolutionary' incident. This reversal of verdict seemed to imply that 'the masses' had the right to make their views known and to criticize their leaders.

Most of the activists who edited or wrote for the unofficial journals wanted democratization within a framework of socialism; they were not opposed to the party as such. However, the most famous figure, Wei Jingsheng, was critical of both the communist system as a whole and Deng Xiaoping in particular. He was a 30-year-old electrician at the Beijing Zoo who was the son of a party cadre but had made the mistake of joining a Red Guard faction opposed to Mao's wife, Jiang Qing, and had suffered as a result. His essay *Democracy – The Fifth Modernization* went beyond criticism of the Cultural Revolution system and Mao to suggest that the current leaders were no better. He attacked Deng for having thanked Mao for restoring him to office in 1973, but for failing to thank the Chinese people whose efforts had restored him in 1977. He urged greater democracy for China as a part of its modernization strategy, suggested that the respect for human rights under socialism was not as effective as the leadership maintained and called for sacrifice to bring about democracy (Wei, 1997, pp. 199–212).

In March 1979, Wei was arrested and sentenced to a lengthy prison term in October and a general crackdown on dissent was launched. At its height the 'Democracy Wall' movement probably embraced only 200–300 activists. In the early 1980s, dissent was sporadic and often directed against specific policies rather than the political system itself. However, in 1986 and more particularly 1989, major demonstrations broke out in Beijing and a number of other cities that provided a more fundamental challenge to the leadership. Yet neither of these movements produced the kind of well-thought-out critiques as presented by Wei Jingsheng, for example.

Both rounds of demonstrations have to be seen in light of the unfulfilled promises for political change that had been presented by Deng Xiaoping as an important part of the reform programme; a part he was prepared to sacrifice to more orthodox party leaders to keep his economic reforms on track. Here we shall just focus on the 1989 demonstrations (for the 1986 demonstrations, see Munro, 1988). These demonstrators were different from those of the earlier Democracy Movement; the participants were not the victims of the Cultural Revolution but those who stood to gain most from the newly emerging system. As a consequence they wanted to place their concerns for a better future on the agenda.

The student-led democracy movement of 1989 was one of unprecedented scale that rocked the party to its foundations and came within a few days of bringing the leadership down (see, for example, Saich, 1990; Calhoun, 1994). Unlike the previous movements, shortly before it was crushed it began to bring together students, intellectuals and workers into one movement. The coming together of workers with students and the creation of an autonomous workers' federation was more than the leadership was willing to tolerate. The fact that the federation and the students had taken over Tiananmen Square, the political heart of China and the symbol of communist power caused them to retaliate with massive force to try to crush once and for all the growing demands for greater democracy (Apter and Saich, 1994, chapter 9).

The immediate catalyst for the student demonstrations was the death of the former general secretary Hu Yaobang on 15 April 1989. The students' demands were simple and were not articulated in an elaborate, systematic way. Essentially, the students called for a significant relaxation of regime practice, with greater freedom of speech and the press and the curtailing of the corrupt practices of the leadership and their children. The simplicity of the demands perhaps partly explains why they found such a massive following, a following that included many party members themselves. The students portrayed themselves as patriots who simply wanted to enter into a dialogue with their own leadership. For the most part, the movement began with the idea of reform from within. It was only later that more radical demands were made. Some of the students began to call for the formation of a nationwide citizens' organization that could deal openly and directly with the government. In this respect, it is clear that much of the inspiration for the students derived from reforms in Poland and Hungary and from the reform programme launched by Gorbachev in the Soviet Union.

This does not explain why the students received such massive support by mid May from the citizens of Beijing. This is explained by the fact that both the political atmosphere and the economic situation had declined noticeably since 1986 and the reservoir of discontent in the urban areas had risen greatly. Indeed, the manner of Hu Yaobang's dismissal caused many intellectuals who had previously been willing to set aside their doubts and accept their newfound prestige to become disillusioned with the top party leadership. Further, it was clear to many that the party had no clear idea over the future direction of the reforms. The economic problems in the urban areas, particularly inflation, caused further erosion of acquiescence to party rule, particularly among those government employees on fixed incomes and the industrial working class.

Despite such factors, it is important to note that the students had been demonstrating a full month before the intellectuals and workers actively supported them. In particular, the hunger strike of mid May brought the students enormous support. This combined with the feeling that the movement had reached a crucial phase encouraged many ordinary citizens to take to the streets. Also, by now the student movement had unwittingly become part of the power struggle within the top party leadership between Zhao Ziyang and his opponents. The massive increase in the size of the demonstrations, and particularly the appearance of workers and government employees on the streets between 15 and 18 May, prompted the orthodox party members to take harsh action, culminating in the massacre on the night of 3–4 June 1989. The suppression of the movement revealed in brutal fashion just how far the orthodox party leaders were from allowing any significant political activity to take place outside their control.

Spontaneous movements are seen as undermining the ruling party's hegemonic position. Indeed, the ruling party has no mechanism to explain such a direct challenge to its 'leading position' within state and society. The existence of an autonomous workers' organization, for example, directly challenges the ruling party's claim to represent the highest form of working-class consciousness. Such a clear challenge cannot be accepted and the party will seek to crush the autonomous organization and denounce it as a 'counterrevolutionary' organization.

Similarly, once the movement gains momentum it is difficult to pursue any course other than one that will result in conflict. Strong emotions, once released, are notoriously difficult to bring back under control. The movement tends to develop a life of its own and often tends towards a fundamental critique of the state itself. If the state cannot see the necessity to redress the 'just grievances', then there must be something wrong with the state itself. The critique tends towards the moral and often assumes an iconoclastic form. The strength of the opinions held often closes off the solution of compromise through negotiation.

This highlights the key problem of non-sanctioned political and social movements in a state-socialist context. The political space in which they must act is extremely limited and any noticeable increase in activity is liable to lead to confrontation. The capacity to develop is restrained by the fact that to expand they must confront highly centralized political institutions whose incumbents will repress or otherwise try to control collective action when it arises. Whether original intent or not, the outcome is to seek the overthrow of the system itself.

Chapter 9

The Chinese State and Society

Chapters 5–8 have revealed the extent to which state and society have changed since the death of Mao. This chapter takes a broader view of these changes by analysing the changing nature of state–society relations. First, it reviews the Mao years and the legacies it inherited from traditional China. Second, it looks at how the reforms have impacted on state-society relations and how researchers have tried to categorize the changes.

The Maoist period: an autonomous state and a state-dominated society

The CCP took over from the traditional political culture the notion of an omnipresent, penetrative view of the state. Unchallenged by other organizations (there was no organized church as in the West), the state assumed an all-embracing role that included defining correct ethical values on the basis of the prevailing interpretation of Confucianism. The local official was to embody and proselytize these values and the 'masses' were expected simply to follow the examples provided for them. The recurrent campaigns launched by the CCP in the 1980s and 1990s to combat 'spiritual pollution' and to 'build a spiritual socialist civilization' were just the latest manifestations of this phenomenon. Hu Jintao has been even more explicit with his use of quasi-Confucian notions such as 'building a harmonious society'.

The state thus assumed the role of educator. In the same way that couplets hung in public places in Imperial times exhorting Confucian values, so huge billboards in the PRC beam out messages for the people to love the party, the army and the nation. This approach is strengthened by the traditional view that people possess innate goodness, and that the proper education will enable them to achieve their full potential. In practice, however, 'goodness' was equated with those attributes that the imperial authorities deemed desirable for the maintenance of the existing social order, and the use of education to inculcate 'correct' ideas was fully accepted as part of government policy. Communist China has promoted role models in the same way that the village lecturers of the Qing dynasty were required to use examples of virtuous behaviour for purposes of emulation. Equally, those deemed guilty of antisocial behaviour were criticized; their names were posted in public places and remained there until they showed contrition for their acts. Thus the communist glorification of moral exemplars and vilification of 'negative examples' has an Imperial tradition. A stroll through a village during a major vilification campaign will reveal not just posters denouncing the villains, but also sets of creative cartoons lampooning them.

As discussed in Chapter 5, this tradition lent itself to the use of mass mobilization and campaign movements combined with a distrust of independent intellectual criticism, which was thereafter associated with a lack of loyalty. The concept of 'loyal opposition' was unknown. Historically, the state did not acknowledge the legitimacy of an opposition as a necessary part of the political system. This sharply defined the role of intellectuals within traditional society, with political control of literature and other such pursuits being widely perceived as legitimate. The scholar-officials who were the product of this system often possessed great political power and social stature. In turn, because most scholars were officials, it worked against the striving for intellectual autonomy. Intellectual autonomy was dangerous and would most probably end up in loss of position or even moral and social exile. In the same way as the dynasties built up their armies of scholars to write up their official histories and to provide arguments for their legitimacy, so too has the CCP built up its coterie of 'establishment intellectuals' (Hamrin and Cheek, 1986).

Most writers agree that the leaders of the post-1949 state not only inherited China's traditional statist disposition but also sought far greater control over and penetration of society than their Imperial and Nationalist predecessors (Wittfogel, 1957; Tsou, 1986). This desire for control derived in part from pre-1949 experiences but also from the process of power consolidation in the 1950s. The result was what Tang Tsou (1983) has termed 'feudal totalitarian'. While for Tsou the CCP was the 'monistic' centre of power, it was not a monolith. Importantly, Tsou highlights the distinction between personal leadership combined with mass mobilization and the totalitarian tendency of the party. The former is a more extreme form, as the system has even less restraint in terms of formal rules or norms.

Not surprisingly, Western scholarship in the 1950s and 1960s focused on the structures of the new state and how they were used to penetrate society, an approach heavily influenced by studies of the Soviet Union (see Schurmann, 1968). However, it is worth cautioning that state penetration was never as consistent or extensive as may have appeared from the outside. The swift revival of social networks and traditional practices once reforms began and the public expression of heterodox ideas suggest that popular culture and local networks of resistance were more pervasive than initially thought. Further, as the sociologist Wank (1998) has noted, the local consequences of structures and policies promulgated by the Central state could create incentives at the 'grass roots for behaviour and actions that deviated significantly' from their intent.

The first and foremost feature of the new state was its relative autonomy from the forces and classes in Chinese society (see Chapter 3). Second, the new state assumed the traditional role as the provider of society's moral framework and compass. This was completed in the Shaan-Gan-Ning Border Region where Mao Zedong consolidated his leadership over the party and cajoled acceptance of his brand of pragmatic Marxism through the Rectification and Rescue Campaigns of 1941 to 1944. Third, the central organizing principle of the state was hierarchical, with parallel vertical structures that made horizontal relationships almost impossible to maintain. In addition, the system of household registration (*hukou*) ensured that a sharp distinction was maintained between the relatively privileged urban dwellers and their disadvantaged rural cousins.

Fourth, authoritarian tendencies in the CCP were brought to the fore by the autonomy of the post-1949 state and the lack of influence by society over its apparat. Selden (1971), in his path-breaking study of the communists in the Shaan-Gan-Ning, argued that there was a democratizing potential in the CCP and that there was an effort at community-building with a genuinely participatory ethos. However, in his later work he acknowledges that a fine line separated popular mobilization in the Shaan-Gan-Ning from repressive commandism (Selden, 1995), and Keating has argued convincingly that the populism which Selden observed was always combined with the authoritarian and state-strengthening ambitions of the CCP cadres (Keating, 1994).

Authoritarianism was always present in the CCP's drive to establish power. Not surprisingly, this became more apparent once the party assumed national power and lost its privileged role as agent of the progressive forces of history. As Friedman, Pickowicz and Selden (1991) discovered in their study of Raoyang in the North China plain, features of socialist dynamics and structures could produce brutal outcomes as the system became stronger. Seeds planted well before 1949 in such systemic factors as a security force set up to crush arbitrarily and mercilessly those dubbed 'counterrevolutionary', and a notion of socialism that treated all accumulated wealth as resulting from exploitation, could be used against society in extreme and arbitrary fashion after 1949.

While official CCP history and some Western accounts portray peasant support as crucial to CCP success, the peasantry was only a short-term beneficiary, through land reform, of the revolution. The need to build up capital quickly led the CCP to collectivize the peasantry's recently awarded lands because the CCP leadership viewed the peasantry as the main source for extraction to fuel urbanization and the rapidly expanding state apparatus. Their economic gains of the early years of the revolution were soon lost and collectivization culminated in the disasters of the GLF (see Chapter 3).

By the mid 1950s, CCP policy clearly saw no significant role for the market in allocating goods and services. This not only had a detrimental effect on the quality of rural life but also led to the eradication of inter-mediary organizations that operated within the market economy and in the spaces between the local state and family. The CCP vigorously sought to suppress lineages, clans and other organizations that might have presented a moral alternative or different organizing principle to the state in the countryside.

While industry was favoured over agriculture and industrial workers over farmers, the CCP retained a contradictory attitude towards the urban. Cities represented the home of the proletariat and the advanced production forces, but they were also the home of sin and temptation that could lead to the sapping of the moral vigour of the revolutionary forces. In part, this ambivalent attitude derived from the fact that CCP rank and file, if not party leadership, was overwhelmingly rural and not only had qualms about entering the urban arena but also brought along a strong anti-intellectual bias. This anti-intellectual bias enjoyed senior party lead-ership support, as witnessed through the extreme personal attacks in the Shaan-Gan-Ning on critical intellectuals such as Wang Shiwei and the attempts to manufacture ideological conformity through the various campaigns. This, in part, accounts for the ferocity of many of the post-1949 urban campaigns, especially those directed against intellectuals.

Research by Perry (1997) reveals that even if the working class was relatively privileged, it did not universally approve of the socialization of industry. By early 1957 reforms had led to a decline in real income for workers and loss of input into decision-making. Thus, the socialization drive of the new state had begun to run against the material interests of both the peasantry and the proletariat. The CCP's rise to power afforded it considerable autonomy from all classes and social forces, an impor-tant factor influencing its policy choices after 1949.

In a number of studies of the developmental state in East Asia and Latin America, it has been argued that especially during the initial phase of industrialization a strong and autonomous state is an advantage as it can push ahead with contentious but necessary policies. It will not be captive to vested forces domestically or external pressures that would work against the national interest. The Chinese state was certainly strong and autonomous but its practice in the late 1950s and 1960s reveals the economic and social carnage that can ensue if the bureauc-racy pursues injudicious policies without any countervailing social forces or controls.

The creation of a dual rural–urban society was solidified by the household registration system (*hukou*) that ensured state resources were channelled primarily to the cities at the same time as substantial portions of the rural surplus were transferred to urban industry, the military and other state priority projects. The post-1949 origins of the system derived from the desire to get many of the refugees in the urban areas back to the countryside. The programme proved successful both because it was voluntary and because the state was able to offer land and/or money to many to leave the cities and return to the countryside. In addition, the state did not announce that it would effectively close the cities to its rural population (Cheng and Selden, 1997, pp. 28–9).

As the country moved from restoration to reconstruction of the economy, the CCP began to adopt more specific regulations about the need to control migration flows. Urban residents, following the 1953 census, were issued with registration books and directives began to appear to control rural–urban movement. Finally, in June 1955 regulations were promulgated for a permanent system for household registration that covered both the urban and the rural areas. Importantly, the new regulations made movement from rural to urban areas extremely difficult and even strengthened monitoring of movement within the countryside and from city to city. While the GLF saw one last major exodus to the urban areas, in 1960 the household registration system was invoked to return people to the countryside. As Cheng and Selden (1997, p. 45) remark, the system as it evolved from 1960 onwards was quite distinct for both China and socialist systems more generally. People were now registered permanently to a particular place on the basis of their birth, or for women the place of the person they married. It 'established and reified a permanent spatial hierarchy of positions that were transmitted across generations'.

Migration up the spatial ladder from rural to urban or from a small city to a major metropolis was hardly ever granted. This locked the population into vastly different socio-economic structures in terms of remuneration and the provision of public goods and services. With the exception of the Cultural Revolution when many urban dwellers were 'sent down', a significant phrase that reveals much about how the state viewed the countryside, most Chinese rarely travelled and knew little about the world outside their own neighbourhood. The system was reinforced not just by the registration controls but also by the elaborate system of ration coupons for grain and other basic goods that were place-specific. Unless one had national grain coupons, which were reserved for only very special Chinese and foreigners, one could buy food only in one's own administrative jurisdiction. The lack of an open urban food market meant that it was difficult to migrate spontaneously.

As the 1950s progressed, the Chinese state concentrated ever more welfare resources on urban inhabitants while enforcing the countryside to practise self-reliance. The associated structures formed a system that exerted control over China's population and locked them into a dependency relationship based on the workplace. In the countryside this was the lowest level of the collective, normally the production team within the commune. This structure had the advantage of fragmenting the society and dividing it into a honeycomb of local communities that would make organization to oppose the CCP all but impossible. The CCP with its network of local members and vertically integrated command system could sit astride and control the local communities.

In urban China, the workplace (*danwei*) became a system to ensure social control (Walder, 1986; Lü and Perry, 1997). Housing was allocated through the workplace as would be welfare benefits, holidays and even, later, the permission for when to have children and how many. Lü and Perry (1997) define five basic features of the *danwei*: it controls personnel, provides communal facilities, operates independent accounts and budgets, has an urban or industrial role and is in the public sector. The system eschewed horizontal contact between workers, students and farmers thus contributing to a system of vertically defined control and the cellularization of society for many functions (Shue, 1988). While the cellular structure of Chinese rural society was long apparent (Skinner, 1964–65), CCP organizational structure and pre-1949 operations dramatically influenced the notion of using this as the organizing principle for society as a whole post-1949. The cellularization of life as reflected in the *danwei* system was inherent in the cell system of the CCP developed before 1949 when horizontal contact was eradicated for fears of discovery and betrayal leading to the destruction of the organization as a whole.

The workplace system became the defining system for urban organization and remained as such well into the reform period. The system also entailed a hierarchy of benefits and quality of life. First, the elite were those workers who had a job in the state-owned sector or the government bureaucracy. Secondly, within the state sector itself there was a very uneven provision of goods and services dependent on the wealth and status of the enterprise. Employment in a large Shanghai state enterprise would provide one with better housing, schools for children and retirement prospects than work in even a large factory in a small city in the hinterland. Labour mobility was not encouraged and one was likely to work one's whole life in the work-unit to which one was assigned upon graduation from school or college. In fact, an employee had to get permission from the workplace to change jobs, giving great power to the personnel department of the work-unit. This power of control was strengthened by the fact that each employee had a dossier (*dang'an*) kept by the department of personnel that contained not just biographical detail but also information about political attitude and performance in campaigns. For women, biological information on their menstrual cycle was also kept so that family-planning quotas could be implemented better. The notion of *danwei* and one's own identity was so pervasive that on answering the phone or on meeting someone for the first time, almost always the first question would be 'Which *danwei* do you belong to?' The reply would help one gauge whether the interlocutor was superior, equal, or of inferior status. In fact, when the reforms began, a number of young urban Chinese who desired to shock put the affiliation on the ubiquitous name card as 'No *danwei*'. This was seen as a sign of rebelliousness and non-conformity to existing norms and structures. As discussed in Chapters 10 and 11, reform of this workplace system is crucial to the CCP leadership's attempts to restructure the urban economy successfully.

The lack of a need to be responsive to social forces and the eradication of all potential opposition outside the party meant that policy-making became increasingly monolithic and less grounded in socio-economic reality. Once ideology began to dominate policy-making, disastrous policy choices were made, which brought the authoritarian trend within the CCP to the fore. The coincidence of state and village interests during the war years hid the tension between state-strengthening and popular sovereignty, and the overall statist thrust of the CCP left some room for local independence. Not surprisingly, this became more apparent once the party assumed national power.

The tendency towards coercion was heightened by traditional statist culture, the dominance of the party over all other institutions and the tendency towards individual domination by Mao Zedong over the decision-making process. China's traditional culture viewed state and society as constituting a moral and ethical unity inseparable from one another. Cadres were expected to define those official values that would 'regulate all social relationships, with rule conceived of as much in terms of preaching and setting moral examples as of administration' (Whyte, 1991, p. 255). This fitted well with the form of Marxism-Leninism developed by Stalin and Mao that claims the unique capacity to interpret the linear progress of historical development and to be able to develop correct policy prescription on that basis (Saich, 1995). By the time the Cultural Revolution broke out, this 'unique capacity' effectively belonged to Mao Zedong alone.

These factors further strengthened the paternalistic nature of the authoritarian party and its state *apparat*. While Mao Zedong was referred to as the 'great teacher' and the party took on the role of political socialization, a policy of 'infantalization' of society was pursued. That is to say, individuals were treated as children who did not know what was in their own best interests. This has persisted down to the present. In the run-up to the March 2007 NPC meeting, the party secretary for Tibet stated that the party was 'like the parent to the Tibetan people, and it is always considerate about what the children want' (Reuters, 2 March 2007. Senior and local officials felt it their role not only to represent the population, but also to think on their behalf and take all important decisions in their interests. Since the party and its leaders were 'infallible' because of their capacity to analyse the unilinear flow of history, policy failure was traced either to deliberate sabotage by class enemies or the inability of the 'masses' to respond properly or because of their low educational quality (*suzhi taidi*). Ultimately, this system also removed individual responsibility from the officials, as they were merely acting on behalf of the masses.

The system of intense bureaucratic control over distribution, the increasing arbitrary control over personal life and the concentration of power in individual hands undermined social cohesion and trust in officials and laid the basis for the corrupt behaviour by officials that dogs the system to this day. So much control over so many resources made it inevitable that officials would use their positions to extract benefits from their local communities. Walder (1994; see also Oi, 1989a, 1989b) and others have noted that party authority was founded upon a citizen dependence upon officials for satisfaction of material needs and for access to career opportunities. One of the most abusive forms was for the commune or brigade party secretary to demand sexual favours from 'sent-down' educated young women who wished to return to the urban areas for study. Often the communes had a shortage of qualified people or there was lack of interest among the local farmers, meaning that it was difficult for local officials to meet quotas. Not surprisingly, such activities increased cynicism towards officialdom and a disrespect for those in authority, who were seen as self-serving rather than 'servants of the people'. Paradoxically, perhaps, the structure led to an expansion in the use of connections to obtain goods, often those to which one was entitled, and an increased reliance on the immediate and extended family. These tendencies that became more pronounced during the Cultural Revolution persisted into the reform era and provide the underlying basis for the more spectacular corruption witnessed in recent years.

The new institutions of the state were not institutionalized and operated primarily to implement party policy. Indeed, one can even speculate to what extent, especially from the mid 1950s, they functioned as institutions to implement the political will of one person, Mao Zedong. A completely Mao-centred approach to Chinese politics leaves many gaps in our knowledge of the workings of the political process, but Mao's role cannot be ignored. It is ironic that although Mao played a crucial role in devising the 'rules of the game' and associated institutions, it was he who was instrumental in causing their breakdown when he resorted to alternative channels of communication and a more personalized form of politics. One of the most crucial tensions in post-1949 politics was the position of Mao Zedong among the 'collective leadership'. His dominance prevented the institutionalization of political structures that could have regularized policy-making. The most extensive analysis of Mao's dominance in policy-making and institutions has been provided by Teiwes (Teiwes, 1990) and Teiwes and Sun (Teiwes and Sun, 1997, pp. 151–90; 1999). This work demonstrates that even at the best of times there was a tension between Mao's supreme position and the demands of party documents that a collective leadership style be practised. Their analysis reveals that for the most part when Mao was committed to a particular policy no one dared to resist, or at least not for long. Politics at Mao's court seemed to go no further than second-guessing Mao. Teiwes and Sun reject attempts to explain the politics of the period as shaped decisively by institutional interests (see, for example, Bachman, 1991). They point to Mao's unchallenged authority and claim that the leadership followed him into the new venture with an extraordinary degree of enthusiasm. However, this does not entirely resolve the issue of how much was Mao's own view, and how much was impressed on him by various bureaucratic interests.

While the emergent system appeared as a strong state, it undermined the capacity of the CCP to rule effectively and to inspire strong bonds of loyalty from its citizens. Not only did the attacks of the Cultural Revolution lead to economic stagnation, but it also actually weakened the capacity of the state to maintain effective control for any extended period of time. In the most radical phase of the Cultural Revolution (1966–69), the party effectively substituted the state and with the party taking over many state functions, there was only the party to blame if, and when, things went wrong. The system, while high on coercion, was low on information flows. This meant that feedback on policy was inefficient and inaccurate, with those lower in the hierarchy passing up only information that those in higher positions wanted to hear. Yet, paradoxically, even though this was not Mao's intention, the Cultural Revolution enabled the young people of China to read and learn more about the inner workings of the system than had been the case before. In addition, the travels that many had undertaken as Red Guards and the periods spent forcibly in the countryside by many had revealed to them the harshness of rural life, a harshness that clashed dramatically with the Maoist images of the rural idyll with which they had grown up. Further, Mao's inspiration to attack the party-state authorities, and indeed all authority, bred disrespect for authority among the people. Subsequently, the savagery with which the radical movement was squashed, the manner in which Mao seemed to turn his back on the 'revolutionary youth' once they had destroyed his party colleagues, and his attempts to rebuild the party-state apparatus, caused many a young rebel to become disillusioned with the 'Great Helmsman'. These factors combined with the stagnating economy meant that there was a population receptive to a radical shake-up of the system once Mao died, the 'Gang of Four' were arrested and Deng Xiaoping returned to power. It also explains the energy of reform ideas that poured out in the late 1970s and early 1980s, both from the official press and in the unofficial journals. While Deng's decisions to squash the Democracy Wall Movement of 1978–79 and the recurrent campaigns against 'bourgeois liberalism' showed that there would be limits to the extent of significant political change, the economic reforms have radically reduced the capacity of the state to intervene in society. Slowly but surely the key features outlined in this section have come under pressure. Chapter 13 looks at whether these challenges fuelled by economic growth will lead to significant political change and eventual democratization of the state and society.

State–society relations under reforms: a negotiated state

The economic reforms launched by the CCP in December 1978 have led to a relaxation of party control over the economy, society and ultimately over public discourse, in part by design and in part by default. Reforms have led to a major transformation of urban and rural society (see Chapter 2). Once social spaces were opened up by the party and state's tactical withdrawal, this led to both the pressure for a further opening up of space and the filling of it with unorthodox ideas.

The reforms in China share certain features with those in other former state-socialist systems. There has been a progressive decline in the state control of the economy, with powers devolved from state agencies to enterprises, and a decrease in the use of mandatory planning mechanisms and a concomitant increase in the use of market forces to guide distribution and, increasingly, production choices. The role of the market has been gradually extended beyond goods and services to labour, now increasingly seen as a commodity (Tomba, 2001), and capital. By contrast, there has been concerted resistance to allowing the development of a market in political ideas. The process has been accompanied by debates over diversification of the ownership structure of the economy, with a marked increase in the collective and private sectors. In addition, there has been an increasing appreciation that law can play a role in moderating official excesses and governing relations between state and society, and that there should be increased accountability of officials not only to the party but also to society.

The economic changes have redefined the social structure and are changing the distribution of power between state and society, have altered the principles on which society is organized and the ways in which it interacts with the state apparatus. Chinese society has become more complex as a result in terms of both structure and attitudes and at the same time has become more fluid and dynamic than at any time since the early 1950s. There is greater social and geographical mobility and horizontal interaction, and integration has developed as the vertical and cellular boundaries of the traditional Leninist system have become more porous. Finally, there has been a significant redistribution of economic power away from the state and its ancillary agencies and towards groups, new or reformed institutions, households and perhaps even individuals.

Over time, the political consequences of these changes, including the rise of an educated middle class, are liable to be considerable. The partial withdrawal of the state and party from people's lives has led to a revival of many traditional practices, the emergence of new organizations to fill the institutional void and the appearance of new trends in thought to fill the spiritual void. However, this does not necessarily mean that the party's power will be eaten away, as a mixed picture emerges if we look at the 'moral resources' possessed by those who either oppose or do not fully support the party-state. While it is true that public discourse is breaking free of the codes and linguistic phrases established by the party-state, it is also clear that no coherent alternative vision has emerged that would fashion either a civil society or a rapid construction of a democratic political order. From the party's point of view, what is lurking in the shadows waiting to pounce on any opening that would allow freedom of expression is revivalism, religion, linguistic division, regional and non-Han ethnic loyalties. A scan across the messages on various bulletin boards and websites reveals that many in the Chinese virtual space are far from democratic and harbour strong nationalist not to say zenophobic views.

What we have seen is a progressive undermining of the party's own heroic narrative of its central role in the revolution and re-emergence of popular religion, class and even secret societies providing not only alternative sources for belief but also as sites for reciprocity and welfare distribution. In the urban areas, there is also the emergence of a focus on individual desires and wants, something that will be enhanced further by the single-child policy. This is reflected in material culture, music and much more hedonistic literature, all of which conflict with the party's traditional collectivist ethos. Thus, while party propaganda tells us that 'women hold up half the sky', Shanghai writer, Wen Hui, tells us women 'have much more freedom than women fifty years ago, better looks than those of thirty years ago, and a greater variety of orgasms than women ten years ago' (Hui Wen, 2002, p. 90). Individuals are rejecting the collectivist ethos and believe that they have more to gain through the pursuit of their own self-interest rather than supporting the collective.

This is problematic for the CCP as it still professes belief in socialism and all socialist systems are based on some variant of collective individualism (Apter and Saich, 1994).

To some extent, the party is right to be afraid. At present, the most clearly emerging alternative foci of identity are ones that tend to weaken central allegiance. The most obvious are the re-statement of Tibetan and Uighur cultural identities that have led to a number of clashes between local demonstrators and the internal security apparatus and the PLA. Similarly, coastal China is not only moving away from Beijing in terms of its economic policy but also in terms of cultural identity. In Guangdong, this is reinforced by the use of the Cantonese language and the interactions with Hong Kong. In Fujian, this is strengthened by the ties across the Taiwan straits.

With the 'belief vacuum' at the centre, traditional belief systems and organizations are beginning to re-emerge, such as popular religion, clans and even secret societies. Not only in the countryside but even in the suburban areas, temples are once again becoming sites for worship and hubs in an intricate system of reciprocity and welfare distribution. In southern China particularly, clans and lineages have reappropriated the role of local self-organization that was partly taken away from them after the communist conquest swept down from the north in the late 1940s. Secret societies are once again flourishing in China and contacts have been established with their counterparts based in Hong Kong and farther afield. There has been a rising concern about alliances being formed between these triads and local officials and worries that in some localities the 'gangs' have taken over (Chapter 13).

In urban China, while the party's official discourse has ceased to be hegemonic and the voice of alternative discourses is readily heard, no new dominant discourse has emerged. What is emerging is the individual as focus. This is impossible for party veterans to contemplate with their stress on a discourse of the 'collective'. The new emphasis might all too easily lead to the realization of oneself as an individual citizen of China rather than as a subjugated element of the masses of the PRC. At present, for many the most important binding factor is the desire to make as much money as quickly as possible and to live a relatively untroubled life.

One result of the reforms and the uncertainty of where boundaries lie is the dynamism in certain art forms and intellectual discussion about where China is heading or should be heading. It is true that much of the best literature has been produced by those in exile or outside China and challenging films are frequently banned, yet there has been a blossoming of the arts, some of which pokes fun at the authoritarian strands of the state. There are artist enclaves in a number of major cities and in Beijing there is 798 Dashanzi where a range of contemporary artists can exhibit.

Among the more famous activist artists is Ai Weiwei who after a lengthy stint in the US returned to Beijing. He was an artistic consultant to the construction of the National Stadium for the 2008 Olympics, although he was highly critical of the opening ceremony. Together with Feng Boyi in 2000, to parallel the Shanghai Third Biennale, he ran an exhibition for 46 avant garde artists entitled 'Fuck Off'. The son of Ai Qing, a writer persecuted in Yan'an and again in the Cultural Revolution, his fame seems to have afforded him some protection for his outspoken views. For example, he has been leading efforts to establish how many children died in the Sichuan 2008 earthquake as a result of the shoddy buildings. Music has also been flourishing, both classical and modern. One well-known jazz musician claimed his preference for the style was because it enjoyed certain protection from the authorities. It was considered to have revolutionary roots but more importantly as much of the music had no vocals, they did not have to run the words by the sensors before performing them. Bloggers such as Shanghai's Han Han have attracted a large following and while they are cautious about delving too deeply into politics many of the blogs are critical. In addition to being a racing car driver, Han keeps up a steady stream of commentary. After a major fire had destroyed the new building for CCTV, he criticized those who had responded online with glee by reminding them that it was the people's money that had gone up in smoke and that as citizens they should feel concerned.

The broader public sphere that reform has created has led to inquiry about China's future and a changing role for intellectuals. However, those who combine theorizing with activism are still liable to find arrest and or abuse awaiting them. New ideological trends run the gamut from liberalism through neo-conservatism to populist nationalism. There has also been a change in the traditional role of the intellectual as providing wise moral counsel to the regime. Commercialization, consumerism and the increased professionalization have combined to offer intellectuals a range of opportunities through which to promote their ideas. Liberalism, which has dominated in the economic sphere, has been losing ground in the political. Thinkers such as Liu Junning have been dismissed from their official positions, and being absent from such a stage have found it difficult to project their views effectively. The decline of political liberalism that had reached its heyday in the late 1980s has been analysed by post-modernist, Wang Hui. Wang argues that its appeal faded in the 1990s because the reforms did not deliver what had been promised. Market influences increased in the economy and China became increasingly integrated in the world. However, the outcome was not an increase in equity and social justice (and certainly not political democracy) but rather polarization, an increase in corruption and the fusion of economic and political power (Wang Hui, 2003).

With the CCP also searching for a deeper source of legitimacy than economic growth alone, space has been filled by many alternative perspectives. Neo-conservatives such as Wang Huning and Xiao Gongqin argue that China is not ripe for a democratic transition and lacks the middle class that would be necessary to promote this and ensure stability. They argue that, in fact, it is the state that must take the place of the middle class in development. However, there are still proponents for a gradual transition to democracy such as Keping Yu (2008). The book and his earlier article from 2006 article argued that while there were many flaws in democracy it still represented the best path to move forward on.

The economic rise of China has given rise to popular nationalism. Western criticism of China has fuelled this trend, especially in online forums, and it has been promoted by official policy. Following the student-led demonstrations of 1989, the party strengthened patriotic education in schools and colleges. By its very nature this reinforced the narrative of China's humiliation at the hands of foreigners, especially the Japanese and the US. In the mid 1990s, a group of poets and writers latched onto this tendency to launch their book *The China That Can Say No* (Song, 1996). While written in a strongly polemical style, it caught a rising trend in society. It criticized the pro-Western values of the 1980s and the neglect of China's traditional culture. The sentiments were heightened by Western criticism of China post-1989, the rejection of China's 1993 bid to host the Olympics, opposition to WTO entry and what was seen as a policy of containment pursued by the US. More articulate arguments have been promoted by Wang Shan and Wang Xiaodong. The latter joined one of the original authors to publish a further book, *China is Unhappy,* in 2009 (Song, 2009). This put forward the claim that China should become a superpower and stand up to the US, an implicit criticism of the Chinese leadership. Although it sold well, it did not have the impact of the original.

The inequality that has been part and parcel of the reforms has drawn criticism from a group loosely termed the 'new left' (Cui Zhiyuan, Hu Angang, Wang Shaoguang). In fact, it is unfair to call them a group because their interests range widely, as do their points of criticism, but they all share the common view that the government has not done enough to curb the inequalities and corruption that have arisen as a part of the reform process. Their voice began to strengthen in the mid 1990s as the reform of the SOE sector began to bite and the rural urban inequalities began to be noticed. Criticism has centred on three main areas. First, the corruption that was associated with the large-scale privatization of SOEs that started from the mid 1990s. Second, financial liberalization and allowing foreign purchase into China's financial institutions has been criticized as compromising China's sovereignty. Third, they focused on the failings of rural healthcare provision as a way of highlighting the pro-urban bias of China's policy. In each of these areas the criticisms have had an impact on moderating subsequent policy, although it is hard to tell whether this came from the writings or because Hu Jintao and Wen Jiabao already had a different approach to policy.

Last but not least, there have been those who are seeking salvation in China's traditions, best represented by Neo-Confucians. Many have presumed that the current leadership is sympathetic to Neo-Confucianism but there is little concrete evidence to support this. The most famous promoter has been Yu Dan whose self-study book (2007) has sold millions of copies and is a frequent panellist on television. More acceptable academically has been the work of Jiang Qing (for a fascinating analysis of the work of Yu and Jiang see Bell, 2008, pp. 163–91). Jiang (2003) argues that future political transition must have roots in China's historical cultural repertoire to gain legitimacy.

The social trends of diversity are best seen away from the political centre where concerns with political conformity are less stringent. In some ways, China at the non-central level begins to resemble descriptions of the traditional. Official vertical reporting is in Marxist terminology (rather than Confucian) and economic statistics will be cooked to conform to centrally set targets. Traditionally, officials passed up Confucian accounts of their locality while many were themselves practising Buddhists, Daoists or whatever. In many areas of China, party organs have atrophied or have become economic service organs. Central officials often mention that half or more of party organizations at the local level do not function well. With the party's withdrawal, as we have seen, traditional belief systems and organizations – popular religion, clans and even secret societies – are beginning to make a comeback. In Sichuan and Yunnan, I have met local party officials who are shamans or Daoists, combining party rule with local spiritual leadership.

Of civil society, corporatism, predation and negotiation

It is not surprising that these tumultuous changes have prompted both Chinese and Western scholars to reconceptualize the relationship between state and society. The problem of definition is compounded by the fact that we are trying to deal with a moving target, a state and society in transition. We are dealing with not only the dynamics of the interaction and how this has changed over time, but also with the changes within the state sector and society. What appeared as a predatory local state may evolve later into one of social partnership. We are also dealing with a country where multiple models of state-society relations may be operating at the same time. It is clear that the local state apparatus in Wenzhou,

Zhejiang Province, with its privatized economy operates in quite a different way from a neo-Maoist showcase on the north China plain. The tendency for both Chinese and Western scholars has been to dwell on the fusion of political and economic power at local government levels. This has been accompanied in Western writings with an emphasis on property rights relationships. In this approach the local state is catalogued in terms of the property rights relationships that evolve from the financial decentralization and the strategies that are taken to deal with this. The resultant structures are 'path dependent' on the economic structure that existed on the eve of reform. Out of this approach comes a categorization of local government forms: entrepreneurial, developmental, predatory, and varieties of corporatism. As Baum and Shevchenko (1999, pp. 333–4) have pointed out, there is considerable ideological confusion concerning the analysis of the state in China.

While social space has opened up, the state has continued to retain a great deal of its organizational power and has moved to dominate the space and reorganize the newly emergent organizations. This is resulting in new hybrid forms of public/private that are difficult to define precisely. That the public clearly dominates in most cases is reflected in the growing interest in the ideological sphere in China by younger intellectuals with statist ideologies of neo-authoritarianism and neo-conservatism.

Given this phenomenon, China's traditional culture and the previous practice of CCP rule, it is surprising that the concept of civil society received so much scholarly attention during the 1990s. The rise or re-emergence of civil society was seen as an important component or even precursor of democratization in China. This search for the signs of civil society was sharpened by the large-scale, student-led demonstrations of 1989 in China and the collapse of the former Communist regimes of Eastern Europe. The number of people who participated and the rapidity with which they formed autonomous organizations caused some to argue that the movement heralded the emergence of a civil society in China (Sullivan, 1990).

Initial literature on civil society and contemporary China focused on the areas of conflict between society and the state. Almost all types of nonconformity or anti-regime behaviour were cited as evidence of an emerging civil society. This, however, is too simplistic. One of the major reasons that the 1989 protests failed was the absence of a framework of a civil society on to which they could graft. In addition, it is clear that to thrive, a lively civil society needs a competent state structure and impartial legal system. Without this, the free-for-all is more likely to produce an uncivil society, as in Russia.

Subsequent writing has taken a more nuanced view but still emphasizes the need for organizations of civil society to enjoy autonomy *vis-à-vis* the state. This includes social groups that want to operate independently of the party and state structures such as private business enterprises, trade or professional bodies and religious organizations (Gold, 1990; Whyte, 1992; Dean, 1993). While such accounts provide useful descriptions of what might constitute elements of a civil society, and where one might look for them, they run the risk of viewing civil society as inevitably pitted against the state and developing *against* the state.

Such approaches underestimate the role the party and the state are playing in sponsoring significant changes that lead to organizational innovation which could be a precursor to civil society. State entities have given birth to many of the new social organizations in China, known as GONGOs. Many of the original briefcase companies (*pibao gongsi*), that is, small mobile businesses where all the paperwork could fit in a briefcase, were set up by state employees who were moonlighting from their state jobs. For example, researchers from the Chinese Academy of Social Sciences, the nation's premier think-tank for the social sciences, have to report for work only two mornings a week and publication requirements are minimal. Their housing is subsidized by the work-unit, as are their medical expenses, basic salary and other costs. Thus, costs are minimal should they wish to go into business and they can use state-subsidized offices and facilities to pursue entrepreneurial goals. Should the company fail, they can simply walk away and start again. This phenomenon has also occurred at an institutional level. One of Beijing's largest SOEs runs about 30–40 enterprises under its umbrella, ranging from collectives, through private companies, to joint-ventures. At its peak, 25–30 per cent of FDI in China is estimated to have been 'round-trip capital' exported to Hong Kong and then reinvested in China.

To try to address this complexity, Frolic (1997, pp. 48, 56) uses the notion of a 'state-led civil society'. This seeming contradiction in terms accounts for Chinese authoritarianism that is creating change from the top down as an adjunct to state power. This civil society is created by the state to help it govern, co-opt and socialize potentially politically active elements in the population. This helps Frolic to avoid the pitfalls of portraying civil society as against the state and it permits a dynamic interaction between society and the party and state structures. It also suggests a potential in the relationship that proponents of corporatism as an explanatory model run the risk of missing.

As we have seen in Chapters 7 and 8, there has been a significant redistribution of power, a revitalization of 'mass organizations' and the creation of new entities. Some suggest the structures arising under this reordering may not amount to a civil society but instead resemble 'state corporatism'. Their continued existence not to mention degree of influence and well-being depend on the whim of the party and the state. In one way or another, all these authors are trying to get to grips with state-dependent interpenetration. As Baum and Shevchenko (1999) point out, the principal attraction of corporatist models is their ability simultaneously to acknowledge the pluralizing socio-economic changes induced by market reforms and the continued dominance of the Leninist party-state. This allows writers to explore the opening up of social space while explaining continued control through more indirect mechanisms of coordination and co-optation.

Applications of corporatism to China have come in various forms. The work of Chan (1993), Saich (1994c, 1994d) and Unger and Chan (1995) have used it to refer to the co-optation of the mass organizations as their roles have changed during the reform period. By contrast, Oi (1999) has used the notion of local state corporatism to explain the process of explosive rural economic growth that took off in the 1980s and continued into the 1990s. This model seems appropriate for those areas such as in southern Jiangsu that have a legacy of collective-run industries that formed the basis for TVE development. Oi shows how the change in incentives allowed local communist officials to play the key role in fostering this growth through local government entrepreneurship. The loss of agricultural revenue from decollectivization, combined with hardened budget constraints, while granting local governments greater rights over any surplus, were crucial. This meant that for those leaders willing to take up the challenge there was a major opportunity to develop the rural industrial economy. In Oi's view (1999, p. 11) 'collectively-owned industrial enterprises served better both the political and the economic interests of local cadres during the initial stages of reform'. In this process, local officials acted like a board of directors in their management of village affairs. Walder has explored this idea in his analysis of local governments as industrial firms (Walder, 1995a, pp. 263–301; 1998a, pp. 62–85). In Walder's view, the key question for a transitional economy is not whether the government should play a role, but what that role should be. A number of other writers have taken up similar themes in looking at the local state as developmental (Blecher and Shue, 1996) or entrepreneurial (Duckett, 1998).

However, as we saw in Chapter 7, the resources available to the local state vary enormously and this affects the nature of entrepreneurialism. Local leaders with no industrial base have either had to build one, often with disastrous results, or have been predatory. Sargeson and Zhang (1999, pp. 77–99) challenge Oi's and Walder's findings even for more developed areas on the basis of their study of a sub-district of Hangzhou, capital of Zhejiang Province. They question the general applicability of the assertion that local governments with strong property rights have acted as entrepreneurs fostering economic development and meeting social demands through the development of collective industries. Their study shows that local government officials put their own objectives above not only the aims of the central government but also those of the local community. They assert that the notion of 'local state corporatism' mistakenly 'conflates the interests of local governments, individual officials and the members of local communities, and also fails to consider the broader implication of concentrating property and power in the hands of lower-level governments and officials' (1999, p. 79). With the lack of accountability the local community is excluded from the decision-making process and has no choice other than to go along with the decisions of the 'board of directors', whether they benefit the local community or not.

The situation is worse in resource-deficient localities or those that are dependent on one product. The work of Guo (1999, pp. 71–99) in Jinguan township in northwest Yunnan reveals this. It is a poor township where the local administration forced the farmers to plant tobacco. This generated revenue for the township government because of a good revenue-sharing agreement with the county-level government. For the province as a whole the tobacco industry provides 70 per cent of the revenues. Since 1991, the local county has obliged 11 of the 18 townships to grow tobacco and excluded only those in the mountainous areas where the conditions were clearly not conducive. Not surprisingly the farmers were unhappy as the tobacco took land away from their capacity to grow rice and they earned less from tobacco. The county government derives enormous revenues, however, as it operates a sales monopoly and has the highest agricultural tax at 38 per cent. To buy the compliance of the township authorities, the county signed a revenue-sharing agreement that allowed the township to keep two-thirds of the tobacco revenue. This cosy agreement ran into problems at the end of 1993 when a bad harvest combined with the government's harsh extraction policy to cause public protests. Compulsory tobacco production was abandoned in 1994 but Guo surmises that this was because of the general 1994 fiscal reform that adjusted the sharing of tobacco revenues between higher and lower levels of government. When the county reintroduced the tobacco quota in 1996, there was no coercion, with the result that only 10 per cent of the quota was met (Guo, 1999, p. 77, n. 16).

The picture is different again in areas with a high degree of privatization. Unger and Chan (1999, pp. 45–74), in their work on Xiqiao township in Guangdong, show how the criteria for success in private enterprise and public office are beginning to converge. The local township government does not need to levy any general taxes on village households and has been strongly in favour of local private business. As they conclude (1999, p. 73), this experience counters the general writing on local government in two significant ways. First, local officials do not give priority to publicly owned industry over the private sector and, secondly, they do not insist on relationships in which private enterprises are subordinate to and dependent on them. Saich and Hu (forthcoming) confirm these findings with their research on Yantian, Dongguan in Guangdong Province, where private business is highly developed. They found that the enterprises were guided by the market and the local administrations did not interfere with their production of business activities. The village government had reinvested substantial funds in developing social services

Thus, empirical research questions the general applicability of the notion of corporatism. Corporatism as a theory captures well the top-down nature of control in the system and how citizens are integrated into vertical structures where elites will represent their perceived interests. However, such explanations risk obscuring both important elements of change and oversimplifying the complexities of the dynamics of the interaction. It can mean that researchers pay less attention to the benefits that members of the 'subordinate' organizations derive. What are the attractions and benefits of participation, or at least acquiescence, with this process? New social organizations, for example, can have considerable impact on the policy-making process by retaining strong linkages to the party and state, far more than if they were to try to create an organization with complete operational autonomy. The interrelationships are symbiotic rather than unidirectional. Those social organizations with close government links often play a more direct role in policy formulation than in other developing counties as they do not have to compete in social space with other NGOs for dominance and access to the government's ear on relevant policy issues (Saich, 2000a).

In the same way that the local state in China shows enormous variation in its nature, each social organization in China has negotiated with the state its own niche that derives from a complex interaction of institutional, economic and individual factors. In some cases the outcome may be a close 'embedded' relationship with the state (Evans, 1995), in others it may entail formal compliance while operating strategies of evasion and circumnavigation of the state.

These kinds of explanations come close to allowing for the complexity of the current system, and the institutional fluidity and ambiguity that operates at all levels is even more pronounced at the local level. A focus on vertical integration and lines of administrative control, while ignoring the way in which the relationship is negotiated, ignores important horizontal relationships in society. As government downsizes further, citizens have greater responsibility for their own welfare and more functions are devoted to national and especially local social organizations; people will look more to the local provider of public goods than the central party and state directives and regulations. This will become more important as the wealthy business class is given more freedom over how it chooses to dispose of its money.

As the historian Timothy Brook (1997, p. 23) has noted, emphasis on the vertical 'minimizes the capabilities and opportunities that people exercise regularly to communicate horizontally and form cooperative bodies'. He suggests that we should be more aware of 'auto-organization' as a more cooperative principle of social integration at the local level.

Social scientists tend to dislike open-ended theories and to seek to close down the range of options available for interpretation through a process of imposing order and logic. The idea of each organization and the nature of each local state being the result of a process of negotiation tries to do justice to the complexities of social reality in China. In the field of state–society relations, we need to develop explanations that allow for the shifting complexities of the current system and the institutional fluidity, ambiguity and messiness that operate at all levels in China, and that are most pronounced at the local level.

Chapter 10

Economic Policy

Chapters 10–13 look at the policy areas of the economy, social development, foreign affairs and at future policy challenges. First, we introduce a few key issues related to the institutional environment for policy-making and implementation.

Policy-making and implementation

Most literature on policy-making in communist systems has highlighted the monolithic and top-down nature of the process. The prime concern has been with the monolith and its totality, and the actions of a cabal of key leaders who transmit policy direction through the party to be implemented by a subservient bureaucracy. As White *et al.* (1990, p. 216) commented, until the late 1980s it 'was not generally believed that the communist states possessed anything that could properly be called a "policy process"'. The overriding policy demand was to build up heavy industry and to achieve the highest possible rate of economic growth. That different parts of the bureaucracy might pursue different interests or that there might be significant variation in input or even that groups might have an input was not taken very seriously. Despite this dominant view of a monolithic and closed decision-making process, even before the reforms there has been significant policy variation and experimentation throughout China. While this was less visible under Mao's rule, it has become more apparent as China has tried to introduce market influences into a centrally planned economy.

The start of the reforms had the added advantage that sources became more readily available, data improved and fieldwork and interviews with those working in China became possible. This made it easier to locate the effect of the bureaucratic setting on Chinese politics and to investigate how these structures affected the policy process.

The most important analysis of the institutional setting remains that of Lieberthal and Oksenberg (1988) with their study of policy-making in the initial development of large-scale energy projects. They conclude that the policy-making process is not entirely rational, they do not see a direct relationship between the problem and the solution, and the policy outcome may not be an actual response to the problem that triggered the decisional process. Rather, the connections are more likely to be 'complex, loose and nearly random' (1988, p. 14). They argue persuasively that it is necessary to understand the bureaucratic structure as it creates or compounds the problems and is a necessary ingredient for understanding typical policy outcomes (1988, p. 17). Their study leads them to conclude that the bureaucratic structure in China is highly fragmented, making consensus-building central and the policy process protracted, disjointed, and incremental. This leads to three operational consequences (1988, pp. 22–3). First, problems tend to get pushed up the system to where supra-bureaucratic bodies can coordinate response and have sufficient leverage to bring together the different parties. Second, the fragmentation of authority means that at each stage of the decision-making process strenuous efforts have to be made to maintain a basic consensus to move forward. Third, for a policy to be successful, it needs the concerted support of one or more top leaders. This fragmentation is accentuated because the party is no longer able to perform the vital role of integrating the bureaucracy to improve both the formulation and implementation of policy.

This structure and the energy needed to keep a policy on track reveal why it is unwise to pursue too many strong policy objectives at the same time. On his appointment as Premier, Zhu Rongji announced a dazzling array of policy priorities for reform, ranging from cutting the bureaucracy to revamping the grain system to restructuring social welfare. With energy dissipated across so many policy areas, it was impossible for him to keep on top of all of them and, with a recalcitrant bureaucracy and considerable vested interests digging in, his most ambitious schemes were diverted. Consequently, Zhu had to pull back, set his sights on one or two main priorities and try to keep the momentum moving forward while making grand statements about the remaining objectives. When Premier Wen Jiabao took over he did not announce a grand strategy but rather concentrated on trying to use the state to improve the lot of those who had not benefited so well from the reforms. The rural sector has been a particular area of concern and a number of initiatives have been introduced to improve health, education, and economic development opportunities. However, even his and Hu's attempts to shift the focus of policy to sustainable development have met with resistance from local administrations that have been more concerned with maintaining economic growth.

Lieberthal (1992) has developed the idea of bureaucratic fragmentation further with his concept of 'fragmented authoritarianism'. This highlights that while the system may be pluralist in terms of interests and highly fragmented, with each level having to negotiate horizontally and vertically, it is certainly not a democratic process. For Lieberthal (1992, p. 8), authority just below the apex of the political system is fragmented, disjointed and structural and has increased as a result of the reforms pursued since 1978. This means that bargaining is a crucial element of the political process (see Lieberthal and Oksenberg, 1988; Lampton, 1992). We have seen in Chapter 7 the complex relationship between the centre and the localities, especially related to financial questions, and how adept lower levels have become at protecting their own interests against higher-level institutions and those at the same administrative levels. This process of bargaining and negotiation makes it difficult to accept one particular approach to policy-making or to be able to predict accurately policy outcome, as each organization will attempt to bend policy to its own advantage. The resultant system is extremely complex with enormous institutional fluidity, ambiguity and messiness as Chapter 9 demonstrated.

The complexity is increased by the challenges of policy implementation. There is no doubt that the implementation phase of the policy process is critical yet it is often ignored by researchers, bureaucrats and national and local policy-makers. However, it is precisely this phase that determines the nature and success of a policy reform initiative and implementation may often lead to an outcome quite different from that intended and anticipated by analysts and policy-makers (Grindle and Thomas, 1991, esp. pp. 121–50). Grindle and Thomas note that many assume a linear model of implementation where a proposed reform gets on the agenda for government action, a decision is made and a new policy or institutional arrangement is implemented either successfully or unsuccessfully. Failure usually results in a call for greater effort to be made to strengthen the institutional capacity or to blame it on the lack of political will. However, a 'policy reform initiative may be altered or reversed at any stage in its life cycle by the pressures and reactions of those who oppose it' (1991, p. 126). These responses can happen either through the reactions of society in a more public arena or in the more closed bureaucratic arena where opposition from vested interests may be mounted. Further, the government simply may not apply enough resources to ensure a successful policy outcome.

Fukuyama (2004) points out that in policy implementation a basic conceptual failure to unpack different dimensions of the state can lead to different outcomes for economic development. He stresses the need to distinguish between the scope of government activity and the strength or capacity of government institutions. On balance it would seem that the strength of state institutions is more important and this would mean that it is unwise to set out too many policy objectives at the same time, as Zhu Rongji discovered. China's economic reform has revealed that the market is a superior way to organize transactions but this does not negate the role of government intervention and regulation (Naughton, 2007, p. 7). However, on the whole, in the economic sphere, the Chinese economy has fared best when the government has limited its interventions but this has not been the case in the social sector where the absence of government action led to a precipitous decline in medical provision in rural China, for example. *poor follow up*

Despite the strength of the Chinese state and its ability to bring enormous resources to bear for limited periods of time in a narrow range of policies, China has suffered from all the problems with implementation and has been especially poor in monitoring and follow-up. As noted above, bargaining and negotiation are key features of the Chinese policy process. Lampton (1992, pp. 57–8) sees bargaining as a fundamental form of authority relationship, and outlines five consequences. First, decisions are generally arrived at slowly because the process of consensus-building and negotiation is protracted. Second, it is difficult to say precisely when a decision has been finalized: most decisions are made 'in principle' and then are still open to amendment. Third, even once a policy is adopted, negotiations among and between various levels of the hierarchy can result in significant adaptation. This is what Naughton (1987) refers to as the 'implementation bias', whereby all central policies will be bent in favour of the organization or locality responsible for implementation. Fourth, it is a mistake to set too many high-priority goals simultaneously. Fifth, because bargaining is so extensive, the legal framework is poorly developed.

Most of the problems that China faces with implementation are not unique to China and plague all systems, but some are more acute. In particular, China's size and diversity makes it especially important that policy remains flexible to account for variation and that policy-makers receive accurate information for policy design and on feedback once policy begins to be implemented. A number of problems have hampered this process in China, ranging from the logistical to the political.

Politically, the party still does not welcome dissenting views. While the principle of democratic centralism may not be applied as rigorously as in the past, the party still has very weak mechanisms for providing feedback on policy implementation. There has been a growth in internet chatrooms associated with party and state organizations for citizens to express views to complement the traditional system of letter writing, but these remain constrained. The use of informal surveys on the performance of local officials is also increasing. The absence of a free academia and media seriously restricts the quality of feedback that the party can gather on how their policies are being received by the population. The party has loosened up somewhat, especially in the realms of reporting on environmental affairs and consumer rights, but it is still virtually impossible to address the systemic nature of the problems to encourage a genuine public debate. The leadership may have put a premium on improving the population's education, but it still does not trust them to use it creatively.

While there is a more pluralistic input to decision-making, with different think-tanks or agencies preparing reports, the limit on the range of views they can put forward is still restricted. Local experimentation has been an important mechanism for introducing policy reform. This experimentation can either occur spontaneously in a locality or may be initially licensed by the central government. Once a consensus has been achieved on the value of the local experimentation it may be adopted as national policy. In fact, raising a problem too soon, even if the analysis is correct, can have adverse consequences. It is more judicious to wait until a consensus emerges that a policy is not working before offering alternatives.

General outline of economic policy

There can be no doubt that in economic terms the reforms launched by Deng Xiaoping and his allies have achieved considerable success. Since 1978, the economy has been growing at some 10 per cent per annum and during 2010, the Chinese economy should become the second largest in the world behind the US. Rising per capita incomes and massive increases in foreign investment all tell the same positive story. However, one should be careful not to be dazzled by these headline figures. In 2005, China's GDP was only one-fifth of that of the US with a GDP per capita of $1700, which compared to the US in 1850 (Naughton, 2007, p.3). Even if China maintains its current rate of growth, which is unlikely over the long term, by 2020 the per capita income will equal that of Malaysia in 2007 (not in purchasing power parity (PPP) terms). By 2030, China will have reached the level achieved by Hungary and the Czech Republic in 2007 and in 2010 it was around the same level as South Africa, Botswana and Jamaica!

   The growth in China has been spurred by two main transitions (see Chapter 1) that have provided a unique opportunity for development. The first was the benefits that came from shifting from a centrally planned economy to one that was more market influenced. The second is a general development story of shifting people from low productivity agricultural labour to higher productivity manufacturing jobs. This has been accompanied by an unprecedented opening of the economy to foreign investment, initially driven by capital from Hong Kong and overseas Chinese looking for cheaper manufacturing outlets. These latter two elements follow the successful development patterns elsewhere in East Asia. Reforms were also able to build on the physical and human investment that had taken place during the Mao years, especially those in the rural areas. What has given China its particular development path was that this 'normal' development pattern was overlain by the struggle to get free of the grip of the old planning system. In Naughton's view (2007, p. 5) much of this legacy has been dealt with and challenges of transition are gradually being replaced by those of development. However, the statist predisposition remains strong and the desire to protect the SOE sector and to privilege funding for this sector and the locally managed enterprises has worked to the detriment of the private sector, which creates jobs more efficiently.

In December 1978, the CCP CC decided that the focus of future work would be economic modernization and that all other work must be subordinated to meeting this objective. The CCP's legitimacy was shifting effectively to the capacity of the leadership to deliver the economic goods. This approach resulted in significant changes in the relationship between the plan and the market, and the party and the economic decision-making apparatus, with previous regime practice significantly liberalized. This new focus had specific causes. First, living standards for much of the population in the late 1970s had barely risen from those in the late 1950s. The government's overconcentration on accumulation at the expense of consumption meant that rationing, queuing and hours spent on laborious household chores were the daily fare for most. Second, the failure of the initial ambitious post-Mao strategy to improve economic performance significantly caused the leadership to focus more sharply on the need for fundamental economic reform. Third, the party was faced with a serious problem of legitimacy. The continual twists and turns of policy since the mid 1950s left the party's claim to be the sole body in society capable of mapping out the correct path to socialism looking a little thin, to say the least. Nor could Mao's name any longer be invoked to legitimize policy. Thus, the party began to promise a bright economic future for all within a relatively short space of time. Legitimacy is now tied more than ever before to the ability to deliver the economic goods.

The new policies revolved around the promotion of market mechanisms to deal with the inefficiencies of allocation and distribution that occurred within the central state planning system. Awareness of the 'new technological revolution' increased the Chinese leaders' desire to make their system more flexible and thus more amenable to change. To take advantage of market opportunities, more power of decision-making was to be given to the localities and in particular to the units of production themselves. Production units now have more autonomy to decide what to produce, how much and where to market the products. At the core of this system lay the ubiquitous contracts that were expected to govern economic activity. Correspondingly material incentives are seen as the major mechanism to stimulate people to work harder, and the socialist principle of 'to each according to his work' is to be firmly applied. Egalitarianism is attacked as a dangerous notion that retards economic growth. This is best reflected in Deng's much-quoted dictum 'to get rich is glorious'. These reforms of the domestic economy have been accompanied by an unprecedented opening to the outside world in a search for export markets and the necessary foreign investments, technology and higher-quality consumer goods.

Importantly, in terms of initial success, the reforms did not have a blueprint, and the centre often appeared to be responding to policy innovation at the local level. The Chinese themselves referred to this as a process of 'Crossing the River by Feeling the Stones'. However, as Rawski (1999) points out, this dignifies the approach somewhat as it implies that there is a bank on the other side that it is the objective to reach. Even in the initial stage, however, the state played a key role. Once the central leadership had decided that a local experiment was suitable, it would try to enforce it throughout the country. As explained below, this was the case with the introduction of the rural household responsibility system.

China's gradual approach to reform has been hailed by many observers as a sound transitional strategy, certainly when compared to reforms in Russia. However, one should remember that the kick-start for reforms was hardly gradual. The collective structures in the countryside were almost completely dismantled and the focus was on household-based farming. Rawski (1999) and others such as Naughton (1999 and 2007) have demonstrated how transitional systems in which the market is not yet fully established can generate very high growth levels. In fact, a gradual transition will provide an opportunity for the development of new or reformed institutions that can help guide the process to a market economy. Both arguments contain elements of truth and, in certain respects, the Chinese government has moved towards a form of economic management that resembles models of state-led growth familiar to students of East Asia. With China now in the WTO, whether approximation to the kind of market-based institutions that have been successful elsewhere is the cause of growth in China has a particular relevance. If the 'gradualists' are correct then WTO membership could create problems as it will constrain the leadership's capacity for exceptionalism and experimentation (Woo, 2001). The economist Jeffrey Sachs and his main collaborator, Wing Thye Woo (Sachs and Woo, 1994; Woo, 1999, pp. 115–37), have suggested that China's success has come in those areas where reform has been most radical and where institutions have begun to resemble those in a regular market economy. Thus, China's approach may not necessarily be better than that of Russia and, no matter what else, they argue that it is not and cannot be a model for other transitional economies given its particularity. In their view, performance to date merely reflects the different starting points of the two countries, with Eastern Europe and the former Soviet Union being over-industrialized while China is an economy based on peasant agriculture. Thus, while in their view, growth in China has occurred in spite of 'gradualism', 'shock therapy' in Russia and the former Eastern Europe was inevitable as other attempts at gradual reform and dual-track reforms had already failed repeatedly.

Three factors were important among China's initial conditions (see among others Boone, Gomulka and Layard, 1998). First, even under Mao the Chinese economy was highly decentralized and this allowed for the varied experimentation to take place, for the take-off of the TVEs, and for certain areas to encourage foreign investment. Second, this did not mean that the state itself was weak and China did not suffer from the kind of implosion of the state witnessed in Russia. Third, as Sachs and Woo note, China was overwhelmingly agrarian and thus there was much capacity for growth just through 'normal development'. Eastern Europe and Russia could not simply redeploy people from the rural to the industrial sector; they had to redeploy within an already overloaded and inefficient industrial sector. In Russia, privatization was rapid and contributed to market collapse rather than its development. Last, but not least, the changes and the end of the Cold War led to a massive collapse in production for the military sector. This altered the pattern of government spending and delivered a further blow to the heavy industrial sector.

To some extent, the argument is not about whether these are alternative modes of transition but rather whether there is a third way between capitalist markets and state planning. In fact, it might be more correct to recast the debate in terms of questions of the speed of the transition and the sequencing of reforms. Kornai, the Hungarian economist, has highlighted the fact that different reforms might need to be conducted at different speeds (Kornai, 2000). In his view, macroeconomic stabilization needs to be carried through quickly, whereas privatization might take a much longer time.

The success of the transition in China to date should not be taken to mean that the economy is without problems as there are indeed some which stem from delayed reform, giving some weight to the views of Sachs and Woo. Deng Xiaoping was very successful at ensuring that there were no significant losers in the first phase of reform and that those who did lose out were small in number and politically marginalized. Thus, while it might have been easier economically to push through the reform of the state sector in the 1980s, the political will was lacking. CCP leaders did not wish to affect adversely the privileged working class that they had created after 1949. This made reform in the late 1990s more difficult. Gradualism allows opposition to further reform to develop. A hybrid system that is neither fish nor fowl provides ample opportunities for the officials who run it to engage in corrupt practices, exploiting the disjunctures between the plan and the market. The SOE lobby in China still has considerable residual strength, not just from the workers affected and the ministries created to run it but from the fact that the vast majority of state revenue (perhaps 80 per cent) comes from the SOE sector and consumes 60 per cent of household savings through bank loans.

The main drivers of growth for the Chinese economy have been state investment and foreign trade. Even before the financial and economic crisis that hit in 2008, the leadership had come to the conclusion that it would be necessary to reform the economic model that had proven so successful over the first three decades of reform. Policies need to be devised that can boost domestic consumption as a major engine of growth while ensuring macroeconomic stability. This shift to consumption as a major driver means that growth will slow over time but this is not necessarily a bad thing. If we look to the future, investment, especially in infrastructure and industry will remain important but there is no room for the ratio of investment to GDP to rise significantly over the long term. While China's exports are likely to continue expanding given the current scale, the rate of increase is bound to diminish. China's total trade is already around 70 per cent of GDP, a ratio usually only found in small, export-driven economies (Association of Southeast Asian Nations (ASEAN) and Taiwan) and not in continental economies. Meanwhile, with its growing production, imports are booming and the overall trade surplus will be small if not eroded all together.

This leaves consumption as the main driver of economic growth. Effective expansion of consumption has been held in check by the high rates of savings because of people's legitimate needs to save for retirement, medical care and education. If these were provided by government, consumption would greatly increase as savings declined. Government sterilization of incoming funds from the export surplus also has stunted consumption. The savings rate in China climbed to over 43 per cent of income in 2004 from about 26 per cent in 1985 and this is not likely to increase further. In major OECD economies, the household savings rate averages around 10 per cent (with the notable exception of the US under 1 per cent). China is on a par with Singapore but much of Singapore's savings consists of mandatory contributions to a social security programme. To meet the consumption objective, China will have to integrate its domestic market with the outside world and to develop more effective financial instruments and credit arrangements. Before the financial crisis, there was clear evidence that this was beginning to happen. In January 2008, *Xinhua* (30 January 2008) reported that consumption had replaced investments as the most powerful engine of growth in 2007. The 11.4 per cent growth rate was broken down into 4.4 per cent from consumer spending, 4.3 per cent from investments and 2.7 per cent from net exports.

Over the short-term, this shift was affected by the response to the financial crisis. The leadership resorted to state investment as the focus of a major stimulus package. In November 2008, China announced a 4 trillion *yuan* ($570 billion) stimulus and at the March 2009 NPC meeting, Premier Wen pledged to speed up delivery and announced that more funding could be made available if necessary. One major concern for Hu and Wen has been to ensure that development is sustainable and more efficient in terms of its consumption of resources. The growth rates are putting pressure on energy and water supplies. The demand for electricity supply is increasing by around 15 per cent per annum, and this is unlikely to decline, oil imports have surpassed those of Japan, and there are clear water shortages leading to the massive project to divert water from the south to the north of China. The development has led to significant environmental damage (see Chapter 13).

One problem in generalizing about the Chinese economy is not only its size but also the variance in conditions from place to place and sector to sector. For example, while there can be chronic deflation in some sectors there may be inflationary pressures in others. While in 2007–08, there was overheating in real estate in Beijing and Shanghai, this was not true for all cities and by 2009 prices were rebounding. Below we look at rural, industrial and financial policy.

Rural policy

Economic reforms began in the agricultural system and have been the most radical. Yet the two most dramatic policy developments, the household responsibility system and TVE development, were unexpected, deriving more from spontaneous local initiatives than government planning. However, many problems have remained, with stagnating incomes and problems concerning land tenure and access to credit. The rural sector has been a major focus of attention for the Hu-Wen leadership. The importance that they attached to the sector is shown by the fact that from 2004 the first state council document of the year is focused on rural issues, as had been the case in the early 1908s. From 2006, the leadership has promoted building a 'new socialist countryside' that comprises policies to improve the quality of life for rural residents and to boost agricultural production while making it more efficient.

While the industrial reforms of the 1980s and early 1990s presented very little that had not been tried in the Soviet Union and Eastern Europe, the agricultural reforms represented a 'big bang' and radical new departure, throwing up the question of whether there was still a socialist agricultural system in China (on this period, see Watson, 1984; Hartford, 1985). However, the success of the early 1980s had soured by the end of the decade and has remained a policy headache since.

At the time of Mao's death, the Chinese countryside was organized on the basis of communes (set up during the GLF, 1958–60). These communes functioned as the highest level of economic organization in the countryside and as the basic level of government there. Below the communes were production brigades and teams. For most farmers, the teams were the most important unit, as they made the final decisions concerning both the production of goods and the distribution of income in accordance with the work-points accumulated. While the radicals of the Cultural Revolution tried to force this level of accounting upwards (see Zweig, 1989), the reforms of the 1980s placed many of the functions in the hands of the individual household. The old commune system lent itself to central planning, large-scale production and unified distribution, precisely those aspects of rural policy that the reforms set out to undermine.

Initial post-Mao policy sought to encourage growth in agricultural production by substantially raising procurement prices and by modernizing agriculture through brigade and team financing. At the same time, policy was relaxed to let different regions make use of 'the law of comparative advantage'. Also, private plots of land and sideline production were stressed as playing an important role in agricultural growth. To allow the peasants to sell their products – for example, their above-quota grain – private markets were again tolerated. This policy was firmly based on the collective and represented nothing radically new.

In December 1978, it was decided that the procurement price of quota grain would be increased by an average of 20 per cent, above-quota grain by 50 per cent and cotton by 30 per cent. The impact was immediate; this single act did more than anything else to lift large numbers of peasants out of poverty. However, the result of this policy was to increase massively state expenditures on agriculture. The Ministry of Finance and the provinces began to spend well over 1 billion *yuan* per year subsidizing grain supplies in urban areas, helping to account for the state budget deficits of 1980 and 1981. In addition, the policy of agricultural modernization did not bear fruit. A new strategy had to be found that would raise agricultural incomes, permitting modernization but without significantly increasing state investment.

The most important subsequent reform was the introduction of the household responsibility system. Although this was introduced in December 1978, initially it did not entail any significant undermining of the collective. However, by 1980 the more radical form, contracting various activities to the household, was becoming commonplace despite official denials. The household was clearly becoming the key economic unit in the countryside. This household contracting system makes the rural household the nucleus of agricultural production, working on a clearly stipulated piece of land for a specific period of time. The contract includes all raw materials and means of production except land-use rights and access rights to irrigation facilities, the latter rights being made available by the collective. Later legislation confirmed this situation and extended the cropping contracts to 15 years, encouraged the concentration of land with the most productive households, encouraged capital flow across regions for investment and reduced the funds that the collective could demand from the peasantry.

The lack of security around land tenure led to further increases in the length of the contract and in 1993 it was announced that new contracts would be for 30 years, something confirmed in both the Land Management Law (August 1998) and the Rural Land Contract Law (effective in March 2003). The two laws also sought to protect against the illegal seizure of land by local officials who then sell it for commercial development, while providing derisory compensation. Farmers are empowered to transfer land-use and to derive income from its use while local authorities are banned from revising the contract or confiscating the land during the contract period. This law marks a massive step forward in recognizing farmers' rights but it is still weak in terms of how to deal with local authorities that refuse to issue contracts.

Yet problems have continued and the Ministry of Land Resources stated that, in 2007, in some cities in central and western China almost 80 per cent of new land projects were illegal. In particular, the regulations did not stop the major source of problems in the countryside, the reclassification of land by local authorities from agricultural use to commercial or residential development. A problem for local governments is how to raise sufficient revenue to meet their fiscal obligations. Previously many had raised illegal fees and levies and relied on the agricultural tax to fund their activities. However, since becoming Premier, Wen Jiabao has cracked down on the use of illegal fees and levies and in 2006 announced that the agricultural tax would be abolished in its entirety. However, the money has to come from somewhere and many local governments have been engaged in converting agricultural land to commercial development land and making huge windfall profits.

In comments made in December 2005 but only published in January 2006 in the *People's Daily*, Wen Jiabao criticized illegal land seizures to raise public funds and claimed that all levels of government and party should take this seriously. On 27 January, Hu Jintao picked up the theme at a Politburo meeting and urged resolution of the major 'contradictions and problems' faced in the countryside. Unless this was done he said the party would not be successful in building a comparatively prosperous society. Guangdong, home to some of the biggest problems, began the process of trying to clean up land transactions. In February 2006, the provincial leadership announced that they would set up requisition rules to introduce uniform compensation standards with funds paid directly to affected farmers using a real-name compensation scheme to avoid different levels of government siphoning off the monies. These new rules would require project developers to pay into designated compensation accounts before seeking provincial approval to requisition land. Also, verification documents had to be obtained from farmers' organizations after paying funds to the farmers. They called for public hearings to discuss compensation standards with farmers unless the farmers chose to opt out. However, a verification document was to be signed by no less than two-thirds of the farmers' representatives.

In October it was announced that the State Council had authorized the Ministry of Land Resources to supervise and overhaul land use by local governments. A national office was to be set up to oversee land use with nine regional bureaus. This followed the issuance in September of an urgent notice on controlling land supply. This noted that local leaders would be penalized if they failed to stop or investigate illegal land sales and officials would be prosecuted if they sold land below its minimum price. These land transactions were also seen as being behind the huge surge in fixed asset investment: 30 per cent in the first half of 2005.

It was clear that some kind of policy needed to be promulgated but divisions existed over just how much authority farmers should be given over the land they farmed. Privatization and sale could not be mentioned as this would undermine the notion of land being collective in the countryside. In the first half of 2008, officials noted 25,231 cases of illegal land use nationwide (Reuters, 20 October 2008). Thus, in October 2008, the CCP issued rather unclear new regulations that allowed farmers to lease their contracted farmland or transfer their land-use rights. This was intended to make farming more efficient by increasing the scale, allowing more agribusiness, and was seen as a crucial part of policy attempts to double farmers' incomes by 2020. The development of more effective agribusiness was seen as crucial to guaranteeing China's food supply with more efficient enterprises replacing the fractured household farms. Markets for land leases and land transfers were set up to allow exchanges and sub-contracting to take place. However, the document was careful not to imply that land could be bought and sold. The notion of collective ownership of land was maintained and farmers were just allowed to 'sublet, lease, swap and transfer' land rights. In addition, it was stated that such actions should not change the land use, thus trying to restrict the large amounts of rural land that are converted to urban use each year (*Caijing*, 20 October 2008). It is not clear that these new regulations have improved the situation.

Economists have stressed the necessity of clear individual property rights for China's farmers but it is not clear that this is what many of them want. Interesting research by Kung and Liu (1997, pp. 33–63) reveals a more nuanced picture. Their study of eight counties reveals that 62 per cent preferred the situation under which land was periodically reassigned among families in response to changing demographics.

In fact, only 14 per cent of those surveyed said that they supported *de jure* land ownership. It was true that a majority (65 per cent) favoured longer contracts, but those from more affluent villages consistently preferred shorter-term contracts. A 2003 Ministry of Agriculture survey found that 86 per cent of the families in their survey had participated in land reallocations.

This and other anecdotal evidence seem to challenge the conventional view of the security of property rights and the relationship to family investment in agriculture. A number of factors are important. Kung and Liu stress the desires of the farmers for a more fluid system. This they trace to the persistence of the strong egalitarian spirit that has remained in many villages despite the inegalitarian reforms launched from 1978. With no social security system for the overwhelming majority of farmers, land is an important guarantee and periodic redistribution can help deal with demographic fluctuations. This has become more pressing with the migration of many away from the village, often meaning that land is left fallow or other farmers are brought in to work the land. Third, it clearly reflects general practice in many rural villages. In many villages that I visited down to the present day, land was periodically reassigned irrespective of the existence of contracts. Kung and Liu (1997, p. 54) note that at the end of 1996 barely over half of China's villages had renewed land contracts in line with 1993 policy, and only 20 per cent were contracts for 30 years. Most of the contracts were signed for 10, 5 or even fewer years. They attribute this also to farmers' desires based on their survey. However, it is clear that village authorities are reluctant to relinquish such a major mechanism for exerting power and patronage. As we have seen earlier, state power in the countryside remained strong throughout the reforms.

In fact, even the introduction of the household responsibility system was more complex than some authors have suggested; these see it as a case of farmers exerting their power over hesitant and obstructive bureaucrats (Zhou, 1996). In 1979, a mere 0.02 per cent of production teams had adopted the household responsibility system, but by the end of 1983 this figure had risen to 97.8 per cent (Yiping Huang, 1998, p. 158). In many areas the new system was not the result of spontaneous farmer dismantling of the collective agricultural structures but enforcement of a new policy line from above. This was especially the case in Heilongjiang where the mechanized grain-farming appeared to favour collective structures. Unger (1985–6, pp. 585–606) conducted a survey of emigrants to Hong Kong from 28 villages in China. Of the 28 villages, 26 had decollectivized to family-based agriculture by the end of 1982; 24 claimed that the type of system adopted was decided above the village level and only in two villages had village cadres and farmers taken the initiative themselves. With the massive extension of the policy through 1983, direction from above can only have increased.

In January 1985, in a further radical move, the state announced its intention to abolish its monopoly over purchasing and marketing of major farm products. Instead of the state assigning fixed quotas for farm products to be purchased from farmers, a system of contract purchasing was to be introduced. All products not purchased in this way could be disposed of on the market. Clearly, the aim of this reform was to improve the distribution of commodities and further reward efficient producers. It was hoped that this would encourage wealthier peasants to reinvest capital and labour in the land. Essentially, the contract procurement system was intended to establish a market relationship between the state and the peasantry and between the urban and rural areas.

This new measure was a massive shock to the agricultural system and challenged the old economic assumptions on which it was built. It led to the breakdown of the unequal terms of trade between the rural and urban areas under which an estimated 600–800 billion *yuan* had been extracted from the peasantry over a 30-year period. New channels opened for the circulation and marketing of surplus grain and other agricultural products. However, the state could not increase the price of grain to the urban dwellers and thus returns on grain production began to decline and in some instances money could even be lost on grain production. For example, between 1983 and 1985, average prices paid for chemical fertilizers rose by 43 per cent and those for pesticides by 83 per cent, reducing net income gained from 1 hectare of grain by about 30–40 per cent. In comparison with cash crops, grain production was no longer a lucrative activity.

The initial agricultural reforms had thus provided a major boost to the rural sector, but by 1985 were beginning to falter. Grain production increased from 305 million tons in 1978 to 407 million tons in 1984, only to fall back to 379 million tons the following year, the second largest fall in grain production in PRC history. Further growth in rural incomes began to slow, from 17.6 per cent per annum from 1978–84 to only 5.5 per cent by 1987. Finally, the income gap between rural and urban areas that had been coming down began to widen again, and by 1986 it was 2.33: 1, worse than it had been at the beginning of the reforms. It was not really until 2003–04 that the leadership made another concerted attempt to deal with rural problems. In the meantime, especially after the demonstrations of 1989, policy focused on rapid economic growth in the urban and coastal areas in order to buy support from the urban populations.

From 1985 onwards policy vacillated primarily over what to do about grain production and procurement. This was an essentially statist perspective as the government was concerned primarily to ensure adequate food supply to the urban areas at a reasonable cost. It did little to boost rural incomes but the system of state control did allow for state grain agencies to make a tidy profit. Until the late 1990s rural policy was left in a never-never land that was governed neither by the market nor the central plan. Also affecting rural production was the state's decision to cut its investment in the agricultural sector from 10 per cent of the capital construction budget in the period 1976–80 to 3.9 per cent for 1986–90. In part, this cut was to make up for the massive subsidies that were necessary to cover the increased price of grain. CCP fear of urban unrest made it impossible to pass on the price rises to residents. The expectation was that the collectives and/or individuals would take up the investment, thus offsetting the reduction in state funds. The effective collapse of the collectives as powerful economic entities sealed off one of the alternative sources of funds. The newly emerged townships used their funds to invest in the TVEs, a point returned to below. Initially, individual households were wary of reinvesting profits because of their uncertainty about how long it would be before policy would change yet again. When they did begin to invest, it was not in grain production but in more lucrative cash crop or sideline production. These problems led the state to abandon the contract procurement system before the reform had been properly carried out. Under the system there was dual pricing, with the state buying the grain needed for urban consumption and state industry at artificially low prices, while allowing surplus grain to be sold at free-market prices. Eventually, the difference between the two price systems was to be eliminated.

The grain procurement bureaus were kept afloat by loans from the Agricultural Development Bank that had to be repaid only once the grain was sold. This produced a large empire that profited from the old system. It controlled 80 per cent of the grain wholesale trade and 50 per cent of the retail trade through 52,000 urban retail enterprises. There were over 1 million employees. They were often able to arm-twist the state into lending more money as maintaining grain self-sufficiency was a key priority. Most of the subsidies were never passed on to the farmers. In Anhui Province, the central government provided procurement bureaus with around 4 billion *yuan* each year, but only around 400 million *yuan* was passed on to the farmers. The agencies were also a source of corruption, buying grain at low state prices and then selling on once market prices moved higher.

Premier Wen signalled an end to this system and in June 2003 the government announced that it would pay subsidies directly to the farmers. The farmers were to decide what to plant based on market circumstances and would receive government subsidy if the market slumped. The state grain bureaus had to compete with private grain merchants without their preferential loans. This policy was based on experiments carried out in 2002 in two counties in Anhui, often a rural reform leader. In one county, the reform resulted in laying off half of the staff and the official responsible thought that with loans cut off it was debatable whether it could compete.

These kinds of problems and the unrest that has come from stagnating incomes and rising local levies have moved rural policy back to the centre of the policy stage and under Premier Wen it has become a key priority. The land concentration, the loss of work in grain-farming and the recognition of the link between poverty and exclusive engagement in agricultural, especially grain production, will cause even more people to move off the land in the future. In fact, this has been promoted by the government with its tolerance of increased migration (see Chapter 11), its desire to boost rural enterprise development and push on with urbanization.

In 2006 in the run-up to the NPC session the leadership began to talk of the need to build a 'new socialist countryside' and this was pulled together at the meeting. The seeds of the new policy were planted in 1998 with the discussions of the 'three-dimensional rural problem' (*sannong wenti* – agriculture, village and farmer). From 2004, the leadership revived the tradition of the CC and State Council Document Number One addressing rural affairs: e.g. 2004, raising farmer's incomes; 2006, building a new socialist countryside; 2008, consolidating the foundations of agriculture; 2010, boosting job growth and rural consumption. The crux of the policy was to maintain farmers' income through agricultural productivity gains and improvement in village governance. Governments at all levels were instructed to make sure that they took rural issues as a top priority. An important December 2005 CCP CC and State Council document that paved the way for the 2006 discussions and the NPC meeting noted 'agricultural and rural development are still arduously crawling uphill, basic infrastructure is weak, rural social service development is backward and the contradictions of a widening urban-rural income gap remain stark'. The intention was also to redirect finances from the urban areas and the coast.

The policies pulled together involved the elimination on restrictions on labour migration and the eradication of discrimination against migrants and increased government spending on education, health and infrastructure (see Chapter 11 for rural social policy). In addition, the aforementioned protection of land rights was pursued and grain and livestock subsidies and price supports were regularized to boost rural income. Last but not least, the agricultural tax was abolished. This followed earlier attempts to consolidate all fees into taxes that had been experimented with in Anhui province. Heilongjiang and Jilin had already abolished the tax in 2004 and by early 2005, 22 provinces had abolished it. Overall, the share of the agricultural tax in the fiscal budget was small (1.7 per cent) but in some provinces it played an important role. In Anhui, it amounted to 12.1 per cent and 11.3 per cent in Henan. For these provinces and those where the agricultural tax amounted to over 5 per cent, the centre agreed to provide support.

Developing off-farm employment has provided a vital income source. While urbanization is a conscious policy choice, the massive migration was not foreseen nor was the expansion of township and village enterprises (TVEs) that have employed in excess of 100 million during the reform period. TVEs have been hailed as one of the wonders of the reforms by Chinese and foreigners alike. By the mid 1980s with farmer income stagnating, one of the best ways to increase it was to stimulate non-grain and non-agricultural production. In 1978 TVEs employed around 25 million but between 1984 and 1997 they created nearly 100 million non-farm jobs. After a shake-out in the late 1990s, employment began to rise again and stood at 154.5 million in 2008. In 1990, those working in this sector surpassed the number of employees in SOEs. The development of these enterprises, as we have seen in Chapter 7, also meshed with the political requirements of local governments, who saw them as a regular source of revenue in a resource-constrained environment.

The TVEs built on one of the enduring legacies of the GLF, the commune and brigade-run industries that had been set up to serve the rural areas. However, these were not little budding sprouts of entrepreneurship and were restricted to the production of the 'five products' of iron and steel, cement, chemical fertilizer, hydroelectric power and farm tools. Their role was limited and in 1978 the rural areas accounted for only 9 per cent of industrial output, while 90 per cent of the rural labour force was engaged in agriculture. However, it is true that employment in rural industry was increasing at 20 per cent per annum from 1970 to 1978 (Naughton, 1995, pp. 144, 146). The reforms changed this and while initial policy measures were intended to use rural industry to divert more resources to the countryside and strengthen the collective, policy changes had a dramatic effect on its role. The results were unexpected, as Deng Xiaoping noted: 'what took us by complete surprise was the development of TVEs ... All sorts of small enterprises boomed in the countryside, as if a strong army appeared suddenly from nowhere. This is not the achievement of the central government ... This was not something I had thought about. Nor had the other comrades. This surprised us' (*Renmin ribao*, 13 June 1987).

Of special importance was the decision to relax the state purchasing monopoly on agricultural goods, making them available to local rural industry. It soon became the most vibrant part of the economy, soaking up excess rural labour, processing agricultural products and diversifying production into a range of consumer goods and products for export. The growth rate was explosive, with rural industrial output growing at 21 per cent per annum from 1978 through to the early 1990s. By 1997 they produced almost 28 per cent of China's GDP and nearly 50 per cent of all industrial exports (Johnson, 1999, p. 11).

The presence of a ready labour force was crucial to the expansion of the TVEs and the introduction of the household responsibility system made this available. Moreover, it was a relatively cheap labour force compared to what industry had to pay in the urban areas. At the same time, costs were at or near market prices for water, electricity and raw materials, unlike for the SOEs that received their inputs at heavily subsidized rates. While taxes on TVEs were low (indeed, they were granted an initial three-year tax break), budget constraints were much harder than in the SOE sector. This meant that there was a greater incentive to produce things that would have a market and that would produce a good rate of return on investment. Finally, these TVEs were extremely flexible in terms not just of what they could produce but also in terms of their organizational structure (Naughton, 1995, pp. 156–7). They ranged from those run by local governments to ones that were more genuinely independent in nature. However, as Wong (1988, pp. 3–30) has shown, through the 1980s most of the supposedly collective TVEs operated in practice as private enterprises. The use of the term 'collective' became a flag of ideological convenience to what was becoming the wholesale privatization of rural enterprise. Huang (2008) has challenged the conventional view that TVEs were collectively run or were covered with a 'collective hat' and that it was the economic pressures of the late 1990s that caused most to be privatized. Huang notes that the Chinese definition of a TVE is defined by location but that if one looks at ownership even in 1985, of the 12 million TVEs, 10 million were actually private and every single net entrant between the mid 1980s and the mid 1990s was a private TVE. TVEs were most vibrant in the poorest and most agricultural provinces of China (Huang, 2008, p. xiv and 31–2).

The growth of these rural enterprises was also strong in areas such as Southern Jiangsu (*Sunan*), around peri-urban Shanghai, and in the Pearl River Delta (Naughton, 2007, pp. 282–4). In fact, the enterprises in Southern Jiangsu gave the name to the *Sunan* model of development based on the profusion of small-scale rural industry. In these areas, their growth was closely linked to the proximity of urban SOEs. With the shift to the taxation system for SOEs from the previous profit transfer system, they had money to invest and many began to outsource their production to the rural enterprises where land and labour were considerably cheaper. For example, in 1988, Jiangsu, Zhejiang and Shandong, while accounting for just 17 per cent of the rural population, had 43 per cent of rural industry, with half of all township and village-level industrial output (Naughton, 2007, p. 279).

However, in the later part of the 1990s dramatic changes took place in the TVE sector. First, the retrenchment of the economy caused many

TVEs to go under; some estimates have suggested that 30 per cent went bankrupt. Second, they became more capital-intensive, and as a result little new employment was created. Third, their limited and dispersed distribution networks and poor management became more of a liability. Fourth, the tendency noted by Wong of TVEs to hide effective privatization became more apparent. Research by Park and Shen (2000) on 15 counties in Jiangsu and Zhejiang revealed a massive trend towards privatization. In 1994 only 92 of the 415 enterprises surveyed were private, but by 1994 the total was 231 and it has risen since. The magazine *Caijing* reported that by the end of 2001, 93.2 per cent of the 85,000 TVEs in Southern Jiangsu had switched to private or stock companies. If Huang is correct about the 1980s, private enterprise has played an even more important role in China's development than is generally recognized and certainly this is clearly the case by the turn of the century.

Industrial policy

Unlike the rural areas, the state has continued to be the dominant player in urban China but gradually even here economic pressures compounded by China's entry into the WTO have forced significant changes on the nature of industrial production. Reforming the industrial sector has been the most difficult challenge for the central leadership as it goes to the core of the economic system that was set up under the central plan. Reform undercuts the interests of powerful bureaucracies that were set up to run the system and the working class of whom the CCP was to represent the most advanced elements. As a result, reform has been stop-go. Throughout the 1980s and the early 1990s, leaders generally backed off from reforms whenever representatives of the heavy industrial sector squealed loudly enough or when the fears of social instability arose. This changed by the latter half of the 1990s when it was clear that difficult reforms could be delayed no longer. The earlier strategy was in Naughton's (1995) memorable term to 'grow out of the plan' by adding capacity in the collective and private sector and opening up the economy to significant foreign direct investment and international trade.

Delay in fundamental reform also initially derived from the lengthy learning process that the leadership underwent in grappling with this sector. It took a long time for central leaders to realize that simply stressing technological upgrading, improved management, limited autonomy and expanded market forces did little to improve the health of SOEs unless the external environment was significantly reformed and a proper sequencing of reforms introduced. Indeed, as the work of Steinfeld (1998) has shown, tinkering with these aspects could actually make the situation worse. As he argues (1998, p. 4), China lacked the key institutional mechanisms needed to make corporate governance, and by extension property rights, function for producers in complex market settings. The problem was compounded by the fact that many SOEs had become net destroyers of assets, with what they consume being of far greater value than what they produce. The dilemma for the government is that they still provide significant revenue for all levels of government: in 1995 amounting to 71 per cent of total revenue.

Just as the reforms of the agricultural sector began to run out of steam in 1984, the leadership turned its attentions to reform of the urban industrial sector. By 1984 pressure had increased for further reform of the industrial sector as it was clear that the industrial system was unable to meet properly the needs of the increasingly commercialized, decentralized agricultural system. Indeed, the reformers used the successes of the rural sector to argue for the implementation of similar measures in the industrial sector. However, it was much harder to transfer these experiences to the urban environment where production was more socialized and bureaucratized. The need for further reform and the reform experiments to date were recognized in the CC 'Decision on Reform of the Economic Structure' of October 1984 that offered a more thoroughgoing vision than the piecemeal experimentation that had previously taken place. However, in 1985–86, 1988 and again in 1990 when problems became apparent, orthodox leaders tried to bring the reforms to a halt by reasserting the levers of administrative controls at the expense of market forces.

The key to the industrial reform programme was to make enterprises more economically responsible, and most important was the introduction of enterprise profit retention. In 1983, a system of tax for profit was introduced and this was adopted in the 1984 Decision as a policy for all enterprises. This new system replaced the old system of requisition of profits or covering losses and the initial reform experiments of profit contracting. The intention was that the tax system would stabilize state revenues and force enterprises to become more fiscally responsible. To ensure that enterprises could take proper advantage of the limited market opportunities, managers of factories and other enterprises were given greater power of decision-making with respect to production plans and marketing, sources of supply, distribution of profits within the enterprise and the hiring and firing of workers. While this provided the carrot, it was recognized by some that there should be a stick with which to beat inefficient enterprises and thus, after some delay, bankruptcy legislation was introduced in 1988, as was the Enterprise Law.

While opposition to the bankruptcy law centred on whether this had a place in a socialist economy, opposition to the enterprise law focused on the relationship of managerial authority to party control. The enterprise manager not only had constraints from the external environment in terms of decisions on key factors such as sourcing of inputs, sales of products, mandated staffing and wage levels, but had authority problems within the enterprise itself *vis-à-vis* the party committee. The passage of the Enterprise Law, by adopting the 'managerial responsibility system', seemed to resolve the debate by moving the party committee out of direct management. The events of 1989 did not lead to repudiation of the Law but opponents used the demonstrations to insist again on the paramount position of the party committee in the enterprise and have reiterated this periodically since.

As with the farmers, the main incentive to make workers work harder and raise labour productivity was to be a material one. Wage rises, bonuses and piece-rate systems were all tried to increase worker productivity, although the results were not remarkable. The politics within enterprises often have meant that the same bonuses are handed out to all and are seen as a part of the basic wage, thus undermining their purpose. Along with the carrot there also came a stick – the 'iron rice bowl', the name given to the system under which it was impossible to fire workers, was abolished. Lifelong tenure was replaced by a system of fixed-term labour contracts. In October 1986, a new labour contract law and supplementary regulations were introduced to cover the recruitment and dismissal of undisciplined employees. This new system was intended to reward those who worked well, provide the basis for dismissal of bad workers and, at the same time, cut down the costs of social security and welfare. Resistance to this new contract system was strong. Essentially urban workers were being offered a deal that involved giving up their secure, subsidy-supported, low-wage lifestyle for a risky contract-based system that might entail higher wages at the possible price of rising costs and unemployment. Leadership vacillation on the reforms persuaded workers to reserve judgement.

The overheating of the economy in 1993–94 and the increasing pressures for SOEs to become more profitable caused then Vice-Premier Zhu Rongji and his supporters to push for a more dramatic set of reforms to break China out of its stop-go industrial reform cycle. The question arose as to whether reform would be pursued any more vigorously this time. There were strong political reasons for central leaders not to pursue swift enterprise restructuring. The first and foremost remained the capacity of other sectors of the economy to absorb the absolute numbers of redundant workers and to develop an adequate social welfare programme. Over the years, the overblown staffs of many of these enterprises proved to be a viable political and social solution to the problem of inefficient industrial production, but now this was no longer financially feasible. However, economic pressures made it impossible for the centre to sit on the fence while the localities were pursuing *de facto* privatization. The World Bank (1997b, p. 1) estimated that in 1996, 50 per cent of SOEs lost money (unofficial estimates are higher). For the first quarter of 1996 the SOE sector slid into the red for the first time since the establishment of the PRC, with a net deficit of around $850 million. Two important reforms were introduced to attempt to help reform this sector. The first was the establishment of a social welfare system independent of the individual enterprises and regulated through the government (see Chapter 11). The second was to harden the budget constraints by gaining control over bank loans, trying to introduce better discipline over lending and commercializing loans.

It must have become apparent that over the long term government resources would be insufficient to pay depositors and bondholders if SOEs were unable to service bad debts. At the same time the state, with a declining revenue base, was unable to offer the same kind of bail-out, and subsidies declined. This made it virtually impossible for many SOEs to meet their full range of social obligations and even salary payments, thus in turn speeding up the need for pension, medical and housing reform. It is not surprising, then, that bankruptcies in 1996 rose by 260 per cent on the year before and that lay-offs rose despite official concern: the total of 6232 bankruptcies exceeded the total for the previous seven years combined.

Such statistics led the party leadership to decide, in a risky venture, to cut themselves loose from the working class that they had created in the 1950s and to reduce working-class expectations about what the state could provide. Rhetoric is still paid to the importance of the leadership of the working class, and policy is to give priority to finding work for laid-off workers. The reality, however, was that many were on their own to find new work in an economy that was increasingly unfamiliar to them and that required very different skills than those they learned under the Soviet-inspired system.

The ground for these changes was laid down in 1993–94 when the central leadership decided that a more coherent set of central policies was necessary to prevent the economy from overheating, and to prevent runaway inflation and local initiative and growth from escaping from central macroeconomic control. For the first time, the centre drew up a comprehensive statement of its reform plans and articulated them again in 1997–98. As Naughton (2000, pp. 56–7) has perceptively pointed out, by 1994 the reform agenda of the 1980s was basically completed and now the leadership had to deal with the tough parts of reform, such as the SOE system, the institutional impediments to rural–urban labour flows, the banking system and the integration of domestic markets with foreign competition.

In November 1993, the Third Plenum of the Fourteenth Party Congress adopted a crucial decision on the 'Establishment of a Socialist

Market Economic System', the details of which were thrashed out at a meeting held in Dalian in June 1993. The back-drop was the feeling that excessive decentralization had caused the centre to lose control over key macroeconomic levers of the economy and that prudent recentralization was necessary. Much of the devolution had been by default rather than by design, with some real decisions on fiscal, monetary, financial and foreign exchange issues residing with the localities. For the state to meet its reform objectives, it became clear that both prudent recentralization and institution-building was necessary. The decision had a number of components. First, a 'modern enterprise system' was to be established that would include reform of the organizational and managerial systems. Clearly defined property rights would be central, with each enterprise becoming genuinely responsible for its profits and losses and bankruptcy as a real option. Government interference would be reduced to enable the enterprises to function properly in the marketplace. Second, it fleshed out the extension of the market in the Chinese economy that had been raised at the Fourteenth Party Congress. Crucially, for the first time, a CC document saw that economic reform required reform of the financial system – including taxation, banking and monetary systems – and laid out objectives. A rational division of taxes between the centre and local authorities was to be devised to replace the annual tug-of-war that currently existed. In monetary policy, the major reform was to allow the People's Bank of China to function as central banks do in other countries. It was to implement monetary policies in an independent manner and to distance itself from provincial political interference by letting the head office take responsibility for the regulation of the scale of the loans. Further, the document recognized that more flexibility needed to be introduced into the social security system and that serious problems existed in the agricultural system.

Subsequent policy has marked a clear commitment to a mixed economy, with theoretical continued dominance of the state sector and with attempts to shift to a more regulatory state. The first reform was to reduce the number of SOEs starting with a policy to reorganize state-owned assets and the formation of large enterprise groups was still to be the focal point, under the policy of 'grasp the large and release the small' (*zhuada fangxiao*). This meant that small- and medium-sized enterprises (SMEs) would be turned into a variety of non-state forms through the expansion of shareholding systems, formation of joint-ventures or sale to interested parties (see Huchet, 2000). The number of SOEs to be kept under state control was progressively reduced from 1000 to between 80 and 100. Surprising as it may seem, these large enterprise groups were to be modelled on the conglomerates of the *keiretsu* in Japan and the *chaebols* of South Korea. Senior Chinese officials feel that during the initial developmental phase such industrial conglomerates can play a positive role, and they claim that they will abandon the model before it has outlived its usefulness. There may indeed be some efficiency benefits to derive from the formation of larger entities. As Huchet (1999, p. 5) pointed out at the time of the reform, China held some unenviable records for the fragmentation of its industrial structure. For example it had 8000 independent cement producers against 1500 throughout the rest of the world. China's leading company had only 0.6 per cent of the national market; it had 123 manufacturers of cars and 1500 steel works. Thus, in part the drive for mergers came from the enormous surplus production capacity in Chinese industry as well as the demands of WTO entry. The leadership felt the need to build up a certain number of world-class, major conglomerates to compete in the global economy: the dream of being in the Fortune 500 list seems irresistible! In 1997, China announced its hope to develop 120 such worldbeaters, i.e. companies such as Changhong in Sichuan, already the seventh-largest producer of televisions in the world. These conglomerates would get priority not only with access to loans but also when listing on the stockmarket, including those overseas. They were also allowed to set up finance companies for internal use and trade overseas without going through state training companies (*FEER*, 21 May 1998, p. 12).

This formation of large enterprise groups was a core element of the September 1999 CC decision on the further reform of SOEs; not surprisingly, it represented a compromise that sought to steer a middle course. Thus, it did not mention radical local practices such as the sale of the large number of state firms, nor did it cite targets for converting large state firms into shareholding companies. However, it did encourage SOEs to pull out of certain sectors of the economy where there were adequate alternatives and once again stressed a mixed ownership system. Yet, the question of managerial autonomy was still ambiguous, as the document stressed the importance of guidance of enterprises by party committees. Party organs were described as the political nucleus within enterprises. At the same time, it called for a modern corporate system to be established with clear ownership and the separation of the enterprise from government administration. Enterprises were to enjoy full management authority and assume full responsibility for profits and losses.

The other important points were that the market was to ensure the survival of the fittest through the encouragement of mergers, standardization of bankruptcy procedures, lay-offs and the encouragement of re-employment projects. To soak up the unemployed, greater political coverage was given to the non-state sector of the economy. These serious reforms have produced a dramatically transformed industrial landscape. Local leaders saw the policy of promoting shareholding as a great opportunity to shed responsibility for the state sector and to raise some much-needed capital as well. However, the big sell-off also increased the potential for corruption and official speculation was great and clearly a number of local officials saw this as a major windfall or one last chance to get rich at the state's expense. 'Insider privatization' was rife. While state assets were diverted into individual pockets, the state was left to cover the debts. An equally severe problem was local authorities forcing workers to buy shares in enterprises so that they qualified as share-holding cooperatives. It is unclear how pervasive this practice has been. For already failing institutions, these one-time infusions of cash did not turn such enterprises around and local officials were often confronted by angry workers who had lost their life's savings. In addition, workers have been frustrated when they have discovered that their buy-in has not bought them a seat at the decision-making table; the majority of shares are held by the old management or local officials, who received them as a reward rather than through purchase.

The problems with corruption that accompanied this policy thrust and the tendency for powerful ministries and enterprises to develop monopolies that rely on political connections to ensure privileged funding caused reform to be slowed. Also, some of the major SOEs had become extremely profitable but the leadership under Hu and Wen were unable to access a sufficient amount of their profits to support their redistributive and welfare policies. The 1990s had seen a restructuring of the SOEs but it also saw the state maintaining and even expanding its role in the urban economy. Huang (2008, p. 173) has described the Shanghai model that held sway in the 1990s as one of 'substantial urban biases, huge investments in state-allied businesses, courting FDI by restricting indigenous capitalists and subsidizing the cosmetically impressive boom by taxing the poorest sections of the population'. This produced high GDP growth but lower growth in household income and massively disfavoured the rural sector. This clearly did not mesh with Hu and Wen's policy priorities.

The policy of 'grasping the large and releasing the small' was later supplemented by the policy of ownership transformation (*gaizhi*). This transformation of the system of ownership covered any structural change to the firm including public offering of shares, internal restruc-turing, bankruptcy, employee shareholding, open sales, leasing and joint-ventures. An interesting study by Garnaut, Song and Yao (2008) of 683 enterprises in 11 cities found that increasingly restructuring became more oriented to privatization with an increase in share ownership by private investors. There was a 'loss of state assets' in the process that derived mainly from price discounts and land-use rights by local govern-ments to new owners in exchange for them agreeing not to sack too many workers. However, restructured firms did sack more workers in a year of change but then had a lower rate than the SOEs subsequently. The process significantly improved profitability but did not raise investment rates or labour productivity. The authors conclude that this amounted to a new business model which abandoned the expansionary SOE model in favour of a new one gaving top priority to cost savings.

In May 2003, General Secretary Hu Jintao decided to launch a new approach to streamlining and improving the performance of the SOE sector. While Jiang's report to the Sixteenth Party Congress (2002) reiterated prior policy, including calling SOEs 'the pillar of the national economy' while continuing to diversify the nature of public ownership, Hu's approach differed. It abandoned the primary focus of selling off smaller SOEs that had produced much corruption: some estimates put the loss of state assets at $41 billion. The new plan separated ownership and management of SOEs, with ownership transferred from various ministries to a central State Asset Supervision and Administration Commission (SASAC, set up in June 2003). The Commission initially took over 196 of the largest SOEs with combined assets of $834 billion, including the national airline Air China, national oil companies and major telecommunications, steel and auto companies (Economist Intelligence Unit, 28 May 2003). The new Commission hoped to enhance management, reduce corruption and try to restructure 30–50 SOEs to become internationally competitive. By the end of 2007, the number had dropped to 152 and the commitment was to reduce this number further.

These SOEs became increasingly profitable and a major issue arose over who should control the profits of these enterprises. In April–May 2005, the role of the State-owned Assets Supervision and Administration Commission (SASAC) was strengthened with new regulations that prohibited management buy-outs at large SOES, closed loopholes and set out terms for these at smaller enterprises. It also launched a policy to deal with how to convert non-circulating shares of companies listed on the stock exchange into circulating shares. The statist thrust of policy was shown in the announcement in December 2006 by the State Council that in seven strategic industries state capital would have absolute control (armaments; oil and petrochemicals; civil aviation; power; coal; shipping; telecommunications). Earlier in September 2006, the Ministry of Commerce was given expanded power to block foreign purchases of Chinese companies. As the Vice-Minister commented, 'foreign companies ultimately aim to eliminate competition and monopolize the domestic market'.

Most important was the move to gain greater control over the profits and dividends of the SOEs (this is based on Naughton, 2008). SASAC engaged in battle with the Ministry of Finance, which claimed that it would be able to disburse the funds in a more effective manner than SASAC. The funds were significant. The 152 SOEs that were under SASAC in 2007 earned profits of 1 trillion *yuan* (4 per cent of GDP) up from 300 billion *yuan* (2.2 per cent of GDP) in 2003 when SASAC was established. The combined profit had risen by some 223 per cent (*Financial Times*, 16 March, 2008). While profits declined by 10 per cent in 2008 as the financial crisis began to be felt and only began to settle down in the third quarter of 2009, the sums involved are still considerable. The SOEs under SASAC showed profits of 679.7 billion *yuan* ($98.5 billion) and returned taxes of 1.44 trillion *yuan* ($210 billion). In January 2010, profits amounted to 74.33 billion *yuan* ($10.9 billion). Since the reforms of 1994, enterprises had not returned profits to the state-only taxes. Given the parlous state of most enterprises this was not especially important. Further, listing on the stock exchange did not return any dividends to the state. In December 2006 it was announced that an asset management committee would be set up to deal with the sale and merger of up to one-half of the remaining SOEs and to help with the payment of dividends to the state. In September 2007, SASAC won its battle to gain control of a revenue stream but it had to give up control over the finances and received a lower share of the profits than it originally requested. This outcome reveals the emergence of major corporate entities in China as strong political players. Instead of the 20 per cent of profits that SASAC had hoped for, the enterprises were divided into three bands. Thirty-two SOEs returned nothing and these were mainly military industrial and research institutes. Ninety-nine SOEs (those seen to be in competitive industries) were requested to give up 5 per cent of profits with 17 firms (including the state tobacco monopoly) being required to remit 10 per cent. However, this last group did contain the most profitable enterprises and the initial remittances amounted to 2 per cent of enterprise profits. In fact, in 2006 nine firms had been responsible for 69 per cent of all the profits of SASAC-managed enterprises and seven of these were expected to pay at the 10 per cent rate. To sweeten the pill for the SOEs, the corporate income tax was reduced from 33 per cent to 25 per cent.

Some of China's SOEs are now becoming major players on the international stage making major overseas investment and trying to acquire overseas assets. This trend has been through their own initiative but also through a government-sponsored programme to 'go global' (see Alon et al., 2009). A number of major successful and failed deals woke up the international community to this new trend. For example, in February 2008, the Aluminum Corporation of China acquired a 9 per cent stake in Rio Tinto while the 2005 unsolicited bid by China National Offshore Oil Company for US oil company Unocal was rebuffed. By mid 2009, SOEs had overseas assets amounting to over $1 trillion and this was becoming an increasing management challenge for SASAC (ChinaStakes.com 12 May 2009). It has also developed into a challenge for the political authorities, with corporate players becoming major players on the global stage. For example, some have complained about the activities of the major company PetroChina in Sudan. One Chinese scholar even spoke of the company as having 'hijacked China's foreign policy in Sudan', something he deemed to be 'truly worrisome' (*Financial Times*, 16 March 2008). Investments in countries as far afield as Zambia, Peru and the Philippines have created problems that foreign ministry officials found embarrassing. As a result, SASAC and the Ministry of Commerce have begun a number of training sessions and are in the process of drafting regulations for the activities of SOEs overseas.

In addition, to marketization and decentralization, diversification of ownership has been an important part of the industrial strategy. The expansion of the non-state sector and also the growth of the service sector have been important in expanding employment opportunities, especially at a time when the SOE sector has been shedding jobs to enhance efficiency. In the late 1990s, if one included early retirees, perhaps 50 million jobs were lost in the SOE sector. We have seen above the major role that rural industry has played in China's recent development, but the private and non-state sectors in the urban areas have also been expanding and gaining increasing political acceptability. Diversification of ownership with the collective and private enterprise sectors providing competition is also seen as a way to improve the SOE sector. The entry of foreign firms, first through joint-ventures and subsequently as wholly foreign-owned enterprises, was seen as providing both the necessary capital, technological upgrading and enhanced management.

It is very difficult for definitional reasons to get an accurate picture of the private sector in China's economy (see Huang, 2008, pp. 13–19). The economist, Fan Gang, stated that the private sector accounted for 70 per cent of GDP in 2005 (*Business Week*, 22 August 2005) up from 22.4 per cent in 1978. According to official statistics in 2007, the gross value of industrial output from private enterprises was 26.9 per cent of that of the state-owned and state-holding industrial enterprises. The official number of private enterprises in 2008 was 6.6 million employing 79.0 million people with another 57.8 million said to be self-employed. The largest number of private enterprises are in Shanghai, Jiangsu and Zhejiang, with 29.2 per cent of the total, and Guangdong with 11 percent. Huang (2008, pp. 13–14) tries to calculate the size of the sector based on the assignment of key control rights such as those to appoint management, dispose of assets and set the strategic direction of the firm. This leads him to conclude that, in terms of industrial value-added, indigenous private enterprises contributed 22 per cent of the total and foreign enterprises 28.8 per cent, making a combined total of 50.8 per cent.

The figures suggest that there is still plenty of room for expansion of the private sector, especially in the service sector. China employs a low percentage of employees in comparison with other countries at a similar developmental level. With better protection and access to adequate credit the private sector could expand further. Laid-off state workers and even many college graduates look towards the sector for future employment. To many young Chinese it offers the attractions of a wealth that was unimaginable for their parents and a freedom from bureaucratic procedures and state intrusion into one's life that SOE work offers. While this might be true for some of China's new million-aires and middle management, reality is far more complex and many labour in sweatshop conditions with minimal labour protection and little chance for financial advancement.

The growth of the sector has been accompanied by grudging accept-ance and a battle over constitutional reform that sought to give the private sector better recognition, legal protection and to reduce political interference, thereby providing better access to credit and other neces-sary resources (see Box 10.1). Policy has moved far from the Seventh NPC (1988) that allowed private enterprises with more than eight employees to enjoy legal status for the first time since the early 1950s (Parris, 1999, pp. 265–6). During the 1990s after Deng's relaunch of economic reforms the sector grew rapidly. In addition to the need to provide employment, it became clear that those provinces with a higher level of private enterprise were also those that enjoyed a higher growth

---

Box 10.1: Measures to Improve the Status of the Private Sector

1986 Private share-holding first adopted in three Guangdong firms when employees bought 30 per cent of the firm's shares
1990 Shenzhen Stock Exchange opens
1991 Shanghai Stock Exchange opens
1997 15th Party Congress effectively adopts partial privatization policy and a mixed economy
1998 Banking system shifted from quota lending to profitability
     Banking shift from enterprise to consumer funding
1998 More export licenses granted to private firms
1999 Constitutional amendment is adopted to give private firms equal standing
2000 IPOs were opened to firms that were not SOEs
2001 Jiang Zemin's July 1 speech on admitting entrepreneurs into the CCP
2002 State Development and Planning Commission abolishes a number of restrictions on private firms
2003 March, All-China Federation Industry and Commerce proposes amendment to the Constitution to protect private property
2004 March, NPC approves the amendment
2007 March, NPC approves new Property Law after one-year delay
2009 October, Shenzhen opens Nasdaq-like board that will help private companies raise capital

and standard of living. For example, in Wenzhou and Taizhou, where the private economy is dominant, there is very little unemployment in contrast with towns like Mudanjiang in the Northeast that are dominated by old SOEs.

As noted, the sector was provided with political legitimacy in 1997–98 (see Chapter 4) and in 1999 the State Constitution was amended to record that the non-state sector of the economy was an 'integral part of the socialist economy' replacing the previous formulation that it 'supplements' the state sector. Politically, of course, acceptability was granted on 1 July 2001 when Jiang Zemin welcomed private entrepreneurs to join the party. Policy changes have also been introduced to boost the sector. For example, in 1998 the banking sector was instructed to shift from lending quotas to using profitability as the main criterion and this was accompanied by attempts to shift lending away from enterprise financing to consumer financing. More export licences have been granted to private firms, allowing them to acquire foreign exchange; in 2000, IPOs were to be allowed not just for SOEs while in 2002 the State Development and Planning Commission abolished a number of restrictions on investments by private firms.

Despite progress, problems still exist for the sector and the tax evasion and extravagant lifestyles of a few of the very rich have damaged the reputation of the sector and played to traditional prejudice against private entrepreneurs. Zhu Rongji was said to have become apoplectic when he discovered that some of the wealthiest people in China paid less taxes than he. Measures to promote the sector have been accompanied by a crackdown on corruption and tax evasion by individuals and an attempt to improve tax collection. The main complaint, apart from insufficient political recognition, is that of access to good business opportunities and credit to develop. The main state banks still tend not to lend to private enterprises and only one private bank exists in China. At the same time, it is very difficult for private companies to raise capital on the stock market. Opportunities for expansion are constrained and while lucrative sectors such as telecommunications are open for foreign investment, they are effectively closed to domestic private enterprise. In 2004 at the NPC meeting, a further constitutional amendment was passed to establish equal treatment for state and private property. This amendment recognized the 'right of citizens to own lawfully earned income, savings, houses and other lawful property'. This was followed at the 2007 NPC meeting by the passing of the Property Law, an Act that was delayed from the 2006 session because of strong opposition from groups on both the left and the right of the political spectrum. Those on the left, including some 3000 who signed a critical petition, claimed that private property had no place in a socialist economy. Some on the right complained that the law would protect and provide a legal basis for the corrupt gains of officials during the transition. This could now be passed off as legitimate property. Finally, in a measure designed directly to help private and smaller businesses, in October 2009 Shenzhen opened a Nasdaq-like enterprise board (ChiNext) to help companies raise capital (*China Daily*, 24 October 2009).

Financial sector reform

A key component for the success of economic reform in general, and SOE reform in particular, is the restructuring of the banking and financial sectors (see Huang et al., 2005). In the 1980s, financial reform was not really thought of as a part of economic reform, and if considered it was interpreted in the very narrow sense of banking reform. With a weak fiscal system banks were essentially used to meet the state's development objectives. However, by the mid 1990s reformers recognized the need for the overhaul of the sector and the necessity of cleaning up the banks' bad debts. This was given extra urgency, first by the Asian Financial Crisis and then by WTO entry that threatened a meltdown of Chinese banks unless they could improve their accounts. The changes have been dramatic and in just 15 years China has built up the framework of institutions that are necessary to run a modern financial sector. Given the short period and the lingering influences of the pre-reform system it is not surprising that there are still many problems that need to be resolved but nonetheless progress has been impressive. The banking system is diversified with a central bank, commercial banks, policy banks and a banking regulatory structure. Capital markets have developed in Shenzhen and Shanghai. However, as Naughton (2007, p. 451) points out, while the financial system has deepened, it remains 'narrow' in the sense that it is still dominated by the banking system.

With the main role of state banks being to feed the SOE sector, they built up a huge portfolio of non-performing loans, the true extent of which no one really appeared to know; estimates ranged up to 25 per cent of GDP. The situation with rural credit cooperatives is even worse. When Zhu Rongji took over responsibility for reform of the sector, he set in motion a number of reforms that have changed the sector beyond recognition, even though the remaining problems are huge, the largest unresolved reform issue in the eyes of some (see, for example, Lardy, 1998b). Zhu set in motion a series of reforms designed to free state banks from local politics, to allow the Central Bank to play more of a regulatory role and to get the non-performing loans off the books of the banking system. In 1994, the banking system was divided into three types of banks: commercial banks, policy banks and cooperative banks, with a limited but increasing role for private banks. The four major banks remained under the authority of the state but were given greater capacity to make loans on a commercial basis. These four banks (the Industrial and Commercial Bank, the Bank of China, the China Construction Bank and the Agricultural Bank of China) account for up to 70 per cent of the domestic banking business. It is important to remember that in China financial assets are essentially concentrated in the banking system as capital markets are small and bank loans are the most important source of capital for enterprises. The state's capacity for direct lending for its priority objectives was entrusted to three newly created 'policy banks' (China Development Bank, the Agricultural Development Bank and the Export–Import Bank of China) that would look after government-mandated lending. Despite this intent, the division has not been so clean in practice. The four commercial banks are still directed to lend to SOEs and they will also purchase bonds from the policy banks.

The next major steps were taken in 1998. With the onset of the Asian Financial Crisis and the realization that China's banking system was as perilously placed as many of those that collapsed in the surrounding countries, reformers were able to push ahead with financial sector reform. The first measure to be unveiled was an overhaul of the banking system, the centrepiece of which was the reorganization of the local branches of the People's Bank along regional lines to reduce political interference by powerful provincial party chiefs in lending decisions. The former 31 provincial branches of the People's Bank of China were reduced to 9 regional centres. As Zhu Rongji noted, the 'power of provincial governors and mayors to command local bank presidents is abolished as of 1998' (Lardy, 1998a, p. 86). 'Reduced' rather than 'abolished' is probably a more accurate assessment. The People's Bank of China was to strengthen its regulatory functions and operate more as a central bank, an authority it was granted only in 1995. However, central leaders remain ambivalent about commercializing the banking system. The extent to which and the speed with which the financial system should be opened has remained a key subject of debate. The Asian Financial Crisis and the Financial Crisis of 2008–09 convinced many that China's cautious approach and not opening the capital accounts prematurely was the right choice. The launch of the stimulus package has also urged caution and a more statist approach than some reformers would like. The package has certainly favoured the state sector over the private sector and thus one may presume that while experimentation will continue it will be very cautious on key questions such as openness of the fiscal system, the level of foreign engagement, and currency revaluation.

In 2003 at the NPC it was decided to set up a new oversight organization for the state banks, the China Banking Regulatory Commission, to help them improve corporate governance, shift lending to commercial criteria and intensify the effort to recover non-performing loans (NPLs). Resolution of China's NPL problem was seen as crucial to the future health of the financial system. A number of reform attempts have been made that have proved successful but the lack of transparency has caused some to worry still about the level of NPLs and the loosening of policy in the wake of the global financial crisis has furthered this concern that bad lending might again slip out of control. Official figures claim that in April 2009, the NPL ratio was 2.04 per cent of lending down from just over 6 per cent at the end of 2007 (*China Daily*, 14 April 2009). This does not include the historical legacy.

The first main measure to get NPLs off the books was the creation of an Asset Management Committee (AMC) for each of the four commercial banks. A write-down of the losses would have been impossible given their magnitude. The capital was provided by the Ministry of Finance and they are owned by the central government, not the banks themselves. To help clear up the problem of SOE debts, the AMCs acquired, at face value, loans from banks to SOEs. Initially 600 SOEs were selected to receive these benefits, later expanded to 1000. These SOEs were selected on the principle that they could become solvent once their debt was cleared, that there was a future market niche for them and that they were well managed. However, it is inevitable that some must have got onto the list because of local politics and connections rather than because of objective criteria (see Steinfeld, 2005).

The programme did not work in the sense of clearing up the bad loans but it did delay the problem until China's finances were healthier. In 1999 and 2000 some $169 billion worth of bad loans were transferred to AMCs, about 18 per cent of China's GDP in 1998 (Ma and Fung, 2002). This was funded through a mixture of cash and 10-year bonds. The AMCs never regained the 30–40 per cent value that was hoped for. The AMCs ran into problems with the cash recoveries that were below their interest obligations, thus creating cash flow pressures. As a result, the government tried to speed up asset recovery and this led to China's first international NPL auction. The banks also had difficulty resolving their own NPL problem as their customer base had not changed; it is still the major SOEs (Woo, n.d.). The AMCs, through the debt-for-equity swaps, were expected to gain a role in restructuring SOEs. However, Steinfeld (2000, pp. 22–7) in late 1999 found that the AMCs had little capacity or power genuinely to reorganize the SOEs. In fact, he notes that enterprise managers felt that the purpose of reform was to preserve assets as they were currently deployed in the existing firm. Many enterprise leaders felt that the fact that they had been put on the Commission's list was proof enough that they were a good company and required no further interference in their management affairs. However, the delay of repayment by purchasing 10-year bonds did mean that when payment fell due in 2009, the bill was a considerably smaller percentage of GDP than was initially the case. It amounted to less than 20 per cent of government revenue (Arthur Kroeber, ft.com/dragonbeat, 6 October 2009). The success of this strategy caused the China Construction Bank to roll over 247 billion *yuan* in debt for another decade (to 2019), a measure that one would expect other banks to follow.

The second measure was to remove 1300 billion *yuan* from three of the main four banks in 2004–05 as a part of the preparation for listing on the international stock markets. In October 2005, the China Construction Bank raised $9.32 billion in the first such initial public offering (IPO). This was followed by similar support for some smaller banks in 2007 and the support of 816 billion *yuan* for the fourth of the major banks (Agricultural Bank of China) in 2008. This means that a considerable tide of NPL has been built up that will fall due in the future. However, Kroeber has calculated that the net fiscal NPL costs would be substantial but not catastrophic by 2019. At most they would amount to 8.7 per cent of GDP depending on the growth rate. He writes 'there is no reason why existing NPLs, even including bad loans arising from the 2009–10 monetary stimulus should threaten the viability of the system'. Yet, this presumes that no more bad loans will be added over the next decade. Should this happen, Kroeber is less sure of the outcome. In major part, this is related to the shifting demographics that turn unfavourable and the naturally slowing growth rate that might decline from 10 per cent per annum to around 5 per cent. This would mean that growth could not write off the prior NPLs, only inflation. As a result, he proposes reforms now that would see banks really lending on a commercial basis rather than continuing to prop up an inefficient SOE sector.

Thus, despite extraordinary progress in economic reform, China's leaders face enormous future challenges. These stem from the problems of delayed reform and will provide a major test for the skills of the next generation of leaders. While there are grounds for pessimism, China has survived remarkably well to date and has avoided the various doom-laden scenarios that have been offered abroad. On the positive side, there is broad recognition that there is no alternative but to move ahead, and from the latter half of the 1990s China's leadership moved to a more comprehensive vision of the nature of reform and began to adopt a better sequencing for the reform programme.

Chapter 11

Social Policy

The impact of reforms on social policy has been no less dramatic than on economic policy. Reforms have produced new inequalities, a dramatic rise in the disparity between welfare provision in rural and urban China and an abandonment of the compact for cradle-to-grave social welfare for the privileged industrial working class. While the reforms may have raised the standard of living for the vast majority and shifted China along the road to a market economy, China's policy-makers have encountered considerable problems devising policies to bridge the social transition. State and collective institutions in rural and urban China that previously carried much of the welfare burden have been dismantled and policy-makers have struggled to devise new policies and institutions to carry the burden. As in other transitional economies, policy-makers have found it difficult to design new welfare systems, mostly because significant institutional change is inherently slower and more complex than macroeconomic stabilization and liberalization measures (see Kornai, 1997; and Nelson, 1997).

Insufficient policy attention persisted through the 1980s and into the first half of the 1990s. Initially, the leadership placed their faith in rapid growth raising all boats, lifting them all out of poverty, and in hopes that the market would provide the necessary services in sufficient quantities. In certain respects, by the late 1990s, the social welfare system had begun to resemble those of other countries in East Asia where the state has been reluctant to take on too great a responsibility for fear of creating a culture of dependency and diverting resources from investment in economic development. In the early-1990s, the central government began to focus on financial reforms and a more thoroughgoing reform of the state sector to prepare for WTO entry. During the boom years of the early 1990s little attention was paid to the social consequences of the reforms and there was a general assumption that high levels of economic growth would resolve all problems. However, by the end of the 1990s it was clear that not all had benefited equally from reforms and that inequality and differential access to services had become a major problem. It was clear that the social costs of restructuring and the attendant rise in unemployment could be significant and potentially destabilizing to the socio-political system as a whole. Consequently, the central leadership began to pull together local experiments with reform into a comprehensive policy framework for the privileged groups in urban China. This involved transferring responsibility for

297

social welfare from the workplace to local governments. However, the reformed system still left most people in rural China and those working in the informal sector to their own devices.

A third phase was launched when Hu Jintao and Wen Jiabao came to power in 2002–03. From the start, their rhetoric implied that they wished to redirect more resources to those who had not benefited from the reform programme to date. There was a wider recognition that some of the problems posed for social development would not be solved by growth alone. This realization led to a more coherent policy framework based on identification of vulnerable groups that were provided with targeted support. Policy is moving from thinking in terms of short-term safety nets to trying to weave the fragmented systems into more integrated, comprehensive systems. The policy agenda was presented at the October 2006 Sixth Plenum of the Sixteenth CC. The plenum, remarkable for its focus on social development, drew policy together under the slogan of 'building a harmonious society'. Among the policy measures were attempts to reduce income inequality, improve access to healthcare and education for those in the rural areas and for migrants, improve and extend the social security system, and invest more heavily in basic infrastructure for the western and northeastern regions of the country, and the rural areas in general.

Recognition that the state and its agencies can no longer handle their welfare obligations has led to the emergence of new service providers, some of which are operating on strict market principles, while others are taking a more philanthropic approach (see, for example, Wong and Flynn, 2001). Reforms have also changed notions of entitlement, with access to services much more tightly tied to financial capacity than in the past. The linkage of service provision to ability to pay has produced new inequalities and exacerbated old ones. In particular, there has been a dramatic rise in the disparity between welfare provision in rural and urban China and an abandonment of the old cradle-to-crave social compact for the privileged urban working class. Not only has this led to policy challenges to devise new institutions and mechanisms for service provision but it also raises more fundamental questions about citizenship and entitlement. To whom does the state have an obligation to provide welfare, and at what level?

The challenge is different for the urban and rural areas. In urban China the challenge is to shift from a system of severely frayed safety nets for the urban working class and officials to a clearer articulation of what China's citizens can expect in terms of welfare guarantees. In rural China, it is more a question of putting basic systems in place that can cover healthcare and education. The resultant policies should address the dualistic development strategy that privileges the urban over the rural. The literal fencing off of the rural from the urban during the Mao years made it easier for the city dwellers to enjoy their privileged position. The reforms have begun to tear down this fence and, as a result, it is increasingly difficult to justify this privilege in political terms. With increased market reliance and with the huge influx of rural migrants to the cities, the two worlds are now inextricably linked and they often share the same neighbourhood. The inequity of providing education and medical services to one while denying it to the other has become a source of tension, especially at a time of economic slowdown. Migrants and those who remain in the countryside need a clear indication from the central leadership as to whether citizenship, in terms of access to social welfare, will be extended to them through a gradual increase of access to social security and insurance schemes or whether they will be left to their own devices, private sector provision and family-based support. There have been encouraging signs of recognizing these problems.

This chapter looks first in general terms at the question of social policy and the transition in China, and then discusses a number of specific policy areas. As it is impossible to cover everything, it highlights a number of representative challenges: the difficult policy area of family planning, the attempts to cut the Gordian knot of urban workplace-based welfare, healthcare provision in the rural areas, the situation of migrants and poverty alleviation programmes.

Social policy and the transition in China

China shares two basic points of departure with all other countries in terms of how the welfare system is structured. First, the ideology and value system provide the basis for decisions about who gets what level of welfare support, and for how long. Second, the structure of the economy and the level of economic development affect the kind of welfare choices that can be made. Welfare is a crucial part of the institutional framework of the economy and attempts are being made to coordinate the two to meet the regime's objectives. Under Mao, the welfare system was seen as subservient to the demands of the economy and to the pursuit of socialism. In practice, this meant that social policy was closely tied to a development strategy that kept the rural and the urban separate, and privileged provision of the urban and industrial sectors over the rural and the agricultural. At the same time, the organization of the collective in the countryside and the inconsequentiality of cost meant that, for its developmental level, rural Chinese enjoyed a good preventive healthcare and basic education system. While they were subsequently derided, the paramedics of the Cultural Revolution known as 'barefoot doctors' do seem to have provided decent vaccination programmes and preventive care for many who would not have received them in other developing countries. This redressed somewhat the urban bias of the system.

There are a number of key features to social policy. First, in both the Maoist years and during the reform period, welfare policy has been subordinate to the demands of economic development, with policy structured to encourage greater participation in the workforce and to reduce the burden of the vulnerable populations on the state. The government has been unwilling to spend significant resources on what it sees as unproductive investments. This was reinforced by the adoption of a quasi-Stalinist approach to industrial development that did not see key public goods as comprising part of the productive forces (Lu Mai, 1999). The underlying premise that the best way to alleviate poverty and improve welfare is to boost production has been accepted by the post-Mao leaderships. They have eschewed policies of significant income redistribution to the poor and welfare will be expanded only as production increases. The obsession to boost production figures has never been seriously challenged by a need to divert resources away from immediate investment in production. Mao rejected any notions of 'welfarism' for the new workers' state and this has been faithfully adhered to by his successors. As Deng Xiaoping pointed out in 1980, while China had to increase education spending because it was among the 20 countries in the world that spent the least relative to GDP, this did not mean that China should become a welfare state. He noted that 'developing production without improving the people's livelihood is not right' but 'calling for an improved livelihood without developing production is not right either and cannot be attained'. However, before the reforms began, ideology did act as a constraint on too great an increase in inegalitarian distributional policies. This made the policy shift to a more inegalitarian wage policy and to an openly inegalitarian development strategy more difficult to accept. It has also provided the basis for Hu Jintao and Wen Jiabao's attempts to rectify the most obvious inequalities.

Thus, like its neighbours in East Asia, China spends relatively little on the provision of public goods and services, and out-of-pocket expenses for healthcare and education have been rising rapidly. This subordination has enabled the CCP to institutionalize its development priorities and reflect the vested interests of the communist *apparat*. Even under Mao these have not been redistributional in nature and post-Mao there has been no attempt to eliminate social inequalities and to build a classless society. Policy has provided selected targeting of state assistance and has shunned an elaborate system of universal entitlements.

The reforms have also eroded the full, or near-full, employment policy operated by the CCP, which was an important element of the production-oriented development strategy. Until the late 1990s, social policy was designed to encourage as much participation as possible in the labour force through providing support that would allow women with children to work. Second, unemployment relief was hard to come by, thus forcing those who could work into the labour force. Third, as many people as possible were encouraged to work. Before the reforms, urban China had a string of factories in which those who were physically handicapped worked. This increased production but also provided them with a wage, making them useful to the family and integrated them into a social network. With the financial bottom line now paramount, many of these factories have closed down, with negative consequences for many of the handicapped. With no effective welfare system to support them, they are now seen as a burden on the family and make up one group of the new urban poor.

Second, the underinvestment by the government has been accompanied by an emphasis on self-reliance and resolving problems *in situ* rather than looking to the higher levels of government for support. Although this has often been written of as a strategy for production, it was also a strategy for consumption. Localities could only consume the goods and services that they were able to produce locally. Thus, whereas intra-locale inequalities might have been limited, inequalities of service across locales could be quite significant. This had a lasting impact on the reform programme to date. As the main providers of public services, sub-national level governments in China have expenditure responsibilities that are quite out of line with international practice (World Bank, 2002, p. ii). The Maoist notion of 'self-reliance' reinforced the idea that each locality should minimize 'dependence' on support from higher levels. Throughout the reform period, the local levels of government have retained major responsibility for financing infrastructure and providing social welfare. In the pre-reform period, self-reliance was focused on the collective and the family, but now it is more likely to be seen as the responsibility of the family alone. Only very recently have there been attempts to spread a rights-based consciousness that sees access to a wider range of public goods and services as a key component of citizenship. What has dominated has been the caricature of quasi-Confucianism that stresses self-help, the support of the family, and the avoidance of seeking help, except as a very last resort.

Third, this has meant that the market and alternative suppliers have begun to play an increasing role in service provision. The form of *de facto* privatization that has been dominant in China has been supply-driven but there has been experimentation with demand-driven approaches. However, China's leaders have placed greater trust in the market (although this is viewed with suspicion by some) than in genuine non-governmental providers. Despite the natural Leninist resistance to an autonomous sphere of civil society actors, a controlled sector providing vital public service functions has emerged, with the church or temple becoming the key points for reciprocity for many.

Fourth, social welfare provision has reflected the bias of the official ideology, with preferential treatment for those living in the urban areas and employed in SOEs as well as for government officials. These key groups were seen as crucial to the industrialization drive and as important constituents for the CCP. The extensive array of benefits through the workplace compensated in part for the low wages paid in the pre-reform era. Such a reliance on the provision of public services through the workplace has provided an important policy challenge for the leadership, especially from the mid 1990s, as it has had to roll back benefits without undermining regime support. The kind of company support that existed in China and still exists to some extent has parallels to the company-based programmes in Japan and Korea. Esping-Andersen (1990) dubs this 'corporatist welfare'. It is even more pervasive in China. In fact, the heavy reliance on the workplace for service provision is a major distinction from other Soviet-style systems. It was at this level that most welfare was managed, with local government agencies only playing a residual role. One of the major challenges of reform has been to weave these fragmented systems into a more coherent whole by transferring welfare obligations to local state administrative agencies (Saich, 2008a).

This system exhibits two major differences from other countries in East Asia. First, it is difficult to speak of simply one system for public service delivery and second, the system is marked by even greater inequalities of service provision. Rural and urban China have operated under quite distinct systems, with the urban being consistently privileged over the rural. Even within urban China, the system is fragmented as those in government employment or working in SOEs enjoy types of support that are not available to those working in other sectors of the economy, especially in the informal sector that is home to increasing numbers of migrant labourers. In Esping-Andersen's term (1990), it is a truly 'Bismarkian' system, with relatively privileged sectors, underprivileged sectors, *and* totally excluded sectors. This system by its very design has institutionalized inequalities in a way that is absent from other systems in East Asia. The main division is between rural and urban, but there are also significant regional variations. China's inegalitarian development strategy deviates considerably from those of its East Asian neighbours whose economic development China is so keen to follow. Calculations regularly cite a Gini coefficient of at least 0.45 as against 0.33 back in 1980 and it may have risen to 0.50. While China is not as unequal as countries such as Brazil (0.61) or Mexico (0.52), normally thought of as highly unequal, it has surpassed other large developing countries such as India (0.38) and Indonesia (0.32). Welfare policy has been used as a safety net in the urban areas to catch those thrown aside by the economic juggernaut that is under constant pressure to produce more with increased efficiency.

A number of problems that have stemmed from this system are covered below. The cost of even the limited welfare provided became too high for the state to cover. Welfare costs rose from 3.1 per cent of Gross National Product (GNP) in 1978 to 6.2 per cent in 1990. Of this amount, 85 per cent went to cover costs for employees in urban enterprises. The costs of medical and pension provision rose the most rapidly and amounted to 50 per cent and 21 per cent of these expenditures, respectively (Leung, 1995, p. 221). The financial crisis in the SOEs meant that they could no longer carry the economic burden of providing the previous levels of social welfare for their workers. The abandonment of the commune meant that the collective health structures all but collapsed and have not been adequately replaced. The introduction of market incentives and a regard for profitability that did not exist previously has led basic-level institutions to shed their social costs or to turn them over to a fee-for-service system. The impact of this is seen particularly with respect to healthcare. In the mid 1970s China was frequently praised by international organizations for the level of healthcare provided given its low income level, yet in the *World Health Report 2000* the World Health Organization (WHO) ranked China 188 out of 191 countries in terms of the fairness with which its healthcare operates, 144th for overall performance and 139th in terms of healthcare per capita. While ranked above most African countries, it is ranked below other large developing countries such as India, Bangladesh and Indonesia. In terms of health quality achieved, it ranks somewhat better (61), but this may be because of the residual impact of the old collective medical system.

The bifurcation of development strategy into rural and urban components has set different starting points for reform and presents different challenges for policy resolution. Up until 1979, most had some kind of minimum guarantee, either through a job in the urban areas or the use of communal land in the countryside. In the urban areas, for those in SOEs there was social insurance provision and the workplace supplied housing and medical benefits. For the rural population, the government offered relatively little but there were provisions through the collective agreements. The support provided by the state was through the local offices of the Ministry of Civil Affairs. This was to provide the 'five guarantees' (to food, fuel, clothes, healthcare and burial) to the destitute with no family to care for them. This was subsequently extended to the urban areas. Those in the urban areas who worked in the non-state sector did not qualify for social insurance but did have access to social relief and welfare services, dependent on a means test. These are dispersed in two ways, either through the firm to laid-off workers or through the Ministry of Civil Affairs to those families whose income falls below a set minimum. Receipt of the first is especially unpredictable as it depends on the willingness and ability of the firm to pay. The second is more predictable but the numbers in receipt have been rising rapidly. When the system was adopted nationwide, some 4 million were receiving support under the minimum living standard scheme and the number stabilized at a little over 22 million by 2006 (23.3 million in 2008, for details see Saich, 2008a, pp. 174–83). The level is decided locally and ranged in 2005 from a high in Guangzhou (330 *yuan*) to a low in Yining (165 *yuan*) and Shenyang and Guiyang (170 *yuan*). However, the highest payout was in Beijing (234 *yuan*) with the lowest payout in the north-west – Xining and Yinchuan (66 *yuan*).

Redressing these problems has been a major challenge for Hu and Wen, coming at a time when the urban proletariat already sees its status and benefits being eroded by reform. Further, any significant shift of resources adversely affects the urban professional health and education networks that have resisted. Like most regimes, the Chinese leadership reflects the political bias of the most powerful, vociferous and visible groups and ignores the needy (Graham, 1997). As a result, policy has focused on the needs of state officials, has been receptive to the policy prescription of its professional classes and has sought to soften the blows of the market transition for the urban proletariat. By contrast, policy has left the rural poor, the migrants and the non-state-sector employees to their own collective devices and has ensured that they have remained politically marginalized.

Family planning: problems of policy coordination and policy evasion

The lack of policy coordination across different line ministries and the adoption of conflicting policies are familiar problems. For example, the quotas that each local bureau of a ministry sets for local farmers are decided independently of one another, with the result that the individual household becomes the point for reconciliation of conflicting demands to produce grain, plant trees and raise livestock. Here we look at the conflicting policies of the promotion of the 'one-child policy' and the household responsibility system as well as the unintended policy challenges that it has created.

The introduction of the household responsibility system set up incentives for households to increase family size rather than comply with the tightening of family-planning policy. Two primary reasons accounted for this. First, when land was initially parcelled out, it was allocated on the basis of household size and thus there was a benefit in having a larger family. Demographics played a major part in who got rich first in a village, with those families having a larger labour force of working age benefiting more than those families with both very young children and old grandparents. Second, the desire to increase family size was derived from the dismantling of the collective welfare system in the countryside. The policy message appeared to be that if you wanted to get rich and be looked after in your old age you needed more children. This was clearly true, but it was not what policy-makers had intended and they were concerned about the baby boom that Mao had set in motion in the late 1950s. They feared that the rapidly increasing population would undermine the economic gains that they hoped would come from the reforms.

In the 1970s, policy encouraged fewer and later births but this was tightened in 1979 under what became known as the 'one-child family policy', although for rural dwellers the policy was more relaxed (see Table 11.1). It has been one of the most unpopular and contested policies in China, especially in the countryside. In the urban areas not only is political control easier but also there are stronger economic incentives for families to consider a smaller family size. While many in China recognize the need to control population and may even feel that the policy is a correct one, many also have specific reasons about why it should not apply to them. The state set up an elaborate administrative framework throughout the system to monitor programme implementation. There are around 400,000 officials at the township level and 1 million in the villages. The State Family Planning Commission sets the national birth-rate and the provincial quotas; it is then the responsibility

Table 11.1 *Family Planning Policy in the 1990s*

Policy regulation	Group covered
One-child policy with few exceptions	All urban residents and rural couples in Jiangsu and Sichuan
Two children if first-born is female	Most rural families
Two children with a spacing of four years	Most rural families
Two or three children permissible	Rural ethnic minorities residing in minority autonomous region
No restriction	Tibetan rural population

Source: Based on Peng (2002).

of local family-planning officials to set out the birth quotas for their administrative jurisdiction. The burden for family planning falls on women and little attempt is made to involve men in the process. In each work-unit or administrative jurisdiction, there is a list kept of whose turn it is to conceive and often lists are kept of the menstrual cycle of women to facilitate control.

The fact that family planning was given the highest priority as a task for local officials meant the implementation often became coercive, even if this was not the intent of central policy-makers. For local officials one can meet all other quota targets but if that for family planning is missed then promotion is not possible. This and the general pressures generated by a quota-driven system have led to the frequently reported abuses of forced abortions and the forced sterilization of women.

However, even with such attention there has been policy evasion and ultimately policy amendment. In fact, the policy was not applied to minority households and in most of the countryside *de facto* policy was for 2 children or even 3. With increasing financial opportunities, those families no longer dependent on the state for grain and other basic products could afford to raise more children. In addition, they could afford to pay the fines that would be imposed on them. There have also been many cases cited of local officials who also preferred to pay the fine rather than reject the child. Other strategies have been used to evade this, such as not registering births of female children, or parking children with friends and relatives when officials may come round, or the repugnant use of female infanticide.

These demographic choices will weigh heavily on China's future social policy. The family planning programme has led to two major long-term consequences: aging of the population and a badly skewed male–female ratio in the population. The ageing burden will weigh heavily on China and the economy and society will feel the negative effects of higher dependency ratios and greater expenditures on elderly care. Overall, China will age 13.8 years during the first half of this century as opposed to the US, which will age 3.6 years (Hewitt, 2004, p. 103). This ageing during the process of industrialization and urbanization will keep up the pressure to maintain rapid and sustainable growth.

By 2030, China's population will be nearing its peak of around 1.52 billion (it will rise to 1.54 billion in 2040 before starting to drop) but it will be seriously skewed in terms of dependency ratios. At the end of the twentieth century, China officially entered the ageing stage in terms of internationally recognized criteria, with 10 per cent of its population over 60 years of age. The ageing population will set serious policy challenges in terms of dependency ratios and pension obligations that the state will have to meet. The structure of the population will be based on what Chinese researchers refer to as a '4-2-1 family', with four grandparents, two parents, and one child. The burden of support that this is placing on the current children is already leading to shifts in government family planning policy and some have even raised the question of whether China should give up on the 'one-child' policy for most urban families. The Population and Family Planning Law (2001) made it clear that the current population policy would remain in place but, in fact, policy now allows parents to have two children if both are from single-child families themselves. One major obstacle to reform is the Family Planning System itself. The officials represent a major obstacle to the lifting of the policy and it is common to find the Minister making public statements on the need to keep the policy in place for the time being.

The problem for policy-makers who wish to reform the system is that there is significant regional variation, making the preference for a 'one-size-fits all' solution less practical. Hussain has pointed out that an exclusive focus on the elderly dependency ratio, which is the focus of the debate around pension obligations, can be misleading. It ignores the large economic gains that come from the declining child dependency ratios (23.68) and these will accrue before the costs of ageing really begin to be felt. The regional variation is considerable. The 2008 total dependency ratio nationally was 36.72, with a variance from a low of 24.99 per cent in Beijing to a high of 51.94 in Guizhou. The highest child dependency ratio is in Guizhou at 39.57 per cent, with the lowest in Shanghai at 10.00 per cent. Conversely, Shanghai has the highest elderly dependency ratio at 16.50 per cent, with Tibet (9.34) and Ningxia (9.16) the lowest. The Northwest and the Northeast provinces tend to have the lowest elderly dependency ratios, while poorer provinces in the Northwest and Southwest, such as Guizhou, tend to have the highest child dependency ratios. Furthermore, the nature of support for these two groups differs (Hussain, 2002). For children, much of the financial cost and care falls on the household, with the state picking up a large part of the external education costs, for example. For the elderly, the household carries the main burden, especially in rural China, with the workplace and the local state carrying the pension burden for many.

Certain consequences arise from these demographics. First, China will have a significant pension obligation to deal with amid a declining workforce to cover the costs. Unless policy is changed, which it certainly will, contribution rates for workers that are currently around 20 per cent of payroll will rise to around 40 per cent by 2030. This would be economically intolerable and thus policy shifts will have to be made, such as raising the retirement age significantly and cutting the amount of benefit available. Second, ageing and especially the increase in the oldest old will lead to a significant increase in medical costs. China will have to hope that the economy keeps growing fast enough to generate the revenues to cover these costs. Third, with the lower fertility rate there will be a lower domestic savings rate but there will also be a higher return to labour because of its relative scarcity and a lower return to capital.

In addition to ageing, another adverse consequence of the family-planning policy is the distortion in the male–female ratios. Essentially, there are three ways to meet the strong demand for male offspring: have more births (and pay a fine); engage in female infanticide and generally discriminate against the girl child; or carry out induced abortions following prenatal sex identification. In some counties the reported differential between female and male children is alarmingly large. However, it is not at all clear how reliable the statistics are. For example, one early study shows that an underreporting of births accounts for between 50 and 70 per cent of the differential sex ratio at birth (Zeng et al., 1993). The current census (2000) shows that the sex ratio of males to females is 106.74:100, resulting in 41.27 million more men than women. However, at birth the ratio is 119.92:100 and by age four it is 120.17:100. Jiangxi and Guangdong have ratios of 138:01:100 and 137.76:100 respectively with rural Guangdong at a rate of 143.7:100 (Zhang Yi, 2003). One group of researchers has suggested that there could be as many as 100 million Chinese bachelors by the year 2020 (*SCMP*, August 25, 2003, internet edition). Such skewed ratios will have significant consequences for family structures and also for the capacity of families to take care of the elderly, perhaps requiring the state or civil society organizations to take on greater responsibilities. Other consequences are the increase in dowry price in the rural areas and the increased illegal trade in women and in prostitution. The thought of large numbers of males who cannot find a bride and drifting into cities looking for work is a potential cause for concern and the increase in clientele for commercial sex workers will increase the potential for the spread of HIV/AIDS.

Those pushing for reform have pointed out that other countries in Asia and elsewhere have also experienced a decline in fertility through the process of industrialization and modernization without resorting to the quota-driven and often coercive policy adopted by China. In addition, further integration with other policy areas is necessary for the problems to be overcome. First, China needs to develop a pension scheme not only for the urban areas but also for rural China that will alleviate reliance on the family as the primary source of support. Second, the family-planning programme needs to be integrated with rural development policy more broadly so that the kinds of policy conflicts noted above are smoothed over. Third, and most importantly, the work method of the family-planning agencies needs to be changed from a quota-driven, top-down operating agency to a service-oriented organization that relies more on participatory and educational approaches than in the past. There is evidence that this is beginning to happen through experimentation at the local level.

Reform in the SOEs: cutting the Gordian Knot

In urban China, the main concern of China's leaders has been how to move from a system of enterprise-based welfare to one where the government is the main provider and upholds minimum support levels. This has involved dismantling the hierarchy and privileges that existed within the planned economy and smoothing out the inequalities that existed between the units under the plan and those outside the system. This involves challenges to develop mechanisms to include the private sector and a question as to whether to integrate the large migrant populations into the urban systems. If the answer is 'yes', which services, and how? This is causing a diversification of service providers in urban China, with increasing acceptance of the role of the market in providing service, a demand for cost recovery rather than highly subsidized provision and an increasing space for non-governmental organizations to operate.

The move to a more market-influenced economy revealed the high costs that welfare provision placed on the SOEs and the increasing incapacity of this sector to bear those costs. In addition, the existing institutional structure inhibited the further development of a labour market. Labour mobility was highly restricted by the fact that pensions, medical care, but most importantly housing belonged to the work-unit. One of the most important days of the year was when enterprises announced the division of new housing units or reallocations for the next year. Many people would time their weddings to coincide with this division, while others might rush back from a trip overseas so as not to be left out. Many families have adopted the approach of '1 family, 2 systems'; one would work in the state sector to ensure maximum state benefits while the other would work in the private sector where financial rewards could be higher but where there would be no housing provided. Not surprisingly, the system also became prey to ever-increasing demands. While the workers made no direct contribution to benefits and paid little in rent, the improvement of benefits was a continual bargaining point at the workplace. Before stricter financial discipline was instituted, it was relatively easy for enterprise leaders to cede on this in return for industrial peace (Walder, 1986). Yet this created a culture of dependence on the workplace that was relatively hard to break.

The fiscal problems of the SOEs changed all this. Research by the Labour and Social Security Research Institute found that by 1998, 58 per cent of the total payroll comprised social security expenses, compared with 19 per cent in collective enterprises and 18 per cent in private ones (in Nielsen et al., 2005, p. 1762). Reforms have been experimented with since the mid 1980s, but it was in 1998 that Premier Zhu announced an end to the enterprise-based, cradle-to-grave care that the Chinese industrial working class and government employees had come to expect.

Policy thrust was to ensure greater individual responsibility through contributions to pension and medical and other insurances, and the privatization of workplace housing stock. At the same time, the old 'iron rice bowl' of permanent employment was smashed. The basic policy objective was three-fold: first, to reduce the welfare burden on the SOEs and redistribute the burden across enterprises and to individuals working in other ownership categories; second, to try to provide equal rights and levels of protection across all ownership categories; third, to establish linkage between the contributions an individual makes to his or her own benefits and what he or she actually receives (Nielsen et al., 2005, p. 1763). Certainly the burden on the SOEs has been reduced but the burden has not been picked up fully by other sectors of the economy. Attempts to extend benefits beyond the state sector have not been entirely successful. Here we shall concentrate on the policy challenge of building a new urban pension scheme.

China does not have a current pension problem, but unless it acts soon, demographics will turn unfavourable after 2010 and then it will have a major policy headache on its hands. In terms of policy priorities, the leadership recognizes it has a problem but not necessarily one of the most urgent to be solved. However, as discussed below, procrastination on this reform will carry very high costs in a decade or so. This was recognized by the head of the People's Bank of China in November 2006 when he called for the problem to be addressed while the finances were sufficiently buoyant to resolve it. He suggested that those with adequate savings should be encouraged to buy pensions and those who could not afford it should be helped with loans. He also recognized the problem of low returns on pension investments – only 2–3 per cent at a time when real wages were rising by about 10 per cent. Consequently, he suggested that greater use be made of capital markets (*Financial Times*, 21 November 2006).

During the Cultural Revolution, the enterprises inherited the responsibility for the management and payment of pensions, when the trade unions, which had previously managed them, were dismantled. Current policy is developing a more integrated system out of the former fragmented parts, together with the introduction of market elements, albeit rather tentatively. Once reforms began to bite, evasion of pension payment by SOEs became more common and compliance in many cities dropped from 90 per cent at the beginning of the 1990s to 70–80 per cent by 1995 (World Bank, 1997d, p. 2). Further, the demographics are not good. In 1995, there were ten workers for every pensioner, five among urban workers, but there would be only three by 2050, with some even suggesting that the ratio may drop as low as 2:1 by 2040 (Jackson and Howe, 2004, p. 6). This would make the contribution rate unaffordable. As in other areas, unitary policy implementation is made more complex

by the varied environment. In a city like Shanghai, where the family planning programme has been especially successful, the population is ageing
fast. Industrial provinces such as Liaoning in the northeast also have a
very high percentage of retirees. Whereas Shanghai has 5.72 per cent of
all retirees, it has only 1.36 per cent of China's population. Liaoning has
7.5 per cent of all retirees but only 3.23 per cent of the population.

The attempts to reform the enterprise pension system were drawn
together in a State Council document of 1997 that was influenced not
just by domestic experimentation but also by input from World Bank
staff. This called for the unification of public-pillar benefits, the standardization of the size of individual contributions, and unified management of the funds (Zhao and Xu, 1999, p. 1; see also Box 11.1). The
first two pillars would provide a replacement rate of around 60 per cent,
redressing the generosity of the existing system that was becoming
increasingly difficult for SOEs to pay. The lack of a unified system and

---

Box 11.1: Designing a New Pension System

The new pension system constructs individual pensions from three pillars.
The first pillar is a defined-benefit public pillar for redistribution. This is to
be funded by a payroll tax of 20 per cent drawn from pre-tax enterprise
revenues and would guarantee a replacement rate of 20 per cent of the
average wages at the time of retirement, if a minimum of 15 years was
contributed. The second pillar is a mandatory-funded, defined-contribution
pillar for each worker. This is funded through a payroll tax of 11 per cent,
initially comprising both enterprise and individual contributions. Subsequently, this was amended to include only individual contributions and was
reduced to 8 per cent. On retirement, the worker would receive a monthly
payout that equals the account balance divided by 120, the factored annuity.
This assumes a life expectancy of 70 and a wage growth rate that equals the
interest rate. If 35 years of contribution are made, then this pillar is expected
to provide a replacement rate of 38.5 per cent. The third pillar is a voluntary
supplemental pillar managed by each enterprise separately or through an
insurance company.

Importantly, the first two pillars would provide a replacement rate of
almost 60 per cent, the figure that the World Bank suggested as being a
realistic target. It would also bring China in line with practice elsewhere in
the world. Previously, Chinese pensions had been very generous in relative
terms by providing a replacement rate of 80–90 per cent. This was already
untenable for many enterprises on the pay-as-you go system that predated
reform. The only source for paying the pensions of retired workers was from
current operating funds. To protect cash-strapped SOEs, enterprise contributions to the new plan were not to exceed 20 per cent of the total enterprise
wage bill, but because of local practice this was raised to 30 per cent.

Source: See State Council Documents 35 and 36, 2006.

the regional variance on contribution rates caused some enterprises to withhold payment. For example, the Sichuan iron and steel producer, Panzhihua, joined the local pooling system in 1986 but in 1992 the iron and steel sector began its own pooling system (11 industrial sectors were allowed to form a pooling system) with lower rates. As a result, Panzhihua refused to pay the higher rates in the geographic pool and accumulated a debt to the local pension fund of 300 million *yuan* (Zhao and Xu, 1999). This practice was quite common.

A number of further steps were taken to provide the policy framework for this new system. First, in the March 1998 restructuring of the State Council, a new Ministry of Labour and Social Security was established to provide more effective coordination and to oversee implementation. Second, in August 1999 a new State Council document building on the previous reforms was issued. The 1997 document had called for pooling of pension accounts at the provincial level but now it was specified that the provinces should have a unified contribution rate and a unified management of funds by the year 2000. It also sought to clarify who took what responsibilities at the local level. Most importantly, it confirmed that responsibility for the collection and distribution of pensions was removed from the enterprises themselves to municipal social insurance bureaus. To ease the way towards provincial management, each province was to set up a 'readjustment fund' to backstop pension obligations and to iron out inequalities among the different municipalities within the province. In a major disincentive for local officials, the document announced that any surplus would be disposed of at the provincial level and most of the money would be invested in central government bonds.

Third, in January 1999 the State Council issued regulations to expand the contribution base to take account of the diversified urban economy. By the end of 1997, while 93.9 per cent of SOEs were in social pension programmes, only 53.8 per cent of urban collectives and 32 per cent of joint-ventures, private enterprises and the self-employed were in such a scheme. Migrant workers were also to be brought into the programme and the 11 industrial sectors that had their own social pooling systems were to be folded into the provincial system. This expansion of the system was to be completed by the end of June 1999 and the number of workers participating in the pool would be increased by 26 million (31 per cent) to reach a total of 110 million (Zhao and Xu, 1999). The rationale for this is obvious. First, if the non-state sectors could escape the payroll tax, then workers would have even fewer incentives to stay in the SOEs and would move to other sectors where their monthly costs would be lower. Second, the state needed increased participation to be able to cover the bills of the current retirees and the large numbers who would retire from the SOE sector in the coming years.

In making this transition, the government needed to deal with the thorny question of how and when to fund the individual accounts as part of the new pension plan. This meant that policy needed to strike a balance between the three goals of meeting the obligations of current pensioners, not placing too heavy a tax on the workforce and minimizing the payment requirements to future generations. As a result, fourth, to act as a government guarantor, in September 2000, the National Council for Social Security was set up to oversee the National Security Fund. The fund's purpose is to provide a long-term strategic reserve that can cover future social security needs (Salditt et al., 2007, p. 17).

Policy has been clarified dramatically in the last few years but implementation still lags and a number of serious problems exist. First, encouraging a unified rate is one thing but enforcing compliance is another. Most provinces have acquiesced in allowing the municipalities to set their own rates based on current obligations rather than risking raising the rate. Yet, in many instances, rates were already above the stipulated 20 per cent, especially in the old industrial areas of the northeast and Sichuan. For example, in Jiamusi (Heilongjiang province), the contribution rate was often above 33 per cent of the total wage bill (Kennedy School of Government, 1999). As a result, in 2000, the State Council raised the contribution rate for enterprise payments to the social security fund to 30 per cent but no longer required enterprises to pay into personal accounts, thus raising employee contribution to 11 per cent but later dropping it to 8 per cent.

The decentralized functioning of the fiscal system has not helped. Pension funds can be major sources for investment funds for the localities and thus the incentive has been to find ways to make it difficult to integrate pooling at a higher administrative level. A 1998 survey revealed that local governments had diverted over 10 billion *yuan* from social security funds to projects that had nothing to do with pensions. Since then the situation has become worse. According to the head of the National Audit Office, 7.1 billion *yuan* of social security funds were misappropriated in 2007, 4.78 billion since 2000 and 2.34 billion prior to this (*SCMP*, 28 June 2007). Corruption scandals concerning social security funds have become commonplace and in the summer of 2006 led to the dismissal of Shanghai party secretary, Chen Liangyu. Shanghai officials were said to have illegally funnelled 6.32 billion *yuan* into the stock market between 2003 and 2006. This included 100 million *yuan* that had been diverted from the municipal social security fund (*SCMP*, 21 June 2007). The fact that this happened in Shanghai does not bode well as the Shanghai programme is seen as one of the better managed programmes.

Further, many of those in a financially healthy pool have not seen the incentive of being merged at a higher administrative level that would include a town with high levels of unemployment and a weak financial base. There has been resistance to joining provincial pools and some towns have refused to contribute to the adjustment funds. If there is no alternative the perverse incentives encourage the spending of any surplus before joining and even running up a deficit before joining. Enterprises have also been reluctant to contribute, even those that have the funds to pay. By the end of 1999, non-payment by enterprises amounted to 38.3 billion *yuan,* with over 200 enterprises owing in excess of 10 million *yuan* (*SCMP,* 16 December 1999, internet edition). Lack of payment has been the source of a number of demonstrations and unrest and the government has usually moved quickly to make up payments. At the end of 1999, a joint statement of the Ministry of Labour and Social Security, the State Economic and Trade Commission (SETC), the Finance Ministry, the China Securities Regulatory Commission and the State Industrial and Commercial Bureau announced new penalties for defaulters. This included a ban from listing on stock markets, setting up joint-ventures and subsidiaries, setting up new branches and expanding the scope of business. However, as with other admonitions, the impact has been limited, as evidenced in the statement by the minister of labour and social security in June 2000 that non-payment would not be tolerated. He acknowledged that another 1.45 billion *yuan* had been added to the unpaid total in the first five months of the year and that payment delay had occurred in 19 provinces (*Xinhua,* 22 June 2000).

The move to integrate the non-state sector into the programme has also met with mixed results, as there has been ambivalence on the part of not only companies themselves but also local authorities about imposing what amounts to an extra 30 per cent cost on these businesses through the payroll tax. A number of provinces have thus allowed cities to set lower rates for the private sector. In Shanghai, the employer has to pay 27 per cent of the previous year's average wage of the workforce into the individual pension accounts, whereas in Shenzhen the company has to pay only 9 per cent (Salditt et al., 2007, p. 8). This is not surprising as Shenzhen has boomed on the expansion of private industry and foreign-invested companies. By contrast, Shanghai has a significant legacy of heavy industry from before the economic reforms began.

Progress to date has been mixed. The major question for the future is the pension system's long-term financial viability. In part, this depends on how high a priority the central leadership places on funding pension reform. The answer appears to be high but not high enough, given other pressing issues. Resolution will also be affected not only by increasing returns on investments from the social security fund but also by improving coverage, raising the retirement age, and thinking about the level of benefits paid out. By 2006, the system was actually receiving more in revenues than it was paying out but demographics could easily cause this situation to change. Despite this, perhaps the greatest problem of all is that the system remains one of pay-as-you-go, despite the new pillars that are to be constructed to provide greater long-term viability. 'Real money' is not being accumulated as there is nothing in them. All along, local governments have been drawing from the individual accounts, a practice that is legal. This means that current pension obligations are still being financed out of current revenues, while the financing for the future is not being accumulated. By about 2025 the system will be overwhelmed and contributions from the contemporary workforce will not meet pension obligations. There is also the tendency to set contribution rates at a low level in order to reduce the future pension obligations and if rates of return are lower than the opportunity cost of the capital, evasion and non-compliance will follow. Estimates of the implicit pension debt vary greatly.

Economic necessity is forcing a faster pace of market-driven change. In 2000, it was reported that the pension system was running a $4.3 billion deficit. Partly in response, the Ministry of Labour and Social Security together with the Boshi Management Company announced that perhaps as much as 15 per cent of pension funds could be invested in stocks with another 10 per cent in treasury and corporate bonds (*China Daily*, 25 May 2001). This marks a significant shift away from the practice that allowed investment only in bank deposits and government bonds. Most important was the establishment in September 2000 of the National Council for Social Security to oversee the social security fund with investment management delegated to qualified asset managers with the exception of investment in bank deposits and the purchase of government bonds in the primary markets. The fund is expected to cover the shortfalls in provincially managed pension funds.

Further reforms have followed including the establishment of enterprise annuities. The World Bank estimates that the annuities should grow to $1.8 trillion by the end of 2030. This would make China the third largest scheme in the world, and this new pension market will generate at least $29 billion for trustees, custodians, and investment managers (*SCMP*, 28 May 2007, internet edition). In perhaps the most significant step towards fund investment, in October 2006, the National Council for Social Security signed overseas investment partnerships with two global investment trustees: Northern Trust Corporation and Citigroup Inc. These agreements will allow the council to move its investments beyond low-yielding government bonds and wildly unpredictable Chinese stocks. In total, the amount for overseas investment cannot exceed 20 per cent of the total fund managed by the council but is still a considerable amount.

Inequality and healthcare in rural China

As we have noted, China has operated a dualistic development strategy with more resources dedicated to the urban areas and with the countryside expected to fend for itself. This has resulted not only in a significant disparity in household income but also in markedly different outcomes in social indicators. This is especially noticeable in the area of healthcare. Healthcare coverage in urban China has suffered from the same kinds of problems as the pension system. However, experiments with a new system were begun in 1994 and in 1999 the government put into operation a 'basic health insurance scheme' for all cities, and all enterprises and employees were expected to participate. This included non-state enterprises and those working in foreign enterprises and joint-ventures. While the government recognized universal coverage is beyond current capacity, the coverage rate has been rising steadily from just 1.4 per cent in 1993 as local experiments began to around 45 percent in 2006. The Hu-Wen leadership have made it clear that healthcare reform is a priority for both urban and rural dwellers and, as a result, local officials have become more serious about implementing suggested reforms. Experimentation has been launched for a medicare-style network in urban centres with an expansion in the role of community healthcare centres to support the basic medical insurance scheme. Beijing and Shanghai were the first two municipalities to launch this programme with 5 per cent coverage in 2008 expanding to coverage of all in the basic medical insurance scheme in Beijing in 2008 and Shanghai by 2010.

In contrast with the urban areas, the challenge in the countryside has been much more significant. Most in the countryside had been left to depend on the family and, in times of desperation, on collective funds. However, this does not mean that reforms have not benefited the countryside, and one of the most remarkable effects has been to lift more than 200 million people out of dire poverty. Yet, it is also true that inequality has risen, collective rural health services were paralysed by the initial reforms and some 23 million still remain below the official poverty line. New policies will be necessary to resolve these problems. The outbreak of SARS in 2003–04 brought home to the leadership just how weak the medical system was in the countryside and the potential for economic disaster that a major pandemic might cause. This refocused attention on improving access in the countryside to medical care. Before turning to these measures, we first discuss briefly the challenge of urban–rural inequality.

While there is significant variation across regions, within the cities and within the rural areas, the most significant inequality is between the urban and the rural. This has fluctuated under the reforms and in the initial period income inequality actually declined. At the start of the reforms official statistics showed a variation in the income of urban and rural households of 2.57: 1 (1978). This declined to 1.85:1 with the pro-rural policies of the early 1980s but rose again in the second half of the 1980s to 2.2:1 in 1990 and has continued to rise since reaching 2.78:1 in 2000 and 3.33 in 2008. While China as a whole is not among the most unequal countries in the world, this urban–rural ratio is the highest in the world, according to the International Labour Organization (ILO). Most countries do not exceed 1.6: 1. Brazil and the Philippines, often thought of as very unequal countries, have ratios of 2.3:1 and 2.1:1 respectively. The urban–rural gap is most pronounced in the poorer areas of China. Thus, while it is 2.26:1 in Shanghai, it is 4.34:1 in Guizhou and 4.09:1 in Gansu.

The Gini coefficient has also been rising during the reform period from 0.33 in 1978 to around 0.45. *Xinhuanet* (21 February 2008) even reported a figure of 0.47 for 2006, while some suggest that it might even be higher. The US, not the most egalitarian of countries, has a Gini of 0.41; Japan, by contrast is 0.25. This makes China quite distinct from the other economies in East Asia such as Japan and South Korea that progressed economically with relatively low levels of inequality during their transition from a rural to an urban, industrialized nation.

It seems certain that as the Chinese economy continues to grow, inequality will increase. Basically, all societies become rich by moving people out of low-productivity agriculture and basic production to higher-productivity urban-based employment and the service sector. Kuznets sees the inequality as a curve that rises in the initial phase of transition that then declines later in the process. East Asia seemed to negate this trend. In Japan and South Korea, where the population is relatively small, the transition can occur within a generation but the size of China means that the transition will probably take several generations. Current policy is focused on slowing the rate of increase rather than actually reversing it. It is worth pointing out that the reality of Mao's China was not as equal as some have portrayed it and Zhao Renwei has argued that the high degree of equality seen in the pre-reform period was largely illusory and that the urban–rural income gap was wider than in other Asian low-income countries. Subsidies and in-kind supplies disproportionately favoured the urban population. In his view the current inequities are visible manifestations of pre-existing but disguised disparities. The most important structural feature was tying people to their place of birth through the household registration system (*hukou*). The existence of these inequalities was hidden by the lack of labour and capital mobility.

Within the countryside, Khan and Riskin's fascinating study (1998, p. 238) shows that the Gini ratio of rural income distribution in 1995 (0.416) is at the high end for developing countries in Asia. The most important factor accounting for this inequality is income from wages, making up 40 per cent of the overall inequality (on this, see also World Bank, 1997e). Other factors are access to receipts from private and other enterprises, and non-farm household activities. This leads Khan and Riskin (1998, p. 240) to conclude that income composition for the rich and poor in the countryside is very different. The rich enjoy wage employment, non-farm entrepreneurship and transfers from the state and collectives. By contrast, the poor derive most income from farming, the rental value of owned housing and, to a lesser extent, private transfers. This description still holds true.

Income alone does not account for all the inequality and costs of healthcare take a higher percentage of rural disposable income than for urban residents while insurance has been less readily available and, despite the promotion of the new insurance scheme, the treatments covered are limited. Under Hu and Wen, government health expenditure has been rising again, now accounting for 20.3 per cent of total health expenditure in 2007 up from a low of 15.5 per cent in 2000 but still below the 36.2 per cent of expenditures that it made up in 1980. Not surprisingly, personal health expenditures have risen from 21.2 per cent of the total in 1980 to 45.2 per cent in 2007 (down from a high of 60 per cent on 2001). The per capita health expenditure in 2007 was 1480 *yuan* for urban China (2007) and 348.5 *yuan* in rural China. Personal expenditure seems to have dropped as a component of total health expenditures through the introduction of the new cooperative medical insurance scheme for the countryside. In the author's own survey spending on insurance for rural families had dropped from 643 *yuan* to (9.65 per cent of household expenditure) to 132.7 *yuan* (1.12 percent of household expenditure). Spending on medical treatment and medicines was still much higher at 1194 *yuan* in 2007 (9.1 per cent of household expenditures). Medical expenses comprised a higher component for lower income families (17.2 per cent) than for the highest earners in the countryside (4.37 per cent). Spending across regions also varies significantly. The World Bank (2005) notes that although Beijing spent 360 *yuan* per capita, Shanghai 220 *yuan* and Tianjin 150 *yuan*, all other provinces and equivalents spent under 100 *yuan*, with Anhui, Hunan, Jiangxi, Chongqing, Guizhou and Henan each spending under 50 *yuan* per capita. In fact, one-quarter of all government health spending occurs in the rich municipalities and provinces of Beijing, Shanghai, Zhejiang and Jiangsu.

Given the situation it is not surprising that health indicators are worse for those in rural China (see Table 11.2). The indicators for both urban and rural China have improved consistently but those for rural China, not surprisingly, lag behind. Especially infant and child mortality indicators are three times worse for rural inhabitants. The quality of healthcare and access in the rural areas has also been affected by broader policy changes. The effective abolition of the collective institutions in the countryside meant that most rural families had to rely on their own resources for medical care and there was *de facto* privatization of much of the medical care. The first impact was the drop in medical insurance coverage from almost 80 per cent in 1979 to only 2 per cent in 1987 before improving a little to 6.57 per cent in 1997. From 1997 the situation began to improve steadily as the leadership began to pay more attention to the problem.

This drop in coverage led to a rise in medical costs for families and became a significant cause of poverty. A 2003 Ministry of Health survey revealed that among the rural poor, 22 per cent attributed their poverty to unmet medical needs. The survey revealed that the percentage of farmers who had sunk into poverty because of illness rose from 21.6 per cent in 1998 to 33.4 per cent in 2003. This has meant that fewer people have sought medical help when needed. The survey revealed that of the 47 per cent of rural inhabitants who left hospital early, 67 per cent did so because of financial problems, 38.6 per cent did not even seek medical help when needed.

One final important factor in addition to the change of ownership is the change in incentives for healthcare providers. Some analysts have blamed the health problems on the *de facto* privatization of health facilities in the villages (UNDP, 1998, pp. 36, 38), but the change in incentives has been more important than the question of ownership of the health facilities (Eggleston et al., 2006). Not only was the financing of most healthcare decentralized but also from 1981 healthcare facilities

Table 11.2 *Rural–Urban Health Indicators, 2008*

Category	Total	Urban China	Rural China
Neo-natal mortality per 1000 live births	10.2	5.0	12.3
Infant mortality per 1000 live births	14.9	6.5	18.4
Under-5 mortality per 1000 live births	18.5	7.9	22.7
Maternal mortality per 100,000 live births	34.2	29.2	36.2
Medical personnel per 1000 citizens	3.59	5.57	2.21
Doctors per 1000 citizens	1.57	1.98	0.68

Source: Ministry of Health website at http://www.gov.ca/publicfiles//business/htmfiles/web/index.htm.

were instructed to cover recurrent costs from user charges (with the exception of those of staff). Beginning in the mid 1980s, preventive care facilities were charged on a fee-for-service basis. The private practice of healthcare was legalized in 1985 and by 1989 healthcare providers were transformed into fee-for-service organizations and active competitors in the healthcare market. Government support was not related to perform-ance-based criteria but rather to the number of staff and beds, thus skewing the incentives further (Eggleston et al., 2006, p. 7).

Given these pressures, the insufficient state funding, and reliance on the extended family for support, it is not surprising that criticisms were made of the rural health system. Dr. Marcel Roux, then China head of Médécins sans Frontières commented before the new push for health-care reform began in 1996:

> Healthcare is better in Africa, for sure. There, people are organized and there are good African physicians and health workers but in China, they don't have the knowledge, the structures or people to make it work. (*SCMP*, 19 October 1999, internet edition)

It seems the Chinese leadership agreed as they came under increasing pressure to re-engage with the health sector and not leave resolution to the market and family support. In December 1996 a National Confer-ence on Health in Beijing was convened to try to fix the broken system. The change of tone was remarkable as the leadership shifted from presenting its healthcare system as a shining example to other devel-oping countries to one of concern about its collapse (discussion with participants; for the joint CC and State Council Decision, see *Jiankang ribao*, 18 February 1997). The central government was clearly alarmed at the social consequences of financial decentralization and it tried to put forward a coherent policy to restore standards and access to health-care. First, it was declared that spending in the national budget would be raised from 2 per cent to 5 per cent, something that has not been achieved. Further measures sought to revive preventive healthcare and public hygiene awareness through education. The proportion of the government's budget for spending on preventive care dropped from 23 per cent in 1978 to 18 per cent in 1994 (Hu and Jiang, 1998, p. 192). Village doctors were to receive a pay boost to bring them in line with government officials and to stop the reliance on kickbacks and other non-sanctioned revenues.

The most important measure was the reconfirmation of the 1994 decision to restore the cooperative medical system. The fact that the need to build a cooperative medical system was reiterated once again suggests that little progress had been made. Variation and non-compli-ance were widespread and the frequent requests by the Centre to reduce financial burdens on farmers were interpreted by some as meaning that they should not have to contribute to medical schemes. In rural health China was suffering from 'state withdrawal' and the lack of public funding, training, and regulation. Evidence clearly shows that where there is a functioning cooperative medical system, utilization rates of the medical services increase, especially the demand for clinic care and hospitalization. This is one clear case where the 'public good' argument would appear to apply and the government needs to tighten the regulatory framework to ensure that guidelines on health are followed and that in poor areas better provision is provided at central government expense.

In 1996, the Ministry of Health launched an important study of the rural cooperative medical care experiments that formed the basis for a new policy launch in 2003 which fitted well with Hu Jinatao and Wen Jiabao's stress on building a 'harmonious society'. The new rural cooperative medical scheme is defined as voluntary public medical insurance. The household forms the basic unit, for participation, with the fee set at 10 *yuan*. The government initially contributed 20 *yuan*, which was raised to 80 *yuan* in 2008. This payment is divided equally between the central and the local government. In addition, it was suggested that the individual contribution could be raised to 20 *yuan*.

The programme has expanded rapidly from 333 participating counties in 2004 with a 75 per cent enrolment rate (80 million people) to 2729 counties in 2008 with a 91.5 per cent enrolment rate (815 million people). The per capita premiums had risen from 50.4 to 96.3 *yuan*. The number of beneficiaries rose from 76 million in 2004 to 585 million with the payout rising from 2.64 billion to 66.2 billion *yuan*. Despite problems, satisfaction seems reasonable. Our 2007 survey showed that 51.6 per cent of rural residents felt that the new system could protect them against major illnesses and 72.8 per cent said that they would continue enrolment in the following year, while only 5.5 per cent said that they would not.

A number of problems exist with the system. In the individual accounts, in 2008 there was an average allocation of 96 *yuan* but the rural per capita medical expense was 348.5 *yuan*. Van Dalen (2006), using data from the 2004 China Health and Nutrition Survey, shows that health insurance was actually not affecting the demand for healthcare in any significant way. The problem is clear, despite progress – insurance does not offer real protection against high healthcare expenditures. Thus, we see the continuation of a large percentage of people declining health service provision when it is needed. Second, the scheme also suffers from those problems normally associated with voluntary insurance schemes. Many of those who are better off or consider themselves healthy might not participate or might withdraw.

However, some poor households forgo treatment because of the high additional costs, meaning that those receiving the reimbursements tend to be concentrated in the higher-earning households. The system has also been prey to coercion. In western China, it is considered an important political achievement to increase participation in the scheme – thus some farmers have been forced to join, or local governments have required officials and teachers to pay fees to boost the participation rates (CHED, 2005, p. 20). The counties carry the costs of the medical insurance schemes and this leads them to seek ways to deflect costs. Many design conservative plans that limit coverage and benefits. Some shrink the risk pool by developing responsibility to the township or by limiting the payout level or the kinds of treatments that can be covered.

To improve infrastructure, on 29 August 2006 the 'Construction and Development Plan for the Rural Health Service' was promulgated. This called for the central government to invest 21.7 billion *yuan* to construct health facilities, with 14.13 billion *yuan* dedicated for township hospitals and 4.9 billion allocated for county-level hospitals to improve outpatient facilities and to buy key equipment. However, little is allocated to the villages. The objective is that in 2010, 8 per cent of the county budget will be dedicated to healthcare and each village will have a clinic.

Migration

One of the main ways to improve income for rural families is to generate off-farm employment. The development of township and village enterprises has been very important for this as has migration to China's booming cities. The rural and the urban are more closely linked than in Maoist days, despite the lingering obstacles to the integration of labour markets, and this is seen most visibly by the huge number of migrants in the cities (for an excellent early study, see Solinger, 1999). Restricted by the household registration and grain-rationing systems, migration began slowly in the early 1980s but with the emergence of a market in grain for migrants (legalized in 1986) and the provision of other goods and services outside of the plan it began to take off in the mid 1980s. This pull factor was complemented by the push factor once the initial rise in agricultural incomes began to decline from 1984. Migrant labour has been crucial to the urban economic boom, whether in supplying the labour to the foreign-invested factories in coastal China, providing the construction crews for the massive building expansion, or feeding the burgeoning service sector, ranging from hotel and restaurant workers to the more unseemly services of prostitution and bar hostesses. It has also been crucial to rural development, in terms of remittances and also because migrants have returned to the villages and brought back with them capital, new skills and social networks that extend beyond the narrow village confines (see Murphy, 2002).

The 2000 census noted 144 million (12 per cent of the population) living away from their registered abode. Of these 79 million were long-distance migrants, up from 7 million on 1982 and 22 million in 1990. In a province such as Guangdong, migrants make up 25 per cent of the population, whereas in Shanghai, they constitute over 10 per cent (Naughton, 2007, pp. 129–30). Migrant workers have probably surpassed urban workers as the main Chinese industrial workforce. Uprooted from the land, these migrants have not been effectively integrated into the new or pre-existing systems for health and education, for example. While their economic benefit to the urban areas has been significant, their social status is extremely low, and only in the late 1990s did urban authorities begin to consider integrating the migrants into social service provision. The shift in thinking was primarily stimulated by central leadership concerns that they might be a source of instability and that falling outside urban administrative jurisdiction they might be evading family-planning regulations. Migrants have been subject to the same abuse and caricature as in other parts of the world and have been blamed, not only by the permanent urban residents but also in the official press, for the breakdown in law and order, the increased messiness of the urban areas and the difficulty for laid-off SOE employees to find new work. However, in terms of the labour market, most evidence suggests that they are not in direct competition with laid-off SOE workers, taking jobs that the latter would not consider.

Debates over their role also have an institutional and political dimension. Basically, the old Ministry of Labour (now Labour and Social Security) favoured keeping tight controls on migration and wanted to keep as many as possible down on the farms, whereas the Ministry of Agriculture has been more positive about the role of migration and the benefits it brings to rural development. Migrant communities have been easy targets for the national and local authorities concerning the problems of urban China and there have been occasional movements to reduce their numbers or eliminate their communities. Xinjiang village in Beijing has been a source of concern for security reasons as it was suspected to house terrorists who favoured independence for the province. As a result, it has been heavily policed and the authorities have tried on a number of occasions to break it up. In contrast with these negative views, there are cases where the large influx of migrants has turned around stagnant urban district economies such as in Fengtai in Beijing, home to Zhejiang village, or has created new cities, such as Dongguan in Guangdong. The economy of Dongguan has grown 20 per cent per annum since 1990 and, as a result, its 50 enterprises employing 5000 residents grew by the mid 1990s to comprise 20,000 foreign-invested enterprises with a population of 500,000, of whom over 90 per cent were migrants (World Bank, 1997e, p. 56).

Increasingly policy has shifted from trying to control and manage the flow of migration to improving the situation of migrants and integrating them into urban services. As Zhao (2006) has perceptively remarked policy in the 1980s and the 1990s was dedicated to delinking employment from one's *hukou* status, under Hu Jinatao and Wen Jiabao policy has been to de-link social services and welfare benefits from *hukou* status. The notion that migrants did not need welfare support because they had land as insurance in their home villages has become untenable. Many migrants are now permanent fixtures in the urban areas together with their families and may no longer have any land back in their place of registration. While *hukou* reforms of the earlier period until 2002–03 benefited mainly investors and those who are well educated, the Hu-Wen leadership shifted policy focus to providing training, and social welfare coverage to migrant workers.

The ability of the authorities to control labour flows is restricted by the 'push' factor from the villages where surplus labour is massive. The main resource for finding jobs is through village and local networks rather than through the state agencies. Most of those working as nannies (*baomu*) in Beijing found work either through personal introductions from someone already employed or by making their way to the informal labour market that grew up beside Beijing's main railway station. A high percentage came from Anhui province. Zhejiang village is a good example of the process and also of the complexity of many migrant communities. It comprises around 100,000 residents and has set up its own schooling system and clinics and hospital, staffed by those from Zhejiang with medical licences, has its own security forces and essentially pays a large annual fee to the local authorities to leave it alone. Recruitment for workers to come to the village, which has cornered much of the clothing and leather business in Beijing, takes place in Zhejiang and those selected are sent on to Beijing. This includes many from outside of Zhejiang itself (about 50 per cent). For example, many of those engaged in the most menial tasks are recruited in Anhui and sent to Zhejiang for initial training before being sent to Beijing to work. The village originated by outsiders renting space from locals, who saw this as an easy way to make some quick money. Subsequently, the migrants began to buy run-down buildings that they used for the workshops and dormitory sleeping quarters. By 1992, the district leaders allowed groups in the 'village' to construct some 40 new buildings (interviews in Zhejiang village, 1997 and 1998; and Xiang, 1996).

Although the wages of migrant workers are lower than those for urban residents, their main problem is the lack of access to social services and welfare facilities. This only started to receive policy attention in the late 1990s (see Fan, 2007; and Cai, 2003). If accommodation is provided, it tends to be very rudimentary, either in the form of segregated dormitories or tents or temporary shacks. The sanitary conditions are poor, creating significant problems as migrants generally do not have health coverage. Those who do will probably be covered only for direct work-related injuries and not infectious diseases or other sicknesses. This places the burden on the already weak rural social infrastructure as when one gets sick the only way to avoid expensive urban treatment is to return to the village to be looked after by the family. Until the end of the 1990s, migrant children were not allowed to enrol in state schools, thus meaning that they missed out on education, were returned to the village on reaching school age, or their parents had to pay for their education in private schools. While state regulation requires local authorities to provide education for all school-age children, urban local authorities have interpreted this as meaning only those with a residence permit and thus migrant children have been excluded. From 1998 to 1999, some Beijing districts, for example, began to recognize migrant-run schools and issue them licences. However, the children attending these schools are still not allowed to take the high school entrance examination and have to return to the rural home to participate (Ming, 2009). It is not surprising that a survey conducted by Shanghai's Fudan University found that only 7.6 per cent of migrants were satisfied with their social status in the city (*China Daily*, 7 January 2008).

The leadership under Hu and Wen pulled together experimental reforms in the first State Council document of 2003 that acknowledged the problems of migration but confirmed that it was an inevitable part of China's progress. In March 2001, the central government had decided to promote reforms in small towns based on prior experiments. The reform of the household registration system had begun in 1997 for 450 small towns (Yu, 2002, p. 379). This allowed residency in small towns and townships for all those from rural areas who could demonstrate legal employment and a place to live. Although restrictions have subsequently been eased for some larger cities, major municipalities have sought to control the flow. Importantly, in November 2002 migrants were given the political status of being a part of the working class. In January 2003, the State Council confirmed that unfair restrictions on migrants were to be lifted and they were to be accorded equal treatment with urban residents when applying for work. Their wages were to be paid in full and on time, while living and working conditions were to be improved. Perhaps most significantly, urban education departments would have to recognize schools for migrant children and provide them with equal education access. Many of these demands are honoured more in the breach than the observance, but the official recognition is important. Finally, the beating to death by police of a university graduate in Guangzhou (in March 2003) because he did not have his temporary residence permit with him led to criticism of police powers to detain and search migrants. As a result, in June the State Council passed new regulations that mandated local governments to set up shelters that fell under the Ministry of Civil Affairs. The new regulations expressly forbid extortion, abuse and forced labour.

In terms of participating in various insurance and pension schemes a major disincentive for migrant workers is the lack of portability. If migrant workers move back to the rural areas or to a different administrative jurisdiction in search of work, it is highly unlikely that they will be able to take the savings (in any case often nominal) in their individual accounts or make a claim against their local pension funds. This problem, affecting the flexibility of the labour market, means that in old age the migrants will be reliant on their own savings and/or family support. As a result of these concerns, in June 2007, a vice minister of the Ministry of Labour and Social Security announced that a new pension plan had been drafted to try to incorporate the huge migrant population. Those with stable jobs are expected to join the pension plan where they work; for others, an individual account is established, the contents of which will be transferred to their home towns each year. Employers and employees both contribute, with employee contribution capped at 5 per cent of the monthly salary. These individual accounts follow the migrant worker from job to job. Self-employed migrants are also allowed to join the scheme if they pay the premium (*SCMP*, 12 June 2007, internet edition). This is as an important step but, as in so many other areas, the main concern is implementation. Profit margins are low in the jobs where migrants work and it is unlikely that employers will want to increase their business costs. There is also the question of trust. There are many stories of migrants being cheated out of their due wages and benefits, thus it may be difficult for them to trust the new system to deliver on its promises.

In a remarkable event to coincide with the 2010 sessions of the NPC and the CPPCC, 13 regional newspapers published a joint editorial calling for the abolition of the household registration system. In so doing, they clearly thought that they were in tune with the policy direction of the leadership. The editorial called the system a product of the planned economy and a bad policy that was unsuitable for the present and was in urgent need of reform. In this, the editors misjudged the leadership that was clearly shaken by this joint policy appeal. At least one senior editor lost his job and the newspapers were sanctioned for their actions.

Poverty alleviation

China's approach to dealing with poverty has undergone significant evolution during the reform period. For rural areas, the initial policy interventions, which were not well targeted or focused, were based on funding to poor counties. This geographic targeting, which was based on the county until 2001, meant that poor households often did not benefit from funding that was disbursed. With the poor now more dispersed, policy will have to focus increasingly on the household to be effective. The focus on the development of the poor region as a whole anticipated that 'trickle down' would work. Urban areas were not considered at all, despite the growing numbers of urban poor. Although the number of poor declined dramatically, the effectiveness of specific poverty interventions was increasingly questioned by domestic and international critics alike. These criticisms led to a significant shift in policy. Already from 1997, micro-credit programmes were being expanded to reach poor households and from 2001, with the completion of the 'Eight-Seven Poverty Reduction Plan', policy was focused on poor villages, even though key poverty reduction counties were still designated. In 2001, the policy was reoriented from 592 poor counties to 148,000 poor villages. Under the Hu Jintao–Wen Jiabao leadership, new programmes have been introduced to provide more focused support for education, health, and infrastructure. Support for the poorest in rural China was brought more into line with that in the urban areas through the introduction of the Minimum Living Support Scheme (MLSS). Unlike rural China, policy for urban China did not suffer from the problems of regional targeting and was household-focused, first through the elaborate system of benefits provided by the workplace and latterly through the revamped social insurance schemes backed up by the MLSS for the very poor.

Poverty alleviation is one area where the market, rather than government intervention, has clearly had a major impact. The return to household farming and the effective abandonment of the rural collective structures meant that the pent-up energies of the rural population were released, with farmers able to produce for and sell their produce on the market. This, combined with the state's decision to raise the purchasing price for staple goods such as cotton and grain in the early 1980s, led to a significant rise in farmers' incomes, pulling tens of millions out of poverty. Producer prices had been held artificially low so as to transfer resources from the rural to the urban areas and to contribute to the programme of urbanization and industrialization. The numbers of those in absolute poverty dropped from 250 million in 1978 to around 125 million in the mid 1980s. By contrast, the state interventions to deal with poverty alleviation that were introduced from the mid 1980s were less successful in raising significant numbers out of poverty. Poverty reduction slowed considerably until the pro-growth policies of 1993 took effect. However, from 1996 until 2001, poverty reduction slowed once again and in 2003 the number of absolute poor rose for the first time. This led to renewed attention to interventions, focusing on the household, to support education and health. As of 2007, official figures record a total of 14.79 million or less than 2 per cent of the rural population. However, the poverty line that is used for Chinese calculations is very low and does not even cover adequately basic food and other essential needs. Using international standards the numbers are higher but nonetheless those brought out of poverty remains impressive. The World Bank calculates that using the new international poverty standard of $1.25 per day per person (using 2005 purchasing power parity), the levels of those categorized as poor declined from 85 per cent in 1981 to 27 per cent in 2004. In 2005, this would leave 254 million people consuming less than $1.25 per day, meaning that China has the second largest number of poor people in the world after India (World Bank, 2009).

The rate of those in absolute poverty shows significant variation across the various provinces in China. As one would expect, the highest percentages are in the west of the country. In 2005, Qinghai had the highest rate of absolute poverty with 11.5 per cent, followed by Guizhou (9 per cent), Gansu (8.1 per cent), Tibet and Shaanxi (both 7.2 per cent). The heavy investment in Tibet seems to have brought benefit as in 1998 the poverty rate was 19 per cent. Only Inner Mongolia had a poverty rate in 2005 that was higher than in 1998 (6.6 per cent as opposed to 6.4 per cent) that was caused by the problems with the death of livestock in 2000 and 2001 (CDRF, 2007, p. 39). In 2001, the poverty rate had risen as high as 13.3 percent.

What these figures show is that, despite tremendous progress, there is still a significant group in the countryside that has not been helped by government policy, a very large group living just above the poverty line who are still very vulnerable, and a smaller but increasing group of urban poor who are the creation of the reforms. The basic view of the government has been that people are poor because of physical disadvantage (such as living in remote areas) or lack of reform. The Jiang Zemin–Zhu Rongji leadership seemed to follow the 'trickle-down' notion, giving primacy to rapid economic growth accompanied by limited targeted interventions. As inequality became a political concern in the late 1990s, a more pro-active 'Develop the West' policy was promoted. The leadership recognized that this was insufficient and thus has attempted to enhance mechanisms for redistribution while pursuing the urbanization drive. However, policies of redistribution raise questions about targeting, whether such funds will be used optimally, and whether it can work against development of the most productive parts of the economy.

The initial measures to alleviate policy were four-fold. The main strategy was targeting resources on poor areas. The other three programmes were: the subsidized loan programme managed by the Leading Group and the Agricultural Bank of China (responsibility was returned to the Bank in 1998 from the Agricultural Development Bank that was set up in 1994); the food-for-work programme managed by the former State Development and Planning Commission (now the State Development and Reform Commission); and the budgetary grant programme. The impact of these three programmes to help the poorest has not been significant and there have been serious distortions in implementation. Here we shall just focus on the main programme.

In 1984, the government set up a special agency under the State Council, the Leading Group for Poverty Alleviation, with offices at the county and township levels to coordinate policy. It invested a huge amount of funds into this objective, some 274.6 billion *yuan* from 1986 to 2004 (in budget support and subsidized loans), and devised a number of specific policies targeted at the counties where it thought the poor were situated.

From 1986, the central government and the provinces began to identify 'poor counties' that would receive targeted poverty alleviation interventions. For even a moderately poor county, it was beneficial to be listed as one of the counties to receive benefits and dispensations, so intense lobbying took place both at the national and the provincial levels. Of the initial 258 officially designated national poor counties in 1986, only one-third (83) actually met the criterion of below 150 *yuan* in rural net income per in 1985, indicative of the intense politicization of the process. Another 82 had incomes between 130 and 200 *yuan* and 93 had average incomes between 200 and 300 *yuan* (Wang, 2004, p. 20). Included on the list were counties that had been part of the pre-1949 CCP revolutionary base areas, counties that contained ethnic minorities, and pastoral counties. By 1988, there were 328 nationally designated counties and in addition another 370 provincially designated poor counties. The number of national counties increased to 331 in 1993 and after a major overhaul in 1994 the total was expanded to 592. This expansion took place despite the fact that the total number of poor had fallen, according to official statistics, from 120 million in 1985 to 80 million by 1993. In addition, two of the ten poorest counties in China were not among the nationally designated counties (Nyberg and Rozelle, 1999, p. 97). A new poverty line was set at 320 *yuan* in 1993 prices, but only 326 of the counties met this criterion (Wang, 2004, p. 22).

In addition to the fact that targeting has clearly not been very effective, the poverty alleviation programme has two main objectives that sometimes clash. One objective is to help the poor and the second is to promote economic development. Many of the absolute poor live outside the nationally designated counties, so the distribution of funds within the poor counties is not effective in supporting the poorest households. The National Statistics Bureau estimated that one-third of the rural poor lived outside of the 592 counties, and other studies suggest that the number may even be as high 50 per cent (UNDP, 2002, p. 35). The leakage of funds through misappropriations and bad investments and use by the non-poor households has meant that effectiveness is low. Within the counties, the money is not properly directed to poor households; instead it is usually divided out evenly between poor and non-poor townships. The UNDP calculated that some 55–75 per cent of poverty alleviation funds did not reach poor households (UNDP, 1998, p. 102). Thus, spreading the money evenly over the 200 million residents in these counties where only 21 million of the absolute poor lived in 1998 meant that the benefits to the poor were outweighed ten-fold by distribution to the non-poor (World Bank, 2000, pp. xvi–xvii).

For many local leaders, poverty alleviation funds are regarded as general development resources and thus a useful supplement to local state income. With the lack of transparency, the funds can often be siphoned off to support pet projects. This was especially a problem in the early and mid 1990s before central policy shifted back to targeting the household. The World Bank (2000, p. xxiv) calculated that in 1992 and 1993, around half of all poverty alleviation-subsidized loans were lent to industrial enterprises. A survey by the Ministry of Finance came to similar conclusions, finding that the majority of subsidized loans were made to large-scale enterprises or were used for infrastructure. In 2002, it seems that of 750 million *yuan* in poverty-alleviation loans in Jiangxi, only 150 million went to households. According to Wang (2004, p. 48), this diversion of loans to non-poverty-alleviation targets became more serious with the commercialization of the Agricultural Bank of China and the closure of most township bank branches. By the mid 1990s, this strategy of copying the successful counties in developing township and village enterprises had run its course and many were in severe financial difficulty. This may have contributed to the decision in the mid 1990s to again focus subsidized loans to the household.

The problems that have been highly associated with these approaches of regional targeting and poorly directed, subsidized loans have led to a re-think of policy. The World Bank (2009) suggests that in future policy will need to focus on risk mitigation and risk management. New policies have been introduced to complement the general reduction of the burden on the rural household as in the abolition of the agricultural tax and efforts to raise household incomes. For example, between 2004 and 2007, direct subsidies to agriculture, including grain and input subsidies increased 3.5 times. Also, as we have seen above, there have been significant attempts to introduce a range of social protection schemes in both urban and rural China with the expansion of health insurance, pensions and medical assistance schemes. In addition, there has been increased interest in the use of micro-credit that can reach poor households directly and second, there has been a shift of emphasis from targeting the county to targeting the village or the household. In 2001 the central government focused poverty alleviation policy on 148,000 designated poor villages that were said to be home to 80 per cent of those in poverty (*Xinhua* News Agency, 6 October 2006). Third, there has been a move to provide minimum subsistence support for the rural poor, similar to the programme begun in the urban areas in the second half of the 1990s.

The 1996 decision by the Leading Group to focus attention on loans to poor households has led to a boom in interest in micro-credit schemes. In 1997, a number of provinces began to authorize the use of poverty alleviation funds for such schemes and in 1998 the Leading Group emphasized that micro-credit should be expanded to all provinces. Small-scale lending schemes have been very successful in other Asian countries, not only in targeting the poor but also in building up the lending infrastructure and reaping high rates of return, well above those experienced in China. But local groups in China have been highly innovative, and programmes targeting poor rural women have been run by the local offices of the Poverty Alleviation Bureau and the Women's Federation. Programmes modelled on those of Grameen Bank in Bangladesh or Cash Poor in Malaysia have been introduced by international organizations such as the United Nations Development Programme (UNDP) and private organizations such as the Ford Foundation. In 1998 it was also decided that the loans should be distributed through the local branches of the Agricultural Bank of China rather than through the poverty alleviation offices in order to ensure better supervision and repayment. By the end of 2001, the Agricultural Bank had issued 3.8 billion *yuan* to 2.3 million poor households and 10.6 million people (Wang, 2004, p. 29). But this structure reduced incentives for the poverty alleviation offices to ensure a good functioning system and the branches of the ABC have little incentive to manage the programme.

These institutional factors and the enforced low lending rate mean that micro-credit schemes have not provided the 'magic wand' that the Leading Group was hoping for and will not be as successful as their counterparts elsewhere in Asia. The interest rates cannot cover operating costs, which in turn will make it impossible to keep such programmes sustainable. Despite these problems, there have been renewed attempts under Premier Wen to expand micro-credit schemes. A major problem with implementation arises from the way Chinese officials view such programmes. Essentially, officials see them as a welfare programme rather than as one that can be financially sustainable. The traditional top-down approach of planning discourages the kinds of local and community-based networks that are necessary to allow such lending programmes to prosper. Such thinking is hard to shift as is state policy on low interest rates, and without such changes the programmes will not be successful and may create significant financial problems.

A major problem with these poverty alleviation strategies is the fragmented nature of the implementing agencies. A more comprehensive and participatory approach to rural development is needed. Current policies are implemented by different, vertical bureaucratic hierarchies, with little attempt to integrate them effectively. Further, there is very little consultation with farmers about what they actually want in terms of help and little effort to build with them sustainable participatory institutions. The paternalism of CCP rule is evident, with many local officials convinced that the farmers do not know what is in their best interests. The phrase 'their cultural quality is too low' (*suzhi tai di*) is frequently used by local officials to justify why they do not ask farmers for input on the design and implementation of projects.

In an important new departure for China, in June 2006 the State Council Leading Group Office for Poverty Alleviation and Development together with the World Bank launched a two-year $8 million programme to promote villagers' participation in local development. Sixty administrative villages in Guangxi, Inner Mongolia, Shaanxi, and Sichuan with 100,000 poor farmers were chosen for inclusion. The 'Community-driven Development Programme' is expected to improve the targeting of poverty alleviation funds by allowing poor people to manage funds in pursuit of their own priorities. The poor communities are responsible for managing programme funds and for implementing small-scale infrastructure and public service improvements (*Xinhua* News Agency, 6 October 2006).

To resolve the problems of poverty and rural social policy more generally, the Chinese government needs to develop a pro-poor approach that integrates social and economic development policy that is more participatory and inclusive. These interventions need to be part of the broader strategy for development. Obviously, urbanization, if well conceived, will resolve much of the problem, but in the meantime the structure of public finance hugely disfavours the rural areas. The main thrust of economic policy is to achieve rapid growth, often by shifting resources away from the poor and then returning some funds through limited poverty alleviation interventions. Investment patterns, as we have seen, favour the coastal and urban areas. However, any major reallocation of resources is liable to be politically unacceptable. Wang (2004, pp. 56–7) concludes that although poverty alleviation programmes may have stopped the poor areas from falling even farther behind, the efficiency of the investment has decreased and the impact of other investments has been greater. He concludes that investments in agriculture, education, and health would be more effective than the local government preference for investment in industry in poor areas.

In addition to increasing the effectiveness of design and delivery of government programmes, it is also necessary to create conditions that enable the poor to cast off poverty on their own, which is often a matter of ensuring that they are able to secure access to and control over productive resources and credit. Strengthening the rights of farmers and rural communities to manage and derive benefits from the natural resources on which they depend is one of the keys to securing sustained improvements in the lives of the rural poor.

One of the most important policy initiatives has been the introduction of the Minimum Living Standard Scheme (MLSS) first in the urban areas and then extended to the countryside. This marks a clear step in the direction of a modern welfare state and a shift away from a traditional approach of alms and charity for specially identified groups. China resembles other developing countries in the sequencing of social insurance and social assistance programmes. By contrast, the countries of the Organisation for Economic Co-operation and Development (OECD) developed social assistance programmes, such as the poor laws, before putting in place social insurance schemes (Overbye, 2005, p. 312). On the whole, social insurance schemes tend to favour those who are in the formal sector of the economy and the better-off in society. To deal with others who are not so fortunate, the World Bank (1994) suggests that social assistance should be the 'first pillar' of social protection in all countries. Social assistance schemes can more effectively extend social protection to the poor than can the formal social insurance schemes. These kinds of schemes can also reach not only the urban poor but also those in the rural areas who are vulnerable. As we have seen, the social insurance programmes not only cannot cover all at the present time, but also they are heavily biased towards the urban areas. The social assistance category has been a residual in the urban areas, but it has been growing more quickly in recent years. From the mid 1990s on, social assistance schemes have received greater policy attention. This derived from the recognition that the social insurance schemes that had been developed still left significant sections of the population exposed to risk, for example, elderly living alone or the new urban poor such as the recently laid-off state workers. The need has been even greater in the rural areas but again coverage is low.

There are a number of categories of social assistance but policy has been to try to consolidate payments into a means-tested system. The leadership in recent years has been trying to shift to a rural minimum income scheme. This was restated as central government policy at the January 2007 rural work conference. Traditional social assistance

programmes were focused on the 'five guarantee households'. It is clear
that where possible government policy is to shift people onto an MLSS
and, as a result, the numbers rose from 3.05 million in 2001 to 43.1
million at the end of 2008. Because the level of support to those identified is left to the decision of the local authorities, there may be considerable variance in terms of both who is covered and the amount provided.
The MLSS is intended to replace traditional programmes such as the
'five-guarantee' households that receive support if they are unable to
earn income and have no other visible means of support. In fact, in June
2007 one Ministry of Civil Affairs vice minister declared that the rural
MLSS formed the 'foundation for a nationwide social security system'
and that it would be possible to cover all the rural poor by the end of
2007 (*Xinhua* News Agency, 31 July 2007).

This attempt to expand the programme rapidly has caused controversy about whether or not a 'universal' minimum support system is
feasible. Those who prefer not to extend support argue that farmers
have land and housing to provide a minimum guarantee. They fear that
if minimum support is provided, some may give up farming altogether.
Yet land no longer provides an adequate guarantee and large numbers
are vulnerable in rural China. Yu Jianrong (2006) estimates that there
are 64.3 million impoverished in rural areas and within this group there
are 23.6 million with annual incomes below 683 *yuan* who do not have
sufficient food and clothing. This group includes the elderly, sick, and
orphaned who have no means of support. In Yu's opinion, and it would
appear that this is now the government's view, these people should be
provided with the MLSS. Yu has calculated that the extra funding
required would amount to only about 10 billion *yuan* and this is easily
affordable for the state.

As currently structured, the scheme reflects the funding bias of the
urban over the rural areas. In fact, in 2003 even in a municipality such
as Shanghai, the poverty line was 290 *yuan* in the urban districts but
only 150–183 *yuan* in the rural districts (Leung, 2006, p. 191). In 2003,
the average threshold for eligibility for minimum living support in urban
areas was about 2040 *yuan* whereas in rural areas it was 650 *yuan*, a
difference of 3.1 times (Xue et al., 2006). Also, the bias against the rural
areas goes even further since when the family's total income is calculated, all members are counted but spouses who do not have an urban
registration are not included for benefits!

The Chinese leadership has begun the process of moving towards a
modern welfare state by shifting its social assistance programmes from
benefits based on specific groups such as veterans or the disabled to one
that adopts a means-tested approach which provides benefits to those in
financial need. If completed, this will mark a major transformation and
open the possibility for developing a social welfare system based on

citizenship rather than a system that is arbitrarily defined by the leadership at the national and local levels. However, there is still a long way to go to meet this objective and the MLSS exhibits the same urban bias as other social welfare provisions in China. It has had the advantage of recognizing the existence of urban poverty among those who are products of the new economic policies and the profound demographic changes that China is experiencing.

The more traditional relief and poverty alleviation programmes have also undergone significant changes during the reform period. The Chinese authorities have begun to accept a limited role for the market through micro-credit schemes and the gradual adoption of international best-practices, such as bringing NGOs into project implementation as well as enhancing community participation. China's statist predisposition still predominates, with most officials, presuming that they know best what the poor need in terms of support, preferring a top-down approach.

Chapter 12

Foreign Policy

The unprecedented level of China's integration into the global economy, energy markets, and foreign reserves accumulation, its role in climate change and other environmental challenges is forcing fundamental changes in China's relatively passive international position. These factors have added to significant challenges provided by the end of the Cold War at the beginning of the 1990s and the US–China agreement on WTO entry at the end of the 1990s. The disappearance of US–Soviet superpower rivalry meant that China had to reconfigure its international position without the room for manoeuvre that had been offered by the Cold War. It also brought the latent antagonisms in the relationship with the United States to the forefront. China's entry into the WTO builds on the extraordinary economic integration into the world economy that has taken place since the reforms began and shows China's leaders' commitment to being an active member of the world economic community. At the same time, it presents new challenges for the leadership in terms of just how much foreign presence China is willing to tolerate and how destabilizing the foreign presence will be to native industry. The US focus on the 'War on Terrorism' after 11 September 2001 has brought unexpected benefits for China as it has quietened the 'China as a threat' voices, but has raised fears about potential US unilateralism following the 2003 war with Iraq. The emergence of the Chinese economy as a key element in the global production chain has meant that many countries and companies have reorganized their own production strategies to adjust to China's development. It is clear that any significant global challenge needs China's participation to resolve. Thus, it is not surprising that the leadership under Hu Jintao has been more energetic in promoting an independent foreign policy based on China's strategic interests. At the same time, they are trying to assure neighbouring countries that China's increased economic strength will bring benefits to all concerned. This is marking a major departure from Deng Xiaoping's view that China should not get involved in global politics and Jiang Zemin's essentially pro-US position. This chapter considers first China's perceptions of global integration and how this may hamper or contribute to success. Second, it reviews China's position within the region. Third we look at the crucial US–China relationship before concluding by looking at the economic dimension of China's foreign relations.

China and globalization

The November 1999 agreement between China and the United States on China's terms of accession to the WTO, following its signing of the two UN covenants on human rights in 1997 and 1998, signalled the Chinese leadership's intent to be a part of the global community. By signing these agreements, China has implicitly acknowledged that international monitoring is justifiable, not only for domestic economic practice but also for political behaviour. However, in practice, while China clearly wants to be a respected member of the international community, it is deeply conflicted about how active it should be and what kind of a role to play in international governance (Saich, 2000b). Like other countries, China wishes to derive the macroeconomic benefits of globalization but is uncomfortable with the costs of social, political and cultural readjustment. Similarly Western observers have been ambivalent about how to deal with the rise of China's economic power and its integration into global frameworks of governance. Some, taking their cue from historical parallels with the rise of new powers such as Germany and Japan at the turn of the twentieth century, see conflict as inevitable; others argue that the changed international situation makes successful accommodation feasible. The strongest expression of the conflict school is Bernstein and Munro (1997) while a more balanced assessment is presented by Nathan and Ross (1997) and Johnston (2003). The value and nature of US–China engagement is debated by Mann (2007) and Lampton (2007). Certainly it has been the approach of all US presidents from Nixon on that the more China could be engaged with the international community the better. The Obama administration is wrestling with what kind of relationship it wants with China that promotes cooperation but does not negate criticism of China's human rights' record and its actions in Tibet. The difficulty in steering this course was shown during Secretary of State Hillary Clinton's 2009 first visit to Beijing when she was criticized for downplaying human rights' problems in order to get more traction on other issues. Successive US administrations have consistently taken the view that engaging China is better than confronting it as this will lead over time to acceptable political change. The jury is still out on this assessment.

Xenophobic outbursts and leadership manipulation notwithstanding, withdrawal from deeper integration into the world economy and its evolving structures of governance is impossible. This point was made emphatically when, despite significant domestic opposition, Jiang Zemin and Premier Zhu Rongji pushed ahead with a deal with the United States on the terms of accession for WTO. This reflected the leadership's need to deliver further economic progress to strengthen its legitimacy and this progress can be delivered over the long term only through the increased trade, foreign investment and a more disciplined domestic economy that WTO membership would bring. Entry in 2001 was not only important for national pride and to fulfil Jiang's desire to steer China to great power status, but also for very pragmatic economic reasons. In 1999 with FDI dropping, foreign interest in China waning and domestic reforms stumbling, early entry was seen as the best way to stimulate the economy. This was compounded by fears that barriers to entry might rise subsequently, especially as the next round of talks would cover two issues of vital interest to China – agriculture and trade in services. By joining early, China was hoping to forge alliances to secure policies more beneficial to its own national concerns. This has proven to be extremely successful with a massive increase in trade, foreign investment, and accumulation of foreign reserves. China is extremely open to foreign engagement in its economy and according to Steinfeld (forthcoming) has even outsourced to foreign organizations the design of the institutional structure to oversee its economic development.

Despite this more accommodating approach to foreign trade and capital, in crucial respects China's policy approach has mirrored that of their nineteenth-century predecessors in the 'self-strengthening movement' that sought to import Western techniques and equipment while keeping out new cultural and political values. This previous policy of selective adaptation proved shortsighted. The Chinese did not comprehend the interrelated nature of Western societies and failed to see that Western technology could not be easily disentangled from the social and cultural matrix in which it was embedded. It remains to be seen whether the CCP will be more successful in gaining the benefits of globalization without accepting its underlying premises. For example, WTO membership seems to presume not only a liberal trading order, but also an independent legal system that constrains government as necessary, transparency, accountability and a relatively pluralistic political order.

Since Mao Zedong initiated contacts with the United States and engineered the PRC's entry into the United Nations (UN) in the early 1970s, the general consensus has been that China has moved from rejection of the international status quo to acceptance. However, it is more correct to say that China has acquiesced in the international order and while it has been a joiner, for the first thirty years of reform it has not been a doer or rule-setter for international governance. In major part this has been because the main priority has been for China to develop its own economic strength and it has seen international organizations as helping it meet this objective. From 1977 to 1996, China's membership in international government organizations rose from 21 to 51 and in international NGOs from 71 to 1,079 (Kim, 1999, pp. 46–7). As Ikenberry (2008) has written: 'Today's Western order is hard to overturn and easy to join.' This has made China reluctant to challenge the existing rules of the game unless they directly confront Chinese claims to sovereignty or economic interests. In addition, coming out of a period of self-imposed exile, China had very few administrative personnel who could work in international organizations to advance China's interests effectively.

Second, as a latecomer to all international governmental organizations, China did not participate in the drafting of the 'rules of the game'. The incapacity of China to change significantly these 'rules of the game' to suit its national conditions has reinforced its perception that international governance is structured essentially to pursue the agenda and interests of the West, especially the United States. China's self-told history of 150 years of shame and humiliation at the hands of foreigners, the anti-imperialist thrust of Leninism, the party's own legacy of distrust and betrayal and the leaders' tendency to interpret decision-making in terms of a 'zero-sum' game mitigate against constructive engagement and interaction with the existing international governing structures.

Compounding this is the fact that the CCP has never been successful in transnational governance. Its attempts in the 1960s and 1970s to lead a loose coalition of nations to oppose 'US-hegemonism' and 'Soviet revisionism' failed, as did its attempts to fund pro-Maoist groups to destabilize neighbouring governments in Asia. Not surprisingly, Deng Xiaoping's advice to his colleagues and successors was not to take the lead in international affairs, lean towards the United States, and concentrate on economic development. However, this is difficult for a nation with a psychology that emphasizes the superiority of Chinese culture and that sees an international leadership role as a right to be reclaimed.

Such sentiments can lead to instability when combined with the more strident nationalism promoted, or acquiesced to, by Presidents Jiang Zemin and Hu Jintao. While China is currently open for business, distrust of foreigners and significant periods of closure have been common. We have seen that the 'Gang of Four' criticized Deng Xiaoping for his attempts to promote foreign trade (Chapter 3), but Premier Zhu Rongji suffered similar accusations of treason once the United States published what it claimed were the terms he had agreed to for WTO entry during his US visit in April 1999. The head of the People's Bank of China also had to endure similar accusations in 2005. The pro-Mainland Hong Kong press ran articles accusing him of selling off assets cheaply to foreigners and virtually accused him of being a national traitor. The sudden and xenophobic outpouring of anti-foreign sentiment following the accidental NATO bombing of the Chinese Embassy in Belgrade on 7 May 1999 and the downing of the US EP-3 in April 2001 revealed how close to the surface distrust of foreigners still lies.

Since 1989, the Chinese leadership has been fairly successful in manipulating public opinion to instil nationalism as a legitimizing core value. However, the CCP has been careful to set limits to the ramifications of a strident nationalism that might challenge its own position. Thus, while initially supportive of the anti-US demonstration in May 1999, it quickly reined them in once they began to criticize the ineptitude of the government's response. While this appeal to nationalism may aid the regime's short-term stability, it presents two challenges in terms of governance. First, it mitigates against constructive involvement in international organizations as rising nationalism compromises the ability of the nation-state to deal with internationalism. Second, it reinforces the outdated notion of sovereignty that still underpins the current leadership's perceptions of the world. By and large China is an Empire with a Westphalian concept of the nation-state trying to operate in an increasingly multilateral world. In fact, what China wants is an economic order that is international in terms of the benefits it brings but not necessarily global if that means decentring decision-making away from the nation-state.

These trends explain the seeming contradiction in China's international behaviour. The dedication to sovereignty and a territorial definition of China that is the most expansive in history, and China's reluctance to move discussions out of bilateral frameworks, causes uncertainty in the region. It also means that China is more willing to join regimes that govern the international economy, but is less enthusiastic about those regional or global frameworks that would place real restrictions on Chinese military capabilities (Economy and Oksenberg, 1999, p. 21; Swaine and Johnston, 1999, pp. 90–135). The CCP and the military have been adamantly opposed to any attempts to establish an Asian collective security system, primarily because they do not wish to give Southeast Asian nations a forum in which to criticize collectively its claims to sovereignty in the South China Sea (Kim, 1999, p. 56; more generally on engaging China, see Johnston and Ross, 1999). It reaffirmed this view in October 2009 when it stressed that it would not accept a role for ASEAN in resolving such disputes and stated that they must be resolved through bilateral arrangements.

It can also lead to decisions that are described as principled in China but that appear petty to others. Of particular importance in this respect is China's concern to deny international space to Taiwan and to punish those countries that show sympathy towards Taiwan's views. One extreme example was China's veto in the Security Council (February 1999), something almost unprecedented, against the continuation of the UN Preventive Deployment Force in Macedonia, because of the latter's switch of diplomatic recognition to Taiwan in January. Sadly, in light of subsequent events, China's Ambassador to the UN, Qin Huasun, did not mention Taiwan as justification but said that peacekeeping forces were no longer necessary as Macedonia had 'apparently stabilized in the last few years' (*New York Times*, 26 February 1999, p. 11). With the outbreak of SARS on Taiwan, China agreed in April 2003 to allow a two-person

WHO group to visit as a 'humanitarian' gesture but the officials were not allowed to speak with the Taiwanese Minister of Health or other senior officials. However, China was at pains to make sure that this would not lead to a political opening and, as usual, China killed in committee Taiwan's attempt to gain observer status at the WHO.

China needs to be able to feel comfortable with the framework for international governance that it is an increasingly important player in. Many important issues beyond the directly political and economic, such as climate change and environmental protection, drug smuggling, trafficking in women and HIV/AIDS, need China's active participation to resolve. In turn, other major nations need to incorporate China as a more equal partner and to build China's reasonable concerns into the architecture of international governance. China, for its part, needs to reduce its suspicion of hostile foreign intent and adjust its outdated notion of sovereignty to accept that some issues need transnational solutions and that international monitoring does not have to erode CCP power. Without accommodation on both sides, China will remain a rather grumpy, unpredictable player in international governance.

As noted, the strategy of not being overly proactive and not interfering in the affairs of other countries is coming under increasing pressure and there are significant changes beginning to take place. First, while China like most nations prefers bilateral negotiations, it is shifting from suspicion of all multilateral organizations to a realization that rather than ensnaring the country, they can be used to promote the nation's own interest, even if this might mean antagonizing US interests. This is especially important as new institutions are developed to deal with challenges such as climate change and old institutions such as the IMF are restructured to reflect better contemporary rather than post-World War Two realities. In the WTO, China has stressed the organization's regulations that 'regardless of size, all member countries enjoy equal rights' and that labour standards and other non-economic subjects should not enter into WTO considerations. In November 2009, China warned the US that it would use WTO rules to prevent the US from using subsidies to support exports to China. Whether China likes it or not, more countries are likely to lobby it for support on a wide range of global issues and look to China as a leader on some trade and investment-related issues.

Second, China is going to have to define its national interest more clearly and this will mean acknowledging that other principles of its foreign policy may, at times, be overridden. For example, the crisis around nuclear proliferation in North Korea has caused China to moderate or even abandon its principle of non-interference in the domestic affairs of other countries and to take on a more active and public diplomatic role (see below). The actions of its companies overseas and state investments as far afield as Africa and Latin America and the search for energy resources are increasingly pulling China's interests into the internal affairs of these nations. Whether China acknowledges it or not, its commercial activities have become important in the politics of a number of countries in the region and beyond. For example, China's export competitiveness and the volume of exports will severely affect the trade prospects of other countries not just in Asia but in other parts of the world as well. The high levels of foreign direct investment forces other countries also to adopt more hospitable environments for international capital.

China's search for the resources to fuel its economic growth will mean that it will have to become more assertive in pursuing self-interest in foreign policy. Oil is already becoming an important element of foreign policy. This is leading to tensions with the US. Shut out from many mature markets by the US and the EU, China often has no alternative other than to deal with countries such as the Sudan, Iran and Russia. This, in turn leads to criticism from the West for China's support for what they consider 'rogue' regimes. Other environmental consequences are also occurring. In the late 1990s, China implemented a logging ban in Southwest China but this did not quench the domestic thirst for wood products. This has caused extensive stripping of forests in the neighbouring countries of Myanmar and Laos and even as far away as the Amazon.

China and the region

While Taiwan is the major sovereignty issue in the region, China has disputed claims with most of its neighbours including Russia, India and Vietnam, with all of whom it has fought a border war. In addition, it has territorial disputes with Japan and with a number of Southeast Asian neighbours over the demarcation of territorial boundaries in the South China Sea. However, slowly it has moved to resolve these issues so that it can concentrate on economic development. Despite China's seat on the Security Council, China's interests for most of the reform period were overwhelmingly regional (see Hinton, 1994, pp. 348–72). While China claims that it has no hegemonic ambitions in the region, its previous support of liberation movements in Asia, its rapidly growing economy, its relative military capacity and the ongoing territorial disputes make it the major cause of concern for most countries in the region.

Although much of China's foreign policy is rooted in Asia, at the conceptual level in the past it has rarely thought in regional terms at all. This was because its foreign policy was driven by the relationship between the superpowers and by ideological factors. China's leaders are now being forced to develop a regional policy and to think more carefully about engagement with regional institutions such as the Asia Pacific Economic Cooperation Forum (APEC) and the ASEAN Regional Forum (ARF). Increasingly, Beijing has begun to see the development of a 'Greater China' cultural and economic sphere that would include Hong Kong and Taiwan and that would benefit from more open markets in Asia. This was clearly indicated in November 2002 when Premier Zhu Rongji signed a commitment with the ASEAN to form a free trade area by 2010; there is a little irony in China appearing as the leader of economic liberalization throughout the region. A deal was also signed to prevent clashes in disputed areas of the South China Sea. Through the 1980s, China enjoyed considerable success with ASEAN nations, helped by the situation in Kampuchea, and it was noticeably successful in allaying fears about its revolutionary past; this was seen most strongly with the restoration of diplomatic ties with Singapore and Indonesia.

Two main factors have provided China with the opportunity to improve relations in the region and to promote its own interests more explicitly. First, with the US preoccupied with Central Asia and the 'war on terror', it has been able to pay less attention to its post-1945 role in regional economic, diplomatic and security fields. Further it is clear that after 2002 and during the Bush administration, popular support for US policies in the region has declined. Many saw the US as preferring unilateralism in foreign affairs to building partnerships. It remains to be seen whether the Obama administration is able to reverse this trend. Despite intent, domestic issues will take up much of its energy (healthcare reform and climate change) and internationally dealing with two wars in Afghanistan and Iraq, while trying to influence behaviour in Pakistan and the Middle East will take up most of its diplomatic capital.

Second, China has become a lynchpin in the reorganization of the international production chain with many other national economies and companies in the region restructuring their own domestic production strategies and external investment plans to match China's development needs. China has become the most important assembly and manufacturing hub and its growth has been especially important for aiding the recovery of the Japanese and South Korean economies in the early part of this century, and many are relying on China to pull the region out of the downturn caused by the 2008–09 economic crisis. Its need for natural resources has been beneficial to countries such as Australia and Indonesia and it has become the number one trading country for Japan and South Korea. Unlike the US, the countries of ASEAN run a trade surplus with China and countries such as Kampuchea, Laos, and Myanmar are virtual client states because of Chinese investment and aid. China needs to assure the countries of the region that its continued economic growth will continue to benefit them and not come at their expense.

However, difficulties remain in addition to the territorial conflicts, and some countries remain worried about China's growing economic might. Countries such as Vietnam, Indonesia and Thailand are more likely to run into competition with China through their own production of textiles, light manufacturing and basic consumer goods. Indeed, one important reason for Vietnam agreeing to a major trade deal with the United States in July 2000 was its concern about the consequences of the recently signed deal between the United States and China. By contrast, Japan should be a natural partner with its capital, advanced technology and high-quality capital goods; however, this relationship is thwarted by political history, mutual suspicions and the concern of other ASEAN countries that Japan should not commit itself to China to the detriment of others.

These trends are pushing China to develop a more coherent approach to its Asia policy. At the conceptual level, the leadership under Hu Jintao has promoted the slogan of 'peace and development' (first used by Hu at the Baoao Forum in May 2005) as a response to those who see the country's rise as a current and, more importantly, future threat. At the regional level, China has been promoting the idea of regional security. China's increased acceptance of multilateral frameworks to promote its national interest has stemmed from two sets of experiences. First, China has led the Shanghai Cooperation Organization that brings together Central Asian states with China to discuss security and other issues. The importance that China attaches to this organization is shown by the fact that it has moved the headquarters from Shanghai to Beijing. Second, the experience of working with the ARF that it joined in 1994 has also been beneficial. China saw the opportunity to reduce suspicions about Chinese power and to reduce US influence without negating the US relationship. However, military confidence building measures through ARF have not developed far.

There has been much discussion about whether China presents a military threat. Fravel (2008) defines China's strategic goals as being keyed 'to ensure the defence of a continental state, governed by an authoritarian political system, with growing maritime interests and several unresolved territorial disputes, especially over Taiwan's unification'. From China's perspective these are largely conservative and not expansionist aims. However, viewed from the region they appear potentially threatening and could cause arms proliferation. This is compounded by the fact that China defines its military doctrine as preparing to fight 'local wars under modern hi-tech conditions'. China's defence spending while rising rapidly in total terms has stayed constant at roughly 8 per cent of GDP and even the highest Pentagon calculation of military spending ($139 billion in 2007) was not as high as US spending on the navy ($147 billion: Fravel, 2008).

Despite progress, China's relationship in the region faces three general challenges and four specific problems. First, as noted China needs to keep convincing its neighbours that its economic strength will be of benefit to all rather than at the expense of its neighbours. Not all will agree with China's 'win-win' scenarios, especially farmers who are priced out of the market by the import of cheap agricultural products from China. Second, there remains the need to develop new institutions and a framework that will allow the countries in the region to cooperate effectively. Third, China's increased influence in the region needs to be pursued in a manner that does not challenge, at least in the short to medium term, US fundamental interests in the region. For other countries to accept a partial withdrawal of the US would mean that China would have to take their interests into account and even give up its expansive view of sovereignty and enter into new security arrangements so that they would not feel the need to rely on the US security umbrella.

The potential for friction is apparent in all the four specific challenges. First, there are the remaining territorial claims in the South China Sea mentioned above. Second, there is the problem of cross-straits relations. China views reunification with Taiwan as an internal matter left unresolved from the civil war. For many years, the Taiwanese leadership shared Beijing's view but simply disputed who was the legitimate ruler of the one China. As far as China is concerned, this is a domestic matter that the United States should not be involved in, and it has continually pushed for the US to accept its position and to halt weapon sales to Taiwan that it claims makes Taiwan more likely to pursue independence. The latent danger of military conflict was highlighted by the dramatic events of 1995–96. China's leaders reacted angrily to then President Lee Teng-hui's invitation to Cornell University and felt that President Clinton had deceived them. This was a shock to the Chinese foreign policy establishment and made senior leaders wake up to the role of Congress. They had always been used to the US President making China policy, often without consultation with Congress. This had been the case with the secret negotiations opened by Nixon, with moves by Carter to normalization and when Bush senior sent a secret emissary after 1989. Their mode of operation had been that the US executive branch makes China policy, and the legislative goes along with it. It took China's policy-makers a while to realize that in the post-Tiananmen environment this had changed.

Beijing began military exercises in the Straits, suspended talks with Taiwan and showed its diplomatic displeasure. It showed its military teeth in 1996 as President Lee campaigned to become the first democratically elected President of Taiwan. With China launching missiles into the Straits as a warning, the US dispatched two battleships to the area. In a sense, the brinkmanship was useful in clarifying the limits of the possible. For Taiwan, it made it clear that any moves to independence would be harshly met by Beijing and that there were limits to their capacity for diplomatic manoeuvre. For China, it indicated that under certain conditions the United States would intervene to protect Taiwan, something that China had thought it would not do. For the United States, it clarified that its historical involvement remained very much alive and that it would remain actively involved, like it or not. From China's perspective things turned even worse in 2000 when opposition DPP member, Chen Shui-bian, was elected President of Taiwan, defeating the officially backed GMD candidate. While Beijing's rhetoric was loud and harsh, its actions were more calculated and a 'wait-and-see' attitude prevailed despite a number of things that could have been seen as deliberate provocation. This maturity from Beijing in not responding to every perceived slight has improved the atmosphere and the increasing Taiwanese presence in the Mainland economy (over $100 billion has been invested) has integrated Taiwan's economy with that of the Mainland to such an extent that conflict would be very destructive to the island's economy. It seems that leaders in Beijing decided to adopt a similar tactic as with Hong Kong to tie the fortunes of the business elite to the Mainland and hope they would become a pressure group for improved relations and eventual reunification. This has had some success but nationalism may still trump economic rationality.

When the DPP controlled the presidency from 2000 until 2008, the CCP began to court the nationalist party (GMD), inviting them to talks in China. This paid a dividend when Ma Ying-jeou was returned as the new President in 2008, direct flights across the straits began, trade and investment expanded and tourism took off. However, Taiwan's international space continued to shrink as China nibbled away further at the few countries that still accorded Taiwan diplomatic recognition. China did, however, allow Taiwan to send a delegation to the World Health Assembly in May 2009, the first time that it had agreed to Taiwan taking part in any UN activity. Despite this, there has been criticism on Taiwan of President Ma for giving away too much to Beijing with little to show in return.

The third problem is the question of North Korea's nuclear ambitions. China and the United States have a common strategic interest in ensuring that there is no conflict on the Korean peninsula and that North Korea does not become a full nuclear power. The situation is tricky for Beijing, and both rapprochement between North and South and deterioration of relations present problems. Nuclear tests by North Korea in October 2006 and again in May 2009 have placed China in a difficult position. In fact, China has a 1961 Peace Treaty with North Korea that has never been rescinded and that commits China to support North Korea in the case of war, unlikely but still embarrassing. The tests have improved relations between China and Japan as well as cooperation with the US on trying to solve the problem. The US has ceded considerable authority to China to bring North Korea to the negotiating table, primarily through the Six-party talks (also including Japan, Russia and South Korea) but China has discovered, if it did not know already just how difficult it is to deal with North Korea. China is clearly the country with the most influence over North Korea and could bring the country to its knees should it wish to do so. Seventy per cent of North Korea's energy needs are met by China and China accounts for 39 per cent of its imports and exports. In November 2009, North Korea announced that it had completed reprocessing its spent nuclear fuel for use in a bomb and used this to try to push for a break out from the Six-party talks and to engage the US in bilateral talks (see *SCMP*, 4 November 2009). This is not what Beijing wants. China has been at best ambivalent and usually opposed to using sanctions to bring North Korea to heel.

China is clearly frustrated at North Korea's behaviour but is more concerned about regime collapse that would bring migrants flooding into China and the US presence up to its borders. As a result, it has opposed harsh sanctions and has tried to prompt the North Korean leadership to adopt Chinese-style economic reforms that might usher in gradual change. The fear of regime collapse has also been a major concern to South Korea and it has oscillated between attempts to engage and isolate the North. By contrast, the major concern for the US is to prevent North Korea possessing an adequate number of effective nuclear missiles, an objective shared by Japan.

The fourth challenge is the question of leadership in the region and this involves China, Japan and the US and, more specifically, how well China and Japan can accommodate to each other. This latter relationship is highly unpredictable and potentially very volatile. Japan is the most important bilateral relationship in the region. Despite the obvious compatibility of the two economies, two-way trade has suffered a number of problems and Japanese economic involvement in China remains far below its potential. The reasons have included the normal frustrations that foreign investors face, combined with the suspicions that both countries harbour about the other as a result of the Japanese invasion in 1937 and China's view that it has not yet made a satisfactory apology for its treatment of the Chinese during the occupation. The tensions with North Korea and the loss of power by the LDP in Japan may provide an opportunity for improved relations. The historical animosities press on the present and mean that any incident can ignite nationalist sentiments in either country. A functioning working relationship needs to be established in order to prevent long-term uncertainty in the East Asian region. The renewal of the US–Japan security guidelines has caused Beijing concern and heightened its view that Japan plays an important role in the US attempts to constrain China. The presence of US troops in Japan and discussions of the theatre missile defence have increased these worries.

China and the United States

It has become commonplace to refer the US–China relationship as the most important bilateral relationship in the world, commonplace as it is true. It even led the historian Niall Ferguson (2007) to refer to 'Chimerica' as the two economies had become so complementary. As he noted, the Chinese save and the US spends while the Chinese lend and the Americans borrow. However, by 2009, he felt this relationship was breaking up, with the Chinese not only no longer willing to bankroll US debt but also deeply concerned about America's profligate ways. This reality was at best only a temporary arrangement and the relationship has been and will be much more complex. China was one country where the Bush administration was considered very positively, after WTO entry trade expanded significantly, and frictions had been kept to a minimum. The Obama administration has a solid foundation to build on but it will have to deal with traditional issues in the relationship such as human rights and trade as well as building an agenda for new issues such as climate change and global warning.

As China entered the 1990s, two major events significantly affected its foreign policy relations with the US. The first was the fallout from the repression of the 1989 demonstrations that produced a strong backlash from the Western nations. The honeymoon period that China had enjoyed with the West throughout the 1980s abruptly ended and rights abuses that the West had been muted suddenly became the focus of extensive media and political attention. It led to an arms embargo from the US that has not been lifted to the present. Second, the tearing down of the Berlin Wall and the subsequent collapse from power of the Soviet Communist Party dramatically affected Chinese foreign policy. China found it hard to adjust to the new world order, even more so as Chinese leaders were used to thinking in terms of an overarching framework based on ideological premises that provided structure to policy and relationships. China had settled into a foreign policy premised on the notion that international politics would be dominated by the existence of a bipolar relationship between the two superpowers. This afforded China the opportunity to play off one against the other and create more space for itself in international affairs. With the balance upset, China began to feel vulnerable and marginalized in world affairs.

The main advantage to China was that it was now free to pursue more unashamedly its own national interests without reference to ideological considerations. As an internal document published shortly after the failed coup of the hard-liners in Russia (1991) stated, China needed to move away from letting moral judgements and ideological considerations predominate. National interest should be put first and foremost and it was no longer necessary to dress up policies in socialist rhetoric. It concluded:

> China is a great power, it should forthrightly establish a general strategy in keeping with its great power status. Moral foreign relations cannot be conducted any longer, the principle of national interest should take the guiding role. (Translated in Kelly, 1996, pp. 13–31)

This would certainly keep China from repeating the messy involvement resulting from its radical anti-Soviet stance of the 1970s when it provided support to Pinochet in Chile and the National Union for the Total Independence of Angola (UNITA) in Angola. With no superpower rivalry, China had less interest in Third World conflicts as it did not matter so much who won. This may change again over the next 20 years as China begins to become more oil-dependent on the Middle East. Iran and Saudi Arabia are China's two main oil suppliers and imports from the Middle East account for 50 per cent of the total imports. However, in this case engagement will be a result of pragmatic economic need rather than ideological necessity. China, as discussed below, is now heavily involved in Africa with its natural resources and markets primary targets for China's development.

China moved quickly to establish diplomatic relations with both former pro-Soviet regimes in the developing world and with the newly independent states that emerged from the break-up of the former Soviet Union. The reasons were two-fold. First, China wished to deny Taiwan the chance to exploit any possibility to establish diplomatic relations. Second, in recognizing the new Central Asian states, China wished to pre-empt the chance that they might become supporters of Muslim fundamentalists within China.

The first Gulf War (1991) provided China with the chance to improve its standing as a global actor and work to overturn some of the sanctions imposed after 1989. It used its role in the UN Security Council in the offensive build-up to side with the US-led coalition. However, as it became clear that force would be used, it abstained in the crucial Security Council vote that authorized the use of force against Iraq. The overwhelming US military might shocked the Chinese high command and for the leadership more broadly there was the concern that the new multipolar world they were touting would in fact be unipolar and US-dominated.

As a result, through the 1990s no new basis for a relationship between the United States and China was forged. The Chinese leadership sought, despite domestic opposition, to maintain Deng Xiaoping's legacy of a neutral or pro-US international orientation that would help facilitate China's ambitious plans for modernization. This meant that despite attempts to improve the relationship on both sides, suspicions remained and unforeseen events could often set the relationship into a tailspin. On the positive side there were the 1994 Clinton decision to de-link trade and human rights (reversing his 1993 executive order conditioning Most-Favoured Nation status on human rights, protecting Tibet's culture and allowing broadcasts into China); the June 1998 Clinton statement on the 'three nos' (see below); the November 1999 agreement on terms of WTO entry; and the signing into law in October 2000 of provisions for China's permanent normal trading status. The 'three nos' were apparently communicated to Jiang Zemin by Clinton in the summer of 1995 and relayed orally during Jiang's visit to the United States and then mentioned publicly by Clinton in Shanghai in June 1998. They refer to no recognition of Taiwanese independence, no support for two Chinas or one Taiwan and one China, and no endorsement of Taiwan's entry into any international organization for which statehood would be required. This abandoned the two-decades-old policy designed to preserve the right of Taiwan's people to self-determination (Tucker, 2000, p. 251). This has remained policy down to the present.

On the negative side was China's general impression that it did not count in US policy-making and the perception that the United States had an active, if undeclared, policy to contain China. There was the casual way in which President Clinton appeared to deal with the 1995 invitation of then Taiwanese President Lee Teng-Hui to visit his *alma mater*, Cornell University: Chinese foreign minister, Qian Qichen, had been assured that no invitation would be issued, only for President Clinton under pressure from Congress to turn around and relent. The 7 May 1999 accidental bombing by a US aircraft of the Chinese Embassy in Belgrade, causing considerable damage and loss of life, served to only compound the frustration and feeling of helplessness.

The new Bush administration that took over in January 2001 seemed to confirm China's worst fears as it adopted a much more confrontational stance and a seemingly more sympathetic view of Taiwan. The collision between a US spyplane and a Chinese jetfighter (April 2001) resulting in Chinese loss of life and a tense stand-off, marked a new low in the relationship. However, it also had the effect of awakening some in the new US administration to the fact that some kind of constructive dialogue with China was necessary. In diplomatic terms China was a major beneficiary of the 11 September 2001 terrorist attacks on the United States. It was hard to establish a political rhetoric of China as a threat or enemy when Al-Qaeda terrorists had just flown fully loaded civilian aircraft into the World Trade Center and the Pentagon. China has been seen as cooperative in the 'War on Terror' and in many ways this led to a better relationship than at any time since the 1980s. It is debatable, however, whether the relationship would survive another unexpected accident and mutual suspicion is still strong on both sides (for thoughtful sets of essays, see Vogel, 1997 and Rosecrance and Gu, 2009).

The need for cooperation was reinforced by the questions of North Korea and Taiwan discussed above. In addition both countries have a vested interest in preventing an escalation of conflict between India and Pakistan. The economic relationship requires good relations while there are a number of other issues on which collaboration would be beneficial, such as environmental pollution, with the United States surpassed by China in 2009 as the world's biggest carbon emitter. Starting with his February 2003 speech at Tsinghua University, President Bush and the administration made it clear that they wanted a positive relationship with China. President Bush noted that America welcomed 'the emergence of a strong and peaceful and prosperous China'. Strong voices on both sides doubt this, and in China US attempts to remain the one dominant superpower are viewed with alarm. US troops are now stationed in Afghanistan and Central Asia as well as traditional bases in Japan and South Korea and a possible collapse of North Korea, it is feared, would bring US troops right up to the Chinese border.

In December 2005 then Deputy Secretary of State, Robert Zoellick clearly outlined that the strategy of engagement had been correct and encouraged China to become a 'responsible stakeholder', a phrase that initially baffled the Chinese for a good translation but that later they came to find appropriate. Zoellick's idea was that this would encourage China to work with the US and others to sustain, adapt and advance the peaceful international system that has enabled it to succeed economically (for a contrary view see Mann, 2007; for a sympathetic view see Lampton, 2001a). The more China was bound into the existing international architecture, the more likely it is to be a responsible international citizen. It is noteworthy that when Zoellick moved to head the World Bank (July 2007), he appointed the Chinese economist from Beijing University, Yifu Lin, to be the Chief Economist.

The Obama administration is trying to build on this positive legacy but it is confronted by a number of challenges. It is clear that the growth of China's economy and its strong and quick rebound from 2008–09 has made it more assertive in terms of what it seeks from the relationship. China no longer considers itself a junior partner and is not willing for the US to dictate the terms of the relationship. This requires a psychological shift on the part of the US. The Obama administration has developed its own new term to describe what it wants from the relationship; it is using the phrase a 'positive, cooperative and comprehensive relationship'. This indicates that the relationship is multifaceted and no single issue should be allowed to dominate, hence the criticism of Secretary of State Hillary Clinton not paying enough attention to human rights during her May 2009 trip. To maintain the broader focus to the relationship, the two countries have set up the annual Strategic and Economic Dialogue that first met in July 2009, a successor to the Strategic Economic Dialogue begun by the Bush administration in 2006. This broadens out the summit meetings from the earlier focus on discussions of human rights, nuclear proliferation and trade to include a range of global issues. The 'strategic track' is led on the US side by the Secretary of State and covers political and strategic issues and the 'economic track' is led by the Treasury Secretary. President Obama's visit in November 2009 covered a similar broad agenda without resulting in any specific progress. In 2010, the relationship underwent its first serious test with US arms sales to Taiwan and a meeting between President Obama and the Dalai Lama. While China criticized these two actions, it was clear that they did not wish to disrupt the relationship. Yet, as Premier Wen's press conference at the closing of the 2010 NPC session made clear, China was no longer in a mood to give in to US pressure on issues such as currency revaluation.

Despite the generally reasonable relationship, problems remain and there is distrust on both sides. Tsinghua Professor, Yan Xuetong, captures the Chinese perspective well by stating: 'We are business partners who share material interests rather than common values' (quoted in *Wall Street Journal*, 9 November 2009). However, this does mean that there are grounds for discussion and agreement even if these fall short of an ideal relationship. As Douglas Paal (1997), now vice-president for studies at the Carnegie Endowment for International Peace, noted: 'China will be likely at most a source of "problems" for America, not a "threat." And problems can be fixed.' They do require effort and mutual respect.

In addition to the territorial disputes and the North Korean nuclear proliferation problem discussed in the previous section, there are two traditional issues that have caused dispute: human rights practices and trade and related economic issues. The question of human rights has become a major issue in the relationship since 1989. The breakdown in bipartisan support for a constructive engagement with China led to a more powerful voice for human rights activists and religious groups critical of China's record. This included groups focusing specifically on China such as Human Rights in China, groups that have a broader mandate with a particular concern about China such as Human Rights Watch, and labour unions and Christian groups that are concerned about persecution of believers in China. There is also a strong lobby that is concerned about the situation in Tibet and what is seen as the destruction of Tibetan culture and the swamping of Tibet with ethnic Han

Chinese. The United States has tried a number of means to try to force China to shift its stance on human rights and improve its record of governance. These have ranged from private diplomacy to public criticism to the use of international forums and the threat of economic sanctions (Harding, 1997, pp. 165–84). In particular, there was the annual introduction by the United States of a resolution to condemn China for its human rights abuses in Geneva at the meeting of the UN Commission on Human Rights. China worked successfully each year to undermine this resolution and from 1997 onwards was successful in breaking European and Oceanian support. Many nations came to see the resolution as a fruitless exercise that made no progress and only made building relations with China even more difficult. In 2003, the Bush administration took a new approach and did not sponsor a motion critical of China's human rights record. The administration decided to take China's comments that not exerting public pressure but engaging in quiet diplomacy would bring greater progress. It was also intended to give the new leadership a chance to ameliorate the situation without appearing to succumb to US pressure. The previous year, the United States and China agreed that the East Turkestan Islamic Movement operating in Xinjiang was a terrorist organization, thus giving Jiang Zemin something concrete to show for his support of the US 'War on Terror'. With the revival of bipartisan support for trying to develop a more comprehensive relationship with China, the space for human rights' organizations to influence US policy has shrunk and the Obama administration has made it clear that no one issue will dominate the bilateral relationship.

Second, there are a number of frictions around trade and investment and not all of these have been smoothed away by the WTO agreement. Despite the omnipresent McDonald's in urban China, US businesses have complained of the hidden barriers to entry in China and the hope that WTO rules on transparency would clear them from the path have not been fully realized. In particular, US companies have complained about piracy that has resulted in significant annual losses for US companies. The periodic high-profile crushing or burning of pirated materials and collaboration with Pinkerton's in China has not stemmed the growth. Industry groups calculate that piracy runs at around 95 per cent for entertainment software, 90 per cent for records and music, and 62 per cent for business software, resulting in an annual loss to US businesses of around $3.5 billion. By contrast, the Chinese have complained about US restrictions on technology transfer from the United States, with the latter often holding back on the most advanced technology not only for commercial reasons but also because of concerns about military adaptation. Chinese officials regularly claim that if the US wants to reduce the trade imbalance, allowing exports from the US in this area would have a significant impact.

Although China is now the United States' second-largest trading partner, there has been considerable friction about the level of the US trade deficit. This mirrored earlier US concerns with Japan and Taiwan. With these now moving up the development chain, much of the anger has focused on China using its cheap labour to promote exports of goods such as toys, clothing and computer components. Nobody denies that the deficit has risen rapidly as China's exports boom, but there are considerable differences about how the deficit is calculated and whether it is structural and will continue to grow. Trade amounted to just $1 billion when China's reforms began in 1978 and jumped to $5 billion in 1980, the first year that China was covered by most-favoured-nation trading status. It grew steadily and received another boost with China's WTO entry in 2000. Trade with China accounts for 12 per cent of US global trade. Under Obama, trade frictions have begun to grind on the relationship; in September 2009, the US imposed 35 per cent tariffs on Chinese-made tyres and in November 24 to 37 per cent tariffs on steel pipes. China has authorized investigation into the export practices of US car makers to see if there are unfair subsidies. Unless nipped in the bud such frictions can easily escalate.

The problem is that as trade has grown so has the deficit for the US. While the US ran a trade surplus of $2.7 billion in 1980, this has shot up, according to US official figures, to $266 billion in 2008, three times the deficit with Japan. The financial crisis moderated this growth and may even cause a slight decline but the structural problem remains. Chinese estimates of the deficit are much lower. Independent assessments that discount factors such as re-exports through Hong Kong (half of bilateral trade) and discount the value-added that accrues to US companies producing in China, also produce a much lower figure than the US official statistics. The fact that a significant amount of exports to the United States are from US-invested firms is distinct from Japan's exports to the United States, which are made up almost entirely of local products manufactured by their own companies.

There has been a strong voice in the US complaining that a root cause of the deficit is the value of the Chinese currency that makes US exports too expensive and has contributed to the undermining of manufacturing. China does not have a market-based floating currency and from 1994 until 2005, China pegged its currency to the dollar at a rate of 8.28 *yuan*. Some analysts have complained that by 2005, it was undervalued by anywhere between 15 per cent and 30 per cent. The US has consistently pressed China to revalue the currency, something which China's leaders resisted as they feared it might lead to a decline in exports that might cause domestic instability. However, in July 2005, the value was appreciated by 2.1 per cent when China moved to a managed float based on a basket of major foreign currencies (but still dominated by the dollar). By the end of 2008, the value of the *yuan* had risen to 6.83 to the dollar (roughly 17.5 per cent). The Bush administration never cited the Chinese government with currency manipulation and this presumably was a reward for their private discussions and pressure. With the onset of the financial crisis, it is clear that the Chinese government halted this gradual appreciation for fear that it might contribute further to the economic problems that China's export system was facing. It looked as if the Obama administration might break with the Bush policy when Geithner, in his confirmation hearings for Treasury Secretary, claimed that China was engaged in currency manipulation. This was a statement that the administration quickly distanced itself from and in April 2009 when the Treasury released its report on exchange rates it stated 'China's continued large current account surplus and accumulation of foreign exchange reserves suggest the *renminbi* [*yuan*] remains undervalued.' 'Currency manipulator' is conspicuously absent.

The non-convertibility of the Chinese currency has meant that there are high costs of sterilizing the currency and the build-up of massive foreign reserves that China has then reinvested in purchasing US debt. By September 2008, China had overtaken Japan as the largest holder of US Treasuries. By the end of June 2008, China held $1,205 billion of US securities and this had risen as a percentage of total foreign holdings from 3.9 per cent in 2002 to 11.7 per cent in mid 2008. Over the last decade, this system had worked well for US consumers and for Chinese growth. China recycled the money it earned from exports to buy US debt, allowing the US to keep interest rates low and permitting US consumers to keep buying cheaply produced Chinese imports. The 2008–09 financial crisis has disturbed this cycle and has raised concerns from both parties. Some in the US are worried that Chinese control over US debt may give it undue leverage over domestic policy decisions. China's leaders are concerned about US profligacy and the fact that the massive bail-out may lead to inflation in the US over time or a large decline in the value of the dollar both of which would cause a drop in the value of Chinese-held assets. To get better returns on their dollars than buying US Treasuries, China set up a sovereign wealth fund to invest funds more effectively (see below).

To this agenda can now be added climate change and energy development. Together the US and China account for 40 per cent of the world's greenhouse gases, with China taking over in 2009 as the main emitter of carbon gases. It is clear that there can be no meaningful global agreement on climate change without the cooperation of these two economic powerhouses. However, while the Obama administration is taking global warming far more seriously than the Bush administration, it shares the view that America will not agree to cap emissions without similar commitments from developing countries such as China. China, for its part, does not want to be seen to bend to US and Western pressure on this issue and shares the view of other developing countries that it should not be expected to match US actions and that the developed economies should make significant payments to help transfer the necessary technologies to the developing countries. Presidents Obama and Hu will presumably come to some kind of agreement to work together on the problem but it is unlikely to be very specific. The UN climate conference in Copenhagen in December 2009, which was meant to find a successor agreement to the Kyoto Protocol of 1997 (a treaty to cut carbon emissions that the US Congress never ratified), revealed the frictions and produced an inconclusive outcome. The Hu–Wen leadership seems to have come increasingly to understand the serious of the damage that climate change could cause to the country's development but a major problem is that around 70 per cent of its electricity supply comes from coal and the challenge is whether China can introduce new technologies to reduce carbon emissions or develop new energy sources swiftly enough.

The main route for reducing energy effectiveness and energy independence are through increasing efficiency. The Chinese economy produces one-quarter of the economic output of the US, yet uses three-quarters of the energy of the US. Thus, China's legacy of industrial development has an energy intensity three times that of the US. By contrast, the Japanese economy is one-third that of the US yet it consumes only one-fifth of the energy of the US. China has recognized the problem and is now investing heavily in renewable energy with targets not far behind those of the European Union. China ranked second for the amount invested in renewable energy in 2007 ($12 billion, only $2 billion behind Germany). China is developing wind and solar power quickly and intends that these should provide 15 per cent of total power supply by 2020. China is already the world's leading renewable energy producer in terms of installed generating capacity, with the largest hydro-electric sector and the fifth largest wind power sector. Further, it is the world's leading manufacturer of solar photovoltaic technology and is vying to take the lead in other critical renewable and low-carbon technologies such as solar water heaters, energy-efficient home appliances and rechargeable batteries. These developments provide the potential for fruitful US–China cooperation.

By the mid 1990s, the remaining frictions and tensions in the relationship with the United States led the Chinese leadership to try to raise its international profile and knit together its own set of strategic alliances. The leadership desperately want to believe that the world can be multipolar, even though this view is ridiculed by some of the country's own academia. The attempts were begun by Jiang but have been continued by Hu. This lay behind China's 'rediscovery' of Europe and

Africa (see below), both continents having been the target of senior visits since the late 1990s. It also led to attempts to breathe new life into the relationship with Russia but while the leaders of both countries have talked about a 'strategic partnership' to build a multipolar world, it is clear that for both the relationship is secondary to one with the US.

China's foreign economic relations

One of the most striking aspects of the pragmatic post-Mao foreign policy has been the important role that economic factors have played. As late as 1977, the Chinese press was insisting that China 'would never receive foreign loans' and 'never allow foreigners to meddle in the management of our enterprises'. Despite the occasional hiccups and the frustrations of many foreign business investors, the speed of change has been staggering. Starting in 1979 Chinese development strategy shifted from import substitution, the privileging of accumulation over consumption and viewing foreign trade as irrelevant to economic growth, to an active interaction with the world economy in which foreign trade – and, latterly, investment – were seen as major engines of growth. China entered the global markets at a fortuitous time and with its cheap and abundant labour supply benefited from the rapidly unfolding globalization of the manufacturing process, rapid strides in telecommunications and internationalization of capital markets.

The economic figures speak for themselves and the effect of WTO entry has been dramatic. The ratio of foreign trade to GDP rose from 12.6 per cent in 1980 to 39.5 per cent in 1995; from 1990 to 2008 trade rose 22-fold from $115 billion to $2.56 trillion (of which over 60 per cent is concentrated in Asia, with the United States accounting for 17.6 per cent of exports and 7.2 per cent of imports). Exports amounted to 37 per cent of GDP in 2007. In 2008 China's trade surplus was $295.6 billion, up from 22.5 billion in 2001. However, it is worth pointing out that it was only in 1993 that China surpassed its 1928 level of two-way trade comprising 2.6 per cent of the world total; the total had fallen to only 0.6 per cent in 1977 (*The Economist*, 20 November 1999, p. 25). It is moving quickly, however, and by the end of the decade China was the third largest trader. In terms of growth of exports, China is number one from 1998 to 2004 with an annual growth rate of 21.5 per cent. FDI, having appeared to peak in 1998, has moved ahead again, but about 60 per cent comes from Hong Kong and Taiwan. The utilized FDI in 2008 was $92.4 billion up from $46.9 billion in 2001. Of this the US accounted for 3.2 per cent down from a peak of 10.8 per cent in 2000. It is important to note that the nature of this investment changed from the 1980s to the 1990s. In the 1980s the concentration was on light industry, producing labour-intensive products that used simple production techniques and processes. From 1992, the new investors were Asian multinational corporations that invested in infrastructure, real estate and financial services (Yasheng Huang, 1998, pp. 5–6). This represented 40 per cent of FDI flows. China's own FDI has risen dramatically with $150 billion invested, making it the world's sixth largest overseas investor. Foreign reserves (excluding gold) hit a record $2.27 trillion in September 2009 up from $212.2 million in 2000.

The desire for foreign technology combined with the constraints at the end of the 1970s meant that China turned to a variety of methods, both commercial and non-commercial, as well as boosting trade (for the politics of this, see Howell, 1993). The first major step was the adoption in 1979 of the Joint Venture Law, amended in 1990, that not only led eventually to equity joint-ventures but paved the way for the establishment of contractual joint ventures and wholly owned foreign enterprises. This was China's first foray into the world of FDI. China also began to take medium- and long-term loans on generally favourable terms from foreign organizations, governments and international organizations, such as the IMF and the World Bank. In 1986, the passage of the Law on Wholly Foreign-Owned Enterprises marked a further stage in the acceptance of foreign capital as a key plank in development policy.

Especially important was the decision in 1979 to establish four Special Economic Zones (Shenzhen, Zhuhai, Xiamen and Shantou) to function as export processing zones. They were important as pilots of reform for the rest of the Chinese economy and many new laws and regulations were tried out there. The more flexible policies were extended to 14 more coastal cities in April 1984 and Hainan island, which in 1988 became an independent province and was given the same powers as the original zones. The strategy evolved by January 1985 to establish three large development triangles along the coast based around the Pearl River Delta, the Min River and the Yangzi River. The Yangzi development was seen as part of the resurrection of Shanghai as a key financial and trading centre, with the new development of Pudong as the focal point. The zones were to operate as a 'window' for the introduction of technology, management techniques and information. The belief was that 'trickle-down' would benefit the hinterland of China, and at the 1989 NPC meeting Premier Zhao Ziyang's 'coastal-strip strategy' was accepted. However, it was not without critics and even at the NPC meeting 300 voted against and 700 abstained. Essentially, the poorer areas were disgruntled with what they saw as the continued preferential treatment of already wealthy areas. Others criticized the economic benefits as negligible; they complained of the diversion of large amounts of funds to develop infrastructure and communications in the zones in exchange for which little advanced technology was brought in, with only a small fraction of total output being exported. Last, but not least, there were attacks on the zones as carriers of a variety of 'bourgeois' afflictions that would undermine the communist edifice. However, the zones survived such attacks, even those that followed the 1989 crackdown and the removal of Zhao Ziyang. Rapidly, their 'specialness' became commonplace as many provinces and even towns took their own initiative to open free zones for foreign investors, even when there was no legal basis to do so. At the end of the 1990s, in its efforts to develop the western part of the country, the government formally allowed localities to increase the tax benefits for foreign investors.

Many have been dazzled by the levels of FDI going into China and most multinationals have been keen to gain a foothold in the Chinese market, but China's experience with FDI has been more nuanced than the headline figures reveal. This has been persuasively argued by Yasheng Huang (2000, and 2003) that the large amount of FDI reveals a fundamental weakness in China's economy, rather than strength. While there was gradual growth through the 1980s, Huang shows that the real take-off occurred between 1992 and 1994 and that the institutional imperatives on the Chinese side for FDI did not necessarily match the intentions of China's central policy-makers. As noted above, the rationale for opening up to FDI was to bring in advanced technology and capital.

Huang concludes that policy has failed for importing technological hardware but that the picture is mixed with respect to factors such as acquisition of new organizational techniques and managerial skills. Most of the enterprises that have foreign investment are labour- rather than technology-intensive. Even in Shanghai, 80 per cent of such enterprises are judged to be 'labour-intensive'. Certainly large amounts of foreign capital have come in, but this happened at a time of a general significant rise in capital flows to developing countries. As we have seen, the primary use of FDI is often to evade restrictions on domestic enterprises, thus suggesting that it may not be used optimally. The FDI has also not been allowed to flow to the private sector of the economy where more effective use could be made. The last vital component of early policy to open China's economy and integrate it into the world economy was the decentralization of the foreign trade apparatus and the various reforms stimulated a massive increase in foreign trade.

By the end of the 1990s it had become apparent that the success of China's overall reform objectives would be influenced significantly by international factors outside of China's control. This was already the case before the agreements were reached between China and its major trading partners on WTO entry. The policy of raising foreign capital through the production of export goods depends on the health of the international economy and especially the views of the US Congress, while the need for advanced foreign technology imports depends on the status of Western import controls, a fact that was brought home to Beijing's leaders in the brief period of sanctions after 1989. There is no doubt that China is now integrated with the global economy and the fate of its domestic reforms is now more dependent on trends in the international economy than ever before. Previously, as Pearson (1999, pp. 187–8) has noted, the core of the Chinese economy had remained somewhat insulated from the competitive pressures of the world economy and the impact of trade had been more limited on the domestic economy than the figures might lead one to presume. That said, China has escaped the worst impacts of both the Asian Financial Crisis of 1997–98 and the global financial crisis of 2008–09. Despite the greater integration of China's economy by 2008, government leaders were able to use a massive stimulus package to boost domestic demand through infrastructure investment and maintain growth rates of 8 to 9 per cent. While trade and foreign investment are important they should not be exaggerated as China, like the US, is a continental-size economy.

That China agreed to the terms of WTO entry is surprising given the opposition but the results are clear for all to see (see Saich, 2002). First and foremost, China had very little choice as not entering might have afforded protection over the short term for its economy but would have shut it out from the benefits that would accompany membership. For example, if China was outside of the WTO it would more easily fall prey to unilateral sanctions for not just economic but also political behaviour. China's leaders were shocked by the post-1989 burst of Western sanctions and concerned about the US propensity to threaten sanctions against other regimes in the world that it does not like or that do not follow its policy lead.

Second, China's desire to be an important player on the world stage means that it must be a member of key organizations to influence policy-making. Simply being outside was not acceptable and did not fit with Jiang Zemin's desire to project an image of a powerful country that needed to be consulted on major world affairs. Importantly, if China did not gain early entry into the WTO, a number of decisions would be made that would affect its vital interests without it having any input.

Third, a number of senior leaders concluded that without some strong external disciplining mechanism, economic reforms might grind to a halt as vested interests resisted further forward momentum. In essence, there is nothing in the WTO agreement that does not support the leadership's stated desire to move towards a market economy and, especially on the SOEs and the financial system, there was pressure for more fundamental reform. It is always useful for a politician to have someone else to blame for tough decisions and, in China's case, who better than foreigners?

Fourth, WTO entry clearly brought a number of specific economic benefits to China as the statistics above show. With Chinese economic growth slowing during the late 1990s and the state investment programmes showing limited signs of success at best, it was clear that new sources of growth had to be found. In particular, WTO entry improved market access for Chinese goods to major markets in Europe, Japan and the United States, especially for textiles and fashion goods, and telecommunications equipment. Apparel was the fourth in terms of quantity for exports in 2008. Further, as noted, FDI dropped in 1999 and WTO entry was seen as a way to boost FDI and to encourage more US and European FDI to supplement Hong Kong and Asian capital.

China's development has had a number of other important impacts. First, the economic growth has caused major imports and investments in natural resource and the energy sector. Imports of mineral fuel and oil were up 61.1 per cent in 2008 and ore, slag and ash were up 59.9 per cent. The search for raw resources has pushed China into new markets in Africa. Second, there has been a major move for Chinese enterprises to invest overseas under the government's policy of 'go global'. Third, to get better returns on its currency reserves, China has set up the world's largest sovereign wealth fund: the China Investment Corporation (CIC).

China's search for raw materials to maintain its economic growth has had a major impact on rejuvenating its relationship with Africa. Since 2001, there has been an enormous growth in trade, especially with the import of natural resources and the export of Chinese products (for an interesting exploration see *The China Quarterly*, no. 199, September 2009 and also Rotberg, 2008). Of China's five top trading partners in Africa, four of them are crude oil exporters, the one exception being South Africa where crude oil exports only accounted for 3 per cent of exports in 2007. For Nigeria, the top trading nation, it was 87 per cent while for Angola it was 95 per cent (Jiang, 2009, p. 591). Africa now accounts for 32.2 per cent of China's crude oil imports (Angola alone 15.3 per cent), not far behind the Middle East at 44.5 per cent (Jiang, 2009, p. 591). The fact that China is also taking crude oil from the Sudan and the Congo has led to criticisms by some in the West that it is propping up regimes with terrible governing records. This has been heightened by China's expressed commitment not to attach conditionality to its loans and investments and not to criticize the governing practices of recipients. This is, of course, not entirely true as China has made it clear that its benefits will extend to only those countries in Africa that do not recognize Taiwan and are not overly critical of China's own practices. However, as noted above with China as a late developer and with many mature markets already dominated by the West, it has had little choice but to go to countries such as Angola, the Democratic Republic of the Congo and the Sudan to meet its needs.

While some see China's behaviour as neo-colonial, its leaders see its no-strings attached support as beneficial to African development, a view echoed by many on the continent. However, China's leaders have clearly been stung by the criticisms and at the November 2009 Africa–China Summit in Egypt, Premier Wen announced eight major measures to strengthen cooperation over the next three years. These included a partnership to address climate change building 100 clean energy projects covering solar power, biogas and small hydro-electric power; education and science and technology collaborations; some $10 billion in concessional loans and support from Chinese financial institutions to set up a special loan fund of $1 billion for small and medium-sized African businesses. For those heavily indebted countries and the least developed, so long as they did not have diplomatic relations with Taiwan, China was willing to cancel debts associated with interest-free loans due to mature by the end of 2009 (*Xinhuanet*, 8 November 2009). Certainly, China has become an important player in Africa and its interests will have to be taken into account.

As the engagement with Africa shows, China has become a significant investor overseas. In terms of developing countries, it is now the largest overseas investor and is sixth overall with $150 billion committed. However, this outbound investment is still dwarfed by the inbound FDI and it only amounts to 3 per cent of GDP, whereas inbound FDI amounts to 10 per cent. Mining and natural resource investments account for about 14 per cent of the total. We can see an interesting shift taking place in the outbound FDI. In the period 1990 to1995, over 60 per cent of Chinese outbound investment was to developed economies mainly to North America and only 4–5 per cent in Africa and 16–18 per cent in Asia. By 1999–2001, the percentage in developed economies had dropped to 36 per cent and that for developing countries had risen to 64 per cent, with Africa taking 16 per cent and Asia almost 28 per cent. Given the level of China's foreign reserves and its fears that the value of its US holdings may decline, we are likely to see a further expansion of China's overseas investment.

In September 2007, China established the world's largest sovereign wealth fund, the China Investment Corporation. It was issued with special bonds by the Ministry of Finance that enabled it to acquire $200 billion of China's foreign exchange reserves. This dwarfed Singapore's Temasek ($129 billion) on which it is modelled as well as the Middle Eastern funds. This made sense as the return on the US Treasury bond was way below the kinds of returns that Temasek has been able to make. CIC conducts its business through a number of wholly owned subsidiaries and, while it is operating on market principles, its primary objective is to raise money for the Chinese state. After a shaky start and political infighting in Beijing between the Ministry of Finance, the People's Bank of China and the State Administration of Foreign Exchange, it seems to have settled down and has begun an active programme of purchases. In 2007, it took stakes in Blackstone and Morgan Stanley and in 2008 in JC Flowers to build its expertise in financial affairs. It will become a major player in China's overseas natural resource acquisitions. However, people who work in CIC say that it is restricted by the bureaucracy and operates more like a government agency than a major financial institution, and any significant acquisition has to be referred to China's political leaders for a decision.

Chapter 13

China's Future Challenges

There is no doubt that China's economic reforms have been a success in raising hundreds of millions out of poverty and building a new middle class. This has created a confidence among many in China that its model of development is suitable for its own circumstances and may even have relevance for others. At times this tips over into arrogance and assertive nationalism but there is also an underlying uncertainty about the future. The country is still not as strong and wealthy as China's leaders desire. The growth of the economy, China's key position in the global production chain and its permanent seat on the UN Security Council all mean that it is being taken increasingly seriously in world affairs. However, there are considerable challenges ahead with the economic transformation and China has not clearly identified its role in the international community. This final chapter looks at four additional challenges that the CCP must confront if it is to complete the successful transition to a wealthy and strong nation. The first is whether China can develop a sustainable model of development that overcomes the significant environmental damage and can deal with resource constraints. The second is the systemic corruption that has arisen because of economic opportunity combined with the lack of accountability. Third, there are the challenges deriving from new communications technology. Fourth are the dangers that arise from insufficient political reform.

The challenge of constraints: environmental degradation and resource shortages

China's rapid growth has come at significant environmental cost and has put a tremendous strain on the supply of natural resources such as water. A major problem is that the environmental damage has occurred at such low levels of per capita income and, even though the Chinese government is undertaking serious steps to control environmental damage, pollution will continue to grow as incomes rise and urbanization continues apace. China's response to these challenges will have a major bearing on the policy response to global warming.

The impacts of the development strategy are clear in terms of environmental impact (see Economy, 2004). The extensive use of coal causes particulate and sulphur air pollution in China's cities. This has been exacerbated by the rapid increase in the use of cars, and leaded petrol has been a major cause of pollution. Up to 90 per cent of emissions in large cities are attributed to motor vehicles (Donald and Benewick, 2005, p. 48). In China's first pollution report (2010) it was calculated that cars were responsible for 30 per cent of nitrous oxide emissions (*Guardian*, 9 February 2010). In 2003, a study showed that over 50 per cent of China's urban population was exposed to annual average levels of particulate matter that are over four times the annual average levels in US cities (Cropper, 2009). Only 1 per cent of China's urban inhabitants were considered to breathe air that the EU would consider to be safe (*New York Times*, 26 August 2007). The health effects of this are significant. A World Bank and State Environmental Protection Agency Study (2007) concluded that outdoor air pollution was causing between 350,000 and 400,000 premature deaths per year, while indoor air pollution contributed another 300,000 (mainly in rural China). The study also concluded that there were another 60,000 deaths that were water-related. These statistics created such a stir that political pressure was exerted to have the figures removed from the openly published version of the report for the fear that it may impact on 'social stability'. The list of environmental woes is endless. An official survey in Yunnan Province revealed that 30 per cent of children under 14 years of age suffered from some degree of lead poisoning (*SCMP*, 29 August 2009).

The pollution survey showed that the main cause of water pollution was caused by the excessive use of pesticides and fertilizer rather than factory effluent. Agriculture was estimated to be responsible for 43.7 per cent of the chemical oxygen demand, 67 per cent of phosphorus and 57 per cent of nitrogen discharges (*Guardian*, 9 February 2010). In addition to water pollution, some 300 million lack access to adequate drinking water and there is the problem of water scarcity in the north of the country. Some of the water is not only unfit for human consumption, but is also not even good enough for industrial use. China's natural endowment is poor to start with, having only 8 per cent of the world's water resources, and the problems are exacerbated by the skewed nature of its distribution. Some 27 per cent of the land mass is desert and 81 per cent of China's water is in the south of the country where 57 per cent of the population live. This means that Beijing has a per capita water use of 210.8 cubic metres (Tianjin, 194.9), against a national average of 446.2 in 2008. Jiangsu has 729.7 and Shanghai 639.5. The water table in the north has been dropping dramatically. In the Beijing area the drop has been over six feet per year and this even led to Beijing's mayor in the late 1980s surmising that perhaps the capital might have to be moved, a conjecture that was excised from the public version of his comments. While the problem is real, as many observers have pointed out (Nickum, 1998 is an early example) the problem is primarily economic and institutional rather than a problem of a finite natural resource. Better water resource management would help, together with the closing of more outdated industrial plants that use water inefficiently and market pricing for use.

The severity of the problems has caught the leadership's attention and Hu Jintao and Wen Jiabao have introduced a number of measures discussed below to try to mitigate the worst effects. The policy attention has also been affected by the development of a larger middle class that is concerned about quality-of-life issues and by social unrest among those who have been deprived of their livelihoods by pollution and environmental accidents. However, with the stress on urbanization and industrialization the situation may still get worse before it gets better. In addition, there are a number of institutional factors that work against better environmental controls and resource management.

Three main factors have created these environmental problems. First, there is the Marxist lack of concern for the environment and the privileging of production over all other factors. This perspective was adopted enthusiastically by Mao Zedong, who saw nature as something to be conquered and tamed and did not appreciate that there are natural limits that resource endowment places on growth (Shapiro, 2001). Not only did the development strategy favour rapid exploitation of natural resources to build up the heavy industrial base but also the associated policy of below-cost pricing for water, coal, and other inputs contributed further.

The desire for the grandiose project to solve problems is evident in the post-Mao leadership, not only with the construction of the Three Gorges Dam but also with the massive project to divert river waters hundreds of miles from the south to the north. Rather than relying on market forces and the punishment of enterprises that pollute water and thus dealing with the problem at source rather than trying to clean up later, this project is expected to provide a technical fix. Both projects were supported by Mao but both have been realized in the post-Mao era. The South–North Water Diversion Project, begun in 2001, is a $60 billion project intended to construct three lines of canals and aqueducts that by 2050 will carry 45 billion cubic meters of water from the water-abundant south to the deficient north. While it will help and if it is actually completed and the bureaucratic hurdles are cleared, it will not alone resolve the problems of water shortage.

The second factor was Mao's promotion from the mid 1950s of population growth as a key factor in boosting economic growth. The population boom aggravated China's already problematic resource-population ratios. As noted, water resources are low, at about one-third of the world average per capita, forests cover only one-eighth of the global average, rangelands per capita are less than half the global average, and about 30 per cent of the world average for croplands.

Natural resources are poorly distributed in terms of population concentrations, with the major fields for oil and natural gas in the northwest and southwest respectively far away from the industrial centres of the cost and the northeast. Similarly, the best areas for the development of hydropower are in the southwest, away from the main customers for electricity. These factors have heightened China's propensity to rely on coal, much of which is of poor quality and highly polluting. In 2006, the coal sector accounted for over 75 per cent of China's primary energy production, and over 80 per cent of electric power production (Cunningham, 2009, p. 61).

Third, the rapid economic growth and urbanization of the last thirty years have added to the environmental toll and natural resource constraints are a potential brake on China's future development. The political economy of the reforms has in many ways been inimical to the development of an effective policy to control environmental pollution. As noted above, the economy is driven by coal and this, together with the rise in the number of cars, has accounted for the problems of air quality and premature deaths. In addition to the air quality problems that coal causes, it is also responsible for some of China's worst industrial accidents, especially in small private mines: China has the highest death rate in the world from mining disasters (4726 in 2006). It also has a low productivity with output per worker at barely over 2 per cent of that in the US.

The number of cars is expanding rapidly from 0.34 per 100 urban households in 1999 to 8.83 in 2008. In January 2009, car sales in China were higher than those in the US for the first time ever. Beijing had the highest ownership at 22.70 per 100 households with Zhejiang second at 19.65, while Gansu had the lowest level of ownership at 2.15. Measures to deal with air pollution caused by car exhaust in Beijing is a good example of the progress that China is making in dealing with the environmental challenges but also shows how huge the problem is moving forward. At the turn of the century, control on car emissions was non-existent yet ten years later the level is now at Euro IV, thus the same standards' emissions level as the European Union. The rest of the country is following suit in 2010. In 2008, Beijing ordered a 90 per cent reduction in the sulphur content of petrol and diesel fuel and one-quarter of the capital's bus fleet run on clean-burning compressed or liquefied natural gas, the largest fleet in the world (*New York Times*, 17 October 2009). Last but not least, access to the roads is registered according to the digits on the number plates taking one-fifth of the registered cars off the road each day, and heavy trucks are banned from entering the city during the day. This and other stringent measures introduced by the government in the run-up to the summer 2008 Olympics have improved air quality, although there is debate about how much. Despite the progress Beijing's air still does not meet the quality standard recommended by the WHO for developing countries and some 1500 new cars are entering the roads every day. Investment in public transport is only now beginning to catch up with new subways and light rail constructions but already many of the new middle class are accustomed to the 'freedom' that car ownership provides. Forecasts from the International Energy Agency and the US Department of Energy calculate that greenhouse emissions will more than double by 2030 (*SCMP*, 10 December 2009).

Even with the development of clean energy technologies and enhanced efficiency, China's energy needs to fuel the growing economy are immense. In 2005, China surpassed the US as the world's largest energy producer and it provided over 94 per cent of its primary energy demand domestically, ranking it among the world's most energy self-sufficient economies. As Cunningham (2009, p. 59) has pointed out, this level of self-sufficiency is remarkable given the 'Chinese state's historical lack of capital, splintered government institutions, and rapid economic growth'. The problem, as noted above, is that China is heavily reliant on coal to meet its needs. Cunningham shows how local collectively owned mines take up much of the production needs in times of rapid growth and indeed while they produced 9 per cent of coal output in 1970, they produced 46 per cent at their peak in 1995 before the percentage dropped to just over 30 per cent in 2002. Future trends are not encouraging; the China National Coal Association estimates that the demand for coal is liable to rise from 2.9 billion tonnes in 2009 to 3.5 billion in 2015 and 3.8 billion in 2030 (*SCMP*, 10 December 2009).

The problem is that these mines are not only dangerous but produce much low-quality coal. There are periodic attempts to close these mines but they clearly expand again as the economy grows and given that many are locally owned they are often protected by officials who see them as a good way to generate necessary income. This reflects a more general pattern of behaviour. Should the central government really be concerned about the large SOEs it would not be difficult to act but much pollution is caused by small-scale township and village enterprises and this is much more difficult. As we have seen in Chapter 7, revenues from such enterprises are of major importance to local governments and, as a result, they are not particularly thorough in their implementation of environmental codes. The Centre has launched occasional campaigns to close down small, inefficient polluting factories in the countryside but they have been short-lived and have often met resistance from local governments. Even local governments that are keen to clean up the environment may not have jurisdiction over the polluting enterprise. In Xinmi municipality (Henan Province), the local people's congress adopted regulations to clean up the terrible pollution from its three main industries: coal, cement and stone blasting. However, two major polluting factories fell under the control of the industrial bureau under the provincial government and they resisted all attempts by the local administration to clean up the pollution.

In the past, the Chinese leadership has been ambivalent about the importance of environmental damage and even now it is clear that growth takes precedence over the quality of that growth. Having created a system where progress and rewards are clearly demarcated in terms of GDP growth, it is hard for China to turn such a system around. The ambivalence is seen with the evolution of the environmental oversight agency. China has developed an extensive environmental protection agency network and adopted a number of policies and regulations that if observed would go a long way to ameliorating the situation. As with other areas, the problem has been in devising incentives to encourage conformity with environmental standards. It was only at the March 1998 NPC meeting after years of lobbying that the environment protection administration was upgraded to ministerial status. Before this the administration ranked below other ministries and provinces, making compliance with its suggestions all but impossible. Its status was enhanced further when it was renamed as the Ministry of Environmental Protection in March 2008. However, it takes a time to ramp up the activities of a bureaucratic agency and, just before it was reclassified as a Ministry, its staff numbered in the hundreds as opposed to the US Environmental Protection Agency that has almost 20,000 employees. This will mean that it is an even weaker bureaucratic player at the local level.

Political support has come from Hu Jintao and Wen Jiabao with their emphasis on sustainable development and the evaluation of local officials has been broadened to include environmental standards in their work assessment. In 2006, in his report on the 11th Five-Year Programme (2006–10) Premier Wen announced the objective of using 20 per cent less energy for each one per cent of GDP in 2010 as compared with 2005. The intention is also to reduce by 10 per cent total emissions of mercury, sulphur dioxide and other pollutants. There has been some progress in this area. In the first six months of 2009, official figures from the Ministry showed that COD (the amount of organic compounds in water) emissions nationwide were down 2.46 per cent and those for sulphur dioxide were down by 5.4 per cent. In Shanghai, the drop was 13.9 per cent and 14.43 per cent respectively.

One initiative that has not taken off was the use of a Green GDP that had been pushed by the state environmental protection agencies. This was intended to reveal just what the cost of environmental damage was to the economy. The idea was endorsed by Hu Jintao in 2004 but was soon dropped by intense lobbying from local leaders and enterprise heads. The first and only report showed that in 2004 pollution had cost just over 3 per cent of GDP, an estimate that many considered too low.

Of the 511.8 billion *yuan* costs, water pollution, air pollution and solid wastes and pollution accidents amounted to 286.28 billion *yuan*, 219.8 billion *yuan* and 5.74 billion *yuan*, accounting for 55.9 per cent, 42.9 per cent and 1.2 per cent of the total costs, respectively. Worse, it indicated that for some provinces there had been no real growth at all once the costs of pollution and healthcare were deducted. This was too much for powerful players at the provincial level to accept along with SOE heads and the idea of a second assessment was dropped.

An additional way to reduce the pollution is to diversify energy sources. This is something that China is working on and is making impressive progress but coal will remain dominant for a long time to come. The plan is for China to increase the proportion of renewable energy in primary energy consumption from 7 per cent in 2005 to 15 per cent in 2020. The estimate is to substitute fossil fuels by 400 million tons of coal equivalent that will cut carbon dioxide discharge by 1 billion tons and sulphur dioxide by over seven million tons (Chen, 2009, p. i). This followed the passing of the 2005 Renewable Energy Law and the Amended Law passed in 2007. There are many other new measures on the books such as the requirement that all power grid companies give preferential purchase to 'green' electricity generated from renewable sources and funding to develop hybrid and electric cars. One official has claimed that China may boost solar power capacity some 13 times by 2011 and the government is already revising the targets for renewable energy that it set in 2007 for 2020. The intention is to invest 2 trillion *yuan* ($293 billion) in the alternative energy industry before 2020 (http://en.in-en.com). The impact on these sectors is becoming clear: China is currently the world's largest solar-panel producer and the fourth largest producer of wind power (13.9 per cent of the total, the US is first with 20.8 per cent). It is possible that by 2030 wind power will be the third main source for electricity after thermal and hydropower (Chen, 2009, p. 6).

One area where the government has been less sure is citizen pressure and collective action to ensure implementation of regulations and to monitor pollution controls. This is not to say that public opinion does not impact on government thinking, after all officials live in China too, but the government is concerned about the kind of environmental activism that they have seen in other countries. Many environmental NGOs have sprung up (see Chapter 8) and environmental protection has become particularly attractive to young people in China. Environmental reporting and documentaries have become very popular. However, despite this progress, Chinese citizens are still less likely to complain about pollution than their counterparts elsewhere. In part this relates to party control over information, meaning that citizens only get to hear what is approved. With few alternative outlets, many citizens have only a very partial view of the problems. It was only in early 1998 that Beijing began to publish air pollution data, the last city to do so, even though it had been collecting the data since 1981. In part, this negligence stemmed from the party's tradition of controlling access to information and its concern about citizen response and also from the fear that it might frighten off foreign investors (interviews with Beijing environment officials, March 1998). Now air quality data is published regularly on national and local websites.

The emissions and other problems of environmental pollution are now a part of the global debate. Acid rain that falls in Japan and South Korea originates in China, people in Hong Kong have complained about the deterioration in air quality caused by factories over the border, Russians were affected by a huge poisonous spill on the Songhua River, and air quality problems in Los Angeles are also said to originate partly in China. Yet, foreigners have also been complicit in the pollution build up in China as multinational corporations have outsourced production to plants in China. This made China a key player in the Copenhagen summit on climate change (December 2009), together with the US it is difficult to reach any kind of meaningful agreement.

Global warming will also impact on China as a World Wildlife Fund (WWF) China report (2009) on the Yangtze Delta warned. The report showed that air temperatures between 2001 and 2005 had risen by 0.71 degrees centigrade. Over the last fifty years, the temperatures in Shanghai had risen at twice the national average and four times the global average. These changes were estimated to cause major impacts on food production and biodiversity. In the Sichuan Basin, it was estimated that corn production would drop by between 25 per cent and 50 per cent by 2090, while rice production in the Yangtze Basin was estimated to decrease by between 9 per cent and 41 per cent. Shanghai itself would be threatened by rising sea levels.

In the build-up to the Copenhagen summit on climate change, China announced that it would reduce carbon intensity between 40 per cent and 45 per cent per unit of GDP from 2005 levels by 2020 (*Xinhua*, 26 November 2009) but at the summit itself its policy position had a mixed reception. Also, within China the policy received a mixed reception with some saying that it was too conservative while others claimed that it was too generous. In February 2010, the Politburo confirmed the policy and 'thought unification campaign' was launched to bring all into line with central policy (*SCMP*, 26 February 2010). At Copenhagen, China's negotiating position was to work with other developing countries to ensure that binding emission targets would be resisted while developed countries would be expected to set compulsory emission reduction targets. This would suit China's domestic development strategy and would avoid the problem of acceding to international verification. For

China this was important not only in terms of its general principle not to allow any foreign oversight of its activities but also to prevent bringing to public light the often significant discrepancies in its own calculations of environmental damage and those of international and US organizations. China did not seem to appreciate fully that the US would not allow any funding for the developing nations to pass unless there was international verification. Domestic pressure in the US would have made this impossible. In the end, while China had an allegiance with developing countries, it also had a significant coalition of interests with the US (together they account for 40 per cent of the emitted greenhouse gases). Finally, China sided with the US in resisting specific targets that might have constrained its growth while at the same time resisting US calls for a regime of international monitoring. The final agreement called for trying to prevent global temperatures rising above 2 degrees centigrade but without forcing any nation to make specific cuts. As *Xinhua* (19 December 2009) noted 'The Copenhagen accord protected the principle of "common but differentiated responsibility" under the climate convention and the Kyoto protocol.' More importantly, the head of China's delegation stated 'For the Chinese, this was our sovereignty and our national interest' (quoted in *The Observer*, 20 December 2009). In March 2010, China together with India wrote to the UN's climate secretariat that they agreed to be listed as parties to the Copenhagen accord but this fell short of association (*Guardian*, 9 March 2010).

The internal challenge: corruption

Corruption has been a problem in all transitional systems and China has not been able to escape its effect. Early in the 1980s, Chen Yun spoke of corruption as a matter of life and death for the party but it has continued making many members wealthy. Subsequently, a string of Chinese leaders have railed against corruption, concerned that it will undermine the party's legitimacy, but none has been willing to promote the kind of structural reforms that might tackle it. Reformers and conservatives alike have used the issue of corruption to push their own agendas. Reformers argue that corruption is caused by the incomplete nature of reform and suggest the best solution is to complete the market reforms and push ahead with political reform to make officials more accountable. Conservatives claim that corruption is caused by lack of party discipline and the increased Western influences that have entered with the economic opening. As Deng Xiaoping commented, you cannot open the door without letting in a few flies, although in China's case it is more like a swarm. Conservatives prefer to combine ideological campaigns with severe restrictions on how far the market should be expanded.

Hu Jintao has tried to toe the difficult line between acknowledging that corruption has become a major problem but not accepting that the system is at fault. He accepts the premise that the party itself can combat corruption through public punishment of a limited number of senior officials, morality campaigns and tightening internal disciplinary mechanisms. Hu was backed up by Premier Wen Jiabao who, in his government work report to the March 2009 NPC meeting, stated that 'corruption remains a serious problem in some localities, departments and areas' and promised concerted (but unspecified) action to promote clean government, something he repeated again at the 2010 session. This follows traditional CCP logic that while the party has made mistakes, it is the party that has corrected them and people should trust it to do so in the future. It is questionable whether this approach can rein-in the current levels of corruption.

The pursuit of economic riches without genuine marketization and democratization and where power remains hierarchically structured with information dependent on position and party membership lies behind the corrupt activities of party members. This is not a new phenomenon; it is just that now with the increased commercialization and monetization of the economy there is more to be corrupt about, and the stakes can be higher. It is not easy to gauge the extent of corruption, but it has clearly increased with reforms and has become much more visible. In the Mao period, most of the corruption was kept hidden behind what appeared outwardly to be relatively plain living. It usually took the form of dining at public expense and travel on the state's ticket. It could take more venal forms of ruthless persecution of villagers under local-party official control. For example, a court proclamation put up in Nanjing in 1977 revealed how vulnerable to the party secretaries people sent down from the cities to work in the communes were. Many wanted to return to the city for education but this could happen only if the party secretary of the commune approved. In this case, the party secretary had used his power to demand sexual favours from some 16 young women in return for processing their applications; showing the hierarchical principles, the deputy secretary had demanded sexual favours from only 12.

The system of intense bureaucratic control over distribution, the increasingly arbitrary control over personal life and the concentration of power in individual hands undermined social cohesion and trust in officials and laid the basis for the corrupt behaviour by officials that dogs the system to this day. Walder (1994, pp. 297–323) and others have noted that party authority was founded on citizen-dependence upon officials for satisfaction of material needs and for access to career opportunities. This system increased cynicism towards officialdom and a disrespect for those in authority, who were seen as self-serving rather than 'servants of the people', as the official ideology claimed. Paradoxically, perhaps, the structure led to an expansion in the use of connections to obtain goods, often those to which one was entitled, and an increased reliance on the immediate and extended family. These trends became more pronounced during the Cultural Revolution and have persisted into the reform era and provide the underlying basis for the more spectacular corruption witnessed in recent years. This has been supplemented by the collusion between individual entrepreneurs and party officials.

The reforms have presented officials with far greater opportunities, political and social controls have relaxed and financial decentralization has provided greater motivation to engage in corrupt activities. An audit office report to the NPC in June 2009 noted that 26.77 billion *yuan* of public money that had been embezzled had been recovered in the past year and that 30 people who had been involved in 116 cases had been arrested and sentenced, and another 117 punished. In its 2009 annual report, the audit office revealed widespread wrongdoing. It audited 54 agencies, the most ever and included for the first time its own books and those of CCP organizations. The audit office itself was found not to have abided by the Budget Law and had misappropriated millions of *yuan*. The Ministry of Foreign Affairs had not turned over 132 million *yuan* in visa and passport handling fees that it had collected from applicants. The Chinese Academy of Sciences had embezzled over 1 million for stock speculations while subsidiaries of the State Development and Reform Commission had forged contracts to transfer 850,000 *yuan* elsewhere (*SCMP*, 3 September 2009).

For such a big country, such figures do not seem particularly large, but it is just the tip of the iceberg. The average size of bribes increased from 2.53 million *yuan* in 2007 to 8.84 million in 2008 (Chen and Zhu, 2009, p. 1; see also Wedeman, 2004). The big cases have been spectacular. Both senior government officials and those running China's SOEs have been arrested. It is estimated that during the 12-year rule of the former corrupt mayor and later party secretary of Beijing, over 18 billion *yuan* disappeared from the municipal coffers. In 2009, it was announced that the former head of Sinopec had taken bribes amounting to 196 million *yuan* and shared the same mistress with the party secretary of Qingdao municipality. The three set up a series of businesses in Hong Kong, Shenzhen and Qingdao before being compromised. In November 2008, the head of GOME Electrical Appliances was arrested and put under investigation for stock manipulation, bribery and insider trading. Subsequent arrests included officials not only from central government agencies but also from local government (including the Mayor of Shenzhen) revealing the interpenetration of business interests and officialdom. It seems that such revelations of the extensive connections between corrupt business practices and local officialdom caused the central leadership to respond more vigorously. In part, this may have been to spruce up the party's image in the run-up to the 60th anniversary of the founding of the PRC (October 2009).

Two examples are exemplary and reveal both the extent of the corruption and the linkage to political power struggles. Pursuit of corruption, especially at senior levels of the party, seems to be more related to factional struggles than the desire to produce a clean administration. Thus, just before the CCP CC Plenum in October 2006, the Shanghai Party Secretary, Chen Liangyu, was arrested in connection with a fraud involving the misuse of the Shanghai social security funds. However, there was clearly a political dimension to this. Chen was known to have clashed with Premier Wen Jiabao over economic policy and was seen as a key member of what is referred to as the 'Shanghai Gang', a group of politicians thought of as close to former leader Jiang Zemin. Chen's demise clearly marked the dominance of Hu in the political system and resembled the purge of Beijing Party Secretary, Chen Xitong, in 1995 that marked Jiang's consolidation of power. With ideological battles as justification for purge a thing of the past, corruption has become the latest weapon of choice to remove political rivals.

The perception of the dangers of corruption have been heightened by incidents in a number of neighbouring countries that drew the leadership's attention to the instability which corruption by leaders and their families can cause. In particular, it seems that the Chinese leadership took note of how the accusations of corruption in Thailand lay behind the *coup* against the Prime Minister, how claims of wrongdoing by Chen Shuibian's family when he was President led to significant protests on Taiwan and how financial scandals in Vietnam led to a shake-up in domestic politics that took some time to work its way through the political system.

It is clear that at the local level, there is a close symbiotic relationship between officials, business leaders, and even gangs. This is clearly shown with the exposé of the massive criminal web that existed in the southwestern municipality of Chongqing. This administrative jurisdiction of 31 million people is the centrepiece of the party's policies to develop the West and presumably the amounts of investment flowing through the municipality must have contributed to the largesse that was to be dispensed. The arrests started in the summer of 2009 and trials continued through the year. Over 1500 people were arrested including 52 government officials and 29 police officers. This latter group included Chongqing's former police chief who had been in his position for some 16 years (*News China*, 5 December 2009, p. 13). The crackdown was overseen by Party Secretary, Bo Xilai, and Wang Wenjun, who was appointed police chief in June 2008. Under Bo's leadership, Wang had overseen a similar clean-up of corruption and collusion between gangs, business people and officials in the northeastern city of Shenyang. The clean-up seems to have been prompted by clashes between rival gangs over the control of lucrative bus routes that had led to 31 deaths and left 20 people wounded. Nationalization of the lucrative bus routes was resisted by the gangs, leading to the crackdown. Earlier friction had been caused when one of those arrested, the billionaire Li Qiang, orchestrated a taxi strike to try to put pressure on the local government. The former police chief was found to have around 20 million *yuan* buried beneath a fish pond while his sister-in-law was found guilty of amassing illegal profits, illegal detention and running a gambling business and providing gamblers with illegal drugs. Six defendants were sentenced to death and others have received prison sentences ranging from one to eighteen years. It is generally accepted that this is not an isolated case and some observers have imputed political motives to the Party Secretary of Chongqing, Bo Xilai, in launching the clean-up. Some have speculated that he has been strident in his activities in order to bolster his chances for promotion at the party congress to be held in 2012.

Certainly, corruption has caused much concern among Chinese citizens. An online opinion poll carried out by the state-run website chinanews.com just before the March 2009 NPC meeting found that 75.5 per cent of respondents ranked corruption and cleaner government as their top concern (*Asia Times*, 26 March 2009). In our survey, corruption is usually singled out as the area of government work that citizens are least satisfied with. In 2007, combating corruption received the lowest evaluation (a rating of 2.5 out of 4.00) above employment creation (2.65) and unemployment insurance (2.65). For those living in rural China the satisfaction rating was a little higher at 2.55 and it was lowest in small town China (2.33). As in other countries, major infrastructure programmes are magnets for considerable corruption. In our 2007 survey, 34.9 per cent answered that they thought it was in major engineering projects that corruption was most likely to occur.

One particular group to have benefited from the opportunities provided by the incomplete reforms and the state's continued control over information and resources has been the children of senior cadres, especially those in the military, referred to as the 'Princeling's party' (*taizi dang*). They formed a focal point of the 1989 student-led protests that criticized 'official speculation' (*guandao*). By the late 1980s many urban dwellers felt that Chinese society had become one 'on the take' where, without a good set of connections and an entrance through the 'back door', it was more difficult to participate in the benefits of economic reform. In this situation, the sight of children of high-level officials joy-riding in imported cars was a moral affront to many ordinary citizens. A stir was caused in 2009 when a report calculated that 91 per cent of the wealthiest in China were children of senior CCP officials. This proved so sensitive that the authorities denounced the report as 'fake' and punished four newspapers that had run accounts of the report. Whatever, the truth is, it is clear that good connections are crucial to business success and there are none better than having a parent in an important position. Much of the money is made in the grey areas or in the underground economy (see Box 13.1).

Spectacular as these major cases may be, ordinary citizens are more concerned about the everyday small corruption that makes their life complicated: the red envelopes filled with money to get to see a doctor or to get the prescription that is one's right; the illegal fees that are paid to the schools to make sure that children get the education they are promised; and so on. Popular displeasure with their officials and the corruption that pervades their lives is shown by the commonplace sayings and jokes. Local people often complained to me that they are required to provide cadres with the best housing, the prettiest women in the village to marry and the fattest pigs to slaughter for the celebrations. They were very upset with the policy to rotate officials more frequently as every two or three years they had to start again.

Generally Chinese people are not very confident in the leadership's capacity to deal with corruption effectively. In our 2007 survey, a

---

Box 13.1: The Rainbow Economy

The underground economy is booming in China with the reforms, and it is estimated that China's gross domestic product (GDP) may be 10 per cent higher if this had been calculated into the official figures. The exposure of corruption in Chongqing revealed the deep links between officials, entrepreneurs and gangland. Millions of dollars were gambled away. One poor official from Guangxi was arrested for accepting bribes after a diary of his sexual adventures was posted online. Officialdom seems to have been 'wedded' not only to mistresses but also to mobsters whose networks reached far and wide. The value of being an official is reflected in the return of the traditional practice of 'buying and selling official posts'. Some have even suggested that money from ill-gotten gains is a major factor causing the increase in income inequality. Researchers at Tsinghua University claim that if one included unpaid taxes and other illegal income the Gini coefficient would have risen in 2001 from 0.42 to 0.49.

So common has illicit economic activity become that some describe the economy in terms of five colours:
1 Black represents money from robbery and theft
2 Blue represents smuggling, often associated with customs and the navy
3 Red represents official corruption, being the colour of the party
4 White represents gains from drug trafficking
5 Yellow represents money from pornography and the sex trade.

majority of respondents did not feel that there had been progress in resolving the problems of bribery and corruption. Of the respondents, 46.8 per cent felt that government officials were not honest (5.2 per cent of these felt they were extremely dishonest). The situation was worst in small towns where 54.3 percent felt that government and its officials were dishonest. Also, in small towns 54.6 per cent of respondents felt that the situation had got worse and overall only 14.2 per cent thought the situation had improved.

Faced with such problems, the leadership has been unwilling to accept that there is a systemic problem and has continued to rely primarily on ideological exhortation and internal mechanisms such as the use of discipline inspection commissions (CDICs). The commissions were abolished in the Cultural Revolution and re-established as the primary mechanism for dealing with discipline and monitoring abuses within the party. The approach has clearly not worked and the commission has often been blocked from carrying out investigations by powerful local party barons. In 2005, to bolster these administrative mechanisms, Hu Jintao launched a rectification campaign that was intended in part to address corruption and to criticize the 'moral degeneration' of some officials. At the 2009 opening ceremony for three key training schools for party officials, the head of the Organization Department railed against the immoral conduct of some members and stated that they should 'resist seduction' and not 'enter vulgar places' (*Xuexi shibao*, 19 October 2009, p. 1).

However, the party is aware that such exhortations are insufficient and has introduced a number of measures to try to deal with the problem. Since 2003, the annual state audit report has been subject to public view and it has expanded to include party organizations in the audit process. In 2007, the government established the National Bureau of Corruption Prevention that reports directly to the State Council. On paper it has an impressive array of powers but it has no authority to investigate individual cases thus reducing its effectiveness (Chen and Zhu, 2009, p. 13). In April 2008, the Politburo passed a five-year anti-corruption plan and it sees regular rotation of officials as one way to break up the kinds of links that can develop with local businesses and gangs.

The party has rejected the idea that there is a role for an independent monitoring authority, but it has given more licence to the media to expose examples of corruption at the grassroots level. In our 2007 survey, respondents saw this as the most effective way to deal with corruption. However, given party control over publishing and especially television, such exposés work under severe constraints and it would be impossible to reveal the wrongdoing of a senior official without Politburo approval. That said, the press has become livelier in this respect and television programmes such as *Law and Society* and *In Focus* do push against the limits, and their reporters are often abused by local powerholders. In fact, it is remarkable how mentioning official corruption moved from being taboo at the beginning of the 1990s to being a major topic of discussion in the media by the end of the decade. This presents the party leadership with a dilemma, as the more corruption is reported, the more people are liable to see the party as lacking credibility. The reluctance to pursue senior figures unless there is political gain only increases this tendency.

The party is pursuing a number of policies to try to improve the situation, but none of them is likely to have the desired effect without broader reforms that removes the structural incentives for corruption. This has not been lost on Chinese analysts, a number of whom have begun to write about the link between corruption and political structure as an unintended effect of economic reform. In addition to the sentencing of key malfeasors and ideological exhortation, the party has tried to improve the quality of the judges, to professionalize the civil service, to raise pay for government officials and to make the financial activities of local administrations more transparent. In late 2009, the CDIC announced that it would step up training for officials from the county and city levels in a programme that would run until 2013. All these measures will help, but as long as there is no systemic reform or independent control over the activities of party officials, the impact will be limited. Political credibility notwithstanding, senior officials at the central and provincial levels should not be that difficult to control; the power elite is not that numerous. If the village elections were made more effective, this would give people greater control over who was elected to local leadership, especially if the party was made more accountable. The big problem is controlling the activities of those at the county and township level who can resist scrutiny from above and below. Moving up the level of direct elections as suggested by some in China would be a start, but it is resisted by many local officials.

The information challenge: blogs, tweets and the internet

The advent of the information revolution and the need for information that is delivered reliably and at high speed provide a major challenge for governance. The embarrassment caused to the CCP by the exposure of its cover-up of SARS during the winter of 2002–03 shows how porous the country's information system is and how vulnerable it can be to cross-border information flows. While the Guangdong authorities were denying that there was anything amiss, 120 million messages were sent in three days by mobile phones warning that there was an unknown disease in the area and that it was killing people (Saich, 2006). The abuses of local officials, demonstrations, and riots have been recorded on mobile phones and quickly placed on the internet providing alternative interpretations to official accounts. The fear of the authorities that protests were being organized online has led to the expansion of the internet police to monitor and delete unacceptable comments. Already in 2005, the number was estimated at over 30,000 (*Guardian*, 14 June 2005). Outside observers claim that China has a more extensive monitoring of the internet than any other country and not only blocks website content deemed unacceptable but also monitors the access of individuals. However, at the same time, the Chinese government has committed itself strongly to the development of the internet and has invested some $50 billion in telecoms and data-processing hardware. China's leaders realize that if their aspirations for major power status are to be realized they have to adopt these new technologies, and they see a great potential for the development of e-commerce despite the obvious current obstacles. There is even an internal information net for party members.

There has been a substantial tradition in China of managing information flows to ensure that the state is the primary, if not sole, provider of information. The CCP has tried to channel information flows so that they are vertically linked and it has eschewed the horizontal flow of information. This has meant that access to information in the Chinese system has formed an important basis for power and the ability to provide the correct interpretation of the past has provided the legitimacy to decide on current policy (Saich, 1995, pp. 299–338). Under such a system, the real basis of exchange is secrets and privileged access to information. However, the advent of the internet makes it much more difficult for the CCP to manage information flows and to ensure that its view of events prevails (see Box 13.2).

This system can starve leaders of the reliable information they need to make appropriate policy decisions. The more coercive the regime, the more that passes up is what leaders want to hear; negative information is suppressed and its agents repressed. What globalization demonstrates better than at any point in the past is that at a certain developmental point – that is, where the need for information becomes very great – it becomes extremely difficult to reduce coercion without inviting vast structural change. In the Soviet Union prolonged coercion and bureaucratization so deprived the state of the capacity to innovate that eventually it broke apart. What appeared at the top as rational public planning was based on a jerrybuilt system of deals and private negotiations (Apter and Saich, 1994, Chapter 9).

It is not surprising that the rapid spread of the internet and new information technology has caused unease among those managing the system as it threatens their monopoly over the flow of information. This does

Box 13.2: Governing in the Age of Information Pluralism

The terrible tragedy of the death of over 40 people, mostly children, in an explosion at a school in Fanglin village, Jiangxi Province (March 2001) provides an early example of how difficult it is to control a story in the world of the internet and information pluralism. In an unusual step, at a press conference at the March 2001 NPC, Premier Zhu Rongji announced that the explosion had been the action of a single madman who had blown up the school. The explosion was an embarrassment to the leadership following a series of accidents that highlighted the poor work safety conditions that existed in China. Coming at the time of the annual NPC meeting in Beijing compounded the problem. It is unusual for a Chinese leader to comment on such an issue and to make such a categorical statement. It is unclear who had advised him on the issue and why he chose to confront it so bluntly. Some have even speculated that he was set up by his political opponents.

The area in Jiangxi is famous for its production of fireworks, and local villagers claimed that not only were fireworks stored at the school but also that the children worked on making them to earn extra income for the school's coffers. The local villagers informed the domestic press, the Hong Kong press and the foreign media of their views and that a major cover-up was under way. Their story was confirmed by county officials reached by phone. A curfew was imposed, the school was bulldozed, preventing any genuine investigation and outsiders were prevented from entering the village. However, Zhu's official version of events was undermined by access to the internet and the foreign media. Chatrooms very quickly filled with alternative versions of what had happened and called on the government for a better response. Interestingly, the local press in China was also assertive in contradicting the centre's account. This caused Zhu the following week to make an apology for the explosion; he stuck to his original explanation but admitted that up until two years before fireworks had been manufactured at the school. This had stopped in 1999 when an explosion at a fireworks factory in a nearby village had killed 35 people. Importantly, Zhu stated that it was the Hong Kong and foreign press reporting of the villagers' version of events that had caused him to check on what had happened. He had sent a six-person undercover team to investigate. However, it is debatable what they could discover and how anonymous they could be in a rural village community. This inability to manage the news as effectively as in the past is indicative of challenges that will increasingly confront the CCP in the future (*New York Times* and Associated Press reports).

not mean, however, that the CCP cannot set up new systems of control or that there will be an automatic progression from more internet users to greater political pluralism. It is widely reported that the party pays for people to post pro-government comments in internet chatrooms and these people have been dubbed the 'Fifty Cents Party'. Yet, it is noteworthy that the Chinese Academy of Social Sciences in their analysis of society in 2009, claimed that the internet together with cell phones had become the most powerful carrier of public opinion (CASS, 2009). In a number of respects, the CCP leadership has treated the internet in the same way as it has traditional print forms. It has tried to institute a system of controls that will allow it to participate in the benefits of faster information flows without having to open up the information system and allowing in the disadvantages of views and information that may challenge the CCP's interpretation of events.

First, it has authorized only four networks for international access in order to control information flows. New regulations issued in October 2000 required internet content providers to obtain Ministry of Information approval for joint-ventures or any business coopera-tion with foreign investors, and are to be held responsible for blocking 'illegal content' and 'subversive content' from spreading through their websites (*Xinhua*, 2 October 2000). In addition to pornographic mate-rials, it has also blocked access to the websites of publications such as the *New York Times*, CNN, those human rights organizations that are critical of China and groups that are pro-Taiwan, pro-Tibet or pro-Falungong. In addition, the state has forbidden China-based websites from using news derived from websites that are situated outside the mainland. This has resulted in a number of service providers in China dropping news services from their menu and concentrating on 'safe' areas of information provision, such as sports and entertainment. In addition, traditional media forms are prohibited from using material derived from any website.

To gain better control over the sector, the CCP has introduced a number of key pieces of legislation and carried through institutional reorganization. In March 1997, the amended Criminal Code included three new articles outlining 'serious crimes' of leaking or misusing infor-mation. At the end of 1997, the Ministry of Public Security published its 'Regulations on Security and Management of Computer Information Networks and the Internet' that made it a crime to damage national security and disclose state secrets. In January 2000, the State Secrecy Bureau published its own detailed regulations concerning state secret protection and the use of computer information systems on the internet. In May 2000, personal websites were banned. In further legislation that was introduced in December 2009, China's citizens were banned from registering personal domain names and those who already had such a domain were likely to forfeit them. Only businesses with operating licences or government authorised organizations were allowed to have websites. The new regulations also implied that foreign websites that were not registered would also be closed down. The authorities justified this in the name mainly of controlling the spread of pornography but a number of observers saw a political motive that was intended to turn China into an intranet system with strong controls and the ability to exclude external information sources if they were deemed problematic (see http://finance.bjmews.com.cn/2009/1222/18388.shtml).

Organizationally, in April 1996 the State Council set up the Steering Committee on National Information Infrastructure to coordinate internet policy until its functions were absorbed by the newly created Ministry of Information Industry. The Ministry was created in 1998 and includes the former ministries of posts and telecommunications, radio, film and broadcasting, and the 'leading group' on information policy. The Ministry is the primary regulator for this sector, thus reducing the potential for bureaucratic fragmentation, and it reports directly to the State Council. The Ministry of Public Security has set up a Computer Management and Supervision Office to deal with crimes involving computers. It has launched the 'Golden Shield Project' that seeks to block content. In February 1999 the State Information Security Appraisal and Identification Management Committee was established directly under the State Council. The work of this system is overseen by the party's Propaganda Ministry supported by the State Council Information Office, which has set up an Internet Affairs Bureau to oversee all websites that contain news and information.

The Chinese leadership is clearly aware that it cannot completely control the flow of information or access to forbidden sites by its citizens. Its intention is to lay down warnings about the limits of the permissible and to deter the casual browser from becoming too inquisitive about the world outside. In this limited respect, it may be successful. For example, with the July 2009 riots in Xinjiang, government censors were able to disable keyword searches for 'Urumqi' (the capital of Xinjiang) and blocked access to Facebook and Twitter as well as local alternatives Fanfou and Youku. Even though China has become extremely porous in terms of information flows, there is scant evidence to suggest that this alone has challenged the CCP's monopoly on political interpretation for the majority.

Usage of new technologies is expanding rapidly, especially among the young. The number of internet users had reached 338 million by June 2009 (up 13.4 per cent from end 2008). At the turn of the century there had been only 22.5 million (for regular updates see China Network Information Centre, http://www.cnnic.cn). The number of users now exceeds the population of the US although penetration is only 25.5 per cent, much lower than America's 74.7 per cent. It is also lower than the penetration rate for Brazil (34.4 per cent) and Russia (27 per cent) but much higher than India (7.1 per cent) and slightly above the world average of 23.8 per cent. Not surprisingly, the preponderance of users is in the more developed areas and urban (71.7 per cent of users) with students accounting for 31.7 per cent. Of those online, 53 per cent are male, 62.8 per cent are 30 or younger, while 85.5 per cent use it for music and 26 per cent for online shopping. Also, 55.4 per cent use e-mail (down 1.4 per cent) and 72.2 per cent of citizens use instant messaging (down 3.1 per cent). There were 3.06 million websites, 16.26 million domain names and 182 million blog users. In the countryside, mobile phone technology has taken off and China is rapidly expanding 3G access. Of those with internet access, 155 million (46 per cent of the total) were mobile users and in urban China at the end of 2008 there were 172.02 mobile phones per 100 households (there had only been 19.5 in 2000) and 96.13 in the rural areas. Mobile phone use is being promoted in the countryside as a part of the programme to build the new socialist countryside. For example, the Ministry of Commerce has developed a website that carries daily prices for key agricultural products for most of the country. Farmers can track prices through the year to see what is the best time to sell and can send questions to Ministry of Commerce staff that have to be answered within a proscribed period of time.

Given the rapid spread of the internet and its commercial potential, it is not surprising that the response of the authorities is differentiated. There are much stricter controls on news and political information and practices and controls that more clearly match international practice for e-commerce dealings. Indeed, there are new opportunities that the internet brings for China. Chinese will be the second language of the internet and may even become dominant. This provides propagandists in Beijing with untold new opportunities to try to shape a Chinese political culture that stretches well beyond its physical boundaries.

The rise of 'virtual communities' that transcend traditional jurisdictions and even sovereign boundaries is difficult for China's current generation of Soviet-trained leaders to contemplate. It is far removed from their notions of modernity where planning, heavy industry and electricity represented progress. Treating citizens as children who need to be spoonfed information and hear only good news is no longer viable when urban elites are part of a global information community tracking down and trading information online. You cannot have a domestic system saying that there is nothing wrong while cyberspace tells China's citizens that there most certainly is a problem. It is not even a question of who is correct, it is dysfunctional. It is also dangerous and threatens to undermine the social stability that the leadership desires in order to ensure economic development. If there is no trust in domestic reporting, people will turn to foreign sources or listen to rumour, leading to greater levels of discontent and distrust. Denial and cover-up can only work against the leadership's long-term interests.

The final challenge: good governance and political reform

While the changes in the economy and society have been far-reaching, political change has lagged far behind. This is not to say that there has been no political reform but the core features of the Leninist party-state remain essentially unchanged and some have begun to ask whether the politico-administrative system will eventually come to act as a brake on further progress.

As we have seen, there are signs of a tentative institutional pluralism, tolerance of a limited public sphere and the emergence of grassroots participation but it is by no means certain that the political system will develop along the lines of China's East Asian neighbours with soft authoritarianism giving way to a democratic breakthrough. In fact, Pei (2006) warns of the risk of a trap in a 'partial reform equilibrium' where incompletely reformed economic and political institutions support a hybrid neo-authoritarian order that serves the needs of a small ruling elite. There is a particular danger in the fusion of economic and political power at the local level as we have seen with respect to corruption.

How the leadership manages the next phase of reform will prove crucial. The Central leadership seems well aware of the problems confronting them and has responded with calls for better and more transparent government and for the party to monitor itself and the actions of government more effectively. The key question is whether the party can develop the governing capacity to deal with the multiple chal-lenges it faces (inequality, social unrest, unemployment, effective urban-ization, environmental degradation) or whether they will rise to a level where they overwhelm the capacity of the administration to deal with them. If the leadership rejects what it terms 'Western-style' political structures, it is incumbent on them to develop the kind of institutions within the framework of one-party rule that can not only maintain economic growth but also deal with social tensions, provide sufficient transparency to reduce corruption, and make officials accountable to citizens who pay their wages. Liberalization will have to be at least a partial substitute for full democratization. This will require further progress in developing the legal system and protecting rights granted to citizens, stricter enforcement of anti-corruption rules, and greater consumer protection. If these objectives are achieved, the CCP will be the first titular Communist movement in world history to manage a peaceful political transition, co-opting the middle class in the process. Yet, there has been little systematic thinking about political reform offered at the Party Congresses and, when confronted by the potential for social unrest, the Chinese senior leadership has preferred to slow down the pace of reform once it bites and perpetuate a system of author-itarian political control.

Despite the enormous changes in the economic base, the policies of the state and its organizational structure still do not reflect fully govern-ance of a mixed economy, with the continuation of preferential policies for the state-owned sector, progress but continuing bias against the private sector and an administrative structure that cleaves too closely to that of the pre-reform era. Many observers expected that with the expansion of the market economy, the role of the state would decline in transitional economies, including China. However, this has not been the case and reform has brought with it state expansion into new areas while old functions have not necessarily been terminated (based on Saich, 2003). Indeed, a withering away of the state may not be the most appropriate approach. One of the primary problems in post-communist Russia has been the lack of an effective state apparatus to guide the process of market transition; a market economy without an effective enabling environment of rules and regulations implemented by a rela-tively impartial judiciary results in an anarchic free-for-all. As Yang (2004) has argued China has undertaken significant reforms to move along the path to a regulatory state. A number of pressures came together to cause the leadership to reform the governmental structures in an attempt to build a more rational, regulatory state that would be more efficient in managing China's increasingly market-influenced economy. These ranged from external causes such as the Asian Financial Crisis that made the leadership think hard about fiscal regulation or domestic causes such as major smuggling and corruption scandals that have enhanced the need for oversight. However, while China seems to be moving in the direction of a regulatory state, implementation has often been ineffective (see Box 13.2).

An optimistic view of the potential for political reform in China is presented by Gilley (2004), who suggests that China has the resources to embark on a process of democratic reform even with its current resources if the leadership were to show sufficient commitment. Commitment is precisely the problem identified by Pei (2006) who, as noted above, esti-mates that the fusion of economic and political power reduces the incen-tive for reform among party members. Political science writing about the relationship between relative wealth in a society and democratiza-tion and the development of the middle class suggests that China might be ripe for a democratic transition around 2025 to 2030 (see Rowen, 2001; and Inglehart and Welzel, 2005). By 2030 China's nominal GDP per capita might be around $9,800 (in terms of purchasing power parity it could be $29,000). In PPP terms, by 2030, China would have surpassed the level of the Czech Republic and South Korea in 2010 and would be approaching the levels of Spain, Italy and Taiwan in 2010.

Box 13.3: The Tainted Milk Scandal

Despite the creation of the State Drug and Food Administration (SFDA), in 2007 and 2008 Chinese and foreign consumers were shaken by a number of food and other scandals that raised concerns about product safety and suggested that the pursuit of profit ruled over concerns about citizens' health. In March 2007, pet food recalls were issued after it transpired that Chinese-produced food had been responsible for a number of pet deaths. In August 2007, a Chinese toy factory owner committed suicide after his export licence was revoked and some 1.5 million products were withdrawn from the market because of fears about high levels of lead. The factory had been a major supplier to Mattel. In July, the former head of the SFDA was executed for taking some $850,000 in bribes, mostly from pharmaceutical companies. No wonder Chinese felt unsafe about the quality of their products. However, in September 2008 there was an even bigger shock with a tainted milk scandal. The melamine-tainted milk caused almost 300,000 babies to become sick, with 51,900 hospitalized. Three deaths were attributed to the tainted milk but some suspect that the real number may have been higher. It is clear that the company and the local officials had engaged in a cover-up after the story began to leak out. The New Zealand Company Fonterra, which held a 43 per cent stake in the Chinese company, Sanlu, were alerted one month before the scandal was made public but their calls for a total recall were ignored. It took the New Zealand Prime Minister to inform Beijing officials before action began to be undertaken. A subsequent investigation revealed that Sanlu had received complaints as early as December 2007 but did not conduct any testing until June 2008. Some suspected that the slow governmental response was caused by the wish not to disrupt the pending Summer Olympics. Eventually, on 15 September the company issued a public apology and it was ordered to halt production and destroy all unsold and recalled products. The event caused public outrage and this even caused Premier Wen Jiabao to make a public apology stating that he felt 'extremely guilty'. By this time he was getting quite good at making public apologies (following those for coal mine deaths, polluted water and those stranded in the snow storms). Two were sentenced to death, the General Manager of Sanlu to life in prison and the mayor of Shijiazhuang, home of the factory, resigned.

A second major driver of democratization is the development of a strong middle class (Moore, 1966) and the creation of an urban, middle class has been a key product of reform. The level of urbanization planned for the next decade will increase further the size of this middle class. The response of this class to policy will be a crucial determinant of China's future direction (see Saich, 2009). The CCP's policy of co-optation of the population has worked very well to date and there is no sign that the middle class demands rapid political reform. Little research has been conducted on the middle class and both its size and opinions are unclear.

The Chinese Academy of Social Sciences in a 2003 survey calculated that the group amounted to 19 per cent of the population and could grow to 35 per cent of the population by 2020 (*China Daily*, 27 October 2004). A report by McKinsey calculated that by 2011 the lower middle class (earning between 25,000 and 40,000 *yuan* annually) would amount to 290 million (accounting for 44 per cent of the urban population). More impressively they calculated that by 2025, the upper middle class (annual income 40 to 100,000 *yuan*) will amount to 520 million (50 per cent of the urban population).

As long as economic growth persists, the growth of this middle class should exert a stabilizing influence if they can be co-opted successfully by the CCP leadership. Following President Jiang Zemin's speech on 1 July 1999 greater numbers of the middle class, including private entrepreneurs, have joined the party, and a law expanding the protection of private property has been passed. If politically cultivated, the middle class will not necessarily be a force to quicken the pace of democratic change. Most research shows that during the process of transition the middle class favours stability and a gradual approach to change within the existing economic and political system. However, they are likely to expect an increase in transparency, particularly at the local level, and a reduction in corruption. They can become a support base for the expansion of civil and political rights if their economic interests so dictate. We have seen, however, a burgeoning social activity around environmental and quality-of-life issues. For example, citizens in middle-class neighbourhoods in Shanghai protested the extension of the Maglev train system to link the cities two major airports. In Xiamen, Fujian province, a largely middle-class protest successfully stopped the opening of a chemical plant. Such protests are not regime threatening in the way that those of the poor or marginalized groups could be but they may lead to calls for greater transparency and accountability in the political system and a more regularized application of the rule of law. This status quo orientation of the middle class at the present time will be reinforced by the ageing of Chinese society. An older society tends to mean a more stable and conservative attitude. This also argues for a gradual approach to change within the Chinese political system. Rocca (2008) has termed this possibility for change 'conservative democracy'.

Political reform remains a divisive issue among the leadership, especially over what the final outcome of such reform might be. Many fear that opening up the system might lead to a collapse of CCP power and the kind of social dislocation that would undermine China's economic growth and produce social chaos rather than social harmony. The weakness of civil society and the systematic eradication of any alternative to CCP rule mean that there is little for an opposition to work with. With no framework of civil society to fall back on, the fear is that there will be the rise of an uncivil society. Last but not least, the CP has been successful in persuading key domestic stakeholders that its form of popular authoritarianism is the best model to continue China's economic rise and is, moreover, a model that suits traditional political culture (this has been dubbed by some as the 'Beijing Consensus').

This might argue for a continuation of the status quo. This is more than possible over the short- perhaps even to medium-term but the status quo does not last for ever. Future scenarios for China's development depend to a large extent on the capacity for the economy to keep developing smoothly (the following draws on Saich, 2008b). Obviously economic growth will slow eventually but over the next ten years at least there is no reason why firm growth cannot be maintained if correct policy choices are made. However, the Chinese economy is more integrated into the world trading system than ever before and this makes it more vulnerable to general trends within the global economy. A continued major slowdown in the US economy or rapidly rising prices for natural resources could cause problems for the Chinese economy. Domestically, the unrest that is local and isolated at the moment could always boil over into a major conflict between state and society. It needs to be remembered that the Chinese economy does not need to slow by too much before the state will lose its capacity to dispense largesse to its followers and for the costs of buying social peace to become problematic. There are a number of potential scenarios for China's political future and one cannot rule out systemic collapse even though this seems least likely. History does not offer much comfort for a peaceful transition as communist regimes unlike some other authoritarian systems have changed only with the collapse of the *ancien regime*. There are two potential causes that could trigger systemic collapse and while both are possible, they are not probable in the foreseeable future. The first would stem from economic collapse. While there are systemic distortions in the economy and an extremely vulnerable banking system, wise policy choice should ensure continued high-level economic growth over the next decade. The second catalyst would be if the social tensions and inequalities led to sufficient unrest to force the leadership to undertake significant political reforms to retain control. Here we shall just sketch three possible scenarios.

As suggested above, the most likely scenario over the short to medium term is a continuation of the politics of muddling through. Bold initiatives are unlikely. An essentially technocratic approach will prevail while the leadership tries to maintain an authoritarian political structure combined with growing economic liberalization. Minimal reform is likely in the political system with a continued focus on strengthening the legal system and building capacity and skills within public administration. The main potential for promoting reform would lie with the ability of people and organizations to exploit the deliberate vagaries of official pronouncements to experiment with cautious reform initiatives. Here the national consensus will be weak and the corruption will continue as will the lack of social cohesion. The party would still flirt with a strident form of nationalism in order to bolster the national consensus. Policy will continue to harbour the tensions between appeasing the new economic elites and trying to provide support for those who have been left behind by the reforms.

The second scenario would see the leadership responding to the increasing diversity in society and the rising protests by moving to accommodation with society and to try to form a new social compact. Instrumental in this process would be a re-evaluation of the events of 1989 and a return to the reform agenda put forward by Zhao Ziyang in 1987. Optimists would like to see China following in the footsteps of its East Asian neighbours with a transition to 'soft-authoritarianism' followed by a democratic breakthrough following as a natural corollary from economic growth. For the reasons outlined above, this does not seem likely over the short to medium term. However, by 2030 a nascent democracy might be possible but a number of conditions would have to be met. A major problem will be the large inequalities across China that might cause the elites to resist introducing democratic reforms. A democratic breakthrough would require a section of the ruling elite to be willing to break with the old system and to form a new compact with progressive forces in society. One could argue that there was such an opportunity in 1989 but that it was rejected by orthodox party members. Some argue that economic growth is creating a middle class that will support change and that the increase of marketization will cause the rule of law to be taken more seriously. However, it is hard to see what would cause the current elite willingly to reject the current beneficial system. This would be a beneficial scenario not only for many in China but also for the international community.

A third scenario would see the current and future leaderships becoming sufficiently disturbed by the potential for unrest and what it interprets as US attempts to isolate it internationally that it would adopt a more xenophobic nationalism combined with an inefficient authoritarianism domestically. Here the party would be dominated by the new elites who would read any opening up of the political system as leading to erosion of their privileges and benefits. The CCP maintains that without it chaos would ensue. By consistently cracking down on alternatives and restricting the growth of a vibrant civil society that could form the basis for a new system, the CCP has created the possibility that the 'uncivil society' might take power. The most probable outcome would be rule by the new economic elites backed by the military in the name of preserving social stability and national sovereignty. A strident nationalism might provide a minimal level of social glue to give the new regime a residue of support. A more likely variant would be the emergence of a pre-democratic Latin American-style political system. Under this scenario the inequalities would continue to rise, with the party becoming the preserve of the elites and with their power backed up by the military. The lack of political reform would produce a permanent underclass in both urban and rural China that would be portrayed as a threat to stability and continued economic progress. The party-dominated state would be in continual friction with society.

Those who have taken power at the Seventeenth Party Congress may not be able to rely on traditional CCP methods for controlling the country and will be under considerable pressure to find new ways to manage the Chinese polity. It is clear that the forces of globalization will require a considerable shift in the way the CCP governs the system and will require political reform that seeks to make the system not only more transparent but also more accountable. They will have to deal with a much more fluid domestic and international political order, where many of the key decisions affecting China will be taken by international organizations that will not respect the CCP's outdated notion of sovereignty. Given its record to date, this will be a significant hurdle for the current leaders to overcome. The ability to deal with the challenges of governance will attest to whether the CCP can retain its leadership over China's development well into the twenty-first century.

Further Reading

Only works that are in English are cited below and the references are for book-length works except when no suitable monograph exists.

With China changing so fast it is difficult to keep up with events. There are two key journals that will help keep readers abreast of developments: *The China Quarterly*, and *The China Journal*. Other useful journals are *China Information, China Perspectives*, the *Journal of Chinese Political Science* and the *Journal of Contemporary China*. An excellent quarterly update is provided in the *China Leadership Monitor*. For economics, see *China Economic Review*. English-language sources from China include the weekly *Beijing Review* and the newspaper *China Daily*. The *China Daily* has a website (http://www.chinadaily.com.cn) and the official Chinese news agency *Xinhua* has an English-language site (http://www.xinhua.org) as does the *People's Daily* (http://english. peoplesdaily.com.cn). An interesting magazine is *News China*. Other useful websites are: http://chinanewsonline.com (for economic and financial information), http://www.cnd.org (for general information) and http://china.scmp.com (Hong Kong's main English-language daily that has extensive China coverage).

2 Diversity within unity

A great visual introduction to the diversity of China is Donald and Benewick (2005), while an interesting set of essays that take us behind the headlines is Jensen and Weston (2006). Hinton (1980; 1986) provides seven volumes of documents covering domestic and foreign relations for the period 1949–1984. The changing geography of China caused by reforms is handled well in Leeming (1993) and Veeck and colleagues (2006). The question of China's ethnic minorities is covered in Dillon (1999), Gladney (1996), and Heberer (1989). Belief is dealt with in the essays in Overmeyer (2003). Dutton (1998) offers a fascinating view of life in China while his view of Beijing (in Dutton et al., 2008) provides a wonderful feel for life in the city. By contrast, Hessler (2001) offers a portrait of life along the Yangzi. Wasserstrom (2008) takes a reflective look at Shanghai.

3 China's changing road to development: political history, 1949–78

Superb introductions that navigate the reader through the complexity of China's history from imperial days down to the reforms are Spence (1990) and Fairbank and Goldman (1998). CCP history before 1949 is documented in Saich (1996).

Selden (1979) provides an excellent documentary collection for the period together with an interesting analysis. The essays in MacFarquhar and Fairbank (1987) provide a state-of-the-art overview of the development of the PRC until 1965, as do the essays in Cheek and Saich (1997). Elite politics from 1949 to 1965 is analysed in masterful fashion in MacFarquhar's trilogy (1974, 1983 and 1997). The politics of the early 1960s is covered in Baum (1975). MacFarquhar's work with Schoenhals (2006) is the most thorough analysis of the Cultural Revolution. A fascinating documentary collection is Schoenhals (1996).

4 China under reform, 1978–2010

The best introduction to the politics of the Deng Xiaoping era is Baum (1994). There are many good books covering the reform period and readers are advised to look at the essays in Dittmer and Liu (2006), and Gittings (2006) provides and interesting reflection on change in China. The changing nature of ideology is covered in Brugger and Kelly (1990) and Bell (2008) provides an interesting reflection on Confucianism in contemporary China. Key documents concerning the student-led demonstrations of 1989 can be found in Han (1990), Nathan and Link (2001) and Oksenberg, Sullivan and Lambert (1990), analysis in Calhoun (1994), Saich (1990) and Cunningham (2009). Fewsmith (2001) provides a fine overview of elite politics post-1989. Zhao Ziyang's memoirs (2009) provide a fascinating insiders' view of the 1980s. Shirk (2007) provides a good analytic review of China's strengths and frailties. Fewsmith (2010) contains essays covering the reform and their implication for future development. Peerenboom (2007) contains a stimulating discussion about the nature of China's reform experience.

5 The Chinese Communist Party

Shambaugh (2008) provides an excellent account of how the CCP responded to the domestic challenges of 1989 and the collapse of the Soviet Union. Lieberthal (1995/2004) provides an excellent introduction to the way China is governed. Schurmann's work (1968) remains a classic analysis of the interrelationship of the role of ideology and organization in China. See Brødsgaard and Zheng (2009) for the most recent set of essays on the party's changing role.

6 The central governing apparatus

To understand the nature of the state as it has evolved historically and the implications for contemporary China readers would be well advised to start with Schram (1985, 1987) and the essays in Brødsgaard and Strand (1998). An interesting set of essays on governance is in Howell (2004) and Yang (2004) reviews the institutionalization of the state apparatus. The most comprehensive overviews of legal developments under reform are Lubman (1999) and Peerenboom (2002). Potter (2001) interestingly handles the domestic and international interplay. Detailed reports on various aspects of rights in China are published by Amnesty International, Human Rights in China and Human Rights Watch.

For the PLA under Mao see Gittings (1967) and these should be supplemented by Joffe (1987) for the later period. More recent accounts are Finkelstein and Gunness (2007), Mulvenon and Yang (1999) and Shambaugh (2002).

7 Governance beyond the centre

Reforms have led to a revival of interest in the province as a unit of study. Detailed analyses are contained in Goodman (1997), Hendrischke and Feng (1999) and Fitzgerald (2002), while the 'develop the west' campaign is covered in Goodman and Edmonds (2004).

The nature of the local state is analysed in terms of local state corporatism by Oi (1989b, 1999). Blecher and Shue (1996) have been attracted to notions of the entrepreneurial and developmental state. Saich and Hu (forthcoming) explore the politics and economy of one of China's more developed regions.

8 Political participation and protest

Whyte (1974) explains the important role of small groups and political ritual. Nathan (1986) explores the concept of democracy in Chinese political culture. Yusuf and Saich (2008) look at the process of urbanization while Tang and Parish (2000) examine how reform has affected urban China, while Shi (1997) has provided a fascinating review of participation in Beijing. Information on the village election programme in China and elections more generally can be found at http://www.chinaelections.org, a site managed jointly by the Carter Center.

In addition to the works on the 1989 demonstrations a number of other works are important for understanding protest in China. Benton and Hunter (1995) translate and introduce significant documents on China's struggle for democracy from 1942 to 1989. Moody (1977) analyses dissent and opposition under Mao. Perry and Selden (2000) edit a set of essays that tackle change and resistance in China. Perry and Goldman (2007) reviews grass-roots political change and Hsing and Lee (2010) provide essays on the new social activism. Mertha (2008) looks at citizen impact on water policy.

9 The Chinese state and society

The essays of Tsou (1986) provide some of the most perceptive analysis of the nature of the Chinese state under Mao, while Womack (1991) provides a set of essays that relate contemporary state-society relations to longer-term historical trends. Shue (1988) provides a sophisticated analysis of the nature of the relationship while Walder (1986) provides the classic account of communist neo-traditionalism and workplace dependency under Mao. Bian (2005) and Bray (2005) both provide interesting analyses of the urban work-place.

10 Economic policy

Three of the most important works dealing with policy-making and implementation in China are Lampton (1987), Lieberthal and Lampton (1992) and Lieberthal and Oksenberg (1988). Riskin (1987) provides a good overview of economic development from 1949 to 1985. Two essential works are Naughton (1995), which shows how the Chinese economy gradually outgrew the plan and Naughton (2007), which provides an excellent introduction to China's development. For a more critical view of the urban, state centric model of development see Huang (2008).

Unger (2002) has a stimulating set of essays on rural transformation. Zweig (1989) provides the best view of agrarian radicalism in the Cultural Revolution and Zweig (1997) shows the role of farmers in restructuring rural production under the reforms, a theme also central to the work of Zhou (1996).

Steinfeld (1998) provides the best analysis to date of the problems of reforming the state-owned sector of the economy. Huang, Saich and Steinfeld (2005) contains essays on various aspects of financial sector reform. The development of the private sector of the economy is covered well in Guthrie (1999) and the private entrepreneurs are analysed in Dickson (2003 and 2008).

11 Social policy

Saich (2008a) provides a general overview of reform and its impact as does China Development Research Foundation (2009). Family planning is the subject of Milwertz (1997) and Sharping (2003). Issues of poverty and wealth are covered in Davis and Wang (2009). Whyte (2010) contains a fascinating study of the response of Beijing's citizens to the increasing inequality. The World Bank (2009) contains an excellent study of the shift in China's poverty alleviation strategy. A number of works have appeared concerning the question of migration, and among the best are Solinger (1999) and Ming (2009).

12 Foreign policy

Excellent works that provide a general orientation are Lampton (2001b) and Sutter (2009). Whether China's rise is a threat to the United States and the West is argued in Bernstein and Munro (1997, most probably), Gertz (2000, most certainly) and Nathan and Ross (1997, not necessarily). Whether engagement is good or indifferent is argued by Mann (2007) and Lampton (2007). Ross (2009) provides the best analysis of security policy. Two thoughtful sets of essays on the US–China relationship are Vogel (1997) and Rosecrance and Gu (2009). Huang (2003) looks at the role that FDI more broadly has played in China's development. Zweig (2002) provides an excellent account of the internationalization of China's reforms. *The China Quarterly* (September 2009) dedicates a special issue to China's relations with Africa and Taylor (2010) provides an interesting background. Dittmer and Yu (2010) provide a good set of essays on China's interaction with the developing world.

13 Challenges in the twenty-first century

A good introduction to the environment in China is Edmonds (1998). The legacy of Mao's policies on the environment is covered in Shapiro (2001) and the impact of reforms is covered in Economy (2004). China's energy policy and needs are covered in Cunningham (2009). Corruption and its threat to CCP rule is the topic of Lü (2000). How the media has changed is the topic of Lynch (1999), and Hughes and Wacker (2003) cover the development of the internet in China. An optimistic view of reform is presented by Gilley (2004) while a more pessimistic picture is painted by Pei (2006).

Bibliography

Alon, I. Chang, J. Fetsherin. M, Lattemann, C. and McIntyre, J. (2009) *China Rules. Globalization and Political Transformation* (Basingstoke: Palgrave).

Apter, D. and Saich, T. (1994) *Revolutionary Discourse in Mao's Republic* (Cambridge, MA: Harvard University Press).

Bachman, D. (1991) *Bureaucracy, Economy, and Leadership in China: The Institutional Origins of the Great Leap Forward* (New York: Cambridge University Press).

Baum, R. (1975) *Prelude to Revolution: Mao, the Party, and the Peasant Question, 1962–1966* (New York: Columbia University Press).

Baum, R. (1994) *Burying Mao: Chinese Politics in the Age of Deng Xiaoping* (Princeton, NJ: Princeton University Press).

Baum, R. (1998) 'The Fifteenth National Party Congress: Jiang Takes Command?', *The China Quarterly*, 153 (January).

Baum, R. (2000) 'Jiang Takes Command: The Fifteenth National Party Congress and Beyond', in Hung-Mao Tien and Yun-Han Chu (eds), *China Under Jiang Zemin* (Boulder, CO: Lynne Rienner).

Baum, R. and Shevchenko, A. (1999) 'The "State of the State"', in M. Goldman and R. MacFarquhar (eds), *The Paradox of China's Post-Mao Reforms* (Cambridge, MA: Harvard University Press).

Becker, J. (1996) *Hungry Ghosts: Mao's Secret Famine* (New York: The Free Press).

Bell, D. (2008), *China's New Confucianism. Politics and Everyday Life in a Changing Society* (Princeton, NJ: Princeton University Press).

Benewick. R. and Wingrove, P. (eds) (2005) *China in the 1990s* (Basingstoke: Palgrave Macmillan).

Benton, G. and Hunter, A. (eds) (1995) *Wild Lily, Prairie Fire: China's Road to Democracy, Yan'an to Tian'anmen, 1942–1989* (Princeton, NJ: Princeton University Press).

Bernstein, R. and Munro, R. H. (1997) *The Coming Conflict with China* (New York: A. A. Knopf).

Bian, M. (2005) *The Making of the State Enterprise System in Modern China. The Dynamics of Institutional Change* (Cambridge, MA: Harvard University Press).

Bird, R. and Wong, C. (2008), 'China's Fiscal System: A Work in Progress', in L. Brandt and T. Rawski (eds), *China's Great Transformation: Origins, Mechanism, and Consequences of the Post-Reform Economic Boom* (New York: Cambridge University Press).

Blecher, M. (1997) *China Against the Tides: Restructuring Through Revolution, Radicalism, and Reform* (London: Pinter/Cassell).

Blecher, M. and Shue, V. (1996) *Tethered Deer: Government and Economy in a Chinese County* (Stanford, CA: Stanford University Press).

Blum, S. D. (2000) 'China's Many Faces: Ethnic, Cultural, and Religious Pluralism', in T. B. Weston and L. M. Jensen (eds), *China Beyond the Headlines* (Lanham, MD: Rowman & Littlefield).

Bo, Z. and Chen, G. (2008) *China's 11th National People's Congress: What's New* (Singapore: East Asian Institute Background Brief No. 374).

Boone, P., Gomulka, S. and Layard, R. (eds) (1998) *Emerging from Communism: Lessons from Russia, China, and Eastern Europe* (Cambridge, MA: MIT Press).

Bray, D. (2005) *Social Space and Governance in Urban China. The Danwei System from Origins to Reform* (Stanford: Stanford University Press).

Breslin, S. (1995) 'Centre and Province in China', in R. Benewick and P. Wingrove (eds), *China in the 1990s* (Basingstoke: Palgrave Macmillan).

Brødsgaard, K. E. and Zheng, Y. (eds) (2009) *The Chinese Communist Party in Reform* (New York: Routledge).

Brødsgaard, K. E. and Strand, D. (eds) (1998) *Reconstructing Twentieth-Century China: State Control, Civil Society, and National Identity* (Oxford: Clarendon Press).

Brook, T. (1997) 'Auto-Organization in Chinese Society', in T. Brook and B. M. Frolic (eds), *Civil Society in China* (Armonk, NY: M. E. Sharpe).

Brugger, B. and Kelly, D. (1990) *Chinese Marxism in the Post-Mao Era* (Stanford, CA: Stanford University Press).

Cai, F. (ed.) (2003) *Zhongguo renkou yu laodong wenti baogao: Zhuanggui zhong de chengshi pinkun wenti* [Report on China's Population and Labour: Urban Poverty in Transitional China] (Beijing: Social Sciences Document Publishing House).

Cai, Y. (2008) 'Local Governments and the Suppression of Popular Resistance in China', *China Quarterly*, 193.

Cabestan, J.-P. (2000) 'The Relationship Between the National People's Congress and the State Council in the People's Republic of China: A Few Checks but No Balances', *French Centre for Research on Contemporary China*, Working Paper 1.

Calhoun, C. J. (1994) *Neither Gods nor Emperors: Students and the Struggle for Democracy in China* (Berkeley: University of California Press).

CASS (2009) *Zhongguo she hui lanpi shu* [China Society Yearbook] (Beijing: Chinese Social Sciences Publishing House).

CDRF (2007) *Zhongguo fazhan baogao 2007: zai fazhan zhong xiaochu pinkun* [China Development Report 2007: Eliminating Poverty Through Development] (Beijing: China Development Publishing House).

Chan, A. (1993) 'Revolution or Corporatism? Workers and Trade Unions in Post-Mao China', *The Australian Journal of Chinese Affairs*, 29 (January).

CHED (2005) *2005. China's Healthcare Reforms and Challenges* (Beijing: unpublished manuscript).

Chen, G. (2009) 'Carbon Intensity: China's Card for Climate Politics', *EAI Background Brief* No. 489.

Chen, G. and Zhu, J. (2009) 'China's Recent Clampdown on High-Stakes Corruption', *EAI Background Brief* No. 490.

Cheek, T. and Saich, T. (eds) (1997) *New Perspectives on State Socialism in China* (Armonk, NY: M. E. Sharpe).

Cheng, Tiejun and Selden, M. (1997) 'The Construction of Spatial Hierarchies: China's *Hukou* and *Danwei* Systems', in T. Cheek and T. Saich (eds), *New Perspectives on State Socialism in China* (Armonk, NY: M. E. Sharpe).

Cheung, P. T. Y. (1998) 'Introduction: Provincial Leadership and Economic Reform in Post-Mao China', in P. T. Y. Cheung, Jae Ho Chung and Zhimin Lin (eds), *Provincial Strategies of Economic Reform in Post-Mao China: Leadership, Politics, and Implementation* (Armonk, NY: M. E. Sharpe).

Cheung, P. T. Y., Chung, Jae Ho and Lin, Zhimin (eds) (1998) *Provincial Strategies of Economic Reform in Post-Mao China: Leadership, Politics, and Implementation* (Armonk, NY: M. E. Sharpe).

China Development Research Foundation (2009) *Constructing a Developmental Social Welfare System for All* (Beijing: CDRF).

Chow, Tse-tsung (1960) *The May Fourth Movement: Intellectual Revolution in Modern China* (Cambridge, MA: Harvard University Press).

Christensen, P. and Delman, J. (1981) 'A Theory of Transitional Society: Mao Zedong and the Mao School', *Bulletin of Concerned Asian Scholars*, 13(2).

Chung, Jae Ho (1998) 'Appendix: Study of Provincial Politics and Development in the Post- Mao Reform Era: Issues, Approaches, and Sources', in P. T. Y. Cheung, Jae Ho Chung and Zhimin Lin (eds), *Provincial Strategies of Economic Reform in Post-Mao China: Leadership, Politics, and Implementation* (Armonk, NY: M. E. Sharpe).

Chung Jae Ho *et al.* (2009) 'Assessing the "Revive the Northeast" (*zhenxing dongbei*) Programme: Origins, Policies and Implementation', *The China Quarterly*, No. 197.

Clarke, D. C. (1995) 'Justice and the Legal System in China', in R. Benewick and P. Wingrove (eds), *China in the 1990s* (Basingstoke: Palgrave Macmillan).

Croll, E. J. (1984) 'Women's Rights and New Political Campaigns in China Today', Working Paper 1, Sub-Series on Women's History and Development.

Cropper, M. (2009) 'Measuring the Costs of Air Pollution and Health in China', *Resources*, No. 173.

Cunningham, E. (2009) *A Portfolio Approach to Energy Governance: State Management of China's Coal and Electric Power Supply Industries* (Cambridge, MA: MIT PhD Thesis).

Davis, D. and Wang, F. (eds) (2009) *Creating Wealth and Poverty in Post-Socialist China* (Stanford, CA: Stanford University Press).

Dean, K. (1993) *Taoist Ritual and Popular Cults in Southeast China* (Princeton, NJ: Princeton University Press).

Deng, Xiaoping (1984) *Selected Works of Deng Xiaoping (1975–1982)* (Beijing: Foreign Languages Press).

Deng, Xiaoping (1994) *Selected Works of Deng Xiaoping: Volume III (1982–1992)* (Beijing: Foreign Languages Press).

Derleth, J. and Koldyk (2004), 'The Shequ Experiment: Grassroots Political Reform in Urban China', *Journal of Contemporary China*, 13(41).

Dickson, B. (2003) *Red Capitalists in China. The Party, Private Entrepreneurs, and Prospects for Political Change* (Cambridge: Cambridge University Press).

Dickson, B. (2008) *Wealth into Power. The Communist Party's Embrace of China's Private Sector* Cambridge: Cambridge University Press).

Dillon, M. (1999) *China's Muslim Hui Community: Migration, Settlement and Sects* (Richmond, Surrey: Curzon Press).

Dittmer, L. (1995) 'Chinese Informal Politics', *The China Journal*, 34 (July).

Dittmer, L., Fukui, H. and Lee, P. N. S. (eds) (2000) *Informal Politics in East Asia* (New York: Cambridge University Press).

Dittmer, L. and Liu, G. (eds) (2006) *China's Deep Reform. Domestic Politics in Transition* (Lanham, MD: Rowman & Littlefield).

Dittmer, L. and Yu, G.T. (eds) (2010) *China, the Developing World, and the New Global Dynamic* (Boulder, CO: Lynne Rienner).

Dollar, D. (2007) *Poverty, Inequality and Social Disparities During China's Economic Reform* (Washington, DC: World Bank Policy Research Working Paper) No. 4253.

Donald, S. H. and Benewick, R. (2005) *The State of China Atlas* (Brighton: Myriad Editions).

Duckett, J. (1998) *The Entrepreneurial State in China: Real Estate and Commerce Departments in Reform Era Tianjin* (London: Routledge).

Dutton, M. (1998) *Streetlife China* (Cambridge: Cambridge University Press).

Dutton, M., Lo, H. and Wu, D. (2008) *Beijing Time* (Cambridge, MA: Harvard University Press).

Economy, E. (2004) *The River Runs Black. The Environmental Challenge to China's Future* (Ithaca, NY: Cornell University Press).

Economy, E. and Oksenberg, M. (eds) (1999) *China Joins the World: Progress and Prospects* (New York: Council on Foreign Relations Press).

Edmonds, R. L. (1998) 'China's Environment', Special Issue of *The China Quarterly*, 156 (December).

Eggleston, K. Lindelow, M. Li, L. Meng, Q. Wagstaff, A. (2006) *Health Service Delivery in China: A Literature Review* (Washington, DC: World Bank Policy Research Working Paper) No. 3978.

Esping-Andersen, G. (1990) *The Three Worlds of Welfare Capitalism* (Princeton, NJ: Princeton University Press).

Evans, P. B. (1995) *Embedded Autonomy: States and Industrial Transformation* (Princeton, NJ: Princeton University Press).

Fairbank, J. K. and Goldman, M. (1998) *China: A New History* (Cambridge, MA: Harvard University Press).

Falkenheim, V. C. (1972) 'Peking and the Provinces: Continuing Central Predominance', *Problems of Communism*, 21(4).

Fan, C. (2007) 'Migration, *Hukou*, and the Chinese City', Yusuf, S. and Saich, T. (eds), *China Urbanizes* (Washington, DC: World Bank).

Ferguson, N. (2007) '"Chimerica" and the Global Asset Market Boom' *International Finance*, 10(3).

Fewsmith, J. (2001) *China Since Tiananmen: The Politics of Transition* (Cambridge: Cambridge University Press).

Fewsmith, J. (2003) 'The Sixteenth National Party Congress: The Succession that Didn't Happen', *The China Quarterly*, 173 (March).

Fewsmith, J. (ed.) (2010) *China Today, China Tomorrow: Domestic Politics, Economy and Society* (Lanham: Rowman & Littlefield).

Finkelstein, D. M. and Gunness, K. (eds) (2007) *Civil–Military Relations in Today's China: Swimming in a New Sea* (Armonk, NY: M.E. Sharpe).

Fitzgerald, J. (ed.) (2002) *Rethinking China's Provinces* (London and New York: Routledge).

Fravel, T. (2008) 'China's Search for Military Power', *The Washington Quarterly*, 31(3).

Friedman, E., Pickowicz, P. G., Selden, M. with Johnson, K. A. (1991) *Chinese Village, Socialist State* (New Haven: Yale University Press).

Frolic, B. M. (1997) 'State-Led Civil Society', in T. Brook and B. M. Frolic (eds), *Civil Society in China* (Armonk, NY: M. E. Sharpe).

Fukuyama, F. (2004) *State-Building. Governance and World Order in the 21ˢᵗ Century* (Ithaca: Cornell University Press).

Garnaut, R. Song, L. Yao, Y. (2008) 'Impact and Significance of State-Owned Enterprise Restructuring in China', Fleisher, B. Hope, C. and Pena, A. (eds) *Policy Reform and Chinese Markets: Progress and Challenges* (Cheltenham: Edward Elgar Publishing Ltd).

Gertz, B. (2000) *The China Threat: How the People's Republic Targets America* (Washington, DC: Regnery).

Gilley, B. (2004) *China's Democratic Future. How it Will Happen and Where it Will Lead* (New York: Columbia University Press).

Gittings, J. (1967) *The Role of the Chinese Army* (London: Oxford University Press).

Gittings, J. (2006) *The Changing Face of China. From Mao to Market* (Oxford: Oxford University Press).

Gladney, D. C. (1996) *Muslim Chinese: Ethnic Nationalism in the People's Republic*, 2nd edn (Cambridge, MA.: Harvard University Press).

Gold, T. B. (1990) 'Party-State Versus Society in China', in J. K. Kallgren (ed.), *Building a Nation-State: China after Forty Years* (Berkeley, CA: Institute of East Asian Studies, Center for Chinese Studies, University of California).

Goldstein, L. J. (2001) 'Return to Zhenbao Island: Who Started Shooting and Why it Matters', *The China Quarterly*, 168 (December).

Goodman, D. S. G. (1979) 'Changes in Leadership Personnel after September 1976', in J. Domes (ed.), *Chinese Politics after Mao* (Cardiff: University College).

Goodman, D. S. G. (1980) 'The Provincial Party First Secretary in the People's Republic of China, 1949–1978: A Profile', *British Journal of Political Science*, 10(1).

Goodman, D. S. G. (1986) *Centre and Province in the People's Republic of China: Sichuan and Guizhou, 1955–1965* (New York: Cambridge University Press).

Goodman, D. S. G. (1994) 'JinJiLuYu in the Sino-Japanese War: The Border Region and the Border Region Government', *The China Quarterly*, 140 (December).

Goodman, D. S. G. (ed.) (1997) *China's Provinces in Reform: Class, Community and Political Culture* (New York: Routledge).

Goodman, D. S. G. and Edmonds, R. (2004) *China's Campaign to 'Open the West': National, Provincial and Local Perspectives* (Cambridge: Cambridge University Press).

Graham, C. (1997) 'From Safety Nets to Social Policy: Lessons for the Transition Economies from the Developing Countries', in J. M. Nelson, C. Tilly and L. Walker (eds), *Transforming Post-Communist Political Economies* (Washington, DC: National Academy Press).

Grindle, M. S. and Thomas, J. W. (1991) *Public Choices and Policy Change: The Political Economy of Reform in Developing Countries* (Baltimore, MD: Johns Hopkins University Press).

Grunfeld, A. T. (1985) 'In Search of Equality: Relations between China's Ethnic Minorities and the Majority Han', *Bulletin of Concerned Asian Scholars*, 17(1).

Gui, Y., Cheng, J. and Ma, W. (2006) 'Cultivation of Grassroots Democracy: A Study of Direct Elections of Residents Committees in Shanghai', *China Information*, 20(1).

Guo, Xiaolin (1999) 'The Role of Local Government in Creating Property Rights: A Comparison of Two Townships in Northwest Yunnan', in J. C. Oi and A. G. Walder (eds), *Property Rights and Economic Reform in China* (Stanford, CA: Stanford University Press).

Guthrie, D. (1999) *Dragon in a Three-Piece Suit: The Emergence of Capitalism in China* (Princeton, NJ: Princeton University Press).

Hamrin, C. L. (1992) 'The Party Leadership System', in K. G. Lieberthal and D. M. Lampton (eds), *Bureaucracy, Politics, and Decision Making in Post-Mao China* (Berkeley, CA: University of California Press).

Hamrin, C. L. and Cheek, T. C. (eds) (1986) *China's Establishment Intellectuals* (Armonk, NY: M. E. Sharpe).

Han, Jun (2003) 'Public Finance Crisis in Chinese Counties and Towns: Performance, Causes, Impact and Measures' (Beijing: International Conference Report on Rural Public Finance).

Han, Minzhu (ed.) (1990) *Cries for Democracy: Writings and Speeches from the 1989 Chinese Democracy Movement* (Princeton, NJ: Princeton University Press).

Harding, H. (1997) 'Breaking the Impasse over Human Rights', in E. F. Vogel (ed.), *Living with China: US/China Relations in the Twenty-First Century* (New York: W. W. Norton).

Hartford, K. (1985) 'Socialist Agriculture is Dead: Long Live Socialist Agriculture! Organizational Transformation in Rural China', in E. J. Perry and C. Wong (eds), *The Political Economy of Reform in Post-Mao China* (Cambridge, MA: Harvard University Press).

He, B. (2003) 'Are Village Elections Competitive?' in J. Cheng (ed.), *China's Challenges in the Twenty-First Century* (Hong Kong: City University of Hong Kong Press).

Heberer, T. (1989) *China and its National Minorities: Autonomy or Assimilation?* (Armonk, NY: M.E. Sharpe).

Hessler, P. (2001) *River Town: Two Years on the Yangtze* (London: John Murray).

Hendrischke, H. and Feng, Chongyi (eds) (1999) *The Political Economy of China's Provinces: Comparative and Competitive Advantage* (New York: Routledge).

Hewitt, P. (2004) 'The Geopolitics of Global Aging', *Harvard Generations Policy Journal*, 1.

Hinton, H. C. (ed.) (1980) *The People's Republic of China, 1949–1979: A Documentary Survey* (Wilmington, DE: Scholarly Resources), 5 vols.

Hinton, H. C. (ed.) (1986) *The People's Republic of China, 1979–1984: A Documentary Survey* (Wilmington, DE: Scholarly Resources), 2 vols.

Hinton, H. C. (1994) 'China as an Asian Power', in T. W. Robinson and D. Shambaugh (eds), *Chinese Foreign Policy: Theory and Practice* (Oxford: Clarendon Press).

Howell, J. (1993) *China Opens Its Doors: The Politics of Economic Transition* (Boulder, CO: Lynne Rienner).

Howell, J. (ed.) (2004) *Governance in China* (Lanham, MD: Rowman & Littlefield).

Hsing, Y. and Lee, C. (eds.) (2010) *Reclaiming Chinese Society* (New York: Routledge).

Hu, B. (2007) *Informal Institutions and Rural Development in China* (New York: Routledge).

Hu, Jintao (2007) 'Hold High the Great Banner of Socialism with Chinese Characteristics and Strive for New Victories in Building a Moderately Prosperous Society in all Respects', *China Daily*, 25 October.

Hu, Shanlian and Jiang, Minghe (1998) 'The People's Republic of China', in D. H. Brooks and Myo Thant (eds), *Social Sector Issues in Transitional Economies of Asia* (Oxford: Oxford University Press).

Hu, Shikai (1993) 'Representation Without Democratization: The "Signature" Incident and China's National People's Congress', *Journal of Contemporary China*, 2(1).

Hua, Guofeng (1977) 'Political Report to the Eleventh National Congress of the Communist Party of China', in *The Eleventh National Congress of the Communist Party of China* (Peking: Foreign Languages Press).

Huang, Yasheng (1995a) 'Why China will not Collapse', *Foreign Policy*, 99 (Summer).

Huang, Yasheng (1995b) 'Administrative Monitoring in China', *The China Quarterly*, 143 (September).

Huang, Yasheng (1996) *Inflation and Investment Controls in China: The Political Economy of Central–Local Relations during the Reform Era* (New York: Cambridge University Press).

Huang, Yasheng (1998) *FDI in China: An Asian Perspective* (Singapore: Institute of Southeast Asian Studies).

Huang, Yasheng (2000) 'Why is There So Much Demand for Foreign Direct Investment in China? An Institutional and Policy Perspective', in Chung Ming Lau and Jianfa Shen (eds), *China Review 2000* (Hong Kong: The Chinese University Press).

Huang, Yasheng (2003) *Selling China: Foreign Direct Investment During the Reform Era* (New York: Cambridge University Press).

Huang, Yasheng (2008) *Capitalism with Chinese Characteristics. Entrepreneurship and the State* (Cambridge: Cambridge University Press).

Huang, Y., Saich, T. and Steinfeld, E. (eds) (2005) *Financial Reform in China* (Cambridge, MA: Harvard University Press).

Huang, Yiping (1998) *Agricultural Reform in China: Getting Institutions Right* (New York: Cambridge University Press).

Huchet, J.-F. (1999) 'Concentration and the Emergence of Corporate Groups in Chinese Industry', *China Perspectives*, 23 (May–June).

Huchet, J.-F. (2000) 'The Hidden Aspect of Public Sector Reforms in China. State and Collective SMEs in Urban Areas', *China Perspectives*, 32 (November–December).

Hughes, C. R. and Wacker, G. (2003) *China and the Internet. Politics of the Digital Leap Forward* (London and New York: Routledge Curzon).

Hussain, A. (2002), 'Demographic Transition in China and its Implications', *World Development*, 30(1).

Ikenberry, G. (2008) 'The Rise of China and the Future of the West. Can the Liberal System Survive?' *Foreign Affairs*, January/February.

Inglehart, R. and Welzel, C. (2005) *Modernization, Cultural Change, and Democracy: The Human Development Sequence* (Cambridge: Cambridge University Press).

Jackson, R. and Howe, N. (2004) 'The Greying of the Middle Kingdom: The Demographics and Economics of Retirement Policy in China' (Washington, DC: Center for Strategic and International Studies Working Paper).

Jenner, W. J. F. (1992) *The Tyranny of History: The Roots of China's Crisis* (London: Allen Lane).

Jenson, L. and Weston, T. (2006) *China's Transformations: The Stories Behind the Headlines* (Lanham, MD: Rowman & Littlefield).

Jiang, Qing (2003) *Zhengzhi ruxue: dangdai ruxue de zhuanxiang, tezhi yu fazhan* [Political Confucianism: The Transformation, Special Characteristics and Development] (Beijing: Sanlian Shudian).

Jiang, W. (2009) 'Fuelling the Dragon: China's Rise and its Energy and Resources Extraction in Africa', *The China Quarterly*, 199 (September).

Jiang, Zemin (1991) 'Beijing Rally Marks CPC Anniversary: Jiang Zemin Speech', in *FBIS-CHI-91-1295*, 5 July.

Jiang, Zemin (1997) 'Hold High the Great Banner of Deng Xiaoping Theory for an All-Round Advancement of the Cause of Building Socialism with Chinese Characteristics into the 21st Century', *Beijing Review*, 40(40) (6–12 October).

Jiang, Zemin (2002) Report to the Sixteenth Party Congress at http://www.16congress.org.cn/english/features/49007.htm.

Jin, Qiu (1999) *The Culture of Power: The Lin Biao Incident in the Cultural Revolution* (Stanford, CA: Stanford University Press).

Joffe, E. (1987) *The Chinese Army after Mao* (Cambridge, MA: Harvard University Press).

Johnson, D. (1999) 'China's Reforms – Some Unfinished Business', unpublished paper (November).

Johnston, A. (2003) 'Is China a Status Quo Power?', *International Security*, 27(4).

Johnston, A. and Ross, R. S. (eds) (1999) *Engaging China: The Management of an Emerging Power* (New York: Routledge).

Keating, P. (1994) 'The Ecological Origins of the Yan'an Way', *The Australian Journal of Chinese Affairs*, 32 (July).

Kelliher, D. (1997) 'The Chinese Debate over Village Self-Government', *The China Journal*, 37 (January).

Kelly, D. (1991) 'Chinese Marxism since Tiananmen: Between Evaporation and Dismemberment', in D. S. G. Goodman and G. Segal (eds), *China in the Nineties: Crisis Management and Beyond* (Oxford: Clarendon Press).

Kelly, D. (ed.) (1996) 'Realistic Responses and Strategic Options: An Alternative CCP Ideology and Its Critics', *Chinese Law and Government*, 20(2).

Kennedy, J. (2007) 'From the Tax-for-Fee Reform to the Abolition of Agricultural taxes: The Impact on Township Governments in Northwest China', *The China Quarterly*, 189 (March).

Kennedy School of Government (1999) 'Pension Reform in China: Weighing the Alternatives', Case Program 1547.0.

Khan, A. R. and Riskin, C. (1998) 'Income and Inequality in China: Composition, Distribution and Growth of Household Income, 1988 to 1995', *The China Quarterly*, 154 (June).

Kim, S. S. (1999) 'China and the United Nations', in E. Economy and M. Oksenberg (eds.), *China Joins the World: Progress and Prospects* (New York: Council on Foreign Relations Press).

Kornai, J. (1992) *The Socialist System: The Political Economy of Communism* (Princeton, NJ: Princeton University Press).

Kornai, J. (1997) 'Reform of the Welfare Sector in the Post-Communist Countries: A Normative Approach', in J. M. Nelson, C. Tilly and L. Walker (eds), *Transforming Post-Communist Political Economies* (Washington, DC: National Academy Press).

Kornai, J. (2000) 'Ten Years After "The Road to a Free Economy": the Author's Self-Evaluation', paper presented at the World Bank Annual Conference and Development Economics (April).

Kung, James Kai-sing and Liu, Shouying (1997) 'Farmers' Preferences regarding Ownership and Land Tenure in Post-Mao China: Unexpected Evidence from Eight Counties', *The China Journal*, 38 (July).

Lampton, D. M. (ed.) (1987) *Policy Implementation in Post-Mao China* (Berkeley: University of California Press).

Lampton, D. M. (1992) 'A Plum for a Peach: Bargaining, Interest, and Bureaucratic Politics in China', in K. G. Lieberthal and D. M. Lampton (eds), *Bureaucracy, Politics, and Decision Making in Post-Mao China* (Berkeley, CA: University of California Press).

Lampton, D. M. (2001a) *Same Bed, Different Dreams: Managing US-China Relations, 1989–2000* (Berkeley, CA: University of California Press).

Lampton, D. M. (ed.) (2001b) *The Making of Chinese Foreign and Security Policy in the Era of Reform* (Stanford, CA: Stanford University Press).

Lampton, D. M. (2007) 'The Wrong Question', *Foreign Policy*, May.

Lane, K. (1998) 'One Step Behind: Shaanxi in Reform, 1978–1995', in P. T. Y. Cheung, Jae Ho Chung and Zhimin Lin (eds), *Provincial Strategies of Economic Reform in Post-Mao China: Leadership, Politics, and Implementation* (Armonk, NY: M. E. Sharpe).

Lardy, N. R. (1998a) 'China and the Asian Contagion', *Foreign Affairs*, 77(4).

Lardy, N. R. (1998b) *China's Unfinished Economic Revolution* (Washington, DC: Brookings Institution Press).

Lawrence, S. V. (1994) 'Democracy, Chinese Style', *The Australian Journal of Chinese Affairs*, no. 32 (July).

Lawyers' Committee for Human Rights (1996) *Opening to Reform? An Analysis of China's Revised Criminal Procedure Law* (New York: Lawyers' Committee for Human Rights).

Lee, Ching Kwan (2000) 'Pathways of Labour Insurgency', in E. J. Perry and M. Selden (eds), *Chinese Society: Change, Conflict and Resistance* (New York: Routledge).

Lee, Ching Kwan (2007) *Against the Law: Labour Protests in China's Rustbelt and Sunbelt* (Berkeley, CA: University of California Press).

Lee, Ching Kwan (2010) 'Workers and the Quest for Citizenship' Hsing, Y. and Lee, C. *Reclaiming Chinese Society: The New Social Activism* (New York: Routledge).

Leeming, F. (1993) *The Changing Geography of China* (Oxford: Blackwell).

Leung, J. C. B. (1995) 'Social Welfare Reforms', in R. Benewick and P. Wingrove (eds), *China in the 1990s* (Basingstoke: Palgrave Macmillan).

Leung, J. (2006), 'The Emergence of Social Assistance in China', *International Journal of Social Welfare*, 15(3).

Li, Cheng (2008) 'A Pivotal Stepping-Stone: Local leaders' Representation on the 17th Central Committee', A Landslide Victory for Provincial Leaders', *China Leadership Monitor*, 23.

Li, Wei and Pye, L. W. (1992) 'The Ubiquitous Role of the *Mishu* in Chinese Politics', *The China Quarterly*, 132 (December).

Li, Xiguang et al. (1996) *Zai yaomohua Zhongguo de beihou (Behind the Sene of Demonizing China)* (Beijing: Zhongguo shehui kexue chubanshe).

Li, Zhisui, with editorial assistance of A. F. Thurston (1994) *The Private Life of Chairman Mao: The Memoirs of Mao's Personal Physician* (New York: Random House).

Lieberthal, K. G. (1992) 'Introduction: The "Fragmented Authoritarianism" Model and Its Limitations', in K. G. Lieberthal and D. M. Lampton (eds), *Bureaucracy, Politics, and Decision Making in Post-Mao China* (Berkeley, CA: University of California Press).

Lieberthal, K. (1995/2004) *Governing China: From Revolution through Reform* (New York: W. W. Norton).

Lieberthal, K. and Lampton, D. M. (eds) (1992) *Bureaucracy, Politics, and Decision Making in Post-Mao China* (Berkeley, CA: University of California Press).

Lieberthal, K. and Oksenberg, M. (1988) *Policymaking in China: Leaders, Structures, and Processes* (Princeton, NJ: Princeton University Press).

Lin, Zhimin (1998) 'Conclusion – Provincial Leadership and Reform: Lessons and Implications for Chinese Politics', in P. T. Y. Cheung, Jae Ho Chung and Zhimin Lin (eds), *Provincial Strategies of Economic Reform in Post-Mao China: Leadership, Politics, and Implementation* (Armonk, NY: M. E. Sharpe).

Lippit, V. (1975) 'The Great Leap Forward Reconsidered', *Modern China*, 1(1).

Lu, Mai (1999) 'China's Urgent Challenge – To Provide Public Goods in a Market Environment', unpublished paper.

Lü, Xiaobo (2000) *Cadres and Corruption: The Organizational Involution of the Chinese Communist Party* (Stanford, CA: Stanford University Press).

Lü, Xiaobo and Perry, E. J. (eds) (1997) *Danwei: The Changing Chinese Work-place in Historical and Comparative Perspective* (Armonk, NY: M. E. Sharpe).

Lubman, S. B. (1999) *Bird in a Cage: Legal Reform in China after Mao* (Stanford, CA: Stanford University Press).

Lynch, D. C. (1999) *After the Propaganda State: Media, Politics, and 'Thought Work' in Reformed China* (Stanford, CA: Stanford University Press).

Ma, Guonan and Fung, B. S. C. (2002) 'China's Asset Management Corporations', *Bank for International Settlements*, Working Paper 115 (August).

MacFarquhar, R. (1974) *The Origins of the Cultural Revolution 1: Contradictions among the People, 1956–1957* (London: Oxford University Press).

MacFarquhar, R. (1983) *The Origins of the Cultural Revolution 2: The Great Leap Forward 1958–1960* (London: Oxford University Press).

MacFarquhar, R. (1997) *The Origins of the Cultural Revolution 3: The Coming of the Cataclysm, 1961–1966* (London: Oxford University Press).

MacFarquhar, R. and Fairbank, J. K. (eds) (1987) *The Cambridge History of China, 14: The People's Republic, Part 1: The Emergence of Revolutionary China, 1949–1965* (Cambridge: Cambridge University Press).

MacFarquhar, R. and Schoenhals, M. (2006) *Mao's Last Revolution* (Cambridge, MA: Harvard University Press).

Mann, J. (2007) 'It's Their Party They Do What They Want', *Foreign Policy*, May.

Meisner, M. J. (1996) *The Deng Xiaoping Era: An Inquiry into the Fate of Chinese Socialism, 1978–1984* (New York: Hill & Wang).

Mertha, A. (2008) *China's Water Warriors. Citizen Action and Policy Change* (Ithaca, NY: Cornell University Press).

Miller, A. (2008) 'China's New Party Leadership', *China Leadership Monitor*, 23.

Milwertz, C. N. (1997) *Accepting Population Control: Urban Chinese Women and the One-Child Family Policy* (Richmond, Surrey: Curzon Press).

Ming, H. (2009) *Realities and Dreams of Migrant Workers in Beijing and Shanghai* (Cambridge, MA: Harvard PhD Thesis).

MOCA (2006) *Zhongguo minzheng tongji nianjian 2006* [China Civil Affairs Statistical Yearbook 2006] (Beijing: China Statistics Publishing House).

Montinola, G., Qian, Yingyi and Weingast, B. (1995) 'Federalism, Chinese Style: The Political Basis for Economic Success in China', *World Politics*, 48(1).

Moody, P. R. (1977) *Opposition and Dissent in Contemporary China* (Stanford: Hoover Institution Press).

Moore, B. (1966) *Social Origins of Dictatorship and Democracy: Lord and Peasant in the Making of the Modern World* (Boston, MA: Beacon Press).

Mountfield, E. and Wong, C. (2005) 'Public Expenditure on the Frontline: Towards Effective Management of Public Expenditure by Sub-National Governments in East Asia' in White, R. and Smoke, P. (eds.) *East Asia Decentralizes* (Washington, DC: World Bank).

Mulvenon, J. C. (1997) *Professionalization of the Senior Chinese Officer Corps: Trends and Implications* (Santa Monica, CA: Rand).

Mulvenon, J. C. (2006) 'So Crooked they Have to Screw Their Pants On: New Trends in Chinese Military Corruption', *China Leadership Monitor*, 19.

Mulvenon, J. C. (2009) 'Hu Jintao and the "Core Values of Military Personnel"', *China Leadership Monitor*, 28.

Mulvenon, J. C. and Yang, R. H. (eds) (1999) *The People's Liberation Army in the Information Age* (Santa Monica, CA: Rand).

Munro, R. (1988) 'Political Reform, Student Demonstrations and the Conservative Backlash', in R. Benewick and P. Wingrove (eds), *Reforming the Revolution: China in Transition* (Basingstoke: Palgrave Macmillan).

Murphy, R. (2002) *How Migrant Labor is Changing Rural China* (Cambridge: Cambridge University Press).

Nathan, A. J. (1973) 'A Factionalism Model for CCP Politics', *The China Quarterly*, 53 (January–March).

Nathan, A. J. (1986) *Chinese Democracy* (Berkeley, CA: University of California Press).

Nathan, A. J. (1994) 'Human Rights in Chinese Foreign Policy', *The China Quarterly*, 139 (September).

Nathan, A. J. (1999) 'China and the International Human Rights Regime', in E. Economy and M. Oksenberg (eds), *China Joins the World: Progress and Prospects* (New York: Council on Foreign Relations Press).

Nathan, A. J. and Link, P. (eds) (2001) *The Tiananmen Papers* (New York: Public Affairs).

Nathan, A. J. and Ross, R. S. (1997) *The Great Wall and the Empty Fortress: China's Search for Security* (New York: W. W. Norton).

Nathan, A. J. and Tsai, K. S. (1995) 'Factionalism: A New Institutionalist Restatement', *The China Journal*, 34 (July).

Naughton, B. (1987) 'The Decline of Central Control over Investment in Post-Mao China', in D. M. Lampton (ed.), *Policy Implementation in Post-Mao China* (Berkeley, CA: University of California Press).

Naughton, B. (1988) 'The Third Front: Defence Industrialization in the Chinese Interior', *China Quarterly*, 115 (September).

Naughton, B. (1992) 'The Chinese Economy: On the Road to Recovery?', in W. A. Joseph (ed.), *China Briefing, 1991* (Boulder, CO: Westview Press).

Naughton, B. (1995) *Growing Out of the Plan: Chinese Economic Reform, 1978–1993* (New York: Cambridge University Press).

Naughton, B. (1999) 'China's Transition in Economic Perspective?', in M. Goldman and R. MacFarquhar (eds), *The Paradox of China's Post-Mao Reforms* (Cambridge, MA: Harvard University Press).

Naughton, B. (2000) 'The Chinese Economy: Fifty Years into the Transformation', in T. White (ed.), *China Briefing, 2000: The Continuing Transformation* (Armonk, NY: M. E. Sharpe).

Naughton, B. (2007) *The Chinese Economy: Transitions and Growth* (Cambridge, MA: The MIT Press).

Naughton, B. (2008) 'SASAC and Rising Corporate Power in China', *China Leadership Monitor*, 24.

Nee, V. (1989) 'A Theory of Market Transition: From Redistribution to Markets in State Socialism', *American Sociological Review*, 54(5).

Nelson, J. M. (1997) 'Social Costs, Social-Sector Reforms, and Politics in Post Communist Transformations', in J. M. Nelson, C. Tilly and L. Walker (eds), *Transforming Post-Communist Political Economies* (Washington, DC: National Academy Press).

Nevitt, C. E. (1996) 'Private Business Associations in China: Evidence of Civil Society or Local State Power?', *The China Journal*, 36 (July).

Nickum, J. E. (1998) 'Is China Living on the Water Margin?' *The China Quarterly*, No. 156 (December).

Nielsen, I., Nyland, C., Smyth, R. and Xhu, C. (2005) 'Marketization and Perceptions of Social Protection in China's Cities', *World Development*, 33(11).

Nyberg, A. and Rozelle, S. (1999) *Accelerating China's Rural Transformation* (Washington, DC: World Bank).

O'Brien, K. (1990) *Reform without Liberalization: China's National People's Congress and the Politics of Institutional Change* (New York: Cambridge University Press).

OECD (2002) *China in the World Economy: The Domestic Policy Challenges* (Paris: OECD).

OECD (2006) *Challenges for China's Public Spending: Toward Greater Effectiveness and Equity* (Paris: OECD).

Ogden, S. et al. (eds) (1992) *China's Search for Democracy: The Student and Mass Movement of 1989* (Armonk, NY: M. E. Sharpe).

Oi, J. C. (1989a) 'Market Reforms and Corruption in Rural China', *Studies in Comparative Communism*, 22(2–3).

Oi, J. C. (1989b) *State and Peasant in Contemporary China: The Political Economy of Village Government* (Berkeley, CA: University of California Press).

Oi, J. (1992) 'Fiscal Reform and the Economic Foundations of Local State Corporatism in China', *World Politics*, 45(1).

Oi, J. C. (1999) *Rural China Takes Off: Institutional Foundations of Economic Reform* (Berkeley, CA: University of California Press).

Oksenberg, M. (1968) 'The Institutionalisation of the Chinese Communist Revolution: The Ladder of Success on the Eve of the Cultural Revolution', *The China Quarterly*, 36 (October–December).

Oksenberg, M., Sullivan, L. R. and Lambert, M. (eds) (1990) *Beijing Spring, 1989: Confrontation and Conflict: The Basic Documents* (Armonk, NY: M. E. Sharpe).

Overbye, E. (2005) 'Extending Social Security in Developing Countries: A Review of Three Main Strategies', *International Journal of Social Work*, 14.

Overmeyer, D. (ed.) (2003) *Religion in China Today* (Cambridge: Cambridge University Press).

Paal, D. (1997) 'China and the East Asian Security Environment: Complementarity and Competition,' in Vogel, E. (ed.) *Living with China* (New York: W. W. Norton).

Pairault, T. (1982) 'Industrial Strategy (January 1975–June 1979): In Search of New Policies for Industrial Growth', in J. Gray and G. White (eds), *China's New Development Strategy* (London: Academic Press).

Park, A. et al. (1996) 'Distributional Consequences of Reforming Local Public Finance in China', *The China Quarterly*, 147 (September).

Park, A. and Shen, Minggao (2000) 'Joint Liability Lending and the Rise and Fall of China's Township and Village Enterprises', unpublished paper.

Parris, K. (1999) 'The Rise of Private Business Interests', in M. Goldman and R. MacFarquhar (eds), *The Paradox of China's Post-Mao Reforms* (Cambridge, MA: Harvard University Press).

Pastor, R. A. and Tan, Qingshan (2000) 'The Meaning of China's Village Elections', *The China Quarterly*, 162 (June).

Pearson, M. M. (1999) 'China's Integration into the International Trade and Investment Regime', in E. Economy and M. Oksenberg (eds), *China Joins the World: Progress and Prospects* (New York: Council on Foreign Relations Press).

Peerenboom, R. (2002) *China's Long March Toward Rule of Law* (Cambridge: Cambridge University Press).

Peerenboom, R. (2007) *China Modernizes: Threat to the West or Model for the Rest?* (Oxford: Oxford University Press).

Pei, Minxin (2006) *China's Trapped Transition. The Limits of Developmental Autocracy* (Cambridge, MA: Harvard University Press).

Peng, Xizhe (2002) *Is this the Right Time to Change China's Population Policy?* (Singapore: East Asian Institute Background Brief No. 132).

Perry, E. J. (1997) 'Shanghai's Strike Wave of 1957', in T. Cheek and T. Saich (eds), *New Perspectives on State Socialism in China* (Armonk, NY: M. E. Sharpe).

Perry, E.J. and Goldman, M. (2007) *Grassroots Political Reform in Contemporary China* (Cambridge, MA: Harvard University Press).

Perry, E. and Selden, M. (eds) (2000) *Chinese Society: Change, Conflict, and Resistance* (New York: Routledge).

Pickowicz, P. G. (1989) 'Popular Cinema and Political Thought in Post-Mao China: Reflections on Official Pronouncements, Film, and the Film Audience', in P. Link, R. Madsen and P. G. Pickowicz (eds), *Unofficial China: Popular Culture and Thought in the People's Republic of China* (Boulder, CO: Westview Press).

Potter, P. B. (2001) *The Chinese Legal System: Globalization and Local Legal Culture* (London and New York: RoutledgeCurzon).

Pye, L. (1981) *The Dynamics of Chinese Politics* (Cambridge, MA: Oelgeschlager, Gunn & Hain).

Pye, L. (1995) 'Factions and the Politics of *Guanxi*: Paradoxes in Chinese Administrative Behaviour', *The China Journal*, 34 (July).

Rawski, T. G. (1999) 'Reforming China's Economy: What Have We Learned?', *The China Journal*, 41 (January).

Read, B. L. (2000) 'Revitalizing the State's Urban "Nerve Tips"', *The China Quarterly*, 163 (September).

Riskin, C. (1987) *China's Political Economy: The Quest for Development since 1949* (Oxford: Oxford University Press).

Roberts, M. (trans) and Levy, R. (annot.) (1977) *A Critique of Soviet Economics by Mao Tsetung* (New York: Monthly Review Press).

Rocca, J.-L. (2008) 'Democracy Within the Communist Party is the New Answer', *Le Monde Diplomatique*, 11 August.

Rong, J. *et al.* (eds) (1998) *Cong yalixing tizhi xiang minzhu hezuo tizhi de zhuanbian* [*The Transformation from a Pressurized System to a Democratic Cooperative System*] (Beijing: Zhongyang bianyi chubanshe).

Rosecrance, R. and Gu, G. (2009) *Power and Restraint. A Shared Vision for the U.S.–China Relationship* (New York: Public Affairs).

Ross, R. (2009) *Chinese Security Policy: Structure, Power and Politics* (London: Routledge).

Rotberg, R. (2008), *China into Africa: Trade, Aid, and Influence* Washington, DC.: Brookings Institution Press).

Rowen, W. T. (2001), 'The Growth of Freedoms in China' APARC Working Paper, Stanford University.

Sachs, J. and Woo, Wing Thye (1994) 'Structural Factors in the Economic Reforms of China, Eastern Europe and the Former Soviet Union: Discussion', *Economic Policy*, 18 (April).

Saich, T. (1983) 'The Fourth Constitution of the People's Republic of China', *Review of Socialist Law*, 9(2).

Saich, T. (1984) 'Workers in the Workers' State: Urban Workers in the PRC', in D. S. G. Goodman (ed.), *Groups and Politics in the People's Republic of China* (Cardiff: University College).

Saich, T. (ed.) (1990) *The Chinese People's Movement: Perspectives on Spring 1989* (Armonk, NY: M. E. Sharpe).

Saich, T. (1992) 'The Fourteenth Party Congress: A Programme for Authoritarian Rule', *The China Quarterly*, 132 (December).

Saich, T. (1994a) 'Introduction: The Chinese Communist Party and the Anti-Japanese War Base Areas', *The China Quarterly*, 140 (December).

Saich, T. (1994c) 'Discos and Dictatorship: Party-State and Society. Relations in the People's Republic of China', in J. N. Wasserstrom and E. J. Perry (eds), *Popular Protest and Political Culture in Modern China* (Boulder, CO: Westview Press), 2nd edn.

Saich, T. (1994d) 'The Search for Civil Society and Democracy in China', *Current History*, 83(584).

Saich, T. (1995) 'Writing or Rewriting History? The Construction of the Maoist Resolution on Party History', in T. Saich and H. van de Ven (eds), *New Perspectives on the Chinese Communist Revolution* (Armonk, NY: M. E. Sharpe).

Saich, T. (ed.) (1996) *The Rise to Power of the Chinese Communist Party: Documents and Analysis* (Armonk, NY: M. E. Sharpe).

Saich, T. (2000a) 'Negotiating the State: The Development of Social Organizations in China', *The China Quarterly*, 161 (March).

Saich, T. (2000b) 'Globalization, Governance, and the Authoritarian Westphalian State: The Case of China', in J. S. Nye and J. D. Donahue (eds), *Governance in a Globalizing World* (Washington, DC: Brookings Institution Press).

Saich, T. (2002) 'China's WTO Gamble. Some Political and Social Questions', *Harvard Asia Pacific Review* (Spring).

Saich, T. (2003) 'Reform and the Role of the State in China', in R. Benewick et al. (eds), *Asian Politics in Development. Essays in Honour of Gordon White* (London: Frank Cass).

Saich, T. (2006) 'SARS: China's Chernobyl or Much Ado About Nothing', Kleinman, A. and Watson, J. (eds), *SARS in China: Economic, Political and Social Consequences* (Stanford: Stanford University Press).

Saich, T. (2008a) *Providing Public Goods in Transitional China* (New York: Palgrave Macmillan).

Saich, T. (2008b) 'China: Socio-Political Issues', in Hoffmann, W. J. and Enright, M.J. (eds) *China Into the Future. Making Sense of the World's Most Dynamic Economy* (Singapore: Wiley).

Saich, T. (2009) 'China and the United States as Interacting Societies', in Rosecrance, R. and Gu, G. (eds) *Power and Restraint. A Shared Vision for the U.S.–China Relationship* (New York: Public Affairs).

Saich, T. and Hu, B. (forthcoming) *Rural Governance in China*.

Saich, T and X. Yang (2003) 'Selecting within the Rules: "Open Recommendation and Selection" and Institutional Innovation in China', *Pacific Affairs* (Summer).

Salditt, F., Whiteford, P. and Adema, W. (2007) 'Pension Reform in China: Progress and Reform' (Paris: OECD Social, Employment and Migration Working Papers).

Sargeson, S. and Zhang, Jian (1999) 'Re-assessing the Role of the Local State: A Case Study of Local Government Interventions in Property Rights Reform in a Hangzhou District', *The China Journal*, 42 (July).

Schoenhals, M. (ed.) (1996) *China's Cultural Revolution, 1966–1969: Not a Dinner Party* (Armonk, NY: M. E. Sharpe).

Schram, S. R. (ed.) (1974) *Mao Tse-Tung Unrehearsed: Talks and Letters, 1966–71* (Harmondsworth: Penguin).

Schram, S. (ed.) (1985) *The Scope of State Power in China* (New York: The Chinese University Press and St Martin's Press).

Schram, S. (ed.) (1987) *Foundations and Limits of State Power in China* (Hong Kong: The Chinese University Press).

Schurmann, F. (1968) *Ideology and Organization in Communist China* (Berkeley, CA: University of California Press).

Scott, J. C. (1985) *Weapons of the Weak: Everyday Forms of Peasant Resistance* (New Haven, CT: Yale University Press).

Segal, G. (1994) 'China's Changing Shape', *Foreign Affairs*, 73(3).

Selden, M. (1971) *The Yenan Way in Revolutionary China* (Cambridge, MA: Harvard University Press).

Selden, M. (ed.) (1979) *The People's Republic of China: A Documentary History of Revolutionary Change* (New York: Monthly Review Press).

Selden, M. (1995) *China in Revolution: The Yenan Way Revisited* (Armonk, NY: M. E. Sharpe).

Shambaugh, D. (1991) 'The Soldier and the State in China: The Political Work System in the People's Liberation Army', *The China Quarterly*, 127 (September).

Shambaugh, D. (1996) 'China's Military in Transition: Politics, Professionalism, Procurement and Power Projection', *The China Quarterly*, 146 (June).

Shambaugh, D. (1997) 'Building the Party-State in China, 1949–1965: Bringing the Soldier Back In', in T. Cheek and T. Saich (eds), *New Perspectives on State Socialism in China* (Armonk, NY: M. E. Sharpe).

Shambaugh, D. (2002) *Modernizing China's Military: Progress, Problems, and Prospects* (Berkeley and Los Angeles, CA: University of California Press).

Shambaugh, D. (2008) *China's Communist Party. Atrophy and Adaptation* (Washington, DC: Woodrow Wilson Center Press).

Shapiro, J. (2001) *Mao's War Against Nature: Politics and the Environment in Revolutionary China* (New York: Cambridge University Press).

Sharping, T. (2003) *Birth Control in China 1949–2000. Population Policy and Demographic Development* (London and New York: Routledge Curzon).

Sheng, Y. (2009) *Provincial Leaders in the CCP Politburo* (Singapore: East Asia Institute Background Brief No. 445).

Shi, Tianjian (1997) *Political Participation in Beijing* (Cambridge, MA: Harvard University Press).

Shih, V. Liu, M. Zhang, Q (n.d.) '"Eating Budget": Determining Fiscal Transfers under Predatory Fiscal Federalism', unpublished paper.

Shirk, S. L. (1990) '"Playing to the Provinces": Deng Xiaoping's Political Strategy of Economic Reform', *Studies in Comparative Communism*, 23(3–4).

Shirk, S. L. (2007) *China. Fragile Superpower* (Oxford: Oxford University Press).

Shue, V. (1988) *The Reach of the State: Sketches of the Chinese Body Politic* (Stanford, CA: Stanford University Press).

Skinner, G. W. (1964–65) 'Marketing and Social Structure in Rural China (parts 1–3)', *Journal of Asian Studies*, 24(1–3).

Snow, E. (1972) *The Long Revolution* (New York: Random House).

Solinger, D. J. (1999) *Contesting Citizenship in Urban China: Peasant Migrants, the State, and the Logic of the Market* (Berkeley, CA: University of California Press).

Song, Qiang et al. (1996) *Zhongguo keyi shuo bu* [*The China That Can Say No*] (Beijing: Zhonghua gongshang lianhe chubanshe).

Song, Xiaojun et al. (2009) *Zhongguo bu gaoxing* [China is Unhappy] (Nanjing: Jiangsu Renmin chubanshe).

Spence, J. D. (1990) *The Search for Modern China* (London: Hutchinson).

Spence, J. D. (1996) *God's Chinese Son: The Taiping Heavenly Kingdom of Hong Xiuquan* (New York: W. W. Norton).

State Council AIDS Working Committee Office (2007) *A Joint Assessment of HIV/AIDS Prevention, Treatment and Care in China* (Beijing: n.p.)

State Council Information Office (2007) *White Paper on China's Political System* (Beijing, can be accessed at http://www.china.org.cn/english/news/231852.htm.

Steinfeld, E. S. (1998) *Forging Reform in China: The Fate of State-owned Industry* (New York: Cambridge University Press).

Steinfeld, E. S. (2000) 'Free Lunch or Last Supper? China's Debt-Equity Swaps in Context', *The China Business Review*, 27(4).

Steinfeld, E. S. (2005) 'China's Program of Debt-Equity Swaps: Government Failure or Market Failure?' in Huang, Saich and Steinfeld (2005).

Steinfeld, E. S. (forthcoming) *Playing Our Game: Why China's Rise Doesn't Threaten the West* (Oxford: Oxford University Press).

Su, M. and Zhao, Q. (2006) *The Fiscal Framework and Urban Infrastructure Finance in China* (Washington, DC: World Bank Policy Research Working Paper), No. 4051.

Sutter, R. (2009) *China's Foreign Relations. Power and Policy since the Cold War* (Lanham, MD: Rowman & Littlefield).

Sullivan, L. R. (1990) 'The Emergence of Civil Society in China, Spring 1989', in T. Saich (ed.), *The Chinese People's Movement Perspectives on Spring 1989* (Armonk, NY: M. E. Sharpe).

Swaine, M. D. and Johnston, A. I. (1999) 'China and Arms Control Institutions', in E. Economy and M. Oksenberg (eds), *China Joins the World: Progress and Prospects* (New York: Council on Foreign Relations Press).

Tang, Wenfang and Parish, W. L. (2000) *Chinese Urban Life under Reform: The Changing Social Contract* (Cambridge: Cambridge University Press).

Tanner, M. S. (1994) 'The Erosion of Communist Party Control over Lawmaking in China', *The China Quarterly*, 138 (June).

Tanner, M. S. (1999) *The Politics of Lawmaking in Post-Mao China: Institutions, Processes, and Democratic Prospects* (New York: Oxford University Press).

Taylor, I. (2010) *China's New Role in Africa* (Boulder, CO: Lynne Rienner).

Teiwes, F. (1987) 'Establishment and Consolidation of the New Regime', in R. MacFarquhar and J. K. Fairbank (eds), *The Cambridge History of China, 14: The People's Republic, Part 1: The Emergence of Revolutionary China, 1949–1965* (Cambridge: Cambridge University Press).

Teiwes, F. C. (1990) *Politics at Mao's Court: Gao Gang and Party Factionalism in the Early 1950s* (Armonk, NY: M. E. Sharpe).

Teiwes, F. C. (1993) *Politics and Purges in China: Rectification and the Decline of Party Norms, 1950–1965* (Armonk, NY: M. E. Sharpe), 2nd edn.

Teiwes, F. C. with Sun, W. (1997) 'The Politics of an "Un-Maoist" Interlude: The Case of Opposing Rash Advance, 1956–1957', in T. Cheek and T. Saich (eds), *New Perspectives on State Socialism in China* (Armonk, NY: M. E. Sharpe).

Teiwes, F. C. with Sun, W. (1999) *China's Road to Disaster: Mao, Central Politicians, and Provincial Leaders in the Unfolding of the Great Leap Forward, 1955–1959* (Armonk, NY: M. E. Sharpe).

Tomba, Luigi (2001) *Paradoxes of Labour Reform: Chinese Labour Theory and Practice from Socialism to the Market* (Richmond, Surrey: Curzon Press).

Tsai, Li. (2001) 'Strategies of Rule or Ruin? Governance and Public Goods Provision in Rural China', Paper presented at the Annual Meeting of the Association for Asian Studies, March.

Tsai, L. (2002) 'Cadres, Temple and Lineage Institutions, and Governance in Rural China', *The China Journal*, 48 (July).

Tsai, L. (2007) *Accountability without Democracy: Solidary Groups and Public Goods Provision in Rural China* (New York: Cambridge University Press).

Tsou, Tang (1983) 'Back from the Brink of Revolutionary – "Feudal Totalitarianism"', in V. Nee and D. Mozingo (eds), *State and Society in Contemporary China* (Ithaca, NY: Cornell University Press).

Tsou, Tang (1986) *The Cultural Revolution and Post-Mao Reforms: A Historical Perspective* (Chicago, IL: University of Chicago Press).

Tucker, N. B. (2000) 'Dangerous Liaisons: China, Taiwan, Hong Kong, and the United States at the Turn of the Century', in T. White (ed.), *China Briefing, 2000: The Continuing Transformation* (Armonk, NY: M. E. Sharpe).

Unger, J. (1985–6) 'The Decollectivization of the Chinese Countryside: A Survey of Twenty-eight Villages', *Pacific Affairs*, 58(4).

Unger, J. (1987) 'The Struggle to Dictate China's Administration: The Conflict of Branches vs. Areas vs. Reform', *Australian Journal of Chinese Affairs*, 18 (July).

Unger, J. (2002) *The Transformation of Rural China* (New York: M. E. Sharpe).

Unger, J. and Chan, A. (1995) 'China, Corporatism, and the East Asian Model', *The Australian Journal of Chinese Affairs*, 33 (January).

Unger, J. and Chan, A. (1999) 'Inheritors of the Boom: Private Enterprise and the Role of Local Government in a Rural South China Township', *The China Journal*, 42 (July).

United Nations Development Programme (UNDP) (1998) *China: Human Development Report: Human Development and Poverty Alleviation 1997* (Beijing: UNDP).

United Nations Development Programme (UNDP) and International Labour Organization (ILO) (2002) *An Integrated Approach to Reducing Poverty in China* (Beijing).

Van Dalen, H. (2006) 'When Health Care Insurance Does Not Make a Difference? The Case of Health Care "Made in China"', Tinbergen Institute Discussion paper, No. 06-091/1.

Van Ness, P. and Raichur, S. (1983) 'Dilemmas of Socialist Development: An Analysis of Strategic Lines in China, 1949–1981', *Bulletin of Concerned Asian Scholars*, 15(1).

Veeck, G, Pannell, C., Smith, C. and Huang, Y. (2006) *China's Geography. Globalization and the Dynamics of Political, Economic, and Social China* (Lanham, MD: Rowman & Littlefield).

Vogel, E. F. (ed.) (1997) *Living with China: US/China Relations in the Twenty-First Century* (New York: W. W. Norton).

Walder, A. G. (1986) *Communist Neo-Traditionalism: Work and Authority in Chinese Industry* (Berkeley, CA: University of California Press).

Walder, A. G. (1994) 'The Decline of Communist Power: Elements of a Theory of Institutional Change', *Theory and Society*, 23(2).

Walder, A. G. (1995a) 'Local Governments as Industrial Firms: An Organizational Analysis of China's Transitional Economy', *American Journal of Sociology*, 101(2).

Walder, A. G. (1998a) 'The County Government as an Industrial Corporation', in A. G. Walder (ed.), *Zouping in Transition: The Process of Reform in Rural North China* (Cambridge, MA: Harvard University Press).

Wang Hui, (2003) *China's New Order. Society, Politics, and Economy in Transition* (Cambridge, MA: Harvard University Press).

Wang, Sangui (2004) 'Poverty Targeting in the People's Republic of China', ADB Institute Discussion paper, No. 4.

Wang, Shaoguang (1995) 'The Rise of the Regions: Fiscal Reform and the Decline of Central State Capacity in China', in A. G. Walder (ed.), *The Waning of the Communist State: Economic Origins of Political Decline in China and Hungary* (Berkeley, CA: University of California Press).

Wang, Shaoguang and Hu, Angang (1999) *The Political Economy of Uneven Development: The Case of China* (Armonk, NY: M. E. Sharpe).

Wank, D. L. (1998) 'Political Sociology and Contemporary China: State-Society Images in American China Studies', *Journal of Contemporary China*, 7(18).

Wasserstrom, J. (2008) *Global Shanghai, 1850–2010* (New York: Routledge).

Watson, A. (1984) 'Agriculture Looks for "Shoes that Fit": The Production Responsibility System and Its Implications', in N. Maxwell and B. McFarlane (eds), *China's Changed Road to Development* (Oxford: Pergamon).

Watson, A., Findlay, C. and Du, Yintang (1989) 'Who Won the "Wool War"? A Case Study of Rural Product Marketing in China', *The China Quarterly*, 118 (June).

Wedeman, A. (2000) 'Budgets, Extra-Budgets, and Small Treasuries: Illegal Monies and Local Autonomy in China', *Journal of Contemporary China*, 9(25).

Wedeman, A. (2004) 'The Intensification of Corruption in China', *The China Quarterly*, 180 (December).

Wei, Jingsheng (1997) *The Courage to Stand Alone: Letters from Prison and Other Writings* (New York: Viking).

Wen, Hui (2002) *Shanghai Baby* (London: Robinson).

White, S. *et al.* (1990) *Communist and Postcommunist Political Systems: An Introduction* (Basingstoke: Palgrave Macmillan), 3rd edn.

Whyte, M. K. (1974) *Small Groups and Political Rituals in China* (Berkeley, CA: University of California Press).

Whyte, M. K. (1991) 'State and Society in the Mao Era', in K. Lieberthal *et al.* (eds), *Perspectives on Modern China: Four Anniversaries* (Armonk, NY: M. E. Sharpe).

Whyte, M. K. (1992) 'Urban China: A Civil Society in the Making?', in A. L. Rosenbaum (ed.), *State and Society in China: The Consequences of Reform* (Boulder, CO: Westview Press).

Whyte, M. K. (2010) *One Country, Two Societies* (Cambridge, MA: Harvard University Press).

Wittfogel, K. (1957) *Oriental Despotism: A Comparative Study of Total Power* (New Haven, CT: Yale University Press).

Womack, B. (ed.) (1991) *Contemporary Chinese Politics in Historical Perspective* (Cambridge: Cambridge University Press).

Wong, C.P.W. (1988) 'Interpreting Rural Industrial Growth in the Post-Mao Period', *Modern China*, 14(1).

Wong, C.P.W. (ed.) (1997) *Financing Local Government in the People's Republic of China* (Hong Kong: Oxford University Press).

Wong, C.P.W. (2000) Central–Local Relations Revisited', *China Perspectives*, 31 (September–October).

Wong, C.P.W. (2007) 'Fiscal Management for a Harmonious Society: Assessing the Central Government's Capacity', British Inter-University China Center Working Paper.

Wong, C.P.W. and Bird, R. (2008) 'China's Fiscal System: A Work in Progress', Brandt, L. and Rawski, T. (eds), *China's Great Transformation: Origins, Mechanism, and Consequences of the Post-Reform Economic Boom* (New York: Cambridge University Press).

Wong, L. and N. Flynn (2001) *The Market in Chinese Social Policy* (Basingstoke: Palgrave Macmillan).

Woo, Wing Thye (1999) 'The Real Reasons for China's Growth', *The China Journal*, 41 (January).

Woo, Wing Thye (2001) 'Recent Claims of China's Economic Exceptionalism: Reflections Inspired by WTO Accession', *China Economic Review*, 12.

Woo, Wing Thye (n.d.) 'Some Unorthodox Thoughts on China's Unorthodox Financial Sector', unpublished paper.

World Bank (1994) *Averting the Old-Age Crisis: Policies to Protect the Old and Promote Growth* (New York: Oxford University Press).

World Bank (1997b) *China's Management of Enterprise Assets: The State as Shareholder* (Washington, DC: World Bank).

World Bank (1997d) *Old Age Security: Pension Reform in China* (Washington, DC: World Bank).

World Bank (1997e) *Sharing Rising Incomes: Disparities in China* (Washington, DC: World Bank).

World Bank (1997g) *Clear Water, Blue Skies: China's Environment in the New Century* (Washington, DC: World Bank).

World Bank (2000) *China: Overcoming Rural Poverty* (Washington, DC: World Bank).

World Bank (2002) *China: National Development and Sub-national Finance: A Review of Provincial Expenditures* (Washington, DC: Poverty Reduction and Economic Management Unit, East Asia and Pacific Region).

World Bank (2005) 'Reforming China's Health Care System', *Quarterly Update* (World Bank Office Beijing) (November), at www.worldbank.org/china.

World Bank (2009) *From Poor Areas to Poor People: China's Evolving Poverty Reduction Agenda. An Assessment of Poverty and Inequality in China* (Washington, DC: Poverty Reduction and Economic Management Department).

World Wildlife Fund (2009) *Summary of the First-ever Yangtze River Basin Climate Change Vulnerability and Adaptability Report* (Beijing: WWF).

Xiang, Biao (1996) 'How to Create a Visible "Non-State Space" Through Migration and Marketized Traditional Networks: An Account of a Migrant Community in China', paper delivered to the International Conference on Chinese Rural Labour Force Migration (Beijing).

Xu, Yong (1997) 'Use Village Self-Governance to Promote the Administration of Village Level Public Finances', paper delivered to the Conference to Mark the Tenth Anniversary of the Organic Law on Village Self-Governance (Beijing).

Xue, Muqiao ([1980] 1982) 'Economic Work Must Grasp the Objective Laws of Development', in Bogdan Szajkowski (ed.), *Documents in Communist Affairs 1980* (Basingstoke: Palgrave Macmillan).

Xue, X. Li, C. Lei, C. and Yu, J. (2006) 'Chengxiang shehui baozhang zhidu de chaju yu tongchou duice' [The Difference in the Urban and Rural Social Insurance System and A Comprehensive Countermeasure], *Nongye guancha* [Rural Investigations] No.3.

Yang, Dali (1994) 'Reform and the Restructuring of Central-Local Relations', in D. S. G. Goodman and G. Segal (eds), *China Deconstructs: Politics, Trade and Regionalism* (New York: Routledge).

Yang, Dali (1997) 'Surviving the Great Leap Famine: The Struggle over Rural Policy, 1958–1962', in T. Cheek and T. Saich (eds), *New Perspectives on State Socialism in China* (Armonk, NY: M. E. Sharpe).

Yang, Dali (2004) *Remaking the Chinese Leviathan: Market, Transition and the Politics of Governance in China* (Stanford: Stanford University Press).

Yang, Zhong (1996) 'Withering Governmental Power in China?', *Communist and Post-Communist Studies*, 29(4).

Yao, Wenyuan (1975) 'On the Social Basis of the Lin Piao Anti-Party Clique', *Peking Review*, 18(10) (7 March).

Yeung, Godfrey Kwok-Yung (1995) 'The People's Liberation Army and the Market Economy', in R. Benewick and P. Wingrove (eds), *China in the 1990s* (Basingstoke: Palgrave Macmillan).

Yu Dan (2007) *'Lunyu' xin de* [Reflections on the *Analects*] (2008) (Beijing: China Publishing House).

Yu Deping (2002) 'Chengxiang shehui: cong geli zouxiang kaifeng: Zhongguo huiji zhidu yu huifa yanjiu' [City and Countryside Societies: From Segregation to Opening: Research on China's Household Registration System and Laws] (Jinan: Shangdong People's Publishing House).

Yu, Keping (2008) *Democracy is a Good Thing: Essays on Politics, Society, and Culture in Contemporary China* (Washington, DC: Brookings Institution Press).

Yu, Jianrong (2006) 'Quanguo dibao jiu shi gei nongmin guomin daiyu' [national Minimum Living Support Gives Farmers the Status of Citizens] at http://paper.cs.com.cn/html/2006-07/25/content_1835590.htm.

Yusuf, S. and Saich, T. (2008) *China Urbanizes. Consequences, Strategies, and Policies* (Washington, DC: World Bank).

Zeng, Yi et al. (1993) 'Causes and Implications of the Recent Increase in the Reported Sex Ratio at Birth in China', *Population and Development Review*, 19(2).

Zhang, Chunqiao [Chang Chun-chiao] (1975) 'On Exercising All-Round Dictatorship over the Bourgeoisie', *Peking Review*, 18(14) (4 April).

Zhang, Le-Yin (1999) 'Chinese Central-Provincial Fiscal Relationships, Budgetary Decline and the Impact of the 1994 Fiscal Reform: An Evaluation', *The China Quarterly*, 157 (March).

Zhang Yi (2003) 'Jingzhong: woguo nuer chusheng xinbie zai chixu shangsheng' (Warning: An Imbalance of Sex Ratio in China), in Ru Xin et al. (eds), *2003 nian: Zhongguo shehui xingshi fenxi yuce* (*2003: Circumstances and Analysis of Chinese Society*) (Beijing: Social Sciences Documentation Publishing House).

Zhao, L. (2006) *Time to Care for Migrant Workers: New Social Initiatives in the Hu-Wen Eva* (Singapore: East Asian Institute Background Brief No. 272).

Zhao, Suisheng (1997) 'Political Reform and Changing One-Party Rule in Deng's China', *Problems of Post-Communism*, 44(5).

Zhao, Yaohui and Xu, Jianguo (1999) 'Alternative Transition Paths in the Chinese Urban Pension System', *China Centre for Economic Research*, Working Paper.

Zhao, Ziyang (1987) 'Advance Along the Road of Socialism with Chinese Characteristics', *Beijing Review*, 30(45) (9–15 November).

Zhao, Ziyang (2009) *Prisoner of the State. The Secret Journal of Premier Zhao Ziyang* (New York: Simon & Schuster).

Zheng, Wang (2010) 'Feminist Networks', in Hsing, Y. and Lee, C. (eds) *Reclaiming Chinese Society* (New York: Routledge).

Zheng, Yong-Nian (1994) 'Perforated Sovereignty: Provincial Dynamism and China's Foreign Trade', *The Pacific Review*, 7(3).

Zheng, Yong-Nian and Lye, Liang Fook (2002) 'Succession Politics, Power Distribution and Legacies: China After the 16th Party Congress', *East Asian Institute Background Brief*, 142.

Zhou, K. (1996) *How the Farmers Changed China: Power of the People* (Boulder, CO: Westview Press).

Zhu, Rongji (2003) 'Government Work Report, Delivered at First Session of Tenth NPC (March)', *FBIS-CHI-2003-0319*.

Zweig, D. (1989) *Agrarian Radicalism in China, 1968–1981* (Cambridge, MA: Harvard University Press).

Zweig, D. (1997) *Freeing China's Farmers: Rural Restructuring in the Reform Era* (Armonk, NY: M. E. Sharpe).

Zweig, D. (2002) *Internationalizing China. Domestic Interests and Global Linkages* (Ithaca, NY: Cornell University Press).

Index